MANAGING TECHNOLOGY-BASED PROJECTS

MANAGING TECHNOLOGY-BASED PROJECTS

Tools, Techniques, People, and Business Processes

Hans J. Thamhain

WILEY

Cover image: Wind Farm © iStockphoto/Estate of Stephen Laurence Strathdee
Display Charts © iStockphoto/Nikada
Computer Chip © iStockphoto/alengoGlobe World Map © iStockphoto/ziggymaj
Cover design: David Riedy

This book is printed on acid-free paper.

Published by John Wiley & Sons, Inc., Hoboken, New Jersey
Published simultaneously in Canada

For general information about our other products and services, please contact our Customer Care Department
within the United States at (800) 762-2974, outside the United States at (317) 572-3993 or fax (317) 572-4002.

Wiley publishes in a variety of print and electronic formats and by print-on-demand. Some material included
with standard print versions of this book may not be included in e-books or in print-on-demand. If this book
refers to media such as a CD or DVD that is not included in the version you purchased, you may download this
material at http://booksupport.wiley.com. For more information about Wiley products, visit www.wiley.com.

Library of Congress Cataloging-in-Publication data is available up on request.

ISBN 978-0-470-40254-2

Printed in the United States of America

10 9 8 7 6 5 4 3 2 1

Contents

Preface

Project management has evolved into a powerful system, used by virtually every enterprise to advance its business and to gain competitive advantage. Although project management has been practiced for thousands of years, only during the past few decades have we begun to understand what drives project performance and what can be done to link the project management system with the enterprise and its business strategy. Yet, on the operational side, many organizations have reached a maturity level that facilitates predictable execution of highly complex projects. Success is no longer random. It is driven by carefully designed and continuously improved project management systems and skill sets that pay attention to both the work process and the human side of project management.

This book focuses on technology-intensive business environments. However today, technology is everywhere, and it is difficult to find a business not affected by technology. Yet, some organizations are more intensely immersed in technology, either to produce new products or to use technology to execute their projects effectively, such as financial or medical services. Managers in these technology-intensive project environments perceive their managerial roles more challenging because of higher levels of dynamics, complexities, and uncertainties that exist in their projects, in comparison to environments less exposed to technology. Many of their technology-based projects require innovative solutions, collaboration with partners and contractor organizations, and expectations by senior management to align the project with the business objectives of the enterprise. Of course, all of this must be accomplished within the defined schedule, budget, and quality constraints. Lots of challenges!

Time after time, managers have told me that the biggest challenge they face is not so much in dealing with the technical issues of applying technology or working out technical solutions but in dealing with the dynamics and uncertainties associated with the complexities of the technology-based work environment, plus adding value to the enterprise. This requires specialized skills in planning, organizing, and guiding multidisciplinary activities. It also requires a great deal of people skills in building cross-functional teams and leading them toward desired results. This involves effective motivation, power and resource sharing, communications both vertically and horizontally, and conflict management. To get results, project managers must be social architects who understand the culture and value system of the enterprise, and who can relate socially as well as technically. The days of managers who get by with only technical expertise or pure administrative skills are gone.

This book is written from the technology manager's perspective, for managers and professionals who must function effectively in complex, technology-oriented business environments. However, as technology crosses virtually all levels and all disciplines of an enterprise, the principles of managing in technology not only are relevant for science, engineering, and R&D but also apply to any organization and business that must effectively deal with the application, integration, and transfer of technology. Financial institutions, hospitals, law enforcement, government services, and media businesses are just a few examples of the vast array of organizations, outside the traditional engineering-scientific community, that see themselves in a high-technology enterprise.

In addition to serving as a professional reference, this book is designed as a text for college courses in project management. In fact, I use it in my own graduate and undergraduate courses at Bentley and Harvard University. It integrates the established body of knowledge in project management (PMBOK) with today's contemporary project management practices and the emerging body of knowledge in management of technology (MOT), all linked with the contemporary concepts of organizational behavior. The lead-in scenarios for each chapter and the questions for discussion and exercises at the end of each chapter should provide food for critical thinking in professional group discussions or academic classroom exercises. Managers and technology-oriented professionals at all levels should find this text useful in gaining an understanding of the organizational process, organizational dynamics, and critical success factors that drive technology-based project performance. Such insight can help in fine-tuning leadership style, resource allocation, and organizational developments—hence continuously improving enterprise ability to compete effectively in today's complex global markets.

The book includes the latest concepts of project management, plus my 40 years of field observations and experiences as researcher, and earlier as manager in RD&E and technology management with ITT, Westinghouse, General Electric, and GTE/Verizon, prior to my current teaching and research career at Bentley University.

I would like to express my appreciation to the many colleagues who encouraged and nurtured the development of this book. Special thanks go to the large number of project professionals, managers, and executives from the United States, South America, Europe, Asia, and Australia who contributed valuable information during various forms of professional engagement and field research, which is now part of the content and professional perspectives presented in this book.

Chapter 1

Challenges of Managing Projects in a Technology World

APPLE IPHONE 5

Photo courtesy of Apple Inc.

When Apple introduced its newest smartphone iPhone 5 at the Yerba Buena Center in San Francisco in late 2012, it was positioned for success. "iPhone 5 is the most beautiful consumer device that we've ever created," said Philip Schiller, Apple's senior vice president of Worldwide Marketing. "We've packed an amazing amount of innovation and advanced technology into a thin and light, jewel-like device with a stunning 4-inch retina display, blazing-fast A6 chip, ultrafast wireless, even longer battery life; and we think customers are going to love it."

The announcement marked the end of an 18-month product development cycle that included intricate collaboration with several software developers, dozens of component manufacturers, partners and the iPhone fabrication at Hon Hai Precision Industry (also known as Foxconn in Zhengzhou, China). Indeed, the new product is state of the art. It is the thinnest and lightest iPhone ever, completely redesigned to feature the new display screen, the world's most advanced mobile operating system, and over 200 new features such as new maps, turn-by-turn navigation, Facebook, Passbook, and more Siri® features.

However, recovering the investment for product development and rollout of the new 16 GB iPhone is not without challenges. For one thing, the cost to produce the phone is high. At over $200 per unit, Apple had to count on wireless companies to subsidize the purchasing price. Nevertheless, business analysts were optimistic that the iPhone 5 would be profitable in the long run—and as it turned out, their optimism was not misplaced. Following up on the impressive success of the iPhone 5, in September 2013, Apple introduced the iPhone 5S and the iPhone 5C.

1.1 PROJECT MANAGEMENT IN A CHANGING WORLD: CHALLENGES AND OPPORTUNITIES

The complexities and challenges faced by Apple in developing the iPhone 5 might look modest by comparison to super projects, such as major aerospace missions, the relocation of Tata's steel plant to the Gulf of Bengal, or the organization of the next Summer Olympics. Yet, the iPhone 5 has all of the characteristics that we find in millions of technology-intensive projects. Project management has become an important variable for success in today's complex business environment, where projects span organizational lines, involving a broad spectrum of personnel, support groups, subcontractors, vendors, partners, government agencies, and customer organizations. Hence, successful execution relies on effective linkages, cooperation, and alliances among various organizational functions, critical for proper communication, and decision making. Top-down control no longer works in most of these environments, but authority must be earned and team commitment must be built as critical conditions to successful project management.

Despite its challenges, this changing environment—especially advances in computers, IT, and communication technology—creates enormous opportunities for enterprises across all industries. It is possible to execute larger, more complex projects, with leaner budgets and more predictable schedules, and to connect with a wide spectrum of resources across the world. However, technology creates its own challenges, requiring additional investment in equipment, software, infrastructure, services, and skill sets. Advances in technology have also accelerated the changes in our business environment, leading to tougher competition, lower barriers of market entry, and shorter product life cycles, requiring more agile and flexible approaches to project management. These changes have shifted the project paradigm with strong impact on business performance. This got the attention of management across all industries, many of them recognizing project management as a critical toolset for providing common language and methodology for executing multidisciplinary ventures.

1.2 GLOBAL DIMENSIONS

The changes in the global business environment have pushed these challenges to an even higher level. To succeed in our ultracompetitive, interconnected world of business, companies are continuously searching for ways to improve effectiveness. They look for partners that can perform the needed work better, cheaper and faster. Speed especially has become one of the great equalizers of competitive performance. In the case of the iPhone, a new product may be obsolete in less than a year, unless provisions for continuous upgrading and enhancement have been built into the system and are implemented in response to evolving market needs. This results in complex project organization and execution processes, involving joint ventures, alliances, multinational sourcing and elaborate vendor relations across the globe, ranging from R&D to manufacturing, and from customer relations to field services.

Project complexity has been increasing in virtually every segment of industry and government, including computer, pharmaceutical, automotive, health care, transportation, and financial businesses, just to name a few of the most noticeable ones. New technologies, especially in computers and communications, have radically changed the workplace and transformed our global economy, focusing on effectiveness, value and speed. These technologies offer more sophisticated capabilities for cross-functional integration, resource mobility, effectiveness and market responsiveness, but they also require more sophisticated skill sets both technically and socially, dealing effectively with a broad spectrum of contemporary challenges, including managing conflict, change, risks and uncertainty.

As a result of this paradigm shift we have seen a change in the dynamics of teamwork and a change in managerial focus from efficiency to effectiveness, and from a focus on traditional performance measures, such as the quadruple constraint, to include a broader spectrum of critical success factors that support innovation, work integration, organizational collaboration, human factors, business process agility, and strategic objectives. Traditional linear work processes and top-down controls are no longer sufficient, but are gradually being replaced with alternate organizational designs, new management techniques and business processes, such as agile processes, concurrent engineering, User-Centered Design, and Stage-Gate protocols (Thamhain 2011). These techniques offer more sophisticated capabilities for cross-functional integration, resources mobility, effectiveness, and market responsiveness, but they also require more sophisticated management skills and leadership.

1.3 PROJECT DESERVE SPECIAL ATTENTION WITHIN THE ENTERPRISE

Projects are different from ongoing operations. They are one-time undertakings, such as the Apple's iPhone development, with a specific mission, purpose, and objective, usually driven by the needs and wants of a sponsor or customer, who could be an individual or an organization, internal or external to the enterprise, or both. In essence, this description identifies the components and uniqueness of projects:

Producing specific deliverables within given time, resource and quality constraints that satisfy the project sponsor/customer.

It also identifies the boundary conditions of time, resources, quality, and customer satisfaction, referred to as *quadruple constraint*, to be discussed in the next chapter in more detail.

By their very nature projects are multidisciplinary, requiring resources and support from many organizational units. This is disruptive to the ongoing operations of the enterprise. It interferes with the mission and objectives of functional departments, and is inconsistent with established central management processes for command, control, and communications.

Thus, to minimize interference with ongoing operations, projects need to be organized and managed separately from the ongoing operations, yet well integrated with the enterprise. With the emergence of contemporary project management, virtually every enterprise with project-related activities established its own project management system with various degrees of formality and sophistication. The aim is to have a common infrastructure with methodologies, supportive processes, tools, and measurement systems that ensures consistent project delivery across the enterprise. Communication is at the heart of any of these management systems for effectively connecting among all team members, including partners, support organizations and other internal and external stakeholder communities.

As it has evolved over the past 60 years, modern project management provides the type of disciplined yet flexible framework for effectively planning, organizing, and executing projects. It has its own body of knowledge, providing a common language and methodology with tools and techniques for managing multidisciplinary ventures, regardless of their size, shape, or industry.

1.4 THE UNIQUE NATURE OF TECHNOLOGY PROJECTS

Technology-intensive projects have their unique characteristics and challenges. By definition, these projects have to deal with *technology*, a fast-changing knowledge area associated with risk and uncertainty. The problems to be solved are often complex and solutions untried, requiring experimental, iterative approaches, innovation and creativity, and highly specialized skill sets. Although one could make an argument that these issues also exist in many low-technology projects, they are amplified as dependence on technology intensifies, such as we see in the iPhone example. Therefore, it is not surprising that managers of technology-based projects see their work environment as different, requiring unique organizational structures, policies, interaction among people, and support systems. Yet the classification of projects along technology lines is not easy. Let's first look into the unique characteristics of technology-intensive projects before suggesting a specific classification based on degree of technology and complexity.

WHAT IS DIFFERENT ABOUT TECHNOLOGY-INTENSIVE PROJECTS?

In our highly connected world, most project managers must deal with technology. They must function in a business environment that uses technology for competitive advantage, and their projects are heavily steeped in technology. Virtually every segment of industry and government tries to leverage technology to improve effectiveness, value, and speed. Traditional linear work processes and top-down controls are no longer sufficient, but are gradually being replaced by alternate organizational designs and new, more agile management techniques and business processes, such as concurrent engineering, design-build, stage-gate and user-centered design. These techniques offer more sophisticated capabilities for cross-functional integration, resources mobility, effectiveness, and market responsiveness, but they also require more sophisticated skills to effectively deal with a broad spectrum of contemporary challenges, both technically and socially, including higher levels of conflict, change, risks, and uncertainty, and a shifting attention from functional efficiency to process integration effectiveness, emphasizing organizational interfaces, human factors, and the overall business process. Taken together, technology-intensive projects can be characterized as follows:

- Value creation by applying technology
- Strong need for innovation and creativity
- High task complexities, risks, and uncertainties
- Resource constraints and tight end-date-driven schedules despite tough performance requirements
- Highly educated and skilled personnel, broad skill spectrum
- Specific technical job knowledge and it competency
- Need for sophisticated people skills, ability to work across different organizational cultures and values, and to deal with organizational conflict, power, and politics
- Complex project organizations and cross-functional linkages
- Complex business processes and stakeholder communities
- Technology used as a tool for managing projects
- Replacement of labor with technology
- Advanced infrastructure
- High front-end expenditures early in the project life cycle
- Low short-term profitability in spite of large capital investment
- Fast-changing markets, technology, regulations
- Intense global competition, open markets, and low barriers to entry
- Short product life cycles affect time to market
- Need for quick market response
- Complex decision-making processes
- Many alliances, joint ventures, and partnerships

1.4.1 Characteristics of Technology-Intensive Projects

Although technology and management practices vary considerably among companies, specific characteristics can be defined to describe technology-intensive projects as part of their dynamic environment and organizational interaction as summarized in 16 categories:

1. **Value creation by applying technology.** Technology-based projects create value primarily by leveraging technology. They exploit or commercialize technology. Examples range from plastics and fiber optics to financial services and e-commerce. The technology-based enterprise competes through technological innovation. Project management provides the process, fueled by technology, for creating new and unique products, services, systems, equipment, or advanced materials. This added value is part of the innovation process, where the final product, such as the Internet service or computer chip, is worth a lot more than its ingredients. Hence, "Innovation is the key driver to competitiveness . . . and long-term economic growth" (US Department of Commerce 2012).

2. **High task complexity, risks, and uncertainty.** Given their technical complexity, market uncertainties, changing technologies, and regulatory ambiguities, technology-based projects can be very risky in terms of economics and technical success. Because of these uncertainties, technology-intensive projects utilize unique organizational structures, work processes, decision-making tools, and leadership styles.

3. **Resource constraints and tight end-date driven schedules despite tough performance requirements.** Because of time-to-market pressures and intense competition typical for technology-based projects, resources and schedules are often very tight despite complex requirements and uncertainties, all adding to the challenges of project managers.

4. **Highly educated and skilled personnel.** Technology-intensive projects require special knowledge, skill sets, and competencies to do the technical work. They also require sophisticated people skills, the ability to deal with organizational conflict, power, and politics, and the ability to work effectively in teams across functional lines toward project integration.

5. **Complex project organizations and cross-functional linkages.** Because of the need to integrate among many disciplines, contractors, and partners, as well as the intricate work processes that often span wide geographic areas, high-tech projects are rarely organized according to conventional structures, such as the matrix or projectized organization. Instead, they are arranged as "studios" where team members organize themselves around tasks, determining their responsibilities, work interfaces, and deliverables, sharing accountability and decision-making among the task owners and their interfaces. The evolving project organizations are usually hybrids of conventional structures

capable of working within established project execution templates, such as stage gate, concurrent, spiral, or agile/scrum, and interfacing with complex business processes and stakeholder communities.

6. **Technology used as a tool for managing projects.** High-tech projects use technology extensively in support of their projects execution. This includes sophisticated communication and reporting systems, computer simulation and modeling, advanced testing, and the latest software for project planning, tracking, and control. Often, these project-specific technologies are integrated with other enterprisewide management systems such as SAP or Oracle to gain operational advantages that lead to more predictable, cost-effective, faster, and market-focused project implementation.

7. **Replacement of labor with technology.** Technology-intensive projects are often part of a technology enterprise, such as computers, automotive, or pharmaceutical, that utilizes a wide spectrum of technology with the objective to gain economic benefits, speed, better quality, and reliability. The added value requires additional resources in the form of more advanced equipment, infrastructure, and software, but reduces labor, explaining the fact that technology-intensive projects and their host companies are mostly *capital* (rather than labor).

8. **Advanced infrastructure.** Technology-intensive projects utilize special state-of-the-art equipment, facilities, infrastructure, software tools, and training in support of the project work to be performed.

9. **High front-end expenditures early in the project life cycle.** The effort and resources needed at the front-end project work, such as planning, feasibility assessment, and R&D, seem to increase with the degree of technology used. For example, expenditures for planning and feasibility assessment of high-tech projects run typically above 10 percent of the total budget, double the average across all projects.

10. **Low short-term profitability in spite of large capital investment.** Technology-intensive projects often need large amounts of cash for capital equipment for reasons just discussed, sometimes more than they can generate. They are the classical "stars" in BCG's Growth-Share Matrix (Grant 2010). As a result, strong financial leveraging and low profitability are quite common, in addition to joint ventures, partnerships, and extensive outsourcing, even for well-established high-tech giants, such as Amazon, Boeing, Intel, Microsoft, Pfizer, and Seagate.

11. **Changing markets, technology, and regulations.** Technology-based projects are likely to operate in continuously changing business environments with fast-changing markets and technologies, low barriers to entry, and high exposure to liabilities and regulations.

12. **Intense global competition, open markets, low barriers to entry.** Traditional barriers to entry, such as infrastructure, brand loyalty, and established supply chains, are virtually nonexistent for high-tech businesses. In particular "new and emerging technologies" can reset the competitive field to "ground zero," whipping out any competitive advantage of established products and services (Andrew and Sirkin 2003).

This reality strongly influences the way projects are organized and managed, leading to more empowerment and autonomy at the project team level to promote the agility and speed needed for optimizing the project value under time-to-market pressure and changing conditions.

13. **Short product life cycles.** Driven largely by changing market conditions, emerging technologies and strong competition, life cycles of technology-based product are shorter, putting pressure on time to market as a critical project performance measure.

14. **Need for quick market response.** High-tech companies are fast, agile, and flexible in responding to business opportunities and threats. This also reflects in their project organizations and management style, empowering teams and relying on more autonomous work processes that enable quick reaction to changing conditions.

15. **Complex decision-making processes.** As a result of high risks, great uncertainties, and the dynamics that technology-intensive projects are exposed to, top-down or centralized management is usually ineffective. To a large extend, it is being replaced by *distributed* (or *team-based*) *decision making*, which promotes risk sharing, collaboration, and commitment at the project team level.

16. **Many alliances, joint ventures, and partnerships.** Because of the potentially high costs, risks, and complexities of high-tech project, virtually no company has the resources to handle all the facets of a technology development, its rollout and field support single-handed. Resource pooling, from cooperative agreements to joint ventures, partnerships and acquisitions are quite common among high-tech projects to raise the resources for implementing the new venture in a timely fashion.

To summarize the areas that are unique and different in managing technology-intensive projects, let us focus on six selected business subsystems, as graphically shown in Figure 1.1 and discussed next.

Figure 1.1   Business subsystems unique to technology-intensive project management

Work

Technology-oriented work is by and large more complex, requiring special skills, equipment, tools, processes, and support systems. The unit of work is often a project, organized and executed by multidisciplinary teams. Cross-functional integration, progress measurements and controlling the work toward desired results is usually more challenging with increasing technology orientation, involving creativity, risks, and uncertainties. Work processes are often nonlinear, with solutions evolving incrementally and iteratively with many cross-functional dependencies.

Impact areas: Organizational structure, work planning, work processes (e.g., project management), personnel recruiting, advancement and careers, skill development, management style, organizational culture, and business strategy.

People

Because of the type of work and its challenges, technology-oriented environments and their projects attract different people. On average, these people have highly specialized skills and can apply them effectively. They are better educated, self-motivated/directed, require a minimum of supervision, and enjoy autonomy and freedom of decision making, while willing to take on responsibilities. Hence, they enjoy empowerment and problem solving, and find challenges such as dealing with resource and schedule constraints to some degree motivating and intellectually stimulating. People in technology-oriented work environments often enjoy a sense of community and team spirit, while having little tolerance for personal conflict, anxieties, and organizational politics.

Impact areas: Because of the relationship between people and work issues, the two impact areas are similar. Organizational structure, work plans, and processes, personnel recruiting and advancement, skill development, management style, and organizational culture are the primary areas affected by people in technology.

Work Process

The nature of high-tech work and its business environment requires the ability to deal effectively with complexities, uncertainties, speed, and innovation. This influenced the evolution of work processes that are less sequential and centrally administered, but more team based, self-directed, agile, and structured for parallel, concurrent execution of the work. New organizational models and management methods, such as the *spiral, Stage-Gate, concurrent engineering, design-build*, and *agile/scrum* processes evolved together with the refinement of time-proven concepts such as the matrix and projectized management structures.

Impact areas: Because of the effect on the people and their work, the work process design affects primarily people issues, management style, and organizational culture. In addition, the work process affects management tools, such as scheduling, budgeting, and project performance analysis, as well as operational effectiveness, such as time to market, cost, and flexibility.

Managerial Tools and Techniques

The unique nature of the work and its business environment creates the need for a special set of tools and techniques for effective administration and management in technology-based projects. Virtually all of the tools and techniques are being used in both high-tech and low-tech organizations, and in many cases, the tools were used long before the high-tech era. However, in their specific application and integration with the enterprise, these tools and techniques often fulfill a unique function and play a unique role. Examples are project schedules that have been tailored to respond to the pressures of a faster, more competitive, and more team-directed work environment. Today these schedules cover a wide spectrum of capabilities and sophistication, from simple milestone charts and bar graphs to PERT charts that show task dependencies and resource requirements, integrated, and trackable throughout the total project.

The wide spectrum of project management tools and techniques can be grouped into five major categories according to their application: (1) project acquisition, (2) project evaluation and selection, (3) project planning and organizing, (4) project tracking, review, and control, (5) contract administration, (6) project support, including legal, human resources (HR), accounting, and training, and (7) strategy. Since the application areas overlap, there is a great deal of overlap among the tools and techniques of the seven areas. In this book we will discuss primarily the first four categories focusing on project management.

Impact areas: The effectiveness of tools and techniques in the enterprise is strongly influenced by the people who use them. Therefore, stakeholder involvement during the tool selection, development, and implementation is critical. The application of many tools involves tradeoffs, such as efficiency versus speed, control versus flexibility, or optimization versus risk. All of these factors must be carefully considered. Getting consensus on specific tools for specific application and stakeholder buy-in for its use is a great challenge.

Organizational Culture

The challenges of technology-driven environments create a unique organizational culture with their own norms, values, and work ethics. These cultures are more team oriented in terms of decision making, work flow, performance evaluation, and workgroup management. Authority must often be earned. It emerges within the workgroup as a result of credibility, trust, and respect, rather than organizational status and position. Rewards come to a considerable degree from satisfaction with the work and its activities. Recognition of accomplishments becomes an important motivational factor for stimulating enthusiasm, cooperation, and innovation. It is also a critical catalyst for unifying project teams, encouraging risk taking, and dealing with conflict.

Impact areas: Organizational culture has a strong influence on people and the work process. It affects organizational systems from hiring practices to performance evaluation and reward systems to organizational structure, teamwork, and management style.

Business Environment

Technology-oriented businesses operate in an environment that is fast changing in terms of markets, suppliers, and regulations. Short product life cycles, intense global competition, and strong dependency on other technologies and support systems are typical for these businesses, which operate in markets with low brand loyalty, low barriers to entry, and fast and continuously improving price-performance ratios. All of these factors strongly influence the type of projects selected for execution and their managerial processes.

Impact areas: The need for speed, agility, and efficiency affects not only the work process design, the organization and execution of work/projects, and the management methods, tools, and techniques, but also business strategy and competitive behavior, which often focuses on cooperation and resource leveling via alliances, mergers, acquisitions, consortia, and joint ventures, spanning part or all of the project life cycle and beyond.

Taken together, the business environment is quite different from what it used to be. New technologies and changing global markets have transformed our business communities and the way we manage projects. Contemporary project leaders who survive and prosper in this environment have the ability to deal with a broad spectrum of challenges that focus on speed, cost, and quality. They have also shifted their focus from managing the effective implementation of specific requirements to a more integrated business management approach that includes attention to human factors, organizational interfaces, business process, and an alignment of their projects with the strategy of the enterprise.

1.5 EVOLUTION AND GROWTH OF PROJECT MANAGEMENT AND TECHNOLOGY

Project management is not an invention of this century, but has been around for thousands of years, as shown in Table 1.1. The same is true for technology. Interestingly, for most of its history, mankind got along fine without sophisticated management tools and techniques. How did we get into such complex work processes and management methods? What role did technology play in this evolution? Technology has been around for a long time. Man's quest for survival led to the development of improved tools and techniques for simple projects, such as gathering food and building shelters, but also more complex projects, such as building monuments, cities, irrigation

Table 1.1   Evolution of Project Management

Time	Project Undertaking (Examples)	Concepts, Advances, Technology
3000 BCE	Pyramids, Damascus, Stonehenge, China Wall, Roman roads, aqueducts, irrigation, military campaigns	Crude projectized organizations, hierarchical structures of command, communication, and control
↓		
0	Colossus of Rhodes	Early methods of project planning, measuring, and controlling performance; autocratic leadership
↓	Ships	
↓	Castles	
↓	Cathedrals, monuments	
1800	Industrialization	
↓	Factories	Evolution of formal organization and management concepts
↓	Research programs	
1900	Movies	Scientific management, behavioral science
1940	Manhattan project	Formal concepts of teamwork, leadership, project management
1960	Sputnik, ICBM, Apollo	
1980	McIntosh computer	Widespread use of computers for project planning, tracking, control
1990	Human Genome Project	
2000	International Space Station	Strong focus on people
2010+	Mega infrastructure programs, (e.g., Brazil's $900 billion PAC-2)	Virtual, agile, collaborative, strategic alignment

systems, and war campaigns. Evidence of highly complex projects dates back more than 4,000 years. Egyptian pyramids, the Great Wall of China, the inauguration of a king, the Trojan horse, waterworks, Roman roads, and war machinery give testimony today of impressive projects completed during those times. Even by today's standards, these were large, complex, multidisciplinary projects. Basic management tools, such as project planning and control techniques, task definition, and scheduling were already known at these early times and eventually formed the foundation for today's project management systems.

Starting in the eighteenth century, the steam engine and Industrial Revolution spawned an enormous growth in technology with focus on mass production and economies of scale, leading to a wide spectrum of increasingly more complex projects in support of these industrial developments. Yet, it was not until the middle of the twentieth century when project management was recognized as a formal discipline, and organizations started to apply project management tools and techniques more systematically to complex projects.

1.5.1 The Onset of Modern Project Management

The classical model of organization and management first proved inadequate for military undertakings during World War II. Early signs of modern project management processes and techniques surfaced with military technology programs, such as the Manhattan Project and the German missile program. However, it was not until the 1950s that many projects, most noticeable defense-oriented engineering developments, such as ICBM-Atlas and Polaris, became too complex to be executed strictly within functional processes. The year 1956 is often identified as the beginning of modern project management. It coincides with the start of the Polaris submarine missile program. At $11 billion, Polaris was the largest undertaken by the US government at the time. The system complexity, the large number of multidisciplinary skill requirements, the number of subcontractors, and the need to reduce lead time, put pressure on the management team to explore project methods different from those previously used. Under the leadership of Vice Admiral William Francis Raborn, a project team of key technical and management personnel was assembled. This team had full authority over all technical, financial, and administrative matters, without the requirement for traditional reviews and approvals through administrative channels and echelons of organizational levels. The new team dynamics gradually changed the concept of hierarchical direction and control. As personnel assigned to projects took directions from both project managers and their functional department bosses, the concept of dual accountability emerged. This sharing of power and resources led to a new charter and definitions of individual responsibility, accountability, authority, and control in support of an integrated project management system, and eventually led to the concept known today as matrix management.

Polaris also adopted the concept of *concurrent engineering*, a method of proceeding with several task phases in parallel, plus other advanced project management techniques from the ICBM-Atlas program, which under the leadership of General Bernard Schriever also introduced a large spectrum of advanced project management methods that contributed to the foundation of modern project management. As the result of the work at Polaris and Atlas, many new tools, such as Program Evaluation and Review Technique (PERT), work breakdown structure (WBS), and methods for formal project planning, organizing and subcontracting were developed, providing the framework for today's body of knowledge and project management process.

The success of Polaris and ICBM-Atlas, and later especially NASA's Apollo space program, left a strong imprint on the evolution of project management. Although Apollo was not the largest US undertaking in terms of dollars or personnel, it was unique in terms of complexity, technological sophistication, schedule pressures, mission risk, and uncertainty. It required the development and integration of thousands of complex subsystems by widely dispersed laboratories, contractors, and technological facilities, involving over 20,000 subcontractors and some 400,000 workers employed by government and private industry, as well as over 200 universities. Managing such an effort was clearly beyond conventionally practiced methods of the time. This drove managerial innovations that shaped modern project management. In fact, it is the Apollo program that is often credited for formalizing cross-functional teamwork and hybrid organizations that became known as the *matrix*, a management concept that was refined and legitimized by NASA. It was also the Apollo program that developed and shaped most of the conventional management tools that we use today for project planning, tracking, and control toward the more mature and stable system that we know today.

1.5.2 Why Did It Take so Long?

Why did modern project management emerge so late, considering that the need for these special work processes and tools existed long before 1950? The answer can be found by examining the evolution of organization and management theories and practices as a whole. Traditionally, managerial power was vested with the owners of the enterprise, who represented the central authority accountable for economic gains or losses, success or failure. Work was performed by executing orders that were handed down in a rigid scalar chain of command.

At the beginning of the Industrial Revolution, these enterprises often modeled themselves after military or church organizations. There was no provision for sharing managerial power, dual accountability, resource negotiations, innovative thinking, agile implementation, or situational leadership. However, during this early era, there was also no need yet for strong project authority, intricate customer interfaces, cross-organizational integration, and extensive collaboration.

These traditional enterprises operated in an environment that was reasonable steady, stable, and predictable, with clear goals and employees that were trained to fit the organization and its values. No one really challenged organizational goals, decisions, or work processes. The central authority had all the wisdom and answers with regard to what should be done and how, and provided clear, top-down directions. It took the complexity and dynamics of a large program, such as Atlas, Polaris, and Apollo, to realize that traditional, centrally orchestrated methods of project management do not work effectively in these situations. They need to be replaced, or at least augmented, by management systems that promote better cross-functional communication, collaboration, and integration, and that can work more adaptable in a changing environment. Today's modern project management systems have this capability.

Although each system is fine-tuned or custom-designed for the specific project to be executed, all systems have the same basic components for project planning, tracking, and control, which have their roots in the early concepts of formal project management of the 1950s. Furthermore, it is interesting to note that while formal project management evolved most noticeably from large military and aerospace programs, it is a toolset that is being applied today to millions of multidisciplinary missions in virtually all enterprises, in all industries, government organizations and NGOs.

1.6 WHERE ARE WE HEADING?

Predicting the future is difficult and risky. Yet there are clear trends and paradigms shifts that give us some reasonable indication of where the field of project management is heading. Look how far we have come just in the past 20 to 30 years. The astounding advances that brought us from a simple, mostly linear process that focused on planning, organizing, and executing projects, to enterprise-integrated project management systems, dashboards, spiral processes, user-centered design, and project portfolio management all happened in the past three decades. Technology, especially computers and communication technology (IT), made much of these advances possible and helped us to take on bigger and more complex projects with fewer resources in less time. In addition to technology, worldwide socioeconomic changes and the resulting globalization of business have transformed project management into a unique multidisciplinary field with its own terminology, standards, body of knowledge, and career paths. The new breed of project managers that evolved with this changing field has had to deal with new challenges, far beyond planning, tracking, and communicating projects. These skills are still important, but they have become threshold competencies. Future project managers must function more like "mini general managers." They must be social architects, leading and orchestrating the many organizations and stakeholder groups that need to collaborate during a typical project execution.

The current trends toward larger, more complex and riskier projects will also require an enhanced project management infrastructure, more effective use of communication technology, and virtual organizations to connect among all team members, including external partners, support groups, and users. Effective leadership and people skills will become critical success factors in this new, contemporary landscape.

Another major challenge will be sustainability, especially regarding large projects, both in terms of carbon footprint and maintenance cost. Project managers will have to take more of a total life cycle approach, and become more creative in optimizing project delivery, as well as in maintaining and decommissioning projects, in order to satisfy increasing concerns of customers, sponsors, and society as a whole.

We also see an increased desire for *agile* management, and for simplifying and expediting validation procedures at various levels of the project life cycle. These trends drive the need for managing change and risk more predictably, a critical factor for project success in the future. We expect that these pressures will lead to new tools that focus especially on iterative and incremental project execution methods.

Project management will be increasingly recognized as a formal management discipline throughout the world, with especially sharp gains in economic growth areas of Asia and Africa, Finally, as project management gains further acceptance as a profession, formal project management knowledge, skill sets, and credentials will play a stronger role in decisions of staffing, rewards and promotion. As a result, skill sets, such as communication, negotiation, gaining commitment and collaboration, change management, conflict resolution and leadership will be equally important to technical competency, and senior managers together with their human resource partners will spend more of their time and resources on managing talent, professional development, and certification.

Looking into the future, it appears "the only constant is change," to quote the Greek philosopher Heraclitus, 500 BCE. For effective role performance, project managers need to adapt to the continuously changing business environments, new technologies, and work processes. Project management will become the principle strategic tool for effectively competing in our crowded global markets. Those who prepared for the future will also benefit from great opportunities. The challenge is to harness these opportunities in spite of shrinking resources and an increasingly complex sociopolitical environment. We can expect these trends to continue, together with pressures toward flatter, leaner organizations, collaboratively networked with higher levels of shared authority, operating-level autonomy, and automated work processes. To survive and prosper in this changing landscape, we have to understand these trends and prepare our organizations and people accordingly.

1.7 KEY POINTS, LESSONS, AND CONCLUSIONS

The following key points were made in this chapter:

- Projects are one-time undertakings with a specific mission, producing specific deliverables within given time, resource, and quality constraints.
- The boundary conditions are the time, resource, and quality specifications, plus the need for customer satisfaction. This set of four conditions is called the *quadruple constraint*.

- Projects are different from ongoing operations and need a unique management system.
- Technology-intensive projects are usually associated with higher risks and uncertainty, but also greater opportunity for profitably leveraging technology in the market.
- Technology-intensive projects often require unique organizational structures, policies, interaction among people, and support systems.
- Low-technology projects have similar issues as high-tech projects. However, the issues and challenges get amplified as dependence on technology intensifies.
- Project management has been practiced for several thousand years. However, it was not until the 1950s that project management emerged as a formal discipline with its own body of knowledge and toolsets, and was finally recognized as a profession starting in the 1970s.
- Six interconnected organizational subsystems uniquely influence managerial leadership style and process for effectively executing technology-intensive projects: (1) work content, (2) people, (3) work process, (4) managerial tools and techniques, (5) organizational culture, and (6) business environment.

1.8 QUESTIONS FOR DISCUSSION AND EXERCISES

1. Find 10 activities reported in your local newspaper that can be identified as "projects." Rank these projects by degree of (a) complexity, (b) difficulty, and (c) technological intensity (a total of three lists). Selecting the most complex project on your list, discuss the challenges of managing the project.
2. Define *project management* in your own words.
3. How do you define project success?
4. What makes technology-intensive projects unique, and why would they require a unique style of management and support system? Or why not?
5. What is the impact of globalization on project management?
6. Why did it take so long for formal project management systems to emerge and for project management to be recognized as a profession?
7. What trends do you see in our world of business that will affect the way we manage project in the future? What managerial changes do you predict?

1.9 *PMBOK®* REFERENCES AND CONNECTIONS

This first chapter introduces the 10 *knowledge areas* and five *processing groups* as defined by *PMBOK®*. It addresses most strongly the *context* of project management. That is, it brings the issues, challenges, and opportunities of project management into perspective with today's global business environment. This broad contextual understanding of project management is necessary for effectively applying the *PMBOK®* standards to the study and practice of project management, and to prepare effectively for PMP® certification (Project Management Institute 2013).

INTERNET LINKS AND RESOURCES

Wikipedia: "Project Management," http://en.wikipedia.org/wiki/Project_management
Project Management Institute (PMI): "What Is Project Management?" www.Pmi.Org/
About-Us/About-Us-What-Is-Project-Management.Aspx

REFERENCES AND ADDITIONAL READINGS

Binder, J. 2007. *Global Project Management: Communication, Collaboration and Management Across Borders*. Farnham, UK: Grower/Ashgate Publishing.
Gale, S. 2008. "The Great Unknown." *pmNetwork* 22(5) (May): 34–39.
Gido, J., and J.P. Clements. 2012. *Successful Project Management*. Mason, OH: South-Western Cengage Learning.
Grant, R. 2010. *Contemporary Strategy Analysis*. Chichester, West Sussex, UK: John Wiley & Sons
Hatfield, M. 2008. "Danger Ahead." *pmNetwork* 22(3) (March): 37–41.
Kerzner, H. 2013. *Project Management: A Systems Approach to Planning, Scheduling, and Controlling*. Chapter 3: "Organizational Structure." Hoboken, NJ: John Wiley & Sons.
Kloppenborg, T. 2012. *Contemporary Project Management*. Mason, OH: South-Western Publishing.
Mantel, S., J. Meredith, S. Shafer, and M. Sutton. 2011. *Project Management in Practice*. Hoboken, NJ: John Wiley and Sons.
Phillips, J. 2010. *IT Project Management: On Track from Start to Finish*. New York: McGraw-Hill.
Pinto, J. 2013. *Project Management: Achieving Competitive Advantage* (3rd ed.). Upper Saddle River, NJ: Prentice-Hall.
Project Management Institute (PMI). 2013. *A Guide to the Project Management Body of Knowledge (PMBOK® Guide)*. Newtown Square, PA: Project Management Institute.
Verzuh, E. 2012. *The Fast Forward MBA in Project Management*. Hoboken NJ: John Wiley and Sons.

Chapter 2

Contemporary Project Management: Concepts and Principles

AMAZON

Source: Courtesy of Amazon

"Amazonians are leaning into the future, with radical and transformational innovations . . . that has become second nature at Amazon, and the pace is even accelerating in many forms . . . with Amazon Web Services, Fulfillment by Amazon, and Kindle Direct Publishing, with AWS, FBA, and KDP, we are creating powerful self-service platforms . . ." explains Jeffrey Bezos, founder and CEO of Amazon.com, at the 2013 annual shareholder meeting. The world's largest online retailer with annual revenues of over $50 billion started with an offline bookstore in 1994. Emerging from the dotcom bubble as one of the few winners, Amazon steadily morphed into a technology company—much like Microsoft and Walmart. The company also produces consumer electronics, most notably the Amazon Kindle e-book reader and the Kindle Fire tablet computer, and is a major provider of cloud computing services.

"What gets us up in the morning and keeps us here late at night is technology," says Jeff Bezos. "Advanced technology is everything." However, the vehicle for transforming this technology into marketable products and services is project management. Amazon plans, organizes and executes hundreds of projects each year, ranging from product developments to data warehousing and business acquisitions, all under pressure for faster, leaner and more customer-focused execution. How do they do it?

"There is an approach called *working backwards* that is widely used at Amazon," says Ian McAllister, product development manager at Amazon. "We try to work backwards from the customer, rather than starting with an idea for a product and trying to bolt customers onto it. This is especially effective when developing *new* products or features." How does it work? Typically, a new product initiative starts by writing an internal press release announcing the finished product, centered on the customer problem. If the customers are not excited about the benefits, then perhaps they're not, and the product manager should keep iterating on the press release until they've come up with benefits that actually sound like benefits. Iterating on a press release is a lot less expensive and quicker than iterating on the product itself!

Innovation in products, work processes, and an agile business model, focused on a changing market, has put Amazon on an impressive growth path. If Bezos's vision works, Amazon could become a service that would allow anyone, anywhere to buy or sell whatever he or she wants. However, trying to be a world-class retailer, a leading software developer, and a service provider simultaneously strikes some observers as a nearly impossible endeavor. Yet, Web services may offer the most expansive potential of all Amazon's tech initiatives. It's still early, but it's possible that Amazon has latched onto one of tech's juiciest dynamics—a self-reinforcing community of supporters. Indeed, it seems to be harnessing the same "viral" nature of the open-source movement that made Linux a contender to Windows.

2.1 THE BIG PICTURE: THE ART OF MANAGING PROJECTS

The spectrum and dynamics of projects at Amazon is typical of the activities and mission complexities we find across virtually all industries and government organizations, including hospitals, universities, and NGOs. Project management is no longer limited to construction, infrastructure programs or large military/aerospace missions, which launched project management as a formal discipline in the 1950s., It is being used everywhere from large defense and industrial programs to smaller, shorter ad hoc missions, such as political campaign management, urban renewal, health, education, and foreign assistance programs. In its fundamental concept, project management is a method for organizing and executing multidisciplinary tasks within budget and on schedule.

Technology has a particularly strong impact on project management. As illustrated in the Amazon situation, it affects everything from the type and magnitude of projects that we can undertake, to the work process, managerial methods, skill sets, teamwork, and leadership. Technology creates unique opportunities, but also challenges that make it often necessary to fine-tune well-established project management tools and techniques, so that they can be adapted to specific situations.

Another aspect that affects project management is complexity, such as the project scope, size, multisystem integration, geographic dispersion and the use of new work processes and technologies, all contributing to the uncertainties, nonlinearity, and challenges of successful project execution.

2.2 PROJECT MANAGEMENT DEFINED

Regardless of the project type or size, project management has specific characteristics that make it unique and different from other forms of management. In its very basic form:

Project management is the art and science of achieving desired objectives within given resource constraints, including time.

This definition implies a specific mission focus, multidisciplinary integration toward deliverables, finite resources, finite duration, specific responsibility identification, and leadership. Formally, these relationships can be expressed in the quadruple constraint illustrated in Figure 2.1. It shows that under the guidance of a project leader, specific deliverables or results (1) should be produced within given budget (2) and schedule limitations (3), and result in customer satisfaction (4). The contemporary interpretation of this definition further implies that the results should be generated regardless of changes in the business environment, such as changing markets, technologies, regulations, or customer requirements, a stipulation that needs some qualification and further discussion in later chapters.

Project management can also be defined as a *process*, providing a common language and methodology—including the tools and techniques—for executing multidisciplinary ventures. Many of these tools and techniques, as well as the process, typically illustrated within the project life cycle (PLC), are well documented and discussed in the literature. They also form the backbone for many of the project management standards, such as PMBOK, PRINCE2, or ISO 21500.

Figure 2.1   Quadruple constraint

2.3 THE PROJECT LIFE CYCLE (PLC)

In contrast to conventional business operations, projects have finite *life cycles* with clearly defined beginning and end points. For the benefit of breaking down its complexity, projects are typically subdivided into stages or phases. These life cycle phases can be arranged in many different forms and operational formats, such as following the stages of a new product development (e.g., feasibility, development, prototype, production, rollout) or the stages of a disaster relief program. While the specific type of phased arrangement usually has considerable flexibility, managers should make an effort to define "natural phases" that divide the project into its logical sets of activities, with inputs, outputs, interfaces, and workflows as they would likely occur during the project execution. To help managers in defining their project-specific phases, many project management standards, such as PMBOK and ISO, suggest several project management process groups for dividing the project life cycle (PLC). These process groups are broadly defined generic project phases that can be used as a framework for developing more detailed project-specific phases, as well as the level-I work breakdown structure (WBS). Consistent with established international standards, the following generic phases are most commonly suggested:

Initiating. Typical, this phase starts with the evaluation of a project idea; defining its basic scope, cost, and baseline; an assessment of its feasibility; its strategic alignment and value; some initial top-down project planning; and go-no/go decision making. Often, the initiating phase also includes bid-proposal and contract definition efforts.

Planning. This includes the detailed project definition, leading to the detailed work breakdown, statement of work, schedules, and budgets. For larger projects, this phase also includes the plan for staffing and organizing the project team, and the managerial guidelines for project integration and control.

Executing. This phase typically begins with organizing and developing the project team. Project execution is usually the largest, most resource-intensive phase. It includes the project implementation, the detailed work and its integration, monitoring and reporting of progress, identifying and resolution issues, and leading the project team toward desired results.

Closing. This final phase often runs concurrent with the tail-end activities of the project execution. It includes final project documentation, lessons learned, resolving/reassigning project team members, performance appraisals and recognitions, administrative closure of contracts, and final sponsor/customer sign-offs.

Although it is normal to expect considerable overlap between PLC phases, each phase defines specific actions in preparation for execution of the next phase, as graphically shown in Figure 2.2. This provides a framework for planning and controlling projects in a systematic, disciplined way, regardless of project size and complexity. The PLC is also a useful starting point for defining the top two levels of the work breakdown structure and a framework for laying out the project plan. However, many project activities span several life cycle phases, while others occur mixed-in with phases that seem to have the "wrong" or misleading label. Examples might be preliminary design work necessary during project initiation, or planning required for a specific test during the execution phase. In fact, planning itself is an ongoing process throughout the project life cycle. Tools such as the PLC are templates, providing a framework for organizing and guiding projects. They are not rigid procedures. Contemporary processes such as agile/scrum, stage-gate, spiral, or concurrent engineering, recognize the challenges of a dynamic business environment and provide a more flexible approach to project planning and execution as an overlay to the conventional PLC template. Yet the PLC is a good and effective model to follow for defining the top-down structure of virtually any project.

As the project moves through its life cycle stages, from start to finish, the managerial focus shifts from planning to organizing, and eventually to controlling. It is further interesting to note that management has most control over the outcome during the early stages of the project that still require low levels of resource commitment. That is, with a small amount of resources, relative to the total life cycle budget, a skilled task group can define the project baseline, conduct simulations, emulations, and tests, establish basic feasibility, and define alternatives of project implementation. Hence, a great deal of options

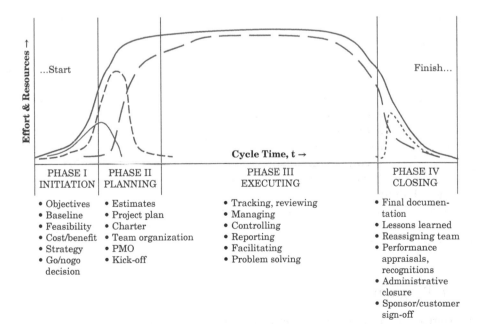

Figure 2.2 Generalized project life cycle

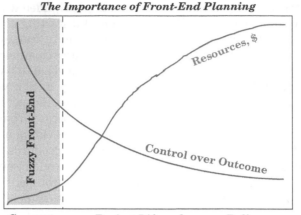

The Importance of Front-End Planning

Concept .... Project Lifecycle .... Delivery

Figure 2.3   Resource commitment and control over outcome

and control over the project implementation and its results exist during the early stages of a project. Later in the PLC the options become more limited, with less ability to influence and optimize deliverables, while larger amounts of resources have been committed or spent, as graphically shown in Figure 2.3.

2.4 PROGRAMS, PROJECTS, TASKS, AND COMMITTEES

Terminology can be confusing and cause communication problems. Let's clarify some common project management jargon. For many years, companies involved in project management have attempted to standardize on a common language, or at least tried to develop a basic metric to differentiate between various project undertakings. Yet to date there is no uniformly agreed-to set of definitions, even for the most commonly used terms, such as *projects* and *programs*. At first glance, there are many similarities among the characteristics of programs, projects, tasks, and committees. This is confusing, especially to newcomers to project management. Yet to the practitioner it might not matter what we call them, as shown by the comments of a senior manager who remarked, "Let's not argue over titles; just define the responsibilities and get the job done."

A closer look tells us, however, that there are benefits to properly establishing and using terminology consistently, at least within the same organization. Based on generally accepted practices, the following terms can be defined.

2.4.1 Program

A program is a goal-focused, multidisciplinary undertaking, established to produce specific results (often called deliverables) within given time and

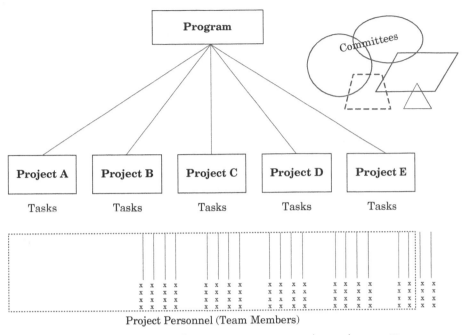

Figure 2.4 Hierarchy of programs, projects, tasks, and committees

resource limitations. Depending on the size and complexity, programs are subdivided into projects and tasks, and usually have committees working imbedded with the program organization. Programs are usually larger in scope and resource requirements than projects. Often they have the characteristics of an autonomous business, such as Boeing's 787 Dreamliner development or a NASA mission or military defense program. Program managers usually report to senior management or operate as a profit center, similar to any other business within the enterprise. Program management responsibilities can be very broad, going considerably beyond just executing a program, but may include future business development, specific market penetrations, and technology developments. If within the same mission, other sets of activities exist (labeled projects or tasks), the program provides the hierarchical umbrella from which all other task sets flow, as shown in Figure 2.4.

2.4.2 Project

A project is similar in structure and work process, but smaller, especially if the project is a subset of a program. However, the basic definition is the same as for programs: A project is a goal-focused, multidisciplinary undertaking, established to produce specific results within given time and resource limitations. The program manager is responsible for achieving the desired results by providing the proper direction and leadership to the project team, and by facilitating the integration of the various subsystems and components throughout the project organization, including its suppliers and partners.

2.4.3 Task

A task is a clearly defined element of work with specific results, time and resource limitations. Tasks are usually on the lowest order in the program-project-task hierarchy. Usually, tasks center on a single function without extensive multidisciplinary involvement. However, they can include multiple activities. Task leaders are most likely associated with the functional segment of the organization that provides the technical expertise and direction to the task team toward achieving the specific results. Task leaders have dual accountability, first to the project or program manager for budget, schedule, and task interfaces and second to the resource manager for the technical execution of the task and its quality. In an engineering or technology organization, task leaders often carry the title of lead engineer, team leader, or task lead. Task leaders are at the front line of the project organization, building the components that will eventually integrate into the system defined as project.

2.4.4 Committees

A committee is a group of appointed or selected people chartered with a specific assignment, such as investigating issues, reporting their findings and making recommendations. Committees are led by a chairperson. A charter defines the committee's authority and responsibilities. The degree of formality of these charters varies. Depending on the complexity of the assignment, committees are often divided into subcommittees or task forces. Committees are extensively used in today's project organizations to carry out major segments of the project administration and support its management. For example, committees are formed and chartered with new projects evaluation and selection, project planning, vendor selection, project teams organization, strategy formulation, project reviews, and capital equipment appropriations, just to name a few. Most committees are multidisciplinary. At first glance, committees look similar to projects. They have specific responsibilities, objectives, deliverables, resource constraints, and schedules. They are formed by borrowing the specific people needed, on a temporary basis, from various resource organizations. Committees or task forces can also develop into permanent parts of an organization, such as licensing or technology review boards.

The hierarchical relationship of programs, projects, tasks, and committees is illustrated in Figure 2.4. The categorization of these entities is just another subdivision of the overall program into its smaller components, similar to that of a work breakdown structure. Although these definitions are independent of the organizational form of the project or its enterprise, such as matrix or projectized structures, they are being defined by their relative position of the activity set within the overall program. For example, in NASA's space shuttle program, the solid rocket booster engine was only one of many subsystems or components, but the contractor of this development, Thiokol Corporation, organized a whole program division around this component. This example illustrates the somewhat-arbitrary use of this terminology, common in project management. However, this is not an issue as long as the terminology is being used consistently within the enterprise, and the hierarchy of program-project-task is consistent with hierarchy of the overall program scope. That is, the program is the largest entity.

2.5 THE ROLE OF THE PROJECT MANAGER

In a nutshell, the project manager is responsible for delivering results according to established objectives. However, accomplishing these deliverables involves a complex array of responsibilities and skill sets. Stating the project manager's role in one sentence runs the risk of oversimplification. Let's explore the role of the project manager from the context of the job.

Projects have always prompted specialized work environments with skilled people, distinct functional capabilities, and special tools and techniques. With advancing technology, projects became even more specialized and challenging, requiring special skills, equipment, tools, processes, and support systems. Today, project leaders have to deal with innovation, risks, uncertainties, and work processes, often characterized as *nonlinear*, iterative, and highly interfunctional. This complex, unique nature of technology-oriented work has raised the competency level and skill requirements even further.

Yet the traditional managerial skill sets, such as the classic model of *technical, human*, and *conceptual* skills defined by Robert Katz in 1956, are still valid. However, they need to be refocused and fine-tuned for today's business world as many of the traditional principles of management have become obsolete, even for ongoing operations. Few organizations are still structured along stovepipe functions with rigid chain-of-command reporting relations and centralized decision making. Instead, they have moved to flatter, more flexible organizations with power-sharing, distributed decision making, and a more self-directed, team-oriented workforce. This is especially true for project operations, and further accelerated for technology-based projects where managers must be skilled in a broad range of disciplines in order to deal with a wide spectrum of complex challenges:

- Leading multidisciplinary project planning and plan validation
- Negotiating resources and lines of authority
- Staffing, organizing, and building the team organization
- Coping with limited resources and end-date-driven schedules
- Reducing project cycle time

- Dealing with complexity, innovation, risk, and uncertainty
- Managing geographically distributed project activities
- Facilitating multiorganizational collaboration and commitment
- Dealing with personnel training, team development, and general HR issues
- Measuring and tracking project performance against plan, in spite of dynamically evolving progress
- Identifying and dealing with risks and contingencies early in their developments
- Dealing with organizational conflict, politics, and power-sharing
- Building alliances among all stakeholders
- Integrating project subsystems among participating organizations, including support groups, contractors, partners, and consultants
- Recognizing emerging technologies and assessing technology changes and their impact on the ongoing project
- Applying and leveraging technology to benefit project implementation
- Identifying, evaluating, and selecting new project business opportunities
- Managing technology transfer and project integration
- Aligning projects with the overall strategy of the enterprise

Looking at these challenges, with their imbedded risks and complexities, it is hard to imagine a job more difficult than managing technology-intensive projects. Yet, this list is just the beginning of exploring the job of a project manager, and to address these questions: What drives project performance? What organizational environment, structures, policies, interactions of people, and leadership style is most conducive to high team performance? and How do all of these factors shape the project management system and affect overall enterprise performance?

While there is no magic formula that guarantees success in managing technology-based projects, or any project for that matter, research consistently shows that high-performing project managers have specific skills in four categories: (1) technical and job-specific skills; (2) people skills and leadership; (3) administrative skills; and (4) strategic/business skills, which will be discussed in more detail in the next chapter.

2.6 CLASSIFICATION OF PROJECTS

Projects come in different sizes, complexities, time durations, and urgencies for execution. They are associated with different locations, applications, technologies, risks, and many other features. Each project has its own unique characteristics, requiring different management focus, style, and methods for optimal execution. Clearly, a construction project of a missile launch facility is different from a residential housing project or the development of the next smartphone product. One-size management style or execution method does not fit all projects. The ability to group projects into separate classes associated with specific characteristics enables managers to analyze, benchmark, and study projects more meaningful in their own category. It sharpens managerial focus and perspective throughout the project life cycle.

Because of its importance, many different classification schemes have been proposed in the past for categorizing projects along various dimensions. More recently, the *Diamond Model*, developed by Shenhar and Dvir (2007), has gained broad recognition as an effective framework for classifying projects along four major characteristics: (1) complexity, (2) technology, (3) novelty, and (4) pace, each being defined as follows:

- **Complexity.** This dimension focuses on the scope of the project along system lines. The magnitude of complexity is defined in three levels: (1) *assembly*, a collection of elements, components and modules, combined in a single unit, such as a laser printer or car engine; (2) *system*, a collection of interactive elements or subsystems, combined into a system, such as a computer or automobile; and (3) *array*, a collection of systems that perform complex, interrelated functions, such as global positioning system or regional mass transit.
- **Technology.** The magnitude of this dimension is defined in four levels: (1) *low-tech*, relying on existing, well-established technologies; (2) *medium-tech*, using mostly existing technology plus some new technologies or technological features that didn't exist in previous products or services; (3) *high-tech*, technologies that are new to project, but already exist elsewhere (most computer products and defense system developments are in this category); (4) *super high-tech*, the technologies that must be developed for the project. Often, super high-tech technologies do not exist at the beginning, but are needed to complete the project, affecting project risk and management style. Many R&D projects fall into this category.
- **Novelty.** This dimension defines how new a product or service is in the market. It impacts especially the front-end of the project, such as requirements analysis and project definition. Novelty is defined in three categories: (1) *derivative products*, extensions or improvements of existing products or services; (2) *platform products*, new developments, upgrades or replacements of existing products in established markets (e.g., a new car model); and (3) *breakthrough products or services* that are completely new and didn't exist before, such as a microwave oven in the 1940s, or the first Sony Walkman in 1979 or the Rubik's Cube in 1980.
- **Pace.** This dimension defines the urgency at which the project must be executed. Pace affects all facets of project organization and execution management. Pace is defined in four levels: (1) *regular*, projects are not end-date driven and results are not time-critical; (2) *fast/competitive*, project performance depends on timely execution and delivery of results; (3) *time-critical*, projects must be completed on a specific date, otherwise they are failures (e.g., Y2K project or Olympic games

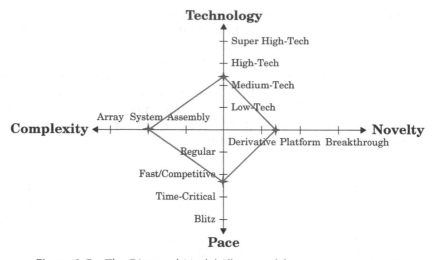

Figure 2.5 The Diamond Model (illustrated for a new car project)

infrastructure); (4) *blitz*, most urgent and time-critical projects, such as disaster responses where speed of crisis resolution is the key success measure.

Classifying projects along the four dimensions helps managers in narrowing the general approach of organizing and executing projects to practices more focused on the specific project at hand. Very few organizations know how to distinguish among their project efforts (Shenhar et al. 2005). These classifications provide a framework for analyzing the specific, most-appropriate means for selecting, organizing, and executing projects of various characteristics. It helps to gain a better understanding of project characteristics and in building more confidence for tailoring project management process and style. The four dimensions of the *Diamond Model* can be graphically displayed as shown in Figure 2.5, which uses a new car model development as an example to illustrate the graphical features.

2.7 PROJECT MANAGEMENT STANDARDS AND GUIDELINES

Ancient monuments, infrastructures, and military campaigns bear witness to projects that were managed quite successfully for thousands of years, apparently without much formality or international standards. At least, that what it seems. However, careful studies reveal that these projects of enormous magnitude and complexity required knowledge of planning, organizing, monitoring, and controlling, and skillful project management in its time. No matter how rudimentary, the basic processes, tools, and techniques of project management were known for a long time and are still the foundation of our contemporary management systems. Yet, it was not until the 1940s that project management began to formalize as a discipline and profession, with slowly emerging procedures, customized mostly to a particular enterprise and application area.

The 1980s and 1990s brought about much change to the way companies do business. Globalization, the Internet, and rapid technological advances drove organizations to work more effectively in all areas. Project management was often seen as an important tool for delivering complex business solutions. It provided a common infrastructure with standardized repeatable methodologies, supporting processes, tools, and measurement systems. Industry and government organizations across the globe began to look for formal procedures and guidelines that ensured consistent project delivery across their enterprises and within their business communities. During this time period, project management standards rapidly emerged from industry and government organizations. However, it was not until 1996 when the first standards aimed at universal project management applications were published, developed in parallel by the Project Management Institute (PMI) and the International Project Management Association (IPMA).

Today, hundreds of project management standards exist. Most of them are focused on specialized applications, such as construction, petroleum, medical, or government sectors.

Three standards emerged with guidelines and rules generally applicable to all projects and programs, by and large acceptable to project management communities across the globe:

1. PMBOK, developed by the Project Management Institute (PMI)
2. PRINCE2, developed by the International Project Management Association (IPMA)
3. ISO 21500, developed by the International Standards Organization (ISO)

Each of these project management standards will be briefly discussed.

2.7.1 PMBOK®—Project Management Body of Knowledge®

Formally known as *A Guide to the Project Management Body of Knowledge®*, or *PMBOK®* for short, this standard was developed by the Project Management Institute (PMI). It was first published as a white paper in 1983, followed by the formal first edition in 1996. PMBOK provides guidelines, rules, and characteristics for project, program, and portfolio management. Following the project life cycle, the standard identifies 47 processes, organized into 5 *process groups* and 10 *knowledge areas*. Since 1999 the *PMBOK® Guide* has been accredited as an American National Standard (ANS) by the American National Standards Institute (ANSI). A newly revised *PMBOK® Guide*, fifth edition, was released in September 2012.

Process Groups

Processes are described in terms of *inputs*, such as documents, specifications, resources, and plans, and outputs, such as products, services, and financial performance. The five process groups are defined as follows:

1. **Initiating.** The process of identifying, selecting, and authorizing a project or program.
2. **Planning.** The process of defining the project and its metrics as a basis for organizing, monitoring, and *controlling* the project toward desired results.
3. **Executing.** The process of leading and managing project personnel and other resources to achieve project objectives.
4. **Monitoring and controlling.** The process of measuring project performance against plan, resolving issues, and taking corrective actions for managing the project to achieve desired objectives.
5. **Closing.** The process of formally closing the project, including customer sign-off, final cost accounting, and personnel reassignment.

Knowledge Areas

Ten knowledge areas cover the discipline of project management. Each of the knowledge areas defines the processes that need to be executed for effectively managing a project across the five major process groups. In essence, each process group relates to several knowledge areas that can be displayed graphically in a 5 × 10 matrix. A description of each knowledge area is provided as follows, excerpted from PMI's *PMBOK Guide* (2012).

1. **Project Integration Management.** Identifies the processes and activities needed to integrate the various elements of project management within the Project Management Process Groups.
2. **Project Scope Management.** Identifies the work needed to accomplish delivery of a product, service, or result-specified features and functions.
3. **Project Time Management.** Identifies the processes required to manage timely completion of the project.
4. **Project Cost Management.** Identifies the processes involved in estimating, budgeting, tracking, and controlling cost according to established project objectives.
5. **Project Quality Management.** Identifies the processes and activities that determine the objectives, policies, and responsibilities for delivering quality results "so that the project will satisfy the needs for which it was undertaken" (PMI PMBOK, 2012).
6. **Project Human Resource Management.** Identifies the processes for selecting, organizing, managing, and leading the project team.

7. **Project Communications Management.** Identifies the processes required to ensure timely and appropriate generation and distribution of information for effective communication among all project stakeholders.
8. **Project Risk Management.** Identifies the processes for planning, identifying, assessing, mitigating, and controlling risks, and to minimize negative impact of risk on project performance.
9. **Project Procurement Management.** Identifies the processes and activities necessary to process and acquire products or services, or results needed from outside the project team, including acquisition planning, source selection, product/service acquisition, and contract administration.
10. **Project Stakeholder Management.** Defines processes and activities necessary to (1) identify stakeholders, (2) plan stakeholder relations, (3) manage stakeholder engagement, and (4) control stakeholder engagement.

2.7.2 PRINCE2®—PRojects IN Controlled Environments

PRINCE2, is a process-based standard, developed by the UK Central Computer and Telecommunications Agency (CCTA). Although the first release in 1989 focused primarily on IT and telecommunication projects, the revised standard published in 1996 is a flexible method aimed at providing guidelines for the management of all types of projects and programs. The latest version of PRINCE2 (2009) was published in two volumes, focusing on (1) projects management professionals who work on projects on a daily basis and (2) projects management professionals who lead or interface with projects as contracting agents or sponsors.

PRINCE2 is based on seven principles that focus on seven themes. Both categories need proper attention for managing the project through the seven phases of its life cycle.

Seven Principles
1. Ensure continued business justification.
2. Learn from experience.
3. Define roles and responsibilities.
4. Manage by stages.
5. Manage by exception.
6. Focus on products.
7. Tailor to suit the project environment.

Seven Themes
1. Business case drives key decision-making in the project.
2. The organization (theme) defines and establishes project roles and responsibilities.

3. Quality focus must be on the project's products and services fit for purpose.
4. Plans are the vehicle for defining how, where, and by whom the project's products will be delivered.
5. Risks are uncertainties that can be either threats or opportunities. Risk management should be proactive, targeting the identification, assessment, and control of uncertainties.
6. Changes should be addressed as part of configuration management, maintaining and controlling the project configuration throughout its life cycle.
7. Progress is an important measurement to monitor and compare actual project performance against the planned values.

Seven Processes

1. **Starting up a project.** Appointing the project manager and team members, defining the project objectives, and planning for the next stage (initiation).
2. **Initiating a project.** Building on the startup process and the business case, the project must be planned to enable proper tracking and controlling over the project life cycle.
3. **Directing a project.** Includes all activities for tracking and managing the project through its life cycle, including reviewing progress against the plan, dealing with issues, and tacking corrective actions.
4. **Controlling a stage.** Projects should be broken into stages that are defined by work packages. Each stage should be individually monitored, managed, and controlled. Project issues should be captured and managed, preferably at the stage level before escalating the issues.
5. **Managing stage boundaries.** Defines the communications, data, and technology transfer processes between and among the project stages, including the key interface personnel.
6. **Managing product delivery.** Focuses on the end product/service and its timely delivery. Effective customer communication are critical to successful product delivery.
7. **Closing a project.** Includes formal processes for closing the project, including final cost accounting, reporting, personnel reassignment, and post-project review.

The PRINCE2 standard is somewhat similar to PMBOK in its focus on project process and life cycle stages. However, in a detailed comparison, PRINCE2 is different and more intricate than PMBOK. Some of the key differences and features of PRINCE2 are the (1) focus on business justification, (2) special attention to project work and team organization, (3) emphasis on product planning, (4) division of the project execution into separately controlled stages, and (5) flexibility of applying the standard to various levels of a project.

2.7.3 ISO 21500—Guidance on Project Management

Developed by the International Organization for Standardization (ISO) and released in 2012, ISO 21500 provides guidelines, rules, and characteristics for project, program, and portfolio management. It can be used by any type of organization, including public, private, or community organizations, and for any type of project, irrespective of complexity, size, or duration. ISO 21500 is the first in a series of planned project management standards. It is designed to align with related International Standards such as ISO 10006 *(Quality Management Systems—Guidelines for Quality Management in Projects)*, ISO 10007 *(Quality Management Systems—Guidelines for Configuration Management)*, ISO 31000 *(Risk Management—Principles and Guidelines)*, and several sector-specific standards in industries such as aerospace and IT. ISO 21500 is also consistent with both PMBOK and PRINC2, and almost identical to PMBOK regarding in structure and context, including in paralleling PMBOK's 5 processing groups and 10 knowledge areas.

Specifically, ISO 21500 is structured along the PMBOK's process-based framework:

- **Five process groups:** (1) initiation, (2) planning, (3) implementing, (4) controlling, and (5) closing.
- **Ten subject groups:** (1) integration, (2) stakeholder, (3) scope, (4) resource (HR), (5) time, (6) cost, (7) risk, (8) quality, (9) procurement, and (10) communication. The subject group identifies the processes.

Except for minor differences, such as the sequencing of the subject groups and use of "resources" instead of "human resources," ISO 21500 is clearly based on the *PMBOK® Guide*, which was discussed in the previous section.

Taken together, these standards provide guidelines, rules, and tools to the professional business community for managing projects, programs, and portfolios consistently and effectively. They also provide a common language. Currently, PMBOK is most widely used throughout the world. However, many other standards are also effectively used and are beneficial for specialized applications in their professional communities.

As project management evolves further and gains more formal acceptance as a profession throughout the world, project management standards will continue to expand and be updated. Karl Best, secretary of the ISO project committee, said, "In an increasingly global economy project managers need guidance to help them understand the basic principles of managing projects."

2.8 KEY POINTS, LESSONS, AND CONCLUSIONS

The following key points were made in this chapter:

- Project management is defined as the art and science of achieving desired objectives within given resource constraints, including time.
- The *quadruple constraint* refers to time, cost, deliverables, and customer satisfaction. It states that projects should be managed to produce specific deliverables or results within given resource budgets and schedule limitations, all resulting in customer satisfaction.
- Projects have finite life cycles with distinct phases or stages, such as initiating, planning, executing, and closing.
- Programs, projects and tasks are similar in context and structure (e.g., a task is a miniature program). But, within the same organization, programs are usually larger in scope and resource requirements than projects, and tasks are the smallest piece of the project's work.
- Committees are similar to projects in context, but their structure and work process is usually less formal and more dynamic than projects.
- Project management standards provide guidelines for establishing a common infrastructure with standardized repeatable methodologies, supporting processes, tools, and measurement systems throughout an enterprise or within an industry.
- Project management standards are important management tools for delivering complex business solutions.
- Among the many application-specific and industry-specific project management standards and guidelines, PMBOK® is most commonly accepted by the project management community worldwide.
- The latest addition of project management standards is ISO 21500, which is part of a family of technology-focused management standards.

2.9 QUESTIONS FOR DISCUSSION AND EXERCISES

1. How can the project life cycle model with its defined stages help in organizing and initial planning of your project?
2. Using the "quadruple constraint," define "project performance" (write a statement) for a project you're familiar with (or use the Kindle product development mentioned in the lead-in scenario at the beginning of the chapter). Write the statement for two separate situations: (1) reviewing project performance at midpoint of the project life cycle and (2) at the end of the project life cycle. Discuss your definition with your group.
3. Why do organizations make distinctions between projects and programs?
4. Discuss the significance of the graphics in Figure 2.3 for project management.

5. What are the benefits of having a project management a monly accepted throughout your industry?
6. Why are there so many different standards for project mana
7. Why do some managers resist accepting project management ₋ards? Do you see any limitations or drawbacks to these standards?
8. From the description given in this chapter, which of the three project management standards would you feel most comfortable using? Why?

2.10 *PMBOK®* REFERENCES AND CONNECTIONS

This chapter introduced PMI's PMBOK standard with its 5 *processing groups* and 10 *knowledge areas*. The general structure and content of the PMBOK is a subject area often tested and should be studied in preparation for the PMP® exam. Further, the project life cycle and program-project-task hierarchy are concepts that should be studied in preparation for PMP® certification.

INTERNET LINKS AND RESOURCES

Amazon Investors Relations. 2013. Website for Letters to Shareholders, Annual Reports and Proxy Statements 1999 to date; http://phx.corporate-ir.net/phoenix .zhtml?c=97664&p=irol-reportsannual

Gasik, Stanislaw. 2013. Analysis of ISO 21500 and Its Comparison with PMBoK® Guide; Sybena Consulting, www.sybena.pl/iso21500pmbok_ang.htm#_Toc294026942

International Organization for Standardization. 2013. "New ISO Standard on Project Management," www.iso.org/iso/home/news_index/news_archive/news.htm? refid=Ref1662

PRINCE2 (official site) www.prince-officialsite.com/

Project Management Institute (PMI), www.pmi.org/default.aspx

Wikipedia. "A Guide to the Project Management Body of Knowledge." http:// en.wikipedia.org/wiki/A_Guide_to_the_Project_Management_Body_of_Knowledge

Wikipedia. "Project Management." http://en.wikipedia.org/wiki/Project_management

REFERENCES AND ADDITIONAL READINGS

Adams, J., and S. Barndt. 1988. "Behavioral Implications of the Project Life Cycle." Chapter 10, *Project Management Handbook* (Cleland & King, eds.). Hoboken, NJ: Wiley.

Amazon.com. 2012. *2012 Annual Report*. Seattle, Washington: Amazon.com, Inc.

Colby, S., and B. Gothard. 2002. "The Enterprise Project Life Cycle—Integrating Project Management into the Business." *Proceedings, PMI Seminars & Symposium*.

Eskerod, P., and B. Blichfeldt. 2005. Managing Team Entrees and Withdrawals During the Project Life Cycle." *International Journal of Project Management* 23(7) (October): 495–503.

Gido, J., and J. P. Clements. 2012. *Successful Project Management*. Mason, OH: South-Western Cengage Learning.

Hormozi, A., R. McMinn, and O. Nzeogwu. 2000. "The Project Life Cycle: The Termination Phase." *SAM Advanced Management Journal* 65(1): 45–54.

International Organization for Standardization. 2012. *ISO 21500 Guidance on Project Management*, ISO Publishing.

Elizabeth Gasiorowski-Denis, ed. 2012. *New ISO Standard on Project Management*. Geneva, Switzerland: International Organization for Standardization Publishing. www.iso.org/iso/home/news_index/news_archive/news.htm?refid=Ref1662.

Kerzner, H. 2013. *Project Management: A Systems Approach to Planning, Scheduling, and Controlling*. Chapter 3: "Organizational Structure." Hoboken, NJ: John Wiley & Sons.

Kloppenborg, T. 2012. *Contemporary Project Management*. Mason, OH: South-Western Publishing.

Mantel, S., J. Meredith, S. Shafer, and M. Sutton. 2011. *Project Management in Practice*. Hoboken, NJ: John Wiley & Sons.

Portman, H. 2009. *Prince2 in Practice*. Zalthommel, Netherlands: Van Haran Publishing.

Project Management Institute (PMI). 2013. *A Guide to the Project Management Body of Knowledge (PMBOK® Guide)*. Newtown Square, PA: Project Management Institute.

Shenhar, A., and D. Dvir. 2007. *Reinventing Project Management: The Diamond Approach to Successful Growth and Innovation*. Cambridge, MA: Harvard Business School Press.

Shenhar, A., D. Dvir, D. Milosevic, J. Mulenburg, P. Patanakul, R. Reilly, A. Sage, B. Sauser, S. Srivannaboon, J. Stefanovic, and H. Thamhain. 2005. "Toward a NASA-specific Project Management Framework." *Engineering Management Journal* 17(4) (December): 8–16.

Van Haren, I. 2013. *Global Standards and Publications*. Zalthommel, Netherlands: Van Haren Publishing.

Chapter 3

The Effective Project Manager: Skills, Values and Agility

PROJECT MANAGEMENT SKILLS EMPHASIZED IN PMI'S ANNUAL REPORT

Under the topic of *Enhancing Business Value around the World*, PMI focuses on the critical importance of effective project management skills for competing successfully in today's uncertain business landscape. As stated by Peter Monkhouse, chair, 2012 PMI Board of Directors: "Project professionals must surpass expectations of the past—delivering results and value that achieve strategic objectives while also positioning their organizations to outpace the competition and secure future gains. And they're challenged with achieving all these objectives with fewer resources, tighter deadlines and more demanding requirements." Four skill sets seem especially critical according to *Career Central*, PMI's hub for knowledge, connections and resources: (1) basic project management skills, (2) business acumen, (3) emotional intelligence and (4) assertiveness. Field research validates the importance of these essential skills and professional preparedness, as explained by Mark Langley, president and CEO of PMI: "Our research indicates that organizations that keep a sharp focus on fundamental project management practices are realizing huge results. By optimizing strengths and improving on weaknesses in the core project management practices, an organization puts far fewer dollars at risk for each project."

3.1 PROJECT-BASED ORGANIZATIONAL CULTURES AND VALUES

Project management is different, and in many ways more challenging from managing ongoing operations, as discussed in chapter 1. These differences have been recognized by professional organizations, such as the Project Management Institute for several decades, who also emphasize the increasingly demanding business environment and need for special skills. Although the recognition of project management as a profession is relatively new in comparison to the thousands of years of practice, project management has always had its unique challenges, which have become more intense with increased competition and dynamics of our global business environment.

Many of these challenges relate to the multidisciplinary nature of projects and the need to organize, coordinate, integrate, and manage activities across the enterprise without much formal authority. The people who have to work together on the project come from different organizational units, reporting to superiors with different management styles and work processes that conform to standards and norms quite different throughout the enterprise, its partners, contractors, and collaborating communities. Unifying the project team across these different cultures and values is one of the biggest challenges faced by project leaders, yet a critical condition for managing any cross-functional project.

Yet organizational culture is one of the more difficult concepts to understand or define. In spite of being widely discussed in the literature it remains an elusive and hazy concept (Gaynor 2013). Nevertheless, we can describe organizational culture when we experience it in terms of people interaction, shared practices, shared believes, values and behavior, or, more simply put, *"It's the way we do things around here."* Culture affects everything from work standards, norms and ethics, to motivation, innovation and tolerance for conflict and risk-taking. In essence, organizational culture defines the work environment and is a key variable in the complex array that determines managerial leadership effectiveness. This is an important connection to managerial skill requirements and effectiveness.

The cultural *impact on leadership style* has two dimensions:

1. The project leader's ability to fine-tune skill sets most suitable for the given multicultural environment
2. The leader's ability to create his/her own project culture for the team working across the enterprise, including contractors and other support organizations

Effective communications and team involvement are some of the most critical tools for developing a unified team culture of shared values, norms, and operational rules (Dennison 2012, Thamhain 2013).

3.2 MEASURING MANAGERIAL PERFORMANCE

Obviously, competency at all levels is vital to project success (Belassi and Turkel 1996; Crawford 2000). However, measuring project performance is complex and challenging, and managers at all levels struggle with defining relevant performance measures, especially for technology-intensive undertakings. Yet, we need some framework for defining project performance before we can address the issues of skill requirements, skill set development, and resource allocation for training, work process support, compensation, and promotion. The intricate mix of timelines, resource allocation, multidisciplinary contributions, value perception, and success criteria often makes it difficult to establish meaningful measures of project performance and to apply them consistently, fairly, and equitably throughout the enterprise. These challenges exist especially in flatter, hierarchically less structured organizations, and in situations where several teams contribute to the overall success or failure of a multistage development with its ultimate success depending on factors not under the control of these teams.

3.2.1 Conventional, Traditional Approach to Measuring Project Performance

In spite of these challenges and the cultural and philosophical differences among managers, some framework for measuring project performance has been established in virtually every organization that executes projects. This performance metric includes at least four basic measures, often referred to as *quadruple constraint:*

1. Schedule-based measures
2. Budget/resource-based measures
3. Technical performance-based measures
4. Stakeholder satisfaction-based measures

These measures are the project performance baseline for many of the project management standards, such as PMBOK (2013), PRINCE2 (2012), and ISO 21500 (2012). Traditionally, these measures were considered sufficient for tracking project performances. However, their adequacy for fully and correctly assessing project performance has been argued by managers for some time.

3.2.2 Contemporary Assessment of Project Performance

In spite of the widely published and accepted *quadruple constraint* of project performance, many project managers insist that in today's complex business environment additional variables are needed to define project performance and success, especially when we consider projects as strategic tools for creating economic value and competitive advantage (Shenhar and Dvir 2007, Maltz et al. 2012). These contemporary concepts suggest that project leaders must take on full responsibility for business results, linking projects to business strategy. That is, aligning projects with the goals of the organization

(Shenhar et al. 2007). This contemporary view suggests four distinct dimensions of project performance and success:

1. Project efficiency (including schedule, budget, and technical performance)
2. Customer impact (including stakeholder satisfaction)
3. Business/enterprise success
4. Preparing for the future (business survival and growth)

The importance of each of these performance measures varies with the strategic time frame considered for the project and its impact on the enterprise as graphically shown in Figure 3.1. Ultimately, each organization can define its own measures, suitable and unique to its specific business environment. This approach is similar to the traditional approach of measuring project performance. In either case, these broadly defined parameters or dimensions provide the basic framework and scope for assessing project performance relevant to the specific business environment. They also provides a framework for developing operational guidelines for managing the various project stages, such as planning, start-up, and execution, and for assessing the effectiveness of these operational systems.

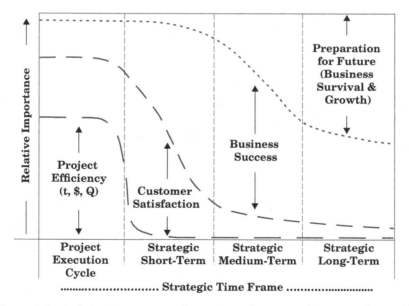

Figure 3.1   Relative importance of project performance measures, short and long term

3.3 SKILL REQUIREMENTS FOR MANAGING TECHNOLOGY PROJECTS

Because of its multidisciplinary nature, as well as resource and power sharing, project management always required more diverse skill sets and the ability to manage with little or no formal authority. These requirements increased further over the past three decades as organizations became flatter, more agile, and more cross-functionally aligned. As a result, many of the principles of conventional management theory and practice, such as clear chain-of-command reporting relations, centralized decision making, and a reasonable predictable business environment, were challenged or became obsolete. Managers who evolve with these contemporary organizations must confront untried problems to handle their complex tasks. Specifically focusing on project management, these new leaders must not only be effective in planning, organizing, and integrating complex, multidisciplinary activities, but also move across various organizational lines, gaining services from personnel not reporting directly to them. They must build multidisciplinary teams into cohesive groups and deal with a variety of networks, such as line departments, staff groups, team members, clients, and senior management; each has different interests, expectations, and charters. They also have to cope with constant and rapid change of technology, markets, regulations, and socioeconomic factors. To get results, managers in technology-based project organizations must relate socially as well as technically. They must understand the culture and value system of the organization in which they work (Badawy 2007, Shenhar and Thamhain 1994, Thamhain 2013a). The days of the manager who gets by with only technical expertise or pure administrative skills are gone.

All of this has implications on managerial skill requirements. In today's project organizations, effective leadership involves a whole spectrum of skills and abilities: clear direction and guidance; ability to plan and elicit commitments; communication skills; assistance in problem solving; dealing effectively with managers and support personnel across functional lines often with little or no formal authority; information-processing skills, the ability to collect and filter relevant data valid for decision making in a dynamic environment; and the ability to integrate individual demands, requirements, and limitations into decisions that benefit the total project. It further involves the manager's ability to resolve intergroup conflicts and to build multifunctional teams. This wide spectrum of skill sets can be grouped into four general categories:

1. Technical or job-specific skills
2. Operational and administrative skills
3. People skills and leadership
4. Strategic/business skills

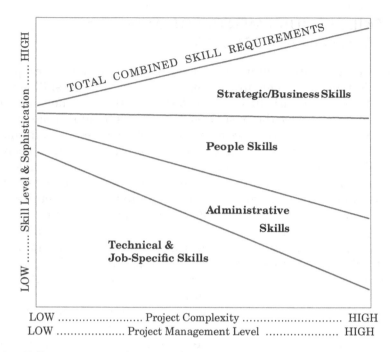

Figure 3.2   Skill requirements change with project management level and complexity

Although there are many ways of organizing the fast array of project management skills, these categories are consistent with other established models, such as Shenhar and Dvir (2011) or Cicmil et al. (2006). They also align with contemporary competency constructs, such as PMI's *Project Management Maturity Model, PM3* (Crawford 2007).

3.3.1 Technical or Job-Specific Skills

This includes the specialized knowledge, analytical ability and proficiency of using job-related tools and techniques; in short, the skill sets required to perform effectively within the assigned discipline, including guiding project personnel and activities toward desired results. However, it is not necessary that project leaders have all the technical expertise to direct the multidisciplinary activities single-handed. This is virtually impossible, especially for technologically more complex or larger projects. It is essential, however, that project leaders understand the technologies and their trends, the markets, and the business environment, so they can communicate effectively with their team members and other stakeholders, assessing risks and cost/schedule/performance tradeoffs, and search for integrated solutions and optimized project performance.

3.3.2 Operational and Administrative Skills

These skill sets involve effective planning, organizing, and administrating the project execution. They include the tools, techniques, and administrative procedures of scheduling, budgeting, staffing, project tracking, performance evaluations, and control techniques, plus information-processing skills and the ability to collect and filter relevant data for decision making. Depending on the project organization and its alignment with the overall enterprise business, these administrative/operational skills also include translating senior management directives and strategic objectives into specific operational plans at the project organization. While all of these skills are important for overall project management effectiveness, it is not always necessary or desirable for the project leaders to get personally involved in the administrative detail. Other resource departments or the project management office (PMO) can be effective in providing administrative support. This frees the project leader from time-consuming administrative tasks.

3.3.3 People Skills and Leadership

Effective leadership involves a whole spectrum of skills and abilities: clear direction and guidance, interactive planning and eliciting commitments, communication skills, assistance in problem solving, interfacing with managers and support personnel across functional lines, resolving intergroup conflicts and building multifunctional teams. It also involves the ability to integrate individual demands, requirements, and limitations into decisions that benefit the overall project. These skills are grounded in the well-known concepts of organizational behavior, motivation, communication, personnel management, and leadership.

3.3.4 Strategic/Business Skills

These skills involve the ability of seeing the project as part of the enterprise, directing and monitoring its overall performance. It includes understanding the nature of the industry, having a general manager's perspective and a business sense. These skills relate to policy decisions, strategic thinking, long-term objectives, and the ability to align the project organization with the overall enterprise and its strategies. These skills are critical for shaping organizational directions and synergizing the contributions of various organizational resources. Knowledge in the area of systems theory, strategic planning, and general business management provides the foundation and supporting tools of this skill area.

3.3.5 The Project Managers Skills Inventory

A more detailed breakdown for each of the four skill sets is provided in Table 3.1, which can be used as a tool for assessing actual skill requirements and proficiencies. For example, a list such as the following could be developed, for individuals or teams, to assess for each skill component, using different assessment criteria as needed:

- Identifying skill deficiencies and development needs
- Assessing the criticality of certain skill sets
- Assessing competencies for position staffing
- Identifying support requirements
- Identifying training and development activities
- Assessing effectiveness of training and development programs

Table 3.1   Project Management Skills Inventory

Technical or Job-Specific Skills	
• Ability to manage the technical work • Aiding problem solving • Analytical skills • Communicating with project personnel • Facilitating project integration • Facilitating tradeoffs • Fostering innovative environment • Guiding/directing project personnel • Integrating technical, business, and human objectives • System perspective • Technical credibility • Understanding and applying work-related tools and techniques • Understanding customer environment and application • Understanding engineering tools and support methods • Understanding market and business environment • Understanding technology and trends	• Unifying the technical team • Working with contractors, customers, and partner organizations • Fostering innovative environment • Guiding/directing project personnel • Integrating technical, business, and human objectives • System perspective • Technical credibility • Understanding and applying work-related tools and techniques • Understanding customer environment and application • Understanding engineering tools and support methods • Understanding market and business environment • Understanding technology and trends • Unifying the technical team • Working with contractors, customers and partner organizations

People Skills and Leadership	
• Ability to manage in unstructured work environment • Action-orientation, self-starter • Aiding group decision making • Assisting in problem solving • Building alliances, coalitions; cooperation • Building multidisciplinary teams • Building priority image • Clarity of management direction • Clear team direction and guidance • Communicating (written and oral) • Creating personnel involvement at all levels	• Eliciting commitment and collaboration • Gaining credibility, trust, and respect • Gaining upper management support and commitment • Human resource management • Interfacing among project team, resource groups, contractors, partners, and customer • Managing conflict • Motivating people • Project leadership • Understanding professional needs • Understanding the organization • Vision and ability to inspire others
Operational and Administrative Skills	
• Attracting and holding quality people • Budgeting and budget control • Communicating effectively (orally and written) • Cost modeling and estimating • Defining clear objectives • Delegating effectively • Estimating and negotiating resources • Information processing • Managing changes • Measuring work status, progress, and performance	• Organizing project team • Planning and organizing multifunctional programs • Project management tools and techniques, including IT tools • Project tracking and reporting • Risk management • Scheduling multidisciplinary activities • Translating management directives into project plan • Understanding policies and operating procedures • Working with other organizations
Strategic/Business Skills	
• Aligning project organization with enterprise and its strategies • Dealing with risks and uncertainties • Entrepreneurial thinking • General manager's perspective • Leveraging resources	• Optimizing project-derived long-term benefits • Strategic thinking and decision making • Synergizing project and enterprise results • Understanding business environment

3.4 HOW LEARNABLE ARE THESE SKILLS?

Formal studies investigating the learnability of project management skills reveal some good news. Many of the skills needed to perform effectively in project management are learnable (Gido and Clements 2012, Morse and Babcock 2013). Several of my field studies (2009a, 2013) show the learnability on average as high as 94 percent, mostly on the job. In fact, we find that 85 percent of all project management skills are derived from experience.[1] Three-quarters are developed strictly by experiential learning, while one-quarter comes from more specific work-related methods such as observations, formal on-the-job training, upper management coaching, and job rotation (Thamhain 2009a, 2013a). Second to experiential learning, skills can be developed by reading professional literature, such as books, magazines, journals, research papers, as well as listening to audio and viewing video on related subjects. A third source for skill development exists via professional activities such as seminars, professional meetings, and special workshops. The fourth distinct category for managerial skill development consists of formal schooling. In addition, managers identify special sources, such as mentoring, job changes, and special organizational development activities, for building technology management skills.

Taken together, research verifies that project management skills, even in technology-based environments, are indeed learnable, and "project managers can be developed"[2] (Thamhain 2013b). The findings are not only encouraging to project management professionals at all levels but also important for designing management training and development programs, allocating resources, and as a framework for comparing the effectiveness of various training methods.

3.5 TRANSITIONING FROM INDIVIDUAL CONTRIBUTOR TO PROJECT MANAGEMENT

How do you get on a project management career path? Or, looking outward from the enterprise, how can managers identify people with project management potential? In either case, the process is more of an art than a science.

---

[1]The percentile was determined by asking 355 technical managers to indicate for the skill inventory shown in Table 3.1, (1) what training methods helped to develop each skill, and (2) how effective was the method in developing these skills relative to other methods employed. The data were evaluated to determine the contribution made by each of the five methods to leadership, technical, and administrative skill development. The distribution of sources was somewhat similar for all three skills. Figure 1 presents an aggregated view of the sources for managerial skill development. For detailed reporting of the study see Thamhain (1992).

[2]This conclusion was reached during a study of 300 managers in 63 technology-based companies (action research between 2000 and 2011). These managers stated almost unanimously in one form or another that technical management skills don't just happen by chance but are systematically developed through formal and informal methods.

However, the indicators are somewhat similar on either side. Professionals aspiring to a career in project management can enhance their chances for management attention and organizational support by taking initiatives in seeking out project-related responsibilities and by engaging in professional activities, such as project management society meetings and conferences, and by enrolling in relevant educational programs.

One of the key criteria for success, stressed by newly promoted project managers and management veterans alike, is the individual's desire to become a project manager. This desire seems to have a positive effect on many of the criteria necessary for transitioning into a project management and up the managerial ladder.[3] Yet despite this favorable field observation, personal desire alone is not enough to gain a promotion. In the final analysis, personal competence and organizational needs are the deciding factors. People who receive promotions usually meet five key requirements:

1. **They are competent in their current assignments.** An individual contributor must master the duties and responsibilities of the current position, must have the respect of his or her colleagues, and receive favorable recommendations from the supervisor.

2. **They have the capacity to take on greater responsibility.** The person must demonstrate the ability to handle larger assignments that have new and more challenging responsibilities. Good time management, the willingness to take on extra assignments, and the expressed desire to advance toward a management assignment are usually good indicators of a person's readiness for advancement.

3. **They have prepared for the new assignments.** A new management assignment requires new skills and knowledge. Candidates who have prepared themselves through courses, seminars, on-the-job training, professional activities, and special assignments will have the edge. Managers perceive such initiatives as evidence that a candidate is committed to the new career path, is willing to develop new skills, and wants to go the extra distance.

4. **They are good matches with organizational needs.** The candidate's ambitions, desire, and capabilities have to match both the current and long-range needs of the firm. Obviously, a new job opening can create an immediate opportunity for advancement, but many companies make detailed, long-range plans for their managerial staffing needs. They also encourage managers to identify and develop future managers. In such environments, people with management ambitions must be recognized early as qualified candidates. Companies then may help them develop management

---

[3]This association was verified statistically using Kendall's correlation: the association between personal desire to become a manager and actual promotion was $\tau = 0.35$; between personal desire and subsequent managerial performance was $\tau = 0.30$. Both statistics are significant at a confidence level of 92 percent or better.

skills with training and special job assignments. When the need for a new manager arises, the company often selects from the pool of prequalified candidates.

5. **They have an aptitude for management.** Taking an integrated look at the qualifications for transitioning into management, we see that the first four criteria are based on behavior in a known environment and on the assumption that the candidate will adapt to the new management situation. If these criteria are met, higher-level managers will have a lot of confidence in the candidate. However, there is yet no guarantee that the candidate will actually perform well in the new assignment. It is quite difficult to evaluate the candidate's readiness for the new challenges of leadership, power-sharing, personnel administration, change, and conflict management. Therefore, technical contributors who want to be considered for leadership positions must show actions and behavior at work that reflect strong aptitudes for management.

3.5.1 Managerial Aptitude Testing

Because of these complexities and intricate sets of variables, I personally do not believe in formal aptitude testing via questionnaires as a tool for selecting project managers. However, for self-testing by individuals, answering a set of aptitude questions can provide some insight and perspective on the person's desires, likes, dislikes, strength, and weaknesses toward project management and help in the process of self-assessment and career development. Such a questionnaire is shown in Table 3.2, designed for project management aptitude self-testing in a technology-based product development environment. To be useful, this sample questionnaire needs to be modified to reflect the specific situation for which managerial aptitude is to be tested.

3.6 IMPLICATIONS FOR SENIOR MANAGEMENT

As more organizations adopt project management across the globe, a talent gap has developed. According to studies by the Project Management Institute (PMI), "There are simply not enough trained or experienced project managers to go around." According to Dr. Edwin Andrews, former director of academic and educational programs at PMI, the issue is further aggravated by the fact that educational institutions are not graduating enough project-skilled professionals to replace even those who retire from the profession. He explains further that "unlike more traditional specializations, such as finance or IT, project management encompasses an array of skill sets spanning marketing, finance, operations, technology and other areas, including critical and strategic thinking, negotiating, networking, problem-solving and working in a culturally diverse environment."

Table 3.2 Questionnaire for Project Management Aptitude Testing (for individual self-testing only)

Score 1–10	Project Management Aptitude Test Use a 10-point scale to indicate your agreement or disagreement with each of the statements (1 = strong disagreement; 10 = strong agreement)
Personal Desire to Be a Manager	
_____	1. Managing people is professionally more interesting and stimulating to me than solving technical problems.
_____	2. I am interested and willing to assume new and greater responsibilities.
_____	3. I am willing to invest considerable time and effort into developing managerial skills.
_____	4. I have an MBA (or am working intensely on it).
_____	5. I am prepared to update my management knowledge and skills via continuing education.
_____	6. I have discussed the specific responsibilities, challenges, and skills required with manager.
_____	7. I have defined my specific career goals and mapped out a plan for achieving them.
_____	8. I would be willing to change my professional area of specialty for an advanced managerial opportunity.
_____	9. Managerial and business challenges are more interesting and stimulating to me than technical challenges.
_____	10. Achieving a managerial promotion within the next few years is a top priority, very important to the satisfaction of my professional needs.
People Skills	
_____	1. I feel at ease communicating with people from other technical and administrative departments.
_____	2. I can effectively solve conflict over technical and personal issues, and don't mind getting involved.
_____	3. I can work with all levels of the organization.
_____	4. I am a good liaison to other departments and outside organizations.
_____	5. I enjoy socializing with people.
_____	6. I can persuade people to do things that they initially don't want to do.
_____	7. I can get commitment from people, even though they don't report directly to me.

(Continued)

Table 3.2   (Continued)

_____	8. People enjoy working with me and follow my suggestions.
_____	9. I am frequently asked by my colleagues for my opinion and for presenting ideas to upper management.
_____	10. I think, the majority of people in my department would select me as team leader.
Technical Knowledge and Job Skills	
_____	1. I understand the technological trends in both my area of responsibility and the business environment of my company.
_____	2. I understand the product applications, markets, and economic conditions of my business area.
_____	3. I can effectively communicate with my technical colleagues from other disciplines.
_____	4. I can unify a technical team toward project objectives and can facilitate group decision making.
_____	5. I have a systems perspective in my area of technical work.
_____	6. I have technical credibility with my colleagues.
_____	7. I can use the latest design techniques and engineering tools.
_____	8. I recognize work with potential for technological breakthrough early in its development.
_____	9. I can measure work/project status and technical performance of other people on my team.
_____	10. I can integrate the technical work of my team members.
Operational and Administrative Skills	
_____	1. I don't mind administrative duties.
_____	2. I am familiar with techniques for planning, scheduling, budgeting, organizing, and personnel administration, and can perform them well.
_____	3. I can estimate and negotiate resources effectively.
_____	4. I can measure and report work status and performance.
_____	5. I find policies and procedures useful as guidelines for my activities.
_____	6. I have no problem delegating work even through I could do it myself even quicker.
_____	7. I don't mind writing reports and preparing for meetings, and I do it well.

_____	8. I can hand change requirements and work interruptions effectively.
_____	9. I am good in organizing social events.
_____	10. I can work effectively with administrative support groups throughout the company.
Business Acumen	
_____	1. I would be good at directing the activities of my department toward the overall company objectives.
_____	2. I am productive.
_____	3. I enjoy long-range planning and find the time to do it.
_____	4. I am willing to take risks to explore opportunities.
_____	5. I feel comfortable working in dynamic environments associated with uncertainty and change.
_____	6. I would enjoy running my own company.
_____	7. I consider myself more of an entrepreneur than an innovator.
_____	8. In social functions, I tend to get involved more in business discussions rather than technical discussions.
_____	9. I enjoy being evaluated, in part, on my contributions to my company's business environments.
_____	10. I have been more right than wrong in predicting the business environment
_____	**Total Test Score (Divided by 5) = Normalized Score** [_____]

These skills cannot be gained readily through traditional training or educational programs. Companies must go beyond the traditional methods of developing managerial talent. Business leaders must recognize the highly multidisciplinary and cross-functional nature of skill requirements, and must establish policies that integrate continuing professional education and project management skill development into the business process, as well as individual performance appraisal and award system consistent with these objectives. For these personnel developments to succeed, _interdisciplinary collaboration_ is vital. Project management is multifunctional, and therefore project management development programs must be, too. Yet this is often a challenge in an enterprise environment of shared resources and power that causes natural tension, anxieties and organizational conflict over cross-functional activities such as project management training and support systems. New ways and strategies have to be found to deal with these issues. An important role of senior management is to provide the leadership and resources for developing project management professionals and for establishing the needed enterprise support systems.

3.7 SUMMARY OF KEY POINTS AND CONCLUSIONS

The following key points were made in this chapter:

- The multidisciplinary nature of projects, operating across different organizational cultures, creates special challenges and requires more sophisticated managerial skills than traditional forms of management.
- Organizational culture is one of the more difficult concepts to understand or define. Yet, it affects everything from work standards, norms and ethics, to motivation, innovation, and tolerance for conflict and risk-taking.
- Project leaders must fine-tune their skills for most effectively interacting with multi-cultural environments. However, they also have the ability to create their own project team culture across the enterprise.
- Project performance measures include at least four basic dimensions, often referred to as quadruple constraint: (1) schedule-based measures, (2) budget/resource-based measures, (3) technical performance-based measures, and (4) stakeholder satisfaction-based measures. More recent approaches to project performance include additional measures of (5) business success and (6) preparation for future business survival and growth, which extend the performance horizon beyond the actual project execution cycle.
- The wide spectrum of project management skill sets can be grouped unto four general categories: (1) technical or job-specific skills, (2) operational and administrative skills, (3) people skills and leadership, and (4) strategic/business skills.
- The skill inventory of Table 3.1 can be used for assessing skill requirements and proficiencies, such as identifying skill deficiencies and development needs, assessing competencies for position staffing, and assessing effectiveness of training and development programs.
- Most of the project management skills are learnable, primarily experientially. Furthermore, experiential learning can be augmented and accelerated by professional readings, seminars, meetings, and special workshops, as well as formal schooling.
- Chances of advancement to a project management or team leadership position are enhanced by five conditions: (1) candidates are competent in their current assignments, (2) candidates have the capacity to take on greater responsibility, (3) candidates have prepared for the new assignments, such as taken courses, on-the-job training and special assignments, (4) candidates are good matches with organizational needs, and (5) candidates have an aptitude for management.

- Questionnaire-based aptitude testing might not be the best tool for selecting project managers. However, for self-testing by individuals, answering aptitude questions can provide some insight and perspective on the person's desires, likes, dislikes, strength, and weaknesses toward project management and may help in self-assessment and career development.
- The highly multidisciplinary and cross-functional nature of project management skill development must be recognized. *Interdisciplinary collaboration* is vital for personnel and organization development efforts to succeed.

3.8 QUESTIONS FOR DISCUSSION

1. Discuss the differences between project environments and functional resource environments, and how these differences affect the managerial skill sets required for effective role performance.
2. Discuss the differences between high-tech and low-tech project environments, and how these differences affect the managerial skill sets required for effective role performance.
3. Select a project environment that your discussion group is familiar with (you could also select a common case study or a news story such as the Boston Big Dig or Boeing 787). Define your team (or subteam) responsibility. Then discuss the performance measures that (a) you as a project leader feel comfortable to be evaluated against by your superiors, (b) you as a project leader would use to evaluate your team, and (c) you as a team would feel comfortable to be evaluated against by your project manager.
4. How would you prepare as an individual contributor for a career in project management? What actions would you take to enhance your chances of "being discovered" as a candidate for advancement into a project management position?
5. What are the benefits, challenges, limitations, and issues of taking a long-term (strategic) look at project performance beyond the project execution cycle?
6. Discuss the importance of each of the four general skill categories of (1) technical or job-specific skills, (2) operational and administrative skills, (3) people skills and leadership, and (4) strategic/business skills. Also, discuss how you could acquire or improve each skill set, and how you could leverage organizational resources to support any of these skills.
7. How would you use the skill inventory in Table 3.1 to identify skill deficiencies and development needs for your project managers?
8. Use the test shown in Table 3.2 to determine your aptitude for project management. (a) How do you interpret the final score points? (b) What conclusions and lessons could you draw from the results? (c) What type

of advantages, disadvantages, limitations, and issues do you see in this instrument for self-testing? (d) What type of advantages, disadvantages, limitations, and issues do you see for companies using this instrument for testing employees?

9. Define a framework of project management training and development for your company or division. What kind of components should such a program include? How could you support the cost-benefits of such a program?

3.9 *PMBOK®* REFERENCES AND CONNECTIONS

The topic of "The Effective Project Manager: Skills, Values, and Agility" focuses directly on the PMBOK® Knowledge Area of project human resource management (#6) with strong connections to the PMBOK® processing groups of planning, executing, and monitoring/controlling. Much of this chapter deals with the context of project executing and monitoring/controlling, discussing the need for managerial skill building to ensure effective project management throughout its life cycle. The managerial perspectives presented in this chapter should be helpful in connecting the PMBOK standards with best practices of project management, and in studying effectively for PMP® certification. In preparing for the PMP® Exam, the following PMBOK sections relate especially to this chapter and should be studied: (1) organizational planning, (2) staff acquisition, and (3) team development.

INTERNET LINKS AND RESOURCES

Project Management Institute (PMI)/ Leadership in PM Community of Practice. http://leadershipinpm.vc.pmi.org/Public/Home.aspx.
Project Management Institute PMI; *2012 Annual Report*. https://www.pmi.org/en/About-Us/About-Us-Annual-Report.aspx.
Project Management Institute, PMI; *Career Central*. http://www.pmi.org/en/Professional-Development/Career-Central/4-Valuable-Skills-to-Break-Into-Project-Management.aspx.

REFERENCES AND ADDITIONAL READINGS

Badawy, M. 2007. "Managing Human Resources." *Research-Technology Management* 50 (4): 56–74.
Belassi, W., and Turkel, O. 1996. "A New Framework for Determining Critical Success/Failure Factors in Projects." *International Journal of Project Management* 14 (3): 141–151.
Cicmil, S., T. Williams, J. Thomas, and D. Hodgson. 2006. "Rethinking Project Management: Researching the Actuality of Projects." *International Journal of Project Management* 24 (8): 675–686.

Crawford, J. K. 2007. *Project Management Maturity Model*. Boca Raton, FL: Auerbach Publications (Taylor & Francis).

Dennison, D. 2012. *Leading Culture Change in Global Organizations: Aligning Culture and Strategy*. Hoboken, NJ: John Wiley & Sons/Jossey-Bass.

Gaynor, G. 2013. "Impact of Organizational Culture on Innovation." *IEEE Engineering Management Review* 41(2) (Second Quarter): 5–7.

Gido, J., and J. P. Clements. 2012. *Successful Project Management*. Independence, KY: CengageBrain.

Elizabeth Gasiorowski-Denis, ed. 2012. *New ISO Standard on Project Management. ISO*. http://www.iso.org/iso/home/news_index/news_archive/news.htm?refid=Ref1662.

Katz, R. L. 1974. "Skills of an Effective Administrator—Retrospective Commentary." *Harvard Business Review* 52 (5): 94–95.

———. 1955. "Skills of an Effective Administrator." *Harvard Business Review* 33 (1): 33–42.

Kerzner, H. 2013. *Project Management: A Systems Approach to Planning, Scheduling, and Controlling*. Chapter 3: "Organizational Structure." Hoboken, NJ: John Wiley & Sons.

Kloppenborg, T. 2012. *Contemporary Project Management*. Mason, OH: South-Western Publishing.

Maltz, A. C., A. J. Shenhar, D. Dvir, and M. Poli. 2012. "Integrating Success Scorecards Across Corporate Organizational Levels." *Open Business Journal* (5): 8–19.

Mantel, S., J. Meredith, S. Shafer, and M. Sutton. 2011. *Project Management in Practice*. Hoboken, NJ: John Wiley & Sons.

Morse, L. C., and D. L. Babcock. 2013. *Managing Engineering and Technology*. New York: Prentice Hall.

Pillai, A., A. Joshi, and K. Rao. 2002. "Performance Measurement of R&D Projects in a Multi-Project, Concurrent Engineering Environment." *International Journal of Project Management* 20(2): 165–177.

Project Management Institute. 2012. *Annual Report*. www.pmi.org/en/About-Us/About-Us-Annual-Report.aspx.

Project Management Institute. 2013. *A Guide to the Project Management Body of Knowledge (PMBOK® Guide)*. Newtown Square, PA: Project Management Institute.

PRINCE2. 2012. *Managing Successful Projects with PRINC2*, Norwich, Norfolk, UK: TSO, The Stationary Office; Office of Government Commerce in the U.K.

Shenhar, A. 2011. "What Great Projects Have in Common." *MIT Sloan Management Review* 52(2): 19–21.

Shenhar, A., and D. Dvir. 2007. *Reinventing Project Management: The Diamond Approach to Successful Growth and Innovation*. Cambridge, MA: Harvard Business School Press.

Shenhar A., D. Milosevic, D. Dvir, and H. Thamhain. 2007. *Linking Project Management to Business Strategy*. Newtown, PA: Project Management Institute (PMI) Press.

Shenhar, A., D. Dvir, O. Levy, and A. C. Maltz. 2001. "Project Success: A Multidimensional Strategic Concept." *Long Range Planning* 34(6): 699–725.

Shenhar, A., and H. Thamhain. 1994. "A New Mixture of Project Management Skills: Meeting the High-Technology Challenge." *Human Systems Management Journal* 13(1) (March): 27–40.

Thamhain, H. 1992. "Developing the Skills You Need." *Research/Technology Management* 35(2): (March/April): 42–47.

———. 2009a. "The Future of Project Team Leadership." In B. Bidanda and D. Cleland (eds.), *Project Management Circa 2025*. Philadelphia, PA: PMI Press.

———. 2009b. "Leadership Lessons from Managing Technology-Intensive Teams." *International Journal of Innovation and Technology Management* 6(2) (June): 117–133.

———. 2013a. "Changing Dynamics of Team Leadership in Global Project Environments." *American Journal of Industrial and Business Management*, no. 3 (May): 146–156.

———. 2013b. "Managing People in Technology." In M. Kutz (ed.), *Mechanical Engineer's Handbook*. Hoboken, NJ: John Wiley & Sons.

Zandhuis, A., and R. Stellingwerf. 2013. *ISO 21500 Guidance on Project Management*. Zaltbommel, Netherlands: Van Haren Publishing.

Chapter 4

Aligning Projects with the Enterprise

SUMMER OLYMPICS, 2016 IN RIO.

When Rio de Janeiro bid for the 2016 Summer Olympics and Paralympics in 2007, it competed with five other cities: Chicago, Baku, Doha, Madrid, Prague and Tokyo. Rio also tried, but failed three times to host the Games in 1936, 2004 and 2012. Regardless, it's hard to predict statistically the chances of winning such a complex bit. However, one thing Is sure. The City of Rio de Janeiro, in collaboration with the Brazilian Olympic Committee, has already spent millions in developing the proposal, and made a $14 billion commitment in its proposal for organizing and hosting the next Olympic Games. The organizers also had to secure commitments from other cities—Barra, Copacabana, Deodoro, and Maracanã—to become satellite venues for the Olympic Games, plus sites for the football matches, which will be held in the cities of Belo Horizonte, Brasília, Salvador, and São Paulo. On January 14, 2008, Rio de Janeiro was shortlisted by the International Olympic Committee (IOC) as a candidate, receiving a score of 6.4 on its proposal. One year later, Rio de Janeiro submitted its Candidature File to the IOC, followed by IOC visits, formal meetings, and on-site inspections validating the proposal and assessing the quality of the bid. Rio city officials supported the final bid with strong statements of commitment. "Brazil represents the safest choice," said Rio secretary general Carlos Roberto Osorio. "The Rio bid is a bid of certainty. Everything in the budget is guaranteed. If we get the games, we can start getting ready from Day 1. There will be no surprises afterward." Other government leaders strongly agreed. "Even in the current difficult global economic climate, we can guarantee that funding for Rio 2016 is secure and that the Brazilian economy is stable. We're the world's 10th largest economy and forecast to be the fifth in 2016. Brazil will be able to support all projected requirements for the games."

The long and intensive bidding process was concluded in Copenhagen, Denmark on October 2, 2009, with the election of Rio de Janeiro as the host city for the XXXI Olympiad and the XV Paralympic Games, which will be the first South American city ever to host the Games.

Sources: BBC Sports (2009); ESPN (2009); Wikipedia (2013).

4.1 MAKING THE CASE FOR ENTERPRISE PROJECT MANAGEMENT

No organization takes a casual approach to a $14 billion project. When Rio de Janeiro supported the Brazilian Olympic Committee in its bid for the 2016 Summer Olympics and Paralympics, the stakes were very high. Decision-making had to reach far beyond the feasibility of organizing and hosting the next Olympic Games, and far beyond the "triple constraint" of cost, time, and deliverables. Conventional performance criteria are just a small part of the long-range socioeconomic-political factors that had to be considered in this complex array of costs and values that justify a go or no-go decision for a multifaceted project of this magnitude. Not every project has such a complex array of stakeholders and cost-benefit-performance criteria. However, for virtually every project, success is more than meeting the triple constraint of time, budget, and technical performance.

What does project success mean? In most situations, efficiency and operational performance are important, and therefore a strong focus on delivering specific results within defined time and budget constraints is appropriate and very common. However, in many cases these are only part of the factors that determine success, and overemphasis of the triple constraint can mask other critical success variables, generating a misleading scorecard and a false sense of value, comfort, and security. Therefore, it is not surprising that in today's rapidly changing global business environment an increased number of organizations consider project management as a strategic tool and define success broadly and long-term. As explained by Aaron Shenhar in *Linking Project Management to Business Strategy* (2007):

> The project management discipline is changing into a new era that is completely different than it has been in the last fifty years. In this new era, projects will be considered as part of the strategic, business related activity of the organization. . . . Organizations of the future will realize that they need to treat their projects in a more strategic way. Similarly, project managers and project teams have to learn how to think more strategically and become responsible for business results, not just for getting the job done. (p. 3)

It is very easy to fall into the "success trap," better known as the activity trap—doing everything right, but failing to do the right thing, focusing on short-term results while missing the long-term picture. Most projects are undertaken with a business purpose. Whether a city bids for the next Olympic games or IBM decides on a new computer development, whether Aérospatiale and the British Aircraft Corporation starts the supersonic transport business, or the federal government launches a supplementary nutrition program, each project is different and so are the success criteria. Defining the metrics for success is a complex undertaking in itself. First of all, it requires defining the performance horizon. Are we looking short or long range? Is success being defined by looking at the deliverables at the end of the project execution cycle, or are we considering the project performance in its user environment? If we buy into the notion that projects are undertaken for a purpose, we have to look beyond the execution cycle. This requires more than just a project plan. It requires a careful assessment of what we want to accomplish with the project. What results do we want to achieve, short-range, long-range, or any time we wish to choose? This requires *strategic alignment* of the project with the business objectives of the enterprise.

In the past, most project managers and their teams did not focus on business results. This is still true today. By and large, their performance is *not* being measured beyond the project execution cycle. Therefore, it is not surprising that project management focus is primarily on the effective execution of projects according to plan with strong attention to producing the required deliverables within given budget and schedule constraints. This does not necessarily lead to desired business results. The Ford Taurus development is an interesting, often cited case (Shenhar 2007) supporting this argument.

The Ford Taurus development was a five-year project started in 1980 and completed with the roll-out of the new model in the fall of 1985. The Taurus was a milestone design that brought many new features and innovations to the marketplace. By 2007, Ford had built over 7.5 million Tauruses, making it the best-selling car in the United States for four consecutive years between 1992 and 1996. Yet when the project was completed, the project manager was fired because the project was six months behind schedule (Shenhar 2007, p. 58).

In contrast, the project manager of the second-generation Ford Taurus, undertaken between 1990 and 1995, took a lesson from the first-generation scorecard, making sure that the project stayed on schedule as established by Ford management. However, Ford paid a price for the shortcuts that were taken to meet the schedule. According to industry analysts, many subtle issues such as team spirit, vendor relations, and component integration led to suboptimal results and a disappointing business performance for the new model car (Shenhar 2007). As reported in the automobile press, the second-generation Ford Taurus suffered from reliability issues, high warranty costs, and low resale value. Many of these issues were blamed largely on the steps taken to reduce project cycle time (Cooper 1999).

The story can be repeated in virtually every industry. It shows that while focus on traditional project performance measures can produce short-term success, it is likely to short-shrift long-term business values and strategic positioning of the enterprise.

4.1.1 Definition

Although the formal framework of strategic alignment is still evolving, many of the pioneers in this field (Milosevic and Srivannaboon 2007, Patanakul and Shenhar 2012, Shenhar and Dvir 2007) have defined the alignment of project management with business strategy as a collaborative state of management where project operations continuously support the strategic goals of the enterprise, bridging the gap between company strategies and project plans. Within the context of this book, the following definition is suggested:

Alignment of projects with enterprise strategies is the effective linkages between project-related operations and the strategic goals and objectives of the enterprise to achieve project results with the highest value and competitive advantage for the enterprise.

Since the enterprise does not operate in a vacuum, the strategic goals and their accomplishments are influences by a broad range of factors from inside and outside of the enterprise, and therefore project performance must be aggregated and measured across all stakeholders. Furthermore, each project must be strategically aligned not only individually but also being managed as part of the overall project portfolio of the company, a critical and necessary requirement of strategic project management.

4.2 CONNECTING WITH THE EXISTING STRATEGY FRAMEWORK

Business strategy is a well-defined concept with its own theory and body of knowledge. Its roots go back to ancient times, such as Sun Tzu's *Art of War*, documented as early as 400 BCE (Hanzhang and Wilkinson 1998). For thousands of years, strategies played important roles in dealing with societies, infrastructure, security, and war. Regardless of its purpose, a strategy is a high-level plan to achieve one or more goals under uncertainty and limited resources. In more modern times, the concept of strategy has been refocused on specific application areas, such as business, where strategy often centers on plans and actions for gaining competitive advantages. The past 50 years produced a wide spectrum of literature in the area of business strategy (Chandler 1962; Conant et al. 1990; Miles and Snow 1978; Mintzberg 1973, 1998; Porter 1980, 1996). These concepts and principles of general business strategy are also applicable to project management. Yet, project management exists within the enterprise construct, even for projectized organizations, and therefore cannot be strategically managed in isolation, but must be aligned with the enterprise, its operational systems, and overall business strategy, as graphically shown in Figure 4.1.

The need for this alignment has been identified for several decades (see Cleland and Ireland, 2002). However, it was not until more recently that project management was recognized as an organizational system that should function as an integrated part of the enterprise and its business processes in the same way as any other organizational subsystem. Therefore, project management should be strategically aligned with the enterprise for optimized resource utilization and value delivery. Driven by this new awareness,

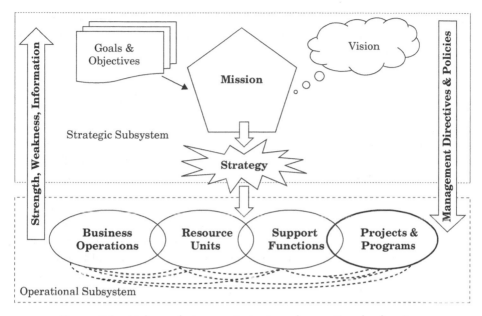

Figure 4.1   Linkages between strategic and operational subsystem

managers and researchers paid more attention to the issues of alignment, resulting in a large number of publications that helped to justify the need for strategic alignment and started to build a conceptual framework for it (Artto and Dietrich 2004; Jamieson and Morris 2004; Milosevic and Srivannaboon 2007).

Although the body of knowledge needs further development, the basic conceptual framework for linking project management with enterprise strategy already exists, which defines the influences, managerial interactions and measurements that impact strategy and project management (Peerasit and Shenhar 2012; Shenhar et al. 2007; Shenhar and Dvir 2007). It should be noted that this linkage or alignment is seen as a two-way process: looking downward, it defines the impact of strategy on projects and their management; upward, it defines the influences of project management on enterprise strategy. Given the dynamics of interaction among organizational components within the enterprise system, alignment can affect everything from project selection, project planning, execution and control, to customer relations and follow-up project acquisitions.

It is interesting to note, however, that while the majority of managers from both the functional and the project side of the enterprise support the concepts and needs for strategic alignment, most projects are not yet managed in a strategic way (Peerasit and Shenhar 2012). True strategic alignment requires a considerable shift from the conventional way projects are being selected and managed today. In addition to the strategic linkage with the enterprise, projects within the same business unit need to be selected and managed under a unified business umbrella, defined as *portfolio management*. They also must have strategic leadership at the project level and top management support.

4.3 PROJECT PORTFOLIO MANAGEMENT (PPM)

Project portfolio management (PPM) is part of the strategic subsystem of an enterprise. It deals with the selection and implementation of projects as a group linked to the strategic objectives of the enterprise. Because of its selection criteria in support of specific enterprise objectives, projects within the portfolio often have similar characteristics, market orientations or business objectives. Examples of such strategic portfolio objectives might be support of specific technologies, market penetration, optimized company resource utilization, product support, mission support, or just growth or profit targets. PPM is a widely used concept. Yet, as a formal discipline, its body of knowledge is still emerging. While there is no formal agreement on one particular definition of PPM, the following statement captures the essence for most situations:

Project portfolio management is the process of managing a collection of proposed or current projects that share similar characteristics and strategic objectives within the same business unit.

In a nutshell, the objective of project portfolio management is to create synergism among a group of projects via optimized resource utilization and mutual support of strategic enterprise objectives. To be successful, this group of projects needs to be managed more collectively and collaboratively than single projects outside such a portfolio. As a result, many special PPM tools and techniques evolved to support project selection and implementation, and to optimize the project portfolio for desired business results. Typically, organizations that adopt PPM establish a project management office (PMO) as a central resource, responsible for developing the PPM support system and for the strategic management of all projects in the portfolio. However, the same body of knowledge and standards, such as PMBOK, Prince2, and ISO 21500 (see Chapter 2), and the same core set of tools and techniques developed for managing single projects, also applies for managing projects in a portfolio. They provide the baseline for managing any type of project, in any kind of business or portfolio setting. They just have to be fine-tuned and supplemented to fit the additional challenges.

Another expansion of the project portfolio concept is *enterprise project management* (EPM). It takes PPM to the next level, a 360-degree strategy-operations integrated way of project management where project managers are directly responsible for selecting and implementing projects in support of enterprise strategy and mission objectives. At the same time, project managers define through their collective vision and leadership the enterprise mission and shape its strategy, goals and objectives, positioning the enterprise for survival and future growth.

Enterprise project management is a management philosophy that integrates all aspects of business management with project management. It relies on the assumption that management can foster an organizational culture supportive to collaboration, commitment, and enthusiasm. This is a culture conducive to organizational learning, collectively sharing the knowledge gained from many projects and interactions with stakeholders, a critical requirement for EPM to work.

Enterprise project management is currently an evolving management philosophy. Many companies across all industries and government are currently exploring the value and feasibility of EPM, and are selectively and cautiously implementing it. It is often seen at the most mature level of the project management maturity model (P3M), with highly advanced management methodologies, processes, and governance structures.

4.4 STRATEGIC PROJECT LEADERSHIP

As projects become more complex, competitive, and uncertain, traditional approaches to project management are often insufficient for guaranteeing success. We have to manage projects strategically, linking them with the enterprise and its business strategy, a case already made earlier in this chapter. A critical part of this strategic alignment is the need for *strategic project leadership*, a term coined by Aaron Shenhar (2004). The concept of strategic project leadership suggests an adjustment to managerial focus and philosophy. While retaining much of the operational approaches to project management as a core competency, strategic leadership requires a shift in managerial perspective from a narrow focus on efficiency to include both efficiency and effectiveness. It also suggests a broadening of managerial attention from focusing on operational issues to include human issues and business results, as summarized from field research (Shenhar et al 2007) in Table 4.1.

Strategic project leadership involves translating enterprise strategy into the project management operations, and vice versa. It's a very intricate and complex process that spreads across the entire project life cycle from project selection and start-up to execution, field application, and new business acquisition follow-on. It involves running the project operation as a business, optimizing its long-term value in a highly dynamic, constantly changing business environment. To do this effectively, David Cleland (2004) suggests that project leaders must consider at least the following seven variables of the project environment in selecting and managing their projects strategically aligned:

1. **Competitive factors.** Understanding markets, users, competitors, and technology in relation to our own enterprise strength and weaknesses is critical to developing a project strategy that creates a competitive advantage and optimizes value.

Table 4.1 Comparison of Traditional Project Management and Strategic Project Leadership Approaches

Characteristics	Traditional Project Management	Strategic Project Leadership Approach
Project definition	Projects are sets of activities which need to be executed to produce specific deliverables on time and within budget	Projects are organizational processes that are initiated to achieve business results consistent with enterprise strategy
Management focus	Efficiency	Effectiveness and efficiency
Management philosophy and emphasis	Executing the project according to established plans	Achieving business results aligned with enterprise goals and objectives
Time horizon	Project execution life cycle (short-range)	Total project life, including its utility (long-range)
Project management style	Universal (one size fits all), but situational adjusted	Adoptive approach
Project selection	Primarily based on short-range enterprise objectives	Based on short and long-range objectives aligned with enterprise strategy
Project definition and planning	Focused on scope, budget, and schedule	Focused on optimizing total value and strategic objectives
Project plan	Roadmap for project execution; plan changes are seen as unfavorable	Initial roadmap for project execution, adjusted to changing conditions
Project reviews and performance measurements	Progress measured against plan, focused on deliverables, schedule, and budget	Same, but dynamically adjusted to achieve project success and strategic objectives
Human side	Teamwork, motivation, and team leadership, collaboration, conflict resolution, cross-functional communication, stakeholder interfaces	Same, plus vision, strategic leadership, top management involvement
Body of knowledge	Well-established theory and standards	Emerging concepts and case studies
Practice	Well-established and accepted	Emerging, new management frontier

2. **Political environment.** Political conditions affect many projects environments, from defense contractors to multinational product developments. These conditions impact many aspects of project management, from the way projects can be executed to customer relations and opportunities for future business, all influencing total project value and the ability for strategic alignment.

3. **Social environment and trends.** Social and cultural conditions and trends are critical inputs to forecasting markets, user environments, and revenue streams, all influencing total project value. They must be considered in the strategic alignment process.
4. **Economic factors.** The availability of sufficient resources for executing the project and sustaining its results in the user environment is one of the most critical factors for overall project success.
5. **Technological factors.** The availability and resourcing of support technologies, from laboratories to test facilities and IT, is critical to both the operational effectiveness and efficiency of project management throughout all of its life cycle phases.
6. **Legal aspects.** This includes a large spectrum of guidelines and constraints, such as contract agreements, environmental laws, antitrust regulations, specific licensing requirements, and ethics standards. This spectrum widens even further for multinational projects that have to deal with different laws, regulations, and standards across their global operations.
7. **Operational competency.** The ability to utilize resources and to maintain the skill sets for effective project execution is critical for strategic alignment and effective strategic project leadership. These are prerequisites for delivering value to the project sponsor.

In summary, management practitioners and scholars have recognized the need for strategic alignment and its importance for effective project management. Research suggests that aligning project management with business strategy can significantly enhance overall project value and the achievement of organizational goals. However, implementing strategic alignment requires more than the willingness of project managers to do it or a corporate policy. It requires a managerial attitude and mindset of strategic project leadership within the enterprise. It also requires a systematic approach, resource commitment, and top management support.

4.5 WHERE ARE WE HEADING?

Project management is still evolving as a formal discipline. While we have an extensive body of knowledge supporting a wide range of project management tools, techniques, and standards for dealing with the "mechanics" of project execution, we are just beginning to understand the complexities and dynamics of project management in a business or enterprise context. We also realize that even the most skillful application of these mechanical tools does not automatically guarantee success or optimize value. In fact, part of the challenge is to define success and project value.

Among the many research efforts, two concurrent studies supported by the Project Management Institute (PMI) underscore these challenges. First, a three-year field study investigated current project management practices and their effectiveness of *linking project management to business strategy*.

The second three-year study focused on *project value*. The results of the first study (Shenhar et al. 2007) concluded that "project management is changing into a new era that is completely different from what it has been in the last fifty years. Projects will be considered as part of the strategic, business related activity in the organization. While this change seems natural, the traditional project management discipline has been slow in responding." Yet, according to Shenhar, organizations in the future have no choice. Their project managers have to learn how to think more strategically and become responsible for business results. The question is not *whether* but *how* to do it. This research clearly highlights the needs, benefits, and challenges of strategic alignment.

The second study on *project value* was published in 2008 (Thomas and Mullaly). It concluded that project management indeed adds value to the organization, discussing how value is actually created. But, the study also shows the difficulties of understanding and measuring value, and the need to go beyond simple financial measures.

Both of these field studies highlight the complexities and challenges of managing projects strategically. Yet the concept of strategic leadership is not a futuristic project management idea. It is a reality that managers in our rapidly changing, ultra-competitive business environment have to deal with. Although each project is unique in its own way, and therefore has unique criteria for success, there are certain factors that effectively managed, strategically aligned projects have in common that make them so uncommonly "great projects." Summarized from their extensive research, Shenhar and Dvir (2007) found the following common conditions in strategically aligned, successfully managed project:

Clearly defined mission. While most projects have a mission statement in their plan, great projects pay special attention to defining the mission objectives and articulate how to achieve distinct competitive advantages and added value to the enterprise.

Extended project definition phase. Great projects invest in the front end of the project selection and definition. They make strong efforts to communicate effectively with their customers, contractors, and partners to ensure realistic and quality inputs to their project plans.

Unconditional management support. Top management support is crucial to project success, especially when aligning with organizational strategy. Adjustments to established project plans might be needed to optimally deal with changes in the business environment. Effective project managers foster an organizational environment conducive to top management involvement and support.

Selection of highly qualified project manager. Top management should select the project manager for strategic projects. In some cases the project manager is a member of the senior management team. The personal qualifications, together with top management's endorsement, provide the project manager with the "earned authority" to deal with resource personnel across functional lines and with customers, contractors, and partners external to the enterprise.

Using existing knowledge. Not only is it cost- and time-effective to use already-available data, components, or off-the-shelf items but also it reduces the risk of failure and rework. Similar benefits are gained from early testing, simulation and rapid prototyping, as well as using open innovation concepts. Overcoming the NIH syndrome requires strategic leadership.

Integrated cross-functional teams. Multidisciplinary work groups need to be unified into project teams. This is a difficult task, as discussed in Chapters 16 and 18 of this text. It is absolutely critical for project success and a great leadership challenge for project managers.

Revolutionizing the organizational culture. Achieving strategic objectives often requires radically new approaches involving new technologies and operational methods. Boeing's 777 development is an often-quoted example of a project that revolutionized the way commercial aircraft were developed and manufactured. For the first time, Boeing used computer simulation and advanced CAD/CAM technology to minimize prototyping and testing of its aircraft components, but move many of these items from the design board to manufacturing.

Cooperating with outside resources. Working with suppliers, customers, and project partners often requires intense collaboration to optimize economic and technological benefits. The working relationships between these outside resources and the internal project team must be cultivated and the efforts strategically aligned, all requiring sophisticated project management skills and leadership.

Ability to adjust to changing conditions. Great project teams have the collective ability to recognize changes in the project environment that require adjustment to the project execution for optimum strategic fit and value. This requires a forward-thinking organizational culture and great project leadership.

Taken together, the issues of linking project management with enterprise strategy are challenging to both senior management and project leaders. The question of strategic fit must be addressed at the project acquisition stage. Inputs to opportunity identification, project evaluation, and selection should come from all segments of future stakeholders of these projects. Collective participative decision making is highly recommended to ensure a project portfolio that represents the best strategic alignment and highest value to the enterprise. Considering all of the challenges of strategic project leadership and strategic alignment, these concepts are still at the frontier of contemporary management practice. However, given the potential for improved project management effectiveness and business value, the alignment concept is gaining management attention, and organizations are using it selectively and successfully.

4.6 SUMMARY OF KEY POINTS AND CONCLUSIONS

The following key points were made in this chapter:

- Most projects are undertaken with a business purpose. Yet, they are not managed strategically.
- Research suggests that aligning project management with business strategy can significantly enhance overall project value and the achievement of organizational goals.
- The alignment of project management with business strategy is defined as a collaborative state of management where project operations continuously support the strategic goals of the enterprise.
- A strategy is a high-level plan to achieve one or more goals under uncertainty and limited resources.
- Each project must be strategically aligned not only individually, but also being managed as part of the company's overall project portfolio.
- Strategic alignment requires a considerable shift from the conventional way projects are being selected and managed today.
- Project portfolio management (PPM) is part of the strategic subsystem of an enterprise. It is the process of managing a collection of proposed or current projects that share similar characteristics and strategic objectives within the same business unit.
- Enterprise Project Management (EPM) is a 360-degree integrated way of project management where project managers are directly responsible for selecting and implementing projects in support of enterprise strategy and also for defining the enterprise mission and strategy, positioning the enterprise for survival and future growth.
- *Strategic project leadership*, a term defined by Aaron Shenhar, requires a shift in managerial perspective from a narrow focus on efficiency to include both, efficiency and effectiveness, plus more attention to human issues and business results.
- David Cleland suggests that project leaders consider at least seven variables in selecting and managing their projects strategically: competitive factors, political environment, social environment and trends, economic factors, technological factors, legal aspects, and operational competency.
- Strategic project leadership and the concept of strategic alignment are still at the frontier stage of contemporary management practice. However, the concept is gaining management attention, and organizations are using it selectively and successfully.

4.7 QUESTIONS FOR DISCUSSION

1. Discuss the differences between traditional project management and strategically aligned project management regarding responsibilities, skill sets, and management style.

2. What kind of strategic objectives would you have as a board member of the Olympic organizing committee in Rio de Janeiro?
3. Who should participate in a bidding decision of a major defense contract acquisition? Who should make the final decision? Why?
4. How would you define (a) project value, (b) project success, and (c) business success for Boeing's 787 Dreamliner program?
5. Why are some project managers and senior executives reluctant to manage projects strategically?
6. Where do you see project management responsibilities going in the future? Toward more strategic alignment or operational focus? What is the basis for your answer?

4.8 *PMBOK®* REFERENCES AND CONNECTIONS

The topic of strategic project management cuts across all of the 10 knowledge areas and 5 processing groups defined by *PMBOK®*. Much of this chapter deals with the context of project management, discussing the need for strategic alignment of projects with enterprise strategy. The managerial perspectives presented in this chapter should be helpful in connecting the *PMBOK®* standards with best practices of project management, and in studying effectively for PMP® certification. In preparing for the PMP® exam, the following *PMBOK®* sections relate especially to this chapter and should be studied: (1) scope planning and definition; (2) risk identification, quantification, and response; (3) organizational planning; (4) stakeholder analysis; and (5) stakeholder management.

INTERNET LINKS AND RESOURCES

BBC Sports (2009). "Rio to stage 2016 Olympic Games," http://news.bbc.co.uk/sport2/hi/olympic_games/8282518.stm
ESPN (2009). "Rio stands by $14.4 billion budget," http://news.bbc.co.uk/sport2/hi/olympic_games/8282518.stm
Wikipedia (2013). "2016 Summer Olympics," https://en.wikipedia.org/wiki/2016_Summer_Olympics

REFERENCES AND ADDITIONAL READINGS

Artto, K., and P. Dietrich. 2004. "Strategic Business Management through Multiple Projects." In P. Morris and J. Pinto, eds., *The Wiley Guide to Managing Projects*. Hoboken, NJ: John Wiley & Sons.
Bigelow Crawford, D. 2012. "Becoming a Business-Focused Project Management Leader." *Proceedings, 2012 PMI Global Congress*, Vancouver, BC, Canada, October 20–23, 2012.
Chandler, A. 1962. *Strategy and Structure: Chapters in the History of Industrial Enterprise*. Cambridge, MA: MIT Press.

Cleland, I. 2004. "Project Management: The Strategic Linkages." In P. Morris and J. Pinto, eds., *The Wiley Guide to Managing Projects*. Hoboken, NJ: John Wiley and Sons.

Cleland, I. and L. Ireland, L. 2002. *Project Management: Strategic Design and Implementation*. New York: McGraw-Hill.

Conant, J., M. Mokwa, and P. Varadarajan. 1990. "Strategic Types, Distinctive Marketing Competencies and Organizational Performance: A Multiple Measures-Based Study." *Strategic Management Journal* 11(5): 365–383.

Cooper, R. 1999. "The Invisible Success Factors in Product Innovation." *Journal of Product Innovation Management* 16: 115–133.

Gido, J., and J. P. Clements. 2012. *Successful Project Management*. Independence, KY: CengageBrain.

Hanzhang, T., and R. Wilkinson, R. 1998. *The Art of War*. Hertfordshire, UK: Wordsworth Editions.

Jamieson, A., and P. Morris. 2004. "Moving from Corporate Strategy to Project Strategy." In P. Morris and J. Pinto, eds., *The Wiley Guide to Managing Projects*. Hoboken, NJ: John Wiley & Sons.

Kloppenborg, T. 2012. *Contemporary Project Management*. Mason, OH: South-Western Publishing.

Microsoft (ed.). 2007. "Project Portfolio Management: Doing the Right Things Right." http://www.epmconnect.com.

Miles, R., and C. Snow. 1978. *Organizational Strategy, Structure, and Process*. New York: McGraw-Hill.

Milosevic, D., and S. Srivannaboon. 2007. "A Theoretical Framework for Aligning Projects with Business Strategy." In Shenhar, Milosevic, Dvir & Thamhain, eds., *Linking Project Management to Business Strategy*. Newtown, PA: Project Management Institute.

Mintzberg, H. 1973. "Strategy-making in Three Modes." *California Management Review* 16(1): 44–53.

Mintzberg, H., and J. Quinn. 1998. *Readings in the Strategy Process*. Upper Saddle River, NJ: Prentice Hall.

Patanakul, P. and A. Shenhar. 2012. "What Project Strategy Really Is: The Fundamental Building Block in Strategic Project Management." *Project Management Journal* 43 (1): 4–20. Project Management Institute. 2013. *A Guide to the Project Management Body of Knowledge (PMBOK® Guide)*. Newtown Square, PA: Project Management Institute.

Porter, M. 1980. *Competitive Strategy*. New York: Free Press.

———. 1996. "What Is Strategy?" *Harvard Business Review* 74 (4) (Nov–Dec): 68–78.

Shenhar, A. 2004. "Strategic Project Leadership: Toward a Strategic Approach to Project Management." *R&D Management* 43(5): 569–578.

Shenhar, A., and D. Dvir. 2007. *Reinventing Project Management: The Diamond Approach to Successful Growth and Innovation*. Cambridge, MA: Harvard Business School Press.

Shenhar, A., D. Milosevic, D. Dvir, and H. Thamhain. 2007. *Linking Project Management to Business Strategy*. Newtown, PA: Project Management Institute (PMI) Press.

Szymczak, C., and D. Walker. 2003. "Boeing—A Case Study Example of Enterprise Project Management from a Learning Organisation Perspective." *Learning Organization* 10(3): 125–137.

Thomas, J., and M. Mullaly. 2008. *Researching the Value of Project Management*, Newtown, PA: Project Management Institute.

Chapter 5

Understanding Project Organizations

GENERAL MOTORS, SHANGHAI

© GM Corp

The second phase of the General Motors China Advanced Technical Center (ATC) remains on track to open at the end of 2012. Adjacent to the GM China International Operations and GM China Headquarters in Shanghai, this is the most-comprehensive advanced auto-motive technology development center in China. "The completion of the Advanced Technical Center is an important milestone for GM in China," says Bob Socia, GM China president and chief country operations officer-China, India and ASEAN (Association of Southeast Asian Nations). "It gives us the most comprehensive automotive technical center in our largest market. It will serve not just China but also GM's operations around the world." The center will focus on advanced design, vehicle engineering, advanced powertrain development, urban mobility and man-ufacturing processes. The first phase of the ATC, which opened in September of 2011, is responsible for research and development of battery cells and lightweight materials, including new battery testing. The lab has been carrying out testing of different submissions from selected Chinese battery suppliers. "The establishment of the ATC is proof of GM's commitment to advanced technology leadership," said GM China Group President and Managing Director, Kevin Wale. "Our local team is cooperating with GM teams around the globe to come up with solutions for sustainable development that will benefit China and the world. The ATC is part of GM's global design center network, which webs from California to Germany to India and Korea and points beyond. We are building a team of talented local designers and modelers that will enable us to deliver world-class work for China and other markets." The 65,000-square-meter ATC will serve as the home of four key GM technical and design organizations: the China Science Lab, Vehicle Engineering

Source: "GM China to Finish Advanced Technical Center in 2012." See GM (2012)

Lab, Advanced Powertrain Engineering Lab, and Advanced Design Center. When complete it will include 62 test labs and 9 research labs, and have more than 300 employees, including engineers, designers, researchers and technicians.

5.1 TODAY'S BUSINESS PROCESSES REQUIRE FLEXIBILITY, SPEED, AND EFFICIENCY

Project organizations have been around in their basic structure for thousands of years. They became more formalized in the mid-1950s when increasing project complexity required more standardized and sophisticated approaches to project execution, leading to the formal structures and management systems, such as the ones we know today as matrix or projectized organizations, to be discussed in detail later in this chapter.

Effective organizational structures are fundamental to business success. However, finding a single, standardized structure, suitable for conducting complex business operations, such as shown in the lead-in scenario for General Motors, is not easy. This challenge exists not only for GM but also for NASA, American Express, and community hospitals, among others. Enterprises must be able to conduct continuous operations and project activities concurrently. Project management provides the process for time-limited missions, such as new product developments or building new power plants. But, it should not interfere with ongoing operations—at least that is what we are aiming for.

As technology changed the competitive landscape, especially over the past 20 years, organizations too had to change to keep up with the demand for greater flexibility, speed, and efficiency. New administrative tools, product development techniques and project management tools evolved, offering better capabilities for executing projects more integrated with the business process, and with greater emphasis on supply chain integration, horizontal decision making, and work/technology transfer. This, in turn, has led to flatter, leaner, and more change-responsive organizations, such as *simultaneous engineering, concurrent project management, design-build, agile, Stage-Gate® and spiral processes*, that can deliver enterprise objectives, such as new products, by integrating resources effectively across multifunctional organizational segments across the globe. However, none of these contemporary organizations can function as a business by itself. They become *overlays to the traditional functional organization*, the baseline of any enterprise from the ancient beginnings of business to this day.

These organizational overlays present major challenges. The drive toward greater cross-functional efficiency and agility weakens the functional organization because it requires *resource and power sharing*, hence diluting central decision making and control toward unified enterprise objectives. It also diminishes the autonomy of functional resource groups to develop and maintain the best functional capabilities needed by the enterprise. When GM China president Bob Socia talked about advanced design, vehicle engineering and powertrain development projects, he also pointed at the importance of supporting GM's operations around the world as part of GM's global design center network. This requires resource alignment, supply chain integration, central organizational focus and senior leadership. The reality is, that even for GM, with its enormous pressure for agility, speed and efficiency, it cannot afford to give up central control. Yet, effective project work is important. Therefore, like GM, most organizations are continuously searching for solutions for better cross-functional, horizontal integration, while maintaining operational efficiency and central control over their operations and strategies for effectively adapting to the changing business environment. Let's take a more formal look at the organizational options that exist for today's enterprises and how they evolved.

5.2 WHY DO WE NEED TO ORGANIZE DIFFERENTLY TO MANAGE PROJECTS?

How can a company be organized to conduct its business most effectively and yield the greatest value to its stakeholders? Different times in history have produced different answers. In 1600 the British East India Company was formed by a group of independent people, joining together for a single business objective: a trading mission to the West Indies. Although the company became one of the most powerful commercial enterprises of its time and took part in the creation of British India, Hong Kong, and Singapore, its stakeholders (the people with a vested interest in the operation) disbanded each time a mission was completed, at least for the first 50 years of the company's existence. Three hundred years later, Henry Ford created quite a different organizational model. He demonstrated that a successful company must be both vertically and horizontally integrated, owning virtually all stages in the supply chain and having strong central control. How does this compare to an Internet startup company, or Intel or General Motors, today? Is there a "norm" of an organizational structure today? "Fitting an organizational approach to a company is like fitting cloth to a person," says Alan Glasser (1982) in his seminal writings on research and development management. "It's a matter of style, personal taste, and circumstances."

How can the activities and functional support systems of an enterprise be organized most effectively to optimize desired results? In today's environment, where companies struggle with issues of complexity, agility, resource efficiency, and interdependence, the need exists for both centralized control *and* decentralized decision making, functional autonomy *and* cross-functional integration. This is a tricky balancing act and a great challenge. Consider the internal work environment of a typical high-tech company. Management has to deal with a broad spectrum of contemporary challenges, including time-to-market pressures, accelerating technologies, innovation, resource limitations, end-date-driven schedules, technical complexities, social and ethical issues, operational dynamics, risk, and uncertainty, all affecting the enterprise and its network of partners, joint ventures, and alliances. Facing such a dynamic environment makes it difficult to manage activities through traditional, linear work processes or top-down controls (Shim and Lee 2001; Thamhain 2011; Zhang, Keil, Rai, and Mann 2003). Many companies and their management have moved from reliance on hierarchy and central control to flatter, more dynamic and more cross-functionally transparent organizations, trying to achieve both vertical and horizontal integration. This creates a classic dilemma: How to organize to ensure unified mission control of the enterprise while providing autonomy and flexibility for horizontal integration and delivery. The answer to this dilemma is a delicate power balance between functional resource units and cross-functional business processes that usually results in some form of hybrid structure. The matrix organization is one of the most common hybrids used for executing projects within a functionally organized enterprise.

5.3 ORGANIZATIONAL LAYERS AND SUBSYSTEMS

The business areas of an enterprise do not operate in a vacuum. They are integrated within the functional support system of the company, which is part of the institutional framework of the enterprise. The three fundamental organizational layers are shown in Figure 5.1 and discussed below.

5.3.1 Institutional Framework

This is the area of "immortality," providing strategic directions, long-range survival and growth plans, policies, and procedures. This layer is staffed with senior management, corporate officers, and directors who provide broad, long-range guidelines and resource allocations for the enterprise.

5.3.2 Functional System

This is the traditional organizational framework of the firm. It is an area of slow change and the provider of stability. It is the functional system that positions the enterprise for competitive advantage, growth, and profitability by advancing methods of operation, markets, and supply lines, and by integrating new technologies into the operating areas of the organization. Typical resource groups of the functional system include R&D, engineering, development, manufacturing, marketing, human resources, legal, quality control, and purchasing, just to name a few of the more common functional subsystems.

5.3.3 Operational Area

These are the contemporary parts of the enterprise that expand and shrink as needed by the business. The operational areas of the firm are often

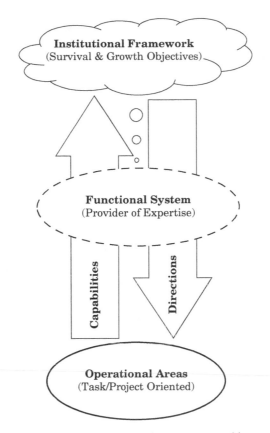

Figure 5.1   Three principal organizational layers

organized as programs and projects, such as new product developments, contracts, off-the-shelf deliverables, internal maintenance, and field support operations. It is the functional system that provides the needed resources to the operational areas, which in the case of project execution leads most often to hybrid organizations such as the matrix. In the extreme, the operational areas expand to absorb the entire functional system, creating a pure product organization or projectized or aggregated organization. In this approach the combined functional-operational system exists for the sole purpose of supporting one operation, such as the development of a new car model at GM, a new commercial airliner at Boeing, or a Mars rover at the Jet Propulsion Laboratory (JPL). In these situations, the operational areas are most visible to the market and customer community and are directly responsible for business results to top management of the enterprise.

Each of the three organizational layers exists in every firm. These layers often overlap significantly and occupy different amounts of space relative to each other. Consider, for example, a high-tech computer assembly plant or a newspaper publisher. These firms can be expected to have a relatively large part of their resources organized along functional lines. Conversely, a consulting firm or aerospace company would be organized with two strong axes, each representing functional and project/operational responsibilities. Yet another situation exists for companies (such as Boeing) that most likely organize the whole company around product lines (such as 747, 767, 777, or 787), hence integrating both functional and operational areas with focus on a particular product or project.

5.4 ORGANIZATIONAL DESIGNS FOR PROJECT MANAGEMENT

With the great variety of products, services, markets, and supply chain scenarios that enterprises have to deal with, it is not surprising to find a large number of organizational structures and processes in today's world of business. Although the resulting organizational structures are often bewildering and confusing, they can be broken down into a few basic components that can be explained in a simple model, such as shown in Figure 5.2. In virtually every enterprise, responsibilities can be divided into two overlapping categories or axes: (1) responsibilities related to the *management of resources* that provide the traditional *functional organization*, such as engineering, manufacturing, and marketing, and (2) responsibilities related to the *management of "mission-oriented" activities, defined as projects or programs with specific results and deliverables*, such as product developments,

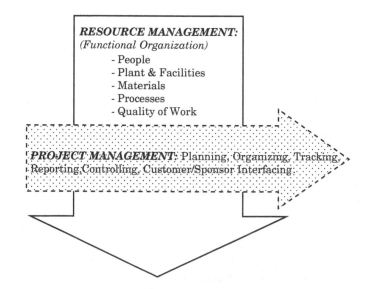

Figure 5.2   Two organizational axes: projects and functional resources

system evaluations or field installation. As shown in Figure 5.2, the project axis is an overlay to the resource axis, well positioned to contract with the functional organization for services needed for the integration of specific projects or programs. This is the essence of matrix management. Every enterprise has these two organizational axes to some degree. However, the organizational construct and managerial processes vary a great deal, depending on the nature of the business, which will be discussed in the next section of this chapter.

5.4.1 Organizational Choices

Fundamentally, companies have two choices for structuring their business operations: *functionally organized* and *project organized*. In a functionally organized operation, resources are grouped by "functional" capabilities and managed via a hierarchical chain of command and control processes. In a project-organized operation, resources are allocated to specific projects that are managed autonomous and independently.

However, virtually no company works as a pure functional or pure project structure. Every company has some functional components that provide support services and infrastructure, and every company has some project activity. As soon as a functionally organized business engages in some project activities, or a project-organized business creates some overhead functions, it operates as a matrix. In a matrix, resources are allocated to specific projects as needed and are shared with other projects and enterprise activities. Managerial control is shared between project leaders and resource managers. The matrix is the most common structure for executing projects.

Although the matrix is a hybrid between pure project and pure functional structures, the degree of projectized versus functional varies a great deal, not only among companies, but also within each company. The matrix provides an effective and convenient framework for structuring any business, because its design depends less on the physical restructuring of organizational components than the management style, policies, procedures, and budgeting processes that determine the sharing of power and responsibilities. Figure 5.3 shows graphically the matrix as part of an organizational continuum, somewhere between the two extremes of pure functional and pure projectized. Further, the "strength" of the matrix, and therefore its location between the two extremes, depends to a large degree on the management style and interaction of people within the organization, as will be discussed next.

5.4.2 The Functional Organization

This is the traditional and most fundamental form of organization and management. It has been successfully used since ancient times by governments,

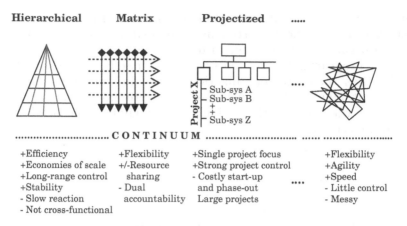

Figure 5.3 The organizational continuum, hierarchal to fishnet

military organizations, churches, and commercial enterprises. The trademark characteristics of the functional organization are (1) the separation of *functional responsibilities*, such as R&D, engineering, product development, marketing, finance, human resources, and so forth, and (2) its *hierarchical structure*, which leads to clearly defined chains of command, controls, and communication channels. As summarized in Table 5.1, the *strength* of this organizational form is in effectively utilizing its resources, taking advantage of economies of scale, developing areas of specialization and expertise, and providing the institutional framework for long-range enterprise planning and control. Still today, the functional organization provides the basic platform of operation for any enterprise, regardless of its business or environment. This concept of organizational structure has been the backbone for companies that are in a single business, especially whose products and services come out of a single operational facility and are marketed through a single distribution and sales network. If decentralization of the enterprise is sought, regional or product divisions can be formed, as is typical for the automobile and aircraft industries (e.g., General Motors, Ford, and Boeing). Or, the company can operate in a number of unrelated conglomerated businesses, such as General Electric, Dow Chemical, ITT, Samsung, Tata, and Mitsubishi. Each of these decentralized businesses has its own organizational systems for development, manufacturing, sales, marketing, and so forth—hence operating its own "functional" business according to its product or regional charter.

Yet, in spite of its robustness and economic benefits, the functional organization has its limitations and weaknesses, as summarized in Table 5.1. In fact, traditional models of organization and management are often ineffective in project-oriented environments. This has been recognized already in the early 1900s, resulting in structural modifications and integration of contemporary systems, tools and techniques that eventually lead to the matrix and projectized organizations used today. However, regardless of these limitations

Table 5.1   Characteristics of Functional Organizations

Strengths	Weaknesses
• Institutional framework for planning, control, and stability	• Difficult cross-functional communications and controls
• Efficient use of collective experiences and facilities	• Limited ability of technology transfer and multidisciplinary integration
• Concentration of expertise, benefiting most advanced developments	• Slow and ineffective decision making at enterprise level
• Long-range preparation for survival and growth	• Limited flexibility in responding to changes in business environment
• Effective utilization of operational facilities and systems	• Risk adverse, limited entrepreneurial capacity
• Career continuity and advancement potential	• Functional structure interferes with business process
• Well-suited for mass production and standardized operations	

and extensions into other organizational forms, the functional structure provides one of the most fundamental and stabilizing layers in any organization, and is the backbone of any company or institution.

5.4.3 The Projectized Organization

The *projectized* structure (also called *aggregated, monolithic* or *pure project organization*) essentially organizes the business activities of an enterprise into project groups. In its purest form, the *projectized* organization is the most extreme departure from the functional organization. The enterprise is partitioned into project units (or programs), with resources allocated to specific projects, managed autonomously and independently. Often, each project is run as a profit center, like a business unit in a conglomerate or division of a large company. In fact, the projectized form of organization and management is similar to the divisionalized structure. It offers a contemporary approach to building an organization for the purpose of executing a single project. Hence, the organization has a limited life. It builds up with the project and terminates with it! As summarized in Table 5.2, the projectized organization represents the strongest form of project authority. Each project manager has complete control over all support functions needed, including people, facilities, and functions necessary to execute the project, start to finish. In its purest form, the projectized business unit contains not only the technical functions, but also the operational and administrative support functions, such as marketing, quality, finance, human resources, and legal.

Table 5.2   Characteristics of Projectized Organizations

Strengths	Weaknesses
• Strong control over all project activities by single authority	• Inefficient use of production facilities and capital equipment
• Rapid reaction time, time-to-market	• Difficulty of balancing and leveling resources
• Schedule, resource, and performance tradeoffs	• Costly project startup and phase-out
• Large project integration capability	• Limited technology development
• Personnel loyalty to project, one boss	• Little opportunity for sharing experiences among projects
• Well-defined interfaces to contractors and customers	• Limited career ladders
• Well suited for large, long-term projects	

The principle advantage of the projectized organization is the high degree of control over each project, its resources and interfaces by a single authority, the project manager. Especially for larger projects this translates into (1) more rapid reaction time to market or customer changes, (2) faster time-to-market, (3) schedule, resource, and performance tradeoffs within each project, and (4) better project integration, in comparison to any other organizational form. Because of the project manager's full authority over all resources, similar to the functional organization, tradeoff decisions between performance, cost, and schedule can be made rapidly and effectively with a focus on the end objectives. All people assigned to the project are loyal to the project and its mission objectives. By definition, there are no competing projects or dual accountabilities, and ultimately there is only one boss, the project manager. This type of project organization is often preferred by the customer, because it can mirror the customer's organization, therefore providing one-to-one people interfaces between customer and contractor.

The principle disadvantages of the projectized organization are: (1) considerable startup cost and time requirement, (2) limited opportunity to share experiences and production elements, and (3) limited opportunity to use economies of scale and to balance workloads. These disadvantages are especially noticeable for smaller project and projects with shorter life cycles.

Because of these disadvantages and limitations, even companies in project-oriented businesses seldom projectize completely, unless their projects are *large enough* to utilize the dedicated resources, and *long enough in duration* to justify the organizational setup and phase-out efforts. What is more common, especially in technology-based companies, is a partially projectized organization. That is, project managers may fully control *some* resources that are particularly critical and can be fully utilized over the project life cycle (resource leveling), while other resources remain under the control of functional managers who share them among many projects as needed. Such resource sharing prevails especially in administrative support functions such as human resources, accounting, and legal. Thus, many enterprises that, at first glance, look projectized are really hybrids of several organizational types and layers. The matrix organization is, in fact, such a hybrid organization that operates across a whole spectrum of organizational entities. Stretched in one direction, it behaves very much like to a functional organization. Stretched in the other direction, it becomes projectized.

5.4.4 The Matrix Organization

The matrix approach offers a compromise solution for project-oriented businesses that cannot *dedicate* the needed resources to projects over their full life cycles, but must share them among many other projects. Matrix organizations are hybrids between functional and projectized structure. When designed right, the matrix combines the strength of both the functional and projectized organization. It provides an effective and convenient framework for structuring any business, because its design depends less on the physical structuring of organizational components than the management style, policies, procedures, and budgeting processes that determine the sharing of power and responsibilities. Ultimately, the managerial process is defined to a large degree by the management style and interaction of people within the organization. Matrix management is a relatively straightforward and simple concept. Yet, it has been surrounded by much mystique and confusion.

Here is how it works. When a functionally organized enterprise has to perform several tasks, missions or programs simultaneously, it automatically operates as a matrix. The matrix is essentially an overlay of contemporary project organizations on the functional resource departments of a company, as symbolically shown in Figures 5.2 and 5.4.

All departments and support units retain their functional, hierarchical characteristics. A clear chain of command and control exists for all units within the enterprise. At the operational level of the enterprise, task leaders or project engineers direct and coordinate the work. They are responsible for the implementation of plans that are directed either from the top down or horizontally via project managers, such as PM(*x*), PM(*y*), or PM(*z*) in Figure 5.4. These task leaders essentially have two bosses, upward they are responsible to their department managers for effective resource utilization and work quality, and horizontally to project leaders for the timely and resource-effective project implementation and delivery of specific results according to established plans. Similar dual-accountabilities often exist at the next level. Department managers share with their task leaders responsibilities along the horizontal axis of the organization for resource-effective implementation of projects plans, while vertically they are responsible to senior management for the maintenance and advancement of personnel, facilities, and support technologies. Project managers, such as PM(*x*), can either

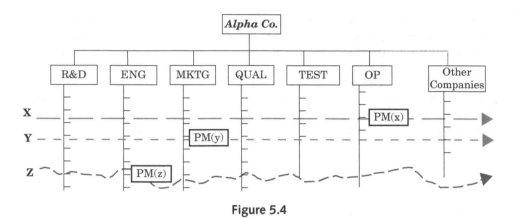

Figure 5.4

report to a functional manager, as shown in Figure 5.4, or into a Program Management Office (PMO), led by a director of programs, responsible for all projects conducted within the enterprise. Further up the organizational hierarchy, senior management is responsible for overall capability coordination and resource allocation, strategic planning, overall corporate direction, and leadership, very similar to top-level responsibilities in traditional hierarchical organizations.

The advantages of the matrix organization, summarized in Table 5.3, are similar to both the functional and projectized organization combined: reasonable reaction time to emerging business opportunities, customer requirements, and changes; effective integration of multidisciplinary activities; efficient resource utilization. The matrix also enjoys a high concentration of specialized resources, positioning the company for creating the best support technologies and most advanced products. The task leaders and project managers within the organization provide effective interface points to other organizational units and externally to the customer, contractor, and supplier communities. Perhaps one of the most important features of the matrix is its ability to start up and phase-out projects quickly and economically, which results in greater agility and flexibility of the enterprise in pursuing emerging business opportunities and in dealing effectively with a mixture of projects that vary in size, duration, and scope.

The weaknesses and limitations of the matrix organization relate to its unconventional structure that relies on resource and power sharing, often a source of organizational conflict, and always a challenge to managerial accountability and control. Furthermore, the additional organizational overlay (two axes) is likely to increase cost overhead, and together with the power and resource sharing, requires a more sophisticated management style than either the traditional functional or the projectized organization.

Yet in spite of its limitations, the matrix, when designed properly, combines some of the best features of both the functional and projectized organization.

Table 5.3   Characteristics of Matrix Organizations

Strengths	Weaknesses
• Effective resource utilization • Quick formation of project teams • High quality of resources and skill sets • Ability of handling complex projects • Ability of working on many projects concurrently • Quick response to business/market needs • Organizational agility • Standardized business processes • Unified business strategy and processes across many operations • Career development and growth opportunities	• Power and resource sharing • Dual accountability • Leading without formal authority • Organizational ambiguity • Complex organizational interfaces and work transfers • Priority conflict and interruptions • Complex cost accounting • Difficulty of project control • Resource multiplexing leads to organizational conflict and inefficiency • Career uncertainty, risk, and anxieties

Therefore, it is not surprising to find some part of the matrix structure in virtually every enterprise that executes projects or has to deal with multidisciplinary task integration. Technology management is, to a large degree, synonymous with matrix management!

Four Matrix Categories

Matrix organizations come in many forms and shapes depending on the specific business processes and operational needs within each company. Formally, matrix organizations are classified into four specific categories, according to their primary purpose and mission objectives:

1. **Project-function matrix.** This represents an overlay of the project structure to the functional resource organization. It is the most common type of matrix organization, used for executing a wide variety of projects, ranging from development to service and training. The project or program manager is responsible for the business results, including project acquisition, planning, organizing, integration, and customer interfacing. Resource managers are responsible for the functionality and quality of the project components, and the management of their departmental resources, including the development and effective utilization of personnel, facilities, and technologies.
2. **Product-function matrix.** This matrix focuses on product-oriented businesses. It is an overlay of the product organization to the functional

or resource organization. Project or product-line managers are responsible for business results. Typically, they have to work across functional lines to achieve the integration of product design, prototyping, fabrication, sales, and marketing. Resource managers are responsible for the development and effective utilization of company resources and the technical implementation of project components, including their functionality and quality.

3. **Product-regional matrix.** This matrix is an overlay of the product organization on the regional network of an enterprise and its operation. This is often a sales-oriented structure where product managers are responsible for business results cutting across geographic-regional lines. This type of business operation also leads to multidimensional matrices with multiple layers of business operations.

4. **Multidimensional matrix.** This organizational structure combines several matrix types, resulting in many layers, such as an overlay of the product organization on the functional organization, within a business division or regional network. Therefore project managers must cross-functional lines in various divisions and geographic regions to achieve the desired business results. Similar to other matrix organizations, resource managers are responsible for the development and effective utilization of company resources and the technical implementation of project components.

Additional Matrix Axes

The relatively simple structure of the project-function matrix, with its two basic axes (see Figures 5.2 and 5.4), can be expanded to reflect the realities of more complex business environments, as shown for the multidimensional matrix. The concept can be expanded even further. Companies that work across geographic, cultural, technological, and industrial boundaries, typical for multinational ventures or large programs, might establish additional matrix axes, which overlap the functional organization. Project charters, management directives, policy directives, and process flow diagrams provide the tools for defining these multidimensional matrices operationally. In addition, personal discussions and interactions, such as team sessions, workshops, focus group meetings, and managerial involvement with the project teams, can help in effectively communicating the matrix process and in clarifying the way the organization actually functions.

5.4.5 Real-World Variations and Hybrids

For real-world technology companies, the choice among functional, divisionalized, projectized, or matrix organization is not simple. A big company such as General Electric operates many unrelated businesses, largely on a high-technology platform, bound together by a common operating system.

Top down the firm looks like a conglomerate, divided into six businesses, each consisting of dozens of related, yet highly diversified, enterprises with very different organizational needs and structures. Take, for example, GE's Technology Infrastructure business group, a $50 billion enterprise consisting of aviation, enterprise solutions, healthcare, and transportation businesses, with products and services ranging from jet engines to locomotives, mining trucks, gas turbines, and medical systems, serving many different markets worldwide. Because these operations involve very large, long-term programs, many of these business groups run their core operations within a projectized structure that helps to concentrate resources and control on single projects or programs with dedicated customer and vendor interfaces, and specialized technology developments and field services. Yet, internally, many resource departments, while dedicated to a single project profit center, operate along matrix lines, executing subprojects that are eventually integrated with the larger program. In addition, there is a layer of traditionally structured administrative and strategic units that provide services and share resources across several businesses. Furthermore, to deal effectively with customers, suppliers, and regulators, each business must cross geographic, cultural, technological, and industrial boundaries, creating a need for additional organizational layers that overlap the core business.

Very few companies are as big as General Electric. Yet, most companies, small or big, have to deal with a spectrum of programs, large and small, short-range and long-term, in different markets and multinational environments. These companies not only have the challenge of choosing the right organizational structure for their project portfolio but must also make these structures congruent with established business processes and consistent with the organizational cultures and value systems of the enterprise.

Creating the proper organizational setting for the management of complex projects requires flexibility and organizational innovation. No single organizational structure has yet emerged to satisfy all requirements that surface in a major technology project. As a result, managers modify the primary structure, such as the matrix or projectized organization, to adapt them to the specific situation and needs. These variations often operate within the formal construct of the enterprise as independent organizational entities, but without much formal authority, yet effectively performing their multidisciplinary roles. Invariably, these new mini-organizations lead to multilayered hybrids, creating their own territorial rights for power and resources and establishing dotted line responsibilities. Some of these structural variations have been formally defined and will be discussed next.

Individual Project Organization

The *individual project organization* is a one-person project office chartered with the coordination and integration of a single project activity across functional lines. It is a mini-matrix within a larger project organization. The degree of authority depends on the specific charter given to the individual, his or her reporting relations to the resource managers and the respect and credibility established within the resource group. Usually, the position power of the task leader is weak, with limited control over the multidisciplinary resources needed to accomplish the task. Yet, authority can be earned via trust, respect, and credibility, which explains some of the differences in effectiveness and role performance of these task leaders. One of the great advantages of the individual project organization is the speed at which it can be established and phased out, and the single point of interface it provides to the customer, sponsor, resource group, and senior management. This organizational structure is especially well suited for the management of smaller projects or subsets of larger projects.

Staff Project Organization

This is another variation of the matrix. Similar to the individual project organization, the manager is responsible for cross-functional project integration. While the staff project charter provides limited authority for directing and controlling cross-functional activities and resources, some staff personnel are reporting directly to the staff project manager, providing that office with additional resources and operating capacity. Since the staff project organization is similar to the individual project organization, it has the same advantages and limitation, and is especially suitable for the management of smaller projects or subsets of larger projects.

Intermix Organization

The *intermix organization* is a special hybrid created by splitting off components from the functional organization of the enterprise by directing personnel from these components to join the new project organization (intermix). This enables large sets of operational capacity to be transferred to the new project together with readily established lines of authority. Therefore, startup time and issues are being kept to a minimum. However, this radical resource transfer creates disruptions and other problems at the functional organization, which explains why intermix organizations are not the first choice for conventional projects, but are formed mostly on a temporary basis to deal with special projects, such as a reorganization, a merger or acquisition, a bid proposal development, or handling a critical short-term assignment. After the assignment (project) has been completed, the intermix organization is resolved and its personnel and other resources returned to their home offices within their functional organization.

The weaknesses of the intermix organization are related primarily to the crippling effects on the host organization. Personnel of an intermix organization view their jobs as temporary and feel uncomfortable if the assignment stretches over longer periods. The organization is not designed for career development, job security, or technology advancement. Further, ineffective utilization of resources, such as limited opportunities for resource leveling, and phase-out difficulties, make the intermix organization often one of the most expensive choices available. Yet, the ability to establish very quickly an operational unit with special skill sets and capabilities, needed to execute a special mission makes the intermix organization a very attractive option for special situations.

5.5 MANAGERIAL PERSPECTIVE

Choosing an appropriate organizational structure is difficult for any company. It is especially tough for firms that are involved with a mixture of functional and project-related activities varying in size, duration, and markets. Since many technology-based companies fall into this category, it is not surprising that most of these enterprises operate, by design or default, as organizational hybrids. The core of these companies is often organized along matrix lines with hierarchically structured core functions, such as R&D, engineering, testing, manufacturing, marketing, field services, legal, and human resources. These resource functions are shared among the various project operations, providing a relatively high degree of organizational versatility and flexibility. In addition to the basic matrix, we find other organizational layers of projectized clusters, mini-matrices, individual project organizations, staff-project, and intermix organizations. These hybrid structures help management to accommodate the widest possible range of business activities with great flexibility, while retaining much of the traditional functional stability and resource effectiveness.

5.5.1 Understanding the Working Environment

Real-world organizations are complex, both on paper and in practice. They must be carefully designed to accommodate the needed infrastructure and support systems for the business process while maintaining effective resource utilization. In many cases, even the managers who "designed" these organizational structures are unable to classify or describe their creations in simple terms, but speak of organizational system overlays, resource sharing, and joint responsibilities.

   In fact, if we look at the organizational description of a typical high-technology company, such as given in an annual report or on a company website, we find that most of today's businesses are very complex in terms of their internal operations and outside interfaces. Many of these companies conduct project-related operations. Therefore, their core structure is some form of a matrix. But, it often also includes an unconventional array of interfaces and reporting relationships.

5.5.2 How to Define Organizational Structure and Environment

To work effectively, people must understand where they fit into the enterprise and what their responsibilities are. Especially with the complex workings and intricacies of modern technology companies, it is important to define the management process together with the command and control structure, which includes responsibilities, reporting relations, and interfaces for all organizational components. The tools come from conventional management practices. They provide the basis for managerial direction, communication, and control, as well as the informational infrastructure for teamwork, technology transfer, and decision making at the operating level of the company. The principal tools are as follows:

- **Policy directive.** This top-level document describes the overall philosophy and principles of managing the business within a particular organizational unit. A sample policy directive is shown in Appendix 1.1 for managing project-related business within an enterprise.
- **Procedure.** This operational guideline describes the various components of the business process, including how specific work and projects are to be executed, and how supporting activities, such as cost estimating, scheduling, testing, and training, are to be conducted.
- **Operating charter.** This policy document defines the operational framework for a particular department, business unit, or program office. It clearly describes its mission, scope, broad responsibilities, authority, organizational structure, interfaces, and reporting relations. Charters should be revised if the scope or mission of the position changes, as is the case for positions within program offices or new product development organizations. Sample charters are provided for a project manager, team leader, director of programs, and R&D project leader in Appendix 1.3, 1.4, 1.5, and 1.6, respectively.
- **Organization chart.** Regardless of the intricacies of the organization, its structure and terminology, a simple organization chart of the core organization defines the major reporting and authority relations, interfaces, and communication channels. In spite of its static nature, the organization chart provides a useful bird's-eye view of key organizational structure and reporting relations.
- **Responsibility matrix.** This chart is especially useful for defining the cross-functional responsibilities and multiple accountabilities for project-related activities. The chart shows who is responsible for what. Its application can be expanded from covering a particular department to the whole company, and even go beyond, to reach into supplier and customer environments. A more detailed discussion of the responsibility chart and some of its derivatives, such as the task roster, will follow in Part III of this book.
- **Job description.** Similar to the position charter, but more detailed and focused on an individual position (or class of positions), the job

description defines (1) principal duties, (2) qualifications, (3) responsibilities, (4) reporting relations, and (5) basic authorities. Job descriptions should be developed for all key personnel, such as managers, lead engineers, scientists, and project managers. Job descriptions are modular and portable among similar positions. Once established, job descriptions become building blocks for staffing, professional development, and performance evaluation and rewards.

While the exhibits in Appendix 1 provide *examples* of policy and procedural tools for defining organizational processes, these tools cannot be used as ready-made templates, but must be modified and fine-tuned to fit the specific organizational needs, specs, cultures, and business processes. The objective of showing these samples is to provide a framework to managers for developing the specific managerial tools as needed by the enterprise.

5.6 BUILDING THE PROJECT ORGANIZATION

Building an effective project organization is complex and difficult. Choosing the right structure and customizing it, or modifying an existing structure to fit special needs, involves many assumptions and the risk of compromising ongoing enterprise operations. In spite of the praise of successful project structures given in the literature, many senior managers remain skeptical, especially of the matrix. Their worries focus on dual accountability and resource and power sharing, which makes it difficult to define clear operating responsibilities. Traditionally, managers are accustomed to working within a single-line command and control system, holding single individuals accountable for business results. While most managers realize that these simplistic concepts no longer hold for managing in today's complex world of business, it is still the background against which contemporary structures, such as matrix or projectized organizations, are measured.

Yet managers have no choice. They have to organize their project work in the best way possible, optimizing their project operations while minimizing any negative impact on their ongoing business. This is an art and a science. No canned recipes. However, the process is not random. Building effective project organizations requires a systematic approaches and a keen understanding of the organization, its people, and the work to be performed. The key is to define precisely what roles and responsibilities people in the various organizations have. The details of the multiple command and control structure will evolve from these primary charter definitions. Let's take a careful look at how to define project organizations systematically.

5.6.1 Key Roles and Responsibilities

To work effectively, people must understand where they fit into the enterprise, what their responsibilities are, and to whom. Regardless of the project structure, five types of management must work together: (1) project/program managers, (2) task leaders, (3) functional or resource managers, (4) project sponsors or customers, and (5) outside suppliers, contractors, and partners. Although position titles and responsibilities vary considerably, Table 5.4 provides typical examples and definitions, suggesting a common language for communicating titles and responsibilities. The formal tool for defining authority and responsibility relations is the *project organization charter*, as mentioned in the previous section as part of the operating charter. Charter examples are shown in Appendix 1, sections 1.2 and 1.3, for three key positions: project manager, resource manager, and task leader.

5.6.2 Organizing the Project Team

Selecting and organizing the project team is crucial to successful project management. If done properly, the team organization defines the project organization. However, this cannot be done in a vacuum. It should be part of a systematic process that includes (1) defining the key functions or positions required and their responsibilities, (2) recruiting the proper personnel needed, (3) establishing reporting relations, and (4) defining the key work interfaces. The project charter, which should exist prior to team organization, provides the executive directive and blueprint for organizing the project team. The process of organizing the project team is similar, whether the team is formed within a matrix or projectized setting or any other project structure. The only difference is the responsibility for staffing, which shifts toward the functional manager in a matrix while residing with the project manager or the project office in a projectized situation. The size and depth of the project team depends on the scope and nature of the project to be executed. Typical positions are shown in Table 5.4. Given a medium-to-large size project, the team might be structured along the following positions: (1) project manager, (2) several task managers or task leaders, (3) technical director or lead engineer or lead scientist, especially for technology projects, (4) project administrator, and (5) individual contributors, project associates or specialists responsible for specific project activities and deliverables. In a matrix environment, most of these positions, except for the project manager and administrator, reside in the functional organization with all the challenges of power, resource and responsibility sharing discussed earlier. For smaller projects, positions are often shared. In the extreme, such as an individual project organization, all functions are performed by one person, the project manager or project leader, as discussed earlier.

The following nine-point process provides some guidelines for organizing a project team. The process described here illustrates who to establish just one layer, for instance the top level of the project team. For smaller projects, this might be the complete team. For larger projects, the process needs to be repeated by each of the subsystem leaders (i.e., task managers), who in turn define the structure for their own cluster team. Many of the tools and

Table 5.4   Project Management Positions and Responsibilities

Project Management Position	Typical Responsibilities	Skill Requirements
• Project administrator • Project coordinator	Coordinating and integrating activities for the total project or for a subset (i.e., work package or cluster). Determining resource requirements (e.g., staff, budget, and schedule). Measuring and analyzing projects performance. Reporting progress. Interfacing with project manager, contractors, and customer.	• Planning • Budgeting • Scheduling • Coordinating • Analyzing • Project coordination
• Task manager • Project engineer • Team lead	Same as above, but stronger role in establishing project requirements and team organization. Directing and controlling the technical implementation for given subsystem according to established plans. Making tradeoff decisions.	• Technical expertise (specialties) • Communicating • Problem/conflict solving • Task leadership • People skills
• Assistant project manager • Project manager • Associate program manager • Program manager	Same as above, but stronger role in project planning and establishing/maintaining overall project control and interface conditions. Overall leadership toward implementing project plan. Maintaining an effective link with senior management and customer community. Responsible for project acquisition and new project business development. Responsible for meeting budget and profit objectives.	• Overall project/program leadership • Team/coalition building • Conflict resolving • Coordinating • Resource allocating • Risk management • Customer/top management interfacing
• Senior program manager • Executive program manager • (These titles are often held by the head of a project management office, PMO)	This title is reserved for very large projects relative to host organization. Responsibilities are same as above, but with strong focus on directing overall program(s) toward established business results, new business development and project organization development.	• Business management and leadership • Project/program management • Coalition building • People skills • Strategic vision

(Continued)

Table 5.4   (Continued)

Project Management Position	Typical Responsibilities	Skill Requirements
• Director of programs • VP program development • (These titles are often held by the head of a project management office, PMO)	Responsible for managing multiprogram business via several project organizations, each led by a project manager. Focus is on business planning/strategizing, business development, technology development and profit performance, plus establishing policies, procedures, personnel and organization development.	• Business management and leadership • Project/program management • Coalition building • People skills • Strategic vision

techniques suggested in this process will be discussed in detail in upcoming chapters of this book:

1. **Work definition.** List all major elements of work or subsystems of your project, plus the key support functions that must be performed. The work breakdown structure, statement of work, requirements document, and administrative procedures provide the basic source of information and some guidelines for defining the principal components of the project work and its supporting services required. A project plan, or at least a preliminary version of it, contains many of these components and is a good starting point.

2. **Reporting relations.** Decide for each major subsystem and support function of your project whether personnel and other resources could be shared or should be dedicated to the project. Also decide whether any of these resources should report directly to the project manager.

3. **Job descriptions.** Prepare job descriptions for all key personnel on the project team. This includes all task leaders and support personnel reporting to you, directly or indirectly, and regardless of whether personnel is fully dedicated or shared with other projects. A summary of these job descriptions becomes a personnel requisition that is needed for staffing the positions, either via company-internal or external sources. In a mature project-oriented business, many generic job descriptions exist already or can be adopted from previous projects, needing only some modification rather than completely new development.

4. **Position staffing.** Using job descriptions and requisitions, advertise the open positions, fill the jobs internally, or negotiate the needed personnel with resource managers. Interview the chosen candidates to ensure mutual interest and fit with the assignment. Negotiate terms and conditions with candidate, and sign on as team member.

Conducting an effective interview and negotiating the assignment is crucial for building a high-performing team. It should be done for staffing, from both outside the company as well as inside.

5. **Functional support.** Negotiate the necessary functional support with resource managers, outside contractors, partner organizations, and other collaborators as needed. In order to discuss and eventually negotiate these support requirements effectively, project leaders must have a description of the work or service to be performed, which at the minimum should include (1) task description, (2) level of effort, and (3) timing. Conventional project planning tools, such as statement of work, work breakdown structure, task matrix, and milestone schedule, are useful for describing and communicating the support requirements.

6. **Requirements analysis.** Team members should familiarize themselves individually and within their task groups with the overall project requirements and their individual assignments. The existing project plan is a good starting point for developing a common baseline of understanding among team members, and to develop a more detailed project plan. This requirements analysis and plan development should be a guided effort, managed by the project leader. As a side benefit of this analysis, the team will identify many of the cross-functional work interfaces and information transfer points.

7. **Reporting relations.** Define the reporting relations of project personnel and their shared accountability between project and resource organizations, plus others, such as contractors, customers, and partners. Reporting relations should also articulate the performance evaluation process and its shared responsibility between project and functional management. Tools such as existing job descriptions, work breakdown structure, project charter, and n-square chart will be helpful in defining the reporting relations.

8. **Project controls.** Define the project evaluation, review, and reporting requirements, together with the review process and basic metrics for assessing project progress and performance. A large array of tools is available to project managers for establishing these controls, including project review meetings, design reviews, status reports, open item reports, process action teams, and focus groups. The basis for establishing these controls is the project plan, with clearly established milestones, resource boundaries, and deliverables. The type and method of controls is also defined to a large degree by the chosen project organization and its management process, such as projectized versus matrix, or concurrent, Stage-Gate®, agile, or spiral. A detailed discussion of these various project management tools and techniques will follow in later chapters of this book.

9. **Project kickoff.** Organize and conduct a formal kickoff meeting with all contributing project personnel present. A brief overview of the project and its importance to the enterprise and its mission helps to unify the team and build team commitment to the project objectives.

An Iterative Process

Building a project team is an iterative process. We have to define some of the key components of the project and its structure before we can begin organizing the team. But project managers need most of their team members before they can complete the project plan and team organization. Therefore, the project team organization evolves incrementally and iteratively. This is especially true for larger, more complex projects, where defining the team and its structure often stretches across the entire project definition phase, or even beyond.

Cross-Functional Coordination

By definition, projects are multidisciplinary and need integration of their components. This can be difficult, especially in matrix organizations where project managers and task leaders must cross functional lines and deal with resource personnel over whom they have little or no formal authority. Regardless of the team structure, project integration is a difficult task in any organization. Virtually any project involves the integration of components. Whether these components are generated within the project organization or across functional lines of a matrix structure, or come from vendors, contractors, or partners, orchestrating all of these activities and resources toward desired results is a great challenge and the source of considerable uncertainty and risk of failure, especially for larger or technologically more complex projects. To facilitate project integration, it is recommended that the project manager designates for each project subsystem a coordinator, often referred to as *gatekeeper*, who becomes the interface point to other subsystems and support functions, responsible for the proper flow of information and other deliverables that interface his or her work package. For smaller projects or at lower levels of the work breakdown, this interface person is the task leader or individual contributor assigned to the task, with only a fraction of his or her time allocated for coordination. For larger projects, or at higher levels of the work breakdown, project integration and functional interface management can be a full-time job. It might even require a dedicated administrator in each of the supporting resource departments or partner organizations.

Some guidelines might be helpful for determining how much interface support is reasonable and justifiable. As a rule of thumb, total administrative project overhead should not exceed 15 percent of the project budget; 10 percent is more common. In my experience, somewhat less than half of this, or approximately 4 to 7 percent of the project budget, might be considered "reasonable" for project interface coordination and integration. This is a relatively small amount, considering the ongoing attention, cross-functional involvement and effort required in dealing with the tough interface issues and project integration challenges.

5.7 WORKING EFFECTIVELY IN RESOURCE-SHARED ENVIRONMENTS

Project-oriented businesses are by definition interdisciplinary, such as matrix-based with shared power and resources. When functional resource personnel are assigned to specific projects, team members are likely to maintain strong ties to their home functions. These ties are very normal and predictable as part of the existing cultural network. They are also desirable and necessary for broad conceptual thinking and ultimately cross-functional integration of the work. Yet, project team leaders often see these functional ties as "disloyalty" and barriers to full commitment of team members to the project effort they are assigned to. However, research shows that fighting these ties to the functional home office is counterproductive. It leads to personal anxieties and mistrust. Project team members realize that their job security and career advancement comes to a large degree via their home office and its management. At the same time, these home-office connections are valuable linkages from the project organization into the functional resource organization that should be carefully cultivated and maintained.

Commitment of assigned personnel to the project is a separate issue that will be discussed in more detail later in this book. Research shows that project ownership has little to do with team member alliance with home offices, but depends instead on the personal involvement and pride team members have in the project, and the professional excitement they experience in the team environment. These are dimensions that can be influenced by the project manager via recognition, project visibility, and management involvement. Further, making accomplishments visible and providing feedback to functional managers will influence the reward process administered though the functional organization. The realization that many of the desired elements that contribute to their professional excitement and career advancement come from the project work will build a strong team member commitment and ownership to the project and its mission objectives.

5.8 SUMMARY OF KEY POINTS AND CONCLUSIONS

The following key points were made in this chapter:

- The need for dealing with larger, more complex projects, pressures for broader business accountability and faster, more-effective market response leads to many new and innovative organizational designs, such as *simultaneous engineering, concurrent project management, design-build, Stage-Gate, spiral,* and *agile processes.*
- Three fundamental organizational layers exist in every enterprise: (1) institutional framework, (2) functional system, and (3) operational areas.

- Companies have two principal choices for structuring their business operations: *Functionally and project organized*. However, virtually no company works in a *pure* mode. Real-world businesses operate as hybrids between functional and project organization, relying on resource sharing among functional units for producing specific project deliverables. This is known as the matrix organizational structure.
- The matrix structure exists within an organizational continuum, somewhere between the two extremes of pure functional and pure projectized structures. Its exact operational location between the two extremes depends on the management style and interaction of people within the organization.
- The projectized form of organization is *similar* to the conventional *divisionalized structure*. It represents the strongest form of project authority and an effective approach to executing large project. It requires considerable startup resources and time, and offers limited opportunity for sharing experiences and support functions.
- Matrix organizations offer a compromise solution for project-oriented businesses. The matrix is an overlay on the functional structure of the firm, combining the strength of both the functional and projectized organization.
- Matrix organizations require resource and power sharing, often a source of organizational conflict, and always a challenge to managerial accountability and control, requiring a more sophisticated management style.
- It is important to define the management process, together with its command-and-control structure, including responsibilities, reporting relations, and organizational. The key tools are policy directives, procedures, charter of key positions, organization chart, responsibility matrix, and job descriptions.
- Commitment of assigned personnel to a project is crucial to team performance. Commitment and project ownership can be enhanced through personal involvement, work challenge, professional interest, and pride in the project activities.

5.9 QUESTIONS FOR DISCUSSIONS AND EXERCISES

1. Describe a business environment that would benefit from a predominately projectized internal organization.
2. What advice would you give to your project managers in a matrix organization to minimize matrix conflict?
3. How do you build and sustain project ownership among the team members assigned from other resource departments?
4. Many managers see the matrix as a messy, sloppy organizational structure that is unworkable. Assuming that you cannot projectize, what alternatives do you see to matrix management?
5. Develop a list of dos and don'ts for effective matrix management.

6. Develop a policy or operational guideline for conducting project activities in your company or a case scenario that you can relate to.
7. Project leaders must often step across functional lines and deal with personnel over whom they have little or no formal authority. How can these leaders "earn" the authority they need to function effectively in a matrix environment?
8. How could senior management help project leaders to manage effectively in a matrix environment?

5.10 *PMBOK*® REFERENCES AND CONNECTIONS

The topic of organizing for project management cuts across virtually all of the 10 *knowledge areas* defined by PMBOK. Most strongly it connects with *project integration management* (area #1), *project human resource management* (area #6), *project communications management* (area #7) and *project stakeholder management* (area #10). It also addresses the first two *processing groups: initiating and planning*. Many of the concepts covered in this chapter address the *context* of project management. That is the way projects are organized and executed within the organizational framework of the enterprise. An understanding of the broader context of project management is necessary for effectively applying the standards to the day-to-day management of projects through their life cycles. *In studying for the PMP*® *Exam,* an understanding of the following concepts will be beneficial: (1) different types of structures for organizing projects, (2) variations of matrix structures, (3) advantages and disadvantages of each organizational structure, (4) types of projects most likely to fit particular structures, (5) responsibilities of the project manager, (6) power sharing and resource sharing, (7) dual accountability, (8) managerial authority and power in each organizational form, (9) job security and organizational form or structure.

INTERNET LINKS AND RESOURCES

GM (2012). "GM China to Finish Advanced Technical Center in 2012." http://media. gm.com/media/us/en/gm/news.detail.html/content/Pages/news/us/en/2011/ Dec/1219_china_tc.html
International Journal of Project Organisation and Management. Inderscience Publishers; in print and online. www.inderscience.com/ijpom/.
Wikipedia. "Organizational Project Management." http://en.wikipedia.org/wiki/ Organizational_project_management

REFERENCES AND ADDITIONAL READINGS

Andersen, E. 2003. "Understand Your Project Charter." *Project Management Journal* 34(6): 4–11.

Anderson, C., and M. Fleming. 1990. Management Control in an Engineering Matrix Organization." *Industrial Management* 32(2): 8–13.

Anderson, Erling. 2003. "Understanding Your Project Organization's Charter." *Project Management Journal* 34 (4): 4–11.

Argyres, N., and B. Silverman. 2004. "R&D, Organization Structure, and the Development of Corporate Technological Knowledge." *Strategic Management Journal* 25(8–9): 929–958.

Bishop, Suzanne K. 1999. "Cross-Functional Project Teams in Functionally Aligned Organizations." *Project Management Journal* 30(3): 6–12.

Bobera, D. 2008. "Project Management Organization." *Management Information Systems* 3 (1): 3–9.

Carroll, T., and R. Burton. 2012. "A Contingency Approach to Designing: Theory and Tools," *Engineering Project Organization Journal* 2(1–2): 5–14.

Cleland, D. 1981. "Matrix Management: A Kaleidoscope of Organizational Systems," *Management Review* 70(12): 48–57.

Cleland, David I. 1991. "The Age of Project Management." *Project Management Journal* 22(1): 21–32.

Crawford, L. 2006. " Developing Organizational Project Management Capabilities." *Project Management Journal* 37 (4): 74–86.

Deschamps, Jean-Philippe, and P. Ranganath Nayak. 1995. "Implementing World-Class Process." Chapter 5 in *Product Juggernauts*. Cambridge, MA: Harvard Press.

Ford, R., and A. Randolph. 1992. "Cross-functional Structures: A Review and Integration of Matrix Organization and Project Management." *Journal of Management* 18(2): 267–294.

Galbraith, J. 1971. "Matrix Organization Design." *Business Horizon* 14 (1): 29–40.

Glasser, A. (1982). *Research and Development Management*. New York: Prentice-Hall.

Gray, C., S. Dworatschek, D. Gobeli, H. Knoepfel, and E. Larson. 1990. "International Comparison of Project Organization Structures: Use and Effectiveness." *International Journal of Project Management* 8(1): 26–32.

Grover, V. 1999. "From Business Reengineering to Business Process Change Management." *IEEE Transactions on Engineering Management* 46(1): 36–46.

Hällgren, M., and E. Maaninen-Olsson 2005. "Deviations, Ambiguity, and Uncertainty in a Project-Intensive Organization." *Project Management Journal* 36(3): 17–26.

Holti, R., and M. Keynes. 2011. "Understanding Institutional Change in Project-based Organizing." *Journal of Applied Behavioral Science* 47(3): 360–394.

Kendra, K., and J. Taplin. 2004. Project Success: A Cultural Framework." *Project Management Journal* 35 (2): 30–45.

Kerzner, H. 2009. "Organizational Structure." *Project Management: A Systems Approach to Planning, Scheduling, and Controlling*. Hoboken, NJ: John Wiley & Sons.

Kloppenborg, T. 2012. "Organizational Capability, Structure, Culture, and Roles." *Contemporary Project Management*. Mason, OH: South-Western Publishing.

Kuprenas, J. 2003. "Implementation and Performance of a Matrix Organization Structure." *International Journal of Project Management* 21(1): 51–62.

Lindkvist, L. 2004. "Governing Project-Based Firms: Promoting Market-Like Processes within Hierarchies." *Journal of Management and Governance* 8(1): 3–25.

Lindkvist, L. 2008. "Project Organization: Exploring Its Adaptation Properties." *International Journal of Project Management* 26(1): 13–20.

Middelton, C. 1967. "How to Set up a Project Organization." *Harvard Business Review* 43(2): 73–82.

Mutch, A. 2010. "Technology, Organization, and Structure—A Morphogenetic Approach." *Organization Science* 21(1): 507–520.

Pywell, H. 1979. "Engineering Management in a Multiple-Matrix Organization." *IEEE Transactions on Engineering Management* 26(3): 51–55.

Shim, D. and M. Lee, M. (2001). "Upward Influence Styles of R&D Project Leaders." *IEEE Transactions on Engineering Management*, 48(4): 394–413.

Sobek, Durwald K., Jeffrey K. Liker, and Allen C. Ward. 1998. "Another Look at How Toyota Integrates Product Development." *Harvard Business Review* (July/August): 36–49.

Sydow, J., L. Lindkvist, and R. DeFillippi. 2004. "Project-Based Organizations, Embeddedness and Repositories of Knowledge." *Organization Studies* 25(9): 1475–1489.

Thamhain, H. 1994. "Designing Project Management Systems for a Radically Changing World." *Project Management Journal* 25(4) (December): 6–7.

———. (2011). "Critical Success Factors for Managing Technology-Intensive Teams the Global Enterprise." *Engineering Management Journal*, 23(3): 30-36.

Thamhain, H., and D. Wilemon. 1998. "Building Effective Teams for Complex Project Environments." *Technology Management* 4: 203–212.

Turner, R. 2001. "Project Contract Management and a Theory of Organization." *International Journal of Project Management* 19(8): 457–464.

Turner, R., and R. Müller. 2003. "On the Nature of the Project as a Temporary Organization." *International Journal of Project Management* 21(1): 1–8.

Whitley, R. 2006. "Project-Based Firms: New Organizational Form or Variations on a Theme?" *Industrial and Corporate Change* 15(1): 77–99.

Zhang P., M. Keil, A. Rai and J. Mann (2003), "Predicting Information Technology Project Escalation. *Journal of Operations Research*, 146(1): 115–129.

Chapter 6

The Project Management Office

IBM WINS PMO OF THE YEAR AWARD

Armonk, NY, September 8, 2010—The Project Management Institute announces that IBM's *Project Management Center of Excellence (PM/COE)* has been selected as *The 2010 PMO of the Year*. The annual award specifically recognizes IBM for "creating global project management standards and enterprise-wide consistency among its 26,000 project managers worldwide; establishing a dedicated project management knowledge repository and communications network; increasing project accountability; improving time-to-market by 65 percent; and decreasing the number of troubled projects by 25 percent." IBM's Center of Excellence was selected from a field of more than 40 applicants from nearly every continent and including state and federal agencies, major nonprofit organizations and Fortune 1000 companies.

"All of this year's award applicants are excellent examples of the incredible impact a mature PMO can make on an organization and of how far the PMO has come over the last decade," said J. Kent Crawford, former president and chairman of PMI and current CEO of PM Solutions, a project management services firm helping organizations apply project management office (PMO) practices. "The vast measures that IBM has taken in this area and its outstanding accomplishments reveal a telling story on how to create a successful PMO that sets the course for the entire enterprise."

"Being honored with this award is a coming of age for our team," said Deborah Dell, PMP, IBM's PM/COE manager. "We've been working toward this level of maturity for years and will continue to do so simply because it is a business model that works. It keeps our enterprise operating efficiently, productively, intelligently. . . and profitably."

According to one award committee judge, "IBM set the stage for other organizations to follow with the creation of its Center for Excellence back in 1996. IBM has continued with its maturity initiatives, career progression, emphasis on portfolio management, its return on investment in knowledge management, and its continuous

Source: Bloomberg News Wire, 2010. "IBM Wins Project Management Office of the Year Award."

emphasis on business benefits." More testimony of the importance and impact of this extraordinary achievement was given by Rommy Musch, executive chair of PMI's *PMO Community of Practice*: "IBM has unquestionably demonstrated the ability to integrate project and program management into the infrastructure, organization, and processes used to execute its business. All PMOs, including the ones represented by our 4,000+ members around the world, can benefit from hearing how IBM's PM/COE was able to accomplish such significant business impact."

6.1 MANAGEMENT PERSPECTIVE

Companies don't have to take the project management office (PMO) concept to a full maturity level, as IBM did, to benefit from it. However, it takes organizational desire, backed by top management support and resources to initiate a major organizational development of this kind, which involves changes in operational procedures, business processes, resource allocation, and power sharing. All of this translates into considerable risk and uncertainty. No organization goes into an organizational change lightly. There is an opportunity, but no guarantee that the new process will work better, yet lots of chances for failure with devastating consequences.

So, why are companies like IBM doing it? There must be benefits. For one thing, the centralized systematic, standardized support of all projects within the enterprise is very appealing. Just by intuition we feel it must have benefits regarding project execution efficiency, synergism among similar projects, and better strategic alignment. Often, there are also competitive pressures that leave the enterprise no choice but to move toward more sophisticated project management systems, such as PMOs. These contemporary concepts have received considerable attention in the management literature and at professional conferences and seminars for several years and have gained the endorsement of many managers and researchers across the global project management community. "In today's economy, every company and organization is struggling to do more with less, and performance is paramount. This is true for the public and private sector. PMOs deliver the most value when they are strategically aligned and can enable competitive advantage without losing sight of project and organizational objectives." This comment, made by PMI's president and CEO, Mark Langley, during the 2012 PMO Symposium in Las Vegas, is typical for the favorable PMO image that is derived from success stories. Some endorsements go even further, arguing that the PMO concept could well be the most important development of the past decade (Kerzner 2013, p. 1097). With these promises for more effective project operations, managers cannot afford to ignore these contemporary concepts that have emerged and are routinely used by companies in all industries. So, let's take a detailed look at PMOs, their functional purpose, cost, benefits, and organizational options of implementation.

6.2 PMO CONCEPT AND FUNCTIONALITY

The true origin of the PMO is somewhat cloudy and imbedded in the evolution of project management (see "Origin and Historic Development of PMOs"). However, the 1980s were probably the years during which PMOs emerged as a formal concept. During this period projects and the business environment became more complex and competitive, and organizations were searching for more effective ways of managing these projects, both single and as a portfolio throughout the enterprise.

ORIGIN AND HISTORIC DEVELOPMENT OF PMOS

Although PMOs as we know it today did not exist before the 1990s, its basic function can be traced back to the dawn of civilization when people started to undertake projects, such as monuments, infrastructure developments, and military campaigns. At these ancient times, the project office was a "command post" responsible for supervising, guiding, and tracking project activities. However, it was not before the turn of the twentieth century that the term *project management* was used and PMO-like organizations evolved. The first record of such an organization was made in the 1930s when the US Army Air Corps used a *project office* to monitor aircraft development contracts. Later, during World War II, between 1942 and 1945, the US Air Force used *project offices* to coordinate the development, production, and deployment of the B-29 bomber. The idea of a *central project management office* developed more formally, but remained primarily in the defense and aerospace domain for the next 40 years. Examples are many of the central offices established by the US government for the coordination and deployment of large projects, such as the *Weapons System Project Office (WSPO)* in 1954, and the *ICBM System Program Office (SPO)*, ICBM *Program Management Office* and *Apollo Spacecraft Program Office (ASPO)* in the 1960s.

Encouraged by research and surveys of the 1980s (e.g., Standish Group and Gartner Inc.), an increasing number of companies from the private and public sector began recognizing the benefits associated with central project support. They started to establish their own project support facilities with the objective of introducing more discipline and professionalism into the management of their projects. By the late 1990s, the PMO concept was well-established and documented in the literature (see Crawford 2007, Letavec and Bolles 2011, Turner 2008, Unger et al. 2012). Today, we find a large variety of PMOs with different structures, scope and services. Two basic classification schemes have emerged: First, the classification distinguishes

PMOs by the number of projects and business areas it supports (e.g., single project support versus portfolio or enterprise support). Second, PMPs are distinguished by the degree of control over business results (e.g., project administrative support versus responsibility for business results and strategic alignment). Currently, most project managers understand the PMO concept, its benefits, and its challenges. However, the concept is not seen by all organizations as the best and most optimal way of managing projects. Today, approximately one-half of project-oriented enterprises have actually established PMOs (see Gartner, Inc. reports) and the number is expected to grow slow but steadily.

1985 through 1995 was especially noticeable for a paradigm shift in the business environment. Rapidly changing technology and globalization drove industry dynamics toward a "faster-better-cheaper" operation. At the same time, project management was seen as a competitive tool for achieving better market position, economic value and mission objectives (DeViney et al. 2012). With this awareness for better, more effective management also came the realization that projects need to be managed for optimized value and better strategic alignment with the business process of the enterprise. All of this prompted a shift toward a more disciplined, standardized approach of project management that also aligned closer with the overall business process of the enterprise (Cleland and Ireland 2007, Morris & Pinto 2004). It also led to new project management models that included more centralized systematic project support, the essence of today's project management office (PMO).

6.2.1 What's in the Name of PMO?

Many different names have been used in recent years to describe the project management support system we defined here as PMO. While I prefer the name *project management office, PMO,* to be consistent with a high level of name recognition and established standards, such as PMI's PMBOK® and ISO's certification 9001, other names are being used in the literature (Wysocki 2012) and by managers: project support office (PSO), project office (PO), project management support office (PMSO), enterprise project management office (EPMO), project control office (PCO), program management office (PMO), and project management center of excellence (PM/COE). In this book I will use the acronym PMO consistently. But, the reader should recognize other names, too.

6.2.2 PMO Definition

While there are many different forms of PMOs, with different structure, scope, operational charter, and functionality, the basic PMO definition can be stated as follows:

A project management office, or PMO, is a central enterprise resource, chartered with the responsibility of supporting the initiation, organization and execution of projects conducted within by the enterprise.

In today's environment, the scope of this support function can vary from simple project coordination and information processing to complete project management with full responsibility for business results. Table 6.2 summarizes the scope and wide variety of services that can be provided by PMOs.

In order to break down the complexity of scope and functionality, we can categorize PMOs in three dimensions: (1) level of project management support and service, (2) target area of support, and (3) services provided. These dimensions are intricately linked as graphically shown in Figure 6.1.

6.2.3 Level of Project Management Support and Service

PMOs can provide resources in form of personnel, technology, advice, or other forms of support at four often-overlapping levels.

Project Administration Support

This is the lowest level of support and responsibility. It is usually provided by the PMO in form of online support with forms, analysis, pm-software, and other IT services available to the project manager. In some cases the PMO

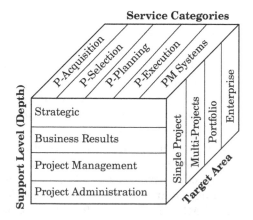

Figure 6.1 Scope of PMO charter

provides project specialized support personnel to the project manager, helping in data collection and analysis, such as for budget and schedule tracking, and in organizing and running review meetings and expediting action items. Such personnel can be assigned on a part-time, as-needed basis or full time for the duration of the project life cycle. Richardson (2010) calls this type of PMO support model metaphorically a "weather station."

Project Management Support

This type of support is provided in the form of an assistant to the project manager or the project manager with full responsiblity for the execution the project or any of the assigned phases. In this support model, the PMO maintains a pool of project management professionals who are assigned to a project within the enterprise as needed. Projects managed by a PMO-based project professional benefit from the latest tools and techniques available within the organization and follow a standard execution method as established for the enterprise. On the down side, PMO-assigned project managers often lack the business-specific knowledge and experience of the project area they are managing. Therefore, projects executed in this mode often have a senior business manager assigned as part of the project management team, responsible for guiding the project to desired business results. If such an arrangement with focus on business results is made, the support mode shifts to the next level, as discussed in Table 6.1.

Table 6.1 Typical Services Provided by PMOs

Service Category	Service Detail
Project acquisition (via competitive bidding)	RFP/RFQ analysis & bid decision support
	Bid proposal support
	Voice-of-the-customer analysis
	Bid strategy development
	Cost modeling and estimating
	Project management plan development
	Vendor/supplier analysis & solicitation
	Contract negotiations
Project evaluation and selection	Evaluation method development
	Risk identification and assessment
	Project proposal evaluation
	Strategic assessment and prioritizing
	Meetings and stakeholders communication
	Computer/IT support
	Decision-making support (i.e., project selection)

(Continued)

Table 6.1 (Continued)

Service Category	Service Detail
Project planning and definition	Baseline definition and documentation
	Definition of scope and deliverables
	Cost modeling and estimating
	Scheduling
	Work breakdown structure (WBS)
	Risk assessment and contingency planning
	Multifunctional resource identification and negotiation, including personnel
	Vendor and contractor selection/negotiation
	Multifunctional interface definition
	Review and control system definition
	Project plan documentation and IT support
	Plan review and signoff
	Website (central portal) development and maintenance
Project startup	Personnel assignment, team development
	Team structure, charter
	Facility development
	Communication network
	Project kickoff
Project execution	Personnel assignment, team development
	Team structure, charter
	Facility development
	Communication network
	Project kickoff
Project closure and follow-up	
Portfolio management	
Project organization development	Same as stated above, but for groups of projects within enterprise portfolio
	Strategic alignment of projects with enterprise business objectives

Project Management Support with Responsibility for Business Results

This support is similar to the previous level, except that the assigned project manager, or assigned project management team, has full responsibility for satisfying contractual requirements to the project sponsor and for achieving expected business results for the enterprise. Since it is often difficult to find project management specialists who also have the business-specific knowledge and experience in the project execution area, a project management team approach is frequently used, involving several senior managers who might come from different functional areas critical to the project success, such as contract administration, new product development, marketing, or general management of a particular business unit. Although this is a common arrangement, especially for large projects, it is a difficult power-shared management system that often leads to conflict over priorities, tradeoffs, effectiveness, and efficiency.

Strategic Support Level

At a high level of maturity, PMOs can provide support to senior management of the enterprise—linking project operations with business strategy, helping to define, adjust and achieve enterprise mission objectives, and optimizing project portfolios for business results. At the same time, PMO leadership must justify its resource allocation and effectiveness, and ensure senior management commitment to PMO funding of its operation and enterprise project management development.

6.2.4 Target Area of Support and Organizational Reach

PMOs can be chartered to provide various levels of project support to different project-oriented groups within the enterprise. That is, support can be limited to just one single project, or it can extend to multiple projects, portfolios, or the total enterprise.

Single Project Support

This type of PMO supports just one project. At the lower level, a single project PMO is just a conventional project office, responsible for the effective execution of the project at hand. However, especially for large projects, organizations establish single-project PMOs with a wide spectrum of support services, including full responsibility for business results. Typically, organizations such as Boeing (aircraft), General Motors (automobile), Samsung (shipbuilding), and NASA (aerospace) establish single-project PMOs with a high maturity level for their large project-based businesses.

Multiproject Support

This type of PMO supports many projects within the enterprise or a particular business division. Similar to the previous category, support services can range from simple administrative support to complete project management with full responsibility for business results.

Project Portfolio Support

Similar to the previous category, this type of PMO supports multiple projects, organized into portfolios of projects with similar characteristics and/or business focus. As in the previous categories, support services can range from simple administrative support to complete project management with full responsibility for business results. However, the emphasis for this type of support is on strategically aligning the portfolio with the business objectives of the enterprise. Therefore, PMOs chartered with project portfolio support are usually operating at a very mature level, providing an extensive range of services and capabilities.

Enterprise Support

PMOs of this category are a central resource for supporting projects throughout the entire enterprise. Usually, PMOs chartered with this responsibility operate at a very mature level. They provide an extensive range of services and capabilities, including the development and maintenance of the most suitable project management tools, techniques, standards and execution method, as well as project management training and career development services, all focused on continuing development of the enterprise project management system.

6.2.5 Services Provided

PMOs can provide a great variety of project support services, targeted to specific activities and processes across the project life cycle. Table 6.1 summarizes these services in eight categories: (1) Project acquisition via competitive bidding, (2) project evaluation and selection, (3) project planning and definition, (4) project startup, (5) project execution, (6) project closure and follow-up, (7) portfolio management, and (8) project organization development. As shown in Table 6.1, each category contains a spectrum of specific services that can be offered to different support areas, such as single of multiple projects. These services can also be offered at various level of management support and sophistication. This overlapping relationship among the three dimensions of PMO support is graphically shown in Figure 6.1.

6.3 REASON FOR ESTABLISHING A PROJECT MANAGEMENT OFFICE (PMO)

No organization goes into an organizational restructuring lightly. I made this comment earlier. With all the potential benefits, favorable image, and press coverage of PMOs, there is still no guarantee that the new process will work better. Therefore, it is not surprising that management is cautious before committing to a new way of executing projects within their organizations.

TOP 15 REASONS FOR ESTABLISHING A PMO

1. More effective project planning and execution
2. Reducing project failures, improving project performance
3. Better project reporting and customer interfacing
4. Improving customer relations and satisfaction
5. Reducing surprises, risks, and uncertainties
6. Setting project standards and disciplines across the enterprise
7. Better alignment of projects with enterprise strategy
8. More enterprise-focused project selection
9. More effective support of portfolio management
10. More effective state-of-the-art tools and techniques, development, and use
11. Better utilization of project management talent and expertise
12. More effective data repository
13. More effective capture of project experiences across the enterprise
14. More effective communication with stakeholders
15. Better support of project management community and career development

The list is rank-ordered by frequency and based on my field observations and discussions with managers across industries.

The reason for establishing a new or upgrading an existing PMO varies considerably from company to company, depending on what management sees as the area that needs improvement most urgently. It is interesting to note that the top five reasons (most frequent observations) for PMO implementation all focus on the need for more effective project management and more predictable outcomes. This is orthogonal to the argument made by researchers that the greatest value of PMOs is in supporting project portfolio management and the alignment of project operations with enterprise strategy. Therefore, this should be the primary reason for establishing a PMO. However, it is not. This might be indicative of the difficulties measuring "strategic benefits." It also reflects the reality of stronger management attention to short-term business performance and survival issues, rather that long-term strategic positioning, regardless of the long-term benefits.

While these observations have little theoretical significance, they are indicative of the realities in the field—that is, the complexities, organizational dynamics, and uncertainty involved in the decision-making process toward a new PMO.

Let's take a systematic approach in exploring why PMOs are being established.

Managers often realize that their projects and business environments have become too complex, to be run effectively by personnel who split their time and efforts among many responsibilities in addition to project management. They also realize that conventional project methods, tools, and skill sets are limited in their effectiveness. They are efficient in tracking and, to some degree, controlling projects to established plans, but weak in dealing with contingencies and adjusting to changing conditions in the market, technology, customer environment, or other areas. Encouraged by favorable reports on PMOs, managers across many industries like to take advantage of these contemporary support systems, which have the potential for providing the best tools and techniques and most experienced project managers, shared throughout the enterprise.

6.3.1 Voices from the Field

The IBM PM/COE discussed in the lead-in scenario of this chapter is an example of how some companies assess the need for more effective project management, and build a rationale and momentum toward establishing a PMO. The turbulent times of the 1990s changed the dynamics of the IT industry, affecting IBM's bottom line, and drove the company to rethink its organizational structure, business model, and management approach. IBM identified project management as key process for delivering complex business solutions to global clients. The lack of good project management was identified as a key factor contributing to project failures, customer issues, and erosion. A group of dedicated project managers wrote an internal white paper describing how IBM could build a competitive advantage by using project management more effectively. In fact, the group suggested turning IBM into a project-based business. IBM's CEO, Louis Gerstner was convinced, and set a goal to transform IBM into a project-based enterprise by raising project management to a core competency. He requested that an executive steering committee (ESC) be established to champion the transformation effort. This committee of senior executives from across all IBM business units laid the foundations for IBM's Project Management Center of Excellence (PM/COE), which became operational in 1998 as a formal PMO and change agent for transforming IBM into a project-based enterprise. Seventeen years after its initial charter, the center has grown to a high level of maturity that is the envy of many project managers across the globe, and earned IBM the PMO of the Year Award in 2010. The center grew from its initial focus on effective, added-value project execution to a much broader support role that includes the continuing development of a consistent career infrastructure, a common project management methodology, including processes, tools, and measurement systems, and provides an interface between IBM's project management community and other professional groups. In 2011, Sam Palmisano, IBM's chairman and CEO, announced that the PM/COE has linked its services to the *Corporate Strategic Roadmap 2015*, supporting continuing growth of the company.

For IBM, the massive undertaking paid off. Testimony given in a 2011 PMI White Paper (PMI 2001, "IBM: Keys to Building a Successful Enterprise Project Management Office") reported the following:

[C]onsistently applying project management disciplines in IBM's service organizations has resulted in a significant decrease in the number of troubled projects with documented root causes in project management since tracking began. The PM/COE enables the practice of project management to become systemic across IBM's global organization through strong and effective communications such as a dedicated intranet site, newsletters, management articles, best practices white papers, conferences, and lunch and learn sessions known as eSharenets. These deliverables provide relevant information to IBM's project managers in the use of project management disciplines to successfully complete projects with higher business and client value.

Yet for IBM, sustaining such an enterprisewide project support capability requires long-term investments of time, people, and funding, plus senior management commitment and collaboration, which is acknowledged and reaffirmed at IBM's COE level.

6.3.2 Four Drivers for Establishing a PMO

Managers are continuously thinking of ways to improve the effectiveness of their businesses operations. However, given the risk and natural resistance to change, the strongest drivers toward a new managerial concept, such as a PMO, come from pressures for survival. The IBM case is a typical example. For many companies, the increased complexity of the business environment with more sophisticated and demanding markets and global competition is continuously putting pressure on market share, profitability, mission success, and the ability to survive and grow as an enterprise. What drives the final decision to establish or upgrade a PMO depends on what management sees as most urgently needing for improvement. It is highly situational and varies from company to company.

The rationale for considering PMOs is driven by many issues, which can be grouped into four categories: (1) effectiveness, (2) capacity to perform, (3) portfolio management, and (4) strategic alignment. In many cases, all or some of the issues are linked, and virtually every case is related to the organization's growth and survival objectives.

Effectiveness

An enterprise experiences increasing pressures for executing projects faster and less costly, typical for today's business environment. Management realizes that a more sophisticated project management system is needed to compete effectively. Upgrading the capabilities for each individual project might be seen too costly and time consuming. However, establishing the needed state-of-the-art capabilities, organized as PMO and shared among all projects enterprisewide, may be a viable alternative for boosting efficiency and value to the enterprise, while delivering projects on time with full customer satisfaction.

Capacity to Perform

An enterprise has the need or opportunity for executing larger and more complex projects, but is limited in its capability, based on the availability of project management skills, tools and techniques. In addition, the company might not have the ability to meet customer requirements for certifications and established standards (i.e., ISO 21500, ISO 9001, PMI/ANSI 99–001–2000), quite common for large project contracts. Upgrading the capabilities for each project individually may be seen too costly and time-consuming, but sharing state-of the-art project management services via an enterprise-wide resource appears a viable alternative.

Portfolio Management

An enterprise finds itself in the situation of managing many related projects, grouped by their characteristics or business areas that should be managed as a portfolio. While project portfolio management is usually treated as a special organization/management system, the management tools, techniques, and disciplines are the same as for project management. In fact, it is difficult to imagine how portfolio management can be achieved without a strong and mature project management support system. The PMO is an effective way to provide the necessary discipline, management tools, and standard methodologies for effective support of project portfolio management. Managers often see the PMO as an important stepping stone to portfolio management.

Strategic Alignment

An enterprise becomes more project-driven with business performance depending increasingly on project performance. Management senses the need for more effective project execution and better alignment of the project operations with the business process, and a stronger linkage with the strategy of the enterprise. A PMO can help in managing projects more strategically with focus on value optimization and business results as compared to traditional attention to delivering contractual results within time and budget constraints.

When we talk with senior managers in organizations that have mature PMOs, they agree with the research (e.g., Norrie 2008, Powell and Young 2004, Richardson 2010, Shenhar 2004) that PMOs have the potential for adding most value in the area of strategic alignment and portfolio management support. However, given the difficulties of measuring the strategic benefits and the realities of priority-focus on immediate survival issues, most PMO initiatives focus initially on short-term performance improvements for their projects, programs and portfolios. That is, improving operational efficiency, effectiveness, and project success. This includes establishing a unified project management discipline, consistent with established standards, across the enterprise. It also relates to the capacity issues of executing larger, more complex projects. Realizing benefits in the area of portfolio management and strategic alignment requires a mature PMO operation, well integrated with the business process of the enterprise and its senior management. These are objectives that are integrated into the PMO charter at the beginning, but will take some time and organizational development to be realized.

6.3.3 Management Concerns

Establishing a PMO is expensive and requires long-term commitment, as we have seen in the IBM PM/COE scenario. Most important, PMOs are no panacea for dealing with the vast challenges of project management in today's complex business environment; they are not quick fixes for management issues or project organizational deficiencies. Moreover, there are no simple metrics for measuring PMO performance, effectiveness, or success. Most of the PMO benefits promised in the management literature—from cost savings to more effective project delivery and strategic alignment—are difficult to benchmark and quantify. Therefore, it is not surprising that management does not rush into such a major organizational development lightly, but has many concerns regarding the cost-benefit and actual success of the PMO in creating value for the enterprise. Another issue is organizational power and politics. PMOs create another layer of management, or another axis to the project matrix. This requires more resource and power-sharing among managers of the enterprise, and has greater potential for organizational politics and conflict. Resistance to any shift toward more power or resource sharing is natural and should be expected. Taken together, many concerns must be satisfied with strong, assuring arguments of potential benefits or needs for survival. Convincing senior management to establish a PMO or upgrade an existing one is a huge undertaking that must be skillfully justified, going beyond intuitive or common-sense arguments. Testimonies of success from other companies in the same industry and collective support for the PMO concept from the project management community of the enterprise are powerful tools for building professional credibility and trust for the a PMO proposal.

Whether you consider the implementation of a basic PMO function aimed at supporting a small group of projects or an enterprisewide initiative, many of the difficulties and concerns relate to the cultural changes required for the development and successful operation of the new organizational system, which requires realignment of responsibilities and authority relations, as well as a different way of cross-functional collaboration and sharing power and resources. "The real issue is not deciding what appears to be a very logical solution to a universal problem, but more of a significant change of organizational culture" (Richardson 2010).

6.4 ESTABLISHING A PROJECT MANAGEMENT OFFICE

Setting up a project management office is a project in itself. After the basic "go-ahead" decision has been made, a project manager must be assigned who is responsible for leading the PMO introduction. That is, working out the detailed implementation plan, negotiating the resources, and developing the facilities, organizational processes, support services, including tools, techniques, and staffing to make the PMO operational. The mechanics of setting up the PMO function itself is a major undertaking that is usually executed by a multifunctional team of stakeholders under the leadership of the appointed project manager. It has the same challenges of coordinating, integrating, staying on budget and schedule, and so on, as any other project. However, in addition, the PMO project leader has to manage change and deal with the issues of organizational culture, politics, and power (Thamhain 2012), which is usually an even bigger challenge that involves a great deal of dynamics and uncertainties that are difficult to plan and to control.

Before embarking on the development of a new PMO, it may be useful to hold focus-group-style discussions with senior managers and future stakeholders across the enterprise to determine whether the key people agree with the basic PMO mandate as it has been established so far, whether managers bought into the objectives that were established, and whether the enterprise is mature enough to benefit from the PMO and ready to make the long-term commitment required for success. These discussions provide valuable inputs for the PMO charter and functional scope of the PMO, and a final reality check on the organizational drive, willpower, and unified long-term commitment, which are critical to the success of this organizational development.

6.4.1 Charter

The objectives, functional scope, roles, responsibilities, and reporting relations must be clearly established and summarized as a charter at the beginning of the PMO implementation. The charter becomes the operating contract for the PMO granted by the enterprise and the basis for funding and its operational existence within the enterprise. For the PMO charter to be recognized and respected by managers throughout the enterprise as a legitimate organizational system, senior management must sign off on it, integrating it with corporate policies and procedures and with management directives.

6.4.2 Implementation Plan

The PMO implementation plan is in essence a project plan, defining the deliverables, budget, cost, and process of establishing the PMO. The plan should also define the type of PMO services to be established and who is responsible for developing them. Since PMOs are service organizations, many of the implementation plan deliverables are services that are often difficult to define in terms of tangible measures of completion. In most cases, a pilot operation is the only way to validate the degree of completion. Given the large variety of PMOs, their operational scopes, and their charters, implementation cycles vary a great deal. However, for a typical PMO, its implementation can easily stretch over 12 months or longer, involving many people across the enterprise and requiring budgets in excess of $1 million. Depending on the scope of the PMO and the size of your organization, the implementation plan should include a launch strategy, such as a subplan describing the way the PMO is to be phased into the current business operations and its management. Taken together, establishing a new PMO is a substantial project that must be professionally planned and executed.

6.4.3 Sponsorship and Senior Management Support

Part of the PMO planning and implementation process is obtaining long-term buy-in from managers across the enterprise, especially at the senior level. Effective communication with all stakeholders during the implementation is important for sustaining interest and commitment. Soliciting advice, invitations to status reviews, open information sessions, Internet home pages, and celebration of milestone achievements are some of the vehicles for keeping the people involved, interested, and supportive to the PMO development. This broad-based management support is critical for ensuring senior management and the PMO sponsor that they made the "right" decision to go forward with the project, and its implementation is organizationally feasible. The role of the sponsor group is to support, promote, and provide strategic guidance for the development, ensuring the people across the company that the PMO is an important organizational development, critical to the survival and growth of the enterprise, and that support to this initiative is valued and rewarded by management. Building and sustaining this long-term commitment is a 360-degree process with senior management providing the vision, direction, and encouragement that leads to interest, enthusiasm, and buy-in by the operational people, which, in turn, is assuring to senior management, refueling their desire for continuing support of the project.

6.4.4 Functional Development

Using the PMO charter and implementation plan as a guide, the PMO structure and service functions must be developed. There is no specific template for structuring PMOs. Each enterprise has its own unique needs and require-ments. The key to determining the right structure is in balancing effective project support with organizational culture and management style. The PMO structure is determined to a large degree by the service functions and other project and portfolio support to be provided by the PMO, consistent with its charter. Examples of these services are summarized in Table 6.1. Part of this functional development is to define the staffing needs for delivering the PMO services, including job descriptions, proficiency levels, skill sets, authority, and reporting relations. In addition, the specific infrastructure requirements for supporting the PMO services must be defined, including facilities, tech-nology support, and externally contracted services.

6.4.5 Operating Budget

The PMO operational budget must be carefully developed, signed off at exec-utive level, and integrated with the annual enterprise budgeting process to ensure that sufficient financial resources are available to sustain the opera-tional mandate.

6.4.6 Performance Measures

Any organization must be able to evaluate its performance, internally as a self-assessment or externally as seen from the users or executive perspec-tive. PMOs are no exception. Specifically, we want to measure the impact of the PMO on the project-driven business of the organization, and ulti-mately the impact on the enterprise as a whole.

Meaningful performance metrics is difficult to define. Many of the mea-sures, such as "satisfaction" are subjective and hard to quantify. Others, such as "project execution time" or "cost-related performance measures," must be interpreted relative to the specific project dynamics (e.g., complexity, contin-gencies, and negotiated changes). They have different meanings in different industry sectors and have different organizational impact, depending on whether projects are managed for enterprise-internal or -external customers. However, regardless of the difficulties and challenges, performance measures should be established and agreed to by key stakeholders of the PMO and senior management of the enterprise, the people who sign off on the PMO charter and its budget.

Different Performance Measures Must Be Established for Different Stages of the PMO

Measures of PMO performance also differ depending on the time period of assessment. Below are four specific examples of performance measures for different stages of PMO operation: (1) PMO implementation, (2) short-term, (3) long-term, and (4) continuous improvement.

- **Performance measures relevant to the PMO implementation stage.** These measures relate to the timely and resource effective implementation of the PMO according to the established project plan, typically measuring deliverables against established schedules and budgets.
- **Performance measures (short-term) relevant to day-by-day PMO operations.** These are simple measures for assessing PMO efficiency and effectiveness on a daily basis. This is different from judging PMO performance against its chartered objectives, which is more long-term and strategically focused, as discussed in the next bullet. The daily operational measures are mostly concerned with the PSO doing the right things, while the long-term performance measures are concerned with doing things right.
- **Performance measures (long-term) relevant to overall PMO effectiveness.** Measuring the effectiveness of PMO performance and its impact on the enterprise is much more difficult and subjective. However, an effort must be made to establish meaningful performance measures so that the value of the PMO relative to the resource commitments can be determined, performance can be benchmarked against the desired maturity and impact level, and continuing performance improvement actions can be taken. PMO performance can be effectively summarized in a scorecard, providing a judgment measure, or quantitative value, against key performance criteria and PMO objectives.
- **Performance measures relevant to the PMO's continuous improvement.** These measures focus on two issues: (1) improving the PMO operation to achieve higher levels of effectiveness and maturity and (2) validating the relevancy and updating of established PMO objectives and governance to ensure alignment with enterprise strategy in our changing business environment. The second part is especially dynamic and strategically focused. Rather than establishing fixed metrics for continuing improvements, I suggest defining processes, such as focus grouping, customer feedback, and executive-level brainstorming, for validating and updating the key objectives, methods, and policies that govern the PMO. The specific performance measures would be an assessment report, to be completed at certain time intervals, stating what was assessed and corrective actions taken, and management controls established.

Type of Measures, Metrics, and Key Performance Indicators

Each PMO is unique, and so are its performance mandates. Therefore, measures of PMO performance, also called key performance indicators (KPI), vary greatly with the scope and objectives established for the PMO, and the industry segment of enterprise operation. Establishing meaningful performance measures is difficult and must consider the specific business environment and organizational context in which the PMO operates. While the wide spectrum of PMO performance measures shared on the Internet can be useful in providing ideas for establishing performance metrics and methods, each PMO manager has to work out his or her own set of performance measures and reach agreement with key stakeholders of the PMO as a basis for future benchmarking and performance assessment.

Performance measures can be categorized by their value judgment into three groups:

1. **Primarily quantitative performance measures.** These are measures that look at "numbers," such as number of PMO-supported projects, number of project managers certified, size of project budget, percent-improvement of profitability (e.g., value added, ROI, IRR, or cash flow), percent of projects performing on time and within budget, $-rework or %-rework reduction, customer satisfaction rate, or percent of portfolio in growth business.

   Quantitative measures have the benefit of producing a clear measure of merit for simple comparison and ranking, but they have limitations. Many performance measures are not quantifiable, such as "quality" or "satisfaction." They are based on judgment. Even if the judgment score is quantified, the source data are qualitative, which should be recognized in subsequent data processing.

2. **Primarily qualitative and intuitive performance measures.** These measures rely on expert judgment, customer feedback, focus groups, benchmarking, or other forms of multifunctional decision making, often relying on broad-scanning and intuitive processes. Typical qualitative performance measures include client satisfaction, strategic alignment of project portfolio, perceived value of project management training and development, and impact of PMO on enterprise performance.

   While qualitative performance measures are often the only way of assessing a particular performance category, such as customer satisfaction, quality or value, their judgmental nature frequently leads to biases introduced by organizational power and politics. This often leads to conflict and disagreement over the interpretation of the performance measure.

3. **Mixed measures, combining both quantitative and qualitative performance measures.** Given the complexity of PMO performance variables, many combine quantitative and qualitative measures. Examples are "project success rates," which often combine financial (quantitative) information with inputs on customer satisfaction (qualitative) and strategic alignment (qualitative). Or, a measure of project portfolio effectiveness, which combines a great deal of financial data (quantitative) with operational efficiency judgment and strategic input (qualitative).

In summary, meaningful and effective evaluation of PMO performance is critical for continuing improvement, organizational support, and funding.

Setting up the metrics and methods for such an evaluation system that has the confidence, trust, and support of the user community and senior management is difficult and challenging. A better understanding of the organizational dynamics and its environment that affects project performance, and the factors that drive cost, revenue, and strategic alignment, will provide a clearer insight into the type of project management support needed by the enterprise. This will help in developing the kind of performance measures that prompt meaningful and fair responses from the PMO user community and PMO sponsor group of senior managers.

6.4.7 Pilot Operation

There is no standardized way or "best practice" of starting up a PMO operation. However, given the changes to the business process, organizational culture, and power structure, caused by the introduction of a new PMO, it is important to launch it properly with the same care as for any other strategic initiative. With this in mind, many companies have chosen an incremental approach to starting up a new PMO function. One option of such a "soft" launch is to start with a pilot operation. This can be done while the PMO is still under development. Quite often, the pilot user groups participated in the PMO proposal and planning phase, and their managers are firm supporters of the PMO initiative. This prior participation ensures some familiarity with the new support function and a positive attitude toward using it. Pilot users should always be chosen on a volunteer basis. Usually there is no shortage of project teams willing to take part in such a pilot operation because it provides opportunities for visibility, recognition, and prestige.

From the PMO developer's perspective, the pilot launch turns the final phase of the PMO initiative into a user-centered design (UCD). The pilot is an excellent opportunity to work with a few committed project teams and senior managers to test the functionality of the new operation, and to obtain early feedback and friendly suggestions from the user groups for fine-tuning and improvement of the PMO system.

6.4.8 Continuous Improvement

As with any enterprise system, and consistent with other quality management efforts, PMOs must have provisions for continuous improvement of their services and processes to achieve the desired level of maturity and to fulfill the chartered responsibilities in our dynamic, continuously changing business environment. As shown in IBM's *Project Management Center of Excellence (PM/COE)*, 17 years after its initial charter, the PMO is still improving its capabilities and adjusting its services continuously to changing corporate needs to remain an effective transformational resource that plays a key role in continuing to improve IBM's project and program management competency.

The starting point for continuous improvement is a regular evaluation of the service delivery processes against the established performance measures, followed by actions for additional improvements. However, the assessment process can't stop at the ongoing service operations, but similar to the IBM example, must examine the objectives and mandates established for the PMO relative to the strategic objectives of the enterprise. In other words, "Are we still doing the right thing? Are our PMO services and resources functioning optimally in aligning project operations with enterprise strategy?" Focus groups, customer feedback, and executive-level steering committees are the management tools for examining the relevancy, maturity level, and performance of PMO services, and, if necessary, redefining PMO objectives and fine-tuning the processes and policies for optimally aligning the project operations with enterprise strategy.

6.5 A FINAL NOTE

If properly designed, integrated in the organization and strategically managed, project management offices (PMO) can be powerful support systems of project-based enterprise operations. This support can be operationally or strategically, ranging from simple project administrative assistance to complete management of single projects or whole project portfolios with full responsibilities for business results. PMOs produce the highest value for the enterprise and the strongest leverage on invested resources in the *strategic area*, such as aligning the project operation of enterprise strategy, starting with more strategic project selection and long-term value focused execution. However, these benefits are difficult to measure with conventional validation methods, and often not fully recognized by management. As a result, PMOs are often underutilized as a strategic tool for creating competitive advantages. One of the biggest challenges to establishing a PMO and fully leveraging its resources is overcoming resistance to change. A new PMO introduces considerable change to organizational culture, authority relations, responsibility realignment, and managerial power. Dealing with the associated issues of fear, trust, respect, credibility, and organizational collaboration is a great challenge that requires strong leadership, supported by effective multidisciplinary planning and skillful execution of the PMO initiative.

6.6 SUMMARY OF KEY POINTS AND CONCLUSIONS

The following key points were made in this chapter:

- Many different names are being used to describe the project support system, which is defined in this chapter as *Project Management Office, PMO*, consistent with established standards, such as PMBOK® and ISO.

- PMOs are powerful management tools for supporting and advancing project-based operations across the enterprise.
- PMOs can be designed for a variety of support services and levels of responsibility, ranging from administrative assistance on single projects to portfolio management with full responsibility for business results and strategic alignment.
- PMOs provide effective interfaces between project operations, senior management, and the customer community.
- PMOs provide effective and consistent project management delivery systems across the organization, especially valuable in supporting large, complex projects and project-based enterprises.
- PMOs can be change agents for transforming an organization into a project-based enterprise.
- PMOs are powerful strategic tools in helping to link project operations with enterprise strategy.
- Defining the mission, roles, responsibilities, and reporting relations are critical to PMO success.
- Establishing a PMO is expensive and requires long-term senior management commitment.
- Establishing a PMO is a major project by itself that needs careful planning, execution, and strong support from management across the enterprise.
- A new PMO introduces considerable change to organizational culture, authority and responsibility relations, and managerial power, resulting in fear and resistance to change. Dealing with these issues requires strong leadership, supported by effective multidisciplinary planning and skillful execution of the PMO initiative.
- An option for launching a new PMO is to start with a pilot operation that might ease the difficulties associated with the cultural changes introduced by the realignment of responsibilities, power and authority.
- An effective PMO performance measurement system is critical to the ability of continuous improvement of its operation and the ability to sustain enterprise support and funding.

6.7 QUESTIONS FOR DISCUSSION

1. Discuss the potential benefits and challenges of establishing a PMO in your organization. (If you wish, you can replace "your organization" with another enterprise you're familiar with from a case study, media report, or other observation.)
2. What approach would you take in proposing a PMO function to your management?
3. Where do you see the highest value added in establishing a PMO in your organization? Is it for project management support, tools/techniques/methods development, training, portfolio management, strategic

alignment, or any combination or other area? Try to be specific. (If you wish, you can replace "your organization" with another enterprise you're familiar with from a case study, media report, or other observation.)

4. How can you minimize the tension and possible resistance to change during the introduction of a new PMO?

5. What measurable milestone would you establish in your PMO implementation plan?

6. How would you define success at the end of a PMO implementation phase?

7. What type of performance measures and methods of collecting these measures would you suggest for assessing PMO performance in supporting (a) individual projects, (b) project portfolios, and (c) strategic issues of the enterprise?

6.8 *PMBOK®* REFERENCES AND CONNECTIONS

The topic of "The Project Management Office" cuts across all of the 10 knowledge areas and 5 processing groups defined by PMBOK®. However, it connects most strongly with project integration management (area #1), project human resource management (area #6), project communications management (area #7), and project stakeholder management (area #10). It also addresses the first two processing groups: initiating and planning. Much of this chapter deals with the context of project management, discussing the way projects are organized and executed within the organizational framework of the enterprise and the need for strategic alignment of projects with enterprise strategy. The managerial perspectives presented in this chapter should be helpful in connecting the PMBOK® standards with best practices of project management, and in studying effectively for PMP® certification. In preparing for the PMP® Exam, the following PMBOK® sections relate especially to this chapter and should be studied: (1) project management office, (2) different types of structures for organizing projects, (3) organizational culture, (4) project life cycle, (5) role of the project manager, (6) human resource planning and management, and (7) project stakeholder relations.

INTERNET LINKS AND RESOURCES

Bloomberg News Wire. 2010. "IBM Wins Project Management Office of the Year Award." Bloomberg (September 8). www.bloomberg.com/apps/news?pid =conewsstory&tkr=ILO:FP&sid=a.HJRkjJ3qpM

CIO. http://www.cio.com/

Dow, W. 2012. *The Tactical Guide for Building a PMO.* www.amazon.com/Tactical-Guide-Building-PMO/dp/098586950X/ref=sr_1_3?s=books&ie=UTF8&qid=137649 3611&sr=1–3&keywords=project+management+Office+PMO#

ESPN. 2009. "PMO of the Year 2010." *pmSolutions.* www.pmsolutions.com/pmoaward.

Gartner, Inc. 2013. http://www.gartner.com/technology/home.jsp

Hobbs, B. 2010. "Project management office: Keynote by Brian Hobbs at 2010 PMO Symposium." http://www.youtube.com/watch?v=-pfsc9iyMFw

MethodCorp. 2011. "Project Management Office." YouTube. http://www.youtube.com/watch?v=AdyGB7i6Wqk

Palermo, J. 2012. "Project Management Office." YouTube. www.youtube.com/watch?v=z-P93T6091U

PMI. Program Management Office Community of Practice. http://pmo.vc.pmi.org/Public/Home.aspx.

The Standish Group. http://blog.standishgroup.com/

Wikipedia. 2013. "2016 Summer Olympics." https://en.wikipedia.org/wiki/2016_Summer_Olympics

REFERENCES AND ADDITIONAL READINGS

Cleland D and L. Ireland (2007). *Project Management: Strategic Design and Implementation*. New York: McGraw-Hill.

Crawford, K. 2007. *Project Management Maturity Model*. Boca Raton, FL: Taylor & Francis.

DeViney, N., K.,Sturtevant, F. Zadeh, L. Peluso, and P. Tambor. 2012. Becoming a Globally Integrated Enterprise: Lessons on Enabling Organizational and Cultural Change. *IBM Journal of Research and Development* 56(6): 2–11.

Gemünden, H. G., C. Killen, and A. Kock. 2013. "A Special Issue of Creativity and Innovation Management: Implementing and Informing Innovation Strategies through Project Portfolio Management." *Creativity and Innovation Management* 22(1): 103–104.

Hamilton, G., G. Byatt, and J. Hodgkinson. 2011. "Seven Keys to Establishing a Successful PMO." *CIO Magazine* (September 26), www.cio.com.au/article/401977/seven_keys_establishing_successful_pmo/

Hill, G. 2013. *The Complete Project Management Office Handbook*. Boca Raton, FL: CRC Press.

Hobbs, B., and M. Aubry. 2010. *The Project Management Office (PMO): A Quest for Understanding*. Newtown, PA: Project Management Institute.

International Organization for Standardization (ISO). 2012. *ISO 21500 Guidance on Project Management*, Geneva, Switzerland: ISO Publishing.

Kerzner, H. 2013. *Project Management: A Systems Approach to Planning, Scheduling, and Controlling*. Hoboken, NJ: John Wiley & Sons.

Kloppenborg, T. 2012. *Contemporary Project Management*. Mason, OH: South-Western Publishing.

Letavec, C., and D. Bolles, eds. 2011. *The PMOSIG Program Management Office Handbook: Strategic and Tactical Insights for Improving Results*. Newtown, PA: Project Management Institute.

Loader, R. 2003. "Lessons Learned from Establishing Project Management Offices in a Corporate Environment." *Australian Project Manager* 23(4): 13–17.

Morris, G., and J. Pinto, eds. 2004. *The Wiley Guide to Managing Projects*. Hoboken, NJ: John Wiley & Sons.

Müller, R. 2009. *Project Governance*. Farnham, Surrey, UK: Gower Publishing, Ltd.

Nir, M. 2013. *The Agile PMO—Leading the Effective, Value Driven, Project Management Office*. CreateSpace Independent Publishing Platform; 3 edition.

Norrie, J. 2008. *Breaking through the Project Fog*. Hoboken, NJ: John Wiley & Sons.

Project Management Institute (PMI). 2011. "IBM: Keys to Building a Successful Enterprise Project Management Office." (White Paper). Newtown, PA: Project Management Institute. http://www.pmi.org/business-solutions/~/media/PDF/Business-Solutions/IBM_CoE_White_Paper.ashx.

———. 2012. "PMI's Program Management Office (PMO) Symposium: Asking Tough Questions, Identifying Solutions." Las Vegas, November 2012. http://www.pmi.org/en/About-Us/Press-Releases/PMIs-Program-Management-Office.aspx.

Powell, M., and J. Young. 2004. "The Project Management Support Office." In G. Morris and J. Pinto, eds., *The Wiley Guide to Managing Projects*. Hoboken, NJ: John Wiley & Sons.

Project Management Institute. 2013. *A Guide to the Project Management Body of Knowledge (PMBOK® Guide)*. Newtown Square, PA: Project Management Institute.

Reiss, G., M. Anthony, J. Chapman, G. Leigh, and A. Pyne. 2008. *Gower Handbook of Programm Management*. Hemshire, UK: Gower Publishing.

Richardson, G. 2010. *Project Management Theory and Practice*. Boca Raton, FL: CRC Press.

Shenhar, A. 2004. "Strategic Project Leadership: Toward a Strategic Approach to Project Management." *R&D Management* 43 (5): 569–578.

Shenhar, A., D. Milosevic, D. Dvir, and H. Thamhain. 2007. *Linking Project Management to Business Strategy*. Newtown, PA: Project Management Institute (PMI) Press.

Standish Group. 2012. *Chaos Report 2012*, http://blog.standishgroup.com/.

Thamhain, H. 2012. "The Changing Role of Team Leadership in Multinational Project Environments." *Revista de Gestão e Projetos (Project Management Journal of Brazil)* 3 (2): 4–38.

Thamhain, Hans. 2009. "Leadership Lessons from Managing Technology-Intensive Teams." *International Journal of Innovation and Technology Management* 6(2): 117–133.

Turner, R. 2009. *The Handbook of Project-based Management: Leading Strategic Change in Organizations* New York: McGraw-Hill.

Turner, R., ed, 2008. *Gower Handbook of Project Management*. Burlington, VT: Gower Publishing.

Tyler, P. 2011. *Leading Successful PMOs*, Burlington, VT: Gower Publishing.

Unger, B., H. Gemünden, and M. Aubry. 2012. The Three Roles of a Project Portfolio Management Office: Their Impact on Portfolio Management Execution and Success. *International Journal of Project Management* 30(5): 608–620.

Wood, A., and M. Shelbourn. 2010. "The Project Management Office: Origins, Definition and Nomenclature." www.aipm.com.au/Documents/AIPM/PMAA_National_Winners_2012/Tony_Wood_paper.pdf.

Wysocki, R. 2012. *Effective Project Management: Traditional, Agile, Extreme*. Hoboken, NJ: John Wiley & Sons.

Chapter 7

Project Evaluation and Selection

MULTIPLE PROJECT SELECTION AT DIRECTV

"We have made considerable progress implementing the strategies we laid out in 2012," says Michael D. White, president and CEO of DIRECTV in the company's annual report. "In addition to the new entertainment package, we've introduced an array of great products and services that will thrill and delight our customers in 2012 and beyond. Our Nomad product allows customers to transfer DVR-recorded content to any portable device. We also will be expanding our TV Everywhere service as a major priority this year, providing online and mobile access to an array of pay-per-view and premium network content on a variety of devices from the PC to the iPad to the iPhone and Android. At the same time, we're accelerating the pace of connecting customers' advanced receivers to the Internet so they may enjoy more DIRECTV CINEMA titles and a wide variety of popular apps, including the DIRECTV iPad App, Facebook, YouTube videos, social TV apps, and Pandora internet radio. We continue to be excited about the growth potential of our alliances with AT&T, CenturyLink, and Verizon. We're making progress on better integrating their services with ours and expect to jump-start sales of bundled services later this year. In 2012, we also are planning to improve the seamlessness of our video/Internet bundles as well as substantially increase the number of fiber and DSL options for our customers. We continue to think outside the box to further strengthen these strategic relationships. As the residential market matures, we are intensifying our focus on three key areas that will produce incremental revenues: our commercial sales, local advertising and DIRECTV CINEMA. We've made good progress growing our commercial business last year and we'll continue to aggressively drive sales in this category in 2012 with new products like our DIRECTV Residential Experience for Hotels and the DIRECTV Message Board, which overlays advertising on live TV in retailers' showrooms. . . . We have set ambitious short and long-term goals, and are excited that 2013 will be another year of growth for DIRECTV."

Sources: DIRECTV company profile and Wikipedia "Direct Broadcast Satellite (DBS) Technology. (For website references see" "Internet Links" section at the end of this chapter.)

The direct broadcast satellite (DBS) ventures are part of the world's most complex and fastest-growing businesses. DIRECTV is the largest US direct broadcast satellite (DBS) system, offering 150 channels of movies, cable TV programs, and sporting events directly to anyone in the United States, Canada, and part of South America. Already in 1997, DIRECTV, then part of Hughes Electronics/General Motors, had secured this market niche by forming an alliance between its PanAmSat subsidiary and SatMex (Satellites Mexicanos), bidding for the strategic satellite position. Other bidders included Primestar and EchoStar. At 77 degrees west longitude, the Mexican slot was the last to allow a satellite to beam full conus coverage of the United States and Mexico.

Today, with nearly $30 billion in annual revenue and 30 million subscribers, DIRECTV does well in a crowded market of increasing competition and a saturating U.S. pay-TV environment. Also, analysts remain positive on the future of DIRECTV. The company that has been smart in responding to changing needs and has demonstrated continued success in the growing Latin American market. Its rivals such as Dish Network and Comcast are doing better than before, but DIRECTV has its ways of continuing growth. However, successfully introducing new products and services is not a random process. It requires skillful evaluation of these opportunities combined with careful planning and implementation. As pointed out by DIRECTV's president White, "Before we reinvent TV it is essential that we do a better job of understanding one size doesn't fit all. Our customers have different tastes, wants and levels of income. Therefore, our first order of business is to make sure we fit each customer's needs."

7.1 MANAGEMENT PERSPECTIVE

Predicting project success has never been easy. The lead-in DIRECTV scenario is a good example of the spectrum of project opportunities, ranging from products and services to broadcasting frequency acquisitions and satellite positioning, that companies have to deal with. All of these opportunities needed to be evaluated to determine their long-range cost-benefits which includes complex market, technological, socio-political and strategic factors, each one associated with enormous uncertainties. DIRECTV was exceptionally successful selecting so many winning projects, a record not easily matched by others. The long list of projects and missions that failed, despite their promises, remind us of this reality. They range from product developments to government social programs, from computers to pharmaceutical and from public transit to supersonic transport (Cicmil et al. 2006; Lemon et al. 2002). Many projects do not live up to their expectations or fail outright even before their technical completion in spite of careful feasibility analysis during their proposal or selection stages (El Emam et al. 2008). Obviously, the ability to evaluate project proposals, assessing future success and organizational value, is critical to overall business performance. In fact, few decisions have more impact on enterprise performance than the resource allocations for new projects. Virtually every organization evaluates, selects, and implements projects. Whether these projects are product developments, organizational improvements, R&D undertakings or bid proposals, pursuing the "wrong" project not only wastes company resources, but also causes the enterprise to (1) miss critical alternatives, (2) operate less flexible and responsive in the market place, and (3) miss opportunities for leveraging core competencies. Yet in spite of pressures to avoid these high-cost errors, predicting project success is difficult and existing models are often unreliable. Especially in today's complex and changing business environment, the process of evaluating and selecting the "best" projects, most suitable and beneficial for the enterprise, has become both an art and a science, strongly influenced by human and organizational factors.

Project opportunities must be analyzed relative to their potential value, strength and importance to the enterprise. Four major dimensions should be considered: (1) added value of the new project, (2) cost of the project, (3) readiness of the enterprise to execute the project, and (4) managerial desire. A well-organized project evaluation and selection process provides the framework for systematic data gathering and informed decision making toward resource allocation. Typically, these decisions can be broken into four categories:

1. Deciding initial feasibility: Screening and filtering, quick decision on the viability of an emerging project for further evaluation
2. Deciding strategic value to enterprise: Identifying alternatives and options to proposed project
3. Deciding detailed feasibility: Determining the chances of success for a proposed project
4. Deciding project go/no-go: Committing resources for a project implementation

Although making these decisions looks simple, logical, and straightforward, developing meaningful support data is a complex undertaking. It is also expensive, time-consuming, and often highly eclectic. Typically, decision making requires the following inputs:

- Specific resource requirements
- Specific implementation risks
- Specific benefits (economics, technology, markets, etc.)
- Benchmarking and comparative analysis
- Strategic perspective, including long- and short-term value assessment

While it is challenging to estimate cost, schedules, risks, and benefits, such as those shown in "Typical Criteria for Project Evaluation and Selection," these measures are relatively straightforward in comparison to predicting project success. The difficulty is in defining a meaningful aggregate indicator for project value and success. Methods for determining success range from purely intuitive to highly analytical. No method is seen as truly reliable in

---

TYPICAL CRITERIA FOR PROJECT EVALUATION AND SELECTION

The criteria relevant to the evaluation and selection of a particular project depend on the specific project type and business situation, such as for a particular product development, custom project, process development, industry, or market. Typically, evaluation procedures include the following criteria and measures:

- Development cost
- Development time
- Technical complexity and feasibility
- Risk
- Return on investment
- Cost-benefit
- Product life cycle
- Sales volume
- Market share
- Project business follow-on
- Organizational readiness and strength
- Consistency with business plan
- Resource availability
- Cash flow, revenue and profit
- Impact on other business activities

Each criteria is based on a complex set of parameters and variables.

---

predicting success, especially for more complex and technologically intensive types of projects. Yet, some companies have a better track record in selecting "winning" projects than others. They seem to have the ability to create a more integrated picture of the potential benefits, costs, and risks for the proposed project relative to the company's strength and strategic objectives. Producing such a composite is both a science and an art. Traditionally, the management literature suggested by-and-large rational selection processes to support project selections. However, purely rational-analytical processes apply only to a limited number of business situations. Many of today's technologically complex business scenarios require the integration of both analytical and judgmental techniques to evaluate projects in a meaningful way, predicting success and making the best choice.

Yet in spite of the dynamics involved in the selection process, systematic information gathering and standardized methods are at the heart of any project evaluation process, and provide the best assurance for reliably predicting project outcome and repeatability of the decision process. Approaches to project evaluation and selection fall into one of three classes:

1. Primarily quantitative and rational approaches
2. Primarily qualitative and intuitive approaches
3. Mixed approaches, combining both quantitative and qualitative methods

Because of the interdisciplinary complexities involved, analyzing a new project opportunity is a highly interactive effort among the various resource groups of the enterprise and its partners. Often, many meetings are needed before (1) a clear picture emerges of potential benefits, costs, and risks involved in the project, and (2) data emerge that are useful for the project evaluation and selection process, regardless of its quantitative, qualitative, or combined nature.

7.2 QUANTITATIVE APPROACHES TO PROJECT EVALUATION AND SELECTION

Quantitative approaches are often favored to support project evaluation and selections if the decisions require economic justification. They are also commonly used to support judgment-based project selections. One of the features of quantitative approaches is the generation of numeric measures for simple and effective comparison, ranking, and selection. These approaches also help to establish quantifiable norms and standards, and lead to repeatable processes. Yet, the ultimate usefulness of these methods depends on the assumption that the decision parameters, such as cash flow, risks, and the underlying economic, social, political, and market factors can actually be quantified and reliably estimated over the project life cycle. Therefore, quantitative techniques are effective and powerful decision support tools, if meaningful estimates of cost-benefits, such as capital expenditures and future revenues, can be obtained, and converted into net present values for comparison. Because of their importance, quantitative methods have been discussed in the literature extensively, ranging from simple return on investment (ROI) calculations to elaborate simulations of project scenarios. Many companies eventually develop their own project evaluation/selection models, customized to their specific needs. However, the backbone for most of these customized models is a set of economic/financial measures that tries to determine the cost-benefit of the proposed venture, usually for some point in the future. Specifically, four measures are especially popular:

- Net present value (NPV)
- Return on investment (ROI)
- Cost-benefit (CB)
- Payback period (PBP)

The calculation and application of these measures to project evaluation/ selection will be illustrated by case examples. Specifically, four project

Table 7.1   Description of Four Project Proposals

Project Option	Description
Project Option P1	Management does not accept any new project proposal. Hence, no investment capital is required, nor is any revenue generated.
Project Option P2	This opportunity requires a $1,000 investment at the beginning of the first year, and generates $200 in revenue at the end of each of the following five years.
Project Option P3	This opportunity requires a $2,000 investment at the beginning of the first year, and generates a variable stream of net revenues at the end of each of the next five years as follows: $1,500; $1,000; $800; $900; $1,200.
Project Option P4	This opportunity requires a $5,000 investment at the beginning of the first year, and generates a variable stream of net revenues at the end of each of the next five years as follows: $1,000; $1,500; $2,000; $3,000; $4,000.

proposals (described in Table 7.1) will be evaluated in this chapter, using the above measures. The results are summarized in Table 7.2.

7.2.1 Net Present Value (NPV) Comparison

This method uses discounted cash flow as the basis for comparing the relative merit of alternative project opportunities. It assumes that all investment costs and revenues are known, and that economic analysis is a valid basis for project selection.

We can determine the net present value (NPV) of a single revenue, or stream of future revenues, or costs expected in the future. Two types of presentations are common: (1) present worth and (2) net present value.

7.2.2 Present Worth, PW

This is the single revenue or cost (also called annuity, A) that occurs at the end of a period n, subject to the prevailing interest rate i. Depending on the management philosophy and enterprise policies, this interest rate can be the *internal rate of return (IRR)* realized by the company on similar investments, the *minimum attractive rate of return (MARR)* acceptable to company management, or the prevailing discount rate. The present worth is calculated as:

$$PW(A \mid i, n) = PW_n = A \frac{1}{(1+i)^n}.$$

For the examples used in this chapter, we consider the IRR (defined as the average return realized on similar investments) to be the prevailing interest rate.

Table 7.2   Cash Flow of Four Project Options or Proposals

End of Year N		Do-Nothing Option P1	Project Option P2	Project Option P3	Project Option P4
			Given Cash Flow		Calculations
0		0	–1,000	2,000	–5,000
1		0	200	1,500	1,000
2		0	200	1,000	1,500
3		0	200	800	2,000
4		0	200	900	3,000
5		0	200	1,200	4,000
Net Cash Flow	$\sum P$	0	0	+3,400	+6,500
Net Present Value at the end of year 5	$NPV\vert_{N=5}$	0	–242	+2,153	+3,192
Net Present Value for revenue to continue to ∞	$NPV\vert_{N=\infty}$	0	+1,000	+9,904	+28,030
Average annual return on investment	$ROI\vert_{N=5}$	0	20%	54%	46%
Cost-benefit analysis	$CB = ROI_{NPV\vert N=5}$	0	76%	108%	164%
Payback period for MARR = 10%	$N_{PBP}\vert_{i=10}$	0	8	1.8	3.8
Payback period for MARR = 0%	$N_{PBP}\vert_{i=0}$	0	5	1.5	3.3

Note: Given for all four project proposals: (1) a single investment is made at the beginning of the project life cycle (e.g. at the end of year 0; (2) the internal rate of return (IRR), or the minimum attractive rate of return (MARR), is 10 percent

7.2.3 Net Present Value, NPV

The *net present value* is defined as a series of revenues or costs, A_n, over N periods of time, at a prevailing interest rate i:.

$$\text{NPV}(A_n \mid i,\ N) = \sum_{n=1}^{N} A_n \frac{1}{(1+i)^n} = \sum_{n=1}^{N} \text{PW}_n$$

Three special cases exist for the net present value calculation:

1. For a uniform series of revenues or costs over N periods: $\text{NPV}(A_n \mid i, N) = A[(1 + i)^{N-1}]/i(1 + i)^N$
2. For an annuity or interest rate i approaching zero: $\text{NPV} = A \times N$
3. For the revenue or cost series to continue forever: $\text{NPV} = A/i$

Table 7.2 applies these formulas to the four project alternatives described in Table 7.1, showing the most favorable five-year net present value of \$3,192 for project option P3.

7.2.4 Return on Investment (ROI) Comparison

Perhaps one of the most popular measures for project evaluation is the return on investment (ROI):

$$\text{ROI} = \frac{R - C}{I}$$

where
$R = \text{Revenue}$
$C = \text{Cost}$
$I = \text{Investment}$

ROI calculates the ratio of net revenue over investment. In its simplest form the stream of cash flow is *not* discounted. One can look at the revenue on a year-by-year basis, relative to the initial investment. For example, project option 1 in Table 7.2 would produce a 20 percent ROI each year, while project option 2 would produce a 75 percent ROI during the first year, 50 percent during the second year, and so on. In a somewhat more sophisticated way, we can calculate the average ROI per year over a given revenue cycle as shown in Table 7.2:

$$\overline{\text{ROI}}(A_n,\ I_n \mid N) = \left[\sum_{n=1}^{N} \frac{(\text{Revenue } R) - (\text{Cost } C)_n}{(\text{Investment } I)_n} \right] \Big/ [N]$$

We can then compare the average ROI to the minimum attractive rate of return, *MARR*. Given a MARR of 10 percent for our project environment, all three project options (P1, P2, and P3) compare favorable, with project P3 yielding the highest average return on investment (54 percent). Although this is a popular measure, it does not permit a meaningful comparative analysis of alternative projects with fluctuating costs and revenues. Furthermore, it does not consider the time value of money.

7.2.5 Cost-Benefit (CB)

Alternatively, we can calculate the net present value of the total ROI over the project life cycle. This measure, known as *cost-benefit, CB*, is calculated as the present-value stream of net-revenues divided by the present-value stream of investments. It is an effective measure for comparing project alternatives with fluctuating cash flows:

$$\text{CB} = \text{ROI}_{NPV}(A_n, I_n \mid i, N) = \left[\sum_{n=1}^{N} \text{NPV}(A_n \mid i, N) \right] / \left[\sum_{n=1}^{N} \text{NPV}(I_n \mid i, N) \right]$$

In our example of four project options (Table 7.2), project proposal P4 produces the highest cost-benefit of 164 percent under the given assumption of i = MARR = 10 percent.

7.2.6 Payback Period (PBP) Comparison

Another popular figure of merit for comparing project alternatives is the *payback period (PBP)*. It indicates the time period of net revenues required to return the capital investment made on the project. For simplicity, undiscounted cash flows are often used to calculate a quick figure for comparison, which is quite meaningful if we deal with an initial investment and a steady stream of net revenue. However, for fluctuating revenue and/or cost steams, the net present value must be *calculated for each period individually* and cumulatively added up to the *break-even point* in time, N_{PBP}, when the net present value of revenue equals the investment. Mathematically,

$$N_{\text{PBP}} \text{ occurs when } \sum_{n=1}^{N} \text{NPV}(A_n \mid i) \geq \sum_{n=1}^{N} \text{NPV}(I_n \mid i)$$

In our example of four project options (Table 7.2), project proposal P3 produces the shortest, most favorable payback period of 1.8 years under the given assumption of i = MARR = 10 percent.

7.2.7 Pacifico and Sobelman Project Ratings

The previously discussed methods of evaluating projects rely heavily on the assumption that technical and commercial success is ensured, and all costs and revenues are predicable. Because these assumptions do not always hold, many companies have developed their own special procedures and formulas for comparing project alternatives. Two examples illustrate this special category of project evaluation metrics.

The Project Rating Factor, PR

This measure was originally developed by Carl Pacifico for assessing chemical products and predicting commercial success:

$$\text{PR} = \frac{pT \times pC \times R}{TC}$$

Pacificio's formula is in essence an ROI calculation adjusted for risk. It includes: Probability of technical success ($0.1 < pT < 1.0$), probability of commercial success ($0.1 < pC < 1.0$), total net revenue over project life cycle (R), and total capital investment for product development, manufacturing setup, marketing, and related overheads (TC).

Product Development Figure of Merit

The formula developed by Sobelman represents a modified cost-benefit measure that takes into account both the development time and commercial life cycle of the product:

$$z = (P \times T_{LC}) - (C \times T_{D})$$

It also includes average profit per year (P), estimated product life cycle (T_{LC}), average development cost per year (C), and years of development (T_{D}).

7.2.8 Going Beyond Simple Formulas

While quantitative methods of project evaluation have the benefit of producing relatively quickly a measure of merit for simple comparison and ranking, they also have many limitations, as summarized in Table 7.3. Yet in spite of the limitations inherent to quantitative evaluation and the increased use of qualitative approaches, *virtually every organization supports its project selections with some form of quantitative measures*—most popular are ROI, cost-benefit, and payback period. However, driven by the growing complexity of the business environment, managers are increasingly concerned about these limitations and are exploring alternatives. They often

Table 7.3   Advantages and Limitations of Quantitative Project Evaluation

Quantitative Methods	Qualitative Methods
Benefits	**Benefits**
• Clear and simple comparison, ranking, selection • Repeatable process • Encourages data gathering and measurability • Benchmarking opportunities • Programmable • Useful input to sensitivity analysis and simulation • Connectable to many analytical and statistical models	• Search for meaningful evaluation metrics • Broad-based organizational involvement • Understanding of problems, benefits, and opportunities • Problem solving as part of selection process • Broadly distributed knowledge base • Multiple solutions and alternatives • Multifunctional involvement leading to buy-in and risk sharing
Limitations	**Limitations**
• Many success factors not quantifiable • Probabilities and weights may change • No true measures • Analyses and conclusions often misleading • Masking of hidden problems and opportunities • Stifling of innovative decision making • Lack people involvement, buy-in, commitment • Ineffective in dealing with multi-functional issues, nonlinearities, and dynamic situations • May mask hidden costs and benefits • Temptation for acting too quickly and prematurely	• Complex, time-consuming process • Biases introduced via organizational power and politics • Difficult to procedurelize or repeat • Conflict and disagreement over decision/outcome • Does not fit conventional decision processes • Intuition and emotion may obscure facts • Used for justifying "wants" • Leads to more fact-finding than decision making • Temptation for unnecessary expansion of fact-finding • Process requires effective managerial leadership

augment quantitative methods with additional measures for determining the long-range cost-benefits of a project proposal to the enterprise. Many of these contemporary decision-making methods rely to a large degree on qualitative, subjective decision making. These data-gathering methods cast a wide net and consider a broad spectrum of factors that are often difficult to describe or quantify, but are effective in gaining strategic perspective and a more comprehensive picture on potential benefits, risk, and challenges of the proposed project.

7.3 QUALITATIVE APPROACHES TO PROJECT EVALUATION AND SELECTION

Although quantitative methods provide an important toolset for project evaluation and selection, there is also a growing sense of frustration, especially among managers of complex and technologically advanced undertakings, that reliance on strictly quantitative methods does not always produce the most useful or reliable inputs for decision making, nor are all methods equally suited for all situations. Therefore, it is not surprising that for project evaluations involving complex sets of business criteria, narrowly focused quantitative methods are often supplemented with broad, intuitive processes, and collective, multifunctional decision-making techniques such as: Delphi, nominal group technology, brainstorming, focus groups, sensitivity analysis, and benchmarking. These techniques can be used alone to determine the best, most successful, or most valuable option, or they can be integrated into a comprehensive analytical framework for collective multifunctional decision making, discussed next.

7.3.1 Collective, Multifunctional Evaluations

This process relies on subject experts from various functional areas for collectively defining and evaluating broad project success criteria, employing both quantitative and qualitative methods. The first step is to define the specific organizational areas critical to project success and to assign expert evaluators. For a typical product development project, these organizations may include R&D, engineering, testing, manufacturing, marketing, product assurance, and customer/field services. These function experts should be given the time necessary for the evaluation. They also should have a commitment from senior management of full organizational support. Ideally, these evaluators should be members of the core team ultimately responsible for project implementation.

Evaluation Factors

Early in the evaluation process the team defines the factors that appear critical to the ultimate success of the projects under evaluation and arranges them into a list that includes both quantitative and qualitative factors. A mutually acceptable scale must be worked out for scoring the evaluation criteria. Studies of collective multifunctional assessment practices show that simple scales are most effective for leading to actionable team decisions.

The four most popular and robust scales for judging situational outcomes are as follows:

1. Ten-point judgment scale: This scale ranges from +5 (most favorable) to –5 (most unfavorable)
2. Three-point judgment scale: +1 (favorable), 0 (neutral or can't judge), –1 (unfavorable)
3. Five-point judgment scale: A (highly favorable), B (favorable), C (marginally favorable), D (most likely unfavorable), F (definitely unfavorable)
4. Five-point Likert scale: 1 (strongly agree), 2 (agree), 3 (neutral), 4 (disagree), 5 (strongly disagree).

Weighing of criteria is not recommended for most applications, as it complicates and often distorts the collective evaluation.

The Evaluation Process

Evaluators first assess and then score all of the success factors they feel qualified to judge. Then collective discussions follow. Initial discussions of project alternatives, their markets, business opportunities, and technologies involved are usually beneficial but not absolutely necessary for the first round of the evaluation process. The objective of this first round of expert judgments is to get consensus on the opportunities and challenges presented. Furthermore, each evaluator has the opportunity to recommend (1) actions that could improve the quality and accuracy of the project evaluation, (2) additional data needed, and (3) suggestions for increasing project success. Before meeting at the next group session, agreed-on action items and activities for improving the decision process should be completed. The evaluation process is enhanced with each iteration by producing more accurate, refined and comprehensive data. Typically, between three and five iterations are required before a go/no-go decision can be reached for a given project.

7.4 RECOMMENDATIONS FOR EFFECTIVE PROJECT EVALUATION AND SELECTION

Effective evaluation and selection of project opportunities involves many variables of the organizational and technological environment, often reaching far beyond cost and revenue measures. While economic models provide an important dimension of the project selection process, most situations are too complex to use simple quantitative methods as the sole basis for decision making. Many of today's project evaluation procedures include a broad spectrum of variables and rely on a combination of rational and intuitive processes for defining the value of a new project venture to the enterprise. The better organizations understand their business processes, markets, customers, and technologies, the better they will be able to evaluate the value, risks, and challenges of a new project venture. Further, manageability of the evaluation process is critical to its results, especially in complex situations. The process must have a certain degree of structure, discipline, and measurability to be conducive to the intricate multivariable analysis. One method of achieving structure and manageability calls for grouping the evaluation variables into four categories: (1) consistency and strength of the project with the business mission, strategy, and plan, (2) multifunctional ability to produce the project deliverables and objectives, including technical, cost, and time factors, (3) success in the customer environment, and (4), economics, including profitability. Modern phase management, such as Stage-Gate, processes provide managers with the tools for organizing and conducting project evaluations in a systematic way. The following list summarizes suggestions that can help managers in effectively evaluating and selecting projects toward successful implementation.

Seek out relevant information. Meaningful project evaluations require relevant quality information. The four sets of variables, related to the strategy, results, customer and economics, as identified above, can provide a framework for establishing the proper metrics and detailed data gathering.

Ensure competence and relevancy. Ensure that the right people become involved in the data collection and judgmental processes.

Take top-down look first; detail comes later. Detail is less important than information relevancy and evaluator expertise. Don't get hung-up on missing data during the early phases of the project evaluation. Evaluation processes should be iterative. It does not make sense to spend a lot of time and resources on gathering perfect data, to justify a "no-go" decision.

Select and match the right people. Whether the project evaluation consists of a simple economic analysis or a complex multifunctional assessment, competent people from functions critical to the overall success of the project should be involved.

Define success criteria. Whether deciding on a single project or choosing among alternatives, evaluation criteria must be defined. They can be quantitative, such as ROI, or qualitative, such as the chances of winning a contract. In either case, these evaluation criteria should cover the true spectrum of factors affecting success and failure of the project(s). The success criteria should be identified by seasoned enterprise personnel. In addition, people from outside of the company, such as vendors, subcontractors, and customers, are often included in this expert group and are critical to the development of meaningful success criteria.

Strictly quantitative criteria can be misleading. Be aware of evaluation procedures based on quantitative criteria only (ROI, cost, market share, MARR, etc.). The input data used to calculate these criteria are likely based on rough estimates and are often unreliable. Furthermore, a reliance on strictly quantitative data considers only a narrow spectrum of factors affecting project success or failure. This strategy ignores many other important factors, especially those that influence project success in a dynamic or non-linear way, typical for many complex, technologically sophisticated undertakings. Evaluations based on predominately quantitative criteria should at least be augmented with some expert judgment as a "sanity check."

Condense criteria list. Combine evaluation criteria, especially among the subjective categories, to keep the list manageable. As a goal, try to stay within 12 criteria for each category.

Gain broad perspective. The inputs to the project selection process should include the broadest possible spectrum of data from the business environment that affect success, failure, and limitations of the new project opportunity. Assumptions should be carefully examined.

Communicate across the enterprise. Facilitate communications among evaluators and functional support groups. Define the process for organizing the team and conducting the evaluation and selection process.

Ensure cross-functional representation and cooperation. People on the evaluation team must share a strategic vision across organizational lines. They also must have the desire to support the project if selected for implementation. The purpose, goals, objectives, and relationships of the project to the business mission should be clear to all parties involved in the evaluation/selection process.

Don't lose the big picture. As discussions go into detail during the evaluation, the team should maintain a broad perspective. Two global judgment factors can help to focus on the big picture of project success: (1) overall cost-benefit perspective and (2) overall risk of failure assessment. These factors can be recorded on a ten-point scale, –5 to +5. This also leads to an effective two-dimensional graphic display for comparing competing project proposals.

Do your homework between iterations. Project evaluations are usually conducted progressively in iterative cycles. Therefore, the need for more information, clarification, and further analysis surfaces between each cycle. Necessary action items should be properly assigned and followed up to enhance the evaluation quality with each consecutive iteration.

Take a project-oriented approach. Plan, organize, and manage your project evaluation/selection process as a project. Proposal evaluation, and selection processes require valuable resources that must be justified and carefully managed.

Resource availability and timing. Don't forget to include in your selection criteria the availability and timing of resources. Many otherwise successful projects fail because they cannot be completed within a required time period.

Use red-team reviews. Set up a special review team of senior personnel. This is especially useful for large and complex projects with major impact on overall business performance. This review team examines the decision parameters, qualitative measures, and assumptions used in the evaluation process. Limitations, biases, and misinterpretations that may otherwise remain hidden can often be identified and dealt with.

Stimulate creativity and candor. Senior management should foster an innovative risk-shared ambience for the evaluation team. Especially the evaluation of complex project situations involves intricate sets of variables. Criteria for success and failure are linked among many subsystems (e.g., organization, technology, and business) associated with a great deal of risks and uncertainty. Innovative approaches are required to evaluate the true potential of success for these projects. Risk-sharing by senior management, recognition, visibility, and a favorable image in terms of high priority, interesting work, and importance of the project to the organization, have been found strong drivers toward attracting and holding quality people on the evaluation team, and toward gaining their active and innovative participation in the process.

Manage and lead. The evaluation team should be chaired by someone who has the trust, respect, and leadership credibility with the team members. Senior management can positively influence the work environment and the process by providing guidelines, charters, visibility, resources, and active support to the project evaluation team.

7.5 CONCLUDING REMARKS

Taken together, effective project evaluation and selection requires a broad-scanning process across all segments of the enterprise and its environment to deal with the risks, uncertainties, ambiguities, and imperfections of data available for assessing the value of a new project venture relative to other opportunities. No single set of broad guidelines exists that guarantees the selection of successful projects. However, the process is not random! A better understanding of the organizational dynamics that affects project performance, and the factors that drive cost, revenue, and other benefits, can help in gaining a better, more meaningful insight into the future value of a prospective new project. Seeking out both quantitative and qualitative measures incorporated into a combined rational-judgmental evaluation process often yields the most reliable predictor of future project value and desirability. Equally important, the process requires managerial leadership and skills in planning, organizing, and communicating. Above all, the leaders of the project evaluation team must be social architects who can unify the multifunctional process and its people. The leader must be able to foster an environment professionally stimulating and conducive to risk sharing. It also must be effectively linked to the functional support groups needed for project implementation. Finally, organizational strategy must be aligned and integrated with the evaluation/selection process, early and throughout its evaluation cycle. Senior management has an important role in unifying the evaluation team behind the mission objectives and in facilitating the linkages to the stakeholders and ultimate user community. Senior management should further help in providing overall leadership and in building mutual trust, respect, and credibility among the members of the proposal evaluation team, all critical drivers toward a strong partnership of all team members and the basis for an effective enterprisewide decision-making system. Taken together, this is the environment conducive to cross-functional communication, cooperation, and integration of the intricate variables needed for effective engineering project evaluation and selection.

7.6 SUMMARY OF KEY POINTS AND CONCLUSIONS

The following key points were made in this chapter:

- Predicting success of a promising project opportunity is very complex and difficult, requiring broad, multidisciplinary scanning and the participation of experts from all enterprise functions affected by the project during its life cycle.
- Project evaluation criteria should include at least four categories: technical feasibility, resource requirements and availability, timing, and strategic value to the enterprise.
- Project evaluation and selection approaches can be categorized into three classes: (1) primarily *quantitative* and *rational* approaches, (2) primarily *qualitative* and *intuitive* approaches, and (3) mixed *approaches*, combining both quantitative and qualitative methods.
- Four of the most popular quantitative measures of future value of a proposed project are: net present value (NPV), (2) return on investment (ROI), (3) cost-benefit (CB), and (4) payback period (PBP).
- The major benefits of quantitative evaluation methods are their quantitative results that lead to effective comparison of competing opportunities, repeatability of tests, and benchmarking to selection parameters.
- The major limitations of quantitative methods are in the reliability associated with the source data. Many of the quantitative methods require inputs from the business environment, based on forecasts and assumptions (i.e., market, technology, or competitive information). Strictly quantitative criteria for project evaluation can be misleading.
- The major benefits of qualitative methods are in the more integrated assessment of the opportunity across a wide spectrum of criteria, usually involving multifunctional, collective judgment across the enterprise and its environment.
- The major limitations of quantitative methods are in the personal and organizational biases, and therefore the subjective nature of the judgment-based results.
- Complex project opportunities require sophisticated evaluation and selection methods that consider many variables of the organizational and technological environment, reaching far beyond cost and revenue measures.
- Most technology-intensive project opportunities are too complex to use simple quantitative methods as the sole basis for decision making.

Seeking out both quantitative and qualitative measures incorporated into a combined rational-judgmental evaluation process often yields the most reliable predictor of future project value and desirability.
- Effective project evaluation and selection requires broad scanning across all segments of the enterprise and its environment to deal with the risks, uncertainties, and ambiguities that face the proposed project over its life cycle.

7.7 QUESTIONS FOR DISCUSSION AND EXERCISES

1. Consider any one of the business opportunities mentioned in the chapter lead-in mini case. To implement, each one of them is a project. What methods would you consider appropriate for evaluating future success and performance of that project?
2. Using the calculations summarized in Table 7.2, which option would you recommend for implementation? How would you justify your decision?
3. Look at the various methods of future value calculations. Then look at Table 7.3 and discuss the benefits and limitations for each one of them, going beyond the factors given in Table 7.3.
4. What kind of actions would you take as project manager to foster a work environment conducive to cross-functional collaboration toward evaluating new project opportunities?
5. How would you prioritize the new business opportunities mentioned in DIRECTV's annual report presented at the beginning of this chapter?
6. Why is cross-functional collaboration necessary to assess the potential for success of new project proposals?
7. Why is managerial leadership important for effectively evaluating new project proposals?
8. What is the role of top management in evaluating and selecting project proposals? How can management help?
9. Why must we consider enterprise strategy and its alignment with the new project proposal in the evaluation and selection process?

7.8 *PMBOK*® REFERENCES AND CONNECTIONS

The topic of project evaluation and selection cuts across many of the 10 knowledge areas defined by PMBOK. It connects most strongly however with project risk management (area #8). It also focuses on the first two processing groups: initiating and planning. This contextual understanding of project management is necessary for effectively applying the PMBOK standards to the day-to-day management of projects and to study effectively for PMP® certification.

In preparing for the PMP® exam, the following concepts should be studied together with the perspectives of the context of project management: (1) scope planning and definition, (2) risk identification, quantification and response, (3) schedule development, (4) resource planning, (5) procurement management, (6) stakeholder analysis; and (7) stakeholder management.

INTERNET LINKS AND RESOURCES

Center for Civic Partnerships. "Quantitative and qualitative evaluation methods," www.civicpartnerships.org/docs/tools_resources/Quan_Qual%20Methods%209 .07.htm

DIRECTV company profile: http://www.directv.com/DTVAPP/content/about_us/our _company;

UNODC, United Nations Office on Drugs and Crime. "Independent project evaluations step by step." www.unodc.org/unodc/en/evaluation/independent-project-evaluations-step-by-step.html

Wikipedia. Boeing 2707, Supersonic transport. http://en.wikipedia.org/wiki/Boeing_2707

Wikipedia. Direct Broadcast Satellite (DBS) Technology: http://en.wikipedia.org/wiki/Direct-broadcast_satellite

REFERENCES

Baker, N. R. 2012. "R&D Project Selection Models: An Assessment." *R&D Management* 5(1): 105–111.

Chapman, C., and S. Ward. 2003. *Project Risk Management*. Hoboken, NJ: Wiley & Sons.

Cicmil, S., T. Williams, J. Thomas, and D. Hodgson. 2006. "Rethinking Project Management: Researching the Actuality of Projects." *International Journal of Project Management* 24(8): 675–686.

Cook, W. D., and R. H. Green. 2000. "Project Prioritization: A Resource-Constrained Data Envelopment Analysis Approach." *Socio-Economic Planning Sciences* 34(2) (June): 85–99.

Craig S., A. Guilfoyle, C. Lin, and P. Love. 2006. "The Attribution of Success and Failure in IT Projects." *Industrial Management & Data Systems* 106(8): 1148–1165.

Ghasemzadeh, F., and N. P. Archer. 2000. "Project Portfolio Selection Through Decision Support." *Decision Support Systems* 29(1) (July): 73–88.

Hadad, Y., B. Keren, and Z. Laslo. 2012. "A Decision-Making Support System Module for Project Manager Selection According to Past Performance." *International Journal of Project Management*.

Henriksen, A.D., and A. J. Traynor. 2002. "A Practical R&D Project-Selection Scoring Tool," *IEEE Transactions on Engineering Management* 46(2): 158–170.

Kavadias, S., and C. H. Loch. 2004. *Project Selection under Uncertainty: Dynamically Allocating Resources to Maximize Value*. Norwood, MA: Kluwer Academic Publishers.

Khorramshahgol, R., H. Azani, and Y. Gousty. 1998. "An Integrated Approach to Project Evaluation and Selection." *IEEE Transactions on Engineering Management* 35(4): 265–270.

Kulkarni, R. B., D. Miller, R. M. Ingram, C-W. Wong, and J. Lorenz. 2004. "Need-Based Project Prioritization: Alternative to Cost-Benefit Analysis." *Journal of Engineering Transportation* 130(2) (March–April): 150–158.

Kumar, P. D. 2006. "Integrated Project Evaluation and Selection Using Multiple-Attribute Decision-Making Technique." *International Journal of Production Economics* 103(1): 87.

Larson, E., and C. Gray. 2011. "Organization Strategy and Project Selection." Chapter 2, *Project Management: The Management Process*. New York: McGraw-Hill, pp. 22–63.

Loch, C. H., M. T. Pich, C. Terwiesch, and M. Urbschat. 2001. "Selecting R&D Projects at BMW: A Case Study of Adopting Mathematical Programming Models." *IEEE Transactions on Engineering Management* 48(1): 70–80.

Mantel, S., J. Meredith, S. Shafer, and M. Sutton. 2011. "Selecting Projects to Meet Organizational Objectives." Chapter 1.5 in *Project Management Practice*. Hoboken, NJ: John Wiley & Sons, pp. 10–22.

Meade, L.A., and A. Presley. 2002. "R&D Project Selection Using ANP . . . The Analytic Network Process." *Potentials* (IEEE) 21 (2): 22–28.

National Science Foundation (NSF). 2010. *The 2010 User-Friendly Handbook for Project Evaluation*. Arlington, VA: National Science Foundation, Division of Research and Learning in Formal and Informal Settings.

Oral, M., O. Kettani, and P. Lang. 1991. "A Methodology for Collective Evaluation and Selection of Industrial R&D Projects." *Management Science* 37(7): 871–881.

Remer, D. S., S. B. Stokdyk, and M. Van Driel. 1993. "Survey of Project Evaluation Techniques Currently Used in Industry." *International Journal of Production Economics* 32(1): 103–115.

Schmidt, R.L., and J. R. Freeland. 1992. "Recent Progress in Modeling R&D Project-Selection Processes." *Transactions on Engineering Management* (IEEE) 39(2) (May):189–201.

Shakhsi-Niaei, M., S. Torabi, and S. Iranmanesh. 2011. "A Comprehensive Framework for Project Selection Problem under Uncertainty and Real-World Constraints." *Computers & Industrial Engineering* 61(1): 226–237.

Shenhar A, D. Milosevic, D. Dvir, and H. Thamhain. 2007. *Linking Project Management to Business Strategy*. Newtown, PA: Project Management Institute Press.

Shtub, A., J. F. Bard, and S. Globerson. 2005. *Project Management: Processes, Methodologies, and Economics*. Englewood Cliffs, NJ: Prentice Hall.

Thamhain, H., and T. Skelton. 2007. "Success Factors for Effective R&D Risk Management." *International Journal of Technology Intelligence and Planning (IJTIP)* 3(4): 376–386.

Thamhain, Hans. 2011. "Critical Success Factors for Managing Technology-Intensive Teams in the Global Enterprise." *Engineering Management Journal* 23(2) (June): 30–36.

Thamhain, Hans. 2013. "Evaluating and Selecting Technology-Based Projects." Chapter 25, *Handbook of Measurements in Science and Engineering, 1*, Chapter 25, pp. 819–832. Hoboken, NJ: John Wiley & Sons.

Wang, C. 2001. "Application of Real Options in Project Portfolio Selection." Proceedings, *IEEE International Conference on Industrial Engineering and Engineering Management*, pp. 848–853.

Ward, T. J. 1994. Which Product Is BE$T? *Chemical Engineering* 101(1): 102–107.

7.9 APPENDIX: SUMMARY DESCRIPTION OF TERMS, VARIABLES, AND ABBREVIATIONS USED IN THIS CHAPTER

7.9.1 Terms

Cross-functional: Actions that span organizational boundaries.

Phase management: Projects are broken into natural implementation phases, such as development, production, and marketing, as a basis for project planning, integration, and control. Phase management also provides the framework for concurrent engineering and Stage-Gate® processes.

Project success: A comprehensive measure, defined in both quantitative and qualitative terms, which includes economic, market, and strategic objectives.

Stage-Gate® process: Framework originally developed by R. Cooper and S. Edgett for executing projects within predefined stages with measurable deliverables (at "gates") at the end of each stage. These gates also provide the review metrics for ensuring successful transition and integration of the project into the next stage. (See also *phase management*, above.)

Weighing of criteria: A multiplier associated with specific evaluation criteria.

7.9.2 Variables and Abbreviations

A	Annuity is the present worth of a revenue or cost at the end of a period n.
CB	Cost benefit, is the net present value of all ROIs in dollars.
i	Prevailing interest rate.
I	Investment.
IRR	Internal rate of return, the average return on investment realized by a firm on its investment capital.
MARR	Minimum attractive rate of return on new investments acceptable to an organization.
NPV	Net present value of a stream of future revenues or costs.
PBP	Payback period, the time period needed to recover the original investment.
PR	Project rating factor, a measure developed by Carlo Pacifico for predicting project success.
PW	Present worth (also called annuity) is the present value of a revenue or cost at the end of a period n.
ROI	Return on investment.
z	Project rating factor, a measure developed by Sobelman for predicting project success.

Chapter 8

Setting Up an Effective Planning and Control Cycle

PROJECT MANAGEMENT FOR NASA

Photo courtesy of NASA Jet Propulsion Laboratory

When President Barack Obama, calling from aboard *Air Force One*, congratulated the *Curiosity* team on their successful Mars rover landing, he reached a jubilant Peter Theisinger, project manager for NASA's Mars Exploration Program. And rightly so. Success did not come easy, nor by luck. It was the result of a carefully planned and executed, billion-dollar eight-year program that culminated in the successful landing at Gale Crater on August 5, 2012, after seven months of space flight. Yet, this is only the beginning of *Curiosity*'s Martian mission.

One of the most ambitious space programs to date, the Mars Science Laboratory mission is part of NASA's Mars Exploration Program. During the next 23 months *Curiosity* will act as a mobile science laboratory on Mars to investigate whether life could exist on the Red Planet and even help scientists and engineers plan for future human missions to Mars. Although *Curiosity* will not be the first rover ever sent to Mars, it will certainly be the most advanced. Eight years in the making, the rover carries the most advanced payload of scientific gear ever used on Mars' surface, a payload more than

---

The Mars rover *Curiosity* is part of the *Mars Science Laboratory (MSL) program*, managed by JPL for NASA's Science Mission Directorate, Washington, DC. The Jet Propulsion Laboratory (JPL) is a division of the California Institute of Technology in Pasadena. At NASA Headquarters, David Lavery is the Mars Science Laboratory program executive and Michael Meyer is program scientist. In Pasadena, Peter Theisinger of JPL is project manager and John Grotzinger of Caltech is project scientist. For more information about MSL/Curiosity, go to: www.nasa.gov/msl.

10 times as massive as those of earlier Mars rovers. *Curiosity* is equipped with 17 cameras, a handful of instruments, and an innovative landing system. Two of the mast-mounted megapixel color cameras will provide 360-degree, stereoscopic, humanlike views of the terrain. The robotic arm will be capable of movement in much the same way as a human arm with an elbow and wrist, and will place instruments directly up against rock and soil targets of interest. In the mechanical "fist" of the arm is a microscopic camera that will serve the same purpose as a geologist's handheld magnifying lens. The rock abrasion tool serves the purpose of a geologist's rock hammer to expose the insides of rocks.

The Challenges of Getting to Mars. Two-thirds of all missions to the Red Planet have failed. One reason there have been so many losses is that there have been so many attempts. "Mars is a favorite target," says Dr. Firouz Naderi, director for Solar System Exploration at NASA's Jet Propulsion Laboratory. "We—the United States and former USSR—have been going to Mars for 40 years. The first time we flew by a planet, it was Mars. The first time we orbited a planet, it was Mars. The first time we landed on a planet it was Mars. However, getting there is hard." *Curiosity*, the Mars exploration rovers, had to fly through about 300 million miles of deep space and target a very precise spot to land at Gale Crater. Adjustments to their flight paths can be made along the way, but a small trajectory error can result in a big detour or even missing the planet completely. The space environment isn't friendly. Hazards range from what engineers call "single event upsets," as when a stray particle of energy passes through a chip in the spacecraft's computer causing a glitch and possibly corrupting data, to massive solar flares, such as the ones that occurred this fall, that can damage or even destroy spacecraft electronics.

A Complex Project. The road to the launch pad is nearly as daunting as the journey to Mars. Even before the trip to Mars can begin, a craft must be built that not only can make the arduous trip but can complete its science mission once it arrives. Nothing less than exceptional technology and planning is required.

If getting to Mars is hard, landing there is even harder. "One colleague describes the entry, descent and landing as six minutes of terror," says Naderi. *Curiosity* entered the Martian space traveling 19,300 kilometers per hour. "During the first four minutes into descent, we used friction with the atmosphere to slow us down considerably," says Naderi. "However, at the end of this phase, we're still traveling at 1,600 kilometers per hour, but now we had only 100 seconds left and were at the altitude that a commercial airliner typically flies. Things need to happen in a hurry. A parachute opened to slow the spacecraft down to "only" 321 kilometers per hour; the rover capsule separates from the parachute. Now, the retro rockets fired to bring the spacecraft down to zero velocity, then the rover capsule lowered it with a 20-meter (66 feet) tether from the "sky crane" system to a soft landing— wheels down—on the Mars surface.

Mars doesn't exactly put out a welcome mat. Landing is complicated by strong winds and difficult terrain. The Martian surface is full of obstacles—massive impact craters, cliffs, cracks, and jagged boulders. Yet, no matter how hard it is, getting to Mars is just the beginning. "The challenge after we land," says Rob

Manning, chief engineer for the rover mission, "is how to get the vehicle out of its cramped cocoon and into a vehicle roving in such a way as to please the scientists." After the rover touched down it waited 2 seconds to confirm that it was on solid ground then fired several pyros (small explosive devices) activating cable cutters on the bridle to free itself from the spacecraft descent stage. The descent stage then flew away to a crash landing, and the rover prepared itself to begin the science mission.

The rewards are great. "Mars is the most Earth-like of the planets in our solar system," says Naderi. "It has the potential to have been an abode of life." The risks are also great. "We did everything humanly possible to avoid human mistakes," says Naderi. "That's why we did check, double check, test, and test again, and then have independent eyes check everything again. Humans, even very smart humans, are fallible, particularly when many thousands of parameters are involved. But even if you have done the best engineering possible, you still don't know what Mars has in store for you on the day you arrive. Mars can get you. We are in a tough business," says Naderi. "It is like climbing Mt. Everest. No matter how good you are, you are going to lose your grip sometimes and fall back. Then you have a choice—either retreat to the relative comfort and safety of the base camp or get up, dust yourself off, get a firmer grip and a surer toehold, and head back up for the summit. The space business is not about base camps. It is about summits. And, the exhilaration of discoveries you make once you get there. That's what drives you on."

8.1 PLANNING THE CORNERSTONE TO EFFECTIVE PROJECT MANAGEMENT

Planning is the cornerstone to effective project management not just for large organizations as NASA. It is a threshold requirement for most technology-intensive projects. Consistent with Benjamin Franklin's popular statement, "By failing to prepare, you are preparing to fail," even the best plan does not guarantee success, but it puts the project at least on an even playing field against tough technical challenges and today's pressures for better, cheaper, and faster performance. The good news is that project managers today have a set of powerful tools available, with proven capabilities for effectively planning and controlling multidisciplinary activities. Let's explore the rationale for this important, but also labor-intensive front-end activity.

8.1.1 The Importance of Project Planning

Effective planning and control techniques are helpful for any undertaking. They are absolutely essential, however, for the successful management of large, complex technology projects. There is probably little argument when we look at a program as big as the Mars Science Laboratory. However, for smaller projects, "absolutely essential" may seem a strong statement, especially to the action-oriented executive who may find charts and analysis burdensome or even stifling to the project start-up process. Realistically, however, project managers have no choice. Management studies and field experts have pointed out repeatedly the strong correlation between quality planning and overall project performance. Quality, however, means more than just generating paperwork. It requires the participation and collaboration of all project stakeholders, including support departments, contractors, top management and, ideally, the customer community, to generate a realistic plan that has the commitment from all team members. If done properly, project planning fosters a sense of community and project ownership that is pervasive toward the goals and objectives of the project. Proper planning makes everyone's job easier and more effective, because it provides the basis for:

- A comprehensive roadmap for the project undertaking
- Creating the big picture and perspective of the total project and its mission
- Showing how activities interact and subsystems integrate
- Articulating the goals and objectives
- Defining tasks and responsibilities
- Directing, tracking, and controlling the program
- Reviews and issue resolutions
- Organizing and building project teams
- Minimizing paperwork
- Minimizing confusion and conflict
- Dealing with changes
- Helping managers at all levels to accomplish optimal results within the given project parameters.

Done properly, project planning must involve all stakeholder organizations engaged over the project lifecycle. This includes support groups from the enterprise as well as external contractors, partners and the customer community. This involvement creates a comprehensive and realistic view of the project and its challenges. In addition, it is this involvement at all organizational levels that stimulates interest in the project, a sense of realism and the desire to succeed. All of this fosters a pervasive reach for excellence that unifies the project team. Most important, it leads to commitment toward reaching desired results and to a self-managed system where team members want to work toward established project and mission objectives.

8.1.2 The Quandaries of Project Planning

With all these benefits, why is there often so much resistance to proper project planning and sometimes an outright rejection of the formal planning process?

The problem centers on four issues: start-up delays, stifled creativity, insufficient flexibility and agility, and lack of funding. To the first issue, formal planning often irritates action-oriented managers who want to start the work and show some results. Second, planning is often perceived as "paperwork," stifling creativity, flexibility, and agility of organizing the work and adjusting the process to changing conditions of the project environment. The comment of one project manager might be typical for many situations:

> My team feels that we spend too much time planning the project; it takes productive time away from the project, it's based on a lot of assumptions, not necessarily consistent with reality; it creates a rigid environment that stifles innovative solution. We feel that these plans benefit our management more that they help us. Especially, milestones are often used rather arbitrarily to establish criteria for reward or punishment, disregarding the difficulties and true team accomplishments.

This comment reflects the frustration of many project leaders, especially in technologically complex situations. It also illustrates another quandary, the misuse of planning to establish unrealistic controls and penalties for deviations from the project plan, rather than using the plan for identifying problems in their early stages and helping to find solutions. It is often the perception of coercion that turns people against planning. Whether these fears are real or fantasies does not change the team behavior. People who see certain policies as threatening will not support them. Finally, the issue of funding can be a barrier to planning. Proper project planning is serious work that requires time and resources. Unless this activity is planned and approved as part of the front end of the project, such as the project definition phase, it is difficult to get the project planning effort funded as an afterthought to an already established contract.

8.1.3 Climbing out of the Quandaries

Few companies have introduced new or updated project planning procedures with ease. Most have experienced problems ranging from skepticism to sabotage of the planning system. Realistically, however, project managers have not much of a choice, especially for larger and more complex projects that are typical for technology-related undertakings. Interestingly, managers most supportive of formal project planning are often those who came with reservations, but learned from painful experience the necessities and benefits of establishing effective project plans.

Clearly, one type of approach to planning does not fit all projects. Some projects expect minimum changes during the execution phase, and therefore can be planned quite accurately at the beginning. Others, such as R&D, can only be planned as a broad outline of activities and targeted results, leaving the details to be developed during the execution when specific development options and work details become available. Yet other approaches call for incremental development of the project plan. That is, planning the project while getting the work started concurrently. This is also consistent with the *phased approach* to project management, which divides projects into stages. A broad-brushed plan is established for the total project, with the plan for each phase refined and detailed before execution, while looking ahead to the next phase on a rolling basis. In fact, for many projects that fall into the "exploratory" or "advanced development" category, it is not only unnecessary but often impractical to plan in great detail at the beginning. The incremental approach is a way to demonstrate operational efficiency while preparing the project plan. This process—showing early results while establishing enough of a roadmap and measurability to roll out the project in manageable steps—is referred to as *incremental-dynamic planning*.

Regardless of the approach, project planning requires cross-functional participation, collaboration, and commitment to the desired results and mission objectives. To achieve such a state of ownership among project team members requires effective administrative skills and leadership, a topic discussed in the next section.

8.1.4 Gaining Support and Commitment

"Unless commitment is made, there are only promises and hopes, but no plan," pointed out by the late Peter Drucker (1999) describes it well. A plan is only a plan if agreed on by all stakeholders. These are tough statements that go beyond the description of a "good project plan" defined as a roadmap articulating the work, resources, responsibilities, and deliverables. Effectiveness is a missing, critical component in this description. To be effective, several other conditions must be met. First, involvement and participation of all stakeholders is necessary for the development of a *realistic plan*, the basis for any commitment. Planning is the dynamic process of gathering information from stakeholder groups, including the assigned project team, support functions, contractors, partners, and, if possible, the customer community. No single person or group of people has all the information needed for developing a detailed project plan. Nor would such a plan have credibility with the people who have to implement the plan, unless they were directly involved in the planning process. Second, an effective plan must have measurable milestones, each with specific deliverables or results defined. These milestones and deliverables must be collectively defined and agreed upon, providing the basis for status assessment and project control. They also provide the metrics for meaningful commitments to specific results.

Developing a quality project plan, agreed on and committed to by all key players of the greater project team, requires extensive managerial skills far beyond writing a statement of work with schedules and budgets. As summarized in "Project Planning Skills" (p. 154), it requires communication and information-processing skills for defining and negotiating the resources

---

PROJECT PLANNING SKILLS

Effective project planning requires skills in the following areas:

- Communicating
- Information processing
- Resource estimating
- Scheduling
- Budgeting
- Incremental dynamic planning
- Defining measurability
- Creating excitement and interest in project mission
- Developing team spirit and mutual respect
- Facilitating senior management involvement
- Teambuilding
- Collaborating and coalition building
- Gaining and sustaining commitment
- Working across functional lines with little or no formal authority

---

and project support needed from various resource groups over whom the project leader often has little or no formal authority. Above all, it requires the ability to foster a professionally stimulating environment where people want to work on the project and achieve its mission. What makes it even more challenging is that much of this coalition and teambuilding needs to be done across organizational boundaries with little or no formal authority.

8.1.5 Concerns and Issues

Each project is unique. The tools, techniques, and processes used for project planning are often rooted in procedures or directives, designed for many organizational units and projects. Experienced project leaders realize that each project calls for its own unique planning process, assessing feasibility and establishing an effective execution roadmap that focuses on the specific situational needs.

Going to Extremes

Managers who take an extreme position create problems for the project. On one side, a project leader might completely ignore established guidelines because they are not specifically aligned with his or her project. This is a very dangerous way of planning as it pushes aside generations of collective experiences that provide useful guidelines, standards, and checklists for project planning, regardless of the specific situation for which the procedures have to be adjusted for. On the other side, the concern is that project planning can be overdone. Trying to get every detail right at the beginning can lead to "paralysis by analysis." Planning can become an end in itself with excessive front-end studies and too much detail that might prove to be irrelevant at a later stage of execution.

On a similar issue, plans can stifle innovation. In the extreme, team members might *not* be willing to "step outside the box," take innovative actions, or dealing with risk, "because it is not in the plan."

Flexbility

Project plans must have enough flexibility to deal with changes and contingencies that are uniquely associated with each project. Nothing outlives its usefulness faster than an obsolete or irrelevant plan. Experienced project leaders understand their operating environment and recognize the possibility of changes in scope, timing, and other parameters. They build into their plans the flexibility to adjust the plan as needed to accomplish their mission effectively. Properly scheduled reviews, stage-gates, tests, user-centered design, beta sites, and built-in design iterations are examples of managerial tools and techniques that can be integrated with the project plan to ensure flexibility and the capability to cope with changes and contingencies.[1]

Not every planning tool, technique or guideline is appropriate for all projects. This is especially true for the more complex and technologically advanced projects. This also includes computer-supported planning procedures and models. Management tools are seldom too simple, but often too complex and irrelevant. Warning signs of inappropriate tools are as follows:

- Team members spent disproportioned amount of time in preparing plans or support material.
- Plans are confusing or only a few people can interpret "the plan."
- The information of the plan or any of its modules is too late or irrelevant for the ongoing planning or execution process.
- The tools are perceived as not contributing to the planning or execution process.

Leadership

Project plans or management tools are no substitute for managerial actions and leadership. Competitive pressures toward "better, faster, cheaper" can produce unrealistic plans. Especially with the help of computers and information technology, plans can look good and integrate well, in spite of unrealistic

---

[1]The following lessons from field studies (Bryson and Bromiley 1993, Collyer et al. 2010, Globerson and Zwikael 2002, Thamhain and Kruglianskas 2000) provide perspectives on the issues of project planning and offer some guidelines to project managers for effective project planning.

assumptions and poor data. These issues propagate further into the execution phase when project administrators try to manage the tools rather than the project. The comment of a senior manager is typical for the frustration experienced: ". . . too often the program office spends a lot of time to determine where and why certain schedule variances occurred; they are very good in re-scheduling and writing reports, rather than catching problems before they get messy so the program is getting back on track again."

Planning is the responsibility of the project manager. It is time-consuming, and it is tempting to delegate project planning to staff personnel. Although convenient, this can lead to unintended consequences. For example, these planning groups often develop their own identity and charter. Many of these groups become institutionalized, using their own jargons, techniques, and standards. Frequently, these staff planners are seen as isolated from the actual project situation, hence lacking credibility and therefore making it difficult to get the project team and functional resource groups on board to participate in the plan development. Ultimately, this leads to weak buy-in and commitment to the plan.

Only the project manager has the respect, credibility, and formal authority to organize and lead the planning effort, including searching for integrated solutions, assessing risks, negotiating resource personnel, and making tradeoffs among cost, schedule, and technical issues. This does not mean, however, that the project manager cannot get assistance from competent support staff or a project management office. On the contrary, proper support is important and often essential, particularly for larger, more complex projects that require more time, effort and administrative planning skills than the project manager can single-handedly provide. However, to be sure, the final responsibility for leading the planning effort, evaluating the tradeoffs and risks, integrating the plan, ensuring agreement with the baseline, and obtaining commitment to the plan among all stakeholders is the ultimate responsibility of the project manager.

Senior management must provide overall direction, support, and leadership. Top management direction, authority delegation, and overall involvement and support are essential for creating a collaborative environment among all resource groups necessary for effective project planning. This senior management involvement also creates strong visibility and priority images at all organizational levels, a favorable condition for stimulating excitement and interest for the project and its mission among the project team and its support groups. It builds the collective desire for success, a pervasive reach for excellence that unifies the total project team and leads to commitment—the keystone in the project planning system.

8.2 AN INTEGRATED APPROACH TO PROJECT PLANNING

Projects are assemblies of intricately connected components, subsystems and work packages. Planning the multifunctional activities and their integration throughout the project lifecycle is one of the most important and challenging responsibilities of the project leader. Before discussing the specific tools and techniques of project management in the next chapters, an integrated approach to project planning is presented here to provide overall managerial perspective.

Successful project management, whether it is in response to an in-house mission or customer request, must utilize effective planning techniques. Yet, equally critical, these tools and techniques must be integrated with the enterprise system, external support groups, and project partners. Planning is not an activity with an end in itself. It must clearly focus on its purpose and objectives to (1) define a blueprint for assessing feasibility, negotiating resources and organizing the project team, (2) communicate the project scope, objectives, and constraints, including time and resources, among all stakeholders, (3) establish the basis for tracking, analyzing, and controlling the project through its lifecycle, (4) establish a system for dealing with risks, changes, contingencies, and (5) establish the basis for assessing and rewarding performance, and motivating the project team.

Competitive pressures, fast-changing technologies and budget realities have shifted the focus of from creating a "complete and perfect" plan that can be executed with a minimum of changes, to creating a more flexible and agile plan that can accommodate inevitable contingencies. The reality is that in today's environment it is virtually impossible to identify every contingency in advance. Therefore, plans must be flexible to accommodate changes, and to include early warning systems, alerting management of changing conditions that require adjustments to the original plan for optimizing project objectives.

Yet, despite these shifting paradigms in the business environment, certain principles of project planning remain unchanged. Any project plan should include and integrate the following 11 topics and components:

1. **Goals and objectives.** Specific results, targets, or quota to be achieved, stated in perspective to enterprise strategy and mission objectives. Although similar to deliverables, these objectives are normally stated in general strategic terms.

2. **Management strategy.** Project execution strategy to be followed. This includes ways to deal with risks, market dynamics, requirements changes, and technology uncertainties.

3. **Project summary.** Thumbnail sketch of overall scope, budget, timelines, responsibilities, and key deliverables.

4. **Deliverables.** Specific results to be achieved during the project execution. Part of the deliverables includes the specifications and quality measures that define the results. Regardless whether the deliverables are hardware, software, processes, systems or services, their performance characteristics must be defined.

5. **Work breakdown structure (WBS).** The backbone of the project plan. It represents the hierarchical decomposition of the project into its subsystems

and tasks. Each component contains at least the "triple constraint" information of delivery, schedule, and budget.

6. **Schedule.** The timeline of the project and its subsystems.

7. **Budget.** Resource requirements for the total project, broken down into its subsystems.

8. **Responsibilities.** Listing of key responsibilities for overall project management, project administration, major tasks, and subsystems.

9. **Project charter.** Description of basic project organization structure and management scope, including major responsibilities, authorities, and reporting relations of key personnel.

10. **Team organization.** Often derived from the project charter, the team organization defines who is responsible for what task, including task and subsystem leadership. Task rosters, task matrices, work breakdown structures, and project charters provide the administrative templates for communicating the team organization.

11. **Interfaces.** Description of interdisciplinary communications, data, and workflow from the project team to support groups, senior management, contractors, partners, and customers.

8.2.1 Integrating Project Performance, Schedule, and Cost Variables

Overall project performance has many variables that include much more than just the triple constraint, as already discussed in Chapter 1. Yet, it is this set of three parameters—budget, schedule, and deliverables—that defines the "technical performance" of the project, and therefore receives much of the attention from all stakeholders during the project planning and execution phases. These parameters or variables also need to be treated as one interdependent set in all managerial activities, such as project planning, tracking, and controlling. Changing one parameter requires a bigger budget and quality shortcuts on deliverables. There are yet additional influences to project performance that must be considered. To be effective, the project plan must go beyond the triple constraint, but include customer satisfaction and influences of the broader business environmental. This introduces additional dynamics and challenges. Yet, this intricate and semi-stable blueprint, called the project plan, has to be acceptable to all stakeholders: project team, management, support functions, contractors, partners and customers, which is an even bigger challenge. Figure 8.1 shows these multifaceted interrelationships that make up the project planning system, as a three-dimensional model that groups the array of variables into three sets: project performance, project execution phases or process groups and influences to the planning process across the project lifecycle. The interrelationship of components was formally studied in the Apollo space program by Hopeman and Wilemon (1973) who presented their findings in a model, similar to the one shown in Figure 8.1.

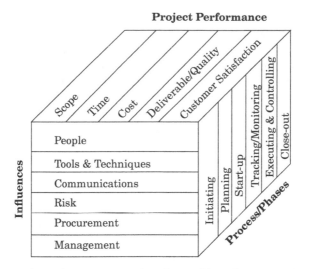

Figure 8.1   Three dimensions and multivariables of integrated project planning system

Today, this model is an important cornerstone for all project planning and control systems. The enhanced version of Figure 8.1 shows the influences of six key organizational subsystems (management, procurement, risk, communications, tools and techniques, and people) to project performance (measured by scope, time, cost, deliverables, and customer satisfaction), across six major phases of the project lifecycle: (1) project initiating, (2) project planning, (3) project organizing and startup, (4) project tracking/monitoring, (5) project executing and controlling, and (6) project closing.

Initiating defines and authorizes the project. This phase often overlaps with the planning phase. It may include bid proposal efforts, feasibility assessments, and formal project evaluation and selection activities.

Planning is a multidisciplinary, collaborative activity that establishes the roadmap and its parameters for technical, schedule, and cost performance of the project. All three of these variables are interdependent, and tradeoffs among them are part of the planning process to optimize overall benefits and project performance. Project planning is one of the fundamental functions of the project leadership team.

Startup includes establishing the project organization, staffing it and getting the team ready for project kickoff.

Monitoring and tracking refers to the process of measuring key project parameters, such as technical results, timing, cost and customer satisfaction, during the execution. This provides the basis for determining an integrated performance measure for comparing actual against planned performance.

Important tools for tracking project performance are (1) performance index, an overall project performance measure, (2) cost variance, (3) schedule variance, (4) estimated cost at completion, (5) estimated completion dates, and (6) deviations of technical performance of deliverables. Accurate tracking is critical to the ability of assessing project performance on an ongoing basis, determining managerial actions for controlling the project according to established plans, and assessing viable alternatives or changes in the project direction, necessary for optimizing overall results.

Executing and Controlling refers to corrective management actions to achieve agreed-on results in spite of changes or contingencies in the project environment. The effectiveness of project control depends to a large degree on the ability to track project performance, root-cause deviations, and to take corrective actions.

Closing refers to the formal termination of the project. This final phase includes customer sign-offs, final documentation, post-project reviews of lesson learned, reassignment of team members, and closure of project offices and facilities.

These six phases represent a consistent but expanded version of the project lifecycle discussed in chapter 2 and the five process groups suggested by PMI's *Project Management Body of Knowledge* (PMBOK®).

8.2.2 The Dynamics of Project Planning

Project plans can seldom be created monolithically, start to finish. They evolve in scope and depth. There are too many dependencies, assumptions, and data to be gathered. It is virtually impossible to write a procedure for developing a perfect project plan, although many have attempted it. Moreover, planning requires data. Gathering and analyzing these data require people. But, to request and assign people, we need data. This is a bit of a vicious circle. How do we get out of these quandaries? This brings us to the dynamics of the planning process. Most project plans start small, with the vision of a few people. As data and basic concepts emerge, more people from multiple disciplines get involved. Support functions and customer communities participate. This is a highly dynamic and iterative process that generates the plan in incremental steps, building in scope, depth, and detail until consensus is reached that the plan provides the type of a roadmap needed for project kickoff. Then planning continues as needed. In fact, planning might never stop during the entire project lifecycle—refining validating, and occasionally revising. The process is not only highly dynamic but also iterative, as shown graphically in Figure 8.2. Hence, the project gets defined in more depth and detail as it goes through its definition phase. Project definition quite commonly includes more than just paper planning, but may also include feasibility studies, concept developments, tests, and simulations.

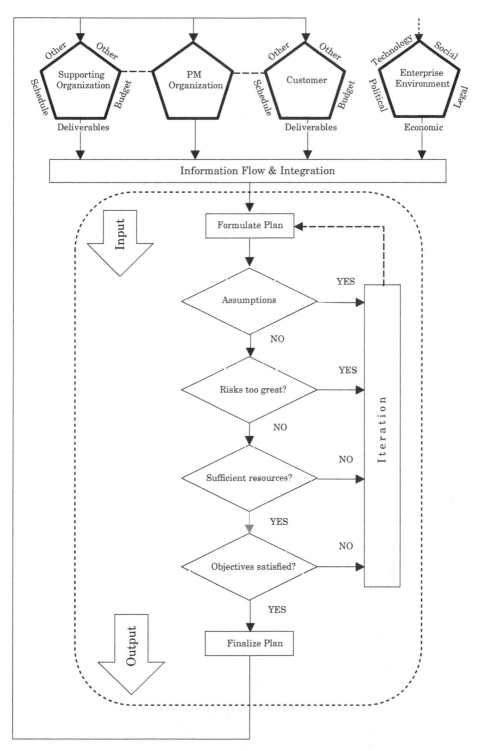

Figure 8.2 Iterations within the project planning process

8.3 MANAGING THE PLANNING PROCESS

Project planning is the art and science of charting a course toward desired objectives within a changing environment characterized by a lot of uncertainties, forecasts and assumptions. The final plan is a management tool for project implementation. The quality of this plan depends largely on the ability to create a realistic roadmap for achieving desired results within given time and resource constraints. This includes the ability of foreseeing the constraints and contingencies of the environment that will affect the project over its lifecycle. Early involvement and participation of key personnel from the greater project community and strong project leadership will help to foster the right work ambience conducive to a realistic, multidisciplinary assessment of the project and its resource requirements. Especially for more complex projects, this multidisciplinary, cross-functional participation is necessary to interpret the requirements, create specifications and interface documents, assess options and alternatives, estimate resources and timing realistically, and ultimately to reach an agreement among all stakeholders on the project plan and its workability.

Once agreed upon by all stakeholders, the project plan becomes a contract, binding to all parties. It also becomes a roadmap that will guide the team through all project implementation phases. Yet, it should be emphasized that, except for very simple and short-range projects, the plan must remain flexible to accommodate changes, contingencies, and opportunities that surface during the project execution. The directions for implementing a project plan come from five areas that guide and influence the project execution, as shown in Figure 8.3: (1) technical, (2) budget, (3) schedule, (4) procedures, and (5) general management and enterprise operations. All components of the project plan and its managerial processes of planning, tracking and control flow from the work breakdown structure (WBS), which is the backbone of any project and its management system. The specific tools and techniques available to facilitate project planning and control will be discussed in the following chapters.

8.4 SUMMARY OF KEY POINTS AND CONCLUSIONS

The following key points were made in this chapter:

- Planning is the cornerstone to effective project management.
- Project planning provides the basis for up front project feasibility assessment and selection, as well as for project organizing, tracking, and controlling during the execution phase.
- Effective planning requires the participation and collaboration of all project stakeholders, including support departments, contractors, top management, and the customer community. This multifunctional involvement fosters a sense of community and project ownership and

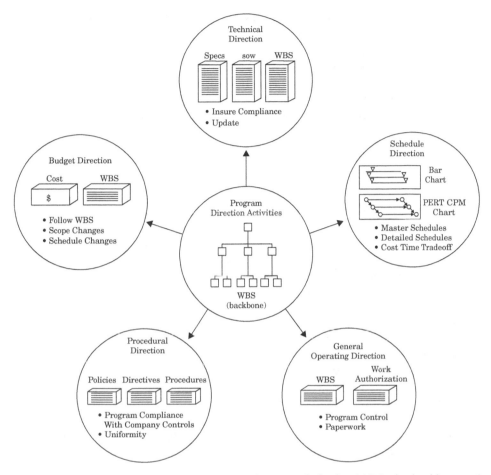

Figure 8.3 Project/program management directions linked to WBS, the backbone of project information

helps to unify the project team behind the goals and objectives of the project.

- A plan is only a plan if agreed on by all stakeholders.
- Project planning is often seen as unproductive paperwork. Resistance to formal project planning is natural and should be expected. Developing a quality project plan, agreed-on by all stakeholders, requires extensive managerial skills far beyond writing a document with schedules and budgets. It requires communicating, information processing, and negotiating skills for securing the support needed from various resource groups over project leaders often have little or no formal authority.
- Each project is unique. Not every planning tool, technique, or guideline is appropriate for all projects, but must be fine-tuned to fit the specific situational need.

- Project plans are no substitute for managerial actions and leadership. Plans are tools designed to help assessing project status and performance. Project control relies on management actions, which are the responsibility of the project manager.
- Senior management must provide overall direction, authority delegation, overall support, and leadership for creating a collaborative environment among all resource groups necessary for effective project planning.

8.5 QUESTIONS FOR DISCUSSION AND EXERCISES

1. Characterize an organizational environment conducive to effective project planning.
2. What are the major barriers to effective project planning, and how can these barriers be removed or minimized?
3. How can project leaders get support and collaboration for their planning efforts from resource groups over whom they have little or no formal authority?
4. How do you characterize or describe a "quality project plan?"
5. What skills do project managers need to develop quality project plans? How can they develop these skills?
6. What do we mean by "integrated approach to project planning?"
7. What advice would you give to a project manager who has difficulties convincing her team and senior managers of the necessity to invest some time and resources for up-front planning?
8. How can senior managers help and support project leaders in their project planning?

8.6 *PMBOK®* REFERENCES AND CONNECTIONS

The topic of project planning cuts across most of the 10 knowledge areas defined by PMBOK. It connects most strongly with project integration management (area #1), project scope management (area #2), project time management (area #3), project cost management (area #4), project communications management (area #7) and project stakeholder management (area #10). It also addresses the first two processing groups: initiating and planning. Many of the topics covered in this chapter address the *context* of project management. That is the way projects are planned and organized in preparation for project execution. This broad contextual understanding of project management is necessary for effectively applying the PMBOK standards to the day-to-day management of projects and to study effectively for PMP® certification. In studying for the PMP® exam, an understanding of the following concepts will be beneficial: (1) elements of the project plan, with more details covered in the following chapters (e.g., work breakdown structure, scope statement, schedule and budget), (2) project plan development, (3) scope planning and definition, (4) schedule development, (5) resource planning, (6) stakeholder analysis, and (7) stakeholder management.

INTERNET LINKS AND RESOURCES

Carnegie Mellon University. "Detailed project plan." www.cmu.edu/computing/ppmo/ project-management/life-cycle/planning/detailed-project-plan.html
ComputerWeekly.com. "How to create a clear project plan." www.computerweekly .com/feature/How-to-create-a-clear-project-plan
Haughey, Duncan. "Project planning a step by step guide." www.projectsmart.co.uk/ project-planning-step-by-step.html
Wikipedia; "Project planning," http://en.wikipedia.org/wiki/Project_planning

REFERENCES AND ADDITIONAL READINGS

Boehm, B. 2002. "Get Ready for Agile Methods, with Care." *Computer* 35(1): 64–69.
Bonnal, P., G. Didier, and L. Germain. 2002. "The Life Cycle of Technical Projects." *Project Management Journal* 33(1): 12–19.
Bryson, J. M. and P. Bromiley. 1993. "Critical Factors Affecting the Planning and Implementation of Major Projects." *Strategic Management Journal* 14(5): 319–337.
Collyer, S., C. Warren, B. Hemsley, and C. Stevens. 2010. "Aim, Fire, Aim—Project Planning Styles in Dynamic Environments." *Project Management Journal* 41(4): 108–121.
Drucker, P. (1999). *Management Challenges for the Twenty-first Century*. New York: HarperCollins.
Garvin, J. B., O. Figueroa, and F. Naderi, 2001. "NASA's New Mars Exploration Program: The Trajectory of Knowledge." *Astrobiology* 1(4) (Dec): 439–446.
Gido, J. and J. P. Clements 2012. "Initiating a Project." Part 1 in *Successful Project Management*. Mason, OH: South-Western Cengage Learning.
Globerson. S, and O. Zwikael. 2002. "The Impact of the Project Manager on Project Management Planning Processes." *Project Management Journal* 33(3): 53–64.
Hopeman, R. J. and D. L. Wilemon 1972. *Project Management/Systems, Management Concepts and Applications*. Syracuse, NY: Syracuse University.
Kerzner, H. 2011. "The Changing Landscape for Project Management." Chapter 1 in *Project Management Metrics, KPIs, and Dashboards: A Guide to Measuring and Monitoring Project Performance*. New York: International Institute of Learning (IIL).
Kloppenborg, T. J. 2012. "Planning Projects." Part 2 in *Contemporary Project Management*. Mason, OH: South-Western Cengage Learning.
Kovács, G. L. and P. Paganelli 2003. "A Planning and Management Infrastructure for Large, Complex, Distributed Projects—Beyond ERP and SCM." *Computers in Industry* 51(2) (June): 165–183.
Lewis, J. 2011. *Project Planning, Scheduling, and Control: The Ultimate Hands-On Guide to Bringing Projects in On Time and On Budget*. New York: McGraw-Hill.
Musser, G. 2004. "The Spirit of Exploration." *Scientific American* 290(1): 52–57.

Naderi, F. 2001. "Mars Exploration." *Robotics & Automation Magazine* (IEEE) 13(2): 72–82.

Platje, A., Seidel, H. and S. Waldman 1994. "Project and Portfolio Planning Cycle: Project-based Management for the Multiproject Challenge." *International Journal of Project Management* 12(2) (May): 100–106.

Project Management Institute (PMI). 2013. *A Guide to the Project Management Body of Knowledge (PMBOK® Guide)*. Newtown Square, PA: Project Management Institute.

Rad, P. F. and V. S. Anantatmula. 2006. *Project Planning Techniques*. Tysons Corner, VA: Management Concepts Press.

Thamhain, H. and I. Kruglianskas 2000. "Managing Technology-based Projects in Multinational Environments." *IEEE Transactions on Engineering Management* 47(1) (February): 55–64.

Chapter 9

The Tools for Integrated Project Planning and Control

2012 LONDON SUMMER OLYMPICS

On July 6, 2005, London was selected by the International Olympic Committee (IOC) as the host city for the 2012 Olympic Games, outscoring the competing cities of Paris, Madrid, New York and Moscow. After the successful bid, the *London Organizing Committee of the Olympic and Paralympic Games (LOCOG)* was formed to continue the work started by the proposal team, and to oversee many of the developments needed for successfully hosting the games in 2012. This included everything from the site preparation and construction of the Olympic Park, to the Aquatics Centre, Velopark, and Stratford-Channel rail link. The need for considerable redevelopment created many environmental concerns regarding sustainability that required highly innovative solutions, such as utilizing a former industrial site in East Landon for the Olympic Park. The initial budget estimates of $3.75 billion (£2.4) for preparing and hosting the Olympic Games grew eventually to $14.5 billion (£9.3), not even including the 70,000 volunteers who supported many of the operations.

The scope of this undertaking is staggering (Edworthy 2012). Twenty-six Olympic sports and 21 paralympic sports across 29 venues in 27 days, plus 11,000 athletes, 1,000,000 spectators, worldwide media attention and urban impact. Managing such a mega-project required highly structured, yet detailed planning. LOCOG decided to use as the backbone for their overall project planning the same "master schedule concept" that had been used for the 2000 Summer Olympics in Sydney, Australia. As explained by Gilbert Felli, IOC executive director for the Olympic Games (Glick 2012), "the master schedule is a timeline of milestones that need to be met for the Games to be delivered on time." Eventually, a robust master plan had to be developed, broken into mission-specific modules, each identifying the technical requirements, timelines and budgets necessary to implement each module. This is a daunting task. Not only must all the

---

For additional details on the London Summer Olympics see Wikipedia (2012).

components of an event mission or support system fit together, but the deliverable components must meet the end user needs. "The devil is in the details when it comes to planning such a complex project," said Sally Ormiston, Deloitte's lead consultant to LOCOG. "LOCOG wanted to be sure we focus on providing high-value experience to our Olympic visitors. No unnecessary razzmatazz. We used focus group techniques, interviewing members of previous Olympic organizing committees and over 450 elite athletes and coaches, collecting inputs on visitor expectations. We had thousands of Post-it® Notes with ideas, recommendations and aspirations. Then we checked them against LOCOG benchmarks of *impact, ease of implementation* and *cost*. These findings provided directions to the project teams for refining their deliverables and developing their detailed plans."

9.1 MANAGEMENT PERSPECTIVE

Clearly, some discipline is needed to arrange this bewildering array of needs, conditions, and constraints that define the "blueprint" of the 2012 Summer Olympics. That is, the requirements must be organized properly. Even for smaller projects, especially technology undertakings, managers have no choice but to use formal project management tools and techniques. It's just too complicated to keep everything in one's head and to communicate it among all the stakeholders. In addition to the conventional project planning and control requirements, there are many other factors that drive managers toward the use of formal project management tools, as we can glean from the Olympics scenario. Specifically, managers are using these tools so that they can better deal with:

- Contract requirements communications
- Requirement changes
- Negotiating resource requirements
- Work in progress measurements
- Adjusting to changing technology or market conditions
- Managing 'agile'
- Expediting/shortening product development cycles
- Organizing project teams
- Assigning task responsibilities
- Assuring individual and team accountability
- Individual and team appraisals and rewards
- Resolving conflicts and confusions
- Personnel changes and resource leveling
- Priority shifts
- Contractor interfaces
- Client communications
- Project integration

All of these challenges amount to pressures for effective, predictable and repeatable project execution. The good news is, project managers today have a large array of tools available for defining, organizing and directing their work, and equally important, providing the foundation for accountability, managerial performance assessment, rewards and building team spirit.

9.1.1 Expanding Tools Respond to New Management Challenges

With the increasing complexities of projects in today's business environment, companies have moved toward more sophisticated tools and techniques for effectively managing their multidisciplinary work. These tools and techniques range from computer software for sophisticated schedule and budget tracking to intricate organizational process designs, such as concurrent engineering, stage-gate protocols and agile methods. Even conventional project management tools, such as schedules, budgets and status reviews, are being continuously upgraded and effectively integrated with modern information technology systems and overall business processes. As part of this evolution, organizations must also shift their focus from simply tracking schedule and budget data, to integrating human factors and organizational interfaces into their management processes. The new generation of project management tools is designed to deal more effectively with the today's challenges business and realities that include highly complex sets of deliverables, as well as timing, environmental, social, political, regulatory and technological factors.

9.1.2 One Size Doesn't Fit All

The large number of available tool and techniques also presents issues. Projects come in many forms, shapes and sizes. No one tool fits all project management needs. Project managers must carefully choose the right tools that best suits their needs and fine-tune them to the specific situation.

Just keeping inventory of all the tools is a challenge. The literature often groups project management tools according to primary application areas, either focusing on lifecycle stages (i.e. initiating, planning, executing, controlling, closing) or management activities (e.g. scope management, time management, cost management, etc.), which in many cases follow standardized project management processes, such as *process groups* or *knowledge areas* defined by PMI's *PMBOK® Guide*. Overall, this is a good way to organize. However, there is a great deal of overlap among the various tools and application areas, and grouping or classifying can send a misleading message of restricted usage. Further, there are multiple applications for almost every project management tool as shown in Table 9.1. For example, schedules are useful in many phases of the project lifecycle, and can be used for planning, monitoring and controlling. So are budget tools. Therefore, in this book I chose to discuss the principal tools with focus on management applications,

Table 9.1 Popular Project Management Tools Across Application Areas and Project Life Cycle

Application Area[1]	Tool and Technique	Principle Usefulness Across Project Lifecycle[2]				
		Initiating	Planning	Executing	Monitoring	Closing
1. Project Integration	Project plan	H	H	H	H	M
	Work breakdown structure (WBS)	H	H	H	H	L
	Project integration plan	M	H	H	M	L
	Interface chart (e.g. N^2-Chart)	M	M	H	M	o
	Configuration management plan	M	H	H	H	L
	PM information system (PMIS)	L	H	H	H	L
	Stage-Gate® process	L	M	H	H	L
	Gate review	o	o	H	H	o
	Project review	o	o	H	H	L
	Spiral project management (SPM)	M	M	H	L	o
	Agile/Scrum	M	M	H	L	o
2. Scope management	Statement of work (SOW)	H	H	H	H	M
	Scope statement	H	H	H	H	M
	Work breakdown structure (WBS)	H	H	H	H	L
	Work package	H	H	M	M	L
	Task authorization	H	H	L	L	
	Specifications	H	H	H	H	L
	Requirements matrix	M	H	H	H	L
	List of deliverables	M	H	H	H	M
	Performance measurements	o	L	H	H	M
	Corrective action plan	o	L	H	H	o

	Col 1	Col 2	Col 3	Col 4	Col 5
	Configuration management plan	M	L	H	H	o
	Design review	o	o	H	H	o
3. Time management	Schedules	H	H	H	H	L
	Bar graph/Gantt chart	H	H	H	H	L
	Network diagram (PERT, CPM, GERT)	M	H	L	H	L
	Estimating (parametric, rough, detailed)	M	H	H	o	L
	Project review	o	o	H	H	M
	Computer model, simulation, tracking	L	M	H	H	o
	Project dashboard	o	H	H	H	L
	Schedule management plan	o	M	M	M	o
	Schedule compression analysis	o	o	L	L	L
4. Cost Management	Budget	H	H	H	H	L
	Cost account	L	M	H	H	L
	Work breakdown structure (WBS)	H	H	H	H	L
	Cost estimating (parametric to detailed)	M	H	L	o	o
	Cost baseline	H	H	M	L	L
	Cost modeling	M	H	L	o	o
	Earned value, variance analysis	o	o	M	M	L

(*Continued*)

Table 9.1 (Continued)

Application Area[1]	Tool and Technique	Principle Usefulness Across Project Lifecycle[2]				
		Initiating	Planning	Executing	Monitoring	Closing
	Change management	o	L	**H**	L	o
	Project review	o	L	**H**	**H**	M
	Computer model, simulation, tracking	o	L	**H**	**H**	o
	Project dashboard	o	M	**H**	**H**	L
	Cost management plan	o	M	M	L	L
5. Quality Management	Project plan	o	M	**H**	**H**	L
	Quality management plan	o	L	**H**	M	L
	Benchmarking	o	L	**H**	M	L
	Design review, audit	o	o	**H**	M	L
	Root-cause analysis	o	o	M	M	o
	Six Sigma	o	L	M	M	L
	Kaizen	o	L	L	L	L
	Pareto	o	o	L	L	o
6. Human Resource Management	Charter, task description	L	**H**	**H**	L	o
	Task roster, task matrix, team roster	L	**H**	M	M	L
	Staffing plan	o	**H**	M	o	L
	Teambuilding	o	M	**H**	o	o
	Organization interface chart	L	M	**H**	L	o
	Performance review	o	o	**H**	L	**H**

Process area	Item					
7. Communications Management	Stakeholder analysis	o	M	M	L	o
	Design review, project review	o	o	H	H	L
	Status meeting	o	L	H	H	o
	Progress report	o	o	H	M	M
	Schedule-budget-performance analysis	o	o	H	H	M
	User-centered design (UCD)	o	L	H	L	L
	Computer-supported monitoring & tracking	o	L	H	H	o
	Project dashboard	o	L	H	H	L
8. Risk Management	Risk management plan	o	M	H	M	L
	Project plan	o	M	M	M	L
	Risk analysis: stat methods, judgment	L	M	H	M	o
	Design review, project review	o	o	H	H	M
	Modeling, simulation	o	M	H	M	o
	Risk strategy	L	H	M	L	M
	Redundancy	o	o	M	o	o
	Teamwork	o	o	M	M	o
	Lessons learned	L	M	M	M	H

(Continued)

Table 9.1 (Continued)

Application Area[1]	Tool and Technique	Principle Usefulness Across Project Lifecycle[2]				
		Initiating	Planning	Executing	Monitoring	Closing
9. Procurement Management	Project plan	o	H	H	H	L
	Procurement management plan	o	M	H	M	L
	Make-buy analysis	L	H	L	o	o
	Request for proposal (RFP)	L	H	L	o	o
	Bid proposal, negotiation	L	H	L	o	o
	Contract	L	H	H	H	M
	Project review, progress report	o	L	H	H	L
	Progress payment	o	o	H	L	L
10. Stakeholder Management	Stakeholder management plan and strategy	L	H	H	L	L
	Project plan	o	H	H	H	L
	Project review/progress report	o	o	H	H	L
	User-centered design (UCD)	L	L	M	M	L
	Project charter	L	L	L	o	o
	Stakeholder register	L	H	M	L	L

[1]The application areas are consistent with the knowledge areas suggested by PMI's PMBOK Standard
[2]The project lifecycle stages are consistent with the five progress groups suggested by PMI's PMBOK Standard
The applicability of the tools in each stage is indicated by the following symbols:
  H   Tools/technique are highly applicable to this stage
  M   Tools/technique are often or mostly applicable to this stage
  L   Tools/technique are sometimes or less applicable to this stage
  o   Tool/technique are rarely or not applicable to this stage

benefits, limitations and challenges, rather than emphasizing categories or creating a "tool book" that exists quite comprehensively already (Milosevic 2003). The specific focus of this chapter is on the management tools useful for project planning and controlling.

9.1.3 Quality and Effectiveness

What determines the quality and effectiveness of a project management tool? Much of management effectiveness is about communications. However, most tools are "templates" of a sort. Some are just pieces of paper, such as a schedule form, others are more interactively connected via sophisticated computer software, such as Microsoft Project, Oracle Primavera, Artemis, or PeopleSoft, just to name a few. Although many of these systems are labeled as collaborative, project tracking, enterprise management, or project portfolio management, they are still just elaborate templates. The effectiveness of any management tool depends by-and-large on the way they are integrated and used within the business process and are communicated among the project stakeholders. Many of the effectiveness criteria relate to the softer side of project management, such as providing any benefit or threat to the team. Much of this perception depends on how the tool is used to generate and communicate the project data among the team members. Some criteria for using project management tools effectively are stated below.

- *Mutual understanding and buy-in on the tool or technique*. If the team is supposed to participate actively with the tool, such as providing data input, analysis or decision-making, it is essential that all stakeholders understand the purpose, scope, and objective of the tool.
- *Standard format*. If at all possible, the information communicated among team members should be in a format that that is recognized as standard within the enterprise, or better yet, an established industry standard (i.e. PMBOK, PRINCE2 or ISO). Even simple documents, such as schedules and budgets, can be confusing and cause conflict if the data is presented in an unusual format not familiar to the project team. These issues expand with larger and more interactive tools. The data formats for most of these larger, computer-based project support systems can be customized to conform to the established standards used by the team.
- *Multi-company teams*. Additional challenges exist with the use of tools and techniques among project teams that are dispersed across several organizations or companies with different standards, cultures, and operational processes. Establishing a common, mutually accepted format and process for project management tools is a major organizational development effort. A compromise to getting the whole team on one uniform project management system is to have independent local management systems that conform to established local standards and

processes. Then integrate the information at the project management office (PMO) or headquarters location into a master control system. This is not an ideal method of management, since it requires translating and interpreting data between the master and local system in both directions. However, this might be a necessary compromise, given tough time and resource constraints for the team and system development.

- *Modularity of project plan.* The project plan and all of its components (e.g., budget, schedule, statement of work) should be organized in a modular fashion. That is, the complexity of the total project should be broken down into sub-systems or work packages. The same breakdown is reflected on all components of the project plan (e.g., budget, schedule, etc.) and tracked throughout the project lifecycle. All sub-systems should flow from and connect with the project work breakdown structure (WBS).
- *Flexibility and dynamics.* Keep the project plan and work process flexible. Regularly scheduled reviews, reassessments, and validation of project objectives, assumptions, and performance should help in assessing the project plan against realities of the business environment. This will ensure that the project management tools work with realistic, current data, and produce valid information for monitoring, tracking and controlling the project execution.
- *Keep project status current.* Nothing outlives it usefulness faster than an outdated document. Plans need to be reviewed regularly and updated. This includes the data files of the monitoring and tracking systems. The best project management systems are perceived as useless if they produce information that cannot be validated or is based on assumptions that no longer hold.
- *User friendliness.* Project management tools and techniques should be user-friendly. This includes the user interfaces and information formats. Simplicity is king! Clarity is quality. The easier it is for project leaders and team members to work with the tool, the more likely the tool will be used effectively, producing the intended benefits.
- *Central system.* A single central system, Internet accessible, representing the most current information and status, is preferred over paper-based tools that easily lead to redundant documents with questionable time status.

9.2 THE BASIC TOOLS AND TECHNIQUES FOR PROJECT MANAGEMENT

Although managers can choose from a large number of tools and techniques to support the difficult task of planning and controlling their projects, these tools must fit the specific operational and organizational needs. Each project is unique in terms of objectives, resource constraints, timing, priorities and organizational culture, and the tools must be carefully chosen and fine-tuned to fit the specific requirements. Yet regardless of these differences, good project management tools are useful across a wide spectrum of projects and their life cycle stages.

To bring some structure into the discussion, this chapter organizes the large array of available tools and techniques into four groups, based on the triple constraint (see chapter 2) and organizational relations. That is, each group focuses on one constraint or project parameter, with primary focus on defining and managing the following:

1. Project scope
2. Project timing
3. Project resources
4. People and organizations.

These groups include many of the tools and techniques listed in Table 9.1. They also cut across several knowledge areas and all of the process groups defined by internationally recognized standards, such as PMI's PMBOK (2013). Further, a great deal of overlap exists among the various groups, application areas, and lifecycle stages, which are linked by these tools into a broad and almost seamless management system.

9.2.1 Scope Management Tools

These work-specific tools focus on *what* needs to be done. These are usually templates that define the work in various detail useful for (a) top-down project definition, (b) time and resource estimating, (c) project planning, (d) work assignments, (e) project monitoring, tracking and reporting, and (f) executing the project according to established objectives.

A wide variety of tools and formats exists for defining, communicating and tracking task-related components of the project. These tools must be fully integrated with the overall project management system in order to manage the project according to its performance parameters of work quality, timing and resource utilization. The following tools are most commonly used for defining tasks and work-related dimensions: (1) work breakdown structure (WBS), (2) scope statement, (3) statement of work, (4) work authorization, (5) work package, (6) specifications, and (7) deliverables. A brief description of each of these management tools is provided next.

Work Breakdown Structure

The work breakdown structure (WBS), sometimes called the *project breakdown structure* (PBS), is a hierarchical family tree of project elements. It is a delivery-oriented grouping of project sub-systems and task elements that define the various hardware, software, and service components of a specified project or program. An example is shown in Figure 9.1 for part of

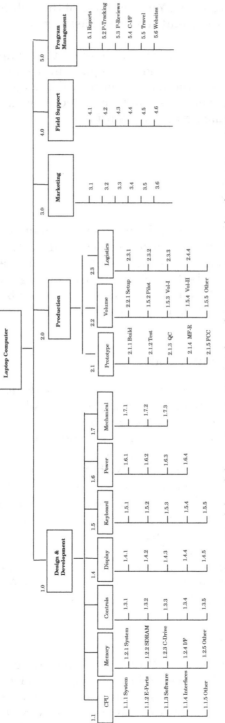

Figure 9.1 Work breakdown structure (WBS) for a laptop computer development project

an engineering development for a laptop computer. The WBS provides the framework for dividing the total program into manageable subsystems and tasks. It must include all the tasks necessary to conceptualize, design, fabricate, test, and eventually deliver the project as defined under the project scope statement. The WBS provides the framework for all program planning, budgeting, and scheduling. It becomes the *cost model* for project budgeting and the framework for the project scope and integration. The WBS is also the central reference point for the project. All other program management tools, such as schedules, task descriptions, and budgets, should clearly correspond to the work breakdown structure.

The level of detail depends on the project complexity. Obviously, larger and more complex projects require more depth and detail for their work breakdown. As a guideline, the total project should not be broken down further than the individual task contributor level. Of course, the individual responsible for the task can develop a mini-WBS for his or her own guidance of the work. However, in the interest of saving overhead and clutter, this additional detail does not have to be formally integrated with the overall project plan. Another consideration is the number of levels presented on a single sheet of paper or electronic screen. Normally, three levels of breakdown, as shown in Figure 9.1, is the maximum detail that should be displayed in a single cluster. Anything more detailed clutters the chart and destroys its flow and simplicity. The work breakdown structure in Figure 9.1 provides sufficient detail to the program manager for integrating the new laptop development. As an example, the program office (level zero) is not really concerned about the specifics of designing the SDRAM unit and integrating it with the computer system. However, someone is—the task leader for the SDRAM subsystem must develop his or her own project plan, starting with a work breakdown structure for the SDRAM subsystem that dovetails into the overall product development plan. This leads to the modular concept of work breakdown. That is, specific elements of work are subdivided on a separate sheet (module) into smaller components, until the level of detail, scope, and complexity is sufficiently defined for proper project execution.

Numbering the tasks. In order to reference specific tasks consistently throughout all planning and control documents, a decimal system is commonly used. The system is illustrated by listing the Level I and II tasks from the WBS of Figure 9.1, in Table 9.2. Such a listing is called a WBS index. If in addition to the index each element is described with a brief statement of work to be performed, the listing in Table 9.2 becomes a WBS directory. Lower levels can be included by breaking the decimal system down further. Alternatively, a modular approach to the WBS directory can be chosen by selecting specific elements and providing a detailed work breakdown just for those elements of interest in a separate list.

Grouping of program elements. This is a critical step. If the WBS has been structured properly, the various tasks integrate logically along the hierarchical lines of the work breakdown structure. Therefore the WBS should be

Table 9.2   WBS Index Based on the Breakdown shown in Figure 9.1

WBS Level	WBS #	WBS Task Element
0	—	Laptop Computer NPD
I	1	Design/Development
II	1.1	CPU
II	1.2	Memory
II	1.3	Control
II	1.4	Display
II	1.5	Keyboard
II	1.6	Power
II	1.7	Mechanical
I	2	Production
II	2.1	Prototype
II	2.2	Volume
II	2.3	Logistics
I	3	Marketing
II	3.1	Task A
II	3.2	Task B
II	3.3	Task C
II	3.4	Task D
II	3.5	Task E
II	3.6	Task F
I	4	Field Support
II	4.1	Task A
II	4.2	Task B
II	4.3	Task C
II	4.4	Task D
II	4.5	Task E
II	4.6	Task F
I	5	Project Management
II	5.1	Reports
II	5.2	P-Tracking
II	5.3	P-Reviews
II	5.4	C-I/F
II	5.5	Travel
II	5.6	Websites

arranged to satisfy two criteria: (1) it should flow according to the planned integration of the program, and (2) the tasks should be grouped to minimize cross-functional involvement for each subset of activities. Accordingly the work breakdown structure shown in Table 9.2 would be most appropriate if the laptop company has organizational resource groups responsible for the activities shown at level I of the WBS, such as design and development, production, marketing and field services. A different structure might be advisable if the company is structured along product group lines for different laptop applications. In this case, the level-I integration is probably most effectively performed at the product group level. However, it should be emphasized that the work breakdown structure is not an organizational chart. Attempts to force congruency often result in a confused and suboptimal WBS.

Regardless of how carefully the work breakdown structure has been fine-tuned to accommodate the existing organization, specific responsibility and authority relationships must be defined with a task matrix and the statement of work, which are described in the next sections of this chapter. Finally, it should be noted that a specific work breakdown structure may be given by the customer, forcing the program office to organize, integrate, and manage the project along a pre-established structure.

The work breakdown structure as cost model. Because the WBS breaks down the overall program into its subsystems, tasks, and deliverable items, it provides an effective and convenient model for estimating the program cost at various task levels. It is equally useful for top-down parametric estimating as well as for bottom-up estimating. As a cost model, the work breakdown structure further provides a management tool for defining the cost drivers, supporting budgetary estimates and economic feasibility studies.

In summary, *the work breakdown structure is the backbone of the project*. It has benefits for both the customer and the contractor because it:

- Defines program building blocks
- Breaks down program complexity
- Allows further expansion via modules
- Resembles a cost model of the program
- Provides a basis for all program planning and controlling: (1) specifications, (2) responsibility, (3) Budget, and (4) schedule

Scope Statement

The scope statement is usually the top-level document for articulating the overall project goals, objectives and mission-critical parameters, such as overall timing and resource constraints. The scope statement creates the big picture for the project. It defines the project baseline for all other documentation and management actions. To ensure conciseness and clarity of this top-level document, the scope statement should not exceed one page. Typical categories within the scope statement include: (1) project name and sponsor/customer data, (2) project mission and key objectives, (3) statement of work to be performed, (4) key deliverables, (5) key milestones, (6) key interfaces, and (7) key resources and constraints.

Statement of Work

The statement of work (SOW) is similar in structure and purpose to the scope statement. Its specific focus is on the base line description of the actual work to be performed. Together with the specification, it forms the contractual basis for most technical projects and programs. While the statement of work can be used to define the project work top-down, it is also a useful format for defining and communicating work at any other project level or work module. The SOW is usually related to a particular work package or task elements in the work breakdown structure, describing precisely what is to be accomplished. Typically, the statement of work includes: (1) The project name and definition of the task module with reference to the corresponding work breakdown structure element, (2) a description of the task, (3) the results and deliverable items to be produced, such as the system concept, hardware, software, tests, documentation and training, (4) references to specifications, standards, directives, and other documents, and (5) all inputs required from and to other tasks. Top-down, the statement of work is often a key document as part of a customer's request for proposal. Similar to the scope statement, the development of the SOW, especially for large programs, is a project by itself. It is a major effort that requires a considerable amount of interfacing with all stakeholders from the user, customer, and supporting organizations.

Specifications

Specifications ("specs") describe the metrics of the project elements to be delivered. Specs form the baseline for developing, producing, and controlling the technical part of the project or program. Good specifications relate to the work breakdown structure. They describe the desired characteristics of the various subsystems in a modular fashion. Depending on the size and complexity of the project, specifications come in different dimensions and modules, such as specification for the overall system, subsystems, components, hardware, software, tests, manufacturing and quality. In order to define and verify the end product, specifications should be developed with focus on measurability. However, there should also be flexibility to accommodate changes that inevitably evolve, particularly during a development program.

Work Package

A work package is a subset of an overall project. Work packages relate to specific elements of the work breakdown. Referring to the WBS of Figure 9.1, the power module (WBS # 1.6), the prototype module (WBS # 2.1) or the production module (WBS # 2.0) are typical examples of task-sets that could be defined as work packages. In order to provide a useful framework for project management, the work package must define (1) the work to be performed, including reference to the corresponding statements of work and specifications, (2) the responsible organization or individual, (3) the resource requirements, and (4) the schedule. The *task authorization* is the proper tool for summarizing and communicating work package data to the project team.

Task Authorization

All work must be properly defined and authorized by the project manager. This also applies to subcontracted items. The task authorization is a convenient way to summarize the requirements, as well as the budget and schedule constraints, for a particular project subsystem, which is often a work package. As shown in Figure 9.2, the format of a task authorization provides

Figure 9.2 Task Authorization Form

for summary and reference data in four major categories, (1) responsible individual organization, (2) schedule, (3) budget and (4) work statement. A one-sheet task authorization form is recommended, regardless of the task magnitude. The form is intended as a summary of key data, referencing pertinent documents for details specifications, statement of work, deliverable items, and quality standards.

The task authorization is the written contract between the project manager and the task leader or the performing organization in general. To be meaningful, the task authorization must have been developed together with the key personnel who will perform the work. Moreover, an agreement on the task feasibility, its schedule, and budget must exist within the team, to have any basis for team commitment to the established objectives.

Deliverables

Deliverables are specific outputs or results from the project activity, such as plans, prototypes, documentations, software, decisions, and approvals. They are tangible, measurable accomplishments, usually associated with a specific milestone. Deliverables can be "hard," such as an installed antenna or "soft," such as a license, but they must be verifiable. An FCC license, a budget decision or a test signoff are soft, but very specific deliverables that can help in tracking and validating project progression and potential problems. Deliverables are also useful measures in determining progress payments, and in providing visibility and recognition for team accomplishments. Deliverable items should be defined for each major milestone. The responsibility for defining deliverable items rests with the project leader. Close cooperation with the performing organizations is necessary in order to ensure meaningful deliverables with measurable parameters. A list of key deliverables is often part of a project summary plan or contract document. Such a list can provide useful focus for detailed project planning, tracking, and management.

9.2.2 Time Management Tools

Time is one of two major constraints on the project. The other is resources. They define the project boundaries and directly affect its scope and quality. The old saying, "any project is possible given unlimited time and money" reminds us that these are luxuries that we don't have in today's business environment. Most projects are end-date driven and resource-limited. Defining and effectively documenting the time and resource requirements, consistent with the project scope and its objectives, is one of the most challenging responsibilities of the project leader. Today managers have available a wide variety of tools and techniques for dealing with time and resource issues. These tools must be fully integrated with the overall project management system in order to manage the project within its set of performance parameters of work quality, timing and resource utilization. This section focuses on the time dimension. Resource management tools will be discussed separately in the next section.

Schedules are the cornerstones in any project planning and control system. They present a time-phased picture of the activities to be performed and highlight the major milestones to be tracked throughout the program. Although schedules come in many forms and levels of detail, they should be related to a master schedule and their activity structure should be consistent with that of other project planning and control documents, particularly the work breakdown structure. For larger programs, a modular arrangement is a necessity to avoid cluttering, as suggested in Table 9.3 for the laptop project discussed earlier.

Schedules are working tools for project/program planning, evaluation, and control. They are developed via many iterations with project team members and the sponsor. Schedules should remain dynamic throughout the program life cycle. Every program has unique management requirements. The most comprehensive schedule is not necessarily the best choice for all programs. Selecting the right schedule is important. There are three principal schedule types that are most commonly used in project management. Milestone charts, Gantt charts (bar graphs) and networks.

Milestone Chart

A good way to start any schedule development is to define the key milestones for the work to be performed. Once agreed upon, the milestone chart

Table 9.3   A Modular Schedule Format

Level-I:	Master Project Schedule			
Level-II:	Design Schedule	Production Schedule	Marketing Schedule	Field Support Schedule
Level-III:	• CPU Schedules • Memory schedules • Control schedules • Display schedules • Keyboard schedules • Power schedules • Mechanical schedules	• Prototype schedule • Production schedule • Logistics schedule	• Market research schedule • Market planning schedule • Distribution schedule • Promotion schedule	• Parts schedule • Service schedule • Training schedule • Support schedule • Remote diagnostics schedule

becomes the backbone for the master schedule and subsequent subsystem schedules.

A key milestone is defined as an important event in the project life cycle, such as the start of a new project phase, a status review, a test, or the first shipment of a deliverable. Ideally, the completion of a key milestone should be easily verifiable. In reality however, most milestones, no matter how crucial, are not easily verifiable. "System design completed," "first article test," and "final design review" are examples of typical key milestones that must be defined in specific detail to be measurable and useful for subsequent project control.

Key milestones should be defined for all major project phases, prior to start-up. The type and number of these milestones must be carefully determined to ensure meaningful tracking of the project/program. If the milestones are spread too far apart, continuity problems in program tracking and control can arise. However, too many milestones can result in unnecessary busywork, confusion, inappropriate controls, and increased overhead cost. As a guideline for multiyear programs, four key milestones per year seem to provide sufficient inputs for detailed project tracking without overburdening the system.

The program office typically has the responsibility for defining key milestones, in close cooperation with the customer and the supporting resource groups.

Selecting the right type of milestone is critical. Every key milestone should represent a checkpoint for the completion of a cluster of activities. Ideally, major milestones are located at strategic time points of a project, encompassing a significant program segment with well-defined boundaries. Examples are:

- Project kickoff
- Requirement analysis complete
- Preliminary design review
- Critical design review
- Prototype fabricated
- Integration and testing
- Value engineering review
- Start volume production
- Promotional program defined
- First shipment
- Customer acceptance test complete

The Bar Graph

The most widely used management tool for project schedule planning and control is the bar graph. Its development dates back to the work by Henry L. Gantt during World War I, which is the reason bar graphs are often referred to as Gantt charts. Figure 9.3 illustrates the basic features of the bar

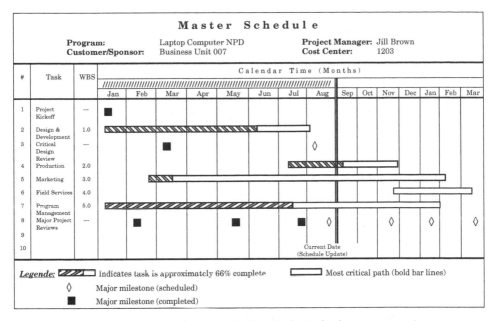

Figure 9.3 Bar graph schedule (Gantt chart) for laptop computer development project

graph by showing a partial master schedule for the minicomputer development of the work breakdown structure of Figure 9.1. The tasks on the left-hand side of the schedule should correspond directly to the work breakdown structure and its numbering system. In fact, there should be no tasks on the schedule that cannot be found in the work breakdown structure.

If it becomes necessary to introduce a new task on the schedule, the work breakdown structure should be revised accordingly, which is part of the iterative nature of project planning. However, it is common practice and appropriate to list milestones, such as project kickoff and critical design review, on the bar graph schedule along with the tasks.

Bar graphs are simple to generate and easy to understand. They show the schedule start and finish of the tasks to be managed. Also, bar graphs can be modified to indicate project status, most critical activity, and so on. The hatched areas in the example of Figure 3 indicate the approximate percentile of project completion, while the bold bar lines indicate that task items 2 (design), 4 (production) and 5 (marketing)are most critical; that is, they are on the longest time path through the project (see also next section, "Network Techniques").

Bar graphs can be further modified to show budget status by adding a column that lists planned and actual expenditures for each new task. Many variations of the original bar graph have been developed to provide more detailed information to project managers. One commonly used method is to replace the bars with lines and triangular markers at the end points. Using different symbols at the end points indicates the original time line and its revisions, thus tracing schedule changes through the project life cycle.

The problem with these additional features is that they take away from the clarity and simplicity of the original bar graph, and often cause confusion interpreting the data. However, in many cases the additional information help in communicating, project status reporting and subsequent control, and are beneficial in spite of the "fog factor" they carry.

The major limitation of the bar graph schedule is its inability to show task interdependence and time-resource tradeoffs. Network techniques, which usually work together with computer data processing, have been developed especially for larger projects. These are powerful (but expensive) techniques, which help project managers plan, track, and control their larger, more complex projects effectively.

Network Techniques

Several techniques evolved in the late 1950s to support planning and tracking of projects with large numbers of interdependent activities. Best known today are PERT (Program Evaluation and Review Technique) and CPM (Critical Path Method). PERT was developed by the U.S. navy in the late 1950s to aid in the management of the Polaris missile program, while CPM was jointly developed by DuPont and Remington Rand, also in the 1950s. CPM originally had an additional feature in comparison to PERT: it could track resource requirements. Originally, each technique had its own unique features; however, today's commercially available project tracking software combines both features, often referred to as PERT/CPM. The concept of PERT/CPM and its features are discussed as part of an example derived from our laptop development. The network diagram shown in Figure 9.4 represents the flow of major

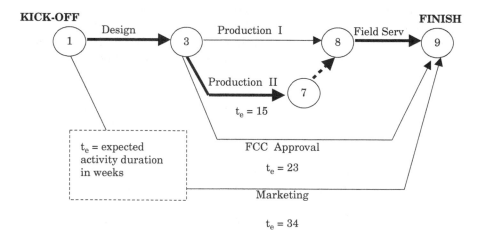

Figure 9.4 Network diagram for laptop development project similar to the WBS in Figure 9.1 and the schedule in Figure 9.3

activities, similar to our laptop development (see WBS of Figure 9.1 and bar graph schedule of Figure 9.3).

It is clear that the network diagram is more powerful than the bar graph in describing the flow of project phases through time and showing task interdependencies. The network provides a dynamic picture of the events and activities and their interrelationships. Yet, this is only the tip of its capability. The main value of PERT/CPM is in its ability to track the timing and cost parameters of the project, and to draw specific conclusions regarding project status and performance.

PERT/CPM Example

PERT/CPM is an excellent system for keeping track of all activities, especially in large projects where there are thousands of interdependent tasks. Moreover, PERT/CPM is a powerful tool for quick impact assessment of what-if scenarios and contingencies during project execution. To explain the quantitative methods and features of PERT /CPM we use an example, similar to the laptop development discussed earlier (see Figure 9.1 and 9.3). The methodology for setting up the PERT or CPM system is shown in Table 9.4.

1. Define the work. The work breakdown structure, such as shown in Figure 9.1, usually provides a good framework for delineating the work or project sub-systems and for deciding the level of detail for the PERT/CPM data base. Let us assume that we want to prepare the network on level-I of the work breakdown. We choose the activities that should be tracked with the PERT/CPM system and list them in the PERT-table (left column) of Table 9.4.

2. Define the resources and time estimates. At the chosen level of detail (i.e., WBS level-I), we have to list all the activities and develop the labor budget (e.g., in staff-hours, staff-weeks or staff-months). Then, based on the available personnel, we have to calculate a time estimate, t_e for each activity duration and record the time estimate in column five of the 5). Many of the commercially available PERT software packages allow the user to calculate an expected time duration for each activity, based on the weighted average of three estimates: most optimistic, most pessimistic and most likely. For simplicity of the example we work here only with one time estimate, t_e. I also like to point out that using a range of estimates, while providing data for interesting statistics, doesn't make the resource estimate any more accurate, nor does it help in getting commitment to a realistic or stretch target date.

3. Establish the skeleton diagram (network). The activities, such as shown in the left column of Table 9.4, must be organized manually into a skeleton diagram or network to reflect their interdependence and resource constraints. Structuring the network diagram is an art that requires a great deal of work process knowledge and judgment, and the unified input of all resource groups across the organization. The result is a PERT/CPM network diagram such as that shown in Figure 9.4. Please note that in our example

Table 9.4 Summary of PERT Calculations for PERT/CPM Example

Activity (n)	WBS Reference (#)	Resource Requirement (staff-weeks)	Available Personnel (P)	Expected Duration (t_e weeks)	Preceding Event (PE)	Succeeding Event (SE)	Earliest Start (ES)	Earliest Finish (EF)	Latest Start (LS)	Latest Finish (LF)	Total Slack (TS)	Free Slack (FS)
Design	1.0	2000	100	30	1	3	1	30	-4	25	-5	0
Production-I	2.0	500	60	10	3	8	31	40	31	40	0	+5
Production-II	2.2	250	20	15	3	7	31	45	26	40	-5	0
FCC Approval	3.0	100	5	23	3	9	31	53	30	52	-1	+4
Marketing	4.0	100	5	34	1	9	1	34	19	52	+18	+23
Field Services	6.0	50	6	12	8	9	46	57	41	52	-5	0
Dummy	–	0	0	0	7	8	45	45	40	40	-5	0

the circles are events, the lines are activities. Therefore, this is an activity-on-arrow (AOA) diagram. While this is the most common form used in industry, PERT/CPM software programs often use an activity-on-node connotation. The skeleton diagram becomes the basis for setting up the PERT/CPM table.

Important rule: when using AOA, all events (the nodes at the beginning and end of each activity) must be uniquely numbered, but the numbers do not have to be sequential. Each activity must be uniquely defined by a *preceding* and a *succeeding* event. For example, the *production-I* activity is uniquely defined by events 3 and 8. In order to define the production-II activity (executed in parallel to production-I) uniquely, an additional *event 7* must be inserted, resulting in the dummy activity 7–8, which is shown as a dashed line in Figure 9.4.

4. Define schedule constraints. Let us assume that the project kickoff cannot take place before January 1 and the total project should be completed by December 31. Therefore, the earliest start (ES) = week 1, and the latest finish (LF) = week 52. These are the schedule limitations or constraints that must be specified, together with the start and finish events (or event numbers).

5. Generate computer inputs and process data. The computer must be instructed regarding (1) how the network is constructed and (2) the time duration for each activity. The network topology is defined by the preceding and succeeding event numbers that tell the computer which activities are executed sequentially and which are in parallel. Technically, the PERT computer software needs only data from Table 9.4, columns 5, 6 and 7 (duration, PE & SE) to calculate all PERT/CPM results. However, to generate more user-friendly outputs, such as shown in Table 9.4, the first seven columns of Table 9.3 should be uploaded to the PERT/CPM software. The computer can now generate a PERT-table, as shown in Table 9.4, based on formulas and calculations summarized in Table 9.5.

Interpretation of results. Looking at the earliest start (ES) and earliest finish (EF) figures, identify the specific week when we plan to start the project and will actually finish. The latest start (LS) and latest finish (LF) figures identify the specific week when we *should* start the project in order to finish as we want to by the end of week 52. Specifically, the following conclusions can be drawn from the computer-generated Table 9.4:

- Project duration: 57 weeks. We find this result by examining the earliest finishing (EF) times. The largest number (week 57) indicates that the field services activity is the last one to finish at the end of week 57. This is 5 week later than we want to finish the program.
- Project start and finish: If we start the project at the beginning of week 1 (as planned), we will finish at the end of week 57 (as discussed above). However, if we want to finish at the end of week 52 (planned), we will have to start the project 5 weeks earlier, at week -4 (please note that "week 0" is the week prior to "week -1." This often causes confusion for manual calculations, but is necessary to make the formulas consistent and workable for both positive and negative dates).

Table 9.5   Formulas used in PERT Analysis

Formulas:	Legend:
$ES = EF_{n-1} + 1$	ES = Earliest start
$EF_n = ES_n + t_e - 1$	EF = Earliest finish
$LS_n = LF_n - t_e + 1$	LS = Latest start
$LF_n = LS_{n=1} - 1$	LF = Latest finish
$TS_n = LF - EF = LS - ES$	TS = Total slack
$FS_n = TS_n - TS_{MCP}$	FS = Free slack
Within the string of networked activities, n – 1 represents the preceding activity, and n + 1 the succeeding activity.	CP = Critical path
	MCP = Most critical path, this is the longest network path
	PE = Preceding event
	SE = Succeeding event
	P = Number of full-time personnel available
	SW = Work effort in staff-weeks
	TS_{MCP} = Total slack of activities on the most critical (longest) path in the network
	t_e = Expected duration (in weeks)

- Total slack (TS): The TS-column indicates the amount of *extra time* we have for each activity before the project exceeds the schedule constraint (becomes late). For example, $TS = -5$ indicates that the design activity is already 5 weeks late, while production-I is just on time (TS = 0) and marketing has 18 weeks of extra time on hand.
- Free slack (FS): The FS-column (also called *float*) indicates the amount of extra time we have for each activity, before it affects the actual project finish date. For example, let's take a look at the FCC approval activity. While this activity is actually one week late, according to the desired project finish time, the field service activity (that enters the same event), finishes even later, exactly five weeks late ($TS = -5$). Therefore we could spend an additional four weeks on the FCC approval before it impacts the overall project schedule.
- Critical path (CP): As a common definition, any activity with a *total slack of zero or less is critical*. That is, activities on the critical path will directly impact the planned finish time of the project, if they experience any delay. Without any other critical path information given, this definition applies. However, project managers can set their own level of criticality, such as TS < 3 weeks, or whatever they deem appropriate.
- Most critical path (MCP): This is the longest activity path through the network. We can quickly identify the MCP by examining the total

slack (TS) or free slack (FS) columns. Under total slack, all activities with the lowest TS (e.g., most negative) are on the most critical path. Alternatively, all activities with *zero free slack* are on the most critical path. By definition, any delay of activities on the most critical path will directly delay the actual finish time of the project.

The Benefits of PERT/CPM

The full benefits of PERT/CPM and other network techniques are only realized on larger and more enterprise-integrated programs that can also utilize the PERT/CPM system for overall contract management, customer reporting, procurement, and contractor management. In our small example, the information gleaned from the PERT-table might not look like a big deal and or seem like it would be much help to project managers. However, when tracking thousands of activities, this type of bookkeeping is very helpful and leads to other types of automatic recordings, checks, and balances.

The more powerful indicators are the slack figures. *Total slack* indicates the number of time units that we can spare and still meet the schedule constraints. In our example, a TS of −5 for the design activity indicates that we will be 5 weeks behind schedule with this activity and any other activity in the same path, unless we shorten the expected duration of t_e. Therefore scanning the TS column assists in identifying which activities need help and where we have the luxury of slack, and therefore could "borrow" resources. Any activity with *negative* total slack is termed a *critical activity*. The activities on the longest path, that is, those activities that are most negative or least positive. are called *most critical*.

Free slack indicates the amount of additional time we have available, without impacting the schedule outcome. For example, the FCC activity will be late by one week, as indicated by TS = −1. However, the field service activity will be late by five weeks (TS = −5). Therefore, the FCC activity really has another four weeks before an impact on the delivery date of the overall project is felt.

9.2.3 Resource Management Tools

Cost, together with time, is one of the major constraints or boundary conditions imposed on most projects. The third variable affecting cost is the project scope. Defining and effectively documenting the resource requirements, consistent with the project scope, its objectives and time constraints, is a difficult task that must be fully integrated with the overall project management system. Four of the most common tools used for project resource management will be discussed in detail: budgets, cost accounts, cost baselines, and earned value.

Project Budgets

Project budgets are important management tools for defining resource requirements in support of project justification, initiations, planning, tracking and execution. Budgets are based on cost estimates, summarized in various detail, formats and formalities. In many cases, the first basic cost estimate is needed to support a feasibility analysis of project selection decision, long before the project baseline is fully defined. Such early cost estimates are referred to as *budgetary estimates* or *rough order of magnitude (ROM) estimates*. Later on, during the project definition phase, when the project requirements are known in sufficient detail, a more accurate estimate (often called a *bottom-up estimate*), can be developed. For these bottom-up budgets, costs estimates are assigned to the lowest WBS-level tasks. Costs are then accumulated to determine sub-system budgets, and eventually the total project budget. Budgets provide a critical input to management decisions on bidding, pricing, new product development, strategic business plans, and the project management process.

For clarity and manageability, project budgets should be modular (similar to the discussion on schedules). That is, budgets should be broken into subsets following established project decompositions, such as execution phases or work breakdown structure (WBS) segments.

Regardless of the specific format chosen, project budgets usually include the following information:

- Cost line items or elements of cost of activities included in the cost breakdown (detail)
- Each line item should include (1) labor, (2) material and (3) other cost
- Each line item should be numbered and referenced to the work breakdown structure (WBS)
- Budgets should include general overheads, either as a separate cost or as part of each line item
- Project budgets should show project administration as a separate line item
- Project budgets should show the accumulate total cost projected for the project

A typical budget template is shown in Table 9.6.

Cost Accounts

The cost account usually is the lowest level at which resources are measured, managed, and reported. However, it can also refer to any project component. Cost accounts represent a specific task, which is referenced to the work breakdown structure (WBS). Aside from resource data, cost accounts often show associated schedule, task, accountability, and organizational information. Resources identified in a cost account are often time-phased over the project life cycle, creating a cost baseline. Especially for larger technology programs, cost accounts become the focal point for project budget planning, cost control, and reporting.

Table 9.6   Project Budget Example Summarizing Level-1 of the Laptop Project shown on the WBS of Figure 9.1

Activity	WBS	Labor (K$)	Material (K$)	Other (K$)	Total (K$)	Remarks
Design and development	1.0	$6,500	2,800	1,000	10,300	
Production	2.0	4,000	5,000	500	9,500	Include only pilot production
Marketing	3.0	3,700	3,200	5,100	12,000	
Field support	4.0	1,100	600	800	2,500	
Project administration	—	1,000	230	200	1,430	
Total Budget		**$16,300**	**$11,830**	**$7,600**	**$35,730**	

A simple but effective cost-tracking mechanism is the conventional *time card system*, or its electronic equivalent, that exists for record-keeping in most organizations. If project personnel, or their supervisors, are required to submit these "time records," the number of hours worked on each task, referenced to a cost account, defines all cost information needed for data processing. Subsequently, cost reports can be generated on a weekly, monthly, or as-needed basis, providing various summaries for convenient cost tracking and control. Examples are:

- Actual total project cost versus planned cost, both in weekly increments and cumulatively
- Variance reports
- Weekly expenditures by task categories and project subsystems
- Listing of project personnel, together with their tasks, budgets, and time allocations

If established properly within the organizational support system, tools such as project dashboards and enterprise cost accounts and their reporting systems, are powerful tools to the project manager for measuring and controlling project cost.

Project Baseline

The project baseline is defined as the original scope, cost, and schedule allocated across the project lifecycle. In a more narrow definition, the *cost baseline* refers only to the time-phased project budget. Either way, the baseline is an important tool for planning, monitoring, and managing projects, including change control. The cost baseline is developed by estimating project cost, or sub-system cost, across specific time periods. Therefore it represents an expenditure profile of costs, showing when they are supposed to occur across the project lifecycle. Quite commonly, the cost baseline is communicated as a chart of project sub-systems, work packages, or tasks against their budgeted expenditures over given time periods. The cost baseline can also be displayed graphically, showing cost projections versus time, which facilitates comparison of planned versus actual expenditures. It can also be expanded to display other cost performance data, such as earned value analysis. Very large projects often have multiple cost baselines, separating different parts of the project with different accounting systems or cash flow models that might account also for revenue flow in addition to expenditures.

Earned Value

Earned value management (EVM), also referred to as earned value project/performance management (EVPM), is a management tool for measuring and tracking project performance. It combines cost, schedule, and scope measurements to calculate technical progress measures and current project performance against an established baseline. The system also forecasts performance for the remaining project lifecycle. Some of the key variables tracked by the EVM system are: planned value (PV), earned value (EV), percent complete (%), cost variance (CV), schedule variance (SV), cost performance index (cPI), schedule performance index (sPI), total estimated cost at completion (EAC), cost performance index (cPI), and schedule performance index (sPI). The earned value measurement (EMS) system has its roots in cost accounting. Its history can be traced back to the factory applications in the 1800s, tracking production targets by comparing planned against actual output, timing, and cost. Later the system became known as line of balance (LOB). In 1967 EVM was introduced by the U.S. government as part of its cost/schedule control system criteria (C/SCSC) and performance measurement system (PMS) for tracking contract performance. Today, EVM techniques find increasing acceptance and use among project managers of all industries, especially for large projects and virtually all major U.S. government contracts. Many contemporary project management systems include EVM as an integrated as part of their computer-supported enterprise system, allowing them to generate sophisticated analysis, statistics, and graphics in support of their project management activities.

How does it work? While some advanced and specialized applications can get complicated, the basic EVM methodologies and calculations are straightforward. They consist of measuring technical progress against an established budget and schedule baseline. However, the crucial and important assumption for EVM to produce meaningful results is the ability to assess technical progress. This is difficult and challenging for most projects, especially for the more complex and technology-intensive undertakings.

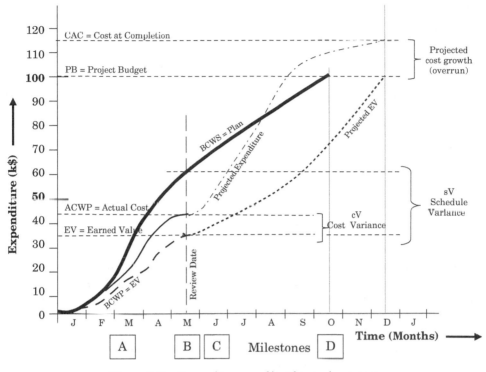

Figure 9.5   Expenditure profile of sample project

The following example will illustrate the system. Let us assume that the spending profile of an engineering project was originally planned as shown in Figure 9.5 and resource expenditures were planned and spent as shown in Table 9.7. The objective is to perform a project status assessment in May, by the end of the scheduled milestone B. The original project plan calls for a project completion by the end of October.

Each of the milestones A, B, C. and D, is associated with specific measurable deliverables, so that a judgment on the "percent of completion" can be made for each milestone at any point in the project life cycle. The budgets originally established for each set of milestone tasks are as follows: $A = \$20,000$, $B = \$40,000$, $C = \$10,000$ and $D = \$30,000$, leading to the "planned" spending profile shown in Table 9.7 with a total budget of $\$100,000$. The cost report, presented at the review time in May, shows an actual expenditure of $A' = \$22,000$, $B' = \$16,000$, $C' = \$1000$, and $D' = \$3000$. These expenditures add up to a total of $\$42,000$ versus a planned expenditure of $\$65,000$, which is shown graphically in Figure 9.5. Although we spent less money than budgeted, obviously we cannot draw any conclusions on project performance, since we do not yet know the technical progress, that is, how much work has been completed.

Table 9.7   Summary Data for Earned Value Calculations

Parameter	Cost and Performance Measures For Each Milestone				Total Project
	A	**B**	**C**	**D**	
Agreed-upon budget	$20,000	$40,000	$10,000	$30,000	$100,000
Actually spent by May	$22,000	$16,000	$1,000	$3,000	$42,000
Percent-complete by May (for each milestone)	90%	30%	20%	10%	
Earned value	$18,000	$12,000	$2,000	$3,000	$35,000
Cost at completion	$24,400	$53,300	$5,000	$30,000	$112,700
Cost to complete	$2,400	$37,300	$4,000	$27,000	$70,700

At this point let us assume that we can actually measure the status of all tasks and their deliverables leading to each of the four milestones: $A = 90$ percent complete, $B = 30$ percent complete, $C = 20$ percent complete, and $D = 10$ percent complete. These measurements are the only subjective data in the earned-value system. All other figures are calculated.

The first important figures which can be calculated are the earned values for each milestone and the project. The formula is

$$\text{Earned Value (EV)} = (\%\text{-complete}) \times (\text{Agreed-on Budget [BAC]})$$

It should be noted that earned value has nothing to do with the actual expenditures, but depends only on the technical performance against the agreed-upon budget. According to this definition the earned values are as follows: $A = \$18,000$, $B = \$12,000$, $C = \$2,000$ and $D = \$3,000$, adding up to a total value of $35,000 for the project. Now we have a basis for assessing project performance. While we spent $42,000, we earned only $35,000. The $35,000 is the amount that can be billed to the customer if we work on a contract.

Now we can compute three performance indices, which are ratios defined as follows:

$$\text{Cost Performance Index (cPI)} = \frac{\text{Earned Value (EV)}}{\text{Actual Cost of Work Performed (ACWP)}}$$

$$= \frac{35}{42} = .83 \, (= 83\%)$$

$$\text{Schedule Performance Index (sPI)} = \frac{\text{Earned Value (EV)}}{\text{Planned Value (PV)}}$$

$$= \frac{35}{65} = .54 \, (= 54\%)$$

$$\textit{Total Performance Index (TPI)} \quad = (cPI)(sPI) = .83 \times .54 = .45 \, (= 45\%)$$

In these formulas, the *actual cost of work performed* (ACWP) is the amount of money spent on the project so far (by May), and the *planned value* (PL) is the amount of money that was budgeted to be spent by May. From the calculations at our May review we can draw the following conclusions:

- Our *cost performance index* (cPI) for the total project is 35/42 = 0.83, indicating that we earned just 83 percent of the value, relative to what we spent; or we are working just 83 percent cost-efficient;
- Our *schedule performance index* (sPI) for the total project is 35/65 = 0.54, indicating that we accomplished just 54 percent of the planned results; or we are working just 83 percent time-efficient;
- Our *overall performance index* (TPI) for the total project is .83 × .54 = .45, indicating that the project is running at an overall efficiency of 45 percent, measured in overall resource utilization.

With the given data on money spent for each milestone so far and each percent-complete estimate, we can also calculate the estimated cost at completion (CAC), cost to complete (CTC), cost variances (cV), and the aggregated percent-completion for the total project as follows:

$$Cost\ at\ Completion\ (CAC) = \frac{Actual\ Cost\ of\ Work\ Performed\ (ACWP)}{Percent - Complete\ (\%)};$$

$$Cost\ to\ Complete\ (CTC) = Cost\ at\ Completion\ (CAC)$$
$$- Actual\ Cost\ of\ Work\ Performed\ (ACWP).$$

$$Cost\ Variance\ (cV) = Earned\ Value\ (EV)$$
$$- Actual\ Cost\ of\ Work\ Performed\ (ACWP).$$

$$Total\ Project\ \% - Completion = \frac{Actual\ Cost\ of\ Work\ Performed\ (ACWP)}{Cost\ at\ Completion\ (CAC)}$$

$$= \frac{42,000}{112,700} = .37\ (= 37\%)$$

The calculated results are shown in Table 9.7 and the definitions for all major EVM variables are summarized in Table 9.8. In the final analysis, the calculations show that the project is only 37 percent complete with 42 percent of its budget spent. The new estimated cost at completion is $112,700 indicates that we will need $12,700 of funding in addition to the originally agreed-on project budget of $100,000.

Project Management Benefits

Project status reviews and subsequent controls focus on measuring actual performance versus expended resources and schedule. The earned-value

Table 9.8   EVM Variables Defined

EVM Variable	Definition
BAC—Budgeted cost at completion	Originally planned and agreed-upon budget for total project
ACWP—Actual cost of work performed	Resources (cost) actually spent to-date
BCWC—Budgeted cost of work completed	Budgeted cost of the work actually completed over time, that is, how much budget did we originally plan and allocate for the work completed so far. BCWC = EV = (BAC) × (% complete)
BCWS—Budgeted cost of work scheduled	Original budget baseline, planned resource expenditure over time
PV—Planned value	Budgeted cost of work scheduled; PV = BCWS
CAC—Estimated cost at completion	Revised total cost estimate (projection) for project at completion time. CAC = ACWP + CTC
CTC—Cost to complete	Estimated cost to complete project, looking forward from a known point in the lifecycle
cV—Cost variance	Difference between earned value and actual cost. cV = EV—ACWP
sV—Schedule variance	Cost measure comparing planned and actual work; sV = BCWS—BCWP
EV—Earned value	Budgeted cost of the work actually completed. EV = BCWP = % BAC
cPI—Cost performance index	Measure of resource effectiveness; cPI = EV/ACWP
sPI—Schedule performance index	Measure of resource efficiency against schedule time line; sPI = EV/PV = EV/BCWS
TPI—Total performance index	Measure of overall resource efficiency; TPI = cPI × sPI

system provides a framework for quantifying and summarizing project performance data, performing variance analysis, re-budgeting and rescheduling, and negotiating changes with the sponsor. Above all, the analysis shows the manager where the project is heading in terms of overall schedule and budget, providing a basis for renegotiations with the sponsor and redirection of the efforts at selected points in the project life cycle. The ability to summarize the performance data in terms of earned value, performance index, estimated cost to complete, estimated cost at completion, cost variance, and schedule slippage is especially useful for multiproject management and large programs that need to be measured and controlled both top-down and at the sub-system level. The validity of the earned value management system hinges, however, on the ability to measure technical progress, which is related to the ability and willingness of the team to define measurable milestones, a topic that will be further discussed in subsequent chapters.

9.2.4 Tools for Managing People and Organizations

All project team members and their support personnel must understand where they fit in the organization. While the traditional organizational chart is a common and useful device to define the command channels of conventional superior-subordinate relations, additional tools are needed to describe the specific authorities, responsibilities, and interfaces associated with each key position within the project organization. Project charters, task rosters, task matrices, and job descriptions are common devices for delineating the roles of key project personnel and for communicating them to all team members. In addition, companies may use management directives to clarify definitions, organizational processes and relations.

Project Charter

The project charter is a particularly useful and powerful tool for identifying and communicating the top-down mission, authority structure and key parameters of a project (Anderson 2003). Eventually these project charters include the names of key personnel, while at the early stages of a project definition the charter serves as a top-down planning document. It is also very useful in identifying and negotiation key team members. Project charters are similar to operating charters, which are more focused on the individual who holds the office. Operating charters were already discussed earlier in the project organizations chapter with examples shown in the appendix of this book.

Project Policies and Procedures

Policies and procedures are sets of management tools for defining the process of managing a project and for describing the inner working of the project organization. They provide operating guidelines for running the business in a proven, standard way. The depth of these documents can range from simply acknowledging project activities, to detailed procedural guidelines that carry the project team through the complete project life cycle. Unless there are extenuating circumstances, project personnel must follow these policies and procedures. At the same time, these documents must be written broadly

Table 9.9 Segment of Task Matrix Based on Work Breakdown Structure (WBS, Figure 1)

TASK MATRIX

Program: Laptop Computer NPD
Project Manager: Jill Brown
Customer/Sponsor: Business Unit 007
Cost Center: 1203

Legend:
P = Prime Responsibility
S = Supporting Responsibility

Task		Resources								
Description	**WBS Reference**	**R&D**	**System Design**	**Engg Section I**	**Engg Section II**	**Testing**	**Quality Assur.**	**Manufacturing**	**Marketing**	**Etc.**
Design and Development	1.0		P	S	S		S		S	
CPU	1.1	S	S	P	S		S		S	
System design	1.1.1	S		P	S	S	S			
E-Parts	1.1.2		S		P		S			
Software	1.1.3		P		S					
Interfaces	1.1.4	S	P	S	S			S		
Other	1.1.5			S	S	P				
Memory	1.2	P	S							
System design	1.2.1	P	S		S					
SDRAM	1.2.2	P	S	S	S					
C-Drive	1.2.3	P	S	S	S					
I/F	1.2.4	P	S							
Other	1.2.5		P							

Controls	1.3	S	S	S	P				
Task A	1.3.1	S	S	S	P				
Task B	1.3.2	S	S		P	S			
Task C	1.3.3	S			P	S			
Task D	1.3.4	S		P		S			
Displays	1.4			S	P		S		
Task A	1.4.1			S	P		S		S
Task B	1.4.2			S	P	S		S	
...	...								
...	...								
Production	**2.0**			S	S	S	S	P	
Prototype	2.1			S	S	S	S	P	
Volume production	2.2				S	S	S	P	
Logistics	2.3			S			S	P	
Marketing	**3.0**		S	S	S				P
Task A	3.1		S						P
Task B	3.2		P		S	S			S
Task C	3.3			S	S				P
Task D	3.4			S	S				P
...	...								
...	...								

enough to leave operating leeway to management and to accommodate the variety of projects that run through the organization. Further, to ensure proper integration of these policies and procedures with the enterprise system, they should be tested and fine-tuned before being formally issued.

Project managers who find themselves without adequate guidelines often develop and issue their own procedures at the project level. This is an excellent way to communicate the established operating standards. Further, these task-level procedures often become test cases for more formal, higher-level directives.

Task Matrix

The *task matrix* is a simple but powerful tool to define responsibility relationships among the various program tasks and the performing organizations. The task matrix, also known as *responsibility matrix* or *linear responsibility chart*, evolved out of frustrations over conventional organization charts, which do not show relationships within and between organizational subsystems—that is, they do not show who is responsible for what at the task level. Equally important, the task matrix has a great amount of flexibility and does not restrain the system by emphasizing status and position, which is an awkward limitation of conventional organizational charts. The task matrix is derived from the work breakdown structure. Therefore all task descriptions should correspond to the WBS. Table 9.9 illustrates this management tool by defining the task responsibilities for the laptop development which we discussed earlier based on the work breakdown in Figure 9.1.

The task descriptions on the left-hand side of the matrix are derived directly from the work breakdown structure and should correspond exactly to its reference numbers and structured hierarchy as shown in the WBS of Figure 9.1. The right-hand side shows either the responsible organizations with their section heads or individual task managers. This structure should correspond to the actual performing organizations, which might be submerged within a functional, projectized, or matrix framework. The relationship between tasks and responsibilities is indicated be a symbol in the matrix. It is common to use P for "prime responsibility" and S for "supporting responsibility." However, quite elaborate schemes for identifying various degrees of responsibility and participation can be devised if needed.

During the program planning phase, the task matrix can be used effectively as a cost model for budgeting. Cost estimating data are collected by recording the working hours, dollar estimates, or budgets needed to perform the task at the crossing points of the task and responsibility. Adding up the rows and columns provides a convenient summary of the estimated cost, for all task and performing organizations.

In summary, the task matrix provides a single framework for planning and negotiating project assignments and resources throughout the enterprise, including support departments, subcontractors, and the customer. Furthermore, the task matrix provides excellent visibility of who is responsible for what, throughout the organizations. It also provides some information on organizational interfaces for integrating particular subtasks.

Task Roster

An alternative to the task matrix is the *task roster*. It's clear and simple format makes it especially attractive for smaller projects. As shown in Table 9.10, the task roster is a listing of the project team members, including their organizational affiliation, telephone number, and email addresses next to their task responsibilities with reference to the WBS. Although the task roster is less sophisticated, it is often preferred over the task matrix because of its clarity and change flexibility. The task roster is, furthermore, a team-building tool. It summarizes in a simple format, usually on one sheet of paper, who is responsible for what. It recognizes the project contributors individually and as a team, regardless of their status and position within the company, and their duration on the project. More than any other management tool, the task roster fosters a sense of belonging, pride, ownership, and commitment to the project. Because of these motivational benefits, the task roster is often used in large projects in addition to the task matrix.

Table 9.10   Task Roster (Based on Laptop Example)

Task Roster Laptop Computer NPD			
Customer/Sponsor: Business Unit 007			
Project Manager: Jill Brown			
Cost Center: 1203 WBS Reference			
Responsible Individual	**Organization/Telephone**		**Task**	**WBS Ref**
Al	Syst Des	x364	Syst Des	1
Beth	Eng-I	x733	E-Parts	1.1.1
Charlie	Mfg.	x445	Vol Prod	2.2
Don	Quality Ass	x233	QC	2
Eric	Testing	x521	Prototype	2.1
Fran	Testing	x633	Test+Integr	2.1
George	Eng-II	x375	Software Des	1.1.3
Helena	Eng-II	x387	Controls	1.3
Ian	Syst Des	x745	Sys D&D	1.2.1
Jeff	Mfg.	x488	Logistics	2.3
Karen	Marketing	x333	Prod Plan	3.1
. . .	. . .		. . .	. . .
. . .	. . .		. . .	. . .
. . .	. . .		. . .	. . .

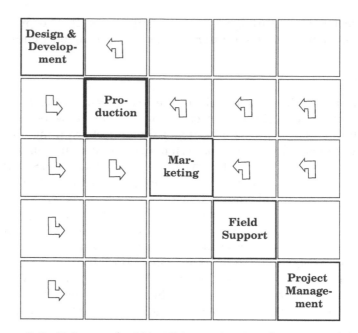

Figure 9.6 N-Square chart identifying project interface responsibilities

N-Square Chart

The N^2 *chart*, also referred to as *N 2 diagram*, is a two-dimensional interface chart showing the input/output requirements among project subsystems. It is used to systematically define the required (1) inputs to each subsystem or task group from any other project group/team, including deliverable data, hardware, software, and other requirements, together with a timetable for each item, and (2) outputs from each sub-system to any other sub-system of the project. The data being transmitted can be defined in each square marked ⇘ = input or ⇖ = output respectively, as shown in Figure 9.6.

The N2 chart is credited to the work of Robert J. Lano (1977), working at TRW in the 1970s. Although originally developed primarily for identifying software project interfaces, today the concept is being used extensively for managing interfaces on all types of projects, especially complex and technology-intensive undertakings.

9.3 USING PROJECT MANAGEMENT TOOLS PROPERTY

Fundamentally, project management tools are communication devices. They have been designed to define and communicate the requirements to all parties involved, to measure performance, and finally to direct and control the effort toward the pre-established requirements. Effective project management tools have the following characteristics:

- They assure measurability of all parameters used
- They use standard formats for all tools throughout the organization
- They use a uniform number system for project elements, consistent with all tools (e.g., a project subsystem number should be the same in the work breakdown structure as it is in the statement of work or cost account).
- They do not clutter the manager's tools with too much detail. They use modular concepts.
- They keep the manger's documents current.

The following suggestions should help in utilizing project management tools effectively and in building a high-performing project organization:

1. An agreed-upon program plan is absolutely essential. The plan defines the requirements in measurable steps and is the key to successful project performance. Measurability of technical status is crucial for engineering projects. If we cannot measure, we cannot control.

2. The use of standard formats for all tools is recommended. Nothing can be more confusing than looking at two different schedule or budget forms for the same project. It is the responsibility of the project manager to issue a standard set of forms if the organization does not have the planning process already proceduralized.

3. Number systems are often another area of unnecessary conflict and confusion. Many of the tools, such as schedules, work breakdown structures, and task matrices, label each task with a number. There is no need to label a particular task differently in the work breakdown structure than in the schedule for example. All tasks should be easily traceable throughout the project plan.

4. Use modular concepts to break down the complexity of our plans. For example, rather than showing all activities in a schedule in detail, partition the schedule in to a master schedule, which provides just an overview, a subsystem. A schedule, a subsystem B schedule, and so on. Or, alternately, use time phasing to break down the complexity, issuing a system design schedule, prototype design schedule, prototype fabrication schedule, and so on.

5. Keep your documents current. Nothing outlives its usefulness faster than an outdated document. Review your plans regularly and make revisions as needed. A document control system should be maintained by an assigned individual such as a secretary, who makes sure that agreed-upon changes get properly recorded and distributed.

9.4 A MODEL FOR PROJECT PERFORMANCE

Based on the preceding discussion, this chapter stressed the import role of project management tools and techniques to establish order and discipline for defining, tracking, communicating and managing projects through their

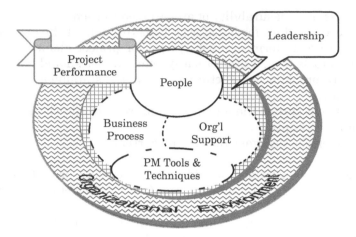

Figure 9.7   Influence on project performance

lifecycles. Yet these tools are just templates and procedures that must be integrated with the organizational system, its people, cultures and value systems. The people in the organization must feel that the documented work processes, tools and techniques in use reflect the way they actually work, and that the tools help them to accomplish their tasks more effectively. While we will revisit the issues of effective project management in later chapters under the topics of project control and team leadership, I would like to establish this important perspective on the proper use of management tools at the end of this chapter.

Performance is the aggregated result of many organizational systems interacting and collaborating effectively as graphically shown in Figure 9.7: (1) the *people* of the project team and their support organizations, (2) *project leadership*, (3) *project tools and techniques*, and (4) *business processes* that power and support the project activities; these four categories are overlapping and intricately affected by (5) *the organizational infrastructure and support systems*, (6) *managerial support*, (7) *project complexity*, and (8) the *overall business environment*. These categories not only determine project performance, but also hold the DNA for the type of leadership style best suited for managing projects though their lifecycles.

The model shown in Figure 9.7 emphasizes the human side as critically important to successful project execution. The project team attitude, effort and commitment, are all influenced by managerial leadership and the work environment, which in turn influences team effectiveness and overall project performance. Research shows consistently and measurably that the strongest drivers toward project performance are *derived from the work itself*, including personal interest, pride and satisfaction with the work, professional work challenge, accomplishments and recognition (see Thamhain 2002, 2011, 2013). Other important influences include effective communications among team members and support units across organizational lines, good team spirit, mutual trust and respect, low interpersonal conflict, opportunities for career development and advancement, and to some lesser degree, job security. All of these factors help in building a unified project team that can leverage the organizational strengths and competencies.

Other critical factors relate to the organizational structure and business process, including the technology transfer system, which by-and-large relies on the tools and techniques of modern project management. These tools are the backbone of any project management system. They must be carefully defined, developed and integrated with the enterprise and its culture and value system.

9.5 SUMMARY OF KEY POINTS AND CONCLUSIONS

The following key points were made in this chapter include:

- The management of complex and technology-intensive projects is supported by a highly diverse set of sophisticated tools and techniques that need to be carefully fine-tuned and integrated with the enterprise and its culture.
- There is a built-in relationship among project management tools that helps to connect the two project management sub-systems of: (1) critical project parameters defining the scope and quality of work, timing, and (2) critical processes for project planning, tracking and control. However, to fully utilize these linkages, project management tools must be custom-fitted to the organizational environment and the specific projects to be managed.
- The work breakdown structure is the backbone of ant project plan and its execution.
- Project planning and tracking systems must be able to measure work quality, timing and resources as an integrated set. For example, the project leader must be able to determine at any given time (1) the amount of work that has been completed, (2) the actual cost of the work completed against budgeted cost, and (3) the schedule of actual work completed against the original schedule.
- Deliverables are specific outputs or results of the project activity, useful for determining progress, and for providing visibility and recognition for team accomplishments. Deliverables must be tangible and measurable, and should be associated with specific milestones.
- The human side is critical to project success. Team involvement in scope definition, resource estimating and scheduling is crucial to the development of realistic project plans, team ownership and commitment.
- Project plans are living documents that must be reviewed on a regular basis and updated to reflect changing requirements, objectives and conditions in the project environment.

- The project information system provides an important tool set for collecting, processing, storing and distributing the information needed for effective project management. Yet, it is the project manager, not the computer, who by skill, experience and team leadership defines the framework of the project and its environment, including scope, work flow, team organization and interfaces.
- Team resistance to the introduction of new project management tools is natural. It can be minimized by involving the people, who will be affected by the new tools, in the selection, testing and fine-tuning of these tools.
- The shift to more sophisticated project management processes requires a radical departure from traditional management practices and leadership styles. The methods of communication, decision-making, soliciting commitment, and risk sharing are continuously shifting away from a centralized, autocratic management style, to a team-centered, more self-directed form of project leadership.
- The strongest drivers toward project performance are derived from the work itself, including personal interest, pride and satisfaction with the work, professional work challenge, accomplishments and recognition.

9.6 QUESTIONS FOR DISCUSSION

1. Why is the work breakdown structure called "the backbone of the project plan?"
2. What is the role and significance of the WBS numbering system?
3. Why is the WBS called a "cost model?"
4. Compare the three popular scheduling tools (1) milestone chart, (2) Gantt chart and (3) PERT/CPM network diagram regarding their strength, weaknesses and limitations.
5. What type of tools would you suggest for summarizing a $100M technology project on one page?
6. Why is modularity within a project plan an important feature?
7. What benefits do you gain from establishing a project management information system?
8. How does modern information technology affect managerial power and leadership style?
9. How do you overcome team member resistance to accept or use a new project management tool, such as following a new design review process or using a new method for reporting progress or changes?

9.7 *PMBOK*® REFERENCES AND CONNECTIONS

In discussing the tools and techniques for project planning and controlling, this chapter focusses on the process groups of planning, executing and monitoring. The tools cut across virtually all of the *10 knowledge areas*. However, it connects most strongly with *project scope management* (area #2), *project time management* (area #3), *project cost management* (area #4) and *project stakeholder management* (area #10) as defined by PMBOK. In studying for the PMP® exam, an understanding of the concept, structure and proper application of the following tools (selected from the large set tools covered in this chapter) might be especially beneficial: scope definition and statement, bar graph, network techniques, especially PERT, budget, cost account, project baseline, and earned value.

INTERNET LINKS AND RESOURCES

Federal Project Manager (authored by Frank O'Mara, Achieva Solutions LLC); www .federalpm.com/

NODIS, NASA Online Directives Information System; http://nodis3.gsfc.nasa.gov /main_lib.cfm

Project Management GURU; "Project Management Tools and Techniques;" www .projectmanagementguru.com/tools.html

Wikipedia; "Project Management," http://en.wikipedia.org/wiki/Project_manage ment

REFERENCES AND ADDITIONAL READINGS

Anderson, E. 2003. "Understanding Your Project Organization's Charter." *Project Management Journal* 34(4): 4–11.

Andler, N. 2011. *Tools for Project Management, Workshops and Consulting.* Erlangen, Germany: Publicis Publishing.

Badir Y, F. Founou, C. Stickerand, and V. Bourquin. 2003. "Management of Global Large-Scale Projects through a Federation of Multiple Web-based Workflow Management Systems." *Project Management Journal* 34(3):40–47.

Cleland, D. and L. Ireland. 2002. *Project Management: Strategic Design and Implementation.* New York: McGraw-Hill.

Edworthy, Sarah. 2012). "Deloitte is the Official Professional Services Provider to London 2012." *The Telegraph* (26 Sep 2012). www.Telegraph.Co.Uk/Sponsored/ Business/Deloitte/9575061/London-2012-Review-Deloitte.HTML.

Glick, Brian 2012. "CIO interview: Gerry Pennell, CIO, London 2012 Olympic Games." www.computerweekly.com/news/2240169116/CIO-interview-Gerry-Pennell-CIO -London-2012-Olympic-Games.

Hopeman, R. J. and D. L. Wilemon. 1972. *Project Management / Systems, Management Concepts and Applications.* Syracuse, NY: Syracuse University.

Jennings, Will. 2012. "The Olympics as a Story of Risk Management." *HBR Blog Network*, http://blogs.hbr.org/cs/2012/08/the_olympics_as_a_story_of_ris.html.

Kendrick, T. 2012. *The Project Management Tool Kit: 100 Tips and Techniques for Getting the Job Done.* New York: AMACOM.

Kerzner, H. 2009. *Project Management: A Systems Approach to Planning, Scheduling, and Controlling.* Chapter 3: "Organizational Structure." Hoboken, NJ: John Wiley and Sons.

Kloppenborg, T. 2012. *Contemporary Project Management*, Chapter 3: Organizational Capability, Structure, Culture and Roles, Mason, OH: South-Western Publishing.

Kruglianskas, I. and H. Thamhain. 2000. "Managing Technology-Based Projects in Multinational Environments." *IEEE Transactions on Engineering Management* 47(1): 55–64.

Lano, R. J. 1977. "The N^2 Chart." *Trw Document # Trw-Ss-77–04* (November 1977). Redondo Beach, CA: Trw, Systems Engineering and Integration Division.

Milosevic, D. 2003. *Project Management Tool Box: Tools and Techniques for the Practicing Project Manager*. Hoboken, NJ: John Wiley & Sons.

Plummer, F. 2007. *Project Engineering: The Essential Toolbox for Young Engineers*. Oxford, UK: Elsevier.

Project Management Institute (PMI). 2013. *A Guide to the Project Management Body of Knowledge (PMBOK® Guide)*. Newtown Square, PA: Project Management Institute

Thamhain, H. 1994. "Designing Project Management Systems for a Radically Changing World." *Project Management Journal* 25(4): 6–7.

Thamhain, H. J. 2002. "Criteria for Effective Leadership in Technology-Oriented Project Teams." Chapter 16 in *the Frontiers of Project Management Research* (Slevin, Cleland and Pinto, Eds.), Newton Square, PA: Project Management Institute, pp. 259–270.

Thamhain, Hans. 2011. "Critical Success Factors for Managing Technology-Intensive Teams the Global Enterprise." *Engineering Management Journal* 23(3) (Sept): 30–36.

———. 2013. "Building a Collaborative Climate for Multinational Projects." *Procedia Social & Behavioral Sciences Journal* 74(1) (Feb 2013).

Thomas, J., C. Delisle, K. Jugdev, and P. Buckle. 2001. "Selling Project Management to Senior Executives." *Pmnetwork* 15(1): 59–62.

White, D. and J. Fortune. 2002. "Current Practice in Project Management—An Empirical Study." *International Journal of Project Management* 20(1) (Jan): 1–11.

Wikipedia 2012. "2012 Summer Olympics." http://en.wikipedia.org/wiki/2012_Summer_Olympics/.

——— 2013. "N-Square Chart." http://en.wikipedia.org/wiki/N2_chart.

Chapter 10

Defining the Project

CHEVROLET *VOLT* ELECTRIC CARS DEVELOPMENT

© GM Corp

Motor Trend magazine named the new Chevrolet Volt the "2011 Motor Trend Car of the Year®." The annual award was one of the most prestigious honors bestowed in the auto industry. "The future is here, and America is back in the game," says General Motors.

As of October 2013, 50,000 Volt electric cars were delivered in the United States since Chevrolet introduced the car in 2010. With combined global sales of more than 60,000, the Volt is the top selling plug-in electric vehicle in the world. However, success did not come by luck or chance. It is the result of a carefully planned project that dates back to earlier GM pilots, such as the EV1 electric car produced between 1996 and 1999. After killing the EV1, GM had to come a long way to earn back the trust of electric-car lovers. But the Volt just might do it. With carefully laid plans and strong resource commitments, GM moved the project from concept to production in under four years. Before developing the vehicle for volume production, Chevrolet introduced its first "series plug-in hybrid car," as a "concept car" at the North American International Auto Show in 2007.

Most of the Volt initial design parameters defined for the concept car (referred to as "iCar"), were kept throughout the design process up to the final production version. However, by comparison to the EV1 of the 1990s, the Volt had significantly enhanced features, such as four doors with a rear liftgate and seating for four passengers. The top speed was increased to 100 miles per hour and the battery pack size was reduced, from about 10.6 cft in the EV1, to just 3.5 cft in the Volt. A key design parameter was the all-electric range of 40 miles, using a lithium-ion battery packs with a storage capacity of 16 kWh. And regenerative braking contributes to the on-board electricity generation. Another key design decision was to standardize

Sources: GM Chevrolet 2011a,b; Walsh 2007; Wikipedia 2013.

the electric powertrain components for future electric vehicles. The new drive system, originally called "E-Flex Systems" but later renamed Voltec, has the potential of adapting the vehicles to pure battery electric, or fuel cell-powered or other sources of energy, such as generators fueled by gasoline, diesel, biodiesel, ethanol fuel, or flex-fuel. According to General Motors, the effective gasoline fuel economy was estimated at 150 mpg for the Volt, based on a 60-mile total daily drive, with 40 all-electric miles included.

However, during these early engineering developments General Motors was cautious, noting that actual production of the Volt would depend on further battery developments to source the required high-capacity rechargeable batteries, which did not exist at that time. Eventually most of these issues were resolved and General Motors started extensive battery testing for two years. Starting in April 2008, the battery packs were tested to an equivalent of 150,000 road miles and 10 years of use, including vibration to simulate potholes and temperatures varying from −40 °F to +116 °F, simulating driving conditions from the Alaska tundra to the Mojave Desert.

In June 2009 the first preproduction car was built in Warren, Michigan, and on November 30, 2010, General Motors held a ceremony at its Hamtramck Assembly Plant in Detroit to celebrate the first Chevrolet Volt rolling off the assembly line under the direction of Tony Posawatz, Volt line director from 2006 to 2012, who had led the team from concept to production.

In 2011, production had to be halted for one month at the Detroit/Hamtramck Assembly plant to complete facility upgrades which increased Volt production to150 units per day, triple the previous rate. A year later, slow sales forced plant shutdowns in the spring and fall of 2012, affecting approximately 1,500 workers. Yet, despite of these challenges, U.S. sales reached the 50,000 unit milestone in October 2013, and GM is projecting strong sales for 2014. However, this favorable projection comes with a price. To compete effectively with the Toyota Prius and Nissan Leaf, GM had to reduce the price of its 2014 Chevrolet Volt by $5,000.

10.1 THE NEED FOR A CLEAR PLAN

Looking at the given scenario, it is clear that an agreed-on project plan is absolutely essential before GM can start executing the project. Although not every project is as broad in scope and complexity as the Chevrolet Volt, the cross-functional challenges, multidisciplinary intricacies, technological difficulties, systems integration, contractor and partner coordination, and market uncertainties are typical for today's technology-driven projects. Even well-defined plans do not guarantee success. But, without them, effective project execution is virtually impossible. Projects must be planned to an appropriate level of detail before they can enter the execution stage. This is also consistent with the guidelines given in established project management standards, such as PMBOK, PPINCE2, and ISO 21500. Typically, project-planning activities occur mostly after project initiation but before project execution as shown in Figure 10.1.

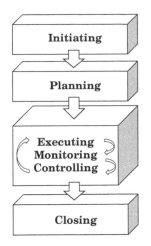

Figure 10.1 Project planning an integrated part of the *Process Groups* within the project life cycle

This model also fits the project life cycle stages discussed in Chapter 8, and the project development stages defined by PMI's PMBOK (2013) as *process groups*. However, in spite of the linear structure of the model, it is quite common for overlaps and iterations to occur between the life cycle stage or process groups.

Fundamentally, project plans are communication tools, designed to define the project requirements for sharing among all stakeholders and useful for effectively organizing, monitoring, and controlling a project toward desires results.

10.2 BUILDING THE PROJECT PLAN

Project plans are not created in a vacuum. They are the end product of an ongoing collaborative process of defining a roadmap for producing specific results within given time and resource constraints. Any project has clients or customers that can be internal or external to the enterprise. These parties, together with all the other stakeholders, need to be included in the planning process to make the project plan realistic and to obtain commitment to its execution.

Although preliminary project planning often starts a long time before the formal project plan is being developed (e.g., bid proposals, strategic planning, customer inquiries, exploratory assessments), formal project planning usually starts with a management decision addressing three areas:

1. Exploration of a particular project endeavor
2. Appointment of a project leader
3. Allocation of resources for exploring the project opportunity and possibly the project plan

10.2.1 The Four-Phase Planning Process

Resource commitment could be for the full planning cycle or any part of it. However, regardless of the funding arrangements, most project plans are developed via a four-phase process:

Phase I Preliminary analysis and feasibility assessment
Phase II Project definition (developing the detailed plan)
Phase III Team organization
Phase IV Project kickoff

A detailed description of the recommended activities for developing the project plan along the four phases is provided next.

Phase I. Preliminary Analysis and Feasibility Assessment

No major project can be organized without first establishing some basic feasibility and desirability for the effort. The starting point for this phase is often the emergence of a new contract opportunity or the need for a new product development, or the redirection of an ongoing project. The objective of the preliminary analysis is twofold:

1. Establish the management decisions basis for committing to and funding of the project.
2. Define the scope and baseline for the project, hence generating the inputs for the project definition phase, which will include detailed plans for the project startup or formal bid proposal.

The preliminary analysis of an upcoming project is a project by itself with specific deadlines, resource allocations, responsibilities, and deliverable results. Like any other activity group, the preliminary analysis varies in scope and deliverables, depending on the nature of the upcoming project. However, a 5 to 15 percent resource requirement relative to the main project is typical. This range can even exceed 15 percent, depending on the scope of the analysis, which might vary from simple brainstorming and calculations to elaborate simulations, field studies, and concept design work. Yet, in principle, the objectives and results expected from a preliminary analysis are very similar for many projects, as summarized in Table 10.1.

The outcome of this preliminary analysis is usually a concise report that scopes the proposed project regarding technical, resource, and timing requirements. This is often referred to as *requirements analysis*. It is also common for the report to discuss the rational for selecting the project, and to compare the requirements with the enterprise capabilities, hence assessing overall business success, including its risks and alternatives. In

Table 10.1   Scope of Preliminary Project Analysis: Objectives and Results

Objective (Type of Effort)	Results
Determine user/sponsor requirements:	• Baseline configuration • Specifications • Functional description • Features • Schedules and deadlines • Budget • Special needs and requirements
Assess technical feasibility:	• Feasibility study • Simulation results • Concept design • R&D report • Prototype
Determine resource requirements: (preliminary, rough order of magnitude)	• Key personnel • Staffing level • Facilities • Support services • Special resource requirement • Budget estimate
Assess risks and opportunities::	• Rational for project undertaking • Technical risk analysis • Project/operational risks • Market/competitive risk • Financial risks (capital requirements, cash flow, ROI) • Political risks
Assess project/program feasibility and success:	• Requirements versus capability assessment (technical, timing, cost, resources) • Competitive assessment • Product acceptance by customer or market • Financial performance • Total project life cycle assessment
Analyze alternatives:	• Different technical approaches & features • Tradeoff analysis (concepts, products, vendors, etc.) • Make-buy analysis • Teaming, partners, joint ventures • Project timeframe

(Continued)

Table 10.1   (Continued)

Objective (Type of Effort)	Results
Define project management approach:	• Project team organization • Key interfaces • Project tracking and control method • Enterprise command and reporting structure • Basic project charter
Define project definition/planning phase:	• Planning process, procedure • Responsibilities, budget, and schedule for project plan development.

essence, the preliminary analysis and feasibility phase addresses the following questions:

- What are the project requirements?
- Can we do it?
- Should we do it?
- What are the alternatives?

The report provides a basis for managerial decision making on whether and how to proceed with the project. Or, in situations of competitive bidding, the report supports the bid decision process.

Performing a preliminary project analysis is hard work and critical to the enterprise's effectiveness in its competitive environment. An inaccurate analysis can lead to the wrong go/no-go decision, costing the enterprise millions in wasted resources or lost opportunities.

Because of its multidisciplinary nature, a single person can seldom do an adequate analysis. It requires the participation of key personnel from the sponsor and all supporting organizations, internal and external, to the enterprise. The leader of this preliminary project analysis (who might also be appointed as project manager) often acts just as facilitator who brings together the right people from the sponsor, functional organizations, contractors, and top management. Moreover, the process of determining, matching, and fine-tuning the sponsor or customer requirements with the performing organization is highly iterative. It usually takes several rounds of meetings and deliberations before an agreement on the project baseline is reached, agreeable to all stakeholders. This process creates involvement at all organizational levels with some important side benefits. It stimulates critical thinking and creates visibility throughout the enterprise. It is a highly pervasive process that unifies the stakeholder community behind the emerging project plan and builds the basis for organizational commitment to the plan.

Phase II. Project Definition

The project definition phase is often the first organized effort of defining *what* needs to be done, *how* we can accomplish the objectives most effectively, and *who* is best qualified to lead the project. The end product of this phase is the formal *project plan*. Although the basic framework and components for the project plan might have been developed already during the preliminary project analysis phase, they need to be formally organized and detailed in a standardized format to serve as a roadmap and effective communications tool during the project execution across the team organization. Project definition is a complex, well-orchestrated "impedance matching process" between (1) customer/sponsor requirements and (2) enterprise capabilities and desires.

Using the tools already described in Chapter 9, the project plan must define the *four key dimensions of the project*:

- Work/Scope . . . . What
- Timing . . . . When
- Cost/resources . . . . . How much
- Responsibilities . . . . Who

In addition, the project plan should define the following:

- Work transfer and integration process
- Project monitoring and controlling process

The specific processes, responsibilities, templates, tools, and techniques required to develop these components of the project plan are summarized in Table 10.2.

Similar to the previous discussion in Phase I, developing the project plan is not a one-person job. This highly multidisciplinary document requires the participation of all key people who will eventually be contributing to the project. Ideally all key personnel, from the core team members to the support organizations, contractors, and customers, should participate in the plan development and its validation. The project manager provides the direction and leadership for orchestrating the planning effort. Especially for complex projects, the plan does not develop linearly, but evolves incrementally and iteratively. That is, one should not expect to produce a perfect scope statement before going to develop a perfect WBS, before going to the schedule, and so on. Typically, all of the components of the project plan evolve incrementally via multiple meetings, estimates, analyses, deliberations, and other forms of communications. This cross-functional involvement leads to a better collective understanding of the plan, which helps to validate its reality and workability and unifies the project team behind the project plan and its objectives.

Especially for larger projects or programs, the project plan can be very substantial in volume. Whether published on paper or electronically, the document should be divided into sections and modules addressing the various

Table 10.2   Components of the Project Plan

Component	Tools and Templates Used for Data Summary and Communications	Organizational Processes
Work/scope Defines the boundaries of work to be completed during the project life cycle	Scope statement Statement of work (SOW) Specifications Work breakdown structure (WBS) Work package Task authorization List of deliverables Quality plan Risk management plan	Requirements analysis Multiorganizational meetings User centered design (UCD) Voice of the customer (VOC) Bid proposal analysis Project feasibility analysis
Timing Defines time duration and sequencing of project tasks, critical for project monitoring, tracking, reporting and controlling.	Milestone schedule Bar graph/Gantt chart Network diagram (i.e. PERT, CPM, GERT) Work breakdown structure (WBS)	Time estimating: • History data • Expert estimates • Parametric • Simulation
Cost/resources Defines the financial resources required for project execution. Processes include cost estimating, budgeting, monitoring, tracking, reporting and controlling.	Budget Cost accounts Project baseline Earned value Work breakdown structure (WBS)	Cost estimating (labor, material, other): • History data • Expert estimates • Parametric • Simulation
Responsibilities Defines specific responsibilities, authorities, reporting relations and organizational interfaces for all project team members, including support organizations.	Project charter Policies and procedures Task matrix Task roster N-square chart Work breakdown structure (WBS)	Established processes for working within organizational structures: • Matrix • Projectized • Hybrid • Project management office • Negotiations

Component	Tools and Templates Used for Data Summary and Communications	Organizational Processes
Work transfer and integration Defines the processes and activities necessary for transferring data and work components among project groups, and for coordinating and integrating the work toward the end deliverable.	Interface definition Work/data transfer protocol Work process definition *N*-square chart Work breakdown structure (WBS) Enterprise project management (web-based, central) Project management dashboard	Cross-functional meetings Cross-functional collaboration Management by wandering around Management and leadership Co-locating team, central workspace
Project monitoring and controlling Defines the processes, activities and techniques for tracking and controlling the project against established plans throughout its life cycle.	Project review Design review Gate review Progress report Action list Prototyping, simulation, testing Enterprise project management (web-based, central) Project management dashboard	Cross-functional meetings, reviews Cross-functional collaboration Management by wandering around Managerial guidance, support and leadership Effective work process and environment Change control Risk management

components of the plan, such as scope, schedule, budget, and risk. Following are content examples of a detailed outline, typical for a major project.

Section 1. Executive Summary

This section provides a top-level overview of the project, summarizing its scope, timing, resource requirements, rationale, and management approach.

- Project overview
- Primary objectives and deliverables
- Enterprise perspective

- Resource requirements
- Key milestones
- Project organization
- Management team
- Technical approach
- Management approach
- Risk assessment
- Customer interface and communications

Templates and tools included: Work breakdown structure (WBS), master schedule, summary budget, project organization chart, requirements analysis, bid proposal.

Section 2. Project Scope

This section describes the work to be performed and deliverables to be produced over the life cycle of the project

- Statement of work (SOW)
- Project objectives
- Deliverables, results
- Listing of subsystems
- Enterprise perspective on project work to overall mission and business strategy
- Financial and schedule boundaries

Templates and tools included: Work breakdown structure (WBS), statement of work (SOW), specifications, technical plans, diagrams, work packages, task authorizations, list of deliverables, quality plan, risk management plan, references to work details

Section 3. Project Schedules

This section discussed the project master schedule with its key milestones and project integration points. It also lists all subordinate schedules and their reference documents.

- Master schedule
- Listing of sub-schedules
- Critical path analysis
- Method of time estimating and assumptions
- Schedule risks and contingency plan
- Schedule control and management

Templates and tools included: Master schedule, milestone chart, Gantt chart, PERT/CPM diagram, work breakdown structure (WBS), risk management plan

Section 4. Resource Requirements and Budgets

This section summarizes the resource requirements for the project, time phased over the project life cycle, and itemized for each project subsystem.

- Overall budget summary

- Project baseline
- Budget details along WBS components
- Contractor and vendor budget
- Overhead costs
- Method of cost estimating and assumptions
- Cost credibility assurance
- Risks and contingency plan

Templates and tools included: Budget charts, weekly labor charts, cost estimating model and software, cost accounts, work breakdown structure (WBS), risk management plan

Section 5. Project Organization Staffing

This section describes the structure of the project organization, including reporting and authority relations, staffing, and team development.

- Project organization/structure within the enterprise
- Authority and reporting relations
- Key interfaces to support organizations, contractors and sponsor
- Key personnel
- Team staffing and development
- Performance appraisals and awards
- Management approach and commitment

Templates and tools included: Organization chart, project charter, job description, task matrix, task roster, staffing plan, work breakdown structure (WBS), master schedule

Section 6. Project Support and Facilities

This section describes the project support requirements, facilities and special resources needed over the project life cycle.

- Facility plan (project team)
- Support organizations
- Outsourced services
- Leasing and renting
- Special resources (e.g., R&D, laboratories, design support CAD/CAM, testing, prototyping, IT, transportation, field support)

Templates and tools included: Organization chart, project charter, department charters, facility plan, plant and office layout, work breakdown structure (WBS), master schedule references to work details

Section 7. Technical Approach

This section describes the work to be performed and the integration processes to meet the project objectives.

- Technical objectives and approach to implementation
- Description (technical) of project entity or mission
- Design and development plan
- Configuration management and document control
- Systems integration and testing

- Quality and reliability
- Risk assessment and management

Templates and tools included: Requirements documents, statement of work (SOW), specifications, diagrams, flow charts, systems interface documents, list of deliverables, design/development policies and procedures, user-centered design (UCD) guideline

Section 8. Project Management

This section describes how the project will be managed, tracked and controlled to achieve the objectives. This section refers to and integrates other parts of the project plan.

- Project management approach
- Project management structure
- Enterprise and customer interfaces and communications
- Progress measurements, monitoring, evaluating and reporting
- Management control systems (i.e. cost, schedule, quality control)
- Leadership team
- Risk management
- Advisory groups and committees

Templates and tools included: Project charter, requirements analysis, work breakdown structure (WBS), master schedule, summary budget, project dashboard, all components of this project plan.

Another way to break down the complexity of large project plans is to divide the total plan into subplans. This can be done by various means. For example, (1) along the project life cycle phases, such as development plan, test plan, production plan, or roll-out plan, or (2) along subsystem lines, such as concept development, central processor development, or software development, or (3) along operational aspects, such as project integration plan, subcontractor plan, configuration management plan, facility plan, quality plan, and logistics support plan. These are just a few examples of how the complexity of a project plan can be reduced while simplifying reading and improving clarity for those responsible for just one specific part of the project.

In parallel to the project plan, the network for customer/sponsor communications must be defined and developed. This is a complex process that defines the key interface personnel between the project team and the customer, sponsor and user community. Initial contact meetings provide the communication vehicle for establishing formal interface relations among all parties of the greater project community. These relations are necessary for developing and validating the details of the project plan, matching and fine-tuning the customer requirements with the contractor capabilities, available resources, and timing. These initial contacts also lead to the involvement of all parties in the project, building interest and potential for greater collaboration and desire for success. It also builds the basis for joint-reviews, collective problem solving, and customer-centered design later during project execution.

Phase III. Team Organization and Startup

The primary objective of this phase is to define the operating environment for the project team. Many of the *team organization and startup* activities overlap with the *project definition phase*, and sometimes continue into the project execution. However, typically the efforts of team organization and startup include the following steps:

1. *Project baseline.* Finalize the project baseline definition, which includes the technical description of the project work, its scope, requirements, specifications, and so on.
2. *Project charter.* Write the project charter and obtain management endorsement (for charter example see Appendix).
3. *Direct reports.* Define all activities and functions that will directly report to the project office or project manager.
4. *Support services.* Define all activities and functions that provide support services to the project. Also define the shared responsibilities, accountabilities and controls between the project office and the functional organization or sub-contractor.
5. *Project organization plan.* Develop a project organization plan, consistent with the project charter and established power sharing, including the team structure, key responsibilities, reporting relations and controls.
6. *Project plan integration.* Integrate the project organization plan with the project plan. Review both plans for consistency.
7. *Direct reports.* Define key team member positions. Write job descriptions for all personnel directly reporting to the project manager. Define candidates and negotiate assignments.
8. *Staff requirements.* Define work-force (team) requirements over the project life cycle. The inputs for these requirements come primarily from the project task leaders who were identified in the previous step, or earlier in the planning process. Develop staffing plan in cooperation with task leaders and functional resource managers. Obtain management approval and commitment to the staffing plan.
9. *Finalize project team.* Organize project team with the help of task leaders (e.g., task managers) and the project manager's direct reports. Establish project task roster.
10. *Task authorizations.* Develop or finalize task authorizations for all major project subsystems (also called work packages or clusters). Preliminary task descriptions should be available from the project plan, providing a good starting point the task authorization development.
11. *Project control.* Extracting from the control system that has already been defined in the project plan, develop a project tracking, reporting, and control system specifically fine-tuned for your project organization.
12. *Kickoff meeting.* Organize and conduct formal project kickoff meeting (although this is a logical point in time for holding the project

kickoff, it can take place earlier or later, or at multiple times, such as a planning kickoff, mission kickoff, or general kickoff). While kickoff meetings are symbolic, they play an important role in unifying the team and demonstrating the importance and management commitment of the effort, benefiting future cross-functional collaboration and support.

One of the key issues in setting up the project organization is the span of control of the project manager or the project management office, all the way down the WBS chain of command. The span of control is conventionally being determined by the number of subsystems or tasks to be integrated under the direction of *one* individual. As a guideline, I suggest aiming for 8, but 10 subsystems should be the upper limit. For larger projects, subsystems or tasks can be clustered, creating an additional activity layer and integrator point. This creates additional overhead and complicates the command and communications structure. But, it might be the only way to get around an unmanageably large number of subsystems to be directed and integrated by one person.

For very large projects, where subsystem layering is unavoidable, additional support personnel can help to make project administration more effective and manageable. Yet, project overhead is an issue that must be taken into account. As a guideline, the overhead for project administration should not exceed 6 to 10 percent of the total project budget. In fact, already 8 percent will be considered generous in most situations. Translating this statistic to staff-level numbers, a small project with 10 full-time team members (let's assume labor-intensive for simplicity), can barely afford one full-time administrator, such as the project manager. That is why we see, for smaller projects, team leaders also taking on technical responsibilities for design, testing, analysis, or other contributions, while allocating only part of their time to the function of project management.

Project Support Staff For larger projects, administrative support staff is not only affordable but also essential for effective management of the project. These project administrators provide vital support to the overall management of the project by taking on time-consuming but important functions, such as collecting and progressing progress data, updating project documents, following up on issue resolutions, organizing review meetings, carrying out liaison activities, maintaining websites, and generating reports. The following administrative positions can provide effective project support and should be considered, depending on actual needs and budget constraints:

Project manager
Deputy project manager
Technical project manager or technical project director
Administrative manager or assistant to project manager

Contracts manager
Configurations manager (change management)
Financial analyst

These position titles vary considerably from industry to industry and are not necessarily indicative of the responsibility, power, or prestige carried by the position. The word *manager* is often replaced by the word *administrator* or *lead* or *engineer*, depending to a large degree on the prevailing organizational culture. However, when used *within the same organization*, the title of *manager* carries more weight and prestige than the *administrator* title. Many of these support functions can also be filled with part-time appointments that are shared among several projects. These services can also be provided cost-effectively by a central project management office (PMO). Cost-effective project administration is still an important issue. The 10 percent rule is a good checkpoint, at least for the initial assessment. Later, the need for a specific support function might emerge, and a cost-benefit–based management decision will be made.

Subplans Somewhere during the project planning process, the leadership team must find time to establish the required subplans, such as quality plan, test plan, systems integration plan, agency certification plan, and so on. Often, it is impossible, however, to develop these plans in detail this early in the project life cycle because of technical detail or staff specialties that will come forward only later in the project execution. In this case, it is important to define at least the type of subplans needed, together with the basic content and schedule for development.

Phase IV. Project Kickoff

The project kickoff meeting is an effective and logical way to transition from the planning to the execution phase. However, operationally, there is no great significance to its timing, and the kickoff can take place earlier or later, or at multiple times, such as a planning kickoff, mission kickoff, or general kickoff. Yet, the kickoff meeting is more than just symbolic. It plays an important role in unifying the team and demonstrating the importance and management commitment of the effort, benefiting future cross-functional collaboration and support. If planned properly, it provides excellent focus on the project objectives and significance of the project to the enterprise.

The advantage of bringing all team members together at the beginning of the execution phase is generating a sense of unity, importance, and commitment, which is further amplified by senior management attendance and comments. A well-organized kickoff meeting will also validate the project plan and its workability in the minds of the people. It will set the stage for the subsequent project execution effort, unifying the project team and building the team spirit for collaborative, committed work toward desired results.

10.3 A LIFE CYCLE APPROACH TO PROJECT PLANNING

Projects evolve. Over their life cycles, project environments and the dynamics of project work and their outcomes change. No one can predict all the contingencies and changes that become essential during the execution of a project. Therefore, project plans must be flexible. This is not to say that front-end accuracy doesn't matter. On the contrary: Project plans are blueprints of the upcoming execution. They provide the roadmap for allocating resources and efforts toward desired objectives. They provide de facto a contractual basis between the project team and its management for delivering specific results. They also provide the basis for individual and team performance evaluation and reward. For that reason, project plans are important management tools.

However, project plans must also be flexible to be relevant in times of change. Flexibility doesn't mean casual, sloppy, or broad-brushed. It means being prepared to cope effectively with a situation that requires a change in plan, such as an unexpected market development, an unfavorable test result, a changing technology, or a new opportunity. As a result, we have to design into our project plans mechanisms for identifying changing situations in their early stages of development and for effectively responding to these situations and requirements.

Many of these mechanisms for identifying change are part of the conventional project management system. They include regular reviews, expert audits, early concept testing, user-centered design (UCD), and design-built processes. Yet, they should also include the people side of dealing with change. One of the important lessons learned from *agile* is to build a collaborative project environment with motivated people who can work as a complex adaptive system. Building such a collaborative team environment where people continuously watch for changes, threats and opportunities, and deal with these situations as they develop requires sophisticated leadership, resulting in a work environment conducive to effective cross-functional communications and collaboration among all stakeholders.

10.4 SUMMARY OF KEY POINTS AND CONCLUSIONS

The following key points were made in this chapter:

- Project plans are blueprints for the upcoming execution. They provide a roadmap for allocating resources and efforts toward desired objectives. Yet, plans have to be flexible to cope with changing situations and requirements during their life cycles.
- Project planning should be a collaborative effort among all stakeholders with consensus to the final document.
- Most project plans are developed via a four-phase process: (1) preliminary analysis and feasibility assessment, (2) project definition (or plan development), (3) team organization, and (4) project kickoff.

- The preliminary analysis and project feasibility assessment are necessary and important activities prior to committing project funding.
- At the minimum, a project plan must define the four project dimensions of (1) work/scope, (2) timing, (3) cost/resources, and (4) responsibilities, plus the processes for work monitoring, integrating, and controlling.
- Dividing the total plan into subplans, such as plans for development, testing, production or rollout, can help to break down the complexity, especially for large projects.
- The project charter, team roster, and work breakdown structure provide the key tools for organizing the project team.
- The span of control of the project manager or any of his/her task leaders should not exceed 10.
- As a guideline, the overhead for project administration should not exceed 6 to 10 percent of the total project budget.
- The project kickoff meeting is an effective and logical way to transition from the planning to the execution phase. However, the kickoff can take place earlier or later during the front-end preparation period.
- A well-organized kickoff meeting will set the stage for the subsequent project execution effort, unifying the project team and building the team spirit for collaborative, committed work toward desired results.
- Although project planning should be collaborative among all stakeholders, it should be performed under the direction and leadership of the project manager, supported by senior management.

10.5 QUESTIONS FOR DISCUSSION AND EXERCISES

1. Describe the characteristics of an effective project plan.
2. Write an outline of table of contents for a project plan of a project you are currently working on. Alternatively, use the lead-in scenario of the Volt electric car development as background to develop your outline. Feel free to make any assumptions.
3. How would you use information technology (IT) for defining and communication your project plan?
4. What can you do as project leader to reduce project-related overhead during the project definition phase?
5. What actions can you take as project manager to create an organizational environment conducive to cross-functional participation and collaboration in your project planning effort? What type of situations and issues would hinder such collaboration?
6. Write an agenda for a project kickoff meeting for a project that you are familiar with (or use the Volt e-car lead-in scenario). What type of kickoff support would you ask from your senior management?

10.6 *PMBOK® GUIDE* REFERENCES AND CONNECTIONS

The topic of project definition cuts across most of the 10 *knowledge areas* defined by PMBOK. Similar to Chapter 8 on "setting up an effective planning and control cycle," it connects most strongly with *project integration management* (area #1), *project scope management* (area #2), *project time management* (area #3), *project cost management* (area #4), *project communications management* (area #7) and *project stakeholder management* (area #10). It also addresses the first two *processing groups: initiating and planning*. Many of the topics covered in this chapter address the *context* of project management. That is the way projects are planned, documented, communicated, and organized in preparation for project execution. This broad contextual understanding of project management is necessary for effectively applying the PMBOK standards to the day-to-day management of projects and to study effectively for PMP® certification. In studying for the PMP® exam, an understanding of the following concepts will be beneficial: (1) activity definition and scope planning, (2) elements of a project plan (e.g., work breakdown structure, scope statement, schedule and budget); (3) change management, (4) project plan development, (5) resource definition, people, facilities, (6) stakeholder participation in project planning, (7) relationship of project planning within the five project management process groups, and (8) human resource plan development.

INTERNET LINKS AND RESOURCES

Carnegie Mellon University. "Detailed Project Plan." www.cmu.edu/computing/ppmo/
  project-management/life-cycle/planning/detailed-project-plan.html
GM Chevrolet. 2011. "Development History of the 2011 Volt." Dailymotion: www
  .dailymotion.com/video/xg4toj_the-development-history-of-the-2011-chevrolet-
  volt_auto
GM Chevrolet. 2011. "Making of the 2011 Chevy Volt," YouTube. www.youtube.com/
  watch?v=s3dZfvTLbBE/
Wikipedia. 2013. "New Product Development." http://en.wikipedia.org/wiki/
  New_product_development
Wikipedia. 2013. "Project Planning." http://en.wikipedia.org/wiki/Project_planning
Wikipedia. 2013. "Chevrolet Volt," http://en.wikipedia.org/wiki/Chevrolet_Volt

REFERENCES AND ADDITIONAL READINGS

Brooke, Lindsay. 2011. *Chevrolet Volt—Development Story of the Pioneering Electrified Vehicle*. Warrendale, PA: SAE International.
Cano, J., and I. Lidon. 2011. "Guided Reflection on Product Definition." *International Journal of Project Management* 29(5): 525–535.
Gido, J., and J. P. Clements. 2012. "Initiating a Project." Part 1 in *Successful Project Management*. Mason, OH: South-Western Cengage Learning.

Gil, N., I. Tommelein, and L. Schruben. 2006. "External Change in Large Engineering Design Projects: The Role of the Client." *IEEE Transactions on Engineering Management* 53(3) (August): 426–437.

Kloppenborg, T. J. 2012. "Planning Projects." Part 2 in *Contemporary Project Management*, Mason, OH: South-Western Cengage Learning.

Lewis, J. 2011. *Project Planning, Scheduling, and Control: The Ultimate Hands-On Guide to Bringing Projects in On Time and On Budget.* New York: McGraw-Hill.

Musser, G. 2004. "The Spirit of Exploration." *Scientific American* 290 (1): 52–57.

Naderi, F. 2001. "Mars Exploration." *Robotics & Automation Magazine* (IEEE) 13(2): 72–82.

Philipenko, R., J. Acharya, and P. Srivastava. 2012. "Define Your Project—Reduce the Risk." *Cost Engineering* 54(4) (Jul/Aug): 25–35.

Platje, A., H. Seidel, and S. Waldman. 1994. "Project and Portfolio Planning Cycle: Project-Based Management for the Multiproject Challenge." *International Journal of Project Management* 12(2) (May): 100–106.

Project Management Institute (PMI). 2013. *A Guide to the Project Management Body of Knowledge (PMBOK® Guide), Fifth Edition.* Newtown Square, PA: Project Management Institute.

Rad, P.F., and V. S. Anantatmula. 2006. *Project Planning Techniques.* Tysons Corner, VA: Management Concepts Press.

Thamhain, H., and I. Kruglianskas. 2000. "Managing Technology-Based Projects in Multinational Environments." *IEEE Transactions on Engineering Management* 47 (1): 55–64.

Walsh, B. 2007. "General Motors Green Leap Forward." *Time* 170(17) (October 22).

Chapter 11

Resource Estimating and Budgeting

AT GOOGLE, TECHNOLOGY PROJECTS ARE DONE ON A RAPID SCHEDULE.

© Google

Since its start-up days in 1995 at Susan Wojcicki's garage in Menlo Park, and founding as a company in 1998, Google has grown enormously. Today, a $50 billion company, Google offers dozens of products from search engines to Gmail and Maps, and keeps continuously searching for new products and better ways to leverage technology. "Our goal is to make it as easy as possible for you to find the information you need and get the things you need to do done," says Larry Page, Google's co-founder and CEO. "We pride ourselves on our ability to develop and launch new products and features at a very fast pace. This is made possible in part by our world-class engineers, but our approach to software development enables us to balance speed and quality, and is integral to our success. Our obsession for speed and scale is evident in our developer infrastructure and tools. Developers across the world continually write, build, test and release code in multiple programming languages like C++, Java, Python, Javascript and others, and our Engineering Tools Team, for example, is challenged to keep this development ecosystem running smoothly. We share technical knowledge and the lessons learned along the way."

At Google most projects have time horizons of just 6 to 12 months. The aim is to deliver results quickly and iterate if necessary. Although some project groups do work on longer-term developments, nearly all projects are "bottom-up" efforts, started by a few Googlers who want to tackle a new problem. We're very light on management. We have more problems than we have people, so there's always a big backlog of problems to be solved.

Sources of chapter introduction minicase: Google (2012); Google (2013); Newsweek (2006).

11.1 WHY WE NEED BUDGETS

Regardless of the type of project, we need to establish budgets to allocate specific resources. Whether Google considers the development of a new search engine or NASA proposes the Mars rover *Curiosity*, we need a resource estimate for many reasons: to (1) determine the desirability, (2) affordability of the project, (3) compare alternatives and support funding decisions of one program over another, (4) determine resource allocation type and timing, and (5) develop a performance measurement baseline.

It is tempting to take shortcuts in the budgeting process, especially when understaffed or under time pressure, like Google developing new products at internet time. However, running projects without a reasonable feeling for the resource requirements can be very costly, ranging from pursuing the wrong opportunity to excessive and unexpected resource requirements, organizational conflict and poor overall enterprise performance. Yet, in many cases it is impossible or impractical to generate a perfect resource estimate. In fact, perfection is not required, and often interferes with effectiveness. In the Google situation, with many projects waiting for resourcing and fast-moving opportunity windows, it is important to minimize front-end estimating, planning, and organizing time. Maybe in the spirit of agile or Tom Peters's "ready-fire-aim," one can develop preliminary results and some feasibility quickly, without much front-end delay, then iterate and fine-tune later if necessary. This is perfectly acceptable and desirable for certain projects. Yet, we should not embark on a project with an open-ended resource plan. There are many effective "quick" or preliminary budgeting techniques, such as using historic cost, parametric estimating, fixed-budget exploratory development, and initial funding via memorandum of understanding, which get you started, but also set resource boundaries. In fact, many projects, especially large ones, need some seed money up front to scope the proposed effort and to determine a rough resource estimate for the new project (rough order of magnitude, ROM), before a preliminary go/no-go decision can be made and the required resources for a formal budgeting effort can be allocated. Regardless how preliminary or final it is, the established project budget is an important management tool to monitor and guide the project, and to serve as an early warning system.

11.1.1 The Role of Cost Estimates

Cost estimates are key components to the project budgeting process. They also provide critical inputs to the front-end project selection, project planning, and overall life cycle cost (LCC) management. Obtaining accurate cost estimates is difficult, especially for large and more complex undertakings that involve new technologies, long life cycles, and lots of uncertainties. Developing accurate cost estimates is often difficult. The challenges range from difficulties of interpreting customer requirements to forecasting technological advances, market trends, competitive reactions and economic conditions, to judging work complexity, schedule requirements, and support needs. Other issues are psychological. Managers might feel pressured to provide optimistic time or cost estimates to influence project approval. However, inaccurate cost estimates will eventually lead to unrealistic project plans that cannot be executed within the established constraints. They are running the risk of feasibility reassessment, replanning, or, worse, cancellation with dire consequences to all parties involved.

Overestimating costs is another problem. Managers might overestimate costs, fearing budget overruns during the execution. Or, the overestimate might just be a result of inaccurate or missing information about the project and its environment, the same issues that caused underestimating. Either way, cost overestimating creates an unnecessarily unfavorable cost image that negatively influences the affordability and ultimately the funding of the project.

Taken together, accurate, reliable cost estimating is critical to realistic project planning, effective project management, and customer/sponsor satisfaction.

11.2 COST ESTIMATING METHODS

Managers have a large number of methods available for estimating cost and resource requirements for their projects. According to PMBOK (2013), it is one of the three activities that need to be performed as part of the cost management function. However, in spite of the sophistication and variety of approaches and computer support, cost estimating is still an art, at least to some degree. Furthermore, the method, extent, and accuracy of the estimate depend on many factors, including the type of the project, time and resources available for the estimate, and the purpose of the estimate. Because of these different needs and approaches, it is useful to establish classes of cost estimating methods. Among the many classification systems in use today, the system developed by the American Association for Cost Engineers (AACE) in the late 1960s has become a national standard, published by ANSI (2012) since 1972. The system divides cost-estimating methods into *five classes*, depending on the level of accuracy and end-use of the estimate as summarized in Table 11.1. The classification acknowledges the fact that different management situations require different levels of budget accuracy, as well as different levels of effort, which according to AACE can vary by a factor of 100 between a "best-judgment" estimate (Class-5) and a "detailed deterministic" estimate of Class-1. The classification also points at different estimating methods, which will be discussed next.

11.2.1 A Variety of Estimating Methods for Different Situations

The ability to select the right estimating method is critical to project management effectiveness. Aiming for too much accuracy early in project definition

Table 11.1 Classification of Cost-Estimating Methods

Estimating Class	Characteristics				
	Level of Project Definition[a]	Typical End-Use of Estimate	Estimating Method	Expected Accuracy[b]	Estimation Effort[c]
Class 5	0–2%	Project screening for feasibility	Stochastic or judgment	10–20	1
Class 4	1–15%	Concept study or feasibility	Primarily stochastic	3–12	2–4
Class 3	10–40%	Budget authorization or contract	Mixed, but primarily stochastic	2–8	3–10
Class 2	30–70%	Contract or bid tender	Primarily deterministic (knowing actual cost)	1–3	5–20
Class 1	50–100%	Final budget or contract payment	Deterministic (knowing actual cost)	1	10–100

(a) Percentile of project definition available relative to a complete project definition. (b) Example: If the accuracy for a Class-1 estimate is 5%, then the accuracy for a Class-5 estimate is 10 to 20 times less accurate, or between 50% and 100% of its expected final value. (c) Example: If a Class-5 estimating effort requires 1 staff-hour, a Class-1 effort would require between 10 and 100 staff-hours.

cycle can be unnecessarily costly and might even be impossible to achieve because of incomplete scope or requirements definition or lacking specialists who are skilled to perform a detailed estimate. In most cases, the question is not to prepare an estimate, but what method to use to estimate the resource requirements for a specific application.

This section discusses seven cost estimating methods, which vary in detail, accuracy, effort, and application. The discussion topics are sequenced somewhat by accuracy, starting from top-down estimates.

Expert Judgment Estimating

This top-down method relies on the subject knowledge and field experience of an individual or group of individuals to estimate the time, resource, or cost of a specific project component or the total project, without going into the task-by-task details. With several experts making an anonymous estimate, which is later averaged, the process is known as the Delphi method. However the technique can also be used in face-to-face discussions, leading to a collective judgment, which is called *estimate-talk-estimate (ETE)* or *mini-Delphi*, a method widely used for forecasting in a wide range of business situations. With the right people, any these forms of expert judgment are very effective and reliable for obtaining a quick cost estimate, especially pragmatic at the very front-end of a new project proposal.

It is also interesting to notice that while an expert judgment is labeled in this section as a "top-down" method, it is the same expert judgment that is used in "bottom-up" estimates, integrating detailed task estimates into the total project cost.

Rule of Thumb Estimating

Rules of thumb are very general measures and ratios among certain metrics. As an example, The US government suggests in its *Cost Estimating and Assessment Guide* that "as a typical rule of thumb, the lower and upper bounds estimated by experts should be interpreted as representing the 15 percent and 85 percent levels, respectively, of all possible outcomes." This doesn't mean that it is always 15 and 85 percent, but it is a good general rule or sanity check. It is also a good starting point if no other information is available. There are rules of thumb for many project-based measures and parameters ranging overhead to profit and meeting duration to risk handling. Rules of thumb are experience-based, common-sense yardsticks that provide both a quick up-front calibration and a benchmark for reality checks.

Past Performance Estimating

Past performance estimating, also known as *analogy estimating*, is a top-down method, which relies on historic cost data of similar projects. It is similar in concept to parametric estimating, but looks more at whole subsystems or even the whole project for cost data, rather than trying to isolate specific parameters for cost modeling. The method builds on the notion that virtually no project, no matter how state-of-the-art, represents a totally new system, but just represents a new combination of existing components. If this assumption holds, we can use the actual costs from a similar project, or its components, adjusted for any differences, to estimate the cost of the new project. This method is often part of continuous improvement processes, utilizing learning curves and experience curves. Past performance estimating is especially effective for projects similar to those already completed.

Three-Point Estimating

Three-point estimating combines expert judgment with analytical methods. Three judgments are made to determine the (a) best-case estimate, (m) most likely estimate and (b) worst-case estimate. The three estimates are combined to calculate a summary statistics of the three-point distribution, such as mean, standard deviation, and percentage points. A triangular distribution is commonly used for calculating the expected cost *(E)*:

$$E = (a + m + b)/3.$$

Alternatively, others calculate the *expected cost (E')* as the approximate mean of an assumed beta-distribution, together with a standard deviation (*SD*):

$$E' = (a + 4m + b)/6$$
$$SD = (b - a)/6$$

The same statistics is also used to determine expected values for Project Evaluation and Review Techniques (PERT).

It should be emphasized, however, that regardless of the distribution used, the accuracy of the estimate can be no better than the accuracy obtained with the three initial estimates, which points at the limitations of this estimating method.

In addition, the method has a built-in psychological bias. Estimators are tempted to go more conservative than justified at the worst-case estimate, and therefore skewing the distribution toward a higher expected value. In statistical terms, the greater the distance between the best-case and worst-case value, the greater is the risks of the cost estimate not being realized. However, in the hands of skilled estimators and in combination with other methods, the three-point method is an effective and popular estimating tool.

Parametric Estimating

In its pure form, parametric estimating is very technical (ISPA 2008). It develops cost estimates by examining statistical relationships among technical, programmatic, and cost data from previously completed (similar) projects to build a cost model which is adjusted for complexity and other factors. The cost derived for a specific parameter, or group of parameters, is then scaled up or down to calculate the cost of the new project. To illustrate, let's assume that in the past we constructed 50 buildings of different sizes, but similar type, and the construction cost for each building, regardless of size, comes to $100 +/–5 percent per square foot floor space, including labor, material, architectural services, permitting, infrastructure, and contingencies, for turn-key delivery. Hence, $100/sq ft +/–5 percent is a reliable parameter for estimating the cost of the next building, if we can determine its floor space. Obviously, determining floor space is a lot simpler and more reliable than estimating the detailed labor and material cost of thousands of items required to construct the new building. The example illustrates the power of parametric estimating, but also its limitations. The assumption is that we can find a parameter, or set of parameters, that provides a good cost model. This seems to be easier for construction and infrastructure projects than for other technology projects, such as product developments, service-based undertakings and R&D. However, in combination with other top-down methods, such as expert judgment and past performance-based methods, parametric estimating can be a very powerful and effective estimating tool. As an example, software developments often use *cost per line of coding* as a parameter to obtain a "rough order of magnitude" cost estimate for a new project. Overall, I find most project managers can identify experientially certain parameters on their specific class of projects for a quick thumbnail resources estimate of a new project.

Detailed Roll-Up Cost Estimating

This method assumes that we can determine the cost for lower level components and subsystems of the project with reasonable accuracy. Then, using a cost model, such as the work breakdown structure (WBS), we can roll up and integrate all the sublevel costs into the total project or program cost. Roll-up estimates do not necessarily have to start at the lowest task or cost element of the project. However, the estimate should be reasonably accurate at whatever level we estimate in order to arrive at a reliable estimate at the top, otherwise we might be better off to rely on a top-down method.

Deterministic Cost Estimating

This method produces by definition the most accurate estimate. But, it is also most time-consuming and costly. *Deterministic cost estimating* requires detailed knowledge of all project tasks and components, so that the actual cost can be determined, and when rolled up, will result in an accurate estimate of the total project. It usually requires detailed estimates at the lowest cost account, including labor time, specific resource requirements, labor rates, material, and other costs. This is a very labor-intensive, time-consuming, and costly effort. Therefore, this type of cost estimate is rarely undertaken early in the project feasibility or initiation stage, but reserved for a later time in the project formation or bid proposal phase when organizational desirability and feasibility of the project has been established with certainty.

11.3 WHERE TO BEGIN?

Eventually, we must define the budget and cost baseline for our project, which shows the type and quantity of resources, when they are needed and how much they cost. We have to do this for all cost accounts, rolled-up through the various subsystems, and integrated at the project level. This is very laborious and time-consuming even for small projects. It can be outright overwhelming for larger projects, especially when attempted in a single step. Therefore, ground rule #1 is to break the budgeting process along two dimensions:

Cost estimating (first) . . .. Budgeting (second)
Top-down (first) . . .. Bottom-up, detailed (second)

To keep the process manageable and effective, we should start with cost estimating *and* with a top-down approach first. Then iterate toward a more detailed estimate and eventually develop the complete project budget, similar to the process diagram suggested in Figure 8.2.

11.3.1 Project Budgeting Step-by-Step

Regardless of the level of estimating detail chosen, the process cannot be performed without a clear project definition at the level of the required estimate and a selection of the estimating method. Therefore, any budgeting process includes four parts or process steps:

Step-I Project definition
Step-II Selection of estimating method
Step-III Cost estimation
Step-IV Budgeting

This is consistent with established standards for project budgeting, such as PMBOK (2013), GOA (2009), and NASA (2008). It follows most closely NASA's guidelines provided in their *2008 NASA Cost Estimating Handbook*.

Step 1—Project Definition

This step defines the project *at the level of required estimating detail*. This includes the project objectives, scope, customer requirements, technical description, timing, and reason for the estimate. The *work breakdown structure (WBS)*, detailed to the desired level of estimate, serves as the *cost model*.

Step 2—Selection of Estimating Method

This step defines the estimating method appropriate for the chosen level of detail. It also includes the ground rules and assumptions, and validates the cost model. This step establishes the framework for the estimate. However, it is likely that the method selection and assumptions needs to be revisited and fine-tuned during the subsequent cost estimating process.

Step 3—Cost Estimation

At this step the actual cost estimates are developed based on the chosen level of detail and estimating method, including appropriate validation and summary documentation. When this step is performed at a detailed project level, specific materials, facilities, and human resource allocations must be considered, including their quantity, skill sets, and time needed.

Step 4—Budgeting

The project budget is the total amount of monetary resources authorized and allocated to a project over its life cycle, providing the basis for resource planning, project monitoring, tracking, and control. Budgets are crucial management tools, not only for the project organization, but also for supporting resource departments throughout the enterprise, contractors, and partner organizations. The budgeting process starts with the cost baseline, that is the aggregation of cost estimates for all cost accounts (e.g., work packages and subsystems), across all stages of the project life cycle. However, budgets usually differ from cost estimates because they should include lessons learned, funding limitations, risk factors, and other business considerations that affect the budged realities beyond itemized cost estimating. Therefore, the cost baseline needs to be reviewed and modified to be consistent with the budget. Because of these dynamics, many of the interdependent project planning activities, such as scoping, scheduling, cost estimating, and budgeting, are being performed concurrently. When working the budgeting process, it is further important for the project manager to collaborate with the team members responsible for implementing the plan regarding scoping the work and schedule to fit the budget constraints and ensure cost-realism. The budgeting process is filled with emotions. Each group is trying to get its "fair share" of the available resources. Matching the scope and schedule with the budget usually requires considerable negotiations among all parties, project leaders, team members, supporting resource managers, senior management and the sponsor organization. While often stressful and time-consuming, this total team involvement has important side benefits of leading to consensus on the budget and ultimately commitment to the project plan that should be an updated document reflecting all adjustment made to the project scope, schedule, cost structure, and other elements that define the project requirements and its performance.

11.4 COST ESTIMATING AND BUDGETING PHILOSOPHY

Cost estimating and budgeting are difficult tasks. Understanding the complexities provides management perspective, a conduit linking the art and science of these intricate processes. Although computers and sophisticated analytical tools provide the "technical" support for the budgeting process, we still need a great deal of intuition, leadership, and judgment to generate meaningful data, integrated into an executable budget, seen as realistic with buy-in from all team members. This takes a lot of experience and specialized skills. From field observations, we find the following *driving forces toward realistic, quality estimates*:

- Estimators have solid knowledge of the project baseline, scope, and requirements
- Estimating team includes experienced, trained cost analysts, and subject experts, individuals assigned to perform project work
- Estimators have prior experience with projects of similar size and complexity
- Specialists from related disciplines (other projects) are involved in the estimating process
- Historic cost data for similar undertakings are available
- Accurate cost model (e.g., WBS) at the level of estimate
- Sufficient funding of cost estimating and budgeting as part of the project planning phase
- Estimating methods are appropriate for the level of estimating detail
- Use of multiple estimating methods
- Integration of analytical and judgmental methods
- Resisting pressures for over- or underestimating
- Costs, budget, and schedule constraints are dealt with via formal design-to-cost or plan-to-cost processes and reflected in adjustments to scope and schedule (cost integrity)
- Avoid estimating at an unknown level of detail
- A rough expert estimate is better than a precise value based on an uncertain cost model
- Use of phased approaches to budgeting and resource commitments
- Project life cycle cost (LCC) management principles are observed
- Risks and uncertainties are identified and considered
- Cost and budget allocations have team agreement
- Work environment is conducive to teamwork, mutual trust, and respect
- Estimates are kept current
- The enterprise evaluates and tracks cost estimating and budgeting performance for continuous process improvement

One especially important criterion for effective estimating is the involvement of the project team in the process, a topic that will be discussed in more detail in the next section. Without such an involvement, the credibility of perceived reality of the estimate and subsequent budget item does not exist. Therefore, soliciting team member participation, input, and cooperation during the estimating process is crucial to obtaining buy-in ultimate commitment to any budget item. It is also critical to developing workable design-to-cost solutions budget cuts or other resource constraints.

11.4.1 Who Should Perform the Estimate?

Ultimately the project manager is the person responsible to senior management for producing the cost estimate, and developing and producing a workable budget. However, there are many stakeholders to the budget, ranging from the core team to the supporting resource groups, outside contractors, customer organization, and senior management. There are also staff groups, such as cost accounting, cost engineering, and specialists from the project management office (PMO) that may support and orchestrate the estimating effort. The critical question is, who should make the estimate, and at what level of detail? The answer depends on the detail of the project concept and its requirements available at the time of the estimate. Ideally, we should have all the information to define the project at the necessary level of detail to completely and accurately estimate the required resources. However, this is seldom possible. Bid proposals, advanced developments, and R&D undertakings are just some of the examples where complete details are usually not available. Also, for most projects, especially complex ones, we need at least a rough estimate, often called *order-of-magnitude*, before we can even make a preliminary funding decision. Therefore, cost estimates are usually made in stages, depending on the life cycle stage the project is in. This also influences who should perform the estimate.

During the early stages of project formation, very little detail is known. The estimate should be performed at a very general project level, top-down by a few senior people who understand the project, its scope and requirements, and ideally, can also relate to previously undertaken similar projects. Dividing the overall project into major subsystems or execution phases, such as documented in a level-1 work breakdown structure, would provide a sufficient and useful cost model.

At a later project phase, or after a preliminary funding decision has been made, a more detailed estimate is needed, maybe as part of a formal project definition and planning effort to establish operating budgets, cost controls or the price of a contract in a bid proposal effort. In either case, the estimating detail depends on the level of intended cost control. The lowest level of project work for which cost is authorized, reported, analyzed, and controlled is called the cost account. Therefore, for most projects it doesn't make sense to estimate resources below the cost account level, although some projects go below this level for additional accuracy and the ability to root-cause performance problems further.

Specific cost estimating requirements and approaches vary to some extent across companies, and even among government organizations, because many of these companies have their own cost accounting system. Furthermore, for contract work and bid proposals the customer often specifies the cost-estimating detail.

Before we can address the question of who should make the estimate at the cost account, we have to clarify what is being estimated. Usually this is *not* the dollar amount, but a complex derivative consisting of task definition, duration, labor categories, skill levels, pay rates, materials, facilities, task integration and other costs. While I already stressed the importance of task specialists to be actively involved in the estimating process, these specialists might not be the best people to develop the estimate single-handed. The task specialist is definitely qualified to estimate time duration, material, and other straightforward cost items. But his or her estimates need to be reviewed, calibrated, and upgraded by someone who has broad organizational perspective, can judge interdisciplinary support and integration efforts, shortcuts, risks, and special needs. Above all, this lead-estimator can motivate task specialists and support personnel to provide realistic resource estimates, and to agree to final budgets. Taken together, resource estimating is teamwork. The effort is led by a senior manager or skilled cost accounting professional, supported by the task specialists assigned to the job and cost accounting analysts preparing the quantitative analysis and cost details.

11.4.2 The Role of Computers

Cost estimating is complex not only in its management process, but also in its data processing. The use of computers is a necessity for virtually every project that goes through a final budget development. First, the measures for labor, time, material, travel, overhead and other items need to be analyzed, risk-adjusted and translated into a currency, such as dollars, so resources can be tracked and controlled in a normalized way. This is a lot of number crunching for just one cost account. A modest-size project with just five subsystems that should be controlled at the work breakdown level-3, might have at least $5 \times 5 \times 5 = 125$ cost accounts. Manual data processing is not a good option, especially in light of over 100 sophisticated computer software programs, available with specialized applications for project resource estimating, tracking and controlling. These applications not only perform all the cost data processing reliably, quickly, and professionally formatted, but also perform a variety of analyses, such as parametric comparisons, relative cost distribution, ranking of cost drivers, and other checks and balances. In addition, once the electronic cost database has been established, any changes in the project configuration—or the original cost estimates or their dependencies—can be assessed very quickly and reliably, together with effective comparisons of different options. These are valuable and powerful features, especially for incremental and iterative cost estimating and budgeting, which is typical for today's complex projects.

11.5 SUMMARY OF KEY POINTS AND CONCLUSIONS

The following key points were made in this chapter:

- Budgets are important management tools for the project selection, planning, and control.

- Cost estimates and budgets are usually developed incrementally and iteratively, matching the evolving management desirability for and commitment to the project.
- Initial cost estimates at the early stage of project evaluation are usually "quick" top-down expert judgments, parametric estimates, or estimates based on comparison with similar undertakings from the past.
- Cost estimating methods are categorized into five classes, ranging from very low accuracy (class-5) to very high accuracy (class-1), each class suitable for a different level of project definition maturity.
- The seven popular cost estimating methods are: (1) expert judgment, (2) rule of thumb, (3) past performance, (4) three-point, (5) parametric, (6) roll-up, and (7) deterministic. They are ranked, with (7) to be most accurate.
- To keep the budgeting process manageable, one should start a new project with top-down cost estimating, Then iterate toward a more detailed estimate and eventually develop the complete project budget.
- Regardless of the project size and level of detail desired, the budgeting process goes through four steps: (1) project definition, (2) estimating method selection, (3) cost estimation, and (4) budgeting.
- The budgeting process is filled with emotions. Each group is trying to get its "fair share." Matching the scope and schedule with the budget requires considerable negotiations among all parties, project leaders, team members, supporting resource managers, senior management, and the sponsor organization.
- While task specialists should be active participants in the estimating process, they might not be the best choice for developing the estimate single-handed.
- Cost estimating is teamwork, led by a senior manager or skilled cost accounting professional, supported by task specialists and cost accounting analysts.
- Cost estimating is very inefficient and unreliable when performed manually. Computer support is strongly recommended. We can choose from over 100 sophisticated computer programs with specialized applications for project resource estimating, tracking, and controlling. These applications perform cost data processing reliably, quickly, and professionally formatted, plus a variety of analyses, such as parametric comparisons, relative cost distribution, ranking of cost drivers, and other checks and balances.

11.6 QUESTIONS FOR DISCUSSION AND EXERCISES

1. Assuming that you are a product manager at Google. You are evaluating a proposal for a new product development similar in complexity to

Google Maps but very different in its application. Your gut feeling is that this development shouldn't cost more than $5 million. What *approach would you take to estimate the total development cost* in support of a project selection and funding decision to be made by Google senior management?

2. How does the classification of the five different cost estimating methods help in managing a cost estimate?
3. How does the budget help in controlling project cost during the execution phase?
4. What are the assumptions for "expert judgment estimating" to work? What are the limitations?
5. What guidelines would your give for performing a parametric cost estimate for the project proposal described in Question #1?
6. What environment is conducive to effective and realistic cost estimating? What are the barriers to effective cost estimating and how can we eliminate these barriers?
7. How can project managers encourage their team members to estimate "realistically?"
8. How can we develop cost-estimating skills? What kind of a professional cost estimator development program would you suggest?

11.7 *PMBOK®* GUIDE REFERENCES AND CONNECTIONS

The topic of cost estimating connects most strongly with the *4th PMBOK Knowledge Area of COST*. It also addresses the first two *processing groups: initiating and planning*. Much of the discussion of this chapter is about the *context* of project planning. That is the way projects are planned, documented, and communicated in preparation for project execution. This broad contextual understanding of project management is necessary for effectively applying the PMBOK standards to the day-to-day management of projects and to study effectively for PMP® certification. *In studying for the PMP® Exam*, an understanding of the following concepts will be beneficial: (1) project planning, (2) cost estimating, (3) budget determination, (4) activity-based cost, (5) cost baseline, (6) should-cost, and (7) risk management.

INTERNET LINKS AND RESOURCES

Google. 2013. "Company overview." http://www.google.com/about/company/
Businessweek. 2006. "Inside Google's New Product Development Process." http://Www.Businessweek.Com/Stories/2006–06–29/Inside-Googles-New-Product-Process (Posted on June 29, 2006).
Wikipedia. 2013. "Project Planning." http://en.wikipedia.org/wiki/Project_planning

REFERENCES AND ADDITIONAL READINGS

AACE International, American Association for Cost Engineers. 2003. *Cost Estimate Classification System (AACE International Recommended Practice No. 17R-97)*. Morgantown, WV: AACE International.

Akintoye, A., and E. Fitzgerald. 2000. "A Survey of Current Cost Estimating Practices in the UK." *Construction Management and Economics* 18(2): 161–172.

American National Standards Institute. 2012. ANSI Standard ASTM E2516–11. "Standard Classification for Cost Estimate Classification System." Washington, DC: American National Standards Institute.

Cano, J., and I. Lidon. 2011. "Guided Reflection on Product Definition." *International Journal of Project Management* 29(5) (July): 525–535.

Garza, J. M., and K. G. Rouhana. 1995. "Neural Networks Versus Parameter-Based Applications in Cost Estimating." *Cost Engineering Journal* 37(2): 14–17.

Gido, J., and J. P. Clements. 2012. "Initiating a Project." Part 1 in *Successful Project Management*. Mason, OH: South-Western Cengage Learning.

Google. 2012. "2011 Annual Report and 2012 CEO Update." Mountain View, CA: Investor Relations, Google Inc.

Hamaker, J. W., and J. W. Componation. 2005. "Improving Space Project Estimating with Engineering Management Variables." *Engineering Management Journal*,vol. 17, no.2 (June), pp. 28–33.

International Society of Parametric Analysts. 2008. *Parametric Estimating Handbook*. Vienna, VA: International Society of Parametric Analysts.

Kendrick, T. 2009. *Identifying and Managing Project Risk: Essential Tools for Failure-Proofing Your Project*. New York: AMACOM.

Kloppenborg, T. J. 2012. "Planning Projects." Part 2 in *Contemporary Project Management*. Mason, OH: South-Western Cengage Learning.

Levin, G. 2008. Project Management Accounting: Budgeting, Tracking and Reporting Cost and Profitability." *Project Management Journal* 39(1) (Mar. 2008): 95–106.

Lewis, J. 2011. *Project Planning, Scheduling, and Control: The Ultimate Hands-On Guide to Bringing Projects in On Time and On Budget*. New York: McGraw-Hill.

Mileham, A. R., G. C. Currie, A. W. Miles, and D. T. Bradford. 1993. "A Parametric Approach to Cost Estimating at the Conceptual Stage of Design." *Journal of Engineering Design* 4, (2): 117–125.

Naderi, F. 2001. "Mars Exploration." *Robotics & Automation Magazine (IEEE)* 13 (2): 72–82.

National Aeronautics and Space Administration. 2008. *2008 NASA Cost Estimating Handbook*. Washington, DC: US Government Printing Office.

Ostwald, P. F., and T.S. McLaren. 2013. *Cost Analysis and Estimating for Engineering and Management*. Old Tappan, NJ: Pearson Education.

Parviz, F. R. 2002. *Project Estimating and Cost Management*, Vienna, VA: Management Concepts.

Philipenko, R., J. Acharya, and P. Srivastava. 2012. "Define Your Project—Reduce the Risk." *Cost Engineering* 54 (4): 25–35.

Project Management Institute. 2013. *A Guide to the Project Management Body of Knowledge (PMBOK® Guide), Fifth Edition*. Newtown Square, PA: Project Management Institute.

Rad, P. F., and V. S. Anantatmula. 2006. *Project Planning Techniques*. Tyson Corner, VA: Management Concepts Press.

Serpell, A. 2011. "Modeling Project's Scopes for Conceptual Cost Modeling." *Cost Engineering* 53(4) (April): 24–34.

Sweeting, J. 1997. *Project Cost Estimating—Principles and Practice.* Rugby, Warwickshire, UK: Institution of Chemical Engineers.

Thamhain, H., and I. Kruglianskas. 2000. "Managing Technology-Based Projects in Multinational Environments." *IEEE Transactions on Engineering Management* 47(1) (February): 55–64.

US Government Accountability Office. 2009. *GAO Cost Estimating and Assessment Guide: Best Practices for Developing and Managing Capital Program Costs.* Washington, DC: US Government Printing Office (publication GAO-09–3SP).

Chapter 12

Monitoring and Controlling
Technology-Intensive Projects

PRAIRIE WATERS PROJECT WINS PMI'S
PROJECT OF THE YEAR AWARD

"When you manage a project, fully compliant *and* $100 million under budget, your stakeholders will be thrilled. Shave another $100 million from the budget and the entire project management profession will take notice," said Cyndee Miller, senior editor of PMI's *PM Network* (2011). This is exactly what happened. On October 23, 2011, the lead team of the Prairie Waters Project of Aurora, Colorado, was named 2011 PMI® Project of the Year in recognition of their outstanding achievements. When asked to explain the superior performance that set this project aside from other well-executed contracts, Larry Catalano, manager of the capital projects division for the city of Aurora, said, "Excellent project management and a little bit of luck." Management, yes. Luck (?) . . . well, it doesn't hurt. However, to execute an $850 million project, involving 5 engineering firms, 7 general contractors, 36 regulatory agencies, 410 permits, and 140 property easements, plus 11 city council members and 4 city project managers; plus meeting or exceeding all requirements ahead of schedule and $200 million under budget, takes more than a "bit of luck." It requires an exceptionally well-planned and organized effort, sophisticated management, and collaboration among all stakeholders.

Six years ago, the city of Aurora, Colorado, located in an arid environment, had to find innovative ways to ensure sustainable, long-term water supply for its population of approximately 300,000. "Our growing population caused an urgent need for more water, while preserving the established high standards for water quality," said Larry Catalano, city manager of capital projects. In order to deliver

---

Sources: PMI Press Release of October 24, 2011, authored by Carey Learnard and Megan Maguire Kelly, "Prairie Waters Project Receives Project Management Institute's Prestigious 2011 PMI Project of the Year Award." Newtown Square, PA: PMI. For more detailed discussion of the Aurora Waters project, see Kevin Allen (2011) and articles of the project published on the website of the CH2M HILL Company (2012).

50 million gallons of drinking water per day, the project required the engineering design and construction of 34 miles of pipeline, four pump stations and the most technologically advanced water-treatment facility. From the project management perspective, the complexities included stringent cost constraints, pressures for fast implementation, stakeholder involvement, and environmental restrictions. The consulting firm *CH2M HILL* of Englewood, Colorado, was chosen among several bidders to lead and manage the project. During the project's design phase, the city council required to cut US$100 million from the initial project budget of US$854 million. Project leaders accomplished these savings during the construction phase by creating contractor incentives for more cost effectively deliveries. Additional savings of $100 million were realized by skillfully managing the project across its interfaces, and by rigorous application of project management standards and processes, and the use of earned value management (EVM) techniques, which also helped to fast-track the project two months ahead of schedule, without compromising quality and safety.

"The City of Aurora's Prairie Waters Project clearly illustrates how project management standards and practices, properly applied and combined with hard work, collaboration and dedication can help deliver a solution that is transformative to a community," said Mark Langley, president and CEO of PMI. "This project demonstrates best practice solutions that show agility and effective stakeholder engagement. PMI commends Aurora Waters and the entire project team for these outstanding results."

12.1 THE CHALLENGES OF MANAGERIAL CONTROL

The word *control* has many connotations. In management, it implies *influencing* the outcome of a process or operation. This can be difficult if the forces that define the outcome are not within our sphere of influence, which is often the case for project management. Satisfying customer requirements within schedule and budget constraints can be challenging, even for small projects, especially when dealing with uncertainties and diverse customer communities, typical for today's projects. Adding complexity, technology, and competitive pressures toward better, faster, cheaper execution, can create mega-challenges for project managers. Especially the dynamics of our business environment and the unknown factors require project leaders to go often beyond conventional techniques of budget and schedule control. Although accurate tracking of project progress is still extremely important, it is the innovative way of dealing with constraints, obstacles and risk factors, and the skillful leadership ensuring team dedication, commitment, collaboration, and stakeholder engagement, that is often even more important to success, as we have noticed in the Aurora Waters project.

I have chosen an infrastructure scenario as lead-in project to this chapter to show that technology and complexity impact not just computers and IT developments, but virtually every major project from healthcare to election campaigns, and from retailing to construction. The challenges presented in the Aurora Waters project are typical for today's undertaking. Resource limitation, end-date-driven schedules, changing requirements, and the need for innovative solutions are quite common together with pressures for cost effectiveness, quality, and implementation flexibility. It is also no coincident that the human side and organizational dynamics were critical factors in the team's success that led to the *Project of the Year Award*. As shown in the lead-in scenario, sophisticated control processes and the latest project management technology are critically important, but no substitute for unified buy-in and commitment of team personnel to the project plan and its mission objectives. Without this collaboration, dedication, and innovative engagement of team members, it is difficult, if not impossible, to maintain control, especially in complex and dynamic mission environments.

12.1.1 Defining Project Control

As a working definition, project control is the process of taking the necessary actions for implementing a plan and reaching its objectives, in spite of changing and often unpredictable conditions. This statement implies many assumptions. First, we must have a plan. Second, we must be able to measure current status and performance in order to determine possible deviations from our plan and to assess their impact. Third, we assume that the root cause of the plan deviation can actually be determined and corrective measures be found. Finally, there is a whole spectrum of assumptions that relate to the organization and its culture, values, and people.

12.1.2 Why Is Control so Difficult?

Project control is no trivial matter. Even with the best preparation, detailed planning, and team involvement, managers find it hard to control projects, achieving desired results. To complicate matters, it seems to be difficult to root-cause these problems. When ask, project managers are likely to blame external factors (e.g., changing requirements, shifting markets, changing technology, or insufficient resources) for performance problems and failures, as summarized in Table 12.1.

These are merely conditions of the project environment, not necessarily the reason for failure. We can certainly find teams that perform well under the same tough conditions that are blamed for performance issues by others. Further, it is interesting to note that while project leaders blame performance problems predominately on "external" factors outside their sphere of control, senior management points at the project leaders. Senior managers argue that projects fail, by and large, because of insufficient planning, tracking, control, poor communication, and weak leadership. Yet, a third perspective can be obtained from observations during field research, which examines the root causes of many of

Table 12.1   Primary Reasons for Poor Project Performance or Failure

Project Managers' Perspective	Senior Managers' Perspective	Field Researcher's Independent Perspective
• Too many changes and contingencies (e.g., requirements, scope, budget, technology, market, etc.) • Unrealistic budgets and schedules • Lacking senior management support • Multinational complexities • Insufficient help in dealing with issues early • Shifting priorities • Lacking specialty skills among team members • Underestimating project complexity • Incompatible administrative processes, power issues and politics	• Insufficient, inaccurate planning • Insufficient performance measurements and tracking • Weak cross-functional communications • Lack of candor and transparency in tracking and reviews • Weak change control • Weak project leadership	• Unrealistic expectations • Unclear requirements • Inability to deal effectively with risks and contingencies • Underestimating required effort, complexities and resource requirements • Insufficient front-end planning • Weak project leadership • Limited ability to sustain support from resource groups • Weak sponsor and top management commitment

the project performance problems and failures (Thamhain 2002, 2008, 2011). It traces the problems to the broader issues of understanding and communicating the complexities of the project. It also points at the limited capacity of project managers to deal with risks and contingencies, to sustain support from resource groups and to engage stakeholders. While the field studies produced a long list of subtle issues related to project performance, we found insufficient front-end preparation and managerial leadership a common denominator to many of these issues, as summarized in part three of Table 12.1.

The challenge is for project managers to apply the available tools and techniques effectively, together with skillful leadership toward collaboration and commitment of the greater project community. These challenges exist for all projects. Yet, they seem to increase with project complexity and the dynamics and uncertainties of the business environment.

12.2   WHAT WE KNOW ABOUT MANAGERIAL CONTROL OF COMPLEX PROJECTS

The concepts and methods of managerial control have been known for a long time (Randolph and Posner 1988). Great philosophers from Confucius to

Aristotle have offered insight and advice to leaders on the art and science of controlling activities, processes, and people. These control philosophies and methods dominated management practices and project control from ancient times up to the twentieth century.

With the onset of modern project management in the 1950s, new tools, such as formal scheduling and budgeting, introduced new, but also very narrow focus to project control. As a result, project control focused, by and large, on tracking of schedule, resource data and deliverables, without too much concern about true project performance, flexibility, and responsiveness to dynamically changing business environments. However, starting with the 1980s, the business environment changed dramatically. New technologies, especially computers and communications, have radically changed the workplace and transformed our global economy to include more service and knowledge work, with a high mobility of resources, skills, processes, and technology itself. Traditional controls, based on central command structures, authority, and narrow performance measures, such as the triple constraint of time, resources, and deliverables, no longer worked effectively. Companies were forced to rethink their management concepts and business practices.

As a result, starting with the 1980s, new project management tools, techniques, and practices evolved that were more agile and integrated with the business process, offering more sophisticated capabilities for project tracking and control in an environment that became not only different in culture, but also had to deal with a broad spectrum of new contemporary challenges, such as time to market, accelerating technologies, innovation, resource limitations, technical complexities, social and ethical issues, operational dynamics, risk, and uncertainty.

In response to these challenges, special processes, such as concurrent engineering, computer-aided design (CAD), computer-aided manufacturing (CAM), information resource management (IRM), manufacturing resource planning (MRP), and design for manufacture and assembly (DFM/A) evolved. In recent years, new highly complex organizational forms and work processes emerged with our increasingly global project environment. These forms support communications, managerial control, and work integration across wide geographic and multinational regions. These concepts gradually replaced many of the traditional, hierarchically structured organizations and their linear work processes. This shift also significantly affected management styles and the tools and techniques for orchestrating and controlling complex projects.

12.3 WHAT DO WE WANT TO CONTROL?

In our highly connected, hypercompetitive world, project success is a complex variable driven by an intricately connected set of factors and conditions. The time-honored *triple constraint* of delivering agreed-on results within given time and budget is certainly a good starting point. However, for most projects success includes a much broader set measures that are often linked to long-term benefits and values of the enterprise and its client organization far beyond the delivery point of the project. Furthermore, customer satisfaction, a key measure of project success, has many dimensions and is a perception of many stakeholders in the customer community. Yet, in spite of very clear signals from the field of project management, the project management literature has been quite divided on this topic, and as of today there is no uniformly accepted set of measures for project performance or project success. However, extensive field studies by researchers, such as Shenhar and Dvir (2008), Milosevic and Srivannaboon (2006), Patanakul et al. (2010), Shenhar et al. (2007) and Thamhain (2011, 2013a) have identified specific variables and organizational conditions that are used by project management professionals for assessing project performance and success during the execution phase and beyond. These contemporary measures of project performance were further investigated in a field survey of 530 project managers (Thamhain 2010). The results are listed here as reference metrics for benchmarking. They may also serve as a framework for designing contemporary project control systems. It should be noticed that, depending on their interpretation, many of these performance measures overlap and appear linked, which is indicative of the intricate nature of project performance.

Contemporary measures of project performance (listed in order of importance and frequency by project managers):
- Producing agreed-on results (deliverables) on time and within budget (triple constraint)
- Innovative, value-added project plan implementation
- Producing benefits and values to client organization beyond triple constraint
- Ability to accelerate project schedule
- Capturing opportunities for time and cost savings via innovative execution
- Quality concerns and enhancements of deliverables
- Technological advances utilized for value added
- Ability to deal with complexity, innovation, and uncertainty
- Ability to work dynamically and incrementally toward objectives and target results
- Ability to deal with risks and contingencies
- Ability to deal with conflict and organizational politics
- Reaching stretch goals
- Recognizing changing environment and responding proactively
- Recognizing new market opportunities and technological trends
- Flexibility toward customer requirements (e.g., change orientation)
- Recognizing and capturing follow-on business
- Minimizing organizational disruptions and interferences
- Engaging stakeholders and building collaborative project environments

- Creating synergism among enterprise units (e.g., leveraging resources)
- Aligning project work with enterprise strategy
- Long-term benefits and values to the enterprise and its client organization beyond the project delivery
- Concern for natural environment
- Capturing experiences for future projects and organizational learning
- Developing project organization and personal skill sets

Clearly, there are great differences among projects in terms of complexity, size, technology, risk, and other variables. Therefore, "one size does not fit all." Performance measures need to be fine-tuned to be relevant for judging project performance and organizational effectiveness, and for determining fair and equitably awards to individuals and project teams.

12.4 AVAILABLE TOOLS AND TECHNIQUES

Driven by the changing business environment, advances in technology and increasing project complexity, managerial methods for project control have expanded continuously. Many companies have invested heavily in new management tools and techniques, promising more effective alternatives and enhancements to traditional forms of project control. The most popular project management tools used today are summarized in the appendix to this chapter. For ease of discussion, these tools are grouped into three categories: (1) analytical tools and techniques, (2) procedural tools and techniques, and (3) people-oriented tools and techniques. This grouping also provides descriptive focus and a convenient way to catalog these control tools (Thamhain 2005). However, it should be noticed that applications overlap a great deal among these categories.

Many of the most popular tools, such as design reviews, and schedule and budget tracking have been around for a long time. However, in recent years virtually all of the traditional project management tools have been redefined and enhanced with information technology and sophisticated computer software to fit the contemporary challenges of today's business environment more appropriately, and to work flexibly and effectively with complex processes, human factors, and cross-functional alliances.

12.4.1 Popularity and Value of Project Control Techniques

Effective project management involves a great variety of tools and methods as summarized in the appendix of this chapter. Table 12.2 lists these tools once more, rank-ordered by popularity. The listing is based on two field studies (Thamhain 2005) and recent action research (Thamhain 2011, 2013b) that together involve over 1,500 project managers. It is interesting to note that traditional project management tools and techniques, such as budget/schedule

Table 12.2 Management Techniques: Popularity, Skill Level, and Value

Management Technique	%	Skill Type & Level Needed					Value
MT	Popularity	Analytical	Business Admin	Team Leadership	Senior Management Support	Project Management	V
Schedule tracking	99	2.00	1.00	3.00	2.00	3.50	3.25
Project definition	98	3.00	2.75	2.00	2.25	3.00	3.75
Project review	93	2.75	3.25	3.25	3.00	2.75	3.15
Budget tracking	92	2.00	1.50	2.50	2.00	1.50	3.25
Design review	87	3.00	2.00	2.75	2.25	3.00	3.50
Prototyping	82	3.50	1.00	1.50	1.00	1.50	3.25
Status assessment	82	3.25	2.50	3.00	2.00	3.00	3.75
Computer software	71	3.75	2.25	2.00	1.50	1.75	2.50
Deficiency report	68	1.50	0.75	0.50	0.50	1.00	2.50
Action Item Report	65	1.00	1.00	0.50	0.50	0.50	3.00
Requirements Analysis	52	3.25	2.75	2.00	1.50	1.50	3.15
Benchmarking	52	3.25	2.50	1.00	1.75	1.75	1.50
PERT/CPM	42	3.00	1.75	2.00	0.75	1.75	1.50
Agile/scrum	40	2.00	2.00	3.75	3.00	3.75	3.20
Earned value analysis	41	2.50	0.50	2.75	0.75	2.00	1.75
Stage-Gate process	40	3.50	3.25	3.25	3.50	3.25	3.15
Variance analysis	39	2.50	1.50	1.50	0.75	1.75	1.50
Core team	38	2.25	2.75	3.25	3.75	3.25	2.35

(Continued)

Table 12.2 (Continued)

Management Technique	%	Skill Type & Level Needed						Value
MT	Popularity	Analytical	Business Admin	Team Leadership	Senior Management Support	Project Management	V
Interface chart	38	2.00	1.50	2.00	2.00	2.00	2.00
Stage-Gate review	35	3.25	3.25	3.00	3.25	3.00	3.15
Critical path analysis	32	1.75	0.50	0.25	0.50	0.00	2.00
Concurrent engineering	32	3.25	3.25	3.50	3.25	3.75	2.00
Rapid prototyping	31	3.50	1.50	1.50	1.25	2.50	3.10
Quality function (QFD)	28	3.25	3.50	3.25	3.25	3.25	2.00
Focus group	28	2.50	1.25	1.50	1.25	1.75	2.00
Voice of the customer	25	2.75	3.00	1.75	2.25	2.25	2.75
Self-directed team	23	2.25	2.50	3.50	3.25	3.50	2.50
Design/build	18	2.75	3.25	3.25	3.50	3.50	3.00
Schedule compression analysis	18	1.75	0.25	0.25	0.50	0.25	1.00
Joint performance evaluation	15	3.00	3.25	2.75	3.75	3.00	2.25
Out-of-bounds review	12	1.50	1.00	2.50	2.75	2.25	2.25

All skill levels and values are perceptions of project leaders and have been measured on a five-point scale, 0–4: 0 = little or no skills or value, 1 = some, 2 = considerable, 3 = high/significant, 4 = very high and critical.

The percentile figures (%) in the Popularity column refer to the number of project professionals actually using the tool or technique.

tracking and project reviews are still very popular and valued. They are among the most frequently used and top-rated tools in the list of 31 items, in spite of their limitations. However, the effectiveness of project management tools cannot be determined by examining them strictly as a single entity. Each tool has its own strength and weakness, which also depends on the type of project and its situation. It is the combination of tools and techniques in a specific project environment that determines collectively the value for managerial control. Nevertheless, Table 12.2 provides some insight into the popularity and value of specific tools, relative to the broad spectrum of available items. The significance of this survey is in identifying the relative use and perceived value of the different control methods, providing awareness and information for benchmarking with implications for training and organization development.

Yet another aspect to popularity is familiarity. We find that for both project managers and team members, lower popularity of certain tools is related to less familiarity, especially for the more contemporary techniques. In fact, familiarity explains 82 percent of the variance between using and not using a particular technique. That is, on average, 82 percent of project leaders who choose not to use a particular technique are also not familiar with its application. The significance of this finding is for judging *value*. Clearly, it would be inappropriate to determine the value of a particular technique from a population that is not familiar with it. Realizing these biases, we used interviews and observations during the field study to ensure that we included only judgments from people who were familiar with the technique and used it appropriately. Interestingly, we found some of the most enthusiastic supporters or rejecters of particular techniques among those who have tried a particular technique with either great success or marginal results, respectively. To minimize biases related to unfamiliarity, we used interviews and observations during the field study to determine the degree of familiarity, proper application, business process integration, and senior management support. Therefore, Table 12.2 includes only carefully screened value judgments from managers who are familiar with the technique and actually use them appropriately. The results show that 85 percent of the tools summarized in Table 12.2 are perceived as having "significant value and importance (or better) for managing their projects effectively." It is also interesting to note that the traditional project-management techniques are not only among the most popular ones, but also among the most valued techniques. Although all of this is clearly an area of further research, it also suggests that project management tools might be underutilized because project managers have insufficient familiarity with them. The finding shows that for over half of the less popular tools, fewer than 25 percent of the project managers interviewed are familiar with these tools.

In summary, the 12 most important techniques, rank-ordered by value, include: (1) project definition, (2) status assessment, (3) design review, (4) project review, (5) schedule tracking, (6) budget tracking, (7) prototyping, (8) agile/scrum, (9) stage-gate process, (10) Stage-Gate review, (11) requirements analysis, and (12) rapid prototyping.

All 12 techniques were rated on average as "significant" and "important" to project success (average score = 3.3), with the top half of these techniques receiving ratings of 3.5 or better, that is close to the rating of "very highly significant and crucial to achieving planned project performance."

12.4.2 How to Use These Tools Effectively

Management tools do not come with a user's manual. Few guidelines have been published in the literature on how and where to use these tools and techniques most appropriately. Perhaps one of the greatest challenges for management is to *seek out* management tools and techniques that meet *three key conditions*:

1. Compatible with the business environment, processes, cultures, and values
2. Conducive to specific problem solving, which usually involves a whole spectrum of factors from innovation to decision making, cross-functional communications, and dealing with risks and uncertainty
3. Useful for tacking and controlling the project according to established plans

The second major challenge is for management to implement selected project control tools and techniques as an integrated part of the business process. For project control to work effectively, it must be congruent with the business process and the human side of management, a conclusion that is supported by other field research (Weisinger and Traut 2003; Davenport 1998; Schultz, Slavin, and Pinto 1987). This involves careful integration of the tools with the various physical, informational, managerial, and psychological subsystems of the enterprise. It also requires a system that is trusted and respected by the users. Therefore, it is not surprising that many of the control techniques depend on a whole spectrum of people issues: clear direction and guidance; ability to plan and elicit commitments; communication skills; assistance in problem solving; ability to deal effectively with managers and support personnel across functional lines, often with only little or no formal authority; information-processing skills, the ability to collect and filter relevant data valid for decision making in a dynamic environment; and the ability to integrate individual demands, requirements, and limitations into decisions that benefit the overall project. It further involves the project manager's ability to resolve intergroup conflicts and to build multifunctional teams. These findings are further supported by other researchers (Doolan and Hacker 2003, McDonough and Leifer 1986) who consistently emphasize the people side of project control, including the important role of organizational and cultural factors, such as mutual trust, respect, candor, risk sharing, and the ability to fail safely. In response to these challenges, an increasing number of companies are focusing on *self-forcing control*, which relies on work challenge, personal pride, and commitment as critical conditions and catalysts to managerial control.

The third major challenge is for management to create and facilitate a learning process so that these tools and techniques become institutionalized. As a result, people in the organization see how these tools help to get projects done more effectively and how they create visibility and recognition for their work.

Many of these contemporary tools also require new administrative skills and a more sophisticated management style. All of this has a profound impact on the way that project leaders must manage toward desired results. The methods of communication, decision making, soliciting commitment, and risk sharing are shifting constantly away from a centralized, autocratic management style to a team-centered, more self-directed form of project control. Equally important, project control has radically departed from its narrow focus of satisfying schedule and budget constraints to a much broader and more balanced managerial approach, which focuses on the effective search for solutions to complex problems, as reflected by the performance metrics in Table 12.2. This requires tradeoffs among many parameters, such as creativity, change-orientation, quality, and traditional schedule and budget constraints. Project control also requires accountability and commitment from the team members toward the project objectives.

12.4.3 Characteristics of Effective Project Controls

Managerial controls have many dimensions and formats. Traditionally, budgets, schedules, and performance appraisals were primarily used in addition to reports, procedures, and directives to control the implementation of managerial plans. These conventional tools still provide the foundation for managerial control. However, given the complexities, dynamics, risks, and uncertainties of technology-intensive work, these conventional tools needed to be upgraded and augmented with contemporary tools that can deal with a broader set of information and the human side of project control.

Every manager has his or her own set of criteria for effective project control. Yet, despite the differences in projects and their environments, to be effective these controls will have these characteristics in common:

- **Realistic plans.** Plans are implemented by people. It is difficult, if not impossible, to control activities toward desired objectives, if these objectives are perceived as unrealistic. People who are ultimately held accountable for achieving the results, should be involved in the planning. This personal involvement leads to a better understanding of the requirements, and hopefully to a commitment of the plan and its objectives. It also results in a more realistic plan because of team-member participation in estimating and validating the elements of the project plan.

- **Commitment.** Control of complex work, such as technology-based projects, depends a great deal on self-imposed control. Personal commitment is a strong intrinsic driver toward self-direction and control. Without this commitment, controls will focus more on the cause and perpetrators of a problem than its correction. Commitment is also expected from senior management regarding resources, priorities, and contingency support.
- **Competence.** The people using the tools and implementing the plan must be professionally competent. The best plan and most sophisticated tools are meaningless unless the people have the capacity to perform. Attracting and holding high-quality people is a primary mission of management. Furthermore, the sign-on process for introducing personnel to a new task or project can help considerably in matching personal skills, capabilities, and interests with the project and its requirements.
- **Measurability.** "If you can't measure it, you can't control it." Any assignment of an activity, project, milestone, or mission must have measurable results. These deliverables should be compared against the plan, including its resources and timing, on an ongoing basis.
- **Appropriate controls.** Management controls must be meaningful and appropriate for the type of project and its mission. This includes both managerial action and timing. For example, close supervision and incentive bonuses might be appropriate for a beta site test operation, but of much less value in R&D. Many controls work only in combination with other methods, such as review meetings, focus groups, reports, and management actions.
- **Focus on key objectives.** According to Peter Drucker, "Control must follow strategy." Managerial control should be related to key objectives. Trivia should not be measured or controlled. It only dilutes the principal objectives and leads into an "activity trap!" That is, we are busy earning Brownie points, following procedures and writing progress reports, rather dealing with risks, implementation challenges, and contingencies, which is the essence of managerial control toward desired results.
- **Simplicity and adaptability.** Management controls must be simple. Their purpose is to identify problems early and to take corrective actions. Good controls produce a quick reaction to potential problems. They have a feedback mechanism. They also have some built-in automatic problem detection system that provides early warnings and adapts dynamically to changing situations and emerging problems. Examples of such in-process controls are *process action teams* and *rapid prototyping*. Further, *Stage-Gate®* and *agile/scrum*-based processes have this kind of adaptability to some degree built into their systems.
- **Early problem detection.** Controls should focus on problem prevention and early detection. Direct management involvement and review meetings are more likely to have this desired focus than reports that

concentrate more on the documentation and analysis of the problem, rather than its resolution.

- **Controlling authority.** Management controls should be in the hands of the people who are accountable for results. As we move up the organization, senior management is responsible for more general business results, and therefore should provide more guidance and support rather than micromanagement.

12.5 RECOMMENDATIONS FOR USING PROJECT CONTROLS EFFECTIVELY

The pressures for improving business performance, combined with the emergence of new tools and techniques that promise more effective project control, have prompted management to cautiously shift their focus away from operational processes that narrowly emphasize schedule/budget performance measures.

To be successful in implementing managerial controls, business leaders must pay attention to three important criteria that are often overlooked: First, tools and techniques must be properly integrated with the business process. Second, the impact on intrinsic project performance must be considered. That is, the impact of a control process on innovation, creativity, quality, customer relations, and the ability to cope with changing requirements must be evaluated and the tools fine-tuned to minimize undesired side effects. Third, the human side of managerial control must be carefully considered. Especially when introducing *new* managerial controls, as minor as a new weekly review procedure or as massive as changing to concurrent engineering, involves organizational change, a process that is often poorly managed or outright ignored.

Any new requirement for project tracking or control is associated with hopes, fears, anxieties, likes and dislikes, plus a good dose of organizational politics. One of the strongest messages from field research points at the fact that people are still the most vital part of any managerial control system. A new system has a chance for consideration if the project team believes in the value of the tool for making their job easier and more effective, helping to produce desired results, visibility, and recognition, while minimizing anxieties and fears over administrative burden, restrictions of freedom and autonomy, and any negative impact on personal growth and security. Unfortunately, research shows that few companies have systematically attacked these softer, more subtle issues of project control and tool implementation, which are crucial for overall business performance, especially in technology-based environments. These issues often need special attention and resources to ensure effective integration of these tools into the business process and effective use by project team members.

A number of recommendations for effective implementation and use of managerial controls for technical projects are summarized. The focus of this section is on the *use* of managerial controls, both for existing systems and for the introduction of new tools. The discussion will be expanded in future chapters to explore the people side of controlling technology-based projects. For this section, the focus is on the tools. These suggestions are based on several decades of field research and observation of project management practices. They should help both project leaders and their managers to understand the complex interaction of organizational and behavioral variables involved in the control of technology-based projects and the implementation of appropriate managerial tools and techniques. The findings should increase the awareness of what works and what doesn't, and help to fine-tune project management systems toward high performance. Finally, the findings should also help management scholars who study these concepts to better understand the complexity and dynamics of project control, and to obtain ideas for further research. The recommendations for controlling technology-intensive work are summarized as follows:

- **Involve the team.** Make your people part of the tool selection and implementation process. Both project team and the project manager should be involved in assessing the project situation and evaluating new control tools. Critical factor analysis, focus groups, and process action teams are good vehicles for such team involvement and collective decision making. These actions lead to ownership, greater acceptance of the selected tool, and a willingness to work toward continuous improvement and effective use.
- **Make tools consistent with the work process.** Management controls should be an integral part of the business process. Particular attention should be paid to the workability of the tools and techniques for integrating tasks and transferring technology across organizational lines.
- **Build on existing tools and systems.** The highest levels of acceptance and success are found in areas where new management tools are added incrementally to already existing control systems. These situations should be identified and addressed first.
- **Connect with established management practices.** Team members feel more comfortable with management procedures that they have familiarity with and can relate to their work. To minimize anxieties, suspicions, and the risk of rejection, management should refer to established project management practices when introducing new tools or techniques. For example, an organization implementing a Stage-Gate process should make an effort to integrate it into the process already established and proven procedures for project definition, documentation, status reports, reviews, and sign-offs. This will make the new management process look evolutionary rather than like a radical change. Thus, if done right, management can use the existing project management system to build on, and incrementally enhance and test, new managerial tools and techniques.

- **Make tools user-friendly.** New project management tools or techniques are more likely to be accepted if they are easy to use and produce results that are helpful to the users and their work, who include the organization's senior management.
- **Anticipate anxieties and conflicts.** Especially when introducing new tools and techniques (e.g., a new concurrent engineering system discussed in Chapter 4), project leaders should anticipate anxieties and conflict among their team members. These negative biases come from uncertainties associated with new working conditions and requirements. They range from personal discomfort with skill requirements to anxieties over the impact of the tool on the work process and personal performance evaluation. These problems should be anticipated and dealt with in a straightforward manner as early as possible.
- **Ensure that there is no threat.** Management must foster a project team environment of mutual trust and cooperation, an environment that is low on personal conflict, power struggles, surprises, unrealistic demands, and threats to personal and professional integrity. Cooperation with a new (or existing) tool or technique, and commitment to it, can be expected only if its use is relatively risk-free to the user. Unnecessary references to performance appraisals, tight supervision, reduced personal freedom and autonomy, and overhead requirements should be avoided, and any concerns dealt with promptly on a personal level.
- **Foster challenging work environment.** Professionally interesting and stimulating work appears to be one of the strongest drivers toward desired results. Verified by several field studies, we find consistently that the degree of interest and excitement derived from work is directly related to personal effort, the level of team involvement, cross-functional communication, commitment toward established plans, and creativity. Work challenge also produces higher levels of cooperation and some tolerance for risk and conflict. Taken together, work challenge seems to foster a desired behavior conducive to exploring new methods and innovatively applying them to project situations. Further, people who are strongly engaged with their work have a more positive attitude toward change. Therefore, work challenge seems to be a catalyst for integrating team members' personal goals with project objectives and organizational goals. All of this fosters a favorable climate toward acceptance and effective use of managerial controls. Project leaders should try to accommodate the professional interests and desires of their personnel whenever possible. One of the best ways to ensure that the work is interesting to team members is to match carefully their personal interests with the scope and needs of the tasks when "signing on" team personnel. In addition, managers should build a project image of importance and high visibility, which can elevate the desirability of participation and contribution.
- **Pretest new tools and techniques.** Preferably, new concept should be tried first with a small project and an experienced, high-performance

project team. Asking such a team to test, evaluate, and fine-tune the new tool for the company is often seen as an honor and professional challenge. Further, it usually starts the implementation with a positive attitude and can create an environment of open communications and candor.

- **Continuous improvement.** Project management tools and techniques are part of the continuously changing business process. Provisions must be made for updating and fine-tuning these tools on an ongoing basis to ensure relevancy to today's project management challenges.
- **Senior management support.** Management tools require top-down support to succeed. Through its involvement and communications, management can stress the importance of these tools to the organization, span organizational and cultural boundaries, and unify objectives.
- **Ensure proper direction and leadership.** Throughout the implementation phase of a new management tool or technique, managers can influence the attitude and commitment of their people toward a new concept by their own actions. Concern for project team members, assistance with the use of the tool, and enthusiasm for the project and its administrative support systems can foster a climate of high motivation, involvement with the project and its management, open communications, and willingness to cooperate with the new requirements and ability to use them effectively.

12.6 CONCLUSION

The proper implementation and use of an effective project management control system, including its tools and techniques, can critically determine the success of any project, especially for technology-based undertakings. Successful application of these management controls involves a complex set of variables. The tools must be consistent with the work process and be an integrated part of the existing managerial control and personal reward system. Most importantly, managers must pay attention to human factors. To enhance cooperation with the evaluation, implementation, and effective use of project management controls, management and team leaders must foster a work environment where people find the controls useful, or at least not threatening or interfering with the work process. Further, professionally stimulating work, refueled by visibility and recognition, is conducive to change and cooperation. Such a professionally stimulating environment seems to lower anxieties over managerial controls, reduce communications barriers and conflict, and enhance the desire of personnel to cooperate and to succeed. It also seems to enhance organizational awareness of the surrounding business environment and the ability to prepare and respond to these challenges effectively by using modern project management techniques. Further, effective use of modern project control techniques requires administrative skills for planning and defining project efforts properly and realistically, as a prerequisite for tracking the project through its life cycle. Effective project leaders understand the interaction of organizational and behavioral variables and can foster a climate of active participation and minimal dysfunctional conflict. They also build alliances with support organizations and upper management to ensure organizational visibility, priority, resource availability, and overall support for the multifunctional activities of the project throughout its life cycle.

In the decades ahead, the ability to effectively manage complex projects, for both internal and external clients, will play a critical role in separating winning companies from losers. Largely because of new technology in computers and communications, project management tools are expected to further proliferate and connect even more broadly across the enterprise. The sophistication and effectiveness with which these tools are used will profoundly influence the way companies (1) do business, (2) utilize resources, (3) handle project complexity, (4) achieve quality, and (5) respond to market requirements with speed and accuracy. These challenges will be true for any enterprise, but they will be especially amplified in technology-intensive business environments.

12.7 SUMMARY OF KEY POINTS AND CONCLUSIONS

The following key points were made in this chapter:

- Managerial control is the process of implementing a plan and reaching its objectives, in spite of changing conditions.
- Effective controls have some common characteristics such as: (1) realistic plans, (2) commitment, (3) competence, (4) measurability, (5) meaningful tracking systems, (6) focus on key objectives, (7) simplicity and adaptability, (8) early problem detection, and (9) controlling authority.
- New organizational forms, such as concurrent engineering, special processes, and self-directed teams, have emerged, gradually replacing traditional, more hierarchically structured organizations and their linear work processes.
- Today's technology projects rely to a considerable extent on member-generated performance norms and evaluations, rather than hierarchical guidelines, policies, and procedures.
- Traditional management tools (e.g., schedules and budgets), designed largely for top-down centralized command, control, and communications, by themselves, are no longer sufficient for managing projects effectively, but need to be augmented with tools that can better deal with the dynamics of our business environment, including risks and changes.
- New project management techniques are often more integrated with the business process, offering more sophisticated capabilities for project tracking and control.
- Driven by business pressures and advances in information technology, many companies have invested heavily in new management tools and

techniques, promising more effective alternatives and enhancements to traditional forms of project control.

- One of the greatest challenges for management is to seek out tools and techniques that meet the three key conditions: (1) compatible with the business environment, processes, culture and values, (2) conducive to specific problem solving, and (3) useful for tackling and controlling the project according to established plans.
- Project control has radically departed from its narrow focus of satisfying schedule and budget constraints, shifting to a much broader and more balanced managerial approach that focuses on the effective search for solutions to complex problems.
- Project management tools are underutilized because of insufficient familiarity on the part of project leaders.
- Project control must be congruent with the business process and the human side of management to work effectively.
- Field research consistently emphasizes the importance of organizational and cultural factors for managerial control, including mutual trust, respect, candor, risk sharing, and the ability to fail safely.
- Self-forcing or self-directed control uses work challenge, personal pride, and commitment as motivators for team self-governance and accountability.
- Project control requires work processes with effective communication channels and cross-functional linkages, interconnecting people, activities, and support functions.
- Few companies go into a major restructuring of their business processes lightly. At best, the introduction of a new project control technique is painful, costly, and disruptive to ongoing operations. At worst, it can destroy existing managerial controls.
- The reasons for underusing or rejecting project controls can be divided into four classes: (1) lack of confidence that tools will produce benefits, (2) anxieties over potentially harmful side effects, (3) conflict among users over method or results, and (4) concern that the method is too difficult or interferes with the work process.
- People are still the most vital part of any managerial control system.
- Effective project leaders understand the interaction of organizational and behavioral variables and can foster a climate of active participation and minimal dysfunctional conflict.

12.8 QUESTIONS FOR DISCUSSION

1. Why is it so difficult to control technology-intensive activities and projects according to established plans? What is different from low-technology projects?
2. Define a very basic (minimal) control system for managing high-technology projects.

3. Why can a narrow focus on budget and schedule parameters be counterproductive to project performance, especially in high-tech work environments?

4. How does a professionally stimulating work environment enhance team self-direction and project control?

5. Discuss the organizational environment and management style most conducive to self-controlled teamwork.

6. What conditions in the work environment are most conducive to personal commitment to project goals and objectives?

7. Define some guidelines for an R&D team for "self-managing" a one-year project.

8. Why are project team members often reluctant to cooperate with a new project control technique, such as a new method for budget or schedule tracking?

9. Discuss the challenges of implementing a new gate review process for a given work environment (select a work environment that you know or can identify with). Could you build on existing tools and make the process congruent with the "old" work environment?

10. How can you make a process for budget or schedule tracking more user-friendly? What issues (barriers) can you identify that cause anxieties, conflict or interference with the work process? What can you suggest to remove these barriers?

11. Discuss risk sharing. What does risk sharing among members of a new product development team mean? How can you encourage risk sharing among these team members?

12. Discuss methods for pretesting of a new design review process.

13. Discuss ways to encourage and engage team members to make continuous improvements in their project tracking and control system.

12.9 *PMBOK®* REFERENCES AND CONNECTIONS

The topic of project monitoring and controlling connects directly with the fourth PMBOK process group of the same name. The topic cuts across virtually all of the *10 knowledge areas*. However, it connects most strongly with *project integration management* (area #1), *project time management* (area #3), *project cost management* (area #4), *project communications management* (area #7), and *project stakeholder management* (area #10) as defined by PMBOK. Although this chapter is consistent with the PMBOK Guide, much of the discussion on tools and methods of project control go beyond the content of PMBOK. Yet, in terms of context it relates strongly to the *five knowledge areas* and directly to the *process group of monitoring and controlling*. That is the way projects are monitored, tracked, and controlled. Communication issues (knowledge area #7) are a strong focus in all discussions. In studying for the PMP® exam, an understanding of the following concepts will be beneficial and is supported by this chapter: (1) monitoring and controlling project work, (2) collecting performance data, (3) performance reporting, and (4) cost, and schedule tracking.

INTERNET LINKS AND RESOURCES

CH2M HILL Company, "Prairie Waters Project at CH2M HILL Company," www
.ch2m.com/corporate/services/program-management/water/prairie-waters.asp
PMI Knowledge Center, www.pmi.org/Knowledge-Center.aspx
Wikipedia. "Project Management," http://en.wikipedia.org/wiki/Project_management

REFERENCES AND ADDITIONAL READINGS

Allen, K. 2011. "PMI 2011 Project of the Year." *Pmnetwork* 25(11) (November): 26–31.

Andler, N. 2011. *Tools for Project Management, Workshops and Consulting*. Erlangen, Germany: Publicis Publishing.

Archibald, R. 2003. *Managing High-Technology Programs and Projects*. Hoboken, NJ: John Wiley & Sons.

Davenport, T 1998. "Putting the Enterprise into the Enterprise System," *Harvard Business Review* 76(4) (July–August): 121–131.

Doolan, T., and M. Hacker. 2003. "The Importance of Situating Culture in Cross-Cultural IT Management." *IEEE Transactions on Engineering Management* 50(3) (August): 285–296.

Dvir, D., S. Lipovetsky, A. Shenhar, and A. Tishler. 2003. "What Is Really Important for Project Success? A Refined, Multivariate, Comprehensive Analysis." *International Journal of Management and Decision Making* 4(4): 382–404.

Dvir, D., and A. Shenhar. 2011. "What Great Projects Have in Common." *MIT Sloan Management Review* 52(3): 19–21.

Gido, J., and J. P. Clements. 2012. "Initiating a Project." Part 1 in *Successful Project Management*. Mason, OH: South-Western Cengage Learning.

Kerzner, H. 2011. "The Changing Landscape for Project Management." Chapter 1 in *Project Management Metrics, KPIs, and Dashboards: A Guide to Measuring and Monitoring Project Performance*. New York: International Institute of Learning (IIL).

Kloppenborg, T.J. 2012. "Planning Projects." Part 2 in *Contemporary Project Management*. Mason, OH: South-Western Cengage Learning.

Learnard, C., and M. Maguire Kelly. 2011. "Prairie Waters Project Receives Project Management Institute's Prestigious 2011 PMI Project of the Year Award." PMI Press Release, October 24, 2011.

Lewis, J. 2011. *Project Planning, Scheduling, and Control: The Ultimate Hands-On Guide to Bringing Projects in On Time and On Budget*. New York: McGraw Hill.

Maltz, A., A. Shenhar, and R. Reilly. 2003. "Beyond the Balanced Scorecard: Refining the Search for Organizational Success Measures." *Long Range Planning* 36(2): 185–201.

McDonough, E., and R, Leifer. 1986. "Effective Control of New Product Projects: The Interaction of Organizational Culture and Project Leadership." *Journal of Product Innovation Management* 3(2): 149–157.

Milosevic, D. 2003. *Project Management ToolBox: Tools and Techniques for the Practicing Project Manager*. Hoboken, NJ: John Wiley & Sons.

Milosevic, D. Z., and S. Srivannaboon. 2006. "A Theoretical Framework for Aligning Project Management with Business Strategy." *Project Management Journal* 37(3): 98–110.

Patanakul, P., B. Iewwongcharoen, and D. Milosevic. 2010. "An Empirical Study on the Use of Project Management Tools and Techniques Across Project Life-Cycle and Their Impact on Project Success." *Journal of General Management* 35(3): 41–65.

Project Management Institute. 2013. *A Guide to the Project Management Body of Knowledge (PMBOK® Guide)*. Newtown Square, PA: Project Management Institute.

Randolph, W. and B. Posner. 1988. "What Every Manager Needs to Know About Project Management." *Sloan Management Review* 29(4) (Summer): 65–73.

Shenhar, A., and D. Dvir. 2007. *Reinventing Project Management: The Diamond Approach to Successful Growth and Innovation*. Cambridge, MA: Harvard Business School Press.

Shenhar, A., D. Dvir, D. Milosevic, J. Mulenburg, P. Patanakul, R. Reilly, M. Ryan, A. Sage, B. Sauser, S. Srivannaboon, J. Stefanovic, and H. Thamhain. 2005. "Toward a NASA-specific Project Management Framework." *Engineering Management Journal* 17(4) (December): 8–16.

Shenhar A., D. Milosevic, D. Dvir, and H. Thamhain. 2007. *Linking Project Management to Business Strategy*. Newtown, PA: Project Management Institute (PMI) Press.

Schultz, R., D. Slevin, and J. Pinto. 1987. "Strategy and Tactics in a Process Model of Project Implementation." *Interfaces* 3(3) (May–June): 34–46.

Thamhain, H. 1996. "Applying Stage-Gate Reviews to Accelerated Product Developments." Proceedings, *PMI-'96 Annual Symposium of the Project Management Institute*, Boston, MA, October 4–10.

———. 1996. "Best Practices for Controlling Technology-based Projects." *Project Management Journal* 27(4) (December): 37–48.

———. 2005. *Management of Technology*. Hoboken, NJ: John Wiley & Sons.

———. 2011. "Critical Success Factors for Managing Technology-Intensive Teams In the Global Enterprise." *Engineering Management Journal* 23(3) (September): 30-36.

———. 2013a. "Changing Dynamics of Team Leadership in Global Project Environments." *American Journal of Industrial and Business Management* 2013(3) (April): 146–156.

———. 2013b. "The Role of Commitment for Managing Complex Multinational Projects." *International Journal of Innovation and Technology Management* 12(3) (May).

Thamhain, H., and I. Kruglianskas. 2000. "Managing Technology-Based Projects in Multinational Environments." *IEEE Transactions on Engineering Management* 47(1) (February): 55–64.

Weisinger, J., and E. Traut. 2003. "The Impact on Organizational Context on Work Team Effectiveness." *IEEE Transactions on Engineering Management* 50(1) (February): 26–30.

12.10 APPENDIX: MANAGEMENT TECHNIQUES FOR PROJECT CONTROL

Part I: Analytical Management Techniques for Project Control

Action item/Report: A memo or report defining specific action items agreed upon with the resolver, necessary to move the project forward or to correct a deficiency.

Elements of control:

- Responsibility identification
- Personal commitment
- Peer pressure

Prerequisites and conditions:

- Individual commitment
- Management support
- Incentives

Computer software: Computer software to support project planning, tracking and control. Provides various reports of project status and performance analysis, and documentation.

Elements of control:

- Schedule
- Budget
- PERT/CPM
- Resource leveling
- Scheduling
- $/t tradeoff

Prerequisites and conditions:

- Ability to measure status
- Valid input data
- Willingness to correct deviations
- Leadership

Critical path analysis: Analysis of the longest paths within a network schedule with the objective of (1) determining the impact of task delays, problems, contingencies and organizational dependencies, (2) finding solutions, and (3) optimizing schedule performance.

Elements of control:

- Schedule
- Budget
- Deliverables
- Cost-time tradeoff

Prerequisites and conditions:

- Accurate estimates of effort, cost, and duration.

Budget tracking: Analysis of planned versus actual budget expenditures relative to work performed. The objective is to detect and correct project performance problems and to deal with projected cost variances in there early developments.

Elements of control:

- Cost
- Budget
- Deliverables
- Project status

Prerequisites and conditions:

- Accurate estimates of effort, cost, and duration

Deficiency report: Description of an emerging deficiency (work, timing, or budget), including impact analysis and recommended resolution.

Elements of control:

- Schedule
- Costs
- Configuration management
- Impact analysis

Prerequisites and conditions:

- Candor
- Commitment to plan
- Management direction

Earned value analysis: Comparison of project completion status to budget expenditure. The regular calculation and analysis of earned value and performance index allows projections of cost variances and schedule slips and serves as an early warning system of project performance problems.

Elements of control:

- Schedule
- Budget
- Deliverables
- Cost-time tradeoff

Prerequisites and conditions:

- Measurable milestones
- Ability to estimate cost and time-to-complete
- Trust
- Risk sharing
- Ownership

Interface chart: A chart of N × N elements defining the inputs, outputs, and timing to and from N interfacing work groups. Chart can also be used as part of QFD to define and manage the "customers" of the business process.

Elements of control:

- Task leaders
- Cross-functional communications
- QFD framework

Prerequisites and conditions:

- Established cross-functional linkages
- Management support and leadership

PERT/CPM: Time-activity network showing task flow, interfaces and dependencies. Used for comprehensive analysis of project schedules and schedule changes.

Elements of control:

- Schedule
- Budget
- Deliverables
- Cost-time tradeoff

Prerequisites and conditions:

- Accurate cost, time, and technical performance data
- Measurable milestones

Schedule compression analysis: Graphical technique for showing compression of overlapping activities due to slippage of earlier or preceding milestones. Serves as early warning system for runaway schedules and costs.

Elements of control:

- Milestones
- Deliverables

Prerequisites and conditions:

- Accurate cost, time, and technical performance data
- Measurable milestones

Schedule tracking: Incremental tracking of activities through time by measuring predefined partial results against plan.

Elements of control:

- Measurable milestone
- Deliverables
- Micro schedule

Prerequisites and conditions:

- Accurate cost, time, and technical performance data

Simulation: Simulation of a technical, business, or project situation based on some form of a model. Applications range from a simple test to computer assisted analysis of complex business scenarios.

Elements of control:

- Advanced results
- Feasibility
- Technology transfer

Prerequisites and conditions:

- Relevant input data and appropriate model
- Meaningful interpretation

Status assessment: Systematic comparison of technical progress with project schedule and budget data. Analysis of status against plan and possible revision of plan, scope, and business strategy.

Elements of control:

- Valid project plan
- Review process
- Earned value
- Variance analysis

Prerequisites and conditions:

- Accurate cost, time, and technical performance data
- Measurable milestones

Variance analysis: Analysis of causes of cost and schedule variances, cost-at-completion, earned value, percent of project completion and performance index. Applied to project status assessment, reporting, and control.

Elements of control:

- Schedule
- Costs
- Configuration management
- Impact analysis
- Management

Prerequisites and conditions:

- Accurate cost, time, and technical performance data
- Measurable milestones

Part II: Process-Oriented Techniques for Project Control

Agile/Scrum: Project execution in highly flexible and interactive manner (in opposite to traditional pm processes, such as "waterfall") providing regular adaptation to changing circumstances.

Elements of control:

- Sustainable development
- Constant pace
- Cooperation among stakeholders
- Negotiations
- Guidelines/method: Agile Manifesto

Prerequisites and conditions:

- Suitable project and environment
- Self-managed motivated teams
- Customer collaboration,
- Management engagement

Benchmarking: Comparing one system, process or practice to another one (usually best-in-class) with the objective to improve performance.

Elements of control:

- Performance metrics
- Business process

Prerequisites and conditions:

- Measurability of comparative metrics
- Ability to diagnose/analyze the cause of differences
- Ability to adopt tool or method

Concurrent engineering: In-parallel/concurrent execution of project phases; "seamless product development." Objectives: reducing project cost and cycle time, increasing responsiveness to customer/market dynamics. Also, an effective tool for multifunctional integration and technology transfer.

Elements of control:

- Input–output definition
- Interface definition
- QFD concepts
- Rapid prototyping
- Structured analysis

Prerequisites and conditions:

- Org interface agreement
- Personal commitment
- Effective communications and organizational linkages

Design review: Review of the project baseline at various stages of development, such as preliminary, critical or final design review. Objective: Examine and predict functionality of the deliverable system early in the project cycle.

Elements of control:

- Baseline
- Design parameters
- Documentation
- Multifunctional reviewers
- Agenda

Prerequisites and conditions:

- Multidisciplinary preparation and participations
- Competence
- Senior management involvement

Out-of-bounds review: Critical review and impact assessment of a situation declared as *out-of-bounds*.

Elements of control:

- Review
- Analysis
- Corrective action plan
- Visibility
- Peer pressure
- Management control

Prerequisites and conditions:

- Mutual trust and respect among team members
- Power sharing among managers and with team

Project definition: Front-end planning of a project and its resource and timing requirements. Objective: project definition/organization, task delegation, project tracking and control:

Elements of control:

- Schedule
- Budget
- Task roster
- Task matrix
- Statement of work
- Task authorization
- Resource leveling

Prerequisites and conditions:

- Team involvement
- Desire to participate
- Risk and power sharing
- Senior management involvement and support

Project review: Technical and contractual review of project status against established plans.

Elements of control:

- Professional review
- C/SCSC
- PERT/CPM
- Variance analysis

Prerequisites and conditions:

- Team involvement
- Risk and power sharing among managers and with team
- Senior management involvement

Prototyping: Advanced build of a design for the purpose of testing functionality and performance prior to production or deployment.

Elements of control:

- Design process
- Simulation
- CAD/CAM
- Project management

Prerequisites and conditions:

- Relevant baseline
- Effective prototype testing and evaluation

Quality function deployment (QFD): TQM concept, known as house of quality. Used for mapping the technology transfer flow throughout an organization and its markets, identifying for each organizational unit: inputs, outputs and specific "internal customers" and their requirements.

Elements of control:

- Organizational interface and input–output definition
- Internal and external customer focus

Prerequisites and conditions:

- Team involvement
- Desire to participate
- Risk sharing and power sharing among managers and with team
- Senior management involvement and support

Rapid prototyping: Quick fabrication of a physical part or assembly, using *solid free-form manufacturing techniques*, such as stereolithography or 3-D printing, using CAD data. In project management, rapid prototyping often refers any method of "quick prototype" for testing and concept validation.

Elements of control:

- Tangible model
- Measurements
- Early testing
- Validation of specs
- Early design validation

Prerequisites and conditions:

- Available digitized design
- Available method or process for rapid prototyping
- Acceptability of results

Requirements analysis: Distinct project planning phase that defines the specific technical, resource, market and timing requirements for the project baseline. Often coupled with voice of the customer and strategic assessment.

Elements of control:

- Needs assessment
- Voice of the customer
- Project planning

Prerequisites and conditions:

- Team involvement
- Customer and management participation
- Risk and power sharing among managers and with team

Stage-Gate® process: Phased approach to project planning and management. Defines "gates" for consecutive stages that check the feasibility, and provide implementation focus and control.

Elements of control:

- Phased planning
- Modular work plan
- Deliverables
- Check points
- Sign-offs
- Gate reviews

Prerequisites and conditions:

- Org interface agreement
- Personal commitment
- Effective cross-functional communications
- Management involvement

Stage-Gate® review: Specific review at the end of a project stage with deliverables and checkpoints, predefined as part of the stage-gate process. Can incorporate other project or design reviews.

Elements of control:

- Stage-Gate® Process
- Focus groups
- Multidisciplinary teams
- Management

Prerequisites and conditions:

- Cross-functional collaboration, commitment
- Management participation

Voice of the customer: Distinct project planning phase that defines the specific technical, resource, market and timing requirements for the project baseline, with focus on the specific customer needs.

Elements of control:

- Needs assessment
- Market analysis
- Focus group
- Survey
- Customer feedback

Prerequisites and conditions:

- Team involvement
- Customer and management participation
- Risk and power sharing among managers and with team

Part III: People-Oriented Management Techniques for Project Control

Core team: A team of resource managers responsible for planning, organization and execution of many projects of a similar nature.

Elements of control:

- Dedicated functional management team
- Minimum cross-functional impedance

Design/build: Typically used in product development projects, new team members are integrated into the project team as it moves from the product design to the product build stages, while retaining key members from the earlier project stages. The term design/build is also used for concurrent design-build processes, similar to rapid prototyping.

Elements of control:

- Shared multifunctional experience
- Project/team ownership
- High technical competence of team

Focus group: A group of stakeholders within a project organization or its support functions, engaging in self-study and analysis of the project management system or the business process with the objective to improve it.

Elements of control:

- Problem ownership
- Pride

- Personal/professional needs
- Will to change status quo

Joint performance evaluation: Both project performance and individual performance are defined in terms of end-objectives, hence including multifunctional measures. The objective is to enhance cross-functional cooperation and team integration.

Elements of control:

- Stakeholder/ownership
- Mutual dependency

- Risk sharing.
- Internal customer orientation

Self-directed team: Individual team members and the project teams as a whole are given high levels of autonomy and accountability (empowerment) toward plan implementation. This forces higher degrees of multidisciplinary decision making and work integration at the operational level.

Elements of control:

- Stakeholder/ownership
- Mutual dependency
- Risk sharing

- Personal commitment and drive
- Team communication and collective decision making

Prerequisites and conditions for all Part III techniques:

- Proper team design and charter
- Effective communication channel, internal and external
- Competent team members and desire to participate
- Risk sharing and power sharing among managers and within team
- Autonomy
- Senior management involvement and support
- Effective conflict management system
- Team-based evaluations and awards
- Minimum fear
- Reasonable job security
- Managerial checks and balances
- Team leadership

Chapter 13

Concurrent Engineering and Other Project Management Systems

THE PENTAGON RECONSTRUCTION PROJECT

When hijacked American Airlines flight 77 slammed in the west face of the Pentagon on September 11, 2001, over 400,000 square feet of office space was destroyed, together with the communications, command, and control technology infrastructure, and an additional 1.6 million square feet of working facilities was damaged. The very same day, project "Phoenix" was formed with the mission of reconstructing the west face of the Pentagon. "Without any preplanning, budgets, or contract approvals; it was an unconventional start of an extraordinary project" says former Phoenix Deputy Program Manager Mike Sullivan. The primary constraint for the completion of this project was a one-year deadline requested by the U.S. government. Fortunately for the Phoenix Project, the nearly completed Wedge 1 Project (part of the 20-year Pentagon Renovation Program, PenRen), was still active. On the very day of the attack, resources from PenRen were quickly reallocated to form the Phoenix integrated project team (IPT). "With all of the stakeholders around the table," says Clark Sheakley, a client liaison with General Dynamics, "it was possible to create and update plans on the fly and to keep everyone informed." The schedule and other parts of the project plan were very informal during the first month after the attack. Virtually overnight the budget to reconstruct the Pentagon was estimated, based on historic cost data from the ongoing PenRen Project, and submitted to the US Congress, which authorized $700 million in emergency funds. Once the Federal Bureau of Investigation released the site, the project plan went through a more formal development.

The project's tight schedule led to concurrent scope and plan development in parallel to project execution. "Before plans are finalized or even in draft form,

---

Background and additional information on this project can be found at The National 9/11 Pentagon Memorial website, "The Phoenix Project," and articles by Natalie Bauer (2004) and Linda Kozaryn (2002).

the project was already under way," says Sheakley. To accelerate the schedule, an "ultra-fast-track schedule" was developed. For example, reconstruction was divided into three horizontal stages. The structure of the three outer rings of the building complex were sequenced independently, allowing early installation of the limestone façade, main electric and communication vaults, and mechanical and roofing systems, concurrently. In addition, smaller sections of concrete were poured so that crews could work simultaneously, rotating through each of the construction sequences rather than waiting for an entire floor to be completed before sending in the subsequent crew.

Due to the fast pace of the project, keeping the schedule current was difficult. Many times it served more as a benchmark than a primary guide. "At times, the schedule could not keep up with the work because it was so far ahead," says Sullivan.

Yet another dimension of the fast-track process included the procurement plan. The Government Program Office was exempt from systems integration responsibilities. Contractors were fully responsible for the integration of systems, subsystems, equipment, and support equipment, and they had to validate full system performance after integration. This approach decreased implementation time, increased product quality, and reduced engineering changes, program office staff, and overall project cost. "It was a challenge to manage all the resources at any specific point in the project, given the number of resources," Sullivan says. "But, the bottom line is that you hire good people, and you let them do their jobs."

The *design-build approach* adopted here allowed design and construction to operate as a single entity under one contract, contrasting with the standard government approach of design-bid-build, which can create startup delays and conflict between contractors and owners.

Taken together, the 3,000-member project team completed the demolition and reconstruction of the damaged west face section of the Pentagon 28 days ahead of schedule and $194 million under budget. The Phoenix management team says that success comes down to two central elements: people and procedure. Project management molded the team into a tangible process conducive to optimum utilization of all available resources. According to Deputy Program Manager Mike Sullivan, "The lesson is that if you get a bunch of people who are dedicated and committed to achieve a clearly defined goal, within a well-defined work process, you can accomplish almost anything!"

13.1 THE NEED FOR EFFECTIVE PROJECT MANAGEMENT PROCESSES

Not every project is as urgent and time-critical as the reconstruction of the nation's center of defense. Yet, many enterprise missions are under similar pressure to perform against end-date-driven schedules. They bear the same necessity for accelerating project execution, utilizing resources effectively, and minimizing implementation risks. The message is clear, virtually every organization in our fiercely competitive business environment is under pressure to do more things faster, better, and cheaper. Speed has become one of the great equalizers in competitiveness and is a key performance measure. New technologies, especially in computers and communications, have removed many of the protective barriers to business, creating enormous opportunities and challenges, and transformed our global economy into a hypercompetitive enterprise system. To survive and prosper, the new breed of business leaders must deal effectively with time-to-market pressures, innovation, cost, and risks in an increasingly fast-changing global business environment. Concurrent engineering has gradually become the norm for developing and introducing new products, systems, and services (Dourado and Silva 2011, Haque et al. 2003). It is also the basis for a wide spectrum of contemporary management systems, ranging from *Stage-Gate®* to agile.

13.1.1 Moving toward Concurrent Execution

Whether we look at the implementation of a new product, process, or service, or we want to rebuild the Pentagon, create a new movie, or win a campaign, reducing project cycle time translates most likely into cost savings, risk reduction, market advantages, and strategic benefits. Bottom line: *"Time is money,"* to paraphrase Benjamin Franklin.

Project management has traditionally provided the tools and techniques for executing specific missions, on time and resource efficiently. These tools and techniques have been around since the dawn of civilization, leading to impressive results ranging from Noah's Ark and the ancient pyramids, and military campaigns to the Brooklyn Bridge and Ford's Model-T automobile. While the first formal project management processes emerged during the Industrial Revolution of the eighteenth century, with focus on mass production, agriculture, construction, and military operations, the recognition of project management as a business discipline and profession did not occur until the 1950s, with the emergence of formal organizational concepts such as the matrix, projectized organizations, life cycles and phased approaches (Morris 1997).

These concepts established the organizational framework for many of the project-oriented management systems in use today, providing a platform for delivering mission-specific results. Beginning in the 1980s, dramatic changes in the business environment required that the process of project management be reengineered to deal effectively with new challenges (Denker et al. 2001; Nee and Ong 2001; Rigby 1995; Thamhain 2002) and to balance efficiency, speed, and quality (Atuahene-Gima 2003). As a result, many new project management tools and delivery systems evolved under the umbrella of *integrated product development (IPD)*. These systems, however, are not just limited to product development, but can be found in a wide spectrum of modern projects, ranging from construction to research, foreign assistance programs, election campaigns, and IT systems installation (Koufteros et al. 2000; Nellore and Balachandra 2001). The focus that all of these IPD applications have in common is the effective, integrated, and often-concurrent multidisciplinary project team effort toward specific deliverables, the very essence of concurrent engineering processes.

13.2 A SPECTRUM OF CONTEMPORARY MANAGEMENT SYSTEMS

Driven by the need for effective multidisciplinary integration and the associated economic benefits, many contemporary project execution methods have evolved akin to both *integrated product development (IPD)* and *concurrent engineering (CE)*. These methods often focus on specific project environments such as manufacturing, marketing, software development, or field services (Gerwin and Barrowman 2002). As a result, many mission-specific project management platforms emerged under what is today characterized as the IPD umbrella, long before IPD had been recognized as a formal concept. These well-established platforms include systems such as *design for manufacture (DMF), just-in-time (JIT), continuous process improvement (CPI), integrated product and process development (IPPD), structured systems design (SSD), rolling wave (RW) concept* (see Githens 1998), *phased-developments (PD), Stage-Gate® processes* (see Cooper 2008), *integrated phase-reviews (IPR)*, and *voice-of-the-customer (VOC)*, just to name a few of the more popular concepts. Other contemporary project management concepts, such as *agile/scrum* (Beck 2001), spiral processes (Boehm 1988; Muench 1994), and *extreme project management (XPM)* (DeCarlo 2004), rely at least in part on the same concept of flexible, concurrent execution of overlapping processes.

Many of these concepts have a specific application focus or managerial philosophy. However, what all of these systems have in common, is the emphasis on effective cross-functional integration and incremental, iterative implementation of project plans with emphasis on strong human interaction and collaboration. For the remainder of this chapter, I will use the terms *concurrent engineering (CE)* and *integrated product development (IPD)* to refer to the broader spectrum of concurrent management processes used in contemporary project management.

13.2.1 Concurrent Engineering—A Unique Project Management Concept

Concurrent engineering, CE, is an extension of the multiphased approach to project management. Although the concept gained formal recognition only during the 1980s, its roots go back to the era of early industrialization at the end of the nineteenth century (Smith 1997). At the heart of its concept is the concurrent execution of tasks segments, which creates overlap and interaction among the various project teams. It also increases the need for strong cross-functional cooperation, integration and team involvement, which creates both managerial benefits and challenges (Wu, Fuh, and Nee 2002).

Although *concurrent engineering* was originally seen as a method for primarily reducing project cycle time and accelerating product development (Prasad 2003, Smith 1997), today, the concept refers quite generally to the many resource- and time-efficient execution of multidisciplinary undertakings. Moreover, the CE concept has been expanded from its original engineering focus on a wide spectrum of projects, ranging from construction and field installations to medical procedures, theater productions, and financial services (Haas and Sinha 2004; Pham, Dimov, and Setchi 1999; Pilkinton and Dyerson 2002; Prasad and Rao 2004). The operational and strategic values of concurrent engineering are much broader than just a gain in lead time and resource effectiveness. They include a wide range of benefits to the enterprise. These benefits are primarily derived from effective cross-functional collaboration, and full integration of the project management process with the total enterprise and its supply chain (Prasad 2002, 2003; Prasad and Rao 2004). In this context, concurrent engineering provides a process template for effectively managing projects. Virtually any project can benefit from this approach, as pointed out by the *Society of Concurrent Product Development* (www.scpdnet.org). As a working definition, the following statement brings the management philosophy of concurrent engineering into perspective:

Concurrent engineering provides the managerial framework for effective, systematic, and concurrent integration of all functional disciplines necessary for producing the desirable project deliverables, in the least amount of time and resource requirements, considering all elements of the project life cycle.

In essence, concurrent engineering is a systematic approach to integrated project execution that emphasizes parallel, integrated execution of project phases, replacing the traditional linear process of serial engineering and expensive design-build-rollout rework. The process also requires strong attention to the human side, focusing on multidisciplinary teamwork, power sharing, and team values of cooperation, trust, respect, and consensus building, engaging all stakeholders in the sharing of information and decision making, starting during the early project formation stages and continuing over the project life cycle.

POTENTIAL BENEFITS OF CONCURRENT ENGINEERING

- Better cross-functional *communication* and *integration*
- Decreased *time to market*
- Early detection of *design problems*, fewer *design errors*
- Emphasis on human side of *multidisciplinary teamwork*
- Greater *power sharing, cooperation, trust, respect,* and *consensus building*
- All stakeholders engaged in *information sharing* and *decision making*
- Enhanced ability to support *multisite manufacturing*
- Enhanced ability to cope with *changing requirements, technology, and markets*
- Enhanced ability to execute *complex projects* and *long-range* undertakings
- Enhanced *supplier communication*
- Fewer *engineering changes*
- High-level of *organizational transparency*, R&D-to-marketing
- Higher *resource efficiency* and *personnel productivity;* more resource-effective project implementation
- Higher *project quality*, measured by customer satisfaction
- Minimized "downstream" *uncertainty, risk and complications,* making the project *outcome more predictable*
- Minimized design-build-rollout *reworks*
- Ongoing *recognition and visibility of team accomplishments*
- Promotion of *total project life cycle thinking*
- A *template or roadmap* for guiding multiphased projects from concept to final delivery
- *Systematic approach* to multiphased project execution
- Shorter *project life cycle* and execution time
- *Validation of work in progress* and deliverables

The concurrent engineering process is graphically shown in Figure 13.1, depicting a typical product development. In its basic form, the process provides a template or roadmap for guiding multiphased projects from concept to final delivery. One of the prime objectives for using concurrent engineering is to minimize "downstream" uncertainty, risk, and complications, and hence make the project outcome more predictable (Aiguier 2012; Guirad et al. 2007; Moffat 1998; Nahm and Ishikawa 2004; Noori, Munro, and Deszca 1997). However, concurrent execution and integration of activities does not just happen by drawing timelines in parallel, but is the result of carefully defined cross-functional linkages and skillfully orchestrated teamwork.

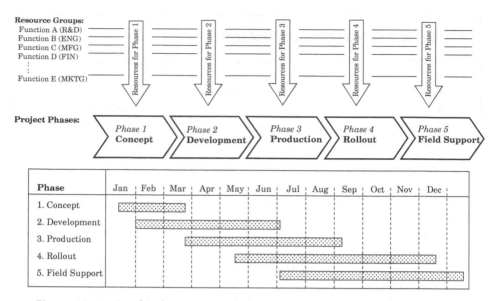

Figure 13.1 Graphical presentation of concurrent execution of project phases

Moreover, concurrent phase execution makes several assumptions regarding the organizational system and its people, as discussed in the next section.

13.3 CRITERIA FOR SUCCESS

For simplicity, concurrent engineering is often shown as a linear process, with overlapping activity phases, scheduled for concurrent execution, as shown in Figure 13.1. However, to make such concurrent project phasing possible, the organizational process must be designed to meet specific criteria that establish the conditions conducive to concurrent, incremental implementation of phased activities. These conditions are very similar to conventional modern project management, which provides the operating platform for concurrent engineering. By its very definition, concurrent engineering is synonymous with cross-disciplinary cooperation, involving all project teams and support groups of the enterprise, internally and externally, throughout the project life cycle. The CE process relies on organizational linkages and integrators that help in identifying problems early, networking information, transferring technology, satisfying the needs of all stakeholders, and unifying the project team. It is important to include all project stakeholders in the project team and its management—not only enterprise-internal components, such as R&D, engineering, manufacturing, marketing and administrative support functions, but also external stakeholders, such as customers, suppliers, regulators and other business partners.

CRITERIA FOR SUCCESSFUL MANAGEMENT OF CONCURRENT ENGINEERING PROJECTS

Concurrent engineering teams and their leaders must be able to:

- Allocate sufficient time and resources for up-front planning
- Identify major task teams, their mission, and interfaces at the beginning of the project cycle
- Work out the logistics and protocol for concurrent phase implementation
- Lay out the master project plan (top level) covering the project life cycle
- Establish a consensus on a project plan among project team members
- Be willing to work with partial, incremental inputs and evolving requirements throughout the team organization, throughout the project life cycle
- Identify all project-internal and -external "customers" of its work and establish effective communication linkages and ongoing working relationships with these customers
- Work flexibly with team members and customers, adjusting to evolving needs and requirements
- Share information and partial results regularly during the project implementation
- Identify the specific deliverables needed by other teams (and individuals) as inputs for their part of the project, including the timing for such deliverables
- Establish effective cross-functional communication channels and specific methods for work transfer
- Establish techniques and protocols for validating the work and its appropriateness to its "customers" on an ongoing basis
- Work with partial results (deliverables) and incremental updates from upstream developments
- Reiterate or modify tasks and deliverables to accommodate emerging needs of downstream task teams and to optimize the evolving project outcome
- Prepare for its mission prior to receiving mission details (e.g., manufacturing is expected to work on pilot production setup prior to receiving full product specs or prototypes)
- Work as an integrated part of a unified and agreed-on project plan
- Have tolerance for ambiguity and uncertainty

(Continued)

(Continued)

- Establish reward systems that promote cross-functional cooperation, collaboration, and joint ownership of results
- Have top management buy-in and support the concurrent engineering process
- Have established a uniform project management system throughout the concurrent engineering team/organization

Taken together, the core ingredient of successful concurrent engineering is the development and effective management of organizational interfaces. For most organizations, these challenges include strong human components that are more difficult to harness and to control than the operational processes of project implementation (Nandedkar and Deshpande 2012, Prasad 2002, Shi-Jie and Li 2004). They involve many complex and constantly changing variables that are hard to measure and even more difficult to manage, especially within self-directed team environments that are often required for realizing the concurrent engineering process (Bauly and Nee 2000, Hull et al. 1996, Yassine and Braha 2003). Procedures are important. They provide (1) the baseline and infrastructure necessary to connect and integrate the various pieces of the multidisciplinary work process, and (2) an important starting point for defining the communication channels necessary for effectively linking the core team with all of its support functions. Yet, it should be realized that the resulting process is only as good as the people who implement it.

13.4 DEFINING THE MANAGEMENT PROCESS—A TEAM-BASED EFFORT

After reaching a principle agreement with major stakeholders, the concurrent engineering process should be defined, showing the major activity phases or stages of the project to be executed. Even more advantageous for future projects would be the ability to define phases that may be common to a class of projects that are being executed by the enterprise over time. To illustrate, let us use the example of a new product development, shown in Figure 13.1. The concurrent engineering process proceeds through five project phases: (1) concept development, (2) detailed development, (3) pilot production, (4) product rollout, launch, and marketing, and (5) field support. Each phase or stage is defined in terms of scope, objectives, activities, and deliverables, as well as functional responsibilities. Each project phase must also include cross-functional interface protocols, defining the specific collaborations and organizational linkages needed for the concurrent development. While the principal cross-functional interfaces can be summarized graphically, as shown

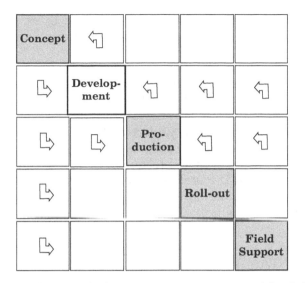

Figure 13.2   Quality function deployment (QFD) matrix, a tool for defining interfaces

in the upper part of Figure 13.1, more sophisticated group technology tools, such as the quality function deployment (QFD) matrix, shown in Figure 13.2, are usually needed for defining (1) the specific cross-functional requirements, (2) the methods of work transfer (often referred to as technology transfer), and (3) the stakeholder interactions necessary for capturing and effectively dealing with the changes that ripple through the product design process.

The best time for setting up these interface protocols is during the definition phase of a specific project when the team organization is most flexible regarding lines of responsibility and authority. To illustrate, Figure 13.2 shows the specific inputs and outputs required during the various phases of a product development process. Each arrow indicates that a specific input/output requirement exists for that particular interface. Most likely, some interface requirements exist from each project phase to each of the others. In our example, the total number of potential interfaces is defined by the 5 × 5 matrix, which equals 25 interfaces (this explains why the QFD matrix is also referred to as *N*-squared chart). The QFD matrix is a useful tool for identifying specific interface personnel and input/output requirements. That is, for each interface, key personnel from both teams have to establish personal contacts and negotiate the specific type and timing of deliverables needed. In many cases, multiple interfaces exist simultaneously, necessitating complex multiteam agreements over project integration issues. An additional challenge is the incremental nature of deliverables resulting from the concurrent project execution. For downstream phases, such as production, to start their work concurrently with earlier project phases, such as product development, it is necessary for all interfaces to define and negotiate (1) what part of the phase deliverables can be transferred early, (2) the exact schedule for the partial deliverable, and (3) the validation, iteration, and integration process for these partial deliverables.

Yet, another important condition for concurrent engineering to work is the ability of "downstream task leaders" to guide the "upstream" design process toward desired results, and to define the "upstream" gate criteria on which they depend as "customers." This interdisciplinary integration is often accomplished by participating in project and design reviews, by soliciting and providing feedback on work in progress, and by cross-functional involvement with interface definitions and technology transfer processes. Interface diagrams, such as the QFD matrix shown in Figure 13.2, can help to define the cross-functional roadmap for establishing and sustaining the required linkages for each task group.

13.5 UNDERSTANDING THE CHALLENGES

Implementing or improving a concurrent engineering process is about organizational development. It's similar to any other business process improvement. Potential benefits, such as higher quality, speed, resource effectiveness and cycle time, are very attractive to management, but they are also associated with high implementation risk, a natural byproduct of the organizational development and change process. Often, the new process does not work as well as the old one, or worse, is a complete disaster. That's why few companies go into a major reorganization lightly. At best, introducing a new system is painful, disruptive, and costly. At worst, it can destroy existing operational effectiveness and the ability to compete successfully in the market place. Seasoned managers understand the many challenges of working with these contemporary business systems:

- Strong autonomy of task teams makes system integration a shared responsibility of all team leaders.
- Power and resource sharing among task leaders and resource managers requires a more sophisticated management style and the ability to deal with inevitable organizational conflict and politics.
- The focus on process templates (e.g., CE) tends to make project execution ridged.
- CE process templates tend to isolates task teams within their program activities
- Objectives focus on phase outputs, such as deliverables, rather than on overall project and mission objectives.
- The need for self-directed teamwork limits top-down and central control.
- The need to work with incremental, partial inputs, and outputs at the task level, makes project planning, measurements, and progress reporting of more difficult.

- Intricate work processes, such as concurrent engineering require additional administrative support, management, and resources.
- Implementing and sustaining concurrent engineering requires senior management involvement and support, and long-term organizational commitment.

Experienced managers evaluate these challenges against current business scenarios. They also root-cause any known problems and failures of *others*, before they dive into reorganizing their own business process.

Some of the toughest challenges of concurrent engineering (CE), and its broader umbrella of integrated product development (IPD), relate to compatibility issues with the organizational culture. Concurrent engineering requires a collaborative culture with a great deal of organizational resource and power sharing. This is often not present to the degree needed for concurrent engineering to succeed. Designing, customizing, and implementing a new project management system usually affects many organizational subsystems and processes, from innovation to decision making, and from cross-functional communications to the ability of dealing effectively with risk and organizational conflict. Hence, integrating concurrent engineering with the business process and its physical, informational, managerial, and psychological subsystems, without compromising business performance, is an important challenge that must be dealt with during the implementation phase. Strong involvement of people across the organization is required for concurrent engineering to become acceptable by the people, and hence to become institutionalized and to succeed as a viable business process in an organization.

13.6 UNDERSTANDING ORGANIZATIONAL LINKAGES AND BENEFITS

While these challenges are more visible to managers, the benefits (i.e., potential benefits of concurrent engineering), are not always obvious just by looking at the basic concept of concurrent engineering. In fact, these benefits are often derivatives of more subtle organizational processes that unfold within a well-executed concurrent project management system. These processes need to be understood and skillfully exploited by project leaders and managers to gain the full benefits of concurrent engineering. Breaking the benefits down and relating them to organizational process might help in gaining additional insight into the workings of concurrent engineering:

1. **Uniform process model.** The concurrent engineering concept provides a uniform process model or template for organizing and executing a predefined class of projects, such as specific new product developments.

   Primary benefit: Time and resource savings during the project/product planning and startup phase.

Secondary benefits: A standardized process model breaks the project cycle into smaller, predefined modules or phases, resolving some of the project complexities, predefining potential risks and areas requiring managerial interactions and support. Standardized platform for project execution provides basis for continuous process improvement and organizational learning.

2. **Integrated product development, IPD.** Because of its focus on cross-functional cooperation, concurrent engineering promotes an integrated approach to product development and other project work.

Primary benefits: Promotes unified, collective understanding of project challenges and search for innovative solutions. Helps in team integration: identifying organizational interfaces, lowering risks, and reducing cycle time.

Secondary benefit: Responsibilities for team and functional support personnel are more visible.

3. **Gate functions.** The concurrent engineering platform is similar to other multi-phased project management concepts, such as Stage-Gate®, structured systems design, or rolling wave concepts, hence encouraging the integration of predefined gates, providing for performance reviews, sign-off criteria, checkpoints, and early warning systems.

Primary benefits: Ensures incremental guidance of the product/ project execution and early problem detection; provides cross-functional accountability; helps in identifying risk and problem areas; minimizes rework; highlights organizational interfaces and responsibilities.

Secondary benefits: Stimulates cross-functional involvement and visibility; identifies internal customers, promotes full life cycle planning, focuses on win-win strategy.

4. **Standard project management process.** The concurrent engineering concept is compatible with the standard project management process, its tools, techniques, and standards. Predefined gates provide performance and sign-off criteria, checkpoints, and early warning systems, ensuring incremental guidance of the product development process and early problem detection.

Primary benefits: Provides cross-functional accountability; helps in identifying risk and problem areas; minimizes rework; highlights organizational interfaces and responsibilities.

Secondary benefits: Stimulates cross-functional involvement and visibility; identifies internal customers, promotes full life cycle planning, focuses on win-win strategy.

5. **QFD approach.** Using the quality function deployment (QFD) concept built into the concurrent engineering process helps you to define cross-functional interfaces and pushes both the performing and the receiving organization toward closer cooperation and "upstream" guidance of the product development.

Primary benefits: Provides an input/output model for identifying workflow throughout the project/product development process, and identifies organizational interfaces and responsibilities.

Secondary benefits: Stimulates cross-functional involvement and vis-ibility; identifies internal customers, promotes full life cycle planning.

6. **Early testing.** Concurrent engineering encourages early testing of overall project or product functionality, features, and performance. These tests are driven by team members of both "downstream" and "upstream" project phases. Downstream members seek assurances for problem-free transfer of the work into their units, and upstream mem-bers seek smooth transfer and sign-off for their completed work.

   Primary benefits: Early problem detection and risk identification, opportunity to "fail early and cheap," less rework.

   Secondary benefits: Stimulates cross-functional involvement and cooperation, assists system integration.

7. **Total organizational involvement and transparency.** Because of its emphasis on mutual dependencies among the various phase teams, strong cross-functional involvement and teamwork is encouraged, enhancing the level of visibility and organizational transparency.

   Primary benefits: Total development cycle/system thinking; enhanced cross-functional innovation; effective teamwork, enhanced cross-functional communications and product integration; early warning system, improved problem detection and risk identification; enhanced flexibility toward changing requirements.

   Secondary benefits: Total team recognition; enhanced team spirit and motivation; conducive to self-direction and self-control.

Taken together, the top benefits of concurrent engineering refer to time, resource, and risk issues, that ultimately translate into increased project performance: (1) reducing project startup time, (2) reducing project cycle time, (3) detecting and resolving problems early, (4) promoting system integra-tion, (5) promoting early concept testing, (6) minimizing rework, (7) handling more complex projects with higher levels of implementation uncertainty, (8) working more resource effective, and (8) gaining higher levels of customer satisfaction.

13.7 RECOMMENDATIONS FOR SETTING UP AND MANAGING CONTEMPORARY SYSTEMS

A number of specific suggestions may help managers to understand the complex interaction of organizational and behavioral variables involved in establishing a contemporary project management system, such as concur-rent engineering, and managing effectively in it. The sequence of recommen-dations follows to some degree the chronology of on organizational system design, its implementation and managerial application. Although each orga-nization is unique with regard to its business, operation, culture, and man-agement style, field studies show a general agreement on the type of factors that are critical to effectively organizing and managing projects in concur-rent multiphase environments (Ainscough et al. 2003, Bowonder and Sharma

2004, Ching-Chow 2007, Denker et al. 2001, Nellore and Balachandra 2001, Nahm and Ishikawa 2004, Pillai et al. 2002, Ratchev and Pawar 2004).

13.7.1 Phase I: Organizational System Design

Take a Systems Approach

The concurrent engineering system must eventually function as a fully interconnected subsystem of the organization, and should be designed as an integrated part of the total enterprise (Haque, Pawar, and Barson 2003). Field studies emphasize consistently that management systems function suboptimal, at best, or fail due to a poor understanding of the interfaces that connect the new system with the total business process (Kerzner 2011, Moffat 1998). System thinking, as described by Senge and Carstedt (2001), Gharajedaghi (2011), and Checkland (1999), provides a useful approach for front-end analysis and organization design.

Build on Existing Management Systems

Radically new methods are usually greeted with anxiety and suspicion. If possible, the introduction of a new organizational system, such as concurrent engineering, should be consistent with already established project management processes and practices within the organization. The more congruent the new operation is with the already existing practices, procedures, and distributed knowledge within the organization, the more cooperation management will find from their people when implementing the new system.

The highest level of acceptance and success is found in areas where new procedures and tools are added incrementally to already existing management systems. These situations should be identified and addressed first. Building on an existing project management system also facilitates the incremental enhancement, testing, and fine-tuning of the new concurrent engineering process. Particular attention should be paid to the cross-functional workability of the new process.

Custom Design

Even for apparently simple situations, a new concurrent engineering process should be customized to fit the host organization, its culture, needs, norms, and processes. For reasons discussed in the previous paragraph, the new system has a better chance for smooth implementation and for gaining organizational acceptance if the new process appears consistent with already-established values, principles, and practices, rather than a new order to be imposed without reference to the existing organizational history, values, or culture (Swink, Sandvig, and Mabert 1996; Kerzner 2011).

13.7.2 Phase II: System Implementation

Define Implementation Plan

Implementation of the new concurrent engineering system is by itself a complex, multidisciplinary project that requires a clear plan with specific milestones, resource allocations, responsibilities, and performance metrics. Further, implementation plans should be designed for measurability, early problem detection and resolution, and visibility of accomplishments, providing the basis for recognition, and rewards.

Pretest the New Technique

Preferably, any new management system should be pilot tested on small projects with an experienced project team. Asking a team to test, evaluate, and fine-tune a new concurrent engineering process is often seen as an honor and professional challenge. It also starts the implementation with a positive attitude, creating an environment of open communication and candor, and a focus on actions leading toward success.

Ensure Good Management Direction and Leadership

Organizational change, such as the implementation of a concurrent engineering system, requires top-down leadership and support to succeed. Team members will be more likely to help implement the concurrent engineering system, and cooperate with the necessary organizational requirements, if management clearly articulates its criticality to business performance and the benefits to the organization and its members. People in the organization must perceive the objectives of the intervention to be attainable and have a clear sense of direction and purpose for reaching these goals.

Senior management involvement and encouragement are often seen as an endorsement of the team's competence and recognition of their efforts and accomplishments (Thamhain 2008, 2011). Throughout the implementation phase, senior management can influence the attitude and commitment of their people toward the new concept of concurrent engineering. Concern for project team members, assistance with the use of the tool, enthusiasm for the project and its administrative support systems, proper funding, help in attracting and retaining the right personnel, support from other resource groups, all will foster a climate of high involvement, motivation, open communications, and desire to make the new concurrent engineering system successful.

Involve People Affected by the New System

The implementation of a new management system involves considerable organizational change with all the expected anxieties and challenges. Proper involvement of relevant organizational members is often critical to success

(Barlett 2002, Nandedkar and Deshpande 2012, Nellore and Balachandra 2001). Key project personnel and managers from all functions and levels of the organization should be involved in assessing the situation, evaluating the new tool, and customizing its application. Although direct participation in decision making is the most effective way to obtain buy-in toward a new system (Pham, Dimov, and Setchi 1999), it is not always possible, especially in large organizations. Critical factor analysis, focus groups, and process action teams, are good vehicles for team involvement and collective decision making, leading to ownership, greater acceptance, and willingness to work toward successful implementation of the new management process (Thamhain 2011).

Anticipate Anxieties and Conflicts

A new management system, such as concurrent engineering, is often perceived as imposing new management controls, being disruptive to the work process, and creating new rules and administrative requirements. People's responses to such new systems range from personal discomfort with skill requirements to dysfunctional anxieties over the impact of tools on work processes and performance evaluations (Sundaramurthy and Lewis 2003). Effective managers seem to understand these challenges intuitively, anticipating the problems and attacking them aggressively as early as possible.

Managers can help in developing guidelines for dealing with problems, and establishing conflict resolution processes, such as informational meetings, management briefings, and workshops, featuring the experiences of early adopters. They can also work with the system implementers to foster an environment of mutual trust and cooperation. Buy-in to the new process and its tools can be expected only if its use is relatively risk-free (Stum 2001, Thamhain 2013). Unnecessary references to performance appraisals, tight supervision, reduced personal freedom and autonomy, and overhead requirements should be avoided, and specific concerns dealt with promptly on a personal level.

Detect Problems Early and Resolve

Cross-functional processes, such as concurrent engineering, are often highly disruptive to the core functions and business process of a company (Denker et al. 2001, Haque et al. 2003). Problems, conflict, and anxieties over technical, personal, or organizational issues are very natural and can be even healthy in fine-tuning and validating the new system. In their early stages, these problems are easy to solve, but usually hard to detect. Management must keep an eye on the organizational process and their people to detect and facilitate resolution of dysfunctional problems.

Round-table discussions, open-door policies, focus groups, process action teams, and management by wandering around are good vehicles for team involvement. They can lead to organizational transparency and a favorable ambience for collective problem identification, analysis, and resolution.

Encourage Project Teams to Fine-Tune the Process

Successful implementation of a concurrent engineering system often requires modifications of organizational processes, policies, and practices. In many of the most effective organizations, project teams have the power and are encouraged to make changes to existing organizational procedures, reporting relations, and decision and work processes. It is crucial, however, that these team initiatives be integrated with the overall business process and supported by management. True integration, acceptance by the people, and sustaining of the new organizational process will only occur through the collective understanding of all the issues and a positive feeling that the process is helpful to the work to be performed.

To optimize the benefits of concurrent engineering, it must be perceived by all the parties as a win-win proposition. Providing people with an active role in the implementation and utilization process helps to build such a favorable image for participant buy-in and commitment. Focus teams, review panels, open discussion meetings, suggestion systems, pilot test groups, and management reviews are examples for providing such stakeholder involvement.

Invest Time and Resources

Management must invest time and resources for developing a new organizational system. An intricate system, such as concurrent engineering, cannot be effectively implemented just via management directives or procedures, but instead requires the broad involvement of all user groups, helping to define metrics and project controls. System designers and project leaders must work together with upper management toward implementation. This demonstrates management confidence in, ownership of, and commitment to the new management process. This will also help to integrate the new system with the overall business process.

As part of the implementation plan, management must also allow time for the people to familiarize themselves with the new vision and process. Training programs, pilot runs, internal consulting support, fully leveraged communication tools such as groupware, and best-practice reviews are examples of action tools that can help in both institutionalizing and fine-tuning the new management system. These tools also help in building the necessary user competencies, management skills, organizational culture, and personal attitudes required for concurrent engineering to succeed.

13.7.3 Phase III: Managing in Concurrent Engineering

Plan the Project Effectively

As with any other project management system, effective project planning and team involvement is crucial to success. This is especially important in the concurrent engineering environment where parallel task execution depends on continuous cross-functional cooperation for dealing with the incremental work flow and partial result transfers. Team involvement, early in the project life cycle, will also have a favorable impact on the team environment, building enthusiasm toward the assignment, team morale, and ultimately team effectiveness. Because project leaders have to integrate various tasks across many functional lines, proper planning requires the participation of all stakeholders, including support departments, subcontractors, and management. Modern project management techniques, such as phased project planning and Stage-Gate concepts, plus established standards such as PMBOK, provide the conceptual framework and tools for effective cross-functional planning and organization of the work for effective execution.

Define Work Process and Team Structure

Successful project management in concurrent engineering requires an infrastructure conducive to cross-functional teamwork and technology transfer. This includes properly defined interfaces, task responsibilities, reporting relations, communication channels, and work transfer protocols. The tools for systematically describing the work process and team structure come from the conventional project management system. They include: (1) project charter, defining the mission and overall responsibilities of the project organization, including performance measures and key interfaces, (2) project organization chart, defining the major reporting and authority relationships, (3) responsibility matrix or task roster, (4) project interface chart, such as the N-squared chart discussed earlier, and (5) job descriptions.

Develop Organizational Interfaces

Overall success of concurrent engineering depends on effective cross-functional integration. Each task team should clearly understand its task inputs and outputs, interface personnel, and work transfer mechanism. Team-based reward systems can help to facilitate cooperation with cross-functional partners. Team members should be encouraged to check out early feasibility and system integration. QFD concepts, N-square charting and well-defined phase-gate criteria can be useful tools for developing cross-functional linkages and promoting interdisciplinary cooperation and alliances. It is critically important to include in these interfaces all of the support organizations, such as purchasing, product assurance, and legal services, as well as outside contractors and suppliers.

Staff and Organize the Project Team

Project staffing is a major activity, usually conducted during the project formation phase. Because of time pressures, staffing is often done hastily and prior to defining the basic work to be performed. The result is often team personnel that are suboptimally matched to the job requirements, resulting in conflict, low morale, suboptimum decision making, and ultimately poor project performance. While this deficiency will cause problems for any project organization, it is especially unfavorable in a concurrent engineering project environment that relies on strong cross-functional teamwork and shared decision making, built on mutual trust, respect and credibility.

Team personnel with poorly matched skill sets for the job requirements are seen as incompetent, affecting their trust, respect, credibility, and ultimately their "concurrent team performance." For best results, project leaders should negotiate the work assignment with their team members one on one, at the outset of the project. These negotiations should include the overall task, its scope, its objectives, and performance measures. A thorough understanding of the task requirements often develops as the result of personal involvement in the front-end activities, such as requirements analysis, bid proposals, project planning, interface definition, or the concurrent engineering system development. This early involvement also has positive effects on the buy-in toward project objectives, plan acceptance, and the unification of the task team.

Communicate Organizational Goals and Objectives

Management must communicate and update the organizational goals and project objectives. The relationship and contribution of individual work to overall business plans and their goals, as well as of individual project objectives and their importance to the organizational mission, must be clear to all team personnel. Senior management can help in unifying the team behind the project objectives by developing a "priority image," through their personal involvement, visible support, and emphasis of project goals and mission objectives.

Define Work Interfaces and Effective Communication Channels

Interdisciplinary transparency is a critical prerequisite for concurrent engineering. Effective cross-functional communication is crucial to the intensive information sharing and joint decision making needed during a concurrent project execution. In addition to modern technology, such as voice mail, e-mail, electronic bulletin boards and conferencing, and process tools, such as the N-square chart, management can facilitate the free flow of information, both horizontally and vertically, by workspace design, regular meetings, reviews, and information sessions (Hauptman and Hirji 1999; Keller 2001; Sarin and O'Connor 2009).

Ensure Senior Management Support and Leadership

You must win the hearts and minds of your work team before it supports and uses a new management system. Senior managers, by their enthusiasm, commitment, sense of purpose, and urgency, provide a strong emotional driver toward acceptance of a new organizational process. This visible management involvement and support also lowers the anxieties and doubts over the organizational value and stability of the new tool and helps to unify the team behind its implementation and effective utilization.

Manage Conflict and Problems

Conflict is inevitable in the concurrent engineering environment, with its complex dynamics of power and resource sharing and incremental decision making. Project managers should focus their efforts on problem avoidance. They should recognize potential problems and conflicts early in their development, and deal with them before they become big and their resolutions consume a large amount of time and effort. Focus team sessions, brainstorming, experience exchanges, and process action teams can be powerful tools for developing the concurrent workgroup into an effective, fully integrated, and unified project.

Encourage Continuous Fine-Tuning and Improvement

In addition to the implementation phase, the actual working process of concurrent engineering provides excellent opportunities for continuous improvement of the system and fine-tuning it to the specific project work at hand and its organizational host environment. Managers can encourage project leaders and their teams to examine the new process for weaknesses and potential improvements. It is important to establish support systems, such as discussion groups, action teams, suggestion systems and post project review sessions, to capture and leverage the lessons learned, and to fine-tune the system as part of a continuous improvement process.

13.8 CONCLUSION

Having the "right" management system is critical to expedient and resource-effective project execution in today's hypercompetitive business environment. The selection, proper implementation, and skillful use of the right system is the foundation for effective project management. Many application-specific contemporary project management concepts share the same philosophy of flexible concurrent execution of overlapping phases, with a great deal of attention to the people side of project work. This chapter used the framework of *concurrent engineering* to discuss the wide range of contemporary project management approaches. Although most of these concepts stress the cost and time advantages, the full range of benefits is in fact much broader than just a gain in lead-time and resource effectiveness. It includes a wide spectrum of competitive advantages to the enterprise, ranging from increased quality of project deliverables to the ability to execute projects of higher complexity and with higher customer satisfaction. These benefits are primarily derived from effective cross-functional collaboration and full integration of the project management process with the total enterprise and its partners, including its customer community and supply chain. However, these benefits do not occur automatically!

Designing, implementing, and managing in contemporary systems, such as concurrent engineering, requires more than just writing a new procedure, delivering a best-practice workshop, or installing new information technology. It requires the ability to engage the organization in a systematic evaluation of specific competencies, assessing opportunities for improvement, and designing a project management system that is fully integrated with the overall enterprise system and its business model. Too many managers end up disappointed that the latest management techniques did not produce the desired result. Regardless of its conceptual sophistication, concurrent engineering is just a framework for processing project data, aligning organizational strategy, structure, and people. To produce benefits for the firm, these tools must be fully customized to fit the specific business process and be congruent with the organizational system and its culture.

One of the most striking findings, from both the practice and the research of contemporary project management systems, is the strong influence of human factors on project performance. The organizational system and its underlying process of concurrent engineering is equally critical, but must be effectively integrated with the human side of the enterprise. Effective managers understand the complex interaction of organizational and behavioral variables. During the design and implementation of the concurrent engineering system, they can work with the various resource organization and senior management, creating a win-win situation between the people affected by the intervention and senior management. They can shake up conventional thinking and create a vision without upsetting established cultures and values. To be successful, both implementing a contemporary system and managing projects through the system requires proactive participation and commitment of all stakeholders. It also requires congruency of the system with the overall business process and its management.

Taken together, leaders must pay attention to the human side. To enhance cooperation among the stakeholders, managers must foster a work environment where people see the significance of the intervention for the enterprise, and personal threats and work interferences are minimized. One of the strongest catalysts to successful implementation and use of the project management system is professional pride and excitement of the people, fueled by visibility and recognition of work accomplishments, a finding that will be further discussed in the following chapters. Such a professionally stimulating environment seems to lower anxieties over organizational change, reduce communications barriers and conflict, and enhance the desire of personnel to cooperate and to succeed, a condition critically important for developing the necessary linkages for effective cross-functional project integration.

Although no single set of broad guidelines exists that guarantees success, project management is not a random process! A solid understanding of modern project management concepts, their tools, support systems, and organizational dynamics, is one of the threshold competencies for leveraging project control. It can help managers both in developing better project management systems and in leading projects most effectively through their execution cycles.

13.9 SUMMARY OF KEY POINTS AND CONCLUSIONS

The following key points were made in this chapter:

- Concurrent engineering is a specific management concept, which focuses on the effective execution of overlapping processes.
- The concurrent engineering process and management philosophy is the basis for a wide spectrum of contemporary management systems, ranging from *Stage-Gate®* to agile.
- Concurrent engineering is an extension of the multiphased approach to project management.
- Concurrent engineering provides the managerial framework for concurrent integration of all activities necessary for producing the desirable results, in the shortest time and best resource utilization.
- Many mission-specific project management platforms, similar to concurrent engineering, emerged under the *integrated product development (IPD)* umbrella. They include: design for manufacture (DMF), just-in-time (JIT), continuous process improvement (CPI), integrated product and process development (IPPD), structured systems design (SSD), rolling wave (RW) concept, phased-developments (PD), Stage-Gate® processes, integrated phase-reviews (IPR), and voice-of-the-customer (VOC), extreme project management (XPM). Spiral processes and agile.
- All of these contemporary systems emphasize effective flexible cross-functional integration, and incremental, iterative implementation of project plans with great emphasis on the human side of project management.
- The top benefits of concurrent engineering refer to time, resource, and risk issues that ultimately translate into increased project performance. However, the benefits include a wider spectrum, ranging from increased quality of project deliverables to the ability to execute projects of higher complexity and with higher customer satisfaction.
- The core ingredient of successful concurrent engineering is the development and effective management of organizational interfaces.
- The best time for setting up these interface protocols is during the definition phase of a specific project.

- The QFD matrix is a useful tool for identifying specific interface personnel and input/output requirements.
- To work effectively, most contemporary project management systems (i.e., concurrent engineering) require a collaborative culture and a great deal of organizational power sharing.
- Strong involvement of people from all organizational levels is required to institutionalize a new project management system, or to upgrade an existing one, and to ensure cooperation of the project team.
- A new project control system is more likely accepted if it is consistent with already established project management processes and practices, and is consistent with the culture, needs, norms, and business processes of the host organization.
- New project controls, such as concurrent engineering, are highly disruptive to the core functions and business process of an enterprise. Conflict and anxieties over administrative, personal, or organizational issues are very natural and can be even helpful in fine-tuning and validating the new system.
- The tools for systematically describing the work process and team structure come from the conventional project management system; they include: project charter, project organization chart, responsibility matrix or task roster, project interface chart, and job descriptions.
- A solid understanding of modern project management concepts, their tools, support systems, and organizational dynamics is one of the threshold competencies for managing projects effectively through any contemporary control system.

13.10 QUESTIONS FOR DISCUSSION

1. What are the reasons behind concurrent engineering's ability to accelerate project execution and increase resource effectiveness?
2. Discuss methods for enhancing cross-functional collaboration and integration.
3. Develop a procedure for defining work interfaces based on the N-squared chart.
4. What are the major challenges of managing projects within a contemporary system, such as concurrent engineering?
5. Discuss some of the barriers to implementing a contemporary project management system such as concurrent engineering.
6. Discuss managerial leadership styles most conducive to concurrent project execution.
7. How can top management facilitate effective project management within a contemporary system, such as concurrent engineering?

13.11 *PMBOK*® REFERENCES AND CONNECTIONS

The topic of Concurrent Engineering and Other Contemporary Project Management Systems addresses three PMBOK® processing groups: planning, executing, and monitoring/controlling. The topic cuts across many of the 10 knowledge areas defined by PMBOK®. However, it connects most strongly with project integration management (area #1), project scope management (area #2), project time management (area #3), project cost management (area #4), project communications management (area #7) and project stakeholder management (area #10). Much of the discussion in this chapter addresses the context of project management. That is the way projects management systems are designed and implemented for effective projects execution. This broad contextual understanding of project management is necessary for effectively applying the PMBOK standards to the day-to-day management of projects and to study effectively for PMP® certification. In studying for the PMP® Exam, an understanding of the following concepts will be beneficial: (1) project phases and project life cycle, (2) Stage-Gates, (3) stakeholder management, (4) organizational culture and influence, (6) elements of project control, (6) project monitoring and control, (7) socioeconomic influences, and (8) customizing management processes.

INTERNET LINKS AND RESOURCES

IT Knowledge Portal. "Extreme Project Management." www.itinfo.am/eng/extreme-project-management

Kozaryn, L. 2002. "Pentagon Reconstruction: Triumph over Terrorism." American Forces Press Service, Department of Defense. www.defense.gov/News/NewsArticle.aspx?ID=44262

National Institute of Standards and Technology: www.nist.gov/.

Product Development Institute. "Stage-Gate®—Your Roadmap for New Product Development." http://www.prod-dev.com/stage-gate.php

Society of Concurrent Product Development. www.scpdnet.org/

The National 9/11 Pentagon Memorial website—The Phoenix Project. http://pentagonmemorial.org/learn/911-pentagon/pentagon-reconstruction-phoenix-project

Watts. S. 2005. Design for Manufacturing & Assembly (DFMA), Aviation & Missile Research, Development, & Engineering Center; Research, Development & Engineering Command (Redstone Arsenal, AL). www.dtic.mil/ndia/2005garm/thursday/watts.pdf

Wikipedia. "Concurrent Engineering." http://en.wikipedia.org/wiki/Concurrent_engineering

REFERENCES AND ADDITIONAL READINGS

Aiguier, M. 2012. "Special Issue on Complex Systems Design and Management." *Concurrent Engineering* 20(3) (June): 83.

Ainscough, M., K. Neailey, and C. Tennant. 2003. "A Self-Assessment Tool for Implementing Concurrent Engineering through Change Management." *International Journal of Project Management* 21(6) (August): 425–431.

Atnahene-Gimo, K. 2003. "The Effects of Centrifugal and Centripetal Forces on Product Development Speed and Quality." *Academy of Management Journal* 43(3) (June): 359–373.

Barlett, J. 2002. "Risk Concept Mapping." Proceedings, *Fifth European Project Management Conference*, Cannes, France (June 19–20).

Bauer, Natalie. 2004. "Rising from the Ashes." *pmNetwork* 18(5) (May): 24–32.

Bauly, J., and Nee, A. 2000. "New Product Development: Implementing Best Practices, Dissemination and Human Factors." *International Journal of Manufacturing Technology and Management* 2(1/7): 961–982.

Beck, K. et al. 2001. *Manifesto for Agile Software Development*. Nashville, TN: Agile Alliance.

Boehm, B. 1988. "A Spiral Model of Software Development and Enhancement." *Computer* 21(5) (May): 61–72.

Bowonder, B., and K. J. Sharma. 2004. "Concurrent Engineering: Basis and Implementation." *International Journal of Manufacturing Technology and Management* 6(3/4): 199–213.

Boyle, T., V. Kumar, and U. Kumar. 2006. "Concurrent Engineering Teams II: Performance Consequences of Usage." *Team Performance Management* 12(5/6): 125–137.

Checkland, P. 1999. *Systems Thinking, Systems Practice*. New York: John Wiley & Sons.

Ching-Chow, Y. 2007. "A Systems Approach to Service Development in a Concurrent Engineering Environment." *The Service Industries Journal* 27(5) (July): 635–644.

Compos, J., and J. Balland. 2012. *The Voice of the Customer in Product Development*. Oshawa, ON, Canada: Multi-Media Publishing.

Cooper, R. 2008. "Perspective: The Stage-Gate® Idea-to-Launch Process—Update, What's New, and NexGen Systems." *Journal of Product Innovation Management* 25(3) (May): 213–232.

Cooper, R., and E. Kleinschmidt. 1993. "Stage-Gate Systems for New Product Success." *Marketing Management* 1(4): 20–29.

DeCarlo, D. 2004. *Extreme Project Management*, San Francisco, CA: Jossey-Bass.

Denker, S., D. Steward, and T. Browning. 2001. "Planning Concurrency and Managing Iteration in Projects." *Project Management Journal* 32(3) (September): 31–38.

Department of Defense 1998. *DOD Integrated Product and Process Development Handbook*. Washington, DC: Office of the Undersecretary of Defense (Acquisition and Technology).

Dixit, J., and R. Kumar. 2008. *Structured System Analysis and Design*. New Delhi, India: Laxmi Publications.

Dourado, J., R. Silva, and A. Silva. 2011 "Concurrent Engineering: An Overview Regarding Major Features and Tools." *Business Excellence* 5(2): 67–82.

Duhovnik, J., M. Starbek, S. Dwivedi, and F. Emery. 1969. *Systems Thinking*, New York: Penguin.

Esra Aleisa, E., N. Suresh, and L. Lin. 2011. "Team Formation in Concurrent Engineering Using Group Technology (GT) Concepts." *Concurrent Engineering* 19(2) (September): 213–224.

Gerwin, D., and N. Barrowman. 2002. "An Evaluation of Research on Integrated Product Development." *Management Science* 48(7) (July): 938–954.

Gharajedaghi, J. 2011. *Systems Thinking, Third Edition: Managing Chaos and Complexity: A Platform for Designing Business Architecture*. Amsterdam, Netherlands: Elsevier.

Girard, P., J. Legardeur, and C. Merlo, 2007. "Product Innovation through Management of Collaborative Design in a Risk Mitigation Approach for Concurrent Engineering." *The International Journal of Technology Management & Sustainable Development* 6(2) (September): 151–163.

Githens, G. 1998) "Rolling Wave Project Planning." Proceedings, 29th Annual Symposium of the Project Management Institute, Long Beach, CA (October 9–15).

Griffin, A., and S. Somermeyer. 2007. *The PDMA ToolBook 3 for New Product Development*. Hoboken, NJ: John Wiley & Sons.

Haas, R., and M. Sinha. 2004. "Concurrent Engineering at Airbus—A Case Study." *International Journal of Manufacturing Technology and Management* 6(3/4): 241–253.

Haque, B., K. Pawar, and R. Barson. 2003. "The Application of Business Process Modeling to Organizational Analysis of Concurrent Engineering Environments." *Technovation* 23(2) (February): 147–162.

Hauptman, O., and K. Hirji. 1999. "Managing Integration and Coordination in Cross-Functional Teams." *R&D Management* 29(2) (April): 179–191.

Hoque, M., M. Akter, and Y. Monden. 2005. "Concurrent Engineering: A Compromising Approach to Develop a Feasible and Customer-pleasing Product." *International Journal of Production Research* 43(8) (April): 1607–1624.

Hull, F., P. Collins, and J. Liker. 1996. "Composite Form of Organization as a Strategy for Concurrent Engineering Effectiveness," *IEEE Transactions on Engineering Management* 43(2) (May): 133–143.

Kayis, B., A. Ahmed, and S. Amornsawadwatana. 2008. "A Risk Mitigation Approach for Concurrent Engineering Projects." *International Journal of Risk Assessment and Management* 9(1/2): 178–189.

Keller, R. 2001. "Cross-Functional Project Groups in Research and New Product Development: Diversity, Communications, Job Stress, and Outcomes." *Academy of Management Journal* 44(3): 547–556.

Kerzner, H. 2011. "The Changing Landscape for Project Management." In *Project Management Metrics, KPIs, and Dashboards: A Guide to Measuring and Monitoring Project Performance*. New York: International Institute of Learning (IIL), Chapter 1.

Koufteros, X., M. Vonderembse, and M. Doll. 2002. "Integrated Product Development Practices and Competitive Capabilities: The Effects of Uncertainty, Equivocality, and Platform Strategy." *Journal of Operations Management* 20(4) (August): 331–355.

Kozaryn, L. D. 2002. "Pentagon Reconstruction: Triumph over Terrorism." *American Forces Press Service* (Washington, March 11, 2002): www.defense.gov/News/NewsArticle.aspx?ID=44262.

Lawson, M., and H. Karandikar. 1994. "A Survey of Concurrent Engineering." *Concurrent Engineering* 2(1): 1–6.

Levandowski C., D. Corin-Stig D. Bergsjö, A. Forslund, U. Högman, R. Söderberg, and H. Johannesson. 2013. "An Integrated Approach to Technology Platform and Product Platform Development." *Concurrent Engineering* 21(1): 65–83.

Moffat, L. 1998. "Tools and Teams: Competing Models of Integrating Product Development Projects." *Journal of Engineering and Technology Management* 1(1) (March): 55–85.

Morris, P. 1997. *The Management of Projects*. London: Thomas Telford, London.

Muench, D. 1994. *The Sybase Development Framework*. Oakland, CA: Sybase, Inc.

Nahm, Y., and H. Ishikawa. 2004. "Integrated Product and Process Modeling for Collaborative Design Environment." *Concurrent Engineering* 12(1) (March): 5–23.

Nandedkar, A., and A. Deshpande. 2012. "Concurrent Engineering, lmx, Envy, and Product Development Cycle Time: A Theoretical Framework." *Journal of Management Policy and Practice* 13(5) (December): 144–158.

Nee, A., and S. Ong. 2001. "Philosophies for Integrated Product Development." *International Journal of Technology Management* 21(3): 221–239.

Nellore, R., and R. Balachandra. 2001. "Factors Influencing Success in Integrated Product Development (IPD) Projects." *IEEE Transactions on Engineering Management* 48(2) (May): 164–174.

Nilsson, A., and T. Wilson. 2012. "Reflections on Barry W. Boehm's 'A spiral model of software development and enhancement.'" *International Journal of Managing Projects in Business* 5(4): 737–756.

Noori, Hami, M. Hugh, and G. Deszca. 1997. "Managing the P/SDI Process: Best-in-Class Principles and Leading Practices." *Journal of Technology Management* 13(3): 245–268.

Paashuis, V., and D. Pham. 1998. *The Organization of Integrated Product Development*, Berlin: Springer Verlag.

Pham, D., S. Dimov, and R. Setchi. 1999. "Concurrent Engineering: A Tool for Collaborative Working." *Human Systems Management* 18(3/4): 213–224.

Pilkinton, A., and R. Dyerson. 2002. "Extending Simultaneous Engineering: Electric Vehicle Supply Chain and New Product Development." *International Journal of Technology Management* 23(1, 2, 3): 74–88.

Pillai, A., A. Joshi, and K. Rao. 2002. "Performance Measurement of R&D Projects in a Multi-Project, Concurrent Engineering Environment." *International Journal of Project Management* 20(2) (February): 165–177.

Prasad, B. 2002. "Toward Life-Cycle Measures and Metrics for Concurrent Product Development." *International Journal of Computer Applications in Technology* 15(1/3): 1–8.

———. 2003. "Development of Innovative Products in a Small and Medium Size Enterprise." *International Journal of Computer Applications in Technology* 17(4): 187–201.

Prasad, G., and B. Rao. 2004. "Concurrent Engineering in a Pharmaceutical Firm: A Case Study of Dr Reddy's Laboratories Ltd." *International Journal of Manufacturing Technology and Management* 6(3/4): 280–290.

Project Management Institute. 2013. *A Guide to the Project Management Body of Knowledge (PMBOK® Guide)*. Newtown Square, PA: Project Management Institute

Ratchev, S., and K. Pawar. 2004. "Critical Company Assessment and Advisory Support for Introduction of Concurrent Engineering Practices." *International Journal of Business Performance Management* 6(1): 69–87.

Rigby, Darrel K. 1995. "Managing the Management Tools." *Engineering Management Review (IEEE)* 23(1) (Spring): 88–92.

Rosenau, M. and G. Githen. 2005. *Successful Project Management: A Step-by-Step Approach with Practical Examples*. Hoboken, NJ: John Wiley & Sons.

Sarin, S., and G. O'Connor. 2009. "First Among Equals: The Effect of Team Leader Characteristics on the Internal Dynamics of Cross-Functional Product Development Teams." *Journal of Product Innovation Management* 26(2): 188–205.

Senge, P., and G. Carstedt. 2001. "Innovating Our Way to the Next Industrial Revolution." *Sloan Management Review* 42(2): 24–38.

Senge, Peter M. P. 1990. *The Fifth Discipline: The Art and Practice of the Learning Organization*. New York: Doubleday/Currency.

Sharma, K. J., and B. Bowonder. 2004. "The Making of Boeing 777: A Case Study in Concurrent Engineering." *International Journal of Manufacturing Technology and Management* 6(3/4): 254–264.

Sherman, J. 2004. "Optimal Modes and Levels of Integration, and the Identification of Cross-Functional Coordination Deficiencies in Concurrent Engineering." *IEEE Transactions on Engineering Management* 51(3) (August): 268–278.

Shi-Jie, C., and L. Li. 2004. "Modeling Team Member Characteristics for the Formation of a Multifunctional Team in Concurrent Engineering." *IEEE Transactions on Engineering Management* 51(2) (May): 111–124.

Smith, R. 1997. "The Historical Roots of Concurrent Engineering Fundamentals." *IEEE Transactions on Engineering Management* 44(1) (February): 67–78

Stum, D. 2001. "Maslow Revisited: Building the Employee Commitment Pyramid." *Strategy and Leadership* 29(4) (Jul/Aug): 4–9.

Sundaramurthy, C., and M. Lewis. 2003. "Control and Collaboration: Paradoxes of Governance." *Academy of Management Review* 28(3) (July): 397–415.

Swink, M., J. Sandvig, J. and V. Mabert. 1996. "Customizing Concurrent Engineering Processes: Five Case Studies." *Journal of Product Innovation Management* 13(3) (May): 229–245.

Thamhain, H. 1994. "A Manager's Guide to Effective Concurrent Project Management." *Project Management Network* vol. 8, no. 11 (November): 6–10.

———. 2002. "Criteria for Effective Leadership in Technology-Oriented Project Teams." In Slevin, Cleland, and Pinto, eds., *The Frontiers of Project Management Research*. Newton Square, PA: Project Management Institute, pp. 259–270.

———. 2003. "Managing Innovative R&D Teams." *R&D Management* 33(3) (June): 297–311.

———. 2004. "Leading Technology Teams." *Project Management Journal* 35(4) (December): 35–47.

———. 2005. "Team Leadership Effectiveness in Technology-Based Project Environments." *IEEE Engineering Management Review* 33(2): 11–25.

———. 2006. "Optimizing Innovative Performance of R&D Teams in Technology-Based Environments." *Creativity Research Journal* 18(4): 435–436.

———. 2008. "Team Leadership Effectiveness in Technology-Based Project Environments." *IEEE Engineering Management Review* 36(1): 165–180.

———. 2013. "The Role of Commitment for Managing Complex Multinational Projects." *International Journal of Innovation and Technology Management* 12(2) (March).

Thamhain, Hans 2009. "Leadership Lessons from Managing Technology-Intensive Teams." *International Journal of Innovation and Technology Management* 6(2) (June): 117–133.

———. 2011. "Critical Success Factors for Managing Technology-Intensive Teams the Global Enterprise." *Engineering Management Journal* 23(3) (September): 30–36.

Valle, S., and D. Vázquez-Bustelo. 2009. "Concurrent Engineering Performance: Incremental versus Radical Innovation." *International Journal of Production Economics* 119(1) (May): 136–146.

Wang P., X. Ming, D. Li, F. Kong, L. Wang, and Z. Wu. 2011. "Modular Development of Product Service Systems." *Concurrent Engineering* 19(1) (March): 85–96.

Wu, S., J. Fuh, and A. Nee. 2002. "Concurrent Process Planning and Scheduling in Distributed Virtual Manufacturing." *IIE Transactions* 34(1) (January): 77–89.

Yassine, A., and D. Braha. 2003. "Complex Concurrent Engineering and the Design Structure Matrix Method." *Concurrent Engineering* 11(3) (September): 165–176.

Chapter 14

Managing Risk and Uncertainty

RISK-TAKING IN NEW PRODUCT DEVELOPMENTS IS PART OF STAYING COMPETITIVE AT INTEL

In 2002 Intel committed some $28 billion to a new product development, including new plant construction and R&D. The company decided that notebook computers needed a boost to ensure sales growth for its own *Pentium*® chips. While *Bluetooth* technology was already available, laptops weren't yet mobile networkable device. Intel saw this as a new market opportunity, deciding to pursue a new product development called Centrino®. It combines Intel's Pentium® processor chip with its other networking systems to create a new OEM product targeting computer companies, enabling them to build the next generation of laptops, using the Centrino® wireless mobile computing platform. The result of this initiative was the first-generation Centrino®, a 130nm, 77 million-transistor chip, based on the Pentium micro architecture (code-named Banias), operating at a bus clock of 400MHz in 2004. This was just the beginning of Intel's highly successful wireless product line. In 2013 Intel introduced the ninth-generation Centrino, code named "Shark Bay." Based on Haswell microarchitecture, this Centrino uses a 22nm chip topology and 3.7 GHz clock rate, faster than existing mobile Celerons. All of this helped Intel to increase its market share in global processor market to 82 percent, a fantastic success story.

However, things did not always look that certain. When Intel decided to go ahead with the Centrino development and committed billions of dollars in 2002, CEO Craig R. Barrett was deeply concerned. Intel management had no idea when the semiconductor industry's longest slump would end. Weak demand could have meant doom as those new semiconductor plants began ramping up production. But Barrett plowed ahead. "The only question was when overall business would begin to pick up. A three-year recession in our industry is about twice as long than the worst I can remember," he said. While things looked pretty dicey for some time, by now it turns out that Barrett put his chips in the right place. Today, Intel is working hard to satisfy demands for its Centrino notebook package. Barrett's push to build highly efficient factories means that Intel can churn out chips at costs

---

Source: Intel's Centrino Mobile Technology website: www.intel.com/products/mobiletechnology/.

way below those of competitors. With 62 percent gross margins, Intel is enjoying earnings of $11 billion on revenues of $53 billion in 2012. Outstanding results in a challenging business environment, as announced by Paul Otellini, Intel president and CEO in his annual report to shareholders: "We continued to execute through a challenging environment. We made tremendous progress across the business in 2012 as we entered the market for smartphones and tablets, worked with our partners to reinvent the PC, and drove continued innovation and growth in the data center. As we enter 2013, our strong product pipeline has us well positioned to bring a new wave of Intel innovations across the spectrum of computing." Intel is also pushing into consumer electronics, set-top boxes, and cell phones. High-risk strategies? Yes. But, also high potential for gains.

14.1 THE ROLE OF UNCERTAINTY IN MANAGING PROJECTS

Looking at a major undertaking, such as Intel's Centrino® technology, risks lurk throughout the project life cycle, affecting everything from technical feasibility to cost, market timing, financial performance, and strategic objectives (Hillson 1999, Loch et al. 2008, Thieme et al. 2003). Uncertainty is both a reality and great challenge for most projects (Chapman and Ward 2003, Hillson 2010). Research groups like Standish (2012) show that on average less than 50 percent of new product development projects succeed, blaming much of the failure on the inability to deal effectively with risks. Other researchers see the ability to deal effectively with risks as a prime factor for predicting project success or failure (Pantil et al. 2012; Shenhar et al. 2001, 2007; Srivannaboon and Milosevic 2006, Buchanan and O'Connell 2006). Yet, for Intel, failure was not an option. In fact, across the world millions of projects, from simple to complex, succeed despite of these challenges, while others see risk even as an opportunity, exploiting it strategically. What lessons can we learn? Unfortunately, there are no quick answers because critical success factors, even for smaller projects, involve a highly complex and intricately linked set of variables (Nellore and Balachandra 2001; Thamhain 2007, 2013).

14.1.1 A Changing Paradigm

Yet, in spite of these complicated processes, most managers understand the critical importance of dealing with risks, and it is not surprising that leaders in virtually all organizations, from commerce to government, spend much of their time and effort to deal with risks-related issues. Examples can be traced back to ancient times. Writings by Sun Tzu articulated specific risks and suggested mitigation methods already 2500 years ago (Hanzhang and

Wilkinson 1998). To be sure, risk management is not a new idea. However, in today's globally connected, fast-changing business world with broad access to resources anywhere, and pressures for quicker, cheaper, and smarter solutions, projects have become highly complex and intricate. Many companies try to leverage their resources and accelerate their schedules by forming alliances, consortia, and partnerships with other firms, universities, and government agencies that range from simple cooperative agreements to *open innovation*, a concept of scouting for new product and service ideas, anywhere in the world. In such an increasingly complex and dynamic business environment, risks lurk in many areas, not only associated with the technical part of the work but also including social, cultural, organizational, and technological dimensions. In fact, research studies have suggested that much of the root cause of project-related risks can be traced to the organizational dynamics and multidisciplinary nature that characterizes today's business environment, especially for technology-based developments (Cooper, Edgett, and Kleinschmidt 2001; Torok et al. 2011).

14.1.2 Why These Difficulties?

The involvement of many people, processes, and technologies spanning different organizations, support groups, subcontractors, vendors, government agencies, and customer communities compounds the level of uncertainty and distributes risk over a wide area of the enterprise and its partners (Thamhain 2004; Thamhain and Wilemon 1999), often creating surprises with potentially devastating consequences. Moreover, contingencies are often *caused by a multitude of issues* that were difficult to predict or could not be corrected earlier in the project life cycle. The resulting problems might be small initially, but often cascade, compound, and become intricately linked. Many of the examples shown in "How Contingencies Affect Project Performance" illustrate the large multiplier effect on performance. As the disturbance propagates through the project organization, it can impact broader performance areas, contributing to schedule delays and system integration problems, time-to-market delays, missed sales opportunities, and ultimately unsatisfactory performance in the market or customer environment. In addition, these contingencies are disruptive to the project organization, causing confusion, conflict, sinking team spirit, and fading commitment, hence creating additional negative influences on project performance.

These new business dynamics led to a changing paradigm of risk management. To be effective in dealing with the broad spectrum of risk factors, project leaders must go beyond the mechanics of analyzing the work and its contractual components of the *triple constraint* of cost, schedules and deliverables. They must also examine and understand the sources of uncertainty before attempting to manage them. This requires a comprehensive approach with sophisticated leadership, integrating resources and a shared vision of risk management across organizational borders, time, and space.

HOW CONTINGENCIES AFFECT PROJECT PERFORMANCE

(Examples of the *Multiplier Effect*: Contingency problems cascade, compound, and interconnect)

- A computer disk drive needed to be reworked at a cost of $2 million at the rollout stage, to incorporate new technologies not foreseeable at earlier development stages.
- A special instrument development, although technically successful, missed the NASA launch date, due to technical difficulties during the assembly and test stage.
- A new ultraportable CD player failed in the market because of higher-than-expected unit production cost.
- A computer chip development resulted in a marginally competitive product, because of unpredictable changes in IC support technologies.
- A new mutual fund product failed in the market, because of changing investor needs and economic conditions.
- A new drug development was terminated during the clinical trial stage, because FDA approval became very unlikely.
- A telecommunications satellite development resulted in a large financial loss due to rework resulting from regulatory changes.
- An automobile industry supplier lost a production contract to a competitor, after investing $5 million in the product development effort.
- A supersonic passenger jet development was canceled after expenditures of $1 billion, because of changing conditions in the airline industry.
- A medical equipment development failed to gain acceptance among doctors because of operational complexities and costly maintenance procedures.
- A new chemical product development, once announced as "critically important to the company's core business and long-range strategy," was terminated because of changing corporate priorities.
- A new Web-based banking support system received only 12 percent satisfaction rating from the bank's customers, resulting in a major overhaul of the system, doubling its original development budget.
- An application software development project failed in the market because of interconnectability problems and user-unfriendliness.
- A new computer operating system failed at the system integration stage, requiring additional design work, resulting in six months' schedule delay and $2 million budget overrun.

- A new oil refinery was delayed by two years at the pilot operation, because of newly discovered environmental concerns.
- A new TV consumer product failed in the market, because of reliability problems that did not surface during the product development or rollout stages.

14.2 WHAT WE KNOW ABOUT RISK MANAGEMENT

Currently, we are quite good in identifying and analyzing known risks, but weak in dealing with the hidden, less obvious aspects of uncertainty, and in proactively dealing with risks in their early stages (Smith and Merritt 2002). Yet, some organizations seem to be more successful than others in dealing with the uncertainties and ambiguities of our business environment, an observation that was explored in several field studies (Thamhain 2013; Thamhain and Skelton 2007), resulting in actionable lessons for effective risk management, summarized at the end of this chapter. Let's take a top-down look how we deal with risk in complex project situations, where we are effective and where we are weak and deficient.

14.2.1 We Are Efficient in Identifying and Analyzing Known Risk Factors

With the help of sophisticated computers and information technology, we have become quite effective in dealing with risks that can be identified and described *analytically*. Examples range from statistical methods and simulations to business case scenarios and user-centered design. Each category includes hundreds of specialized applications that help in dealing with project risk issues, often focusing on schedule, budget, or technical areas (Barlett 2002, Barber 2005, Dey 2002, Elliott 2001). Risk management tools and techniques have been discussed extensively in the literature (Bstieler et al. 2005; Cooper et al. 2005; Hilson 2000, 2003, 2010; Jaofari 2003; Kallman 2006). Examples include critical path analysis, budget tracking, earned value analysis, configuration control, risk-impact matrices, priority charts, brainstorming, focus groups, online databases for categorizing and sorting risks, and sophisticated Monte Carlo analysis, all designed to make project-based results more predictable. In addition, many companies have developed their own policies, procedures, and management tools for dealing with risks, focusing on their specific needs and unique situations. Especially in the area of new product development, contemporary tools such as phase-gate processes, concurrent engineering, rapid prototyping, early testing, design-build simulation, CAD/CAE/CAM, spiral developments, voice-of-the-customer, user-centered design (UCD), agile concepts, and scrum have been credited for reducing project uncertainties. Furthermore, industry-specific guidelines (e.g., *DOD Directive 5000* 2007), national and international standards (e.g., ANSI, CSA and ISO), and guidelines developed by professional organizations (*PMI PMBOK* 2013), have all contributed to the knowledge base and broad spectrum of risk management tools available today.

14.2.2 We Are Weak in Dealing with Unknown Risks

These are uncertainties, ambiguities, and arrays of risk factors that are often intricately connected. They most likely follow nonlinear processes that develop into issues that ultimately affect project performance (Apgar 2006). A typical example is the 2010 *Deepwater Horizon* accident in the Gulf of Mexico. In hindsight, the catastrophe should have been predictable and preventable. In reality, the loss of 11 workers and an environmental disaster of devastating proportion came as a "surprise." While the individual pieces of this risk scenario appeared to be manageable, the cumulative effects, leading to the explosion, were not. They involved multiple interconnected processes of technical, organizational, and human factors, all associated with some imperfection and risk. Even in hindsight, tracing the causes and culprits was difficult. Predicting and controlling such risks appears impossible with the existing organizational systems and management processes in place.

14.2.3 We Are Getting Better at Integrating Experience and Judgment with Analytical Models

With the increasing complexity of projects and business processes, managers are more keenly aware of the intricate connections of risk variables among organizational systems and processes, which limit the effectiveness of analytical methods. Managers often argue that no single person or group within the enterprise has all the smarts and insight for assessing these multivariable risks and their cascading effects. Further, no analytical model seems sophisticated enough to represent the complexities and dynamics of *all* risk scenarios that might affect a major project. These managers realize that, while analytical methods provide a critically important toolset for risk management, it also takes the collective thinking and collaboration of all the stakeholders and key personnel of the enterprise and its partners to identify and deal with the complexity of risks in today's business environment. As a result, an increasing number of organizations are complementing their analytical methods with managerial judgment and collective stakeholder experience, moving beyond a narrow dependence on just analytical models. In addition, many companies have developed their own "systems," uniquely designed for dealing with uncertainties in their specific projects and enterprise environment. These systems emphasize the integration of various tools, often combining quantitative and qualitative methods to cast a wider net for capturing and assessing risk factors beyond the boundaries of conventional methods. Examples are well-known management tools, such as review meetings, Delphi processes, brainstorming, and focus groups, which have been skillfully integrated with analytical methods to leverage their effectiveness and improve their reliability. In addition, a broad spectrum of new and sophisticated tools and techniques, such as user-centered design (UCD), voice of the customer (VoC), and phase-gate processes evolved that rely, by and large, on organizational collaboration and collective judgment processes to deal with the broad spectrum of risk variables that are dynamically distributed throughout the enterprise and its external environment.

14.2.4 The Missing Link

In spite of extensive studies on project risks and its management practices (Wideman 1992; Hilson 2000, 2010; Jaofari 2003; Kallman 2006), relatively little has been published on the role of collaboration across the total enterprise for managing risk. That is, we know little about organizational processes that involve the broader project community in a collective cross-functional way for dealing with risks identification and mitigation. Moreover, there is no framework currently available for handling risks that are either unknown or too dynamic to fit conventional management models. The missing link is the people side as a trans-functional, collective risk management tool, *an area that was investigated in a recent field study* (Thamhain 2013), focusing on the conditions in a project environment that are most conducive to dealing with risk issues, including managerial leadership.

14.3 KEY VARIABLES AFFECTING RISK MANAGEMENT

By definition, risk is a condition that occurs when uncertainties emerge with the potential of adversely affecting one or more of the project objectives and its performance within the enterprise system (ISO 3100 2009; PMBOK 2013). Risk can occur in many different forms, such as *known* or *unknown, quantitative* or *qualitative*, and even *real* or *imaginary* (see Shaw et al. 1999). In any case, risk is derived from uncertainty. It is composed of a complex array of variables, parameters, and conditions that have the potential of adversely impacting a particular activity or event, such as a project. At the minimum, three interrelated sets of variables affect the cost and overall ability of dealing with risk, as graphically shown in Figure 14.1:

1. Degree of uncertainty (variable set #1)
2. Project complexity (variable set #2)
3. Impact (variable set #3)

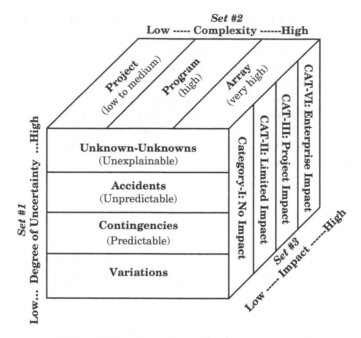

Figure 14.1   Dimensions of risk management

Understanding these variables is important for selecting an appropriate method of risk management, and for involving the right people and organizations necessary for effectively dealing with a specific risk situation.

14.3.1 Degree of Uncertainty (Variable Set #1)

For the purpose of discussion we can divide the degree of uncertainty into four categories (rank-ordered from low to high uncertainty), which may impact various segments of the project or the whole business enterprise.

1. *Variations*. Variations of known variables, such as cost, timing or technical requirements. The degree of risk varies with the level uncertainty and magnitude of the expected variation, and the potential impact on the project. However, by definition, the variables are well understood and the model for project performance impact in known. This is an area where analytical methods, and conventional methods of project planning, execution and control are usually highly effective.
2. *Contingencies*. These are known events that could occur and negatively impact project performance. However the probability of occurrence and magnitude of impact are not known. Or, the cost and effort of determining probable occurrence and impact are too great, or stakeholders

simply have chosen not to deal with this contingency for the time being. Examples are customer changes, design failures and contractor issues that could have been anticipated, but catch project leaders by surprise. This is an area where better management discipline, policies and procedures can be effective. In addition, certain analytical method, such as PERT and computer simulations can help in anticipating and dealing with these risk factors.

3. *Accidents*. These are events that can be identified in principle, but the probability of occurrence and its specific scope and impact on project performance are difficult if not impossible to predict. A somewhat simplified but graphic example might be a motorist planning for a car accident. One could make an argument that a savvy driver proactively deals with this risk factor by carrying insurance, emergency medical kit, flash light, cell phone, and so on and drives carefully to avoid accidents. However, reality is, that car accidents happen even to the most skilled and careful drivers. When they happen, they were not "anticipated," and a contingency plan might be of little or no value. Projecting this example to a complex project venture, such as off-shore oil drilling or outer space exploration, provides the type of scenario, were the possibility of accidents is certainly recognized, but its scope and impact is very difficult to predict.

4. *Unknown-unknowns*. These are event that were not known to the project team before they occurred, or were seen as impossible to happen in a specific project situation. Examples might be the failure of a certified component with proven liability in similar applications, a sudden bankruptcy of a customer organization, or a competitor's break-through invention/innovation that undermines the value of your current project or threatens a major line of business. By definition, unknown-unknowns are not foreseeable and therefore cannot be dealt with proactively.

This classification was developed during an earlier research study (Thamhain and Skelton 2007), were it helped in characterizing various types of uncertainties and in setting specific boundaries for various levels of uncertainty, hence establishing a conceptual framework and basis for further discussion. However, it should be pointed out that the boundaries are rather fluid with a wide range of overlaps among the categories. In fact, these four categories of uncertainty, described above, blend into a continuous spectrum ranging from "predictable and manageable" to "unforeseeable and unpreventable." The degree of overlay among these classifications depends on managerial skill sets, experiences and organizational environments, which is yet another set of variables affecting uncertainty. That is, events that seem to be manageable to one team, might appear as a complete surprise (unknown-unknowns) to another, an interesting reality that will be discussed further in this paper.

14.3.2 Project Complexity (Variable Set #2)

The scope and complexity of the project undertaking is yet another dimension likely to influence the ability of dealing with risk issues (Geraldi 2007, Haas 2009, Thomas and Mengel 2008). Formal studies of project-related complexity have focused on two aspects: "complexity *in* projects" and "complexity *of* projects" (Cooke-Davis, Ciemil, Crawford and Richardson, 2007). The first focus aims by-and-large at the complexities surrounding the project organization, such as its socio-economic and political environment, its dynamics and changes, both internal and external to the enterprise (Ciemil and Marshall 2005; Cooke-Davis et al. 2007; Maylor, Vidgen, and Carver 2008). The second stream of research looks more specifically at the project, trying to characterize and classify its complexity (Geraldi and Adlbrecht 2007, Jaofari, 2003, Shenhar and Dvir, 2007, Williams 2005, Williams and Sumset 2010). Among the many streams of complexity research, the classifications along structural lines, such as the task-project-program-array shown in Figure 14.1, seems to be most common. It is also part of the popular Diamond Model (Shenhar and Dvir 2007, 2010) which suggests a broader scope for characterizing project complexity along four dimensions: (1) *structural complexity* (low: assembly, medium: system, high: array), (2) *novelty or innovation* (derivative-platform-breakthrough), (3) *pace* (regular-fast-blitz), and (4) *technology* (low-medium-high-super high). All of these models help in establishing some metric for classifying the degree of "project difficulty," providing useful parameters for discussing risk in the context of project complexity.

14.3.3 Risk Impact on Project and Enterprise Performance (Variable Set #3)

Although complex projects are likely to have a larger impact on the enterprise, smaller projects or risk issues can also impact large segments of the enterprise. An example is the Toyota acceleration problem, caused by a relatively small component of the automobile. Yet, it impacted the image and financial performance of the whole enterprise. *Four specific categories of risk* have been suggested in prior studies (Thamhain and Skelton 2007) as a framework for discussing the situational nature of risk and its *potential impact* on project and enterprise performance:

- **Category I Risk:** Little or no impact on project performance. Category-I risks are potentially harmful events that can be identified and dealt with before impacting project performance.
- **Category II Risks:** Potential for limited impact on project performance. These risk issues can be dealt with at a lower level of project activity, such as a task or subsystem, before they impact overall project performance. Examples are technical issues that can be solved locally. The impact on

cost, time, quality, and other performance parameters is limited to a subset of the project.

- **Category III Risks:** Potential for significant impact on project performance. The contingency is expected to affect the project significantly, affecting overall project performance, such as causing critical schedule delays and budget overruns.
- **Category IV Risks:** Potential for significant irreversible impact on project and overall enterprise performance. The effects could be immediate or cascading, as we have seen in Toyota's "accidental acceleration issue," which started out as an "unknown-unknown" risk factor that appeared to be limited to some technical issues, but eventually affected overall enterprise performance extensively.

The importance of establishing categories of risks with defined impact boundaries is in describing and comparing the impact of a specific contingency. These four categories are suggested as a measure for communicating the degree of risk impact. As an analogy, this is similar to the use of categories for storms or earthquakes to describe the potential for damages resulting from the event. Similarly, *risk categories* identify the degree of potential problems caused to our projects and enterprise systems. The four risk categories will be used later in this chapter to build a model explaining the dynamics and cascading effects of risk events affecting projects and their enterprise systems.

14.4 A SIMPLE RISK-IMPACT MODEL

"Risks do not impact all projects equally." This observation is strongly supported by formal field research (Thamhain 2011, 2013). The managerial actions of dealing with the event, such as eliminating or working around the contingency, greatly influence the ability to minimize the magnitude of problems and their cascading effects throughout the organization. The dynamics of these processes is illustrated in Figure 14.2, which shows the influences of both the external and internal business environment. The conceptual development of this model goes back to a 2007 study (Thamhain and Skelton 2007) that was further validated in 2013 (Thamhain 2013). The model suggests that contingencies affecting one part of a project have the tendency of cascading throughout the project organization, causing increasingly unfavorable impact on project performance, and eventually affecting the whole enterprise.

14.4.1 Four Risk Categories

Based on the performance impact, the model identifies four distinct risk categories, which were briefly mentioned before.

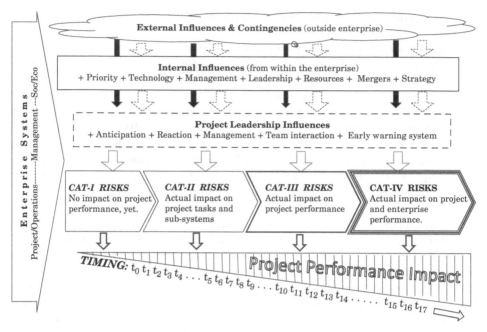

Figure 14.2   Model of risk impact on project performance

Category I Risk: No Impact

A Category 1 risk has no impact on project performance. Two types of risks fall into this category. First, events might occur in the external or internal project environment with a potentially harmful impact on project performance in the future. These contingencies, such as a delayed contract delivery, labor dispute, technical issue or priority change, are lurking in the environment, whether they are anticipated or not. But they have not yet occurred, and therefore have not yet impacted project performance. By anticipating these contingencies, management can take preventive actions to mitigate the resulting impact in case the event occurs. Second, events that actually occurred are identified and dealt with before they affect project time, cost, or other performance parameters.

Category II risk: Impact on Task or Project Subsystems Only

The risk events have occurred in the external or internal project environment with potentially harmful impact on project performance. However, by definition these risk issues occurred at a lower level of project activity, such as a task or subsystem, and have not yet affected overall project performance. Examples are delayed contract deliveries, labor disputes, technical issues, or priority changes that can be solved locally. Although the resolution might require extra time, it is not part of a critical path, and therefore the performance impact is limited to a subset of the project. A similar situation exists for issues that affect cost, quality, or other performance parameters at the local level only. Thus, while these risks are expected to impact the whole project, they have not yet affected overall project performance. Therefore, timely managerial actions could minimize or even avoid such performance impact.

Category III Risk: Impact on Project Performance

Events that occurred in the external or internal project environment did impact project performance, such as schedules, budgets, customer relations, or technical issues. The impact on project performance could have been a direct result of a contingency, such as a failure to obtain a permit, or resulting from an issue at a lower level, but propagating to a point that affects total project performance. Examples are test failure on a critical activity path, or problems caused at a lower-level that propagate to a point where they affect total project performance. However, by definition the impact is still contained within the project, without affecting enterprise performance. Proper timely management actions can lessen the impact on overall project performance, and possibly minimize or avoid any harmful impact on the enterprise.

Category IV Risk: Impact on Project and Enterprise Performance

Events have significantly impacted overall project performance and the performance of the entire enterprise. Similar to Category III, the effects could be immediate or cascading (e.g., Toyota's "accidental acceleration"). Proper management actions can lessen the final impact on both project and enterprise performance, but by definition, a certain degree of irreversible harm has been done to the project and the enterprise.

14.4.2 Example Illustrating the Dynamics and Cascading Effects

Using the model shown in Figure 14.2, we can follow the cascading effects of a contingency through a time cycle. Let us assume that an OEM supplier runs into manufacturing issues now (time t_0) that *could* affect the delivery of a critical component to your system five months from now. However, you learn about the supply issue one month after it occurred and decide on remedial action at month #2. That is, the contingency with potentially undesirable consequences (Category I risk) occurs at time t_0 and is recognized at t_1 = month #1. Its actual impact of the contingency on project performance (occurring at t_5 = month #5) will depend on the managerial actions of dealing with the event at time t_2. These actions could range from (1) eliminating the risk issue (e.g., switching to an alternate supplier), to (2) project replanning, or (3) innovative work-around. Hence, depending on the effectiveness of the project team and its leadership, the contingency occurring at t_0 may or may not impact project performance at time t_5. However, if it does, the situation is classified as a Category III risk.

Assuming this situation is being recognized at t_6, the managerial actions taken between t_7 and t_{14} will determine whether the risk is contained within the project or escalates further, affecting enterprise performance, such as cash flow and future business between t_{15} through t_{17}. If such impact on enterprise performance occurs, the situation would be classified as Category-IV Risk. Depending on the type of contingency, the complexity of the project and the managerial interventions, the cascading of impacts may continue further. These cascading effects of contingencies propagating through the work process and compounding at higher project breakdown levels have been clearly identified and verified during participant observation and interviewing as part of the field study. It also supports the comments frequently heard from managers, that "performance problems caused by contingencies are likely to cascade, compound, and become intricately linked."

Significance

The model underscores the importance of recognizing risk factors and their potential performance impact early in the project life cycle. It also points to the people side of risk management. That is, the attitude and sensitivity of team members toward early warning signs and first-order effects is critically important. The model further provides a framework for integrated enterprise risk management (ERM) by highlighting the importance of collective cross-functional involvement toward risk identification and impact assessment, emphasizing the benefits of cross-organizational collaboration for early risk detection and effective treatment. The model also supports the need for strategic alignment of the project with the enterprise objectives. Only with the help of senior management is it possible to see the potential impact of evolving risk on overall enterprise performance and long-range mission objectives. On the operational side, the model provides a guideline for assessing the project execution process regarding its work flow, interfaces, transparency and effectiveness of providing useful downstream results and upstream guidance, consistent with well-established models, such as voice of the customer (VOC), quality function deployment (QFD), and Stage-Gate® processes.

Robustness and Limitations

Although the risk-impact model is relatively simple in comparison to the complexities, dynamics and nonlinearity of today's project undertakings, it provides critical insight into the dynamics of risk propagation and its effects on project performance, as well as a framework for tracking risk issues impacting project performance and analyzing risk management effectiveness. Some of the positive features of the *risk-impact model* are its simple construct, clarity and robustness, which should be helpful for work process analysis and improvement. However, this is also an area for further research, fine-tuning the model and extending it toward managerial leadership style assessment.

14.5 HOW DO RISKS AFFECT PROJECT PERFORMANCE?

During a series of field studies (Thamhain 2008, 2011, 2013; Thamhain and Skelton 2007) managers identified over 1,000 unique contingencies or risk factors with potential of unfavorably impacting project performance. These contingencies were grouped into 14 sets, or *classes of risks*, based on their root-cause similarities. A graphical summary shows the 13 classes in Figure 14.3, ranked by average frequency as observed over a project life cycle. Typical project performance impact includes schedule slippage, cost overruns and customer dissatisfaction. In addition, risks affect broader enterprise performance, such as market share, profitability, and long-range growth. On average, project leaders identified six to seven contingencies that occurred at least once over the project life cycle. However, it should be noticed that not every contingency or risk event seems to impact project performance, as discussed in the previous section. As a most striking example, project managers reported "the loss or change of team members" (see Figure 14.3, set #6) to occur in 38 percent of their projects, an event described as a major risk factor with *potentially* "significant negative implications to project performance." Yet only 13 percent of these projects actually faced "considerable"

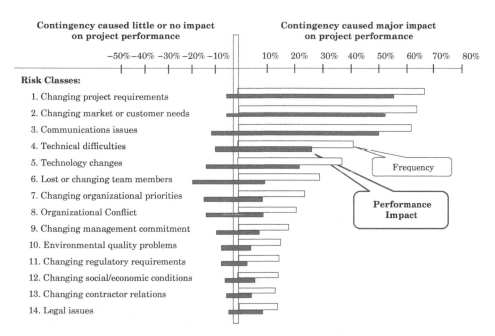

Figure 14.3   Risk classes, frequency and impact on project performance

or "major" performance issues, while 22 percent experienced even less of an issue, described as "little" or "no" impact on project performance. Hence, 60 percent of projects with lost or changed team members experienced little or no impact on project performance. For most of the other 13 sets of contingencies, the statistics is leaning more toward a "negative performance impact." On average, 61 percent of the contingencies observed in the sample of 35 projects caused considerable or major impact on project performance. The most frequently reported contingencies or risks fall into three groups: (1) changing project requirements (78 percent), (2) changing markets or customer needs (76 percent), and (3) communications issues (72 percent). These are also risk areas that experience the highest negative impact on project performance. They include approximately 80 percent of all projects with "considerable" or "major" performance issues.

The specific statistics observed across all contingencies or risks recognized by project leaders in all 35 projects, are as follows: (1) 9 percent of the contingencies had no impact on project performance (Category I risks), (2) 16 percent of the contingencies had some manageable impact on project performance (mostly risk Category II plus some Category III), (3) 14 percent of the contingencies had substantial, but still manageable impact on project performance (Category III risks), (4) 49 percent of the contingencies had a strong, irreversible impact on project and enterprise performance (Category IV risks), and (5) 12 percent of the contingencies resulted in *project failure* (mostly Category IV risks).

14.5.1 Mixed Performance Impact

While the number of risk occurrences (frequency) was approximately equally observed by all project leaders, the reported impact distribution was more skewed, with 20 percent of the project leaders reporting 71 percent of all considerable and major performance problems. This provides also support for observations made in my field research that "contingencies in the project environment do not impact the performance of all projects equally" (Thamhain 2013). It is further interesting to note that while all projects (and their leaders) reported more or less the same amount of contingencies with normal distribution across the 14 categories, some projects were hit much harder on their performance (i.e., those 12 percent that failed). This suggests differences in organizational environment, project leadership, support systems, and possibly other factors that influence the ability to manage risks.

14.5.2 Senior Management Perception

When analyzing the survey responses from senior managers separately, we find that senior managers rate the performance impact on average 30 percent lower than project managers. That is, senior management perceives less of a correlation between contingencies and project performance. Additional interviews with senior managers and root-cause analysis of project failures strongly confirm this finding. While senior managers and project leaders exhibit about the same statistics regarding (1) the number of contingencies and risks occurring in projects and (2) the distribution of risks across the 14 categories (as tested by Kruskal-Wallis analysis of variance by rank), *senior managers perceive fewer performance issues directly associated with these risks.* That is, they are less likely to blame poor performance on changes or unforeseeable events (risks), but more likely are holding project leaders accountable for agreed-on results, regardless of risks and contingencies. The comment made by one of the marketing directors might be typical for this prevailing perspective: "Our customer environment is quite dynamic. No product was ever rolled out without major changes. Our best project leaders anticipate changing requirements. They set up work processes that can deal with the market dynamics. Budget and schedule problems are usually related to more conventional project management issues, but are often blamed on external factors, such as changing customer requirement." This has significance in three areas: (1) perceived effectiveness of project management performance, (2) conditioning of the organizational environment, and (3) enterprise leadership.

First, project leaders should realize that their performance is being assessed largely on the basis of project outcome, not the number and magnitude of contingencies that they had to deal with. Although overall complexity and challenges of the project are part of the performance score card, they are also part of the conditions accepted by the project leader at the beginning of the project, and therefore not a "retrospective" performance measure. Second, less management attention and resources might be directed toward conditioning the organizational environment to deal with risks that specifically affect projects, because senior managers perceive less of a linkage between risk and project performance. This connects to the third area, the overall direction and leadership of the enterprise, which affects policies, procedures, organizational design, work processes, and the overall organizational ambience for project execution and control, an area that probably receives less attention from the top but could potentially influence project performance significantly, an area that should be investigated further in future research studies.

14.6 MANAGING RISKS IN PROJECTS: LESSONS FROM THE FIELD

Seasoned project leaders understand the importance of dealing with project risks. They take their responsibility very serious. However, foreseeing contingencies and effectively managing the associated risks is difficult and challenging (Maylor et al 2008; Thamhain 2007, 2011). It is both an art and a science to bring the effects of uncertainty under control before they impact the project and its deliverables and objectives. Given the time and budget pressures of today's business environment, it is not surprising that project managers focus most of their efforts on fixing problems after they have impacted performance (see field study, Thamhain 2013). That is, while the majority of project leaders understand the sources of risks well, they focus their primary attention on monitoring and managing the domino effects of the contingency rather than dealing with its root causes. It is quite common for these managers to deal with problems and contingencies only after they have impacted project performance, such as schedule delays and budget overruns, and therefore have become Category II or III risks. Field studies show that only one-quarter of these managers feel they could have foreseen or influenced the events that eventually impacted project performance adversely (Hillson 2010, Thamhain 2013). It is further interesting to note that many of the organizational tools and techniques that support early risk detection and management—such as spiral processes, performance monitoring, early warning systems, contingency planning, rapid prototyping, and CAD/CAM-based simulations—readily exist in many organizations as part of the product development process or embedded in the project planning, tracking, and reporting system. Taken together, here are some lessons learned from the field.

14.6.1 Decoupling Risks from Projects: Cause-Effect Dynamics

Field studies, such as those cited in this chapter, provide an interesting insight into the cause and effect of contingencies on project performance, including their dynamics and psychology. Whether a risk factor actually impacts project performance depends on the reaction of the project team to the event, as graphically shown in Figure 14.2. It also seems to depend on the judgment of the manager whether or not a particular contingency is blamed for subsequent performance problems. Undesirable events (contingencies) are often caused by a multitude of problems that were not predictable or could not be dealt with earlier in the project life cycle. During a typical project execution, these problems often cascade, compound, and become intricately linked. It is also noticeable that the impact of risk on project performance seems to increase with project complexity, especially technology content of the undertakings. From the interviews and field observations it was clear that even small and anticipated contingencies, such as additional design rework or the resignation of a key project team member, can lead to issues with other groups, confusion, organizational conflict, sinking team spirit, and fading commitment. All of these factors potentially contribute to schedule delays, budget issues, and system integration problems that may cause time-to-market delays and customer relation issues that ultimately affect project performance. Realizing the cascading and compounding effects of contingencies on project performance, the research emphasizes the importance of identifying and dealing with risk early in the project life cycle to avoid problems at more mature stages. The study also acknowledges the enormous difficulties of actually predicting specific risk situations, their timing, root cause, and dysfunctional consequences, and to take appropriate actions before they affect project performance.

14.6.2 Performance Issues Are Differently Assessed by Project Managers and Senior Managers

Project leaders and senior managers differ in their "true cause" assessment of performance problems, as was shown in the statistical analysis of Figure 14.3. Yet there are additional implications to the perception of what causes performance issues. These perceptions affect the managerial approaches of dealing with risk. Specifically, we learn from the discussions and field interviews that project leaders blame project performance problems and failures predominately on contingencies (risk situations) that originate outside their sphere of control, such as scope changes, market shifts, and project support problems, while senior management points directly at project leaders for not managing effectively. That is, senior management blames project managers for insufficient planning, tracking and control, poor communications, and weak leadership. Even more subtle, many of the project performance problems and failures are root-caused to the broader issues and difficulties of understanding and communicating the complexities of the project, its applications and support environment, including unrealistic expectations for scope, schedule and budget, underfunding, unclear requirements, and weak sponsor commitment.

The significance of these findings is in several areas. First, the polarized perspective between project leaders and senior managers creates a potential for organizational tension and conflict. It also provides an insight into the mutual expectations. Senior management is expected to provide effective project support and a reasonably stable work environment, while project leaders are expected to "manage" their projects toward agreed-on results. The reality is, however, that project leaders are often stretched too thin and placed in a tough situation by challenging requirements, weak project support, and changing organizational conditions. Moreover, many of the risk factors have their roots *outside the project organization*, and are controlled by senior management. Examples are contingencies that originate with the strategic planning process. Management, by setting guidelines for target markets, timing, ROI, and product features, often creates conflicting target parameters that are also subject to change due to the dynamic nature of the business environment. In turn, these "external changes" create contingencies and risks at the project level. Existing business models do not connect well between the strategic and operational subsystems of the firm, and tend to constrain the degree to which risk can be foreseen and managed proactively at the project level (Hillson 2003, Shenhar, Milosevic et al. 2007). It is therefore important for management to recognize these variables and their potential impact on the work environment. Organizational stability, availability of resources, management involvement and support, personal rewards, stability of organizational goals, objectives and priorities, are all derived from enterprise systems that are controlled by general management. It is further crucial for project leaders to work with senior management, and vice versa, to ensure an organizational ambience conducive to cross-functional collaboration.

14.7 CRITERIA FOR EFFECTIVE RISK MANAGEMENT

In spite of the challenges and uncertainties associated with complex projects, success is not random. One of the strong conclusions from empirical research is this: *Risks can be managed*. However, to be effective, especially in complex project environments, risk management must go beyond analytical methods. While analytical methods provide the backbone for most risk management approaches, and have the benefit of producing relatively quickly an assessment of a known risk situation, including economic measures of gains or losses, they also have many limitations. The most obvious limitations are in identifying potential, unknown risk situations and reducing risk impact by engaging people throughout the enterprise. Because of these limitations and the mounting pressures on managers to reduce risk, many companies have shifted their focus from "investigating the impact of known risk factors" to "managing risk scenarios" with the objective to eliminate potential risks before they impact organizational activities. As a result, these companies have augmented conventional analytical methods with more adaptive, team-based methods that rely to a large degree on (1) broad data gathering across a wide spectrum of factors, and (2) judgmental decision making. Examples of such approaches aimed at the reduction or even elimination of risks are: simplifying work processes, reducing development cycles, and testing product feasibility early in the development cycle. Often, companies combine, fine-tune and integrate these approaches to fit specific project situations, their people, and cultures, to manage risks as part of the total enterprise system. The criteria for effective risk management are summarized as follows, together with some recommendations. I have labeled these criteria as *critical success factors (CSF)*, emphasizing the complex organizational processes involved in dealing effectively with project-related risks and uncertainties. This summary is the result of years of collective experiences and formal studies by many researchers, including my own work. It should help management practitioners and scholars to better understand the complex organizational processes, provide benchmarks, and stimulate thoughts for contemporary risk management practices, new tool developments, and future research.

14.7.1 CSF #1: Early Recognition

Early recognition of undesirable events is a critical pre-condition for managing risk. In addition, project leaders must not only recognize potential risk factors in general, but also know when they will most likely occur in the project life cycle. Recognizing specific issues and contingencies before they occur or early in their development is critical to the ability of taking preventive actions and decoupling the contingencies from the work process before they impact any project performance factors. Examples include the anticipation of changing requirements, market conditions or technology.

If the possibility of these changes is recognized, their probability and impact can be assessed, additional resources for mitigation can be allocated, and plans for dealing with the probable situation can be devised. This is similar to a fire drill or hurricane defense exercise. When specific risk scenarios are known, preventive measures, such as early warning systems, evacuation procedures, tool acquisitions and skill developments, can be put in place. This readiness will minimize the impact, in case the risk situation actually occurs. While most managers acknowledge the difficulties of recognizing risk factors ahead of time, it is fundamental to any risk management approach. It is also a measure of team maturity and competency and gives support to the field observation cited earlier that "contingencies do not impact performance of all projects equally."

14.7.2 CSF #2: Unrecognized Contingencies

Unrecognized risk factors are common in complex project environments. Contingencies (even after affecting project performance) often go unrecognized. Field studies show that more than half of the contingencies that occur were not anticipated before causing significant performance issues (*Category III* Risk or higher). Most commonly, the impact is on cost, schedule, and risk escalation.

"Delayed risk recognition is more difficult and costly to correct than contingencies treated early in their development," was a remark often heard during field interviews and in group discussions. To minimize these problems, more collective, team-centered approaches of monitoring the project environment are needed. This includes effective project reviews, design reviews, focus groups, action teams, gate reviews, and "management by wandering around" (MBWA). All of these approaches are catalysts toward making the project organization more transparent, agile and alert to changes and issues in the work environment.

14.7.3 CSF #3: Unchecked Contingencies

Unchecked contingencies tend to cascade and penetrate wider project areas. Contingencies occurring anywhere at a project have the tendency to penetrate into multiple subsystems (domino effect) and eventually affect overall project performance. Many of the contingencies observed in this field study, such as design rework of a component, a minor requirements change, or the resignation of a team member, may initially affect the project only at the subsystem level. These situations might even be ignored or dismissed as issues of no significance to the project as a whole. However, all of these contingencies can trigger issues elsewhere, causing workflow or integration problems, and eventually resulting in time-to-market delays, missed sales opportunities and unsatisfactory project performance. Moreover, surprises, no matter how small, often have psychological effects on the organization, leading to confusion, organizational conflict, sinking team spirit, fading commitment and excuses to change prior agreements.

All of these issues eventually translate into reduced organizational efficiency and lower performance. Recognizing the cascading nature and multiple performance impact of contingencies provides a starting point for devising an effective risk management strategy. It also helps in conditioning the team toward collective monitoring of the potential problem areas and effective early intervention.

14.7.4 CSF #4: Cross-Functional Collaboration

Cross-functional collaboration is an effective catalyst for collectively dealing with threats to the project environment. The project planning phase appears to be an effective vehicle for building such a collaborative culture early in the project life cycle. The active involvement of all stakeholders—including team members, support functions, outside contractors, customers, and other partners—in the project planning process leads to a better, more detailed understanding of the project objectives and interfaces, and a better collective sensitivity where risks lurk and how to deal with the issues effectively. Collaboration is especially essential for complex and geographically dispersed projects with limited central authority, and limited ability for centrally orchestrated control. Throughout the project life cycle, collaboration is a catalyst for identifying risks early. It helps to create transparency throughout the organization, unifies team members behind the requirements, and enhances the team's ability of collectively recognizing and dealing with risks in the broader project environment.

14.7.5 CSF #5: Senior Management

Senior management has a critical role in conditioning the organizational environment for effective risk management. Many risk factors have their roots outside of the project organization, residing in the domain of the broader enterprise system and its environment. Examples are functional support systems, joint reviews, resource allocations, facility and skill developments, as well as other organizational components that relate to business strategy, work process, team structure, managerial command and control, technical direction, and overall leadership. All of these organizational subsystems have their locus outside of the project organization, controlled to a large extent by senior management. In addition, a natural "impedance barrier" seems to exist between the enterprise systems and the project organization, which makes external risks less recognizable and manageable in their early stages.

Since early risk detection and mitigation depends to a large degree on the collective multifunctional involvement and collaboration of all stakeholders, it is important for management to foster an organizational environment conducive to effective cross-functional communications and cooperation. In addition, senior management can unify the project community behind the broader enterprise objectives by clearly articulating business strategy and vision, a contemporary process that is known as strategic alignment (Shenhar et al. 2007). Taken together, senior management—by their involvement and actions—can develop personal relations, mutual trust, respect, and credibility among the various project groups, its support functions and stakeholders, a critical condition for building an effective partnership among all members of the project community. This is an ambiance supportive to collective initiatives and outreach, conducive to early risk detection and management.

14.7.6 CSF #6: People Skills

People are one of the greatest sources of uncertainty and risk in any project undertaking, but also one of the most important resources for reducing risk. The quality of communications, trust, respect, credibility, minimum conflict, job security and skill sets, all of these factors influence cooperation and the collective ability of identifying, processing, and dealing with risk factors. Field studies found that many of the conditions that stimulate favorably risk management behavior are enhanced by a professionally stimulating work environment, including strong personal interest in the project, pride and satisfaction with the work, professional work challenge, accomplishments and recognition. Other important influences include effective communications among team members and support units across organizational lines; good team spirit, mutual trust, respect, low interpersonal conflict, plus opportunities for career development and advancement, and to some degree, job security. All of these factors seem to help in building a unified project team that focuses on cross-functional cooperation and desired results. Such a mission-oriented environment is more transparent to emerging risk factors and more likely to have an action-oriented, collaborative nature that can identify and deal with emerging issues early in their development.

14.7.7 CSF #7: Authority to Adapt

Project leaders should have the authority to adapt their plans to changing conditions. By definition, projects are conducted in a changing environment of uncertainty and risk. No matter how careful and detailed the project plan is laid-out, contingencies will surface during its execution that require adjustment. The project managers and their teams should not only have the authority to adapt to changing conditions but also be encouraged to identify potential contingencies and propose plan changes for eliminating risks before they impact the work process.

14.7.8 CSF #8: Test Early and Often

Testing project feasibility early and frequently during execution reduces overall project risk. Advances in technology provide opportunities for accelerating feasibility testing to the early stages of a project life cycle. Examples are system integration, market acceptance, flight tests, and automobile crash tests that traditionally were performed only at the end of a project subphase or at a major integration point. However, with the help of modern computer and information technology, many of the companies in our study were able to reduce risks considerably by advancing these tests to the front end of the project or to the early stages of a product or service development. Examples are CAD/CDE/CAM-supported simulations, and product/service application modeling. A simulated jet flight or automobile crash test is not only much less costly and less time consuming than the real thing, but also yields valuable information for the improvement and optimization of the product design at its early stages, long before a lot of time and resources have been expended.

Technology also offers many other forms and methods of early testing and validation, ranging from 3-D printing, stereo lithography and holographic imagery for model building, to focus groups and early design usability testing. These technology-based methods also allow companies to test more project and product ideas, and their underlying assumptions for success, in less time and with considerably less resources than with traditional "end-of-the-development" test methods.

14.7.9 CSF #9 Simplification

Reducing work complexity and simplifying work processes will most likely reduce risk. Uncertainties originate within the work itself. That is, the project work together with its complexities and processes, contributes especially heavily to the uncertainties and risks affecting project success. Whatever can be done to simplify the project, its scope, deliverables, and work process will minimize the potential for problems and contingencies, make the project more manageable, and increase its probability of success. Work simplification comes in many forms, ranging from the use of prefabricated components, to subcontracting, snap-on assembly techniques, material choices, and high-level programming languages. Any innovation that reduces complexity, development time, resource requirements, testing, production setup, or assembly also reduces the risk of contingencies to occur over the development cycle. In addition, risk and uncertainties can be reduced by streamlining the work processes. Contemporary project management platforms, such as concurrent engineering, Stage-Gate®

processes, or agile/scrum, in their right setting, can simplify the work process, reduce development time, and enhance organizational transparency.

14.8 A FINAL NOTE

Risks do not affect all projects equally. The actual impact depends on both, the risk event *and* managerial actions taken, including the timing, that influence the magnitude of problems caused and the cascading effects within the project organization. The risk impact on performance provides a framework for describing the dynamics and cumulative nature of contingencies affecting project performance. Because of the complex, intricately linked set of variables, simple analytical approaches are unlikely to produce desired results, but need to be augmented with more adaptive methods that rely on broad data gathering across a wide spectrum of the enterprise and its environment. The methods also have to connect effectively with the organizational process and the people-side of project management.

Some of the strongest influences on risk management seem to emerge from three enterprise areas: (1) work process, (2) organizational environment, and (3) people. Many approaches to effectively reducing risk rely on simplifying the work and its transfer processes, shortening development cycles, and testing project feasibility early. Another lesson from the field is the critical importance of identifying and dealing with risks early in the development cycle. This requires broad scanning across all segments of the project team and its environment and creative methods for assessing feasibilities early in the project life cycle.

Many risk factors originate outside of the project organization, residing in the broader enterprise and its environment. Therefore, it is important for management to foster an organizational environment conducive to effective cross-functional communications and collaboration among all stakeholders, a condition especially important to early risk detection and risk management.

While no single set of broad guidelines exists that guarantees project success, the process is not random! A better understanding of the organizational dynamics that affect project performance and the issues that cause risks in complex projects is an important prerequisite and catalyst to building a strong cross-functional team that can collectively deal with risk before it affects project performance.

14.9 SUMMARY OF KEY POINTS AND CONCLUSIONS

The following key points were made in this chapter:

- Risks and uncertainties exist throughout the project life cycle, affecting everything from technical feasibility to cost, market timing, financial performance, and strategic objectives.

- Risk occurs when uncertainties emerge with the potential of adversely affecting business activities performance.
- In today's globally connected, fast-changing business world risks span across wider areas of the enterprise and its partners, compounding the level of uncertainty.
- Project leaders often understand the sources of risks well, but focus their attention on monitoring the "derivatives of the cause," such as schedules and budgets.
- Managers are good in dealing with risks that can be identified and described analytically, but weak in dealing with unknown risks.
- Project leaders blame performance problems and failures predominately on situations outside their sphere of control, while senior management points at project managers for insufficient planning, tracking, and control, poor communication, and weak leadership.
- Analytical approaches are important tools for risk management and are predominately used for quantifying probabilities of risk.
- The ultimate usefulness of analytical methods depends on the assumption that risks factors and their underlying parameters, such as economic, social, political, and market factors can actually be quantified and reliably forecasted over the project life cycle.
- Many contemporary approaches to risk management go beyond identifying risk factors and try to eliminate the cause of risk.
- The risk DNA consists of a complex, intricately linked array of variables. Simple analytical approaches are unlikely to produce solutions, but need to be augmented with more adaptive methods that rely on broad data gathering across a wide spectrum of the enterprise environment.
- Three sets of variables affect the ability of dealing with risk: (1) degree of uncertainty, (2) project complexity, and (3) impact on project and enterprise performance.
- Degrees of uncertainty can be classified into four categories: (1) *variations* (known uncertainty), (2) *contingencies* (uncertainty is known but difficult to quantify), (3) *accidents* (known or unknown uncertainty with unknown timing and impact), and (4) *unknown-unknowns* (risk is unknown and unexpected).
- The impact of a particular risk event on the project and its enterprise can be classified into four categories: (1) *Category I risk* has no impact on project performance, (2) *Category II risk* has some impact on project performance, limited lower-level project activities, (3) *Category III risk* has significant impact on overall project performance, and (4) *Category IV risk* has irreversible impact on project and overall enterprise performance.
- The most frequently experienced contingencies or risks that cause major project performance problems are: changing project requirements, changing markets or customer needs, and communications issues.
- Not all contingencies cause performance problems. Some teams seem to manage risks better than others.

- Successful risk managers are able to identify and deal with risks early in the development cycle.
- Senior managers rate the performance impact lower than project managers, and blame performance issues on weak project management rather than on contingencies.
- The strongest influences on risk management emerge from three enterprise areas: (1) work process, (2) organizational environment, and (3) people.
- Effective risk managers are capable of more than understanding the tools and techniques of enterprise risk management. They also understand the dynamics of their organizations and can deal with the complex social, technical, and economic issues that determine the culture and value system of the enterprise.
- Effective risk management focuses on risk reduction via simplifying the work and its transfer processes, shortening development cycles, and testing project feasibility early.
- Successful methods of risk management involve effective cross-functional communications and collaboration among all stakeholders.

14.10 QUESTIONS FOR DISCUSSION

1. Discuss the type of risks that may occur in a high-tech product development project of your choice (e.g., computer, pharmaceutical, automotive, etc., or, use the chapter lead-in Intel Centrino® scenario).
2. What kind of similarities and differences do you see in the type of risks between hardware, software, and service product developments? Discuss.
3. What kind of an "early warning system" could you implement to detect the type of risks discussed in question 1?
4. Discuss risk management approaches within the five categories of (a) identifying and managing risk factors, (b) simplifying the product and product design, (c) simplifying the development process, (d) reducing product development time, and (e) testing product feasibility early. Choose a project or mission similar to the one you used in question 1 or select an industry group such as computers, pharmaceuticals, or automotive.
5. Discuss the type of risks that may originate with each of the three areas within the enterprise (a) work and its process, (b) analytical tools and methods, and (c) people. Refer to a specific situation, such as chosen in question 1.
6. Discuss managerial leadership styles most conducive to risk management. What type of team environment would be most effective? How can you foster such an environment?
7. How can top management facilitate effective risk management at the project team level?

14.11 *PMBOK*® REFERENCES AND CONNECTIONS

The topic of *risk management* focuses specifically on the *PMBOK*® Knowledge Area #8 with the same title. The topic also cuts across all five PMBOK® processing groups, connecting most strongly with: planning, executing and monitoring/controlling. Much of this chapter addresses the *context* of project management, discussing the challenges and managerial actions of effective risk management, going beyond the framework set forth in the PMBOK standards. The broader perspective of risk management provided in this chapter should be helpful to effectively applying the PMBOK standards to the day-to-day management of projects and to study effectively for PMP® certification. In studying for the PMP® Exam, an understanding of the following concepts will be beneficial: (1) definition of risk in projects and the notion of risk management, (2) identifying risks, (3) risk analysis, both quantitative and qualitative. (4) tools for risk quantification, and (5) risk management plan.

INTERNET LINKS AND RESOURCES

Academy of program/project and Engineering Leadership (a NASA monthly e-newsletter Publication). www.nasa.gov/offices/oce/appel/home/index.html (updated April 8, 2013)

Intel. "Intel Launches Intel® Centrino™ Mobile Technology" (news release March 12, 2003). www.intel.com/pressroom/archive/releases/2003/20030312comp.htm

PMI Risk Management Professional (PMI-RMP Certification). www.pmi.org/certification/pmi-risk-management-professional-pmi-rmp.aspx (updated 2013)

Project Management Institute. Project Risk Management Community of Practice. http://risk.vc.pmi.org/Public/Home.aspx

Standish Group Chaos Report 2012. http://blog.standishgroup.com/

Wikipedia, Centrino. http://en.wikipedia.org/wiki/Centrino (updated March 23, 2013)

REFERENCES AND ADDITIONAL READINGS

Apgar, D. 2006. *Risk Intelligence: Learning to Manage What We Don't Know*. Boston, MA: Harvard Business School Press.

Barber, R. B. 2005. "Understanding Internally Generated Risks in Projects." *International Journal of Project Management* 23(8): 584–590.

Barlett, J. 2002. "Risk Concept Mapping." Proceedings, *Fifth European Project Management Conference*, Cannes, France (June 19–20).

Besner, C., and B. Hobbs. 2012. "The Paradox of Risk Management; A Project Management Practice Perspective." *International Journal of Managing Projects in Business* 5(2): 230–247.

Bstieler, L. 2005. "The Moderating Effects of Environmental Uncertainty on New Product Development and Time Efficiency." *Journal of Product Innovation Management* 22(3): 267–284.

Buchanan, L., and A. O'Connell. 2006. "Chances Are." *Harvard Business Review* 84(1): 34–35.

Chapman, C., and S. Ward. 2003. *Project Risk Management: Process, Techniques and Insight*. London, UK: John Wiley and Sons.

Ciemil, S., and D. Marshall. 2005. "Insight into Collaboration at the Project Level: Complexity, Social Interaction and Procurement Mechanisms." *Building Research and Information* 33(6): 523–535.

Cooke-Davies, T., S. Ciemil, L. Crawford, and K. Richardson. 2007. "We're Not in Kansas Anymore Toto: Mapping the Strange Landscape of Complexity Theory, and Its Relationship to Project Management." *Project Management Journal* 35(2): 50–61.

Cooper, D., S. Grey, G. Raymond, and P. Walker, P. 2005. *Project Risk Management Guidelines: Managing Risk in Large Projects and Complex Procurements*. Hoboken, NJ: John Wiley & Sons.

Cooper, R., S. Edgett, and E. Kleinschmidt. 2001. *Portfolio Management for New Products*. Da Capo Press.

de Bakker, K., A. Boonstra, and H. Wortmann. 2012. "Risk Managements' Communicative Effects Influencing IT Project Success." *International Journal of Project Management* 30(4): 444–455.

Dey, P. K. 2002. "Project Risk Management." *Cost Engineering* 44(3): 13–27.

DOD Directive 5000.1. 2007. Washington, DC: Government Printing Office.

Elliott, M. 2001. "The Emerging Field of Enterprise Risk." *Viewpoint* 2 (2) (March).

Geraldi, J., and G. Adlbrecht. 2007. "On Faith, Fact and Interaction in Projects." *Project Management Journal* 38(1): 32–43.

Haas, K. 2009. *Managing Complex Projects: A New Model*. Vienna, VA: Management Concepts.

Hanzhang, T., and R. Wilkinson. 1998. *The Art of War*. Hertfordshire, UK: Wordsworth Editions.

Hillson, D. 1999. "Business Uncertainty: Risk or Opportunity." *ETHOS Magazine* 13 (June/July): 14–17.

———. 2000. "Project Risks—Identifying Causes, Risks and Effects." *PM Network*, 14(9): 48–51.

———. 2003. "Gaining Strategic Advantage." *Strategic Risk Magazine* (June 27–28).

———. 2010. "Managing Risk in Projects: What's New?" *PMWorld Today* (*Project Management eJournal*) 12(2) (February), Column #2.

ISO. 2009. ISO 31000, Risk Management: Principles and Guidelines. Geneva, Switzerland: International Organization for Standardization (ISO).

Jaofari, A. 2003. "Project Management in the Age of Change." *Project Management Journal* 34(4): 47–57.

Kallman, J. 2006. "Managing Risk." *Risk Management* 52(12): 46.

Kwan, T., and H. Leung. 2011. "A Risk Management Methodology for Project Risk Dependencies." *IEEE Transactions on Software Engineering* 37(5): 635–648.

Loch, C. H., M. E. Solt, and E. M. Bailey. 2008. "Diagnosing Unforeseeable Uncertainty in a New Venture." *Journal of Product Innovation Management* 25(1): 28–46.

Marle, F., L. Vidal, and J. Bocquet. 2013. "Interactions-Based Risk Clustering Methodologies and Algorithms for Complex Project Management." *International Journal of Production Economics* 142(2): 225–236.

Maylor, H., R. Vidgen, and S. Carver. 2008. "Managerial Complexity in Project-Based Operations: A Ground Model and Its Implications for Practice." *Project Management Journal* 39(1): 15–26.

National Institute of Standards and Technology 2000. *Managing Technical Risk: Understanding Private Sector Decision Making on Early Stage, Technology-Based*

Projects. NIST Publication No. GCR 00–787. Washington, DC: US Government Printing Office.

Nellore, R., and R. Balachandra. 2001. "Factors Influencing Success in Integrated Product Development (IPD) Projects." *IEEE Transactions on Engineering Management* 48(2): 164–173.

Patil, R., Grantham, K., and D. Steele. 2012. "Business Risk in Early Design: A Business Risk Assessment Approach." *Engineering Management Journal* 24(1): 35–46.

Project Management Institute. 2013. *A Guide to the Project Management Body of Knowledge (PMBOK® Guide)*. Newtown Square, PA: Project Management Institute.

"Psychological Impacts on Judgment, Estimation, and Risk Assessment." *Ask the Academy* (NASA publication) 5(2) (February 29).

Shaw, C., K. Abrams, and T. Marteau. 1999. "Psychological Impact of Predicting Individuals' Risks of Illness: A Systematic Review." *Social Science and Medicine* 49(12): 1571–1598.

Shenhar, A. J. 2001. "One Size Does Not Fit All Projects: Exploring Classical Contingency Domains." *Management Science* 47(3): 394–414.

Shenhar, A., and D. Dvir. 2007. *Reinventing Project Management: The Diamond Approach to Successful Growth and Innovation*. Cambridge, MA: Harvard Business School Press.

Shenhar A, D. Milosevic, D, Dvir, and H. Thamhain. 2007. *Linking Project Management to Business Strategy*. Newtown, PA: Project Management Institute Press.

Smith, P. G., and G. M. Merritt. 2002. *Proactive Risk Management*. New York: Productivity Press.

Smith, T. 2013. "Intel's Centrino Notebook Platform is 10 Years Old." www.theregister.co.uk/2013/03/12/feature_intel_centrino_notebook_brand_ten_years_old/. Updated March 12, 2013.

Srivannaboon, S., and D. Z. Milosevic. 2006. "A Two-Way Influence between Business Strategy and Project Management." *International Journal of Project Management* 24(2): 184–197.

Thamhain, H. 2004. "Leading Technology Teams." *Project Management Journal* 35(4): 35–47.

———. 2011. "Critical Success Factors for Managing Technology-Intensive Teams the Global Enterprise." *Engineering Management Journal* 23(3): 30–36.

———. 2013. "Managing Risks in Complex Projects." *Project Management Journal (PMJ)* 44(2): 20–35.

Thamhain, H., and T. Skelton. 2007. "Success Factors for Effective R&D Risk Management." *International Journal of Technology Intelligence and Planning (IJTIP)* 3(4): 376–386.

———. 2009. "Managing Globally Dispersed R&D Teams." *International Journal of Information Technology and Management (IJITM)* 8(1): 107–126.

Thamhain, H., and D. Wilemon. 1999. "Building Effective Teams in Complex Project Environments." *Technology Management* 5(2): 203–212.

Thieme R., M. Song, and G. Shin. 2003. "Project Management Characteristics and New Product Survival." *Journal of Product Innovation Management* 20(2): 104–111.

Thomas, J., and T. Mengel. 2008. "Preparing Project Managers to Deal with Complexity." *International Journal of Project Management* 26(3):304–315.

Torok, R., C. Nordman, and S. Lin. 2011. *Clearing the Clouds: Shining a Light on Successful Enterprise Risk Management*. Executive Report, IBM Institute for Business Value. Somers, NY: IBM Global Services.

Wideman, R. M. 1992. *Project and Program Risk Management: A Guide to Managing Project Risks and Opportunities*. Newtown Square, PA: Project Management Institute.

Williams, T. 2005. "Assessing and Moving from a Dominant Project Management Discourse in the Light of Project Overruns." *IEEE Transactions on Engineering Management* 52(4): 497–508.

Williams, T., and K. Sumset. 2010. "Issues in Front-End Decision-Making on Projects." *Project Management Journal* 41(2): 38–49.

Chapter 15

Managing by Commitment and Collaboration

WIND ENERGY RESEARCH

"If you could close your eyes for just a moment like Rip Van Winkle, and blink them open in 2023, you might see a very different energy world," says Clifford Krauss (2013) in a *New York Times* editorial on energy and environment. Among the many changes, he also foresees "explosive growth" in renewable energy for electricity, with wind generation systems now running at a cost below that of many older power plants. "We are going to see a lot of change in power generation over the next 10 years," he said. However, progress does not come by chance or luck, it is driven by systematic, well-coordinated and collaborative efforts. One of the organizations facilitating, stimulating, and promoting industry-wide efforts of renewable energy development is the National Renewable Energy Laboratory (NREL). Funded by the US Department of Energy, NREL's efforts at the National Wind Technology Center (NWTC) have contributed to numerous successes. In addition to helping its industry partners develop commercially successful wind turbines, NREL has developed award-winning components and modeling software. The Laboratory also engages in deployment activities that help schools, communities, and utilities understand the benefits of wind energy and how it can be successfully integrated into our nation's electrical system to provide for a cleaner, more secure energy future.

Many of NREL's R&D projects focus on reducing the cost of wind technology and expanding access to wind energy technology. "Our specialized technical expertise, comprehensive design and analysis tools, and unique testing facilities help industry overcome challenges to bringing new wind technology to the marketplace," explains NREL's website:

> We also work closely with universities and other national laboratories supporting fundamental research in wind technologies, including aerodynamics, aeroacoustics,

Source: National Renewable Energy Laboratory (NREL). "Success Stories and Accomplishments:" www.nrel.gov/about/accomplishments.html.

and material sciences essential in the development of new blade technologies and advanced controls, power electronics, and testing to further refine drivetrain topology. Specifically, we work with industry to (1) reduce the cost of wind turbine technology, (2) increase wind energy system reliability and operability, (3) lower risk and validate performance and design, (4) improve power transmission and grid integration issues, (5) mitigate wind plant siting and environmental issues, and (6) expand wind energy markets.

Current research includes a wide range of projects from offshore wind energy to wind turbine research, utility grid integration, environmental impacts, and international research collaborations. To be successful, all of these projects require extraordinary collaboration and commitments from many government agencies and the participating companies to overcome key barriers that include the relatively high cost of energy, the mitigation of environmental impacts, technology development, technical difficulties of project installation, and grid interconnection.

15.1 THE CRITICAL ROLE OF COMMITMENT AND COLLABORATION

It's easy to lose sight of what really drives project performance in large, complex projects. While technical skill sets, management tools, and effective work processes are absolutely critical, the work environment and leadership style that fosters commitment and collaboration are equally important. As we can imagine, successfully managing complex, multiagency projects, such as NREL's wind energy technology developments, takes more than a sophisticated project control system. Even the best project management technology and most skillfully applied scheduling and budgeting tools will not be sufficient to orchestrate the various US government departments, nongovernment organizations (NGOs) and participating companies to execute these project according to the established plans and mission objectives. For the conventional project management system to work, we need an *additional system* of "self-forcing control." We have to foster a culture of collaboration and commitment across the whole project community and its support functions. Let's take a specific look at the challenges.

15.1.1 Issues and Challenges

There is little argument: Commitment is critical to project success in today's complex business environment. However, it is also difficult to obtain and to sustain because it deals with many issues outside the framework of traditional managerial control. This is especially true for large, complex, or multinational endeavors that typically require the integration of many activity sets and subsystems across geographically dispersed areas and countries, involving many stakeholders such as contractors, customers, government agencies, and globally distributed work groups with different cultures, enterprise systems, and leadership personnel. It also requires dealing effectively with political, social, and economic processes, resource sharing, multiple reporting relationships, and broadly based alliances across the enterprise and its partners.

15.1.2 Definitions

Although the process for gaining commitment and gaining collaboration is very similar for both, the outcome is different.

Commitment—A psychological contract between individuals or groups to reach an agreed-on goal or objective. In the strongest sense, individuals or groups will try their utmost to reach the goal regardless of any obstacles, personal hardship, or cost. Commitments are difficult and costly to reverse, and they restrict future options for the individuals or groups who committed to a certain act or goal.

Collaboration—An attitude of individuals or groups toward actions that support others to reach a common goal. Although collaboration might also require some personal effort and cost, it is much less intense and less psychologically engaged than commitment.

The process of building commitment or collaboration is similar for both. It involves the conditioning of individuals or groups toward buy-in or accepting certain objectives. This process unifies the team and transforms the goals and energies of all project stakeholders toward specific objectives and desired results.

Commitment and collaboration are characterized by a broad spectrum of components and challenges that define their nature. They are powerful management tools critical to project success, but also difficult to obtain, and the personal efforts are often underestimated.

Characteristics of Commitment and Collaboration

Commitment and collaboration have similar characteristics and affect the project outcome in a similar way. Yet by definition the psychological contract between the parties is much stronger and more costly to reverse for commitments than they are for collaboration. Both collaboration and commitment encompass a broad spectrum of overlapping components that characterize their nature and define the process of transforming the goals and energies of all project stakeholders toward specific objectives. The statements below include the responses of a field study of 500 project leaders characterizing collaboration and commitment.

Characteristics and Dimensions of Collaboration:
- People or organizations work together to realize shared goals
- Involves processes of integrating people (cross-functionally) to achieve common goals
- Strong collective determination to reach a common goal or objective
- Succeeds only is participants' goals are compatible
- Creates expanded vision of issue or mission
- Requires accountability to desired results
- Increases team effectiveness and synergy
- Involves effective communications and feedback
- Involves knowledge sharing, learning and consensus building
- Promote learning, knowledge creation, and knowledge sharing
- Promotes a professionally stimulating environment and makes work more enjoyable
- A mindset, an attitude, and behavior that can be developed and conditioned
- Embedded in the culture and promoted by example
- Different meanings, so definition and expectations must be clear

Characteristics and Dimensions of Commitment:
- An emotionally binding contract or promise to engage in a specific activity or work toward a specific goal
- A collaborative effort with colleagues toward specific goals
- Binding yourself, intellectually and emotionally specific goals or actions
- A moral contract or obligation to a course of action
- Determination to work hard toward an agreed-on goal
- Supporting team decisions, agenda or agreed-on plans, even though these plans may not entirely reflect own position
- Accepting joint responsibilities for team agenda
- Working in partnership with team and management
- Promoting a climate of teamwork and collaboration
- Pursuing the effective use of common resources
- Sharing of information, concerns, and support
- Providing support to others
- Reaching out to deal with and resolve issues
- Helping to share risks with others by supporting decisions
- Full participation, engagement, and dedication in/to a given project
- Open and candid communication

15.2 WHAT DO WE KNOW ABOUT COLLABORATION AND COMMITMENT?

Despite of all the recent attention by management researchers and practitioners, collaboration and commitment are not new ideas. They have been used effectively for thousands of years by emperors, religious leaders, architects, and merchants to create and unify stakeholder communities across geographic borders and cultures. Already 2,500 years ago, the great Chinese military strategist Sun Tzu, who I cited already in Chapter 14 on risk management, utilized collaboration as a powerful tool for "unifying objectives across distance, technology . . . and building committed alliances" (Hanzhang and Wilkinson 1998). In more modern times, starting with some subtle references by Igor Ansoff in 1965 and Walton's classic 1985 article "From Control to Commitment in the Workplace," commitment has become a major building block of organizational theory and management practice.

More recently, much of the theoretical framework for commitment and collaboration has been established under the umbrella of organizational stakeholder relations (Harrison and Freeman 1999), with a good part of the body of knowledge summarized in the writings of Donaldson and Preston (1995), Jones and Wicks (1999), Luoma and Goldstein (1999), and Mitchell et al. (1997). Although most of the earlier research focused on either social or economic implications of stakeholder commitment (Berman et al. 1999; Luoma and Goldstein 1999), or more general aspects of employee commitment grounded in the construct of social exchange theory (Lambert 2000), the increased complexities of today's business environment that changed the project dynamics and work processes have forced management to expand attention from a traditional, trait-oriented focus to a broader spectrum of influences that include the team ambience and overall enterprise environment. Therefore, it is not surprising that in today's multinational and technologically complex business environment, both collaboration and commitment are being recognized as essential management tools for transforming multifunctional groups of individuals with different interests, needs, backgrounds, and expertise into integrated, collaborative project teams (Anconda and Bresman 2007, Hackman 2002, Kruglianskas and Thamhain 2000).

Because of this strong managerial interest and the impact on business results, a substantial body of knowledge evolved in the broader area of project teamwork and team leadership related to both commitment and collaboration. Scholar such as Armstrong (2000), Barkema, Baum, and Mannix (2002), Dillon, (2001), Hilton (2008), Kearney et al. (2009), Kirkman and Shapiro (2001), Sawhney (2002), Shim and Lee (2001), Siders et al. (2001), Sidle (2009), and Thamhain and Wilemon (1999) have studied project teams extensively, root-causing their successes and failures and identifying organizational conditions for effective teamwork, including the critical role of collaboration and commitment (Anconda et al. 2007, Hackman 2002, 2006, Kruglianskas and Thamhain 2000).

Indeed, the existing literature on commitment and collaboration is quite extensive in discussing the broad issues and in establishing a theoretical framework. Yet despite of all this research, *only one in eight project managers feels confident of building and sustaining commitment or full collaboration* among the members of their project community (Thamhain 2013). Many of these managers lament that not enough guidelines, perspectives, tools, and techniques are available to help in dealing with the complex issues of commitment and collaboration.

15.2.1 The Missing Link

Although we have gained sophisticated knowledge and substantial insight into the effects and organizational dynamics of managing project teams, including the role of commitment and collaboration in specific segments of the business process and its support functions, such as manufacturing, marketing, human resources, finance, and accountancy (Hausknecht et al. 2008, Burgess and Turner 2000, Keil et al. 2000), we have been largely unable to define specific commitment-performance relationships (Schmidt and Calantone 2002, Benkoff 1997, Gregersen 1993, Siders et al. 2001). That is, relatively little is known about the effectiveness of team leadership styles and the organizational conditions most conducive to team collaboration and commitment, and their effects on project performance in complex business environments. The missing link is the influence of leadership style, work environment, and project characteristics on the strength of commitment and its impact on project performance, an area that is being discussed in the remaining chapter as part of a recent field study (see Appendix of this chapter, 15.11).

15.3 DRIVERS AND BARRIERS TO COLLABORATION AND COMMITMENT

The initial focus of this discussion is on commitment. As we investigated both commitment and collaboration in parallel, we found that the same conditions that drive commitment also support collaboration. However, obtaining and sustaining commitment is more difficult than collaboration. And once you have commitment, you also get collaboration. Let's focus on commitment first.

Using primarily data from the recent field study, Table 15.1 summarizes the basic drivers of commitment in complex project environments. Specifically, content analysis of the survey data was obtained from three sources: (1) interviews, (2) questionnaires, and (3) observations, to identify the most common components that support and drive individual, as well as team commitment. The data are organized into two categories: *primary drivers* and *secondary* or *derivative drivers*. Primary drivers were obtained during the interviews with project leaders and team members by asking, "What conditions in the team environment are important for getting individual or collective team member commitment?" To learn about secondary drivers, we ask, "For the conditions

Table 15.1   Drivers toward Commitment

Primary Drivers	Secondary Drivers	
Team/project environment has ...	**Team/project environment is high on ...**	
Personal qualities: • Trust • Respect • Competence • Credibility • Charisma • Empathy • Benefits Project characteristics: • Interesting, professional stimulating work • Recognition of accomplishments • Visibility • Priority • Success image • Management Involvement • Low risk • Low organizational and personal conflict	• Accomplishments • Autonomy and freedom, flexibility • Clear project goals and plans • Clear project objectives and directions • Conflict resolution • Contingency planning and handling • Continuous improvement of work process • Cross-functional interfaces • Effective communication channels • Fair, equitable performance measures/ evaluation • Good team spirit and morale • Good work environment • Help/support to problem solving • Job security • Knowledge, skills, skill development	• Personal/team pride and ownership • Professional advancement • Professionally stimulating, interesting, challenging work • Recognition • Rewards and satisfaction of needs • Risk sharing • Smooth project administration • Sufficient resources • Team and work visibility • Team involvement in work • Team member support and cooperation • Unified team environment • Upper management endorsement of pm leadership • Upper management support of work • Winning team image and attitude
	Team/project environment is shielded from ... • Conflict, organizational tension, and politics • Excessive demands and performance pressures • Organizational instability • Unrealistic project requirements and changes	

of commitment just identified, what is necessary, in terms of leadership and organizational support, to create these conditions?"

While the primary conditions are rank-ordered by frequency of reported answers, the secondary conditions are just being listed alphabetically. The alphabetical listing seem to be the best option to avoid false rank-order representation, given the subtitle connections between primary and secondary frequencies and some other interview related issues. The significance of listing both primary and secondary conditions is to show some of the depth and breadth that lies behind the criteria that drive or hinder commitment. Further, it shows that primary conditions cannot be created in isolation, but must be carefully "cultivated and earned." Hence, the primary drivers to commitment, such as trust, respect, and credibility, are only derivatives of a much larger set of conditions that must be present to develop the principle or primary drivers. Another interesting finding is the discrepancy between team leader and team member responses. Team members identified at a 100 percent higher frequency (twice as often) the importance of trust, respect, credibility, accomplishments, recognition, and probability of success than their team leaders. Interestingly, these were also the conditions that were identified in the correlation analysis of this study (see correlation tables in the chapter appendix) as the strongest drivers toward gaining and sustaining commitment. In addition, we noticed that only few of the project leaders are sufficiently familiar with the broad spectrum of components that support or hinder team commitment, which suggests that many of these managers might not be effective in applying commitment processes in their organizations. On average, less than one-third of the project leaders interviewed could name more than half of the components shown in Table 15.1. All of this might explain, at least in part, why many project leaders have difficulties getting commitment from their teams.

Obviously, understanding these drivers, their sources, and secondary influence factors is an important prerequisite for gaining and maintaining commitment from the team, and hence a critical success factor for leading project teams effectively toward desired results.

Many observations from this study point to the importance of a workable plan and "can-do" project situation that is reasonably low on risk, anxiety, and interpersonal conflict, as conducive to team commitment and high project performance. Equally important seems to be interesting, professionally stimulating work, which is high on recognition, accomplishments, and management involvement. These conditions seem to affect motivation of individual team members toward participation in the project and the desire to achieve the necessary results. They also have favorable effects on team spirit, team unification, cross-functional communications, and other components that ultimately support the ability to gain and sustain commitment. These conditions seem to be especially critical for maintaining commitment in situations involving stretch goals. This was also confirmed with the statistical tests. The Kendall tau analysis, summarized in the chapter appendix, measures the association among variables of the work environment, leadership style, commitment, and project performance. The results show indeed that those conditions, which are conducive to risk reduction and a professionally stimulating work environment, also lead to higher levels of (1) initial commitment and (2) sustained commitment. The same conditions also correlate strongly to (3) team performance and (4) an image of project success. Equally important, we find that the same conditions that support commitment also facilitate collaboration. In fact, we find that collaboration is an embedded function of commitment. That is, individuals and teams must buy into a plan and its objectives before they are willing and ready to collaborate. Yet, in comparison to collaboration, commitment requires a much stronger psychological bond or contract, which in turn requires higher levels of risk sharing, management support, personal confidence and trust, to ensure that the psychological cost of commitment is not too high.

15.4 MANAGING BY COMMITMENT

Project managers point out consistently that for today's complex and technology-based undertakings, success is no longer the result of a few expert contributors and skilled project leaders. Rather, project success depends on effective multidisciplinary collaborative efforts, involving teams of people and support organizations interacting in a highly complex, intricate, and sometimes even chaotic way. This is especially true for multinational efforts with widely distributed power and resources, and managerial controls that can no longer be directed top-down but must be shared among team leaders at the local level. This is a process that requires experiential learning, trial and error, risk taking, as well as the cross-functional coordination and integration of technical knowledge, information and components. Yet, in spite of all of these challenges, many project teams are highly effective, producing great results within agreed-on budget and schedule constraints. This suggests that even complex, multinational, and technology-based projects can be managed toward agreed-on results, given the right team environment. One characteristic that these high-performing teams seem to have in common is the commitment to desired results and overall project success.

Based on the lessons learned from this field research and other studies of best practices, we can suggest some answers to two important questions that were raised at the beginning of this chapter regarding the ability to control projects and to drive project performance:

- What conditions in the project environment are conducive to gaining and sustaining team commitment and collaboration?
- How does project leadership style influence commitment and collaboration?

Specific suggestions will be discussed with focus on three categories: people, organizational process, and work/task related influences to commitment.

15.4.1 People-Oriented Influences

Factors that satisfy professional interests and needs seem to have the strongest effect on the ability to obtain and eventually sustain commitment over the project lifecycle. The most significant drivers are derived from the work itself, including personal interest, pride and satisfaction with the work, professional work challenge, accomplishments and recognition, as well as the trust, respect and credibility placed in the team leader. Other important influences include effective communications among team members and support units across organizational lines, good team spirit, mutual trust, low interpersonal conflict and personal pride, plus opportunities for career development, advancement, and, to some degree, job security. These conditions serve as bridging mechanisms, helpful in enhancing project performance, especially in complex project environments that involve technology and multinational settings. All of these factors help in building a unified project team that can leverage the organizational strengths and competencies effectively, and produce integrated results that support the organization's mission objective.

What lessons can effective team leaders take away from this? Creating such a climate and culture conducive to quality teamwork involves multifaceted management challenges, which increase with the complexities of the project and its organizational environment. No longer will technical expertise or good leadership alone be sufficient, but excellence across a broad range of skills and sophisticated organizational support is required to manage project teams effectively. Hence, it is critically important for project leaders to understand, identify and minimize the potential barriers to team development. Leading such self-directed teams can rarely be done "top-down," but requires a great deal of interactive team management skills and senior management support at the local level of the multinational team.

15.4.2 Organizational Process, Tools, and Techniques

Successful management of culturally diverse project teams requires a unified managerial process. This includes organizational structures and technology transfer processes that relies, by-and-large, on modern project management techniques. Although the research did not favor specific project structures and processes over others, it specifically pointed at effective project planning and support systems, clear communication, organizational goals and project objectives, and overall managerial leadership as important conditions for effectively gaining and sustaining commitment. An effective project management system also includes effective cross-functional support, joint reviews and performance appraisals, and the availability of the necessary resources, skills, and facilities. Other crucial components that affect the organizational process and ultimately commitment are team structure, managerial power, and its sharing among the team members and organizational units, autonomy and freedom, and most importantly technical direction and leadership. This requires a skillfully designed management system with enough flexibility and adaptability to local leadership while functioning consistently within established organizational norms and cultures. This is a big challenge, especially for multinational companies; it requires resources and senior management support toward the development of a unified work process. Focus groups, organizational studies, internal and external consultants, process action teams, and professional training and teambuilding sessions all are powerful tools for unifying and optimizing the work flow and managing process.

Many of the variables related to organizational process are primarily under the control of senior management. They are often a derivative of the company's business strategy developed by top management. It is important for management to recognize that these variables affect the team's perception of the work environment, such as organizational stability, availability of resources, management involvement and support, personal rewards, organizational goals, objectives and priorities, and therefore have a direct effect on commitment. Hence, it is important for management to understand the personal and professional needs and wants of their team members, and to foster an organizational environment conducive to these needs. Proper communications of organizational vision and perspective is especially important. The relationship of managers to staff and people in their organizations is critical to building an effective partnership between the project team and its management and sponsor organization, as are mutual trust and respect.

15.4.3 Work and Task-Related Influences

Commitment also has its locus in the work itself. This is highlighted in the correlations of Tables 15.2 through 15.6 in the appendix (section 15.9). The statistical tests, supported by interviews and observations clearly shows that those variables associated with the personal aspects of work—such as interest in the project, ability to solve problems, minimize risks and uncertainties, job skills, and experience—are statistically significant in driving commitment. Many other work-related variables from the structural side, such as project size, complexity, and work process, had no statistically significance for gaining or sustaining commitment.

The managerial significance of this finding is in two areas. First, project leaders must be able to attract and hold people with the right skill sets, appropriate for the work to be performed. They must also invest in maintaining and upgrading job skill and support systems. Second, managers must effectively partition and assign the work. That is, while the total task structure and the development process is fixed and more difficult to change, the way managers distribute, assign, and present the work is flexible. Therefore, promoting a climate of high interest, involvement, and support might be *easier* to achieve than redefining the project or reengineering the work process, yet it might have a *higher* impact on the commitment process.

15.5 CONCLUSION

Taken together, effective project managers understand the nature and power of commitment and collaboration and can foster an organizational ambience that unifies the greater project team behind the established mission objectives. Such collaborative, committed teams are "self-controlling," providing early warning systems and engaging in proactive problem solving. This creates a critical reinforcement of the conventional project management system that is effective in communicating and analyzing information but weak in identifying issues in their early stages and proactively dealing with these issues. Fostering such a self-controlling project environment requires carefully developed skills in leadership, administration, organization, and technical expertise. It further requires the project leader's ability to involve top management, to ensure organizational visibility, resource availability, and overall support for the project throughout its life cycle.

People cannot be programmed to collaborate. Building commitment and collaboration requires a leadership style that relies, to a large degree, on shared power and earned authority. By understanding the criteria and organizational dynamics that drive people toward commitment, managers can examine and fine-tune the work environment and leadership style. Team leaders can also build alliances with support organizations and upper management to ensure organizational visibility, priority, resource availability, and overall support for the project and its people throughout its life cycle. These are some of the important criteria for gaining and sustaining and commitment, and for building a collaborative culture within today's tightly interconnected project teams—conditions that are crucial to project success.

15.6 SUMMARY OF KEY POINTS AND CONCLUSIONS

The following key points were made in this chapter:

- Management by commitment provides a "self-forcing" control environment that reinforces the conventional project management system.
- Commitment is a psychological contract between individuals or groups to reach an agreed-on goal or objective.
- Collaboration is an attitude of individuals or groups toward actions that support others to reach a common goal.
- The same conditions that drive commitment also support collaboration. However, obtaining and sustaining commitment is more difficult.
- The theoretical framework for commitment and collaboration has been established under the umbrella of organizational stakeholder relations. However, relatively little is known about leadership effectiveness and the organizational conditions conducive to team collaboration and commitment.
- The primary drivers toward commitment derive from two sources: (1) management/people: trust, respect, competence, credibility, charisma,

empathy, benefits; and (2) work environment: accomplishments, recognition, visibility, priority, success image, management involvement, low risk, conflict, and anxiety.

- Factors that satisfy professional interests seem to have the strongest effect on the ability to obtain and sustain commitment.
- The most significant drivers to commitment are derived from the work itself, including personal interest, pride and satisfaction with the work, accomplishments and recognition, plus the trust, respect, and credibility of the team leader.
- People cannot be programmed to collaborate. Building commitment and collaboration requires a leadership style that relies, to a large degree, on shared power and earned authority, and a skillfully designed management system with enough flexibility for people to interact effectively.
- Appropriate skill sets and competence of the work force are critical to obtaining true team commitment.
- Many of the variables related to commitment and collaboration connect with organizational processes under the control of senior management (i.e., resource availability, management support, personal rewards, organizational goals, objectives, and priorities). It is important for management to recognize these linkages and to provide favorable conditions if possible.

15.7 QUESTIONS FOR DISCUSSION

1. Discuss why and how commitment and collaboration help in executing/controlling projects according to established plans, on schedule and within budget?
2. Why is commitment especially important for managing complex or multinational projects?
3. What kind of provisions could you suggest to ensure that the organizational structure and work process is conducive to commitment and collaboration?
4. What advice would you give to a newly appointed project manager to build trust, respect, and credibility with the team?
5. Discuss the characteristics of a team leadership style conducive to building a culture of commitment and collaboration. What are some of the dos and don'ts?
6. How can top management help in facilitating a project environment conducive to commitment and collaboration?

15.8 *PMBOK®* REFERENCES AND CONNECTIONS

The topic of commitment and collaboration focuses on three PMBOK® knowledge areas: #6 (project human resource management), #7 (project communications management), and #10 (project stakeholder management). The topic also cuts across three PMBOK® processing groups: planning, executing, and monitoring/controlling. Much of this chapter focuses on the context of project planning, executing, and monitoring/controlling, discussing the need for team collaboration and commitment, and the role for project control. The managerial perspectives presented in this chapter should be helpful in connecting the PMBOK standards to best practices of project management, and to study effectively for PMP® certification. In studying for the PMP® Exam, an understanding of the following concepts will be beneficial: (1) managing stakeholder expectations, (2) project plan communications, (3) managing project execution, and (4) project monitoring and controlling.

INTERNET LINKS AND RESOURCES

National Renewable Energy Laboratory. "Success Stories and Accomplishments." www.nrel.gov/about/accomplishments.html
Project Management Institute. "Welcome to the Leadership in PM Community of Practice." http://leadershipinpm.vc.pmi.org/Public/Home.aspx
Wikipedia. February 26, 2013. "High Commitment Management." http://en.wikipedia .org/wiki/High_commitment_management

REFERENCES AND ADDITIONAL READINGS

Anconda D., and H. Bresman. 2007. *X-teams: How to Build Teams that Lead, Innovate and Succeed*. Boston: HBS Publishing.
Anconda D., T. Malone, W. Orlikowski, and P. Senge. 2007. "It's Time to End the Myth of the Incomplete Leader." *Harvard Business Review* 85(1): 92–100.
Ansoff, I. 1965. *Corporate Strategy*. New York: McGraw-Hill.
———. 1988. *The New Corporate Strategy*. New York: John Wiley & Sons.
Barczak, G., E. McDonough, and N. Athanassiou. 2006. "So You Want to Be a Global Project Leader?" *Research Technology Management* 49(3): 28–36.
Barkema H., J. Baum, and E. Mannix. 2002. "Management Challenges in a New Time." *Academy of Management Journal* 45(5): 916–930.
Becker T. E., R. S. Billings, D. M. Eveleth, and N. L. Gilbert. 1996. "Foci and Bases of Employee Commitment: Implications for Job Performance." *Academy of Management Journal* 39(2): 464–482.
Benkoff B 1997. "Ignoring Commitment Is Costly: New Approaches Establish the Missing Link between Commitment and Performance." *Human Relations* 50(3): 701–726.
Berman, S., A.Wicks, S. Kotha, and T. Jones. 1999. "Does Stakeholder Orientation Matter? The Relationship between Stakeholder Management Models and Firm Financial Performance." *Academy of Management Journal* 42(5): 488–506.
Burgess, R., and S. Turner. 2000. "Seven Key Features for Creating and Sustaining Commitment." *International Journal of Project Management* 18(4): 225–233.
Dillon, P. 2001. "A Global Challenge." *Forbes* 168 (September 10): 73+.
Donaldson, T., and L. Preston. 1995. "The Stakeholder Theory of the Corporation: Concepts Evidence and Implications." *Academy of Management Journal* 38(1): 65–91.

Gregorsen H. B. 1993. "Multiple Commitments at Work and Extrarole Behavior during Three Stages of Organizational Tenure." *Journal of Business Research* 26(1): 31–47.

Hackman, J. 2002. *Leading Teams: Setting the Stage for Great Performance—The 5 Keys to Successful Teams.* Boston: Harvard Business School Press.

Hackman, J. 2006. "The Five Dysfunctions of a Team: A Leadership Fable." *Academy of Management Perspectives* 20(1): 122–125.

Hanzhang, T., and R. Wilkinson.1998. *The Art of War, Wordsworth Editions.*

Hausknecht J. P., N. J. Hiller, and R. J. Vance. 2008. "Work-unit Absenteeism: Effects of Satisfaction, Commitment, Labor Market Condition and Time." *Academy of Management Journal* 51(6): 1223–1245.

Harrison, J. S., and R. E. Freeman. 1999. "Stakeholders, Social Responsibility, and Performance: Empirical Evidence and Theoretical Perspectives." *Academy of Management Journal* 42(5): 479–485.

Hilton, M. 2008. "Skills for Work in the 21st Century." *Academy of Management Perspectives* 2(4): 63–78.

Hoegl M., K. Weinkauf, and H. G. Gemuenden. 2004. "Interteam Coordination, Project Commitment, and Teamwork in Multiteam R&D Projects: A Longitudinal Study." *Organization Science* 15(1): 38–55.

Jones, T. and A. Wicks. 1999. "Convergent stakeholder theory." *Academy of Management Journal* 42(2): 206–221.

Kearney, E., Gebert, D. and Voelpel, S. 2009. "When and How Diversity Benefits Teams." *Academy of Management Journal* 52(3): 350–372.

Keil, M., T. Bernard, and W. Kwok-Kee et al. 2000. "A Cross-Cultural Study on Escalation of Commitment Behavior in Software Projects." *MIS Quarterly* 24(2): 299–325.

Keller, R. 2001. Cross-Functional Project Groups in Research and NPD. *Academy of Management Journal* 44(3): 547–556.

Kirkman, B., and D. Shapiro,. 2001. "The Impact of Cultural Values on Job Satisfaction and Organizational Commitment in Self-Managing Work Teams: The Mediating Role of Employee Resistance." *Academy of Management Journal* 44(3): 557–569.

Krauss, C. 2013. "By 2023, a Changed World of Energy." *New York Times*, Energy & Environment Section, April 26, 2013.

Kruglianskas, I., and H. Thamhain. 2000. "Managing Technology-Based Projects in Multinational Environments." *IEEE Transactions on Engineering Management* 47(1): 55–64.

Lambert, S. J. 2000. "Added Benefits: The Link Between Work-Life Benefits and Organizational Citizenship Behavior." *Academy of Management Journal* 43(5): 801–815.

Luoma, P., and J. Goldstein. 1999. "Stakeholders and Corporate Boards: Institutional Influences on Board Composition and Structure." *Academy of Management Journal* 42(6): 553–563.

Mathieu J., and D. Zajac. 1990. "A Review and Meta-Analysis of the Antecedents, Correlates and Consequences of Organizational Commitment." *Psychological Bulletin* 108: 171–194.

Mitchell, R., B. Agle, and D. Wood. 1997. "Toward a Theory of Stakeholder Identification and Salience." *Academy of Management Journal* 40(6): 853–886.

Project Management Institute (PMI). 2013. *A Guide to the Project Management Body of Knowledge (PMBOK® Guide).* Newtown Square, PA: Project Management Institute.

Sawhney, M. 2002. "Don't Just Relate—Collaborate." *MIT Sloan Management Review* 43(3): 96–107.

Schmidt J. B., and R. J. Calantone. 2002. "Escalation of Commitment during New Product Development." *Journal of the Academy of Marketing Science* 30(1): 103–118.

Shim, D., and M. Lee. 2001. " Upward Influence Styles of R&D Project Leaders." *IEEE Transactions on Engineering Management* 48(4): 394–413.

Shirky C. 2008. "Institutions vs. Collaboration." MIT TED (recorded July 2005, posted May 28, 2009), www.ted.com/talks/clay_shirky_on_institutions_versus _collaboration.html

Siders M., G. Georg, and R. Dharwadkar. 2001. "The Relationship of Internal and External Commitment Foci to Objective Job Performance Measures." *Academy of Management Journal* 44(3): 570–579.

Sidle, S. 2009. "Building a Committed Workforce: Does What Employers Want Depend on Culture?" *Academy of Management Perspectives* 23(1): 79–80.

Thamhain, H. 2002. "Criteria for Effective Leadership in Technology-Oriented Project Teams." In Slevin, Cleland, and Pinto, eds., *The Frontiers of Project Management Research*. Newton Square, PA: Project Management Institute, pp. 259–270.

———. 2008. "Team Leadership Effectiveness in Technology-Based Project Environments." *IEEE Engineering Management Review* 36(1):165–180.

———. 2009. "Managing Globally Dispersed R&D Teams." *International Journal of Information Technology and Management (IJITM)* 8(1): 107–126.

———. 2011. "Critical Success Factors for Managing Technology-Intensive Teams in the Global Enterprise." *Engineering Management Journal* 23(3): 33–41.

———. 2013. "The Role of Commitment for Managing Complex Multinational Projects. *International Journal of Innovation and Technology Management* 12(3): 22–32.

Thamhain, H., and D. Wilemon.1999. "Building Effective Teams for Complex Project Environments." *Technology Management* 5(2): 203–212.

Walton, R.E. 1985. "From Control to Commitment in the Workplace." *Harvard Business Review* 63(1): 77–85.

Wong K. F., M. Yik, and J. Kwong. 2006. "Understanding the Emotional Aspects of Escalation of Commitment: The Role of Negative Affect." *Journal of Applied Psychology* 9(2): 282–297.

Wysocki, R. 2012. "Agile Project Management." In *Effective Project Management*. Hoboken, NJ: John Wiley & Sons.

15.9 APPENDIX: FIELD RESEARCH SUMMARY ON COMMITMENT

This appendix summarizes one of my field studies (2013) in support of the discussions, concepts and recommendations presented in this chapter. (Thamhain 2013). The results provide insight into the dynamics and the specific project management skill sets needed to foster a culture of collaboration and commitment across intricate organizational boundaries connecting support functions, suppliers, customers, and partners.

Research Design

An exploratory field research format was chosen for this empirical investigation. The format involves a combination of questionnaires and two qualitative methods: participant observation and in-depth retrospective interviewing. Specifically, data were captured between 2007 and 2012 from 35 product development teams and their management. These NPD projects were part of large multinational corporations (FORTUNE-1000 category) headquartered in the United States, Brazil, or European Union (EU). The projects involved high-technology product/service developments, such as information system, computer and pharmaceutical products, and financial services with project budgets averaging $1.4 million and life cycles of 1.6 years.

For each of these organizations, the research was conducted in three stages. In the first stage, interviews with project leaders and project team personnel, together with hands-on participant observations, helped to (1) understand the specific nature and challenges of the project work undertaken, (2) gain insight into the multinational nature and strategic linkages of their projects with the enterprise, (3) prepare for the design of the questionnaire and its proper introduction, and (4) design follow-up interviews. During the second stage, data were collected as part of a management consulting or training assignment, using questionnaires, observations, and expert panels. The third stage relied mostly on in-depth retrospective interviewing, providing perspective and additional information for clarifying and leveraging the data captured in stage one and two. As part of the action research, the data collection included other relevant source material, such as project progress reports, company reports, design review memos, committee action reports, financial statements, and information from the public media. This combined method is particularly useful for new and exploratory investigations, such as the study reported here, which is considerably outside the framework of established theories and constructs.

The questionnaire was designed to measure the (1) characteristics of the work environment, (2) leadership style, (3) level of commitment, and (4) project performance. To minimize potential biases that might result from the use of social science jargon, specific statements were developed to describe each of the variables of the work environment and team-performance, such as shown in the correlation tables. The format and process of the specific questionnaires and in-depth semi-structured *interviews* used in this study were developed and tested in previous field studies of R&D and NPD management, similar in context to the current investigation (Kruglianskas and Thamhain 2000; Thamhain 2002, 2003, 2007, 2009b).

Statistical Tests

Tables 15.2, 15.3, 15.4, 15.5, and 15.6 summarize the results of the Kendall tau analysis, measuring the association among variables of the work environment, leadership style, commitment, and project performance. The results show that those conditions, which are conducive to risk reduction and a professionally stimulating work environment, also lead to higher levels of (1) initial commitment and (2) sustained commitment. The same conditions also correlate strongly to (3) team performance and (4) an image of project success.

The strength of variables displayed in Tables 15.2 through 15.6 has been measured with descriptive statements on a five-point Likert scale: (1) strongly disagree, (2) disagree, (3) neutral, (4) agree, and (5) strongly agree, unless indicated differently (e.g., project size and duration). The agreement/disagreement judgment on these descriptive statements was made by team members (T), project managers (PM) or team leaders, or senior management (SM), as indicated.

Inputs were solicited from the individuals who could most appropriately judge the variable under investigation. For example, team members were asked to judge the quality of the work environment, such as communication effectiveness and leadership, and senior management was asked to judge the level of team performance and project success. Both senior management and project managers judged the team's commitment level.

Correlation Statistics

To break down the complexity, the statistical data have been divided into the five tables, showing project-related variables (Table 15.2), team-related variables (Table 15.3), team-leader-related variables (Table 15.4), leadership style-related variables (Table 15.5), and benefit/reward-related variables (Table 15.6). As indicated by the strong positive correlation, conditions that create a favorable image of the project, enhance the projection of success, or fulfill professional esteem needs seem to have a particularly favorable influence on the ability to obtain and sustain commitment from team members. These are also the conditions that produce the highest level of team performance and project success. The four most significant sets of associations are: (1) ability to minimize risks of project failure and uncertainties (Table 15.2, $\tau = 0.55$ and 0.65); (2) ability to develop clear, agreed-on plans with measurable milestones (Table 15.5, $\tau = 0.62, 0.55, 0.78, 0.55, 0.37$ and 0.40); (3) ability to foster a professionally stimulating and challenging work environment that is high on recognition of accomplishments, and opportunities for skill enhancement and career development (Table 15.6, $\tau = 0.43, 0.47, 0.47, 0.49, 0.45, 0.47$ and 0.38), also low on conflict, effective in communications, and high on team morale and spirit (Table 15.2, $\tau = 0.43, 0.48, 0.38, 0.42$ and 0.34); and (4) team leader's image of a sound, experienced project manager who enjoys the trust, respect, and credibility of the team and senior management (Table 15.4, $\tau = 0.37, 0.55, 0.43, 0.51, 0.45$ and 0.40).

Many of the factors that correlate favorably to commitment and team performance appear to deal favorably with the integration of team members'

Table 15.2 Descriptive Statistics and Correlation of Project-Related Variables and Commitment

Variables (Grouped by Categories)	Mean (μ)	s.d (σ)	1.1	1.2	1.3	1.4	1.5	1.6	1.7	1.8	1.9	7.0	8.0	9.0	10.0
1.0 Project [T, PM, SM]															
1.1 Importance	3.2	.5	1.0												
1.2 State-of-the-art	3.1	.6	.37	1.0											
1.3 Size (relative to others)	3.4	.7	.04	−.05	1.0										
1.4 Duration (yrs)	.85	.4	.22	.04	.57	1.0									
1.5 Success image	4.3	.5	.35	.18	.21	−.08	1.0								
1.6 Complexity	4.2	.4	.08	.02	.27	.20	−.07	1.0							
1.7 Uncertainties, risk	2.8	1.6	−.17	.20	.07	.11	−.37	.10	1.0						
1.8 Interruptions and changes	2.1	1.1	−.39	.18	.15	.17	−.43	.21	.54	1.0					
1.9 Professionally interesting	3.7	.7	.41	.37	.33	−.09	.35	.33	−.18	−.23	1.0				
7.0 Initial Commitment [PM, SM]	3.9	1.0	.39	.27	.05	.14	.39	.33	−.55	−.33	.40	1.0			
8.0 Sustained Commitment [PM, SM]	3.1	.7	.42	.20	.12	−.22	.31	.26	−.65	−.38	.42	.38	1.0		
9.0 Project Team Performance [SM]	4.0	.5	.30	.15	.00	.05	.40	.06	.15	−.28	.33	.35	.45	1.0	
10.0 Project Success Projection [SM]	4.2	.3	.25	−.22	−.11	−.24	.32	.20	−.45	−.20	.41	.28	.49	.65	1.0

Table 15.3   Descriptive Statistics and Correlation of Team-Related Variables and Commitment

Variables (Grouped by Categories)	Mean (μ)	s.d (σ)	2.1	2.2	2.3	2.4	2.5	2.6	7.0	8.0	9.0	10.0
2.0 Team Members [T]												
2.1 Co-located	3.7	.9	1.0									
2.2 Low conflict	3.9	1.4	.21	1.0								
2.3 Effective communications	4.2	.8	.24	.27	1.0							
2.4 Competency	3.6	.7	-.08	.13	.20	1.0						
2.5 Self-directed	3.4	.8	.08	-.15	.26	-.04	1.0					
2.6 Moral and team spirit	4.1	.8	.30	.17	.32	.29	.24	1.0				
7.0 Initial Commitment [PM, SM]	3.9	1.0	.28	.43	.38	.24	-.08	.11	1.0			
8.0 Sustained Commitment [PM, SM]	3.1	.7	.31	.48	.42	-.37	-.09	.34	.38	1.0		
9.0 Project Team Performance [SM]	4.0	.5	.03	.19	.32	.55	.13	.38	.35	.45	1.0	
10.0 Project Success Projection [SM]	4.2	.3	-.07	.20	-.27	.50	.07	.22	.28	.49	.65	1.0

357

Table 15.4   Descriptive Statistics and Correlation of Team-Leader-Related Variables and Commitment

Variables (Grouped by Categories)	Mean (μ)	s.d (σ)	3.1	3.2	3.3	3.4	3.5	3.6	7.0	8.0	9.0	10.0
3.0 Team Leader [T]												
3.1 Tenure with team (yrs)	.8	.3	1.0									
3.2 PM experience (yrs)	4.2	1.8	.09	1.0								
3.3 Trust	4.3	.3	.34	.22	1.0							
3.4 Respect and credibility	4.2	.5	.20	.12	.67	1.0						
3.5 Liked by team members	4.1	.4	.08	–12	.57	.22	1.0					
3.6 Gender (F = 0, M = 10)	8.3	—	.03	.29	.12	.10	–.09	1.0				
7.0 Initial Commitment [PM, SM]	3.9	1.0	.21	.37	.55	.51	.40	.10	1.0			
8.0 Sustained Commitment [PM, SM]	3.1	.7	.15	.35	.43	.45	.27	–15	.38	1.0		
9.0 Project Team Performance [SM]	4.0	.5	.10	.25	.32	.17	.20	.01	.35	.45	1.0	
10. Project Success Projection [SM]	4.2	.3	.12	.31	–.15	.15	.10	.12	.28	.49	.65	1.0

Table 15.5 Descriptive Statistics and Correlation of Leadership Style Variables and Commitment

Variables (Grouped by Categories)	Mean (μ)	s.d (σ)	4.1	4.2	4.3	4.4	4.5	4.6	4.7	7.0	8.0	9.0	10.0
4.0 Team Leadership Style [T]													
4.1 Clear plan and objectives	3.2	.8	1.0										
4.2 Agreement on p-plan	2.7	.8	.45	1.0									
4.3 Regular reviews	4.2	.3	.11	.03	1.0								
4.4 Measurable milestones	3.7	.7	.23	.33	.43	1.0							
4.5 Resolves technical problems	2.6	.8	.05	.22	.33	.51	1.0						
4.6 Resolves conflict	2.1	1.3	.35	.09	.46	.37	.32	1.0					
4.7 Good leadership	4.1	.3	.27	.20	.18	.23	.21	.39	1.0				
7.0 Initial Commitment [PM, SM]	3.9	1.0	.62	.78	.28	.37	.30	.60	.43	1.0			
8.0 Sustained Commitment [PM, SM]	3.1	.7	.55	.55	.38	.40	.42	-.62	.49	.38	1.0		
9.0 Project Team Performance [SM]	4.0	.5	.30	.17	.37	.31	.24	.20	.39	.35	.45	1.0	
10.0 Project Success Projection [SM]	4.2	.3	.39	.05	.42	.27	.33	.31	.22	.28	.49	.65	1.0

Table 15.6 Descriptive Statistics and Correlation of Team Benefit-Related Variables and Commitment

Variables (Grouped by Categories)	Mean (μ)	s.d (σ)	5.1	5.2	5.3	5.4	5.5	5.6	7.0	8.0	9.0	10.0
5.0 Benefit of Participation [T]												
5.1 Monetary benefit	1.7	.6	1.0									
5.2 Recognition	4.1	.3	.29	1.0								
5.3 Career development	3.9	.8	.16	.41	1.0							
5.4 Professionally stimulating	4.2	.4	-09	.55	.29	1.0						
5.5 Skill enhancement	4.3	.7	.03	.34	.09	.31	1.0					
5.6 Job security	2.6	.9	-16	.33	.34	.34	.38	1.0				
7.0 Initial Commitment [PM, SM]	3.9	1.0	.38	.47	.38	.45	.32	.29	1.0			
8.0 Sustained Commitment [PM, SM]	3.1	.7	.20	.49	.25	.47	.20	.09	.38	1.0		
9.0 Project Team Performance [SM]	4.0	.5	.12	.36	.21	.39	.20	-.11	.35	.45	1.0	
10.0 Project Success Projection [SM]	4.2	.3	.18	.33	.13	.38	.08	-.08	.28	.49	.65	1.0

All variables were measured with descriptive statements on a five-point Likert scale: (1) strongly disagree, (2) disagree, (3) neutral, (4) agree, (5) strongly agree. Some variables were measures on an absolute scale as notes. Statements were judge by [T] team members, [PM] project managers or team leaders, and [SM] senior management, as indicated. Statistical significance: $p = .10$ ($\tau \geq .20$), $p = .05$ ($\tau \geq .20$), $p = .01$ ($\tau \geq .31$), $p = .01$ ($\tau \geq .36$). Correlation of $p = .01$ or stronger is marked in bold italics.

personal goals and needs with the project goals. In this context, these more subtle factors seem to become catalysts for cross-functional communications, information sharing, and ultimate integration of the project team with focus on desired results. All associations shown as "most significant" (italics), have p-values of $p = .01$ or better. The implications and lessons gleaned from the broader context of this field study are summarized in the next section. The implications of these results to commitment and collaboration are discussed in the main part of this chapter.

Chapter 16

Managing People and Interfaces

AT GE, MANAGEMENT PHILOSOPHY FOCUSES ON PEOPLE

"GE can execute on a scale few can match," says CEO Jeff Immelt in his address to shareowners at the 2013 annual meeting in New Orleans. "It starts with a culture—the foundation for any successful enterprise—a culture that inspires our people to improve every day. Our team is mission-based: We build, move, power and cure the world. We believe in a better way: We constantly learn from our customers, our competition and each other. We seek solutions for our customers and society. And we are a "We Company." We know that strong teams with great people outperform individuals. That is why GE works. It is driving accountability for outcomes. It is fostering smart risk-taking and business judgment. Our ability to create our own future is why GE can win in any environment. We put our scale, industry expertise, technology and—most of all—the ingenuity of our people to work, creating a world that works better."

With close to $150 billion in revenues in 2012 and $16 billion profits, GE is envied by many as an effectively run diversified technology company in global markets. Organized into five business segments of *Energy Infrastructure, Aviation, Healthcare, Transportation, Home and Business Solutions, and GE Capital*, its products and services range from household appliances to aircraft engines, energy generation, medical systems, and consumer financing. All of these businesses depend on project management for effectively executing everything from new business acquisitions to R&D, product developments and roll-outs. GE's leadership team recognizes the importance of people and managerial leadership as critical components that drive organizational performance.

16.1 CHANGING ROLES AND CHALLENGES OF MANAGERIAL LEADERSHIP

General Electric is not the only company emphasizing the human side of business management. Virtually every organization in today's ultra-competitive

Source: GE 2012 Annual Report.

362

environment recognizes the critical importance of people, their attitudes, personal efforts, and collaboration within the enterprise for producing "better, faster, cheaper." This couldn't be more obvious than in project environments where time and resource effectiveness are critical components of performance. Business leaders and scholars agree (Anconda and Bresman 2007, Kruglianskas and Thamhain 2000, Nellore and Balachandra 2001, Nurick and Thamhain 2006; Schmid and Adams 2008, Shenhar 2011, Sidle 2009, Thamhain 2011). Yet, managing people effectively is very difficult. It is especially challenging in today's complex business environment with many operations distributed across the globe. This requires working with people from different support organizations, vendors, partners, customers, and government agencies; it requires effective networking and cooperation among organizations with different cultures, values, and languages (Armstrong 2000, Barkema et al. 2002, Barner 1997, Bhatnager 1999, Dillon 2001, Gray and Larson 2000, Shenhar 2011, Thamhain 2002). Thus, managers today, especially in engineering and technology, must be capable of dealing with not just the technical challenges, but also economic, political, social, and regulatory issues, and the associated uncertainties and risks (Keller 2001, Manning et al. 2008, Newell and Rogers 2002, Thamhain 2009a). In such a challenging, competitive environment, managers have to work effectively with people. In fact, people are our most valuable asset. They are the heart and soul of the company's core competency, critical to the successful implementation of any strategic plan, operational initiative, and especially cross-functional project undertaking. The real value of this human asset is measured in terms of integrated skill sets, attitudes, ambitions, and compassions for the business. Many of the issues overlap between functional and project management since the project organization is, by-and-large, an overlay to the functional organization, depending on establishing the needed resources and developing the required skill sets, which is also emphasized in "Core Management Issues and Challenges."

16.1.1 Core Management Issues and Challenges

Manage technical work content. Any job has technical content. But, especially in engineering and technology, projects are technologically intense and complex. The ability to manage the technical work, on an individual job level and collaboratively throughout the organization, is a *threshold competency*, critically important to the success of any technology-based business. Managerial work issues relate to staffing, task assignments, professional development, support technologies, innovation, and risk management.

Manage talent. While equipment, buildings, and infrastructure are important, businesses succeed because of their people, their ideas, and actions that bring the system alive. For many technology companies, talent is everything! The type of talent, and its fit with the business needs and organizational culture, determines everything from idea generation to problem resolution and business results. Talent does not occur at random. Nor should it be taken for granted. It needs to be searched out, attracted, developed, and maintained. An organization's personal policies and award systems must be consistent with the talent objectives. Losing a top talent is a sin! Companies like GE conduct postmortems on every top talent loss, and hold their management accountable for those losses.

Manage knowledge. Technology companies are knowledge factories. In essence, they buy, trade, transfer, and sell knowledge. Their value lies increasingly in the collective knowledge that becomes the basis for creating new ideas, concepts, products, and services. The emphasis must be on orchestrated management of this collective multidisciplinary knowledge. New products and services usually do not come from a single brilliant idea, but are the result of broad-based collaborative efforts throughout the organization. They are the result of an intricately connected, vast knowledge network with high interconnectivity and low cross-organizational impedance. Setting up effective support systems and managing the development, processing, filtering, sharing, and transferring knowledge toward desired results is a very important and challenging task that requires sophisticated people skills.

Manage information. Similar to knowledge, information management has a strong human side, which often does not receive sufficient attention. Regardless of the available technology, people are involved in gathering, transferring, interpreting, sharing, and acting on information.

Manage innovation and creativity. The important role of technological innovation for business success has been long recognized (Drucker 2006). Innovation can generate competitive advantages for one firm while eroding the market position for another, which is especially true for enterprises that derive their added value from technology. In an address to GE stockholders, Immelt said, "Our technology, reach, and resources aren't enough to make us the global best. It's all about people, nurturing, energizing, and inspiring then to search for ideas and to cooperate. It's about creating a culture that brings everyone into the game across the organization." This statement captures the critical role of innovation in today's ultra-competitive world of business. However, generating such a competitive advantage from innovation is an intricate and risky process. The companies that will survive and prosper in the decades ahead will be those that can *manage* innovation and derive business benefits from it. They must do this in spite of the complex organizational processes, increasing risks, uncertainties, and rapidly changing markets and technology.

Manage communications. Communication is the backbone of a firm's command and control structure. It is the catalyst toward crucial integration of organizational efforts toward unified results. This is especially critical in technology firms with their unconventional organizational structures and strong need for cross-functional coordination. While strongly supported by IT, communication systems are much broader in scope. They include everything from digitized systems to focus groups, task action teams, and old-fashioned group meetings.

Build a supportive organizational environment. Successful companies have cultures and environments that support their people. These companies provide visibility and recognition to their people. They also show the impact of these accomplishments on the company's mission and project-related objectives. This creates an ambiance where people are interested and excited about their work, which produces higher levels of ownership, cross-functional communications, collaboration, and commitment. These are also the conditions for unifying team members behind the requirements and keeping the project effort focused and synchronized.

Ensure direction and leadership. Managers themselves are change agents. Their concern for people, assistance to problem solving, and enthusiasm for the enterprise mission and objectives can foster a climate of high motivation, work involvement, commitment, open communications, and willingness to cooperate across the organization.

All of this has an impact on managerial education, training, and skill development. Not too long ago, managers *could* successfully lead their work groups toward desired results by focusing on the work requirements, timing, and resource constraints. However, these traditional approaches are no longer sufficient. They have become threshold competencies, critically important, but unlikely to guaranty by themselves success.

The mandate for managers is clear: they must weave together the best practices and programs for continuous development of their people toward highest possible performance. However, even the best practices and most sophisticated methods do not guarantee success. They must be carefully integrated with the business process, its culture, and its value system. The challenges are especially felt in today's technology organizations, which have become highly complex internally and externally, with a bewildering array of multifaceted activities, requiring sophisticated cross-functional cooperation, integration, and joint decision making.

Because of these dynamics, technology organizations are seldom structured along traditional functional lines. Rather, they operate as matrices or hybrid organizations with a great deal of power and resource sharing, as discussed in previous chapters. In addition, lines of authority and responsibility blur among formal management functions, project personnel and other subject experts, leading to a more empowered and self-directed workforce with a much higher bandwidth of skills to solve operational problems, responsive to the needs of our ultra-competitive business environment.

New technologies, especially computers and communications, have radically changed the workplace and transformed our global economy, focusing on effectiveness, value, and speed. These new technologies offer advanced capabilities for cross-functional integration, resource mobility, effectiveness, and market responsiveness, but they also require more sophisticated skill sets both technically and socially, dealing effectively with a broad spectrum of contemporary challenges, including managing conflict, change, risks, and uncertainty. As a result of this paradigm shift, the dynamics of how people work together has changed, and managerial focus has shifted from efficiency to effectiveness, and from traditional performance measures, such as the quadruple constraint (deliverables, budget, and schedule), to include a broader spectrum of critical success factors that support process integration effectiveness, organizational collaboration, innovation, human factors, and overall business process effectiveness and strategic objectives. These issues involve great challenges that define a new management frontier.

16.2 WHAT DRIVES PERFORMANCE IN TECHNOLOGY-BASED TEAMS

Project managers in engineering and technology see themselves different from those in less technical environments. Their work requires unique organizational structures, policies, and interaction among people. Their management style and leadership must not only be consistent with the nature of the work and the business process but also conducive to the special needs of the people, and consistent with the unique culture of the technology-based organization and its values.

Responding to these special needs, many technology-based organizations have evolved over time with their own somewhat unique characteristics, as discussed in Chapter 5, making engineering and technology management a specific discipline, different from other types of management. As an extension of the *people-work-process-tools model* introduced in Chapter 1, Figure 16.1

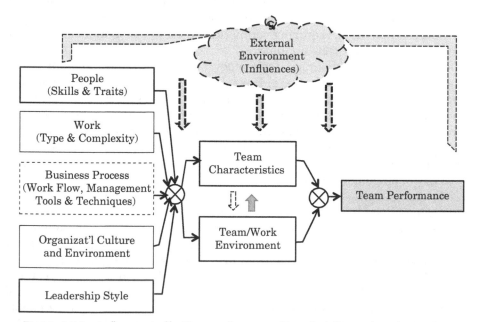

Figure 16.1 Influences affecting work group characteristics and performance in Technology-Intensive Organizations

shows six of the most influential organizational subsystems: (1) people, (2) work, (3) business process, (4) organizational culture, (5) leadership, and (6) external business environment. These affect the work environment, team characteristics, project success, and ultimately enterprise performance as discussed in the following sections.

16.2.1 People (Skill Sets, Traits and Attitudes)

Because of the type of its work and challenges, technology-oriented environments attract different people, with specialized knowledge and skill sets. Usually, they are better educated, self-motivated, and require minimum supervision. They enjoy problem solving and find technical challenges motivating and intellectually stimulating. They enjoy a sense of community and team spirit, while having low tolerance for personal conflict and organizational politics.

Managerial Impact

Because of the complexity of the work and the intricate decision-making processes, these workgroups rely to a considerable extent on member-generated norms and performance evaluations, rather than on hierarchical guidelines, policies and procedures (Anconda et al. 2007, Hilton 2008, Sawhney 2002, Sawhney and Prandelli 2000, Thamhain 2011). As a result, decision-making power and responsibility for achieving specific outcomes are more distributed among team members who function more autonomous. These self-directed workgroup models have become increasingly popular, especially for orchestrating and controlling complex projects (Tomkovich and Miller 2000). As these contemporary teams replace traditional, hierarchical work groups, effective leadership requires a more sophisticated management style that relies strongly on group interaction, resource and power sharing, individual accountability, commitment, conflict handling, cross-functional linkages and cooperation, technology transfer models, top management involvement, and design/build approaches (Debruyne et al. 2002). For example, traditional management tools, such as static project plans and linear performance measures—designed largely for conventional management systems, with clearly defined horizontal and vertical lines of communication, and centralized command and control system—are no longer effective in these contemporary situations (Hackman 2002, 2006). They are being replaced with more team-based and agile management processes, ranging from concurrent engineering to stage reviews and spiral processes. Many of these management systems, tools, and techniques are under continuous review and adjustment to adapt to the changing nature of the business environment, dynamically impacting organizational structure, work process, personnel recruiting and advancement, skill development, management style, and organizational culture.

16.2.2 Work (Type, Nature and Complexity)

The nature of technology-driven work is complex and outcomes cannot always be predicted or achieved with certainty. When describing their work, managers point to technical difficulties, high levels of innovation and creativity, evolving solutions, complex decision processes, uncertainty, and highly sophisticated forms of work integration. Much of technology-intensive work is conducted in *projects*, organized and executed by a multidisciplinary team. This involves additional challenges of resource and power sharing, intricate technology transfer networks, complex support systems, and highly sophisticated forms of performance measurements (Manning et al. 2008; Solomond 1996; Keller 2001; Thamhain 2003, 2008).

Managerial Impact

Because of the complexity and multidisciplinary nature of work, technology organizations look for a broad talent pool, often reaching across time zones and multinational boarders to form joint-ventures, consortia and partnerships. This leads to more organizational complexity and work process dynamics, which, in turn, require more sophisticated managerial skills to facilitate work integration, cross-functional collaboration and control of the work toward desired results.

16.2.3 Business Process (Workflow and Managerial Tools)

Team dynamics is affected by several business processes. The way work is organized, flows through the organization, and connects with its support systems, are examples. In addition, the technologies used for supporting the work, facilitating interdisciplinary communications, and integrating work components affect the effectiveness of the management style. To illustrate, a commercial airplane development results in very different organizational interactions than a pharmaceutical project with multinational R&D partners (Arranz and de Arroyabe 2008). A matrix-organized microprocessor rollout results in different work processes than a projectized electric car development. While many of the managerial processes, tools, and techniques are also used in other environments, the unique nature of technology and engineering requires special tools and application. Spiral planning, stakeholder mapping, concurrent engineering, and integrated product developments are just a few examples of the specialized nature of tools needed to produce team-based solutions to complex technical problems.

Managerial Impact

The *work process design* directly affects people issues, management style, and organizational culture. New organizational models and management methods, such as *Stage-Gate, concurrent engineering*, and *design-build processes* evolved together with the refinement of long-time established concepts such as the *matrix* and project and product management. Furthermore, managerial tools and techniques affect the people and the work process. Matching organizational culture with any of these tools is a great challenge. Stakeholder involvement during tool selection, development, and implementation, and tradeoffs among efficiency, speed, control, flexibility, and risk, are critical to the effective use of these tools and techniques.

16.2.4 Organizational Culture

The challenges of technology-driven environments create a unique organizational culture with their own norms, values and work ethics. These cultures are more team oriented regarding decision-making, work-flow, performance evaluation and work group management. Authority must often be earned and emerges within the work group as a result of credibility, trust and respect, rather than organizational status and position. Rewards come to a considerable degree from satisfaction with the work and its surroundings, with recognition of accomplishments as important motivational factors for stimulating enthusiasm, cooperation and innovation.

Managerial Impact

Organizational culture has a strong influence on the people and work process (Anconda et al. 2007, Cohen 2009). This culture is deeply rooted in the organizational fiber with strong influences on a wide range of managerial processes, affecting everything from hiring practices, performance evaluations, and reward systems to organizational structures and management style.

16.2.5 Managerial Leadership

This is one of the strongest influences on the people and their performance in technology-based work environments. Although technical skill sets, management tools, and effective work processes are absolutely critical, it is managerial leadership that drives team performance. It is the force that guides the work process, unifies the team, and fosters a culture of collaboration and commitment across organizational boundaries that connect support functions, suppliers, customers, and partners (Anconda and Bresman 2007, Hoegl and Parboteeah 2007, Thamhain 2011, Wade 2009).

Managerial Impact

Among the many influences, managerial leadership has the strongest impact on team effectiveness and overall project success. It is also under the direct control of the manager! A better understanding of the criteria and organizational dynamics that motivate people and drive team performance can help managers in effectively integrating workgroups with the enterprise. Effective team leaders are social architects who understand the interaction of organizational and behavioral variables and can foster a climate of active participation, accountability and result-orientation throughout the enterprise and its external partners. This requires an in-depth understanding of the business environment, its dynamics and cultures, plus sophisticated management skills in support of the credibility, trust and respect needed for effective leadership.

16.2.6 External Business Environment

All five previously discussed enterprise subsystems operate within a socially, politically, and economically complex business environment. Especially for technology-intensive organizations this environment is fast changing regarding market structure, suppliers and regulations. Short product life cycles, intense global competition, low brand-loyalty, low barriers to entry, and strong dependency on other technologies and support system are very common. These complexities call for specialized work processes, new concepts of technology transfer, and more sophisticated management skills and leadership.

Managerial Impact

The need for speed, agility, and efficiency has an impact on the work process design, supply chain, organizational structure, management methods, tools, and techniques. It also affects business strategy (Shenhar 2004) and competitive behavior (Dayan et al. 2012, Patanakul and Shenhar 2012) that often leads to collaboration and resource sharing via alliances, mergers, acquisitions, consortia, and joint ventures.

Managers of technology-intensive projects often describe their organizational environments as "unorthodox," with ambiguous authority and responsibility relations. They argue that such environments require broader management skill sets and more sophisticated leadership than traditional business situations. In this more open, dynamic business environment, project success and ultimately enterprise performance is based to a large degree on teamwork. Yet, attention to individuals, their competence, accountability, commitment, and sense for self-direction is crucial for project organizations to function effectively. Such a "team-centered" management style is based on the thorough understanding of the motivational forces and their interaction with the enterprise environment.

16.3 HOW TO MOTIVATE AND INSPIRE

Understanding people, their wants and needs, is important in any management situation. It is especially critical in today's technology-based engineering organizations. Leaders who succeed within these often-unstructured environments must work with cross-functional groups and gain services from personnel not reporting directly to them. They have to deal with line departments, staff groups, team members, clients, and senior management, each having different cultures, interests, expectations, and charters. Transforming these task multidisciplinary groups into cohesive teams is difficult. To get results, these engineering managers must relate socially as well as technically, and understand the culture and value system of the organization in which they work. The days of managers who get by with only technical expertise or pure administrative skills are gone.

What work best? Observations of best-in-class practices show consistently and measurably two important characteristics of high performers in technology organizations: (1) they enjoy work and are excited about their contributions they make to their company and society; and (2) they have their professional and personal needs fulfilled. Specifically, field research studies have identified 16 of these needs that associate particularly strongly with job performance (Thamhain 2004).

16.3.1 Understanding Professional Needs

Sixteen professional needs are strongly associated with engineering job performance. The fulfillment of these needs drives professional people to higher performance; conversely, the inability to fulfill these needs may become a barrier to individual performance and teamwork (Thamhain 2005). The rationale for this important correlation is found in the complex interaction of organizational and behavioral elements. Effective team management involves three primary components: (1) people skills, (2) organizational structure, and (3) management style. All three components are influenced by the specific task to be performed and the surrounding environment. That is, the degree of satisfaction of any of the needs is a function of (1) having the right mix of people with appropriate skills and traits, (2) organizing the people and resources according to the tasks to be performed, and (3) adopting the right leadership style.

The "Sixteen Professional Needs Affecting Individual and Team Performance" provides further insight into the motivational process and the important role of needs graphically shown in the *Inducement-Contribution Model* of Figure 16.2. Similar to Vroom's well-known Expectancy Theory (Isaac et al. 2001), the model shows that people are motivated to work toward personal and professional goals because they satisfy specific needs, such as needs for recognition, promotion, or pay increase. In the process of satisfying their needs, people make a contribution to the organization and its performance. If, on the other hand, employees cannot reach their goals and fulfill their needs through activities within their "primary organization" (i.e., project organization), they may try to satisfy their needs and reach their goals by working through an "outside" organization. They may

SIXTEEN PROFESSIONAL NEEDS AFFECTING INDIVIDUAL AND TEAM PERFORMANCE

1. *Interesting and challenging work*. This is an intrinsic motivator that satisfies professional esteem needs and helps to integrate personal goals organizational objectives.
2. *Professionally stimulating work environment.* An ambience conducive to professional involvement, creativity, and interdisciplinary support. It also fosters team building and is conducive to effective communication, conflict resolution, collaboration, and commitment toward the organizational goals. The quality of the work environment is defined primarily by the organizational structure, its facilities, and management style.
3. *Professional growth* is measured by promotional opportunities, salary advances, the learning of new skills and techniques, and professional recognition. A particular challenge exists for management in limited-growth or zero-growth businesses to compensate for lack of promotional opportunities by offering more intrinsic professional growth in terms of job satisfaction, esteem, and skill building.
4. *Overall leadership* involves dealing effectively with individual contributors, managers, and support personnel within a specific functional discipline as well as across organizational lines. It includes technical expertise, information-processing skills, effective communication, and decision-making skills. Taken together, leadership means satisfying the need for clear direction and unified guidance toward established objectives.
5. *Tangible rewards* include salary increases, bonuses, and incentives, as well as promotions, recognition, better offices, and educational opportunities. While financial rewards in this list are *extrinsic*, they are important and necessary to sustain strong long-term efforts, motivation and commitment. Furthermore, they validate the "softer" *intrinsic* rewards, such as recognition and praise, and reassure people of their value in the organization.
6. *Technical expertise* means that personnel within their work team have all necessary interdisciplinary skills and expertise available to perform the required tasks. Technical expertise includes understanding the technicalities of the work; the technology of underlying concepts, theories, and principles; design methods and techniques; and functioning and interrelationship of the various components that make up the total system.
7. *Assisting in problem solving* includes facilitating and assisting in resolving technical, administrative, and personal issues. It is a very important need, which, if not satisfied, often leads to frustration, conflict, unsustainable commitment, and poor-quality work.

8. *Clearly defined objectives.* Goals, objectives, and expected outcomes of an effort must be clearly communicated to all affected personnel. Conflict can develop over ambiguities or missing information.

9. *Management control* is important for effective team performance. Managers must understand the interaction of organizational and behavior variables in order to exert the direction, leadership, and control required to steer the work effort toward established organizational goals without stifling innovation and creativity.

10. *Job security* is one of the very fundamental needs that must be satisfied before people consider higher-order growth needs. While many of the factors that influence job security are not under the control of engineering managers, through their leadership style and effective communications managers can create more or less of a favorable image, and therefore affect people's attitude and their way of dealing with a given situation.

11. *Senior management support* should be provided in four major areas: (1) financial resources, (2) administrative support, including an effective operating charter, policies, and procedures, (3) work support from functional resource groups, and (4) necessary facilities and equipment. Management support is particularly crucial for larger, more complex undertakings.

12. *Good interpersonal relations* are required especially for effective teamwork they foster a stimulating work environment with low conflict, high involvement, motivated personnel, and high productivity.

13. *Proper planning* is absolutely essential for the successful management of multidisciplinary activities. It requires communications and information-processing skills to define the actual resource requirements and administrative support necessary. It also requires the ability to negotiate for resources and commitment from key personnel in various support groups across organizational lines.

14. *Clear role definition* helps to minimize role conflict and power struggles among team members and/or supporting organizations. Clear charters, plans, and good management direction are some of the powerful tools used to facilitate clear role definition.

15. *Open communication* satisfies the need for a free flow of information both horizontally and vertically, keeping personnel informed and functioning as a pervasive integrator of the overall project effort.

(Continued)

(Continued)

Minimum changes. Although technology managers have to live with constant change, their team members often see change as an unnecessary condition that impedes their creativity and timely performance. Advanced planning and proper communication can help to minimize changes and lessen their negative impact.

Implications for project performance. The significance of assessing these motivational forces lies in several areas. First, Table 16.2 provides insight into the broad needs of knowledge workers who we find to a large extend in technology-intensive projects. These needs must be satisfied *continuously* before the people can reach high levels of performance. This is consistent with findings from other studies, which show that in technology-based environments a significant correlation exists between professional satisfaction and organizational performance (Kruglianskas and Thamhain 2000; Thamhain 2011, 2013). From the preceding list we know now more specifically what areas we should focus our attention. In fact, it provides a model for *benchmarking*; that is, it offers managers a framework for monitoring, defining, and assessing the needs of their people in specific ways, and ultimately building a work environment that is responsive to their needs and ultimately conducive to high performance.

explore other job opportunities or involve themselves in volunteer work or recreational activities. Although this might help to satisfy the employee's need for interesting and stimulating activities, their efforts and energy are directed within a secondary organization, which provides inducement and receives the employee's contributions, which is being "leaked away" from the employer.

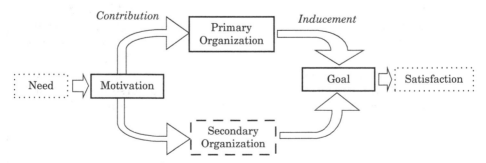

Figure 16.2 The inducement-induction model of motivation

An employee's need satisfaction is as important to the healthy functioning of the organization as it is to the employee. Good project managers are closely involved with their team members and their work. Managers should also identify any unrealistic goals and correct them, change situations that impede the attainment of realistic goals, and support people in reaching their goals and encourage them with recognition. This will help to refuel the individual desire to reach the goal and keep the employees' energies channeled through the primary organization. The tools that help the project manager to facilitate professional satisfaction are work sign-on, delegation, career counseling and development, job training and skill development, and effective managerial direction and leadership with proper recognition and visibility of individual and team accomplishments.

16.3.2 Motivation as a Function of Risks and Challenges

Additional insight into motivational drive and its dynamics can be gained by examining motivational strength as a function of the probability and desire to achieve the goal. We can push others, or ourselves, toward success or failure because of our mental predisposition. This is called *self-fulfilling prophesy* (Biggs 2011). Our motivational drive and personal efforts increase or decrease relative to the likelihood of the expected outcome. Personal motivation toward reaching a goal changes with the probability of success (perception of doability) and challenge (Hoegl et al. 2007). Figure 16.3 expresses the relationship graphically. A person's motivation is very low if the probability of achieving the goal is very low or zero. As the probability of reaching the goal increases, so does the motivational strength. However, this increase continues only up to a level where the goal is still seen as desirable and challenging. When success is more or less assured, motivation often decreases.

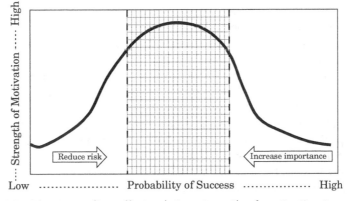

Figure 16.3 The Pygmalion effect, relating strength of motivation to probability of success

This is an area where work is often perceived as routine, uninteresting, and holding little potential for professional growth. The challenge is for team leaders to build an image of low risk and high professional interest. This could include showing the team that the project is well-planned, resourced, and supported, but also emphasizing the importance to the outcome to the enterprise and society, and the excitement of working on this project and its mission.

Success as a Function of Attitude

The saying "the harder you work, the luckier you get" expresses the effect of motivation in pragmatic terms. People who have a "can-do" attitude, who are confident and motivated, are more likely to succeed in their mission. Winning is in the attitude. This is the essence of the self-fulfilling prophecy. In fact, high-performing project teams often have a very positive image of their capabilities. As a result they are more determined to produce the desired results, often against high risks and odds.

16.3.3 Managing at High Levels of Motivation

Applying motivational models to the high-technology workplace suggests that project managers should ensure proper matching of people to their jobs. Further, managers must foster a work environment and direct their personnel in a manner that promotes "can-do" attitudes and facilitates continuous assistance and guidance toward successful task completion. The process involves four primary issues: (1) work assignments, (2) team organization, (3) skill development, and (4) management. Specific suggestions for stimulation and sustaining motivation in technology-oriented project professionals are summarized below:

1. Work assignments
   - Explain the assignment, its importance to the company, and the type of contributions expected.
   - Understand the employee's professional interests, desires, and ambitions and try to accommodate to them.
   - Understand the employee's limitations, anxieties, and fears. Often, these factors are unjustly perceived and can be removed in a face-to-face discussion.
   - Develop the employee's interest in an assignment by pointing out its importance to the company and possible benefits to the employee.
   - Assure assistance where needed and share risks.
   - Show how to be successful. Develop a "can-do" attitude.
   - If possible, involve the employee in the definition phase of the work assignment, for instance via up-front planning, a feasibility analysis, needs assessment, or a bid proposal.

2. Team organization
   - Select the team members for each task or project carefully, ensuring the necessary support skills and interpersonal compatibility.
   - Select the team members for each task or project carefully, ensuring the necessary support skills and interpersonal compatibility.
   - Plan each engineering project properly to ensure clear directions, objectives, and task charters.
   - Ensure leadership within each task group.
   - Sign-on key personnel on a one-on-one basis according to the guidelines discusses in item number 1.
3. Skill development
   - Plan the capabilities needed in your engineering department for the long-range. Direct your staffing and development activities accordingly.
   - Encourage people to keep abreast in their professional field.
   - Provide for on-the-job experimental training via selected work assignments and managerial guidance.
   - Provide the opportunity for some formal training via seminars, courses, conferences, and professional society activities.
   - Use career counseling sessions and performance reviews to help in guiding skill development and matching them with personal and organizational objectives.
4. Management
   - Develop interest in the work itself by showing its importance to the company and the potential for professional rewards and growth.
   - Promote project visibility, team spirit, and upper-management involvement.
   - Assign technically and managerially competent task leaders for each team, and provide top-down leadership for each project and for the engineering function as a whole.
   - Manage the quality of the work via regular task reviews and by staying involved with the project team, without infringing on their autonomy and accountability.
   - Plan your projects up front. Conduct a feasibility study and requirements analysis first. Assure the involvement of the key players during these early phases.
   - Break activities or projects into phases and define measurable milestones with specific results. Involve personnel in the definition phase. Obtain their commitment.
   - Try to detect and correct technical problems early in their development.
   - Foster a professionally stimulating work environment.
   - Unify the task team behind the overall objectives. Stimulate the sense of belonging and mutual interdependence.
   - Refuel the commitment and interest in the work by recognizing accomplishments frequently.

- Assist in problem solving and group decision making.
- Provide the proper resources.
- Keep the visibility and priority for the project high. No interruptions.
- Avoid threats. Deal with fear, anxieties, mistrust, and conflicts.
- Facilitate skill development and technical competency.
- Manage and lead.

16.4 THE POWER PROFILE OF PROJECT MANAGERS

As organizations become flatter, leaner, more agile and self-directed, they share to a greater extent responsibilities, resources, and power. Especially for technology-based enterprises, which rely to an increasing extend on innovation, cross-functional teamwork, intricate multicompany alliances, and complex forms of work integration, success depends to a considerable extent on member-generated performance norms and work processes. Self-directed team concepts are gradually replacing the traditional, more hier-archically structured organization (Cleland and Ireland 2007, Jassawalla et al. 1999, Polzer et al. 2006), requiring a radical departure from traditional management practices of top-down, centralized command, control, and com-munications. To be effective, engineering managers have to direct their per-sonnel and obtain cross-functional support without much organizationally derived power. They must develop, or "earn," their own bases of influence and build their own power spectrum, which derives from personal knowl-edge, expertise, and the image of a sound decision maker. The basic concept of *power and authority* has been known for a long time. Four decades ago, French and Raven (1959) presented a typology that included five bases of interpersonal power—*authority, reward, punishment, expertise* and *referent power* (e.g., friendship, charisma, empathy), summarized in Figure 16.4. To

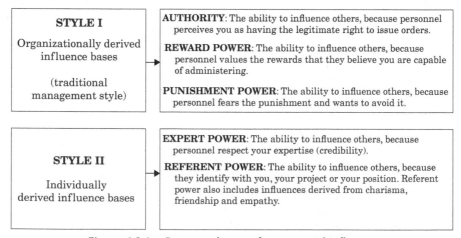

Figure 16.4   Common bases of managerial influence

this day, these are still the most commonly recognized influences of managerial power. For some time, the first three bases—authority, reward, and punishment—were perceived as being derived entirely from the organization. However, more recent studies provide measurable evidence that all bases of power can be individually developed, at least to some degree.

Today's organizations grant power to their leaders in many forms. Some of it is still derived from the organizational construct and vested in the leader via organizational position, status, and other traditional components of legitimacy, including the power to rewards and punishment. However, contemporary engineering managers must *earn* most of their authority and influence bases for managing their multifunctional teams. Since earned authority depends largely on the image of trust, respect, credibility, and competence, it is strongly influenced by the manager's ability to foster a work environment where the team feels comfortable, accomplishes results, receives recognition, and meets the professional and personal needs of its members (Thamhain 2008). This includes images of managerial expertise, friendship, work challenge, promotional opportunities, fund allocations, charisma, personal favors, project goal identification, recognition, and visibility of the work and its importance.

Salary and other financial rewards play a very special role in the managerial power spectrum. It is often over- or undervalued as a motivator. While overvaluation is costly and might set false expectations, ignoring or underplaying the importance of financial rewards can be detrimental to motivation and the morale of the people. It is quite common for engineering and technology managers to argue that salary and other financial rewards fulfill only lower level needs, while recognition, pride and accomplishments are the true motivators of professional people. This is generally true. It is also supported by the writings in this chapter. However, the above argument holds only if personnel perceive the compensation as fair and adequate. Otherwise, salary becomes a barrier to effective teamwork, a handicap for attracting and holding quality people, and a source of subtle conflict.

To illustrate, a person who is motivated to make an extra effort might indeed enjoy the praise and recognition that comes with the well-done job. The person may further conclude that the job was important to the company and he or she is making significant contributions to the enterprise and could expect a better than average raise or be in line for a promotion. Now, suppose a subsequent salary review results in a very small, less than expected increase, the employee would question the sincerity and value of any praise, recognition or other intrinsic rewards received in the past and anticipated for the future. The employee might also feel confused, frustrated, angry or manipulated. Obviously, this is *not* a situation that leads to long-term motivation, sustained personal drive, commitment and high morale. In summary, salary and other financial rewards are very important bases of managerial power. They must be used judiciously, consistent with the employee's output, efforts, and contributions, and fair and equitable across the organization. Effectively employee communication, explaining the rationale for any financial award, supported with well-earned recognition of the accomplishments, is a good starting point for optimizing the motivational benefits of financial rewards.

Taken together, the sources of motivation involve an intricate set of variables that are grounded to a large degree in the work environment, team characteristics, and leadership style. Most importantly, managers must pay attention to human side. To earn the trust, respect, and credibility of team members and support personnel, engineering managers must foster a work environment where people find the work interesting and challenging, leading to recognition and professional growth. Such a professionally stimulating environment seems to lower anxieties over managerial controls and conflict. It promotes cross-functional communication and enhances organizational awareness of the surrounding business environment, favorably affecting collaboration and the ability to unify the team behind the agreed-on objectives and organizational leadership.

16.4.1 Influences on Power and Motivation

Managerial power and motivation is not necessarily fixed or stable, but changes with the work environment and team dynamics. This situational dependency is graphically shown in Figure 16.5. It indicates that intrinsic motivation of professional people in most situations, but especially in engineering and technology environments, increases with the manager's emphasis on work challenge, his/her expertise, and ability to provide professional growth opportunities. On the other hand, emphasis on penalties and authority, and inability to manage conflict lowers personnel motivation. Managers' positional power is further determined by such variables as formal position within the organization, the scope and nature of work, earned authority, and

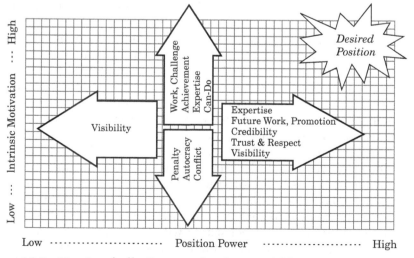

Figure 16.5 Situational effectiveness of environmental factors on motivation and managerial power

ability to influence promotion and future work assignments. Managers who have strong positional power and can foster a climate of high motivation not only obtain greater support from their personnel, but also achieve high overall performance ratings from their superiors.

16.5 CRITERIA AND RECOMMENDATIONS FOR WORKING EFFECTIVELY WITH PEOPLE ON PROJECTS

Focusing on the people-side of project management, this section summarizes the criteria for managing effectively in technology-based project environments. These suggestions integrate many of the broader project management issues of planning, organizing and dealing with risks and commitment, introduced in previous chapters. They are valid for any project situation. However, these suggestions have a stronger impact on project success or failure in technology-intensive situations which are often more complex, nonlinear and uncertain, with solution relying on innovation, risk-taking, collaboration, self-direction and other intrinsic motivators, requiring more sophisticated leadership and a strong focus on the human side of management.

The 12 criteria for working effectively with people are as follows:

1. **Clear task assignment.** At the outset of any new assignment, managers and project leaders should discuss with their staff/team members the overall task, its scope, timing, resources, deliverables, and objectives.

2. **Early project/mission involvement and ownership.** A thorough understanding of the task requirements usually comes with intense personal involvement, which can be stimulated through participation in project planning, requirements analysis, interface definition, or a producability study. Involvement of the people during the early phases of the assignment, such as bid proposals and project planning, can produce great benefits toward plan acceptance, realism, buy-in, personnel matching, and unification of the task team.

3. **Priority image.** Management should clearly articulate the importance of the assignment and its impact on the company and its mission. Senior management can help develop such a priority image by their involvement and by effectively communicating key mission parameters. The relationship and contribution of individual work to overall business plans, as well as of individual project objectives and their importance to the organizational mission, must be clear to all personnel.

4. **Team image.** Building a favorable image for an ongoing project and its team, in terms of high priority, interesting work, importance to the organization, high visibility, and potential for professional rewards, is crucial for attracting and holding high-quality people. Senior management can help develop a "priority image" and communicate clear, top-down objectives, building an image of high visibility, importance, priority, and interesting work.

5. **Effective project planning and team structure.** Formal planning, using proven tools and techniques, early in the life cycle of a project is critical

to any project success. These plans and their methods don't have to be far out, but should be effective in defining the basic team structure and cross-functional linkages for effective project execution. This requires the participation of the entire multidisciplinary team, including support departments, subcontractors, and management.

6. **Work challenge, professionally stimulating work.** Whenever possible, managers should try to accommodate the professional interests and desires of their personnel. Interesting and challenging work is a perception that can be enhanced by the visibility of the work, management attention and support, priority image, and the overlap of personnel values and perceived benefits with organizational objectives. Making work more interesting leads to increased involvement, better communication, lower conflict, higher commitment, stronger work effort, and higher levels of creativity.

7. **Senior management support and commitment.** It is critically important that senior management provide the proper environment for a technology team to function effectively. Early in the project life cycle the project manager should negotiate the needed resources with the sponsor organization and obtain commitment from management that these resources will be available. An effective working relationship among resource managers, project leaders, and senior management critically affects the credibility, visibility, and priority image perceived by the project team.

8. **Clear communication.** Poor communication is a major barrier to teamwork and effective performance. In addition to technology tools, such as voice mail, e-mail, electronic bulletin boards, and conferencing, management can facilitate the free flow of information, both horizontally and vertically, by workspace design, regular meetings, reviews and information sessions. Further, well-defined interfaces, task responsibilities, reporting relations, communication channels and work transfer protocols can greatly enhance communications within the work team and its interfaces, especially in complex organizational settings.

9. **Leadership positions.** Leadership positions should be carefully defined and staffed for all projects and support functions. Especially critical is the credibility of project leaders among team members, with senior management and with the program sponsor, for the leader's ability to manage multidisciplinary activities effectively across functional lines.

10. **Reward system.** Personnel evaluation and reward systems should be designed to reflect the desired behavior and focus of the people on the team. Rewards should encompass the whole spectrum of intrinsic and extrinsic motivators, and reward both individual and team performance.

11. **Problem resolution.** Project managers should focus their efforts on problem identification and early problem solving. That is, managers and team leaders, through experience, should recognize potential problems and conflicts at their onset, and deal with them before they become big and their resolutions consume a large amount of time and effort.

12. **Personal drive and leadership.** Managers can influence the work environment by their own actions. Concern for the team members, the ability

to integrate personal needs of their staff with the goals of the organization, and the ability to create personal enthusiasm for a particular project, can foster a climate of high motivation, work involvement, open communication, and ultimately high team performance.

16.6 CONCLUDING REMARKS

Managerial leadership has significant impact on the work environment, affecting project personnel and performance. Factors that satisfy personal and professional needs—such as professional interest, pride and satisfaction with the work, professional work challenge, accomplishments and recognition—seem to have the most favorable impact on individual and team performance, reducing communication barriers, while enhancing collaboration and the desire to succeed. Other important influences include effective communications among team members and support units across organizational lines, good team spirit, mutual trust and respect, low interpersonal conflict, plus opportunities for career development and job security. These conditions serve as a bridging mechanism between personal and organizational goals, helpful in building a unified project team capable of producing integrated results in support of the organization's mission.

Taking a bird's-eye look at the people side of project management, the following three recommendations seem to stand out as particularly important to effective role performance:

16.6.1 Understand Motivational Needs

Project managers need to understand the interaction of organizational and behavioral elements in order to build an environment conducive to their personnel's motivational needs. Two conditions seem to be especially critical to high performance: professional interest and work support. However, identifying and satisfying these needs across a complex diversified workgroup is challenging and requires special techniques and skills. Conventional tools, such as focus groups, action teams, suggestion systems, open-door policies and management-by-wandering-around, complemented with computer-aided tools, such as PeopleSoft and on-line surveys, can provide a useful framework for identifying and profiling the needs of various segments of the project team.

16.6.2 Accommodate Professional Interests, Build Enthusiasm and Excitement

Project managers should try to accommodate the professional interests and desires of their personnel when negotiating tasks and during the execution. This leads to employee ownership and commitment, resulting in increased involvement, better communication, lower conflict, stronger work effort, and higher levels of creativity. Equally important, factors that satisfy professional interests and needs, strongly effect team unification and overall project performance. Although the scope of the work group may be fixed, the manager has the flexibility of allocating task assignments among various members. Well-established practices, such as front-end involvement of team members during the project planning or proposal phase and one-on-one discussions are effective tools for matching team member interests and project needs.

16.6.3 Adapt Leadership to the Situation

Because their environment is temporary and often untested, project managers should seek a leadership style that allows them to adapt to the dynamics of their organizations, support departments, customers, and senior management. They must learn to "test" the expectations of others by observation and experimentation. Leading a technology team can rarely be done "top-down," but requires a great deal of interactive team management skills and senior management support. Although difficult, managers must be able to alter their leadership style as demanded by the specific work situation and its people.

Effective project managers are social architects who understand the interaction of organizational and behavioral variables and who can foster a climate of active participation, accountability and result-orientation throughout the enterprise and its partners. This requires a keen, in-depth understanding of the organizational dynamics and its cultures, plus sophisticated technology management and leadership skills. It further requires the ability to engage top management, ensuring organizational visibility, resource availability, and overall support for the engineering work across the enterprise.

16.7 SUMMARY OF KEY POINTS AND CONCLUSIONS

The following key points were made in this chapter:

- People are our most valuable asset. They are the heart and soul of the company's core competency.
- Skill sets related to the technical work and administrative part of the project are threshold competencies—critically important, but unlikely to guaranty by themselves success. They must be carefully integrated with the business process, its culture, and its value system.
- Technology managers must not only be technically qualified but also be respected, skilled in dealing with people, and comfortable with the latest business practices and administrative techniques.
- The six most influential organizational subsystems affecting project performance are: (1) people, (2) work, (3) business process, (4) organizational culture, (5) leadership, and (6) external business environment.

- Leaders who succeed within technology organizations must move across various organizational lines to gain services from personnel not reporting directly to them.
- Technical people are a special breed, who do not always follow the conventional motivation and leadership models.
- Sixteen professional needs are critical to technology-based performance: (1) interesting and challenging work, (2) a professionally stimulating work environment, (3) professional growth, (4) overall leadership, (5) tangible rewards, (6) technical expertise, (7) assisting in problem solving, (8) clearly defined objectives, (9) management control, (10) job security, (11) senior management support, (12) good interpersonal relations, (13) proper planning, (14) clear role definition, (15) open communications, and (16) minimum changes.
- These needs must be satisfied *continuously* before the people can reach and sustain high levels of performance.
- Motivation is an inner drive that transforms activities into desired results.
- "What you expect from yourself or others is most likely to happen," is the essence of the self-fulfilling prophecy, also known as the *Pygmalion effect*.
- Many of the true motivators or satisfiers are called "intrinsic motivators." They are derived from the *work content*, while the "hygiene factors" are related to the *work context* and work environment. Intrinsically motivated people are less concerned about hygiene factors.
- The *inducement-induction model of motivation* is similar to Vroom's model, which suggests that motivation is based on three conditions: Individuals must perceive/expect that (1) their effort will actually lead to the goal, (2) the goal will actually produce results, and (3) these results are desirable.
- Motivational strength is a function of the probability and desire to achieve the goal.
- Early leadership concepts focused on personality traits, while contemporary models emphasize the situational nature of leadership, including task, organization, environment, business process, and people relations.
- French and Raven's typology is still the most commonly recognized concept and prime reference to managerial influence. It includes five bases of interpersonal power: *authority, reward, punishment, expertise,* and *referent power.* However, the context and interpretation of the model has changed considerably to be relevant in today's business environment.
- Salary is a very important power base, which must be used judiciously, but it must also be in line with the employee's output, efforts, and salary expectations.
- Extensive use of authority, salary, and coercion as an influence method has negative effects, resulting not only in a lower level of performance but also in less communication and involvement among project personnel.

- Managerial leadership has significant impact on the work environment, affecting project personnel and performance.
- Factors that satisfy personal and professional needs—such as *professional interest, pride and satisfaction with the work, professional work challenge, accomplishments*, and *recognition*—seem to have the most favorable impact on individual and team performance, reducing communication barriers while enhancing collaboration and the desire to succeed.

16.8 QUESTIONS FOR DISCUSSION

1. How can motivational models, such as the Inducement-Induction Model or the Pygmalion effect help in guiding project managers toward effective leadership of technology professionals?
2. Define a management development program for a young team leader in preparation for more advanced management assignments.
3. What leadership skills are learnable in the classroom, and which ones can only be gained experientially?
4. How do you explain the fact that the same manager is being perceived as "autocratic" by some people and "democratic or team-oriented" by others within the same work team?
5. Discuss the role of salary and financial awards for motivating project personnel.
6. How can managers and team leaders "earn" their authority, especially when crossing functional lines and dealing with organizations over which they have no formal authority?
7. Discuss the role of trust, respect, and credibility for effective leadership in technology-driven enterprises (relate also to the previous question).
8. What is the role of technical (job-specific) expertise for managerial effectiveness in technology-driven enterprises? Is there a danger for a manager to have "too much" technical expertise?
9. You have been assigned to lead a product enhancement project. This is a priority project, critically important to your company. The product still produces 30 percent of the company's revenue, but is losing profitability and market share. Your project team is not very excited about the project, perceiving it as "routine work" with little state-of-the-art technology and opportunities for skill enhancement or career advancement. What approach would you take to create an ambience of excitement and professional interest in the project among your team personnel?

16.9 *PMBOK®* REFERENCES AND CONNECTIONS

The topic of managing people and interfaces focuses most strongly on the three PMBOK® Knowledge Areas of project human resource management

(#6), project communications management (#7), and project stakeholder management (#10). The topic cuts across all five PMBOK® processing groups with the strongest connection to planning, executing, and monitoring/controlling. Much of this chapter focuses on the context of project executing and monitoring/controlling, discussing the need for working effectively with people and for building a collaborative project environment. The managerial perspectives presented in this chapter should be helpful in connecting the PMBOK standards to best practices of project management, and in studying effectively for PMP® certification. In preparing for the PMP® Exam, the following PMBOK sections relate especially to this chapter and should be studied: (1) project interfaces, (2) staffing requirements, (3) staff assignments, (4) human resource practices and (5) project communications management.

INTERNET LINKS AND RESOURCES

NASA. "Leadership and Management Development." http://leadership.nasa.gov/Model/Manager.htm

Project Management Institute. "Welcom to Leadership in PM Community of Practice." http://leadershipinpm.vc.pmi.org/Public/Home.aspx

TED (Technology, Entertainment, Design. www.ted.com/; many interesting motivational and leadership speeches, such as Simon Sinek, "How Great Leaders Inspire and Lead." www.ted.com/talks/simon_sinek_how_great_leaders_inspire_action.html

REFERENCES AND ADDITIONAL READINGS

Anconda D., and H. Bresman. 2007. *X-teams: How to Build Teams That Lead, Innovate and Succeed*. Boston: HBS Publishing.

Anconda D., T. Malone, W. Orlikowski, and P. Senge. 2007. "In Praise of the Incomplete Leader." *Research Technology Management* 19(3): 92–100.

Armstrong, D. 2000. "Building Teams Across Borders." *Executive Excellence* 17(3): 10–11.

Arranz N,, and J. de Arroyabe. 2008. "Joint R&D Projects as Complex Systems." *IEEE Transactions on Engineering Management* 55(4): 552–566.

Barkema H., J. Baum, and E. Mannix. 2002. "Management Challenges in a New Time." *Academy of Management Journal* 45(5): 916–930.

Barner, R. 1997. "The New Millennium Workplace." *Engineering Management Review (IEEE)* 25(3): 114–119.

Bhatnager, A. 1999. "Great Teams." *The Academy of Management Executive* 13(3): 50–63.

Biggs, M. 2011. "Self-Fulfilling Prophesies." In P. Hedström and P. Bearman (ed.), *The Oxford Handbook of Analytical Sociology*. Oxford, U.K.: Oxford University Press, Chapter 13.

Cleland, D., and L. Ireland. 2007. *Project Management: Strategic Design and Implementation*. New York: McGraw-Hill.

Cohen, D. 2009. "Interview with Alexander Laufer." *Academy of Sharing Knowledge* 35 (Summer): 23–28.

Dayan M., S. Elbanna, and A. Di Benedetto. 2012. "Antecedents and Consequences of Political Behavior in New Product Development Teams." *IEEE Transactions on Engineering Management* 59(3).

Debruyne, M., R. Moenaert, A. Griffin, and S. Hart. 2002. *The Journal of Product Innovation Management* 19(2): 159–169.

Dillon, P. 2001. "A Global Challenge." *Forbes*, September 10.

Drucker, P. 2006. *Innovation and Entrepreneurship*. New York: Harper Collins.

Fortune 2012. "Fortune 500 Companies." *Fortune*, May 21.

French, J. R., Jr., and B. Raven. 1959. "The Basis of Social Power." In D. Cartwright (ed.), *Studies in Social Power*. Ann Arbor, MI: Research Center for Group Dynamics, pp. 150–165.

GE. 2013. *GE 2012 Annual Report*. Fairfield, CT: General Electric Company.

Gibbert, M., and M. Hoegl. 2011. "In Praise of Dissimilarity." *Sloan Management Review* 52(4): 20–22.

Gray, C., and E. Larson. 2000. *Project Management*. New York: Irwin McGraw-Hill, 2000.

Grossman, R. 2009. "Managing the People Who Manage the Projects." *HR Magazine* 54(8): 8+.

Hackman, J. 2002. *Leading Teams: Setting the Stage for Great Performance—The 5 Keys to Successful Teams*. Boston: Harvard Business School Press.

———. 2006. "The Five Dysfunctions of a Team: A Leadership Fable." *Academy of Management Perspectives* 20(1): 122–125.

Hilton, M. 2008. "Skills for Work in the 21st Century." *Academy of Management Perspectives* 2(4): 63–78.

Hoegl, M., and K. P. Parboteeah. 2006. "Team Goal Commitment in Innovative Projects." *International Journal of Innovation Management* 10(3): 299–324.

———. 2007. "Creativity in Innovative Projects: How Teamwork Matters." *Journal of Engineering and Technology Management* 24: 148–166.

Isaac, R., W. Zerbe, W. and D. Pitt. 2001. "Leadership and Motivation: The Effective Application of Expectancy Theory." *Journal of Managerial Issues* 13(2): 212–226.

Jassawalla, A. R., and C. Sashittal, Hemant. 1999. "Building Collaborate Cross-Functional New Product Teams." *The Academy of Management Executive* 13(3): 50–63.

Keller, R. 2001. Cross-Functional Project Groups in Research and NPD. *Academy of Management Journal* 44(3): 547–556.

Kruglianskas, I., and H. Thamhain. 2000. "Managing Technology-Based Projects in Multinational Environments." *IEEE Transactions on Engineering Management* 47(1): 55–64.

Manning, S., S. Massini, and A. Lewin. 2008. "A Dynamic Perspective on Next-Generation Offshoring: The Global Sourcing of Science and Engineering Talents." *Academy of Management Perspectives* 22(3): 35–54.

McGregor, D. 1960. *The Human Side of Enterprise*. New York, McGrawHill.

Nellore, R., and R. Balachandra. 2001. "Factors Influencing Success in Integrated Product Development (IPD) Projects." *IEEE Transactions on Engineering Management* 48(2): 164–173.

Newell, F., and M. Rogers. 2002. *loyalty.com: Relationship Management in the Era of Internet Marketing*. New York: McGraw Hill.

Nurick, A., and H. Thamhain. 2006. "Team Leadership in Global Project Environments." In D. Cleland (ed.), *Global Project Management Handbook*. New York: McGraw Hill, Chapter 38.

Parker, D., and M. Craig. 2008. *Managing Projects, Managing People*. South Yara, Victoria, Australia: Palgrave Macmillan.

Patanakul P., and A. Shenhar. 2012. "What Is Really Project Strategy: The Fundamental Building Block in Strategic Project Management." *Project Management Journal* 43(1): 4–20.

Peters, S. 2012. "How GE Is Attracting, Developing, and Retaining Global Talent." *Harvard Business Review Blog Network*. (February 8).

Project Management Institute. 2013. *A Guide to the Project Management Body of Knowledge (PMBOK® Guide*. Newtown Square, PA: Project Management Institute.

Polzer J., C. Crisp, S. Jarvenpaa and J. Kim. 2006. "Extending the Fault Line Model to Geographically Dispersed Teams." *Academy of Management Journal* 49(4): 679–692.

Sawhney, M. 2002. "Don't Just Relate—Collaborate." *MIT Sloan Management Review* 43(3): 96–107.

Sawhney, M., and E. Prandelli. 2000. "Communities of Creation: Managing Distributed Innovation in Turbulent Markets." *California Management Review* 42(4): 45–69.

Schmid B., and J. Adams. 2008. "Motivation in Project Management: A Project Manager's Perspective." *Project Management Journal* 39(2): 60–71.

Senge, P., and G. Carstedt. 2001. "Innovating Our Way to the Next Industrial Revolution." *Sloan Management Review* 42(2): 24–38.

Senge, Peter M. 1990. *The Fifth Discipline: The Art and Practice of the Learning Organization*. New York: Doubleday/Currency.

Shenhar, A. 2004. "Strategic Project Leadership: Toward a Strategic Approach to Project Management." *R&D Management* 34 (November): 569–578.

———. 2011. "What Great Projects Have in Common." *MIT Sloan Management Review*, 52(3): 19–21.

Shim, D., and M. Lee. 2001. "Upward Influence Styles of R&D Project Leaders." *IEEE Transactions on Engineering Management* 48(4): 394–413.

Sidle, S. 2009. "Building a Committed Workforce: Does What Employers Want Depend on Culture?" *Academy of Management Perspectives* 23(1): 79–80.

Solomond, J. 1996. "International High Technology Cooperation: Lessons Learned." *IEEE Transactions on Engineering Management* 43(1): 69–78.

Stum, D. 2001. "Maslow Revisited: Building the Employee Commitment Pyramid." *Strategy and Leadership* 29(4): 4–9.

Thamhain, H. 2002. "Criteria for Effective Leadership in Technology-Oriented Project Teams." In Slevin, Cleland, and Pinto (eds.), *The Frontiers of Project Management Research*. Newton Square, PA: Project Management Institute, pp. 259–270.

———. 2003. Managing Innovative R&D Teams. *R&D Management*, 33(3): 297–312.

———. 2004. "Leading Technology Teams." *Project Management Journal* 35(4): 35–47.

———. 2009. "Managing Globally Dispersed R&D Teams." *International Journal of Information Technology and Management (IJITM)* 8(1): 107–126.

———. 2011. "Critical Success Factors for Managing Technology-Intensive Teams the Global Enterprise." *Engineering Management Journal* 23(3): 30–36.

———. 2013. "The Role of Commitment for Managing Complex Multinational Projects." *International Journal of Innovation and Technology Management* 12(3): 22–32.

Thamhain, H., and D. Wilemon. 1999. "Building Effective Teams for Complex Project Environments." *Technology Management* 5(2): 203–212.

Tichy, N. M., and D. O. Ulrich. 1984. "The Leadership Challenge—A Call for the Transformational Leader." *Sloan Management Review* 26: 59–68.

Tomkovich, C., and C. Miller. 2000. "Riding the Wind: Managing New Product Development in the Age of Change." *Product Innovation Management* 17(6): 413–423.

Valikangas, L., M. Hoegl, and M. Gibbert. 2009. "Why Learning from Failure Isn't Easy (and What to Do about It): Innovation Trauma at Sun Microsystems." *European Management Journal* 27(4): 225–233.

Wade H.S., ed. 2009. Special Issue on "Leading Small Groups." *IEEE Engineering Management Review* 36(1): 3–183.

Chapter 17

Managing Conflict in Project Organizations

SUN TZU—THE ANCIENT ART OF LEADERSHIP: MAKING CONFLICT UNNECESSARY

Source: Wikimedia/User 663Highland

There is an interesting story, documented well over two thousand years ago by the mysterious Chinese warrior-philosopher Sun Tzu in his writings on *The Art of War*, that is worth remembering. According to the legend, an emperor in ancient China asked his physician to compare the skills of his medicine-trained brothers to determine who was most skilled in the art of healing. The physician, whose reputation was seminal and synonymous with medical science in China, replied, "My younger brother sees the spirit of sickness and removes it before it takes shape, so his name does not get out of the house. My older brother cures sicknesses when they are still extremely minute, so his name does not get out of the neighborhood. As for me, I puncture veins, prescribe potions, and massage skin, so my name gets out and is heard among the lords." After pondering the facts, the master physician concluded that his youngest brother, who can deal with the onset of illnesses before they impact, is the most skillful healer.

As in the story of the most effective healer, the most effective manager has the knowledge and skills to deploy strategies that make conflict altogether unnecessary. As announced by Sun Tzu: To overcome others' armies without fighting is the best of skills. As a study on organizational conflict, *The Art of War* applies to business competition and conflict on every level from interpersonal to multinational enterprises. Its focus is on victory without battle, and strategic leverage through

Source: Sun Tzu 1988.

understanding of the causes, psychology and politics of conflict. While the healing arts and the world of business or project management may be a miles apart in their issues and challenges, they share in common that "less is more" when it comes to needed interventions and in dealing with disharmony. Further, proper diagnostics and knowledge of the problem are critical to the solution.

As for the master warrior in *The Art of War* who knows the psychology and mechanics of conflict in great detail, and can interpret every move of an opponent, able to act precisely accord to the situations with a minimum of effort, so can the skillful manager in dealing with actual or potential conflict situation before they develop into major issues.

17.1 CONFLICT—GOOD, BAD, AND INEVITABLE

With the complex organizational interactions necessary for executing today's projects, conflict is inevitable and often impacts performance. However, contrary to conventional wisdom, conflict can also be beneficial, producing involvement, new information, and competitive spirit. Conflict cannot be characterized as good *or* bad. It is determined by the interplay of the project organization and its support functions, rather than caused by trouble makers and uncooperative people, which was the prevailing traditional view until the 1960s. Complex organizational relationships, nonlinear work processes, dual accountability, managerial power sharing, multiple constraints, and intricate stakeholder communities are factors that contribute to a work environment where conflict is inevitable.

While there is no single universally accepted definition of conflict, Wikipedia (2013) suggests a good working definition relevant to modern project situations:

> Conflict refers to some form of friction, disagreement, or discord arising within a group when the beliefs or actions of one of more members of the group are either resisted by or unacceptable to one or more members of another group. Conflict can arise between members of the same group, known as intragroup conflict, or it can occur between members of two or more groups, and involve violence, interpersonal discord, and psychological tension, known as intergroup conflict.

This definition is also consistent with broader concept of *conflict in organizations* (Blake et al. 1964, Butler 1973, Kilman and Thomas 1978, Rahim 2010, Van de Vliert et al. 1990, von Glinow et al. 2004), which in turn is a subset of the general body of knowledge on conflict, grounded in the social sciences. This more general theory focuses on the social dimensions of conflict, including political and material inequalities of social groups, emphasizing power differentials and class conflict; the roots of the theory date back to Karl Marx (Marx [1867] 2010), the father of social conflict theory.

Conflict in project situations is special. While connecting with the same macro theory, it has unique characteristics and follows a particular process:

In the first stage, routine group work is disrupted by disagreements over issues, such as schedules, resources or technical specifications. These disagreements are often caused by differences of opinion between members or changes introduced by a third party from the outside of the team. At this stage conflict is subtle and often not fully realized by the group. This situation is being called "initial conflict."

In the second stage, conflict escalates. The team or work group is no longer unified but might split into interest groups and form coalitions. At this point the group realizes that disagreement or conflict exists.

In the third stage, the cause of conflict is being examined and diagnosed. This can be done by the work group or a lead person or a combination of both. This stage has a strong focus toward conflict resolution.

The fourth stage deals with searches for conflict resolution which could range from withdrawal to forcing or finding compromises. This stage could engage the work group, a lead person, or both.

The fifth stage deals with implementation, hence actually resolving the conflict and returning the group to its initial state of routine unified teamwork.

Understanding the determinants of organizational or personal stress and disagreements is important to the project manager's ability to deal with conflict effectively. When conflict becomes dysfunctional, it often results in poor decision making, lengthy delays over operational issues, and a disruption of the team efforts, all negative influences on project performance. However, a new view on conflict emerged from field research in the 1970s (Thamhain and Wilemon 1975, 1977), recognizing that conflict can be both detrimental and beneficial to an organization, a finding that has been widely confirmed in the research literature and is generally accepted today by both management researchers and practitioners (Holahan and Mooney 2004; Khan, Afzal, and Rehman 2009). Field studies also show that conflict is a normal byproduct of innovation and creativity, and should be expected especially in technology-intensive organizations.

The ability to deal effectively with this inevitable conflict is critical to project performance. Seasoned project managers seem to have a "sixth sense" to know when conflict is desirable, what kind of conflict will be useful, and when and how to resolve developing issues.

17.2 CATEGORIZING CONFLICT IN ORGANIZATIONS

To study conflict in project organizations, and to deal with conflict effectively, it is useful to define a common language for describing specific conflict situations. Following the suggestions of the research literature (Hearn and Anderson 2002; Jehn 1995, 1997; Pinkley 1990), conflict in work groups can be characterized along three major dimensions: (1) content, (2) relationship, and (3) organization.

1. **Content-based conflict.** Also called substantive conflict, this type of conflict involves disagreement among team members or groups over the content of project work, such as tasks, performance issues, or work process. Conflict occurs when people disagree on project-related issues, including differences in viewpoints, ideas, and opinions. A special category of content-based conflict is process-based conflict, which deals with issues of how tasks should be completed and integrated as part of the overall project (Hearn and Anderson 2002).

2. **Relationship-based conflict.** Also called affective or interpersonal conflict, this type of conflict deals with interpersonal relationships or incompatibilities in personal interests, objectives, values, culture, attitude, and believes (Barki and Hartwick 2001). Disagreement is the key cognitive component of this interpersonal conflict. It most strongly affects communication effectiveness. It can develop between individuals or organizational groups. Affective conflict is virtually always counterproductive and has the tendency to spread further. It is often difficult to diagnose and is one of the most difficult types of conflict to resolve (Behfar et al. 2008, Amason 1996, Guetzkow and Gyr 1954, Jehn 1995; Jehn and Mannix 2001, Pinkley 1990, Priem and Price 1991).

3. **Organization-based conflict.** This type of conflict can be either content- or relationship-based. It occurs between two or more organizational groups. In terms of organizational footprint and scope of conflict, we can distinguish among three subcategories: (1) interorganizational (or Intergroup), conflict between organizations, including contractors, government and partner organizations; (2) intraorganizational (or Intragroup), conflict within an organization, such as a department or work group; and (3) individual (or interpersonal) conflict. This type of conflict exists on the smallest organizational footprint. It occurs between two or more individuals. If these individuals are part of the same work group, the conflict represents a special type of intragroup conflict otherwise it is a special type of intergroup conflict (Rahim 2002).

All conflict, regardless of its classification, is negatively related to team member satisfaction (De Dreu and Weingart 2003). However, with regard to team and project performance, field research presents a less unified picture. It shows that most relationship-based conflicts (over 90 percent) are negatively correlated to project performance, while content-based conflict produced weaker negative results, and in 20 percent of the field studies showed statistically significant positive correlation between substantive conflict and project performance. This is consistent with my own field research (Thamhain 2004, 2008, 2013). It also confirms the statement made at the beginning of this chapter that conflict can be beneficial, producing involvement, new information, and competitive spirit.

17.3 HOW TO ANTICIPATE ISSUES

Project managers frequently admit that they are unprepared to deal with conflict. Yet understanding conflict and its determinants is critically important for effectively dealing with the multitude of work and personality issues that come into play during the execution of today's complex projects.

Several studies have investigated the sources of conflict. Conflict can originate in many areas, and there are many ways to cluster the issues that cause conflict. Yet, one of my earlier studies (1975), conducted together with David Wilemon, has become a model for investigating conflict (Gobeli et al. 1998, Lam and Chin 2004, Verma 1998) by focusing on seven key sources of conflict in project organizations, which are described as follows. The listing is rank-ordered by the frequency with which these conflicts are likely to occur over the project life cycle (Thamhain 2003), and is graphically summarized in Figure 17.1. While these conflict sources can be further expanded and the frequency may vary among given project situation, the seven conflict sources provide a reasonable framework for anticipating potential conflict in specific areas, and for dealing with the issues effectively.

1. **Conflict over schedules.** Disagreements may develop around the timing, sequencing, and scheduling of project-related tasks.
2. **Conflict over cost.** Frequently, conflict may develop between support areas and project integrators over cost estimates. Another common source of conflict is cost escalation over the project life cycle due to a variety of issues that have their root cause in other areas, such as shifting priorities, technical difficulties, and scope changes.

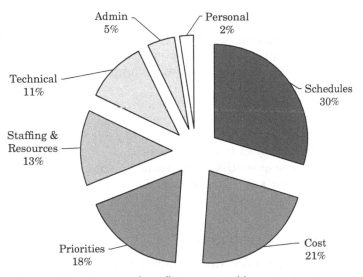

Figure 17.1 Sources of conflict perceived by project managers

3. **Conflict over project priorities.** The views of project participants often differ over the sequence of activities and tasks that should be undertaken to achieve successful project completion. Conflict over priorities may occur not only between the project team and other support groups but also within the project team itself.

4. **Conflict over staffing and resources.** Conflicts may arise over the staffing of the project team with personnel from other functional and support areas or from the desire to use another department's personnel for project support, even though the personnel remain under the authority of their functional superiors.

5. **Conflict over technical issues.** Especially in technology-based organizations, disagreements may arise over technical issues related to performance-cost tradeoffs, specifications, quality, reliability, and broad issues of optimizing results.

6. **Conflict over administrative procedures.** Managerial and administration-oriented conflicts may develop over how the project will be managed, including defining project managers' reporting relationships and responsibilities, interfaces, project scope, operational requirements, plan of execution, negotiated work agreements with other groups, and procedures for administrative support.

7. **Personality conflict.** Disagreements may originate from differences in personality, culture, or attitude. Personality conflicts are often very subtle, not always visible to the outsider. While the frequency of these type of conflict is relatively low, the impact on team performance and overall project success can be significant.

17.3.1 Conflict Among Organizational Units

Several observations can be made regarding the intensity and causes of conflict among various organizational subsystems of the enterprise. In looking at five organizational groups or subsystems, we can rank these subsystems regarding conflict intensity with the project organization as follows (highest conflict level is listed first):

1. Conflict between functional resource departments and project manager
2. Conflict between assigned personnel and project manager
3. Conflict among project team members
4. Conflict between executive-level management and project manager
5. Conflict between subordinate personnel (direct reports) and project manager

Conflict with Resource Departments

Project managers experience the highest level of conflict with functional resource groups supporting the project. It is also the highest frequency of conflict. Much of this conflict can be explained in terms of power and resource sharing. Project managers often do not have the authority to direct the work or priorities in functional support areas. Thus, conflict frequently develops over the timing of activities, which often affects other issues, such as related to integration, testing, and design-build. Conflict with functional departments may also originate over technical details and opinions. Many project managers argue that they have to maintain an overview of the entire project, both from the business and the technical side. They need to understand the specific technical solutions at the subsystem level, as well as how a particular approach affects other components and overall project performance. Since the personnel at the resource department does not have the full project overview, conflict can develop over what decisions are "best" for the project.

Conflict with Assigned Personnel

Conflict between the project manager and assigned personnel ranked second, both in intensity and frequency. Although project managers have a higher degree of authority and control over personnel assigned to the project than over autonomous support departments, assigned employees still have a fair amount of loyalty to their home offices. In addition, many awards, such as salary, promotion and future work assignments, are heavily influenced by their home office managers. As one manager stated:

> My assigned personnel come from our resource departments. They often represent the views of their functional managers. They know, when the project is finished, they need to go back to their home offices. Obviously, they want to maintain good relations with their functional managers.

This statement highlights the dual-accountabilities typical for matrix situations. It also is a source of tension and conflict that makes it more challenging to build a unified project team focused on the big picture and final results.

Conflict among Project Team Members

This type of conflict ranks third in terms of intensity and frequency. However, in comparison to the first two categories, conflict among team members focuses mostly on technical issues with minimum involvement of the project manager. Although conflict over technical issues can get heated and emotionally charged, it seldom leads to personal issues. Yet, project managers must keep an eye on this type of conflict and the group interaction to ensure proper resolution and to avoid conflict escalation.

Conflict with Executive-Level Management

Conflict between the project manager and his/her supervisors and executive management of the enterprise is relatively low and infrequent, accounting for only less than 5 percent of all conflicts. Two facts might explain this finding. First, upper-level management seems to generally more aligned with the project than other organizational components. Second, the power distance between project managers and upper management limits the opportunity and desire for heavy engagement over issues, making project managers more likely agreeable to certain requests or requirements. Although this bias toward withdrawing from a potential or actual conflict situation does not necessarily lead to the best outcome in terms of the project, it is just a reality of organizational life.

Conflict with Subordinate Personnel

Conflict between project managers and their direct reports (i.e., subordinates) ranks lowest among the five groups. It accounts for less than 3 percent of all conflicts reported from the field. The reasons are probably similar to those mentioned in the previous category—alignment of project interest and position power. Most of the issues center on technical, schedule, or budget challenges. They seem to get resolved at low intensity levels and without creating much personal conflict, at least for most cases.

Taken together, conflict can originate in many areas and from many sources. It is interesting to note that in terms of organizational areas, resource departments and assigned personnel contribute about 75 percent of all conflicts in the areas of schedules and personnel resources. On the other side, personality conflict is relatively low, averaging about 5 percent across all organizational areas. However, it should be emphasized that averages are not necessarily good measures of effectiveness or impact. Small conflicts can intensify with devastating consequences. Also, something seen as a small conflict by the project manager might turn out to be a big issue to another party—maybe serious enough to cause the resignation of a key team member as a big surprise to the project manager. Conflict in project organizations is highly dynamic, with complex relations among the various sources of conflict and their causes. Effective project managers keep a watchful eye on their people and activities. They know when conflict is just part of the problem-solving process and the team is handling the issues satisfactorily. Or, on the other side, they recognize when conflict intensifies to a point where it becomes dysfunctional and managerial intervention is required.

17.4 CONFLICT IN THE PROJECT LIFE CYCLE

While it is important to examine the principal determinants of conflict from an aggregate perspective, additional, more specific and useful insights can be gained by exploring the intensity and frequency of various conflicts across the project life-cycle. Consistent with established definitions, the cycle is divided into four stages (also referred to as phases): (1) project formation, (2) project startup and early buildup, (3) main project stage, and (4) phase-out. The discussions in this section are based on three decades of field studies, started between 1975 and 1977 (Thamhain 1991, 2004, 2006, 2011; Thamhain and Wilemon 1997). Figure 17.2 summarizes the intensities for the seven conflict categories, introduced in the previous section.

17.4.1 Conflict during Project Formation

A great deal of conflict from all sources is experienced by project managers during project formation. The project formation phase has unique characteristics. Unlike in other stages, the project manager must launch the project within the larger host organization and build his/her cross-functional team from newly assigned personnel and resource groups over whom he/she has often very limited formal authority and control. The *new* project often competes for resources with ongoing activities and has to establish itself within the intricate system of priorities in the enterprise—a situation especially typical for matrix organizations.

Priorities and schedules seem to cause most issues. Project managers experience not only the highest frequency of conflict in these categories (see Figure 17.1), but also the highest intensity during formation and throughout the project life cycle (Figure 17.2). Many of the priority issues involve disagreements over schedules and administrative procedures, the second and third highest intensity of conflict during project formation.

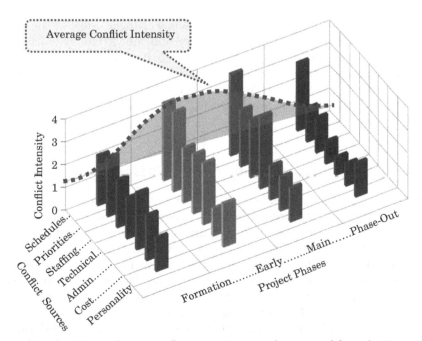

Figure 17.2 Relative conflict intensity over the project life cycle [c]

For example, an urgent issue may receive a low-priority treatment from support groups and/or staff personnel because of a different priority structure in the support organization. In discussing priority conflict with project managers, many indicated that this type of conflict often develops because the new project competes for resources with ongoing activities. Consequently, the changing pattern of priorities requires reallocation of crucial resources, rescheduling or displacing of other activities already under way, a process that can be susceptible to intense disagreements and conflicts.

Further, priority issues can develop into conflict with other support departments whose established schedules and work patterns are disturbed by changed requirements. Priority, schedule, and administrative conflicts often occur with other support departments over which project managers have limited authority and control. Another important observation is on domino effects. Especially schedule issues often overlap with other problems, or are triggered by conflicts in other areas, such as technical, staffing, and resource issues, which are also high in intensity and frequency during the formation stage.

To eliminate or minimize these conflicts and their negative consequences, project managers need to plan and negotiate the support activities properly. This should be accomplished as early as possible in the program life cycle, and ideally involve the key personnel of all interfacing parties. Many of the priority and administrative conflicts center on critical management issues such as: How will the project organization be structured? To whom will the project manager report? What is the authority of the project manager? Does the project manager have control over workforce and material resources? What reporting and communication channels will be used? Who establishes schedules and performance specifications and review criteria? Most of these issues are negotiated between the project manager and the various resource groups needed for project support, and conflict frequently occurs during the process. To avoid prolonged problems over these issues, it is important to establish a mutually-agreed-on resource plan, together with clear procedures and project charters that define the work process, interface protocol, and authority relations.

17.4.2 Project Startup and Early Buildup Phase

The total amount of conflict aggregated from all seven sources seems to reach the highest level during project buildup. Disagreements over *project schedules* and *priorities* continue as important determinants of conflict, followed by staffing, technical, and administrative problems. Some of these conflicts appear as an extension from the previous project phase. By contrast to the formation phase, schedule conflicts develop over the enforcement of schedules and necessary schedule changes. Overall, many of the conflicts occur during negotiations with other resource groups.

Conflict over *technical issues* becomes more pronounced and intensive during project buildup, rising from the sixth to the fourth level and staying a strong source of conflict over the remaining project life cycle (ranking fourth in intensity and fifth in frequency). Most of the technical conflict occurs among functional support groups over system/component interfaces. Second, between functional support groups and the system integrators, and third between the project management team and the "technology providers," such as R&D, engineering, product development, production or field support groups. These technology groups are primarily responsible for delivering their work package according to agreed-on specs and performance standards. The project management team, on the other hand, is accountable for cost, schedules, and overall results. Typically, conflict occurs when the project manager is faced with a need to change some specifications or part of the configuration in response to important changes in the market or customer community, while the technology groups find it impossible to accommodate the change requirements without increasing budgets and/or delivery dates. Similar, conflict occurs when resource teams recommend alternative superior solutions, but get rejected due to cost or schedule restraints.

Personality conflicts start flaring up during project buildup. While personality issues are among the lowest level in terms of overall frequency and intensity throughout the project life cycle, they are more disruptive and detrimental to overall project performance than conflicts over nonpersonal issues. Discussions with project managers indicate that in spite of appearing less intense and frequent than other conflicts, they are often the most difficult type of conflict to deal with. When they occur, they have almost always a strong impact on team communications, team efficiency, team morale, ability to share risk, and to deal with other conflict issues. Personality conflict is often a condition that masks or obscures other problems. For example, a team member, may stress the technical aspect of a disagreement with the project manager when, in fact, the real issue is a personality conflict.

17.4.3 Main Project Phase

The main project phase reveals a conflict pattern similar to that of project buildup with particularly high conflict over schedules and technical issues, followed by staffing and priorities. This makes sense because project plans committed to during earlier phases might turn out to be more difficult to implement, leading to unexpected technical issues and schedule slippages. Yet, meeting deadlines remains critical and conflict develops over this incompatibility. These issues are further complicated by interdependencies of various support groups that can cause a whiplash effect throughout the project. In other words, a slippage in schedule by one group may affect other groups if they are in the critical path of the project.

Technical issues are often subtle and less obvious as a source of conflict. Yet, they can cause many of the other conflicts, especially with cost and schedules. Technical issues are one of the more important sources of conflict in the main execution phase. Many of the technical issues relate to system integration challenges. Due to the complexities involved in the integration process, conflicts frequently develop over system interface definitions, data transfer protocols, and the actual integration of various subsystems that involve people from different resource groups with different organizational cultures, technical norms, and standards. As explained by one project manager: "Just because a component can be designed and prototyped according to specs by one resource group, doesn't always ensure that it will work in the system, or that all the technical anomalies are eliminated." In extreme cases, a component or subsystem may not even be producible. Such problems can severely impact the project and generate intense conflicts. Disagreements also may arise in the main program phase over reliability and quality control issues, various design problems, and testing procedures. All these problems cause conflicts for the project manager and impact overall project performance.

17.4.4 Project Phase-Out

The final project phase shows an interesting shift in the principal causes of conflict, resulting in the lowest level of overall conflict. The exception is schedule conflict, which is double the intensity and frequency of other conflict categories in this final project phase, almost as strong as for the previous two project phases. Project managers frequently indicate that many of the schedule slippages that developed in the main program phase, never get fully resolved as an issue. This typically leads to further schedule compression, cumulates, and is carried over to the end-phase of the project. Personality conflict becomes more pronounced during project phase-out. This can be explained in two ways. First, it is not uncommon for project participants to be tense and concerned with future assignments. Second, interpersonal relationships may be quite strained during this period due to the pressure on project participants to meet stringent schedules, budgets, and performance specifications and objectives. All of this might explain the remaining modest, but still substantial conflict that exists even in the final phase over staffing/ resource issues and priorities as shown in Figure 17.2.

Conflict over priorities in the phase-out stage appears to be directly related to the competition with other project startups. The combined pressure on schedules, workforce, and personality creates a climate that is highly vulnerable to conflicts over priorities.

Technical, administrative, and cost issues rank lowest as conflict sources during this final phase. When a project reaches this stage, most of the technical issues are usually resolved. A similar argument holds for administrative procedures. However, the fact that cost issues do not surface as a major conflict is somewhat surprising. Discussions with project personnel suggest that while cost control can be troublesome in this phase, intense conflicts usually do not develop because cost problems develop gradually and provide little ground for arguments during the final phase. There are various other reasons why conflict over cost is low. First, some of the project components may be purchased externally on a fixed-fee basis. In such cases the contractor would bear the burden of the costs. Second, while cost is difficult to control at an established level, project budgets are often adjusted for increase in material and workforce costs. This incremental cost growth frequently eliminates the "sting" from cost overruns. Moreover some projects in the high-technology area, such as R&D, are managed on a cost-plus basis. In some of these projects precise cost estimates cannot always be rigidly adhered to. The reader should be cautioned, however, that the low level of conflict is by no means indicative of little importance of cost performance. During discussions with top management, it is repeatedly emphasized that cost performance is one of the key evaluation measures in judging the performance of project managers.

Moreover, it is important to note that while a conflict issue may be ranked relatively low by its intensity, it does not necessarily mean that its significance or impact is low. A single conflict over a technical issue can be equally detrimental and jeopardizing to project performance as a series of schedule slippages. This point should be kept in mind in any discussion of managing conflict in projects. Furthermore, problems may develop which appear virtually "conflict-free," but have obscured or hidden issues, such as technological anomalies or problems with suppliers. While the issues were known, its full impact may take time to develop, and therefore the intensity of the conflict may be felt at a later time or phase of the project.

17.5 HOW TO DEAL WITH CONFLICT

An important first step in dealing effectively with a conflict situation is to recognize the potential causes and intensities of conflicts, as discussed in the previous section. This establishes the basis for selecting the proper conflict resolution style and approach most effective for a given situation. Effective conflict management is not necessarily the same as conflict resolution; it is the process of limiting the negative consequences of conflict while increasing its positive aspects. The objective is to improve the work ambience and team performance (DeChurch and Marks 2001, Rahim 2002). Project managers spend much of their time dealing with conflict in the workplace, by some estimates more than 25 percent (Lang, 2009), and often the outcome is unsatisfactory. Therefore, understanding the dynamics of conflict and the options of handling conflict effectively is critical to project management performance. The next section will provide some insight into this complex topic of conflict management.

17.5.1 Conflict Resolution Approaches

Many organizations have established formal systems for arbitrating conflict that cannot be resolved at the project level. However, in most cases project personnel attempt to resolve the conflict at the project level rather than resorting to arbitration by higher management. Typically, they have straightforward meetings with other team members to address conflicts, especially those that are task-oriented. Such direct interventions can dispose of many problems before they become detrimental to the overall project. However, when conflict involves more complex issues, such as organizational or personal issues, people might not feel capable or comfortable resolving the conflict in a direct, straightforward way, but resort to more subtle, intricate approaches, involving a variety of styles and methods that range from autocratic to team-based, and from negotiating resolutions to just walking away.

Many approaches to conflict resolution have been proposed, going back to biblical times and ancient Chinese dynasties (Gagliardi 2003). In the 1920s, one of the pioneers of organizational behavior and early researchers on this subject, Mary Parker Follett (Metcalf and Urwick 2003), found that conflict was managed by individuals in three main ways: domination, compromise, and integration, and to a lesser degree by avoidance and suppression. Later, Blake and Mouton (1964) were among the first to suggest a conceptual framework, classifying five modes for handling interpersonal conflicts: forcing, withdrawing, smoothing, compromising, and problem solving. Although many researchers built on this framework and suggested refinements and alternatives, Blake and Mouton's scheme became the theoretical framework for most conflict management research and discussions, especially in the field of project management. The five modes or methods of conflict handling, defined by Blake and Mouton, are listed here in increasing order of mental involvement. They are further described in Table 17.1.

1. **Withdrawing.** Retreating or withdrawing from actual or potential disagreements
2. **Smoothing (also known as accommodating).** Deemphasizing differences and emphasizing commonalities over conflict issues
3. **Compromising.** Searching for solutions which bring some degree of satisfaction
4. **Forcing (also known as competing).** Exerting one's viewpoint at the potential expense of another
5. **Problem solving or collaborating (originally called confronting).** Facing the conflict directly, actively searching for resolution.

17.5.2 What Conflict Resolution Works Best?

Project managers are quick to point out the highly situational nature of each conflict resolution mode. That is, the effectiveness of a particular resolution mode depends not only on the type of conflict, but also on the organizational culture, team composition, business climate, special circumstances, and most importantly the leadership style of the project manager, including his or her credibility, trust and respect with the conflicting parties. Nevertheless, some of our field studies (Thamhain and Wilemon 1977; Thamhain 2000, 2007, 2011,

Table 17.1 Five General Modes for Handling Conflict

	Withdrawing	
Characteristics	**Potential Benefit**	**Potential Detriment**
Retreating from a conflict issue. Here the project manager does not deal with the disagreement, but ignores it. He or she might withdraw out of fear, may feel inadequately prepared to bring about an effective resolution, or may want to avoid rocking the boat. Withdrawal, by definition, does not resolve the issues, but the conflict may even intensify over time.	Withdrawing can be beneficial either as a temporary strategy to allow the other party to cool off or as a strategy to buy time so study the issues further. Withdrawal may also be effective for the leader if the parties engaged in the conflict are capable and willing to resolve the issues among themselves.	Conflict may increase or propagate into other areas. Team leader is seen as ineffective, unprepared, or incompetent. Polarization of conflicting parties over issues. Withdrawal may result in broader management involvement with fewer options for resolution.
	Smoothing (a.k.a. Accommodating)	
Emphasizes common areas of agreement and deemphasizes areas of differences. Like withdrawing, smoothing may not address the real issues in a disagreement.	Smoothing is often effective in complex conflict situations in separating agreements from disagreements, and therefore focuses energy on the issues that need resolution. Project work can often continue in areas where there is agreement by the parties.	Similar to withdrawing from conflict, smoothing does not address the real issues. Conflict often increases over time. Smoothing often masks the real issues and makes people believe that conflict does not exist or has been resolved. When conflict reoccurs over the same issue, it usually is even more intense. If conflict is not resolved, the team leader is seen as ineffective, unprepared or incompetent which might result in broader management involvement with less options for resolution (similar to withdrawal approach).

(Continued)

Table 17.1 (Continued)

	Compromising	
Characteristics	Potential Benefit	Potential Detriment
Negotiating, bargaining and searching for solutions that offer some degree of satisfaction to the parties involved in conflict. Since compromise yields less than optimum results, the project manager must weigh such actions against project goals and objectives. Compromise is always the outcome of a negotiation, hence part of the fifth conflict-handling mode "Problem solving or confronting."	A compromise can be a win-win resolution. Compromise is often seen as a reality of work or personal life, and the outcome accepted by the parties. Since compromise involves active involvement by all parties in the resolution process, it leads most likely to an outcome that has some buy-in and ownership, and a personal feeling by people that the issues have actually been resolved.	A compromise may lead to a lose-lose scenario (e.g, when parties suddenly realize that the compromise is not workable). Not all conflicts can be solved by compromise (some issues are not negotiable). Compromise, by definition is always suboptimal. The cost of compromising may outweigh its benefits. Compromise should not be used for convenience. Inappropriate use of this conflict resolution affects the project manager's leadership image.

	Forcing (a.k.a. Competing)	
Characteristics	Potential Benefit	Potential Detriment
Exerting one's viewpoint at the expense of another. The ability to force assumes position power and is characterized by competitiveness and win/lose behavior. The effectiveness of forcing is highly situational and also depending on the personal style, credentials, trust, and respect of the decision maker.	Quick way to resolve conflict. Keeps project moving. Effective in resolving issues where the leader has the "right" answer. Effective in emergency situations or decisions with no alternatives. Forcing is part of effective leadership and is expected and wanted by the team in certain situations (e.g., clear directions and objectives).	May lead to resentment, de-motivation, uncooperative behavior and general deterioration of the team environment. Transfers accountability from the team to the decision maker. May escalate the conflict, drawing wider circles and involvement of upper management. Forcing may not work because of insufficient position power or authority in given situation.

	The image of forcing can be modified by explaining the rationale for a decision, and asking for help and collaboration with the implementation.	Forcing is often used as a last resort by project managers since it may cause resentment and deterioration of the work climate.
Problem-solving (a.k.a. Collaborating, originally called Confronting)		
Involves a rational problem-solving approach. Disputing parties solve difference by focusing on the issues, looking at alternative approaches, and selecting the best resolution. Confronting may contain elements of other conflict resolution modes, and virtually always results in a compromise.	Often the only viable mode for resolving complex conflict. People feel included in the problem-solving process with beneficial effects on motivation, collaboration, and overall team spirit. Because of the involvement of the people associated with the conflict, the solutions worked out most likely have mutual agreement and commitment to implementation.	Requires time, personal effort and energy. Therefore, the problem-solving mode might not be suitable, effective or even workable for many conflict situations.

2012) show a clear preference for certain modes among project managers. Figure 17.3 summarizes the results of several field surveys that simply ask project leaders, "Which conflict resolution approaches work or don't work for you in your project environment?" Specifically, each project leader was shown a list of the five approaches discussed in this chapter, together with a brief definition, next to a statement: "I find this conflict resolution mode effective in dealing with certain issues in my project environment." Then, each leader was asked to indicate on a five-point scale his or her agreement to the statement: (1) I strongly agree, (2) I agree, (3) not sure, (4) disagree, (5) strongly disagree. Responses of (1) and (2) were recorded as favoring this mode, and responses of (4) and (5) as rejecting the mode as effective for conflict resolution. The responses of the "(3) not sure" category are graphically accounted for in Figure 17.3 by the difference between 100 percent minus (%-rejected + %-favored). The survey was structured in a way that respondents could favor (or reject) multiple modes. In fact, project leaders seem to favor an average of 2.5 modes and reject 1.5, while on average perceiving approximately 1 out of the 5 modes as "questionable or unsure" regarding effectiveness.

As indicated in Figure 17.3, conflict resolution approaches involving *problem-solving* and *compromise* seem to be most important to project managers and most frequently used, while *forcing* and *withdrawal* seem to be least favored. Even more important is the finding that problem-solving and compromise were found the most effective methods of dealing with conflict in most project situations, while forcing and withdrawal seem to be least effective in the management of multifunctional activities.

The problem-solving (or collaborating) approach seems to hold a special place among the five conflict resolution modes. While time-consuming and requiring intense personal involvement, it is often the only approach that leads to a resolution of complex issues. Collaboration, when approached

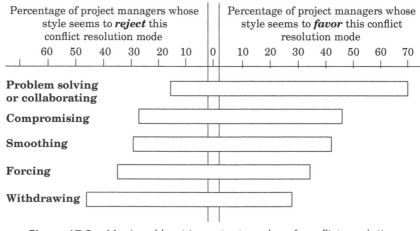

Figure 17.3   Most and least important modes of conflict resolution (project managers' perception)

skillfully, focuses on resolving the problem and depersonalizing the issue. The approach concentrates on delineating the key issues involved in the disagreement, the options available in resolving the differences, and the best alternatives. This might explain why collaboration was perceived the preferred and most effective conflict resolution approach by 70 percent of project managers in our field studies.

The following example illustrates a situation where potentially detrimental conflict was handled effectively: The project manager had a severe conflict with the hydraulic design group over a key component of the project. The design group informed the project manager that they couldn't deliver the subsystem as originally planned. They offered an alternative design with the stipulation that this was the only feasible solution for delivering the subsystem. However, alternative design would increase the project cost, cause additional interface problem, and affect overall technical project performance. The project manager had a series of meetings with the hydraulic design group, joint by some key system's integrators and one hydraulic specialist borrowed from another resource group. Some of these meetings were quite intense and heated. The handling of the issues in a problem-solving style eventually resulted in a substantially better design and improved overall project performance, without affecting the budget.

As shown in this scenario from the field, a potentially detrimental conflict was turned around by the project manager using the problem-solving approach, resulting in a win-win resolution to which several groups contributed, and therefore had ownership and commitment to its implementation, which in this case meant commitment to the subsystem design and its integration with the overall project.

Further investigation into the effectiveness of conflict resolution styles confirmed the situational dependencies stated earlier, including the type of conflict, personnel, and organizations involved. It also showed that because of the complex power and authority relations that often exist among the conflicting parties (maybe as typically illustrated with the conflict scenario regarding the hydraulic design group, described in the two paragraphs above), the problem-solving (or collaborating) approach not only is most frequently used, but also seems to lead to more broadly acceptable outcomes, higher levels of perceived effectiveness, and ultimately to higher overall project performance as judged by senior management. While this conclusion appears to hold for all types of projects investigated, the statistical significance of performance correlation tests is especially high for larger, more complex and technologically advanced undertakings.

In contrast to studies of general management, research in project-oriented environments suggests that it is less important to search for a best mode of effective conflict management. It appears to be more significant that project managers, in their capacity as integrators of diverse organizational resources, employ the full range of conflict resolution modes. While problem solving was found effective under most circumstances, other approaches may be equally appropriate, depending on the situational nature of the disagreement.

Withdrawal, for example, may be used effectively as a temporary measure until new information can be sought or to "cool off" a hostile reaction from a colleague. As a basic long-term strategy, however, withdrawal may actually escalate conflict if no resolution is sought.

In other cases, compromise or smoothing might be considered an effective strategy by the project manager if it does not severely affect the overall project objectives. Forcing, on the other hand, often proves to be a win–lose mode. Even though the project manager may win over a specific issue, effective working arrangements with the "forced" party may be jeopardized in future relationships, and almost certain, commitment to the implementation of a forced decision is lost. Nevertheless, in some situations, such emergencies, critical safety or ethics issues, or strategic decisions, forcing might be the only viable mode. Collaboration (the problem-solving mode) may actually encompass all conflict-handling modes to some extent. For example, in solving a conflict a project manager may use Collaboration in combination with withdrawal, forcing, and smoothing to eventually get an effective compromise resolution to the issue, acceptable by all affected parties.

In summary, conflict is fundamental to complex task management. It is not only important for project managers to be cognizant of the potential sources of conflict, but also to know when, in the life cycle of a project, they are most likely to occur. Such knowledge can help the project manager avoid the detrimental aspects of conflict and maximize its beneficial aspects. Conflict can be beneficial when disagreements result in the development of new information that can enhance the decision-making process. Finally, when conflict does develop, the project manager needs to know the advantages and disadvantages of each resolution mode for conflict resolution effectiveness.

17.6 CRITERIA FOR MANAGING CONFLICT IN PROJECTS EFFECTIVELY

Project managers operate in an environment that is prone to conflict. The nature of project management, its dynamic organizational interfaces, the need to solicit support from various resource departments, the power and resource-shared operations, the frequently ambiguous authority definition of the project manager, and the temporary nature of projects, all contribute to the amount of conflict experienced by project managers. A number of criteria for managing conflict effectively are derived from the field studies quoted in this chapter and from my own observations in project in project environments.

17.6.1 Recognize Situational Nature

Since the ability to manage conflict is affected by many situational variables, a project manager should (1) recognize the primary determinants of conflict and when they are most likely to occur in the life of the project, (2) consider the effectiveness of the conflict-handling approach he or she has used in the past to manage these issues, and (3) consider fine-tuning or modifying the conflict-handling approach used in the past if such action seem to be appropriate.

17.6.2 Use Judgment before Resorting to Forcing or Withdrawing

Project managers need to be aware of the potentially negative side effects of each conflict resolution mode. While appropriate and effective in certain situations, forcing and withdrawing can have strong adverse effects if used inappropriately, especially when dealing with conflict across functional lines. As shown in field studies, project managers who use forcing and/or withdrawal extensively are likely to experience more intense and prolonged conflict.

17.6.3 Ensure Subject Expertise

Project leaders should develop and maintain expertise in the field they are managing. Without an understanding of the technology, markets, work processes and people they are managing, it is difficult to win the confidence of the team and to build credibility, trust and respect needed to manage conflict across the project community.

17.6.4 Use Expertise Judiciously

Somewhat orthogonal to the previous statement, project managers must use their expertise judiciously in facilitating conflict resolution. If overused, it can be intimidating and demotivating to the team. It sends a signal to the participants that their skill sets are not important or relevant to the resolution of the issues at hand, which often leads to team members' withdrawal from active participation. It also biases solutions toward the project manager's ideas, which, in turn, weakens any team buy-in and commitment toward acceptance and implementation.

17.6.5 Ensure Effective Project Planning

Effective planning early in the project life cycle is important to minimize confusion and ambiguity that might lead to conflict later during the project execution phase. Especially conflict with support departments and outside contractors is often blamed on insufficient project planning, which occurs most intensely during system integration.

17.6.6 Catch Conflict in Its Early Development

It is critical to deal with conflict in its early stages. The difficulty is to know when an issue is likely to intensify. The old Machiavellian saying, "Small problems are easy to fix, but hard to detect; when they get big, they are easy to see, but hard to fix!" is so very true and indicative of the challenges. Project managers need a sixth sense to know when conflict is under control as handled by the team, and when some intervention is necessary. Regular project reviews, gate reviews, user-centered design, design-build, open-door policy, suggestion systems, action teams, focus groups, and management by wandering around are some of the tools that can help in assuring transparency across the project environment, recognizing developing conflict in its early stages, and dealing with the issues before they become organizationally and personally tainted.

17.6.7 Avoid the Quick-Solution Trap

Serious issues usually take considerable time and broad team involvement to resolve. A quick agreement on fixing a major problem should be looked at carefully and with suspicion. Often people withdraw from a conflict because it is too time- or energy-consuming, or the psychological cost is too high. For the moment, it might appear that the conflict has been resolved, but the underlying issues are still there and conflict is likely to reappear at a later time, probably even more intensely. To avoid this trap, project managers should follow up on these agreements, making sure that the issues have been addressed and will permanently resolve the conflict, facilitate follow-up meetings and help in working out the details needed for a workable resolution.

17.6.8 Utilize the Power of Collaboration and Consensus

People are more likely to collaborate on conflict issues if they understand the rationale behind the arguments and they accept the logic of differing points of view. Explaining the issues and their impact on the current project, and the importance of finding acceptable solutions, can help in building a sense of collaboration. It is important to search for common grounds, rather than to aim for a win-lose scenario. The initial objective of most conflict resolution intervention is to reach consensus, not necessary unanimity, on how to proceed. This requires mutual respect for everyone's ideas, opinions, and suggestions.

17.6.9 Practice the Art of Listening

Active listening includes questions of clarification and notions of understanding the rationale behind the issues and arguments of the opposing parties.

It is an important catalyst for fostering an environment open to discussing issues and searching for solutions. Careful listening demonstrates respect for the opposing parties and their viewpoints, it helps to depersonalize conflict and to engage the parties in search for common grounds and problem resolution.

17.6.10 Fine-tune Your Leadership Style

Field research shows a definite correlation between the project manager's leadership style and the level of conflict experienced during the project life cycle. Less autocratic, more team-centered management styles, and styles that provide space for autonomy and self-direction seem to foster an environment of lower conflict, both in intensity and frequency. Team members feel more accountable for their actions, and more likely to keep an eye on developing issues trying to resolve them collectively and collaboratively before they intensify.

17.6.11 Foster Professionally Stimulating Work Environment

A professionally exciting, vibrant environment seems to be a strong catalyst for conflict self-management. People who enjoy their work and are motivated and focused toward the end objectives are more likely to reach out, seeking resolutions for developing issues. Professionally motivated people also have a higher threshold for conflict. That is, they take issues less personally but focus on problem solving. Project managers should try to accommodate the professional interests and desires of supporting personnel when negotiating their tasks, matching personal goals with project objectives whenever possible. While the overall scope of a project may be fixed, the project manager usually has a degree of flexibility in allocating task assignments among various contributors. Further, emphasizing the importance of the project to the enterprise, the market, and possibly to society as a whole can enhance the perceived value and desire to participate.

In conclusion, conflict is a fundamental characteristic of project management. The value produced from this conflict depends on the project manager's effectiveness of promoting beneficial aspects while minimizing dysfunctional consequences. Effective project managers seem to have a sixth sense, knowing when conflict is desirable in exploring issues, bringing out new information, and stimulating creativity. They know what kind of conflict is useful and how much is optimal for a given situation. However, they also know when to intervene, facilitate, and manage conflict before it intensifies and escalates into other areas of the enterprise. Managing conflict is both a science and an art, based on skill sets that are difficult to learn. However, field research shows that under the right leadership, project managers and their teams can handle extensive conflict over tough issues and produce great results, in spite of difficult requirements, high project complexities, and tight budget and schedule constraints.

The concepts and observations from the field, discussed in this chapter, should help both project leaders and professionals who must function in these project-based environments to understand the complex interaction of organizational and behavioral variables involved in effective conflict management of today's complex projects. The discussions should increase the awareness of what works and what doesn't, and help to fine-tune managerial leadership style and work process toward high performance.

17.7 SUMMARY OF KEY POINTS AND CONCLUSIONS

The following key points were made in this chapter:

- Conflict is inevitable in today's complex project undertakings. It is determined by the interplay of the project organization and its support functions. Conflict can have positive and negative side effects, but IT usually impacts project performance.
- A conflict resolution cycle can be divided into five stages: (1) routine work is disrupted by disagreements; (2) conflict escalates; (3) conflict is examined and diagnosed; (4) conflicting parties search for resolutions; and (5) proposed solutions are implemented, hence actually resolving the conflict.
- Conflict in work groups can be characterized along three major dimensions: (1) content, (2) relationship, and (3) organization-based conflict.
- Among the many sources of conflict, this chapter identifies two groups of conflict sources: (I) *Work process-related sources of conflict*, such as (1) schedules, (2) cost, (3) priorities, (4) staffing, (5) technical issues, (6) administrative procedures, and (7) personal issues, and (II) *Organizational sources of conflict*, such as conflict between the project manager and (1) functional resource departments, (2) assigned personnel, (3) executives, (4) subordinate personnel, and (5) among project team members.
- Project managers experience the highest level of conflict with functional resource groups and assigned personnel, while subordinates and senior-level personnel cause the least amount and lowest level of conflict. Much of this pattern can be explained in terms of managerial power. The more power is shared and the more ambiguous authority relations are, the more likely conflict will occur.
- Most conflict occurs over work issues rather than personality issues. However, small conflicts can intensify with devastating consequences. Conflict in project organizations is highly dynamic, with complex relations among the various sources of conflict and their causes. Effective project managers keep a watchful eye. They know when conflict is just part of the problem-solving process and the team is handling the issues,

or when conflict intensifies to a point where it becomes dysfunctional and managerial intervention is required.

- Additional insights can be gained by exploring the intensity and frequency of various conflicts across the project life cycle.
- It is important for project managers not only to be cognizant of the potential sources of conflict but also to know when, in the life cycle of a project, they are most likely to occur. Such knowledge can help the project manager avoid the detrimental aspects of conflict and maximize its beneficial aspects. Conflict can be beneficial when disagreements result in the development of new information, which can enhance the decision-making process. Across all phases, conflict over schedules and priorities is highest, while conflict over cost and personal issues is lowest. However, it is important to note that low intensity conflict does not necessarily mean low significance or impact. Further, some problems may appear virtually "conflict-free," but have obscured or hidden issues.
- The five conflict handling modes, defined by Blake and Mouton, have become an accepted framework for investigating and discussing conflict, especially in project environments: (1) withdrawing, (2) smoothing, a.k.a. accommodating, (3) compromising, (4) forcing, a.k.a. competing, and (5) problem solving or collaborating.
- Conflict resolution approaches involving problem solving and/or compromise seem to be most important to project managers and most frequently used, they also produced on average the best results in field studies, while forcing and withdrawal seem to be least favored and least effective, on average.
- The problem-solving (or collaborating) approach seems to hold a special place among the five conflict resolution modes. Although time-consuming and requiring intense personal involvement, it is often the only approach that leads to a resolution of complex issues. It focuses on resolving the problem and depersonalizing the issue.
- In contrast to general management situations, in project-oriented environments it seems less important to search for a best mode of conflict management—rather, that project managers employ the full range of conflict resolution approaches. While problem solving was found effective under most circumstances, other approaches may be equally appropriate, depending on the situational nature of the disagreement. Withdrawal, for example, may be used effectively as a temporary measure until new information can be sought or to "cool off" a hostile reaction from a colleague. As a basic long-term strategy, however, withdrawal may actually escalate conflict in the long-run.
- To gain value from conflict, project managers must promote beneficial aspects while minimizing dysfunctional consequences. Effective project managers seem to have a sixth sense, knowing when conflict is desirable in exploring issues, bringing out new information, and stimulating creativity. They know what kind of conflict is useful and how much is optimal for a given situation. However, they also know when

to intervene and manage conflict before it intensifies and escalates into other areas of the enterprise.

- Managing conflict is both a science and an art, based on skill sets that are difficult to learn. However, field research shows that under the right leadership, project managers and their teams can handle extensive conflict over tough issues and produce great results, in spite of difficult requirements, high project complexities, and tight budget and schedule constraints.

17.8 QUESTIONS FOR DISCUSSION AND EXERCISES

1. Discuss the advantages and disadvantages of the five conflict resolution modes. Identify specific situations where these advantages or disadvantages are amplified.
2. List some early warning signs of a conflict situation becoming dysfunctional.
3. Discuss the characteristics of a work environment conducive to effective conflict handling. Explain why these characteristics are conducive.
4. Discuss the characteristics of an effective leadership style (e.g., project manager) conducive to effective conflict management. Explain why this style will produce favorable results. Any caveats?
5. Why is conflict at the beginning of the project life cycle relatively low? Why does conflict increase, especially for schedule and priority issues, throughout the main phases of the project cycle? What might be the rationale for low conflict over cost and personal issues (as found from field studies)?
6. A conflict developed between you, the project manager, and a component design group over the use of special materials that are superior in terms of weight, strength, and reliability, but are expected to cause problems in the manufacturing process. The manager of the design team just has informed you that the team strongly recommends the new material, and asks you to accept the "minor" change in the original specifications. How would you deal with this conflict situation? What conflict resolution mode(s) would you use? Discuss in your group several options for dealing with this conflict. Anticipate the reaction (effectiveness) of each option regarding acceptance by other affected groups, and overall project performance. Select the best option as determined by your group. Discuss the results with other groups.

17.9 *PMBOK®* REFERENCES AND CONNECTIONS

The topic of managing conflict in roject organizations focuses most strongly on the PMBOK® knowledge areas of project human resource management (#6). The topic cuts across all five PMBOK® processing groups with the strongest connection to planning, executing and monitoring/controlling. Much of this chapter focuses on the context of project executing and monitoring/controlling, discussing the concepts and methods for dealing with the inevitable conflict across the enterprise effectively. The managerial perspectives presented in this chapter should be helpful in connecting the PMBOK standards to best practices of project management, and in studying effectively for PMP® certification. In preparing for the PMP® Exam, the following PMBOK sections relate especially to this chapter and should be studied: (1) project interfaces, (2) staffing requirements, (3) staff assignments, (4) human resource practices, (5) project communications management, (6) managing stakeholder expectations, (7) project plan communications, (8) managing project execution, and (9) project monitoring and controlling.

INTERNET LINKS AND RESOURCES

Academy of Management, Conflict Management Division. http://division.aomonline .org/cm/

Ur, William.2010. "The Walk from No to Yes." Ted Talk. www.ted.com/talks/william_ ury.html

Project management Institute. 2012. Project Management Conference: Leadership Panel on "Conflict Management in 2022." www.youtube.com/watch?v=4He1X__kvFU

REFERENCES AND ADDITIONAL READINGS

Amason, A. 1996. "Distinguishing the Effects of Functional and Dysfunctional Conflict on Strategic Decision Making: Resolving a Paradox for Top Management Teams." *Academy of Management Journal* 39(1): 123–148.

Barki, H., and J. Hartwick. 2001. "Interpersonal Conflict and Its Management in Information System Development." *MIS Quarterly* 25(2): 195–228.

Behfar, K. J., R. S. Peterson, E. A. Mannix, and W. M. K. Trochim. 2008. "The Critical Role of Conflict Resolution in Teams: A Close Look at the Links between Conflict Type, Conflict Management Strategies, and Team Outcomes." *Journal of Applied Psychology* 93: 170–188.

Blake, R., and S. Mouton. (1964) 1994. *The Managerial Grid*. Houston: Gulf Publishing.

Blake, R., H. Sephard, and J. Mouton. 1964 *Managing Intergroup Conflict in Industry*. Houston, TX: Gulf Publishing.

Burke, R. 1969. "Methods of Resolving Interpersonal Conflict." *Personnel Administration* 1969: 48–55.

Butler, A. 1973. "Project Management, A Study in Organizational Conflict." *Academy of Management Journal* 16(1): 84–94.

Cahyono, A., and Y. Hartijasti. 2012. "Conflict Approaches of Effective Project Manager in the Upstream Sector of Indonesian Oil and Gas Industry." *South East Asian Journal of Management* 6(2): 65–80.

Cleland, D. 1968. "The Deliberate Conflict." *Business Horizons* (February).

De Dreu, C., A. Evers, B. Beersma, E. Kluwer, and A. Nauta. 2001. "A Theory-Based Measure of Conflict Management Strategies in the Workplace." *Journal of Organizational Behavior* 22(6): 645–668.

De Dreu, C. and L. Weingart. 2003. "Task versus Relationship Conflict, Team Performance, and Team Member Satisfaction: A Meta-Analysis." *Journal of Applied Psychology* 88(4): 741.

DeChurch, L., and M. Marks. 2001. "Maximizing the Benefits of Task Conflict: The Role of Conflict Management." *The International Journal of Conflict Management* 12(1): 4–22.

Gagliardi, G. 2003a. *Sun Tzu's The Art of War Plus, The Art of Management*. Seattle, WA: Clearbridge Pub.

———. 2003b. Sun Tzu's the Art of War Plus the Ancient Chinese Revealed. Seattle, WA: Clearbridge Publishing.

Gemmill, G., and D. Wilemon. 1970. "The Power Spectrum in Project Management." *Sloan Management Review* 12 (Fall): 15–25.

Gobeli, D., H. Koenig, and I. Bechinger. 1998. "Managing Conflict in Software Development Teams: A Multilevel Analysis." *Journal of Product Innovation Management* 15(5): 423–435.

Guetzkow, H., and J. Gyr. 1954. "An Analysis of Conflict in Decision-Making Groups." *Human Relations* 7(4): 367–382

Hanzhang, T., and R. Wilkinson. 1998. *The Art of War*. Hertfordshire, UK: Wordsworth Editions.

Hearn, J., and M. Anderson. 2002. "Conflict in Academic Departments: An Analysis of Disputes over Faculty Promotion and Tenure." *Research in Higher Education* 43(5): 503–529.

Holahan, P., and A. Mooney. 2004. "Conflict in Project Teams: Gaining the Benefits, Avoiding the Costs." *Current Issues in Technology Management* 3(8): 1–8.

Jehn, K.A. 1995. "A Multi-Method Examination of the Benefits and Detriments of Intragroup Conflict." *Administrative Science Quarterly* 40: 256–282.

———. 1997. "A Qualitative Analysis of Conflict Types and Dimensions in Organizational Groups." *Administrative Science Quarterly* 42: 530–557.

Jehn, K. A., and E. Mannix. 2001. "The Dynamic Nature of Conflict: A Longitudinal Study of Intragroup Conflict and Group Performance." *Academy of Management Journal* 44(2): 238–251.

Kehinde. O. A. 2011. "Impact of Conflict Management on Corporate Productivity: An Evaluative Study." *Australian Journal of Business and Management Research* 1(5): 44–49.

Khan, M., H. Afzal, and K. Rehman. 2009. "Impact of Task Conflict on Employee's Performance of Financial Institutions." *European Journal of Scientific Research* 27(4): 479–487.

Killiam, W. P. 1971. "Project Management: Future Organizational Concepts." *Marquette Business Review*. Summer.

Kilmann, R., and K. Thomas. 1978. "Four Perspectives on Conflict Management: An Attributional Framework for Organizing Descriptive and Normative Theory." *Academy of Management Review* 3(1): 59–68.

Lam, P-K., and K-S. Chin. 2004. "Project Factors Influencing Conflict Intensity and Handling Styles in Collaborative NPD." *Creativity and Innovation Management* 13 (March): 52–62.

Lang, M. 2009. "Conflict Management: A Gap in Business Education Curricula." *Journal of Education for Business* 84(4): 240–245.

Li, J., and D. Hambrick. 2005. "Fractional Groups: A New Vantage on Demographic Faultlines, Conflict, and Disintegration in Work Teams." *Academy of Management Journal* 48(5): 794–813.

Marx, K. (1867) 2010. *Das Kapital*. Translated by Samuel Moore. Seattle, WA: Pacific Publishing.

Metcalf, H., and L. Urwick. 2003. *Dynamic Administration: The Collected Papers of Mary Parker Follett. Vol. 3: Early Sociology of Management and Organizations*. London: Taylor and Francis /Routledge.

Montoya-Weiss, M., A. Massey, and M. Song. 2001. "Getting It Together: Temporal Coordination and Conflict Management in Global Virtual Teams." *Academy of Management Journal* 44(6): 1251–1262.

Pinkley, R. 1990. "Dimensions of Conflict Frame: Disputant Interpretations of Conflict." *Journal of Applied Psychology* 75(2), 117–126.

Priem, R., and K. Price. 1991. "Process and Outcome Expectations for the Dialectical Inquiry, Devil's Advocacy, and Consensus Techniques of Strategic Decision Making." *Group and Organization Management* 16(2): 206–225.

Rahim, A. 2010. *Managing Conflict in Organizations*. Piscataway, NJ: Transaction Publishers.

Rahim, M. 2002. "Toward a Theory of Managing Organizational Conflict." *The International Journal of Conflict Management* 13(3): 206–235.

Rahim, M., D. Antonioni, and C. Psenicka, C. 2001. "A Structural Equations Model of Leader Power, Subordinates' Styles of Handling Conflict, and Job Performance." *International Journal of Conflict Management* 12(3): 91–202.

Sun Tzu 1988. *The Art of War*. Translated by T. Cleary. Boston and London: Shambhala Publications.

Thamhain, H. 1991. "Developing Technology Management Skills." *Research and Technology Management Journal* 35(23): 42–47.

———. 2003. "Managing Innovative R&D Teams." *R&D Management* 33(3): 297–312.

———. 2011. "Studies in Project Human Resources Management and Leadership." In Paul C. Dinsmore and Jeannette Cabanis-Brewin (ed.), *Handbook of Project Management*. New York: AMACOM, pp. 163–172.

Thamhain, Hans. 2004. "Leading Technology-Based Project Teams." *Engineering Management Journal* 16(2): 35–43.

———. 2006. "Optimizing Innovative Performance of R&D Teams in Technology-Based Environments." *Creativity Research Journal* 18(4): 435–436.

———. 2008. "Team Leadership Effectiveness in Technology-Based Project Environments." *IEEE Engineering Management Review* 36(1): 165–180.

———. 2011. "Critical Success Factors for Managing Technology-Intensive Teams in the Global Enterprise." *Engineering Management Journal* 23(3): 30–36.

———. 2012. "The Changing Role of Team Leadership in Multinational Project Environments." *Revista de Gestão e Projetos* (Project Management Journal of Brazil) 3(2): 4–38.

———. 2013. "Building a Collaborative Climate for Multinational Projects." *Procedia— Social and Behavioral Sciences Journal* 74 (March): 21–33.

Thamhain, Hans, and I. Kruglianskas. 2000. "Managing Technology-Based Projects in Multinational Environments." *IEEE Transactions on Engineering Management* 47(1): 55–64.

Thamhain, H., and T. Skelton. 2007. "Success Factors for Effective R&D Risk Management." *International Journal of Technology Intelligence and Planning (IJTIP)* 3(4): 376–386.

Thamhain, H., and D. Wilemon. 1975. "Diagnosing. Conflict Determinants in Project Management." *IEEE Transactions on Engineering Management* 22(1): 35–44.

———. 1977. "Leadership, Conflict, and Program Management Effectiveness." *Sloan Management Review* 19(1): 69–89.

Van de Vliert, E., and B. Kabanoff. 1990. "Toward Theory-Based Measures of Conflict Management." *Academy of Management Journal* 33(1): 199–209.

Verma, V. 1998. "Conflict Management." Chapter 22 in Jeffrey Pinto, ed., *Project Management Handbook*. Newtown Square, PA: Project Management Institute.

Von Glinow, M., D. Shapiro, and J. Brett. 2004. "Can We Talk, and Should We? Managing Emotional Conflict in Multicultural Teams." *Academy of Management Review* 29(4): 578–592.

Walton, R., and J. Dutton. 1969. "The Management of Interdepartmental Conflict: A Model and Review." *Administrative Science Quarterly* 14 (March).

Wikipedia. 2013. "Conflict Process." http://en.wikipedia.org/wiki/Conflict_%28process%29.

Chapter 18

Leading Technology Teams

BOEING 787 DREAMLINER

Everett, WA., April 19, 2013, /PRNewswire/—"Today's FAA approval of battery system improvements for the 787 Dreamliner clears the way for us and the airlines to begin the process of returning the 787 to flight with continued confidence in the safety and reliability of this game-changing new airplane," said Boeing chairman, president and CEO Jim McNerney. "The FAA set a high bar for our team and our solution," said McNerney. "We appreciate the diligence, expertise and professionalism of the FAA's technical team and the leadership of FAA Administrator Michael Huerta and Secretary of Transportation Ray LaHood throughout this process. Our shared commitment with global regulators and our customers to safe, efficient and reliable airplanes has helped make air travel the safest form of transportation in the world today." Boeing, in collaboration with its supplier partners and in support of the investigations of the National Transportation Safety Board and the Japan Transport Safety Board, conducted extensive engineering analysis and testing to develop a thorough understanding of the factors that could have caused the 787's batteries to fail and overheat in two incidents last January. "Our team has worked tirelessly, spending more than 100,000 hours, to develop a comprehensive solution that fully satisfies the FAA and its global counterparts, our customers and our own high standards for safety and reliability," said Boeing Commercial Airplanes President and CEO Ray Conner. "Through the skill and dedication of the Boeing team and our partners, we achieved that objective and made a great airplane even better."

Regardless of the battery issues, an order backlog of over 1,000 Dreamliners puts Boeing's business is in an excellent position. However, success was hard earned. The ten-year development grew out of the Sonic Cruiser project, which was cancelled in 2002, giving the 787 a head start. The aircraft was designed to be the first production airliner with the fuselage assembled with one-piece composite barrel sections instead of the multiple aluminum

---

Source: Boeing press releases (www.boeing.mediaroom.com) and *Wikipedia* (http://en.wikipedia.org/wiki/Boeing_878_Dreamliner).

sheets used on conventional aircrafts. Instead of building the complete aircraft from the ground up in the traditional manner, Boeing decided to assign its global subcontractors more responsibilities for assembly and delivery of completed subassemblies for final assembly in Boeing's Paine Field facilities near Everett, Washington. This approach was intended to result in a leaner and simpler assembly line and lower inventory, with preinstalled systems reducing final assembly cost and time, but it also increased the complexity of this multibillion dollar development project, requiring extensive teamwork and collaboration to achieve the large-scale integration among its 100+ globally dispersed suppliers of components, subassemblies and test facilities. Considering the enormous organizational and technological challenges, the 787 Dreamliner is seen as one of the world's most complex product development projects, also resulting in extensive cost increases and schedule delays of over two years. For Boeing, potential risks and benefits were very high right from the beginning. Yet, given the delivery of over 100 Dreamliners by the beginning of 2014 and order backlog in excess of 1,000 airplanes, the commitments made to this large-scale undertaking by Boeing and its partners seem to pay off. However, continuing emerging technical issue, such as the recent engine icing, need to be resolved before Boeing can claim success These surprises are also constant reminders of the vast challenges associated with such a complex supersize development project.

18.1 TEAM LEADERSHIP—CRITICAL TO PROJECT SUCCESS

Complex megaprojects such as the Boeing 787 Dreamliner development with its 100-plus contractors obviously requires highly sophisticated teamwork. However, all projects big or small require managed teamwork for their multidisciplinary integration. Team effectiveness relates directly to project performance and success in virtually any project situation, from computer development to retailing and medical systems (Ferrante et al. 2006; Keller 2001; Nellore and Balachandra 2001; Thamhain 2006; Shim and Lee 2001; Zhang, Keil, Rai, and Mann 2003). Few managers would disagree, team leadership *is* critically important to project performance and essential for competing effectively in today's global arena (Ferante, Green and Foster 2006; Groysberg and Abrahams 2006). Yet, many project leaders are frustrated by the difficulties to create a work environment that is truly conducive to teamwork.

18.1.1 Where Are the Challenges?

Building and managing a workgroup as a fully integrated, unified team is challenging, even in its most basic form, involving intricately connected organizational systems, behavioral issues and work processes (Bhatnager 1999; Cleland and Ireland 2007; Hilton 2008; Keller 2001; Pellerin 2009. By their very nature, teams must function dynamically in their multidisciplinary environment, interconnecting with people from different functional groups, support organizations, subcontractors, vendors, partners, government agencies, and customer organizations (Keller 2001; Manning et al. 2008; Newell and Rogers 2002; Thamhain 2009a). They also have to deal with technological, economic, political, social, and regulatory factors, which add considerable risk and uncertainty and further increase the challenges of organizing and managing project teams. This process is further complicated by multi-company teaming and partnerships as we noticed in the Boeing Dreamliner development. Companies are continuously looking for partners that can perform the needed work better, cheaper, and faster. This results in alliances across the globe, covering project activities from R&D to manufacturing, and from customer relations management to field services.

Larger, more complex and technologically intense projects especially emphasize the criticality of teamwork and have forced management to expand their attention from the traditional trait-oriented focus to a broader spectrum of critical success factors that include the team ambience and overall enterprise environment. Visionary researchers, such as Deborah Anconda, identified the importance of integrating project teamwork with the external enterprise environment, its stakeholders, support groups and even competitors, which led to the well-known *X-Teams* concept (Anconda and Bresman 2007). Estimates suggest that within the United States alone, more than 10 million employees are part of such distributed project teams. These geographically dispersed workgroups have become an important competitive tool in a business environment characterized by highly mobile resources, skill sets, and technology transfers across global regions and multinational borders.

18.1.2 Teamwork: A New Managerial Frontier

How did modern teamwork evolve? To be sure, teamwork is not a new idea. We can trace the basic concepts of organizing and managing teams back to biblical times. However, as projects became more complex and technologically sophisticated, the work group reemerged as a business management concept. The first formal framework evolved with the *human relations movement* that followed the classic Hawthorne studies by Roethlingsberger and Dickinson (1939). Visionaries such as McGregor (1960; Theory Y), Likert (1961; participating group management) and Dyer (1977; cohesion in the workplace), and more recently Tichy and Urlich (1984), Walton (1985), and Oderwald (1996) have further broadened the understanding of the team and its work processes.

Redefining the Process

In more recent times, declining bureaucratic hierarchies, more complex and geographically dispersed projects and higher levels of technological sophistication required further conceptual refinement and higher levels of management sophistication. As a result, the workgroup reemerged with a broader definition.

Teambuilding can be defined as the process of taking a collection of individuals with different needs, backgrounds, and expertise and transforming them into an integrated, effective work unit.

In this transformation process, the goals and energies of individual contributors merge and focus on specific objectives and desired results that ultimately reflect project performance that is graphically shown in Figure 18.1.

All of this may sound straightforward, but the higher level of complexity introduces many new challenges and new variables. Not too long ago, project leaders *could* ensure successful integration for most of their projects by focusing on properly defining the work, timing, and resources, and by following established procedures for project tracking and control. Today, these factors are still crucial. However, they have become threshold competencies—critically important, but unlikely to guaranty by themselves project success.

Today's complex business world requires *project teams* who are fast and flexible, and can dynamically and creatively work toward established objectives in a changing environment (Bhatnager 1999, Groysberg and Abrahams 2006, Thamhain 2004). This requires effective networking and collaboration among people from different organizations, support groups, subcontractors, vendors, government agencies, and customer communities. It also requires the ability to deal with uncertainties and risks caused by technological, economic, political, social, and regulatory factors.

Supported by modern information and communication technologies, and consistent with the concepts of stakeholder management (Newell and Rogers 2002) and learning organizations (Senge and Carstedt 2001), the roles and boundaries of teams are expanding toward self-direction because of more

Figure 18.1   Characteristics of high-performing teams

open and organizationally transparent processes. Work teams play an important role in realizing projects—from conventional new product developments, systems designs and construction to implementing organizational change and running election campaigns.

Whether Yahoo! creates a new search engine, Sony develops a new laptop computer, or the World Health Organization rolls out a new information system, project success depends to a large degree on effective interactions among the team members responsible for the new development. These teams often include support groups, subcontractors, vendors, partners, government agencies, customer organizations, and other project stakeholders (Armstrong 2000. Barkema et al. 2002. Dillon 2001. Gray and Larson 2000. Hilton 2008. Thamhain 2003. Zanomi and Audy 2004). Globalization, privatization, digitization, and rapidly changing technologies have transformed our economies into a hypercompetitive enterprise system where virtually every organization is under pressure to do more things faster, better, and cheaper. A team working effectively together is seen as a key success factor in deriving competitive advantages from these developments. At the same time, the process of team building has become more complex and more difficult to understand, requiring more sophisticated management skills and leadership ability.

Managers of these teams must not only deal with contemporary technology challenges but must also contend with a wide spectrum of economic, political, social, and regulatory challenges. In fact, current project management literature documents field research that shows managerial challenges are dominated by behavioral and organizational issues, rather than technical difficulties (Anconda and Bresman 2007, Belassi and Tukel 1996, Hartman and Ashrafi 2002). As a result, the leadership styles of project managers working in technology-based team environments have changed considerably, showing an increased emphasis on the human side of project management.

Up to the 1960s, project management was considered, by and large, a management science. To ensure successful project integration, project leaders focused on properly defining the work, timing, and resources; they also followed established procedures for project tracking and control. Although these factors are still crucial in today environment, they are considered threshold competencies—critically important, but unlikely to guarantee project success. To effectively and efficiently execute projects, today's project leaders must build fast, flexible teams that can dynamically and creatively work toward established objectives in a changing environment (Bhatnager 1999, Jassawalla and Sashittal 1998, Thamhain 2002). This requires effective networking and collaboration among all parties involved in the project— the people from the different organizations, support groups, subcontractors, vendors, government agencies, and customer communities. Managing in such an environment requires carefully developed skills in leadership, administration, organization, *and* technical expertise (Shenhar and Thamhain 1994, Thamhain 2003).

All of this has strong implications for organizational process and project leadership. Traditional forms of hierarchical team structure and leadership

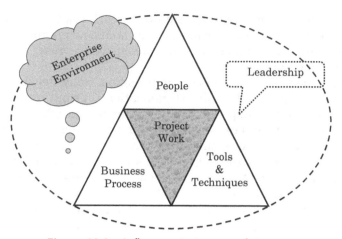

Figure 18.2 Influences to team performance

are no longer effective. and often replaced with self-directed, self-managed team concepts (Bidanda and Cleland 2009, Prokesch 2012, Thamhain 2009b).

18.1.3 A Simple Framework for Analyzing Team Effectiveness

To be effective in these situations, project managers must understand the interaction of organizational and behavioral variables, so that they can foster a work environment conducive to team involvement and commitment, and to transforming a multidisciplinary task group into a unified high-performing project team.

Consistent with the discussions on management style in Chapter 16, four overlapping organizational subsystems seem to influence the effectiveness of project teams especially strongly. These subsystems interact with the enterprise environment, influenced by project leadership, as graphically shown in Figure 18.2. This framework is consistent with team leadership concepts, discussed in the contemporary literature, such as the *X-Teams* (Anconda 2007) and *Keys to Successful Teamwork* (Hackman 2002). Although the five interacting organizational subsystems shown in Figure 18.2 are not necessarily the only influences on project team performance, they represent a simple and reasonably robust model for analyzing and discussing team effectiveness in complex, project environments.

18.2 MEASURING TEAM PERFORMANCE

Measuring team performance is complex and challenging. Its metrics are difficult to define. Yet, team performance influences many organizational decisions, from resource allocations and training programs to compensation and promotion initiatives. In many cases, project managers struggle with relevant measures of team performance, especially for technology-intensive undertakings. The intricate mix of timelines, resource allocation, multidisciplinary contributions, value perception, and success criteria often makes it difficult for companies to establish meaningful measures of project performance. Even more difficult is the application of such metrics, which involves ensuring consistency and fairness across the organization with implications to managerial control and making performance-based awards fair and equitable. These challenges exist especially in flatter, hierarchically less-structured organizations, where the entire workforce is engaged in project execution. This situation is also a challenge in organizations where the project team contributes only a portion to the company's overall success or failure, such as for long-term product developments. Yet in spite of its intricate nature and the fluctuation of specific performance measures with the cultural and philosophical differences among managers, departments, and companies, some framework for measurability can be established by grouping performance measures into six categories:

1. Deliverable-based measures
2. Schedule-based measures
3. Cost/resource-based measures
4. Risk and contingency measures
5. Enterprise benefit measures
6. Stakeholder/customer satisfaction-based measures.

Managers commonly use a limited set of deliverable-schedule-cost based variables to measure team or project performance. For major projects, virtually every project manager includes the first three measures, known as *triple constraint*, for assessing project performance. In addition, risk, enterprise benefits and stakeholder satisfaction expand the scope of team performance toward a more comprehensive measurement system. However, it is also a very broad and fuzzy set of variables that is often difficult to quantify, with many variables residing outside the direct control of the project team. Since project performance will be judged at various points of its life cycle, a mutually agreed on set of performance measures will not only help in defining the responsibilities and criteria for reward and recognition, but also establish guidelines for controlling the project toward its ultimate success. Tools such as the Project Score Card and Stakeholder Matrix can provide useful support in establishing meaningful and agreed-on performance measures early in the project life cycle, which also helps in unifying the project team behind the project objectives and its ultimate success criteria. Within the six broad categories, managers use more specific and detailed measures (or metrics) for judging project performance, which are referred to as *key performance indicators* (KPI) (Table 18.1).

Many of the larger, more complex projects have established very detailed metrics for measuring team performance and project success. They often

Table 18.1   Performance measures and key performance indicators

Deliverable-based measures	• Specific results (i.e., hardware, software, systems, data, processes, equipment, facilities) • Quality of results • Added value • Effectiveness of transferring results • Long-range performance • Overall user impact
Schedule-based measures	• On-time delivery of partial results or end items • Time-to-market • Ability to accelerate schedule over similar projects • Dealing with risks and uncertainties
Cost/Resource-based measures	• Performing within agreed-on budget • Credibility and aggressiveness of cost estimate • Cost reduction over previous/similar project • Dealing with risks and uncertainties • Achieving a unit production cost target • Achieving a return-on-investment (ROI) target
Risk and contingency measures	• Anticipating and identifying contingencies • Preparation for dealing with risks and uncertainties • Handling of risks and contingencies • Networking with other risk stakeholders
Enterprise benefit measures	• Learning from past project experiences • Developing self-directed teams • Establishing continuous improvement process • Benchmarking of others—a best-in-class analysis • Establishing project management norms, standards, and reliable performance measures
Stakeholder/customer satisfaction measures	• Overall quality and performance of project deliverables • Flexibility toward changes in project requirements • Overall benefits of project implementation • Handling of problems, contingencies, and conflicts • Minimum organizational disruptions • Innovative project implementation • Dealing with risks and uncertainties • Satisfaction measured by survey or other feedback • Repeat business • Referrals • Critics' report • Press/media coverage • Professionalism

expand on enterprise benefits and stakeholder satisfaction measures, since from the enterprise perspective, these appear to be the ultimate determinants of project success. However, the six performance categories and measures summarized above are a good starting point and framework for defining and benchmarking team performance.

18.3 FOSTERING CONDITIONS FOR COLLABORATION, COMMITMENT, AND SELF-CONTROL

Field research points out consistently and measurably that, among the many factors of the project environment, those that fulfill professional esteem needs have a particularly favorable effect on team performance. However, a well-functioning work process is a critical precondition. That is, traditional project support, such as clearly defined objectives, project plans, directions, leadership and cross-functional support seem to be equally important to creating an effective, professionally stimulating work environment. The need for balancing "team enablers" from both the people side and the organizational side is emphasized in a recent field study (Thamhain 2012) that finds the strongest drivers to team performance are in the following areas, rank-ordered by their statistical significance:

1. Professionally stimulating and challenging work environment
2. Opportunity for accomplishments and recognition
3. Clearly defined organizational objectives relevant to the project
4. Job skills and expertise of team members appropriate for the project work
5. Clear direction and leadership
6. Trust/respect/credibility
7. Effective cross-functional support
8. Clear project plan and support
9. Autonomy and freedom
10. Career development opportunities
11. Job security
12. Fair salary, raise, bonus

Although many of these factors (e.g., clear objectives, skill sets, and effective business process) deal with conventional project management practices, they also relate to the human side, conditioning the work environment for success. Hence in a complex project environment that relies on commitment, buy-in, and personal drive for success, these influences appear to deal effectively with the integration of goals and needs between the team member and the organization. In this context, the more subtle factors seem to become catalysts for cross-functional communication, information sharing, and ultimate integration of the project team with focus on desired results. Hence, the above correlation data provide a snapshot of the critical importance of both human factors and traditional project management techniques to team performance.

Initially, the datasets were analyzed separately for each "local" team in its own cultural environment using Kendall tau correlation. Then, the cross-team association was tested via Kruskal-Wallis analysis of variance by rank, which shows at a confidence level of 98 percent that an agreement exists among local teams on their rankings. This finding is interesting and important because it shows a similarity among the various local teams in spite of their differences in culture. While specific interpretation and perception of environmental characteristics, such as "needs" and "professionally stimulating work," are differing among teams, the rank-order correlation to project performance metrics is similar. The significance of this finding is for team leaders to realize the critical importance of creating a professionally stimulating work environment. This cannot be accomplished by procedures or formalities, but requires palpable actions, plus credibility, trust and respect earned by the project manager.

It is further interesting to note that the same conditions, which are conducive to overall team performance, also lead to (1) innovation and creative problem solving, (2) change orientation and high response rate of the team, (3) self-directed teams with minimum supervision, (4) effective customer and client interface, (5) effective conflict resolution among team members, (6) ability to deal with risk and uncertainty, (7) stronger personal effort and commitment to established objectives, (8) more effective communications within the team and its interfaces, and (9) favorable schedule and budget performance. Hence, this correlation validates our earlier discussion that the organizational environment influences the team characteristics, which influences team performance.

18.4 BUILDING HIGH-PERFORMANCE TEAMS

The leadership lessons learned from empirical studies and best practices, especially over the past 20 years, show that in spite of the complexities, technologies, and organizational differences, certain conditions of the work environment appear most favorably associated with team performance. These conditions serve as bridging mechanisms that can help technology-based organizations enhance their overall team performance.

To provide focus, the discussion of this section is divided into five parts, consistent with the five sets of performance influences summarized in Figure 18.2: people, work, organizational process, tools and techniques, and leadership. Each of the five influences is affected by the project environment, such as project complexity, organizational support, managerial support, and the general socioeconomic business environment as discussed next.

18.4.1 People-Oriented Influences

Factors that satisfy personal and professional needs seem to have the strongest effect on project team performance. We find that the statistically most significant drivers are derived from the work itself, including personal interest, pride and satisfaction with the work, professional work challenge, and accomplishments and recognition. Other important influences include the ability to resolve problems, especially interpersonal conflict; good team spirit; mutual trust and respect; effective support and communications across organizational lines; and opportunities for career advancement and job security. All of these factors help build a unified project team that can effectively leverage the organizational strengths and competencies and efficiently produce integrated results that support the organization's mission. These factors seem to foster a work environment conducive to open dialogue and to dealing with ambiguities, risks, complexities, and organizational conflict. All of these influences help to ultimately transform the team efforts into tangible results that add value to the enterprise.

18.4.2 Work- and Task-Related Influences

Team performance also has its locus in the work itself. Highlighted by the list of 12 performance-correlated factors, empirical studies frequently show that variables associated with the personal aspects of work—such as interest, ability to solve problems, job skills, and experience—significantly drive team performance. On the other side, many work-related variables from the structural side (e.g., project size, work complexity, and work process) seem to have little significance on influencing team performance (see Thamhain 2012). The importance of this finding is two-fold: first, managers must have the ability to attract and retain the appropriately skilled people needed to complete the project work. Managers must also invest in maintaining and upgrading the project team's skill sets and work support systems. Second, managers must effectively assign the work to leverage their control over work allocation and results. This means that while the total task structure and the development process is fixed and difficult to change, the way managers distribute, assign, and present the work is flexible. This has significant managerial implications: though promoting a climate of high interest, involvement, and support might be easier to achieve than redefining organizational structure or reengineering the work process, it may have an equal or higher impact on project team performance.

18.4.3 Organizational Process-Related Influences

These influences include the organizational structure and technology transfer process that relies, by-and-large, on modern project management techniques. While from my experience, I do not favor particular project structures or processes because they need to be custom-fitted to their applications, researchers point to specific work process-related variables as important to team performance. Influences such as cross-functional cooperation, effective communications, and effective project planning and support systems are seemingly important conditions for high team performance. An effective project management system will also maintain organizational processes for effective functional support, including joint reviews and performance appraisals and processes for ensuring the availability of necessary resources, skills, and facilities. Other crucial components that affect the work process are team structure, managerial power, command and control, the power sharing among team members and organizational units, autonomy and freedom, and most importantly, technical direction and leadership.

These research findings provide top management with food for critical thought. Many of these organizational process variables have their locus outside the project team organization. These variables are often a derivative of the company's business strategy, which is developed and controlled by senior management. Because of this, management must recognize that these variables can directly affect the quality of the work environment.

Furthermore, these conditions of the general enterprise environment will most likely affect team member perception of organizational stability, availability of resources, management involvement and support, personal rewards, stability of organizational goals, objectives, and priorities. Since all of these influences are images of personal perception, management must understand the personal and professional needs of their team members and foster an organizational environment that is conducive to their needs. Management can accomplish this by properly and effectively communicating the company's organizational vision and perspective to the team members. For example, team members could perceive a company merger as an opportunity or as a threat, as a stabilizer or as a destabilizer: Their perception is influenced by the management's ability to communicate. The relationship of managers to the people in their organizations and the people they specifically manage is built on mutual trust, respect, and credibility, all of which are critical factors in building an effective partnership between the project team and its sponsor organization.

18.4.4 Project Management Tools and Techniques as Influences

While, in general, project team members don't show great enthusiasm for management tools and techniques, these tools are enablers of the work process and have a strong influence on team performance. Specifically, the overall team ambience and work process—including the support to problem solving, communication, and technology transfer—is strongly affected by the management tools and techniques that managers employ to support the essential organizational systems, such as budgeting, scheduling, and reviews. The tools and techniques that managers use help run the team's efforts smoothly. As explained by one team member during one of my field studies: "We really don't have time to come to all the meetings and to provide all the paperwork required by management, but we do cooperate because we hope that it will stabilize the funding for this project and help in the cross-functional integration."

As project work and business environments become increasingly complex, project management tools and techniques are adapting by evolving to meet this complexity; managers are now also requiring greater team member involvement. At the same time, modern project management is moving further toward self-directed teams, high market responsiveness, and less formal structures and controls that are based, to a large extent, on commitment, motivation, and team leadership. This evolution has specific implications for managers: Successful project leaders are making an effort to apply management tools as an overlay to the project organization, with minimal interference to their teams and operations. For the team members to use the tools effectively, the team must view these management tools as helpful instruments in supporting and facilitating the project activities.

18.4.5 Leadership as an Important Influence

Leadership is an essential component of project teamwork. Many technical failures can be traced back to bad leadership. I took notice of this fact earlier in my career when the *Hubble Review Board* (NASA 1990) declared the cause of the flawed mirror a leadership failure. Project leadership is the art of creating a supportive work environment. Many of the factors that influence project team performance are derived from organizational processes and systems that have their locus outside the team. Examples range from the functional support units to work transfer processes—as well as the project management system itself with its specialized tools and techniques. Organizational stability, management involvement and support, personal rewards, the availability of resources, and the stability of organizational goals, objectives, and priorities are all factors that influence team performance, yet these are all controlled—by and large—by general management. Therefore, team leaders must work with senior management to ensure that they create an organizational ambience that is conducive to their teams' needs.

In addition, team leaders can influence these organizational systems via their management techniques and their ability to create a team environment through their leadership actions. Although project support or work transfer processes might be defined in terms of procedures and management directives, the way that team leaders organize their plans, involve support function personnel, run meetings, track projects, or recognize team performance is under their own control. In exercising this control, team leaders create and define the team environment through their own actions to build a favorable image of their projects and a team-friendly project environment that is supportive of teamwork and integrated within the overall enterprise system.

18.5 TEAM LEADERSHIP LESSONS

Four areas of the enterprise system—leadership, work, personal needs, and team environment—contribute most of the influences to team performance, with its strongest drivers derived from work challenge. I'm trying to capture the essence of team leadership and the lessons learned from the field in *three propositions*:

- *Four primary areas of influence*: The degree of project success seems to be primarily determined by specific driving forces related to (1) leadership, (2) job content, (3) personal needs, and (4) general work environment.
- *Strongest single driver*: Work challenge, characterized by professionally stimulating, interesting work, visibility and recognition of achievements, seems to be the most reliable predictor of high team performance and project success.

- *Work challenge dividend*: A professionally stimulating team environment is also favorably associated with other desired team characteristics, such as low conflict, high levels of commitment, innovation, team involvement, effective risk management, good communications, and collaboration.

To be effective in organizing, developing, and directing a project team, the leader must have the ability to recognize potential drivers and barriers and know when they most likely will occur during the project's life cycle. Effective project leaders initiate preventive actions early in the project life cycle and foster a work environment that is conducive to teambuilding as an ongoing process.

The effective team leader is a social architect who understands the interaction of organizational and behavioral variables and can foster a climate of active participation and minimal dysfunctional conflict. To effectively perform their role, leaders must possess carefully developed skills in leadership, administration, and organization, as well as technical expertise. The leader is also required to have the ability to involve top management when necessary and to ensure organizational visibility, resource availability, and overall support for the project throughout its life cycle.

18.6 GUIDELINES FOR EFFECTIVE TEAM MANAGEMENT

In addition to the implications to project management discussed so far, several specific suggestions are being made in this section. These suggestions are based on research and shared experiences from many project management professionals, including my own 40 years as manager and researcher of complex project undertakings. Focus on effective team management in environments. The resulting suggestions focus on technology-based projects. They are organized into 13 guidelines sequenced in chronological order following a typical project life cycle.

18.6.1 Guideline 1. Ensure Team Involvement Early in the Project Life Cycle

For most projects, effective project planning and early team involvement is crucial to subsequent high project team performance. This planning and involvement is especially important for technology-based project work, where high levels of complexity, uncertainty, and risk—along with the need for innovation—make it nearly impossible for the project leader to work out a project plan that is seen as realistic, *unless* performance is the result of collective efforts by all stakeholders, including support departments, subcontractors, and management. Modern project management techniques, such as phased project planning and Stage-Gate concepts, plus established standards, such as *A Guide to the Project Management Body of Knowledge (PMBOK® Guide)*, provide the conceptual framework and tools for effective cross-functional planning and for organizing the work toward effective execution. Furthermore, the team's involvement at an early stage in the project life cycle has a favorable impact on the team environment: Such involvement builds the team's morale, its enthusiasm toward the assignment, and its commitment toward desirable results.

18.6.2 Guideline 2. Define the Work Process and Team Structure

Successful project team management requires an infrastructure conducive to cross-functional teamwork and technology transfer. This infrastructure includes properly defined interfaces, task responsibilities, reporting relations, communication channels, and work transfer protocols. The tools for systematically describing the work process and team structure come from the conventional project management system and include the following:

- Project charter, which defines the mission and overall responsibilities of the project organization, including performance measures and key interfaces
- Project organization chart, which defines the major reporting and authority relationships
- Responsibility matrix or task roster
- Project interface chart, such as the N-squared chart
- Job descriptions

18.6.3 Guideline 3. Develop Organizational Interfaces and Communication Channels

A result of the work process—overall project team success—depends on effective cross functional support and integration. All team members should clearly understand their task inputs and outputs, work interfaces, and transfer mechanisms. Management can facilitate the flow of information, both horizontally and vertically, through workspace design, regular meetings, reviews, and information sessions. In addition, modern technology—such as voice mail, e-mail, electronic bulletin boards, and conferencing—can greatly enhance communications, especially in complex organizational settings. In addition, team-based reward systems can promote cooperation with cross-functional partners. Quality function deployment (QFD) concepts, N-squared charting, and well-defined phase-gate criteria are useful tools for developing cross-functional linkages and facilitating interdisciplinary cooperation, alliances, and communications.

18.6.4 Guideline 4. Staff and Organize the Project Team Properly

Project staffing, usually carried out during the project formation phase, is critically important to project success. However, time pressures and budget constraints often lead to shortcuts in the staffing process. Teams that are hastily organized with people who are poorly matched to the job requirements are frequently subject to conflicts, low morale, suboptimum decision making, and ultimately, poor project performance.

Although staffing deficiencies will cause problems for any project, these are especially damaging for high-technology environments with heavy reliance on cross-functional teamwork, shared decision making, credibility, and mutual trust and respect. For best results, project leaders should negotiate the work assignment with their team members in one-on-one meetings at the beginning of the project. Such meetings should focus on the overall task, scope, and objectives, as well as on relevant performance measures. Project leaders can often develop a thorough understanding of the task requirements through personal involvement in front-end activities, such as requirements analysis, bid proposals, project planning, interface definition, or overall product planning. Such early involvement is also conducive to the team's agreement to project objectives, plan acceptance, and unification of the project team.

18.6.5 Guideline 5. Build a High-Performance Image

Project teams that have a clear sense of purpose and confidence in the project mission perform better. The fact that people who have a mission and high esteem perform better has been long known. Already early in my investigations of this topic (Thamhain and Wilemon 1998), my coauthor and I found a strong correlation between the can-do image of a team and its actual performance. Our study also found that the team's self-esteem is a perception that can be enhanced by the visibility of the work, frequent recognition of accomplishments, management attention and support, and the overlap of personnel values and perceived benefits with organizational objectives. Creating such a high-esteem image also leads to increased involvement, better communication, lower conflict, higher commitment, stronger work effort, and higher levels of creativity.

A high-performance image stimulates interest in the project among individual team members, pride of participation, and a sense of ownership. This image also builds professional confidence, a desire to reach out, and the ability to think outside the box. To build such a high-performance image, team members must have a clear sense of the significance of their contributions. All stakeholders must have a clear understanding of the organizational goals and the mission's objectives. A favorable project image can help unify the team, build the team's commitment toward the project objectives, and establish a high-level of project priority. Project leaders and senior managers can help build a favorable project image by making the project visible and stressing its importance through media exposure, management involvement, and budgetary actions, as well as by emphasizing critical success factors and professional opportunities and rewards. All of these factors help create a sense of project ownership among team members and encourage each member's desire to succeed.

18.6.6 Guideline 6. Stimulate Enthusiasm, Excitement, and Professional Interests

Factors that satisfy personal and professional needs have the strongest effect on team performance and overall project results. Many studies show that the most significant performance drivers are derived from the work itself, including personal interest, pride and satisfaction with the work, professional work challenge, accomplishments, and recognition. Whenever possible, managers should try to accommodate the professional interests and desires of their personnel. Interesting and challenging work is a perception that can be enhanced by the visibility of the work, management attention and support, priority image, and the alignment of personnel values with organizational objectives. Interesting work leads also to increased involvement, better communication, lower conflict, higher commitment, stronger work effort, and higher levels of creativity.

Although the overall project scope and workload might stand as a fixed requirement, project leaders usually have considerable freedom in dividing the project and assigning the work packages. Well-established practices, such as front-end involvement of team members during the project planning or proposal phase and in one-on-one discussions, are effective tools for matching each team member's interests and project needs. These practices help—simultaneously—sell the project's benefits and support team leaders in their dealing with the concerns, anxieties, and potential problems of the project team.

18.6.7 Guideline 7. Create Proper Reward Systems

Although salary itself seems to have no significant impact on team performance (as shown by the relatively low correlation in several of my field studies), recognition, accomplishments, career opportunities, and job security are strongly associated with team/project performance. Yet, there is an important connection. Financial rewards are also recognition! Therefore, team leaders should develop an evaluation and reward system that is designed to recognize both individual and team performance. However, creating such a system, with metrics that reflect the desired sharing of responsibility and power, is a great challenge. Several models, such as the Integrated Performance Index proposed by Pillai, Joshi, and Raoi (2002) and the QFD concept (where everyone recognizes the immediate customer), provide some framework for designing a reward system that balances both individual and team rewards.

18.6.8 Guideline 8. Ensure Senior Management Support

The team's perception of senior management support is critically important to project performance. At the outset of a new project, the manager needs to negotiate with the sponsor and support organizations for the required resources; this individual must also obtain a commitment from management that these resources will become available when these are needed. An effective working relationship among resource managers, project leaders, and senior management also favorably affects the credibility, visibility, and priority of the team, and ultimately, project performance. This information also supports the suggestions in Guideline 5 in relation to building a high-performance image.

18.6.9 Guideline 9. Build Commitment

Managers must ensure that the project team's members are committed to their project plans, objectives, and results. If these commitments appear weak, managers should seek a reason for the weak commitments and attempt to modify any possible negative views that team members may have. Anxieties and fear of the unknown are often a major reason for low commitment (Stum 2001; Thamhain 2002, 2013). Managers should investigate the potential for team member insecurities, determine the cause, and then work with the team members to reduce their anxieties and transform their negative perceptions. Conflict with other team members and a general lack of interest in the project are other potential factors that can negatively affect a team member's commitment to the project and its objectives.

18.6.10 Guideline 10. Manage Conflict and Problems

Project management activities are highly disruptive to an organization and conflict is inevitable. Project managers should focus their efforts on problem avoidance. This means that managers and team leaders, based on their experience, should recognize potential problems and conflicts at the project's beginning and deal with these before the conflicts become big and interpersonal, at which stage the resolutions consume a large amount of time and effort.

18.6.11 Guideline 11. Conduct Team-Building Sessions

A mixture of focus-team sessions, brainstorming, experience exchanges, and social gatherings offer powerful opportunities for developing the work group into an effective, fully integrated, and unified project team. Such organized team-building efforts should occur throughout the project life cycle, while intensive team-building efforts should probably occur during the formation stage of a new project. Although formally defined, team-building sessions are often conducted in an informal and relaxed atmosphere to discuss such critical questions as:

- How are we working as a team?
- What are the project's critical success factors?
- What is our strength?
- How can we improve?
- What support do we need?
- What challenges and problems are we likely to face?
- What actions should we take?

18.6.12 Guideline 12. Provide Proper Direction and Leadership

Successful project managers focus their attention on the people—and the roles these individuals play—who are involved with the project. Effective project organizations have cultures that support multidisciplinary work. These organizations have project managers who, by their own actions, influence the attitude and commitment of people toward the project objectives. The project manager's concern for the project team's members and enthusiasm for the project fosters a climate with high levels of motivation and involvement with the project and its management. It also promotes open communications and a collective focus on desired results.

18.6.13 Guideline 13. Foster a Culture of Continuous Support and Improvement

Effective organizations adapt to changing environments. By continually updating and fine-tuning established project management processes and their people, team leaders ensure that their organization is capable of confronting today's business challenges. To accomplish this, team leaders could establish *listening posts*—discussion groups, action teams, and suggestion systems—to capture the voice of the customer and the lessons learned from past projects. These listening posts could serve as a basis for continuous improvement when combined with tools such as project maturity models and the Six Sigma project management process, which provide useful frameworks for analyzing and developing the project team and its management process.

18.7 HOW TO MAKE IT WORK

There are two critically important conditions that need to exist for teams to perform at high-levels: professional interest and work support. Both conditions are influenced by organizational environment and team leadership.

Although nobody has a panacea that guarantees high levels of team performance, project success is not random! A better understanding of the criteria and organizational dynamics that drive project team performance can assist managers in developing a sharper and more meaningful understanding of the organizational process and the critical success factors that drive project team performance.

To achieve project success in our hypercompetitive world of business, project leaders must understand all of the facets of the project management system and its organizational environment. This includes not only the latest tools and techniques, but also the people, business processes, cultures, and value systems of the organization. One of the consistent and most striking findings from field studies is the need for increased involvement from all project stakeholders—both within the organization and among the external partners.

Many of the managers with whom I spoke during my career pointed out that project success in today's technology-based environment is no longer the result of acquiring a few expert contributors and skilled project leaders. While this is a good starting point, project success is, to a large, degree driven by multidisciplinary efforts involving teams of people and support organizations interacting in a highly complex and intricate relationship. Cooperation, collaboration, and commitment are significant drivers to high project performance. Both cooperation and commitment are greatly enhanced when project leaders foster a work environment where people see the purpose and significance of their projects. One of the strongest catalysts to team performance is the professional pride among organizational members who are fueled by visibility and a desire for recognition. Cultivating a professionally stimulating environment seems to lower anxieties over organizational change and reduces communication barriers and conflict, as its simultaneously enhances the desire of those involved to cooperate and to succeed.

Effective project leaders are social architects who can foster a climate of active participation by involving people at all organizational levels in the planning, formation, and execution of projects. They also can build alliances with support organizations and upper management to ensure organizational visibility, priority, resource availability, and overall support for sustaining the team effort beyond its startup phase. Accomplishing these activities requires that project managers possess carefully developed skills in leadership, administration, organization, and technical expertise. These activities also demand that managers possess the ability to engage top management and to ensure visibility for their projects by using organizational media, management reviews, and cross-functional networking throughout the project's life cycle.

The result is that technology-based projects can be managed to accomplish the project goals when the project team works in an environment that helps them thrive. The concepts and empirical data summarized in this chapter show that under the right conditions, project teams can produce great results, in spite of tough requirements, high project complexities, and difficult budget/schedule constraints.

18.8 SUMMARY OF KEY POINTS AND CONCLUSIONS

The following key points were made in this chapter:

- Effective teamwork is critical to project performance for all projects. However, team deficiencies affect project performance more severely in large and technologically complex undertakings that have to deal with people from many different functional groups, support organizations, partners, contractors, government and nongovernment organizations.
- The first formal framework of team management evolved with the human relations movement in the early 1900s, followed by many refinements that led to the current body of knowledge, which connects to five overlapping subsystems: (1) people, (2) project work, (3) organizational process, (4) project tools and techniques, and (5) leadership.
- Project performance consists of a complex array of variables, difficult to define and measure. Most managers include in their project and team performance evaluations some metrics of the following six categories: (1) deliverables, (2) schedules, (3) cost, (4) risk, (5) enterprise benefits, and (6) stakeholder/customer satisfaction. The specific measures selected for determining team/project performance are called key performance indicators (KPI).
- The strongest drivers to high team performance include a mixture of factors derived from managerial leadership, work process, and organizational environment. In the right combination, these factors create a professionally stimulating work environment, which is one of the most reliable predictors of high-performing project teams.
- Effective team leaders know when potential issues occur in the project life cycle and take corrective actions early, before problems escalate.
- Team performance and project success are strongly influenced by effective multidisciplinary efforts involving teams of people and support organizations interacting in a highly complex and intricate relationship.
- Effective project leaders are social architects who can foster a climate of active participation of people at all organizational levels. They can also build alliances across the enterprise and its partners and promote an environment of high visibility, priority, and resource availability.

18.9 QUESTIONS FOR DISCUSSION AND EXERCISES

1. Using the lead-in case scenario for this chapter, identify Boeing's organizational challenges and the issues of effective teamwork on the 787 Dreamliner project.
2. Identify and profile the type of leadership style that is needed for effectively organizing, developing, and managing the 787 development team at Boeing.

3. What are some of the characteristics of a fully integrated team? Develop a list of performance measures or criteria for a specific team you know, and evaluate this team against your benchmark list.
4. Identify a workgroup that you know. Define the metrics for measuring team performance.
5. What are some of the organizational variables that influence project team characteristics? How can you as project leader influence these variables?
6. Is it more challenging to lead project teams today than 25 years ago? Why, or why not?
7. List and discuss some of the task- and people-related qualities of successful project teams. How could you measure these qualities? How can you influence these qualities?
8. Discuss why it is import for project managers to understanding the drivers and barriers to team performance.
9. Do you accept the three propositions stated under "Team Leadership Lessons" (section 18.5) as they relate to team performance and project success? Explain.
10. How do you develop team leadership skills?
11. What means and methods, other than money, would you consider to motivate your team toward high project performance?
12. Why is team commitment and ownership important to team performance?
13. Two team leaders have identical projects in the same organizational environment. One team perceives the project as highly interesting and important with a lot of opportunities for career advancement, while the other team perceives the project as boring, routine work with little opportunity for career advancement. What do these two project leaders do differently?
14. How can the proper application of conventional project management tools and techniques help in building high-performing teams?
15. What kind of changes do you anticipate over the next 10 years, regarding project team challenges, characteristics, and leadership style?

18.10 *PMBOK®* REFERENCES AND CONNECTIONS

The topic of team leadership focuses most strongly on the three PMBOK® Knowledge Areas of project human resource management (#6), project communications management (#7), and project stakeholder management (#10). The topic cuts across all five PMBOK® processing groups with the strongest connection to planning, executing, and monitoring/controlling. Much of this chapter focuses on the context of project executing and monitoring/controlling, discussing the need for working effectively and collaboratively with people across the enterprise. The managerial perspectives presented in this chapter should be helpful in connecting the PMBOK standards to best practices of project management, and in studying effectively for PMP®

certification. In preparing for the PMP® Exam, the following PMBOK sections relate especially to this chapter and should be studied: (1) project interfaces, (2) staffing requirements, (3) staff assignments, (4) human resource practices, (5) project communications management, and (6) team development.

INTERNET LINKS AND RESOURCES

NASA, *aPPEL, Academy of Program / Project and Engineering Leadership.* http://appel.nasa.gov

NASA. "Leadership Model." http://leadership.nasa.gov/Model/Manager.htm

NASA. "Leadership and Management Development." http://leadership.nasa.gov/model/influence.htm

Project Management Institute. Knowledge Center. http://www.pmi.org/Knowledge-Center.aspx.

Project Management Institute. "Welcome to the Leadership in PM Community of Practice." http://leadershipinpm.vc.pmi.org/Public/Home.aspx

TED (Technology, Entertainment, Design), www.ted.com/; many interesting leadership speeches, e.g., Simon Sinek, "How Great Leaders Inspire and Lead." www.ted.com/talks/simon_sinek_how_great_leaders_inspire_action.html

Wikipedia. 2013. "Boeing 787 Dreamliner." http://en.wikipedia.org/wiki/Boeing_878_Dreamliner

REFERENCES AND ADDITIONAL READINGS

Anconda D., and H. Bresman. 2007. *X-teams: How to Build Teams That Lead, Innovate and Succeed.* Boston, MA: Harvard Business School Publishing Company.

Anconda D., T. Malone, W. Orlikowski, and P. Senge. 2007. "It's Time to End the Myth of the Incomplete Leader." *Harvard Business Review* 85: 92–100.

Armstrong, D. 2000. "Building Teams Across Borders." *Executive Excellence* 17(3): 10.

Asgary, N., and H. Thamhain. 2007. "Managing Multinational Project Teams," Proceedings, *Annual Meeting of the Association for Global Business.*Washington, DC, November 15–18, 2007.

Badrinarayanan, V. 2012. "Effective Virtual Product Development Teams: An Integrated Framework." *IEEE Engineering Management Review* 40(4): 80–90.

Barkoma H., J. Baum and F. Mannix. 2002. "Management Challenges in a New Time." *Academy of Management Journal* 45(5): 916–930.

Bhatnager, A. 1999. "Great Teams." *The Academy of Management Executive* 13(3): 50–63.

Belassi, W., and O. Tukel. 1996. "A New Framework for Determining Critical Success/ Failure Factors in Projects." *International Journal of Project Management* 14(3):141–151.

Bidanda, B., and D. Cleland (eds.). 2009. *Project Management Circa 2025.* Philadelphia: PMI Press.

Brown, K., and N. Hyer. 2010. *Managing Projects: A Team-Based Approach.* New York: McGraw Hill/Irvin.

Cleland D., and L. Ireland. 2007. *Project Management: Strategic Design and Implementation.* New York: McGraw Hill.

Dillon, Patrick. 2001. "A Global Challenge." *Forbes* 168 (September 10): 73+.

Dumaine, Brian. 1991. "The Bureaucracy Buster." *Fortune* (June 17).

Dyer, W. G. 1977. *Team Building: Issues and Alternatives.* Reading, MA: Addison-Wesley.

Ferrante C., S. Green, and W. Forster. 2006. "Getting More out of Team Projects: Incentivizing Leadership to Enhance Performance." *Journal of Management Education* 30(6): 788–798.

Gray, Clifford, and E. Larson. 2000. *Project Management.* New York: Irwin McGraw Hill, 2000.

Groysberg B., and R. Abrahams. 2006. "Lift Outs: How to Acquire a High-Functioning Team." *Harvard Business Review* 84(12): 133–143.

Hackman, J. 2002. *Leading Teams: Setting the Stage for Great Performance—The 5 Keys to Successful Teams.* Boston: Harvard Business School Press.

Hackman, J 2006. "The Five Dysfunctions of a Team: A Leadership Fable." *Academy of Management Perspectives* 20:122–125.

Hartman, F., and R. Ashrafi. 2002. "Project Management in the Information Systems and Technologies Industries." *Project Management Journal* 33(3): 5–15.

Hilton, M. 2008. "Skills for Work in the 21st Century." *Academy of Management Perspectives* 22(4): 63–78.

Jassawalla, A. R., and H. C. Sashittal. 1999. "Building Collaborate Cross-Functional New Product Teams." *The Academy of Management Executive* 13(3): 50–63.

Kearney, E., D. Gebert, and S. Voelpel. 2009. "When and How Diversity Benefits Teams." *Academy of Management Journal* 52(3): 350–372.

Keller, R. 2001. "Cross-Functional Project Groups in Research and New Product Development." *Academy of Management Journal* 44(3): 547–556.

Kruglianskas, I., and H. Thamhain. 2000. "Managing Technology-Based Projects in Multinational Environments." *IEEE Transactions on Engineering Management* 47(1): 55–64.

Likert, R. 1961. *New Patterns of Management.* New York: McGraw Hill,.

Manning, S., S. Massini, and A. Lewin. 2008. "A Dynamic Perspective on Next-Generation Offshoring: The Global Sourcing of Science and Engineering Talents." *Academy of Management Perspectives* 22(3): 35–54.

McGregor D. 1960. *The Human Side of Enterprise.* New York: McGraw Hill.

National Aeronautics and Space Administration. 1990. *The Hubble Space Telescope Optical Systems Failure Report,* NASA-TM 103 443.

Nellore, R., and R. Balachandra. 2001. "Factors Influencing Success in Integrated Product Development (IPD) Projects." *IEEE Transactions on Engineering Management* 48(2): 164–173.

Newell, F., and M. Rogers. 2002. *loyalty.com: Relationship Management in the Era of Internet Marketing.* New York: McGraw Hill.

Nurick, A., and H. Thamhain. 2006. "Team Leadership in Global Project Environments." In D. Cleland, ed., *Global Project Management Handbook.* New York: McGraw Hill, Chapter 38.

Oderwald, S. 1996. "Global Work Teams." *Training and Development* 5(2).

Pellerin, C. 2009. *How NASA Builds Teams.* Hoboken, NJ: John Wiley & Sons.

Pillai, A., A. Joshi, and K. Raoi. 2002. "Performance Measurement of R&D Projects in a Multi-Project, Concurrent Engineering Environment." *International Journal of Project Management* 20(2): 165–172.

Project Management Institute. 2013. *A Guide to the Project Management Body of Knowledge (PMBOK® Guide).* Newtown Square, PA: Project Management Institute.

Prokesch, S. 2012. "How GE Teaches Teams to Lead Change." *IEEE Engineering Management Review* 40(4): 31–41.

Roethlingsberger F., and W. Dickerson. 1939. *Management and the Worker.* Cambridge, MA: Harvard University Press.

Rosenbach, W., R. Taylor, and M. Youndt (eds.). 2012. *Contemporary Issues in Leadership.* Bolder, CO: Westview Press.

Sawhney, M. 2002. "Don't Just Relate—Collaborate." *MIT Sloan Management Review* 43(3): 96–107.

Senge, P. and G. Carstedt. 2001. "Innovating Our Way to the Next Industrial Revolution." *Sloan Management Review* 42(2): 24–38.

Shim, D., and M. Lee. 2001. "Upward Influence Styles of R&D Project Leaders." *IEEE Transactions on Engineering Management* 48(4): 394–413.

Stum, D. 2001. "Maslow Revisited: Building the Employee Commitment Pyramid." *Strategy and Leadership* 29(4): 4–9.

Thamhain H. 2002. "Team Management." In J. Knutson, ed., *Project Management for Business Professionals.* New York: John Wiley and Sons, Chapter 29.

———. 2002. "Criteria for Effective Leadership in Technology-Oriented Project Teams." In Slevin, Cleland, and Pinto (eds.), *The Frontiers of Project Management Research.* Newton Square, PA: Project Management Institute, pp. 259–270.

———. 2003. "Managing Innovative R&D Teams." *R&D Management* 33(3): 297–312.

———. 2004. "Leading Technology Teams," *Project Management Journal* 35(4): 35–47.

———. 2006. "Optimizing Innovative Performance of R&D Teams in Technology-Based Environments." *Creativity Research Journal* 18(4): 435–436.

———. 2008. "Team Leadership Effectiveness in Technology-Based Project Environments." *IEEE Engineering Management Review* 36(1): 165–180.

———. 2009a. "Managing Globally Dispersed R&D Teams." *International Journal of Information Technology and Management (IJITM)* 8(1): 107–126.

———. 2009b. "Leadership Lessons from Managing Technology-Intensive Teams." *International Journal of Innovation and Technology Management* 6(2):117–133.

———. 2009c. "The Future of Project Team Leadership." In B. Bidanda and D. Cleland, (eds.), *Project Management Circa 2025*, chapter 11. Philadelphia: PMI Press.

———. 2012. "The Changing Role of Team Leadership in Multinational Project Environments." *Revista de Gestão e Projetos* (Project Management Journal of Brazil) 3(2): 4–38.

———. 2013. "Commitment as a Critical Success Factor for Managing Complex Multinational Projects." *International Journal of Innovation and Technology Management* 10(4) (Aug): 101–118.

Tichy, N., and D. Ulrich. 1984. "The Leadership Challenge—Call for the Transformational Leader." *Sloan Management Review.* (Fall): 59–69.

Tomkovich, C., and C. Miller. 2000. "Riding the Wind: Managing New Product Development in the Age of Change." *Product Innovation Management* 17(6): 413–423.

Zanoni, R., and J. Audy. 2004. "Project Management Model for Physically Distributed Software Development Environment." *Engineering Management Journal* 16(1).

Walton, R. 1985. "From Control to Commitment in the Workplace." *Harvard Business Review* 63(2) (March–April): 77–84.

Zhang P, M. Keil, A. Rai, and J. Mann 2003. "Predicting Information Technology Project Escalation." *Journal of Operations Research* 146(1):115–129.

Chapter 19

Professional Development: Training and Education

DEVELOPING MANAGEMENT TALENT AT GE

"I am very proud of our team," says Jeffrey Immelt, chairman of the board and chief operating officer, in GE's Annual Report. "They are passionate and committed. I spend about one-third of my time with my partners John Lynch (senior VP of human resources) and Susan Peters (VP executive development and chief learning officer). We recruit, we train, we develop, we improve, we think about people constantly. Historically, we have been known as a company that developed *professional managers*. These are broad problem-solvers with experience in multiple businesses or functions. However, I want to raise a generation of growth leaders—people with market depth, customer touch and technical understanding. This change emphasizes depth. We are expecting people to spend more time in business or on a job. We think this will help our team develop 'market instincts,' so important to growth and for growth, and the confidence to grow global businesses. Ultimately, careers should be broad and deep, giving our leaders the confidence to solve problems and the experience to drive growth. But today, to get the right balance, we are emphasizing depth."

"About a year ago, one of our executive development classes suggested that we reformulate our values to capture the spirit of GE as a growth company. Values can't just be words on a page. To be effective, they must shape actions. We looked to make them simpler, more inclusive and aspirational," explains Susan Peters (2012), GE's VP for executive development and chief learning officer. "We recently convened a team of 21 millennials from various GE businesses and functions around the world for a special three-month assignment to identify ways to attract, develop, and retain talent in the future. We named the effort 'Global New Directions.'" She points out that "the generation entering the workforce today is uniquely connected digitally and socially attuned to the forces of change and common purpose. But what's the best way to unleash their potential? Anticipating their needs is one of the great tasks of leadership

Source: GE 2012 Annual Report.

development and an area of sustained inquiry at GE. At Crotonville, our corporate university, we're addressing this challenge through an evolutionary leadership curriculum, breakthrough learning experiences, and a transformational environment. We're essentially reimagining a vision for the global nexus of ideas. And we're always looking to broaden the dialogue."

After weeks of intense effort, the members of the Global New Directions group presented several recommendations to Susan Peters and her team, and ultimately to CEO Jeff Immelt. These recommendations included: (1) creating a personalized suite of benefits, providing greater flexibility and choice to better meet the needs of a global, diverse workforce; (2) enhancing GE's performance-management system to help employees navigate their career at GE; (3) leveraging gaming technology to connects the world to GE in a fun and engaging way, helping to educate prospective employees about the company and its economic and social values; and (4) expanding GE's leadership-development and accelerator programs and connecting participants across those programs in order to support a broader base of culturally adaptive global leaders. GE is now implementing these key recommendations.

With $147 billion in revenues and $ 16 billion in earnings, GE is ranked by *Fortune* (2012) as the 6th-largest firm in the U.S. "GE can execute on a scale few can match," says Jeffrey Immelt at this year's annual shareholder meeting. However achieving these results required substantial investment in capability and people. We have developed and repositioned our leaders to capitalize on growth-market opportunities. So how does GE attract, develop, and retain global talent?

19.1 PROJECT MANAGERS HAVE SPECIAL NEEDS FOR PROFESSIONAL DEVELOPMENT

Project management always required special skill sets and competencies to perform effectively in an environment of unique organizational structures, reporting relations, power and resource sharing. However, the vast changes experienced in our world of business have differentiated project management even further from the practice of conventional management, especially over the past 20 years. The changing business environment and competitive pressures toward "better, faster, cheaper" delivery of products and services have transformed many organizations into project-based enterprises (see Chapter 6), leading to an expansion of project management responsibilities to include not only effective on-time/budget delivery of agreed-on results, but also responsibilities for business performance and alignment of the project operation with enterprise strategy. All of this requires additional skills and competencies, and a career focus quite different from traditional management.

The specialized knowledge and skill sets required to function effectively vary, depending on project size, complexity, and project management maturity of the enterprise. However, especially for more complex and technologically advanced projects at enterprises with high levels of project management maturity, skill requirements can be extensive. Typically, mature project-based businesses look at their development needs in the following areas:

- Effective project management, delivering quality results on time and within budget
- Effective utilization of enterprise resources
- Ability to advance project management organization (methods, standards, tools and techniques)
- Strategically optimized project selection (internally) and acquisition (externally)
- Alignment of projects with enterprise strategy
- Effective management of project portfolio
- Project management career development

Effective role performance in these areas takes a great deal of knowledge and skills, and the ability to apply them in the dynamic real world of project management. We discussed the skill requirements, aptitude testing and learnability already in Chapter 3, so let's focus on the actual development issues.

19.2 LINKING KNOWLEDGE, SKILLS, AND COMPETENCY

Effective project management is a key differentiator driving a competitive advantage for the project-oriented enterprise, and appropriate training and development of project leaders is essential. This is a great challenge, because it involves not only analytical and administrative skills that can be taught and learned in various settings, but also a spectrum of "soft skills," such as leadership, conflict resolution, collaboration, teambuilding, and business management, which are much more difficult to learn, primarily through experience.

Industry experts agree that a broad-based approach to project management development is fundamental to bridge the current gap between training, skill development, and actual competency (Carbone and Gholston 2004). Senior managers share this concern across industries. The statement by GE's CEO Jeff Immelt at the annual shareholders meeting (see GE 2012 Annual Report) reflects the awareness and changing approach to management development:

> Historically, we have been known as a company that developed *professional managers*. These are broad problem-solvers with experience in multiple businesses or functions. However, I want to raise a generation of growth leaders—people with market depth, customer touch and technical understanding. This change emphasizes depth. We think this will help our team develop . . . the confidence to grow global businesses.

Although Immelt's statement reflects on management development in general, it is typical of the new focus on management skills beyond technical, operational, and administrative competencies, to include also business savvy and leadership. It also addresses an important concern and often-heard critique that too many training programs emphasize knowledge and operational skills, while overlooking the importance of on-the-job competency.

Competence is the ability to *apply* the skills to dynamic real-world project situations that also involves issues of management attitude and style that need to complement the organizational culture of the project environment. This competency can only be developed experientially, in the field. Therefore, for project management development programs to be effective, they must combine knowledge and skill building with field-based learning experiences, such as we do in the training of commercial airline pilots and astronauts. Yet knowledge and skill sets are the foundation of competency, linked together and conditioned by the organizational environment, as graphically shown in Figure 19.1. We can build knowledge and skill sets separately or concurrently, but we cannot ignore them in project management development programs that target competency as a major objective.

19.3 BUILDING KNOWLEDGE, SKILLS, AND COMPETENCY

In the previous section I stressed the importance of a balanced approach to professional project manager development with ultimate focus on competency, which is based on knowledge and skills, all linked in a dynamic way, as shown in Figure 19.1. So, we must pay attention to these bases if we want

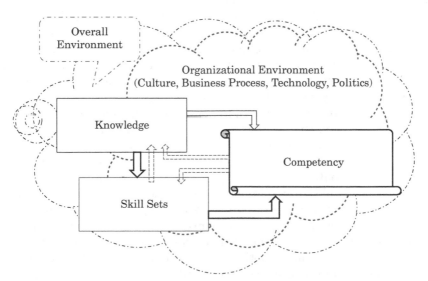

Figure 19.1 Linkage between knowledge, skills, and competency

to develop competency. Knowledge plays a critical role in the path to competency. Some would argue that the focus should be on skill development, not learning of concepts and theories. If you want to learn how to ride a bicycle, you don't take a course. Instead you climb on the two-wheeler, fall off, and climb on again until you've got it. This is a wonderful case for experiential learning. However, it is not too relevant for many of the skill sets needed by project managers. Without proper knowledge of how the system is supposed to work, what drives effectiveness, what approaches work and which don't, experiential learning is very time consuming and risky.

If no prior knowledge exists, we have no choice; we have to build skills by trial and error. But, in project management we have an enormous body of well-documented knowledge, covering a wide spectrum of application areas from administration to strategy and from technology to teambuilding. So, we should take advantage of this knowledge base in preparing future managers and helping practicing project management professionals in the field to enhance their skills and competencies. We use knowledge-to-skill accelerators all the time in our daily lives. Whether we want to learn how to drive a car or fly an airplane, or use a new software application, building some knowledge of how the system is supposed to work prior to using it will save time and reduce the risk of failure in the field. Yet, the reality is that many project managers are left to their own resources to build and upgrade their skill sets on the job with little or no organizational support.

Often, a project manager is promoted into the new position based on technical performance, but is lacking the necessary organizational and people skills necessary to resolve issues and build cross-functional team (Nellore and Balachandra 2001). This can lead to major deficiencies and issues ranging from inefficient execution to project failure. As remarked by a senior manager of a system integration company: "This practice of tossing the best technical person into the project lead position without much additional training might work on smaller routine projects. But, when we install a new system or make major technology enhancements the new lead really struggles."

A 2012 survey by *Computerworld* (Pratt 2013) adds yet another facet: "More than 75 percent executives interviewed indicated that a lack of in-house project management skills is a major workforce issue for them. But relatively few companies offer formal project management training . . ." Yet another concern is on the supply side of project managers. Some of the best and brightest professionals in their field might feel inadequately prepared to take on a project leadership role and do not consider project management as a desirable career path. Available project management training and development programs could minimize these fears and actually stimulate interest in project management as a viable career. "While experience is often quoted as the best teacher, companies must recognize the need to enhance on-the-job training with formal project manager development" (Carbone and Gholston 2004). Today we have many options to educate, train, and develop project leaders, and to build the knowledge and skills needed for managing projects in our demanding business environment.

19.3.1 Building Knowledge

Project management knowledge can be gained in many different ways. For simplicity and effective communication this section summarizes the methods of building knowledge in Five categories: (1) experiential, (2) teaching, (3) self-directed learning, and (4) professional networking.

1. **Experiential knowledge building.** This is an effective way to verify knowledge previously gained, build depth and more complete understanding to it, and transform knowledge into skill sets. On-the-job learning is also the only way to gain new knowledge (i.e. no access to training or knowledge doesn't exist yet). We call this 'learning by trial-and error'. As a primary method of knowledge building, trial-and-error is not very effective or reliable.

2. **Teaching.** Knowledge can be taught in many different ways and forms. Examples are:
   i. *Conventional classroom teaching* by lecturing, discussion, case studies, role play, and other means that often include readings, counseling, testing and feedback. This type of teaching always involves a "teacher" who leads the classroom activities and is responsible for the content and method of instruction. Conventional teaching can be delivered in many forms, such as workshops, seminars, and college and university courses. Classroom teaching can also be augmented with guest speakers, expert panels, field trips and excursions.
   ii. *Virtual Learning Environment (VLE), distance learning.* These learning platforms use information and communication technologies (ICT) to create a virtual classroom that can be visited by learners "online" via the Internet, TV, or other systems. A great variety of learning management systems such as Blackboard and Moodle combined with other ICTs can make the virtual classroom interactive and effective for learning. These technologies include web conferencing enabling students and instructors to communicate via webcam, microphone, and real-time chatting. Discussion boards, text notes, call-in options, and wikies, combined with other technologies, provide the opportunity for student interactions and for working collaboratively in a small groups while instructors can talk with students either individually or in groups, providing feedback and directions.

3. **Synchronous versus asynchronous.** Distance learning can be conducted either *synchronously* (learning occurs in real-time with all participants interacting at the same time) or *asynchronously* (allowing participants to join the learning community on their own schedule). Asynchronous learning is self-paced but somewhat limited in the participants' ability to interact with other students and to participate in the exchange of ideas.

An important feature of the virtual classroom is its ease of recording and storing the session content. This allows students to watch missed classes or review concepts for in-depth study.

i. *e-Learning.* This educational method can be seen as part of a virtual learning or distance-learning environment. However, it is aimed at providing more specific content and instructions for solving a problem or using a new piece of equipment or software, rather than dealing with a broad topic such as team leadership. Similar to the Virtual Learning Environment (VLE), e-learning uses information and communication technologies (ICT) to deliver actionable information via tape, CD-ROM, satellite TV, Internet, intranet, or extranet. Educational content is delivered by a wide variety of media options, such as text, audio, pictures/images, animation, and streaming videos. E-learning is often referred to by other names that reflect a particular aspect of content delivery, such as *multimedia learning, technology-enhanced learning (TEL), computer-based instruction (CBI), computer-based training (CBT), online education, computer-assisted instruction, computer-aided instruction (CAI), Internet-based training (IBT), web-based training (WBT),* and *web-based learning.* E-learning is suitable for classroom or distance learning, set up for either synchronous or asynchronous learning.

4. **Self-directed learning.** In this educational process individuals take the initiative of diagnosing their learning needs, formulating learning goals, identifying the sources for learning, implementing learning strategies, and evaluating outcomes (Merriam 2001). In this context it includes everything from reading of professional journals and books to gleaning knowledge from the Internet. Technically speaking, it also includes any learning initiative that was discussed in the first two categories of experiential learning and learning from teaching. However, in the context of this chapter, self-directed learning is an activity that is pursued without much interaction or guidance from the outside. It is probably one of the most flexible forms of learning and knowledge building, but also requires the greatest degree of self-discipline and self-governance.

5. **Professional networking.** This involves a special learning process that does not fit well into any of the other categories. Networking builds knowledge from interactions with like-minded professionals, such as attending professional meetings, conferences and social gatherings, and keeping in touch with colleagues of your company and your industry. Knowledge can also be derived from participation in web-based communities of practice, weblogs, Twitter, LinkedIn, and Facebook. Professional networking is an effective way of complementing and validating knowledge produced by other means, and gaining insight into the prevailing issues, challenges, best practices, and trends of a given business environment. It is also effective in identifying potential services and partners for future collaboration.

19.3.2 Building Skill Sets

The skill sets needed by project managers can be developed in several ways. But almost always experientially. Skills require the ability to apply knowledge to perform managerial tasks effectively and competently, and therefore have to be acquired by practice. We summarized the skill sets required for effective role performance and competency in four categories: (1) (technical, (2) operational/administrative, (3) people, and (4) strategic/business skills, and discussed the challenges associated with their developments in Chapter 3. The good news is that most of these skills can be developed and will enhance of project managers. Research supports these claims (Baldwin et al. 2012, Carbone and Gholston 2004, Clegg and Ross-Smith 2003, Kerzner 2013). Unlike certain personality traits or attributes, such as IQ, personal drive, temperament, and emotional intelligence, that are innate to a person and difficult to change even over long periods of time, individuals can build and improve their skills in virtually any area through practice, feedback, coaching, and perseverance. This is not a simple process. For one thing, management skills come in clusters, combining many overlapping, intricately connected skills into sets, necessary for managers to interact dynamically and effectively with the project environment, resolving issues and moving the project forward.

Taken together, skills are developed through practice, supported by knowledge and personal attributes such as desire, drive, and persistence. However, to be effective, skill building must consist of more than just a training or internship program. It should include specific knowledge from many sources to support the field-based experience, which should be monitored and updated periodically, based on the lessons learned from self-assessments and senior management observations. After all discussions and debates, the only thing standing in defining competency is the ability to make things happen, which is the ability to apply skills and talents in any combination necessary to move the project forward. It is the art and science of being a catalyst for motivating the team toward focusing their efforts on desired results.

19.4 DEVELOPING PROJECT MANAGERS

While project management is being recognized as a powerful, competitive tool, nearly 75 percent of executives surveyed by PMI believe that more effective project management could improve their company performance. Recognizing project management as a key performance differentiator, many organizations have focused on its systematic development. Yet, company support and investment is not sufficient to guarantee improvement of project management performance. The focus should be on systematic development of *competencies* required for project success (see PMI's "Project Manager Competency Development Framework" 2002). Competency is the ability to make things happen by applying knowledge, skills, and talents in whatever way necessary, driven by courage, to move projects forward. These characteristics can be developed. However, it takes systematic efforts of building and updating knowledge, integrated with practice and mentoring. The development program should align with the specific business needs and strategic objectives of the enterprise. It is a long-term commitment, based on solid needs assessment and planning. This cannot be done in isolation, but should involve the key project management stakeholders of the enterprise. In addition to the specific program features, the plan should define the responsibilities for administering, managing, and leading the development program. It should also include performance measures, evaluations, feedback to participants, and provisions for assessing relevancy and options for plan adjustments as needed. Finally, any development of project managers must be carefully integrated with existing project management support systems such as project management offices (PMO) and human resource (HR) departments.

19.5 PROFESSIONAL EDUCATION

With the growing demand for project management expertise, a broad spectrum of educational offerings emerged to build specialized knowledge and professional recognition. The respective programs vary widely in content and format. Readings, podcasts, seminars, workshops, lectures, and formal degree and certificate programs are some of the typical formats delivered online or in class by various organizations, such as specialized training companies, professional organizations, in-house training at corporations, colleges, and universities. In addition to knowledge building, there are many professional certification programs offered worldwide that often align with the educational programs and vice versa.

19.5.1 A Growing Number of Educational Programs

Professional training companies were the first to recognize the need for project management education. Starting in the 1950s, these companies offered short courses, workshops and seminars, either at their training facilities or in-house at their client organizations. Today, project management education is a billion-dollar business with millions of educational firms, institutions and consultants competing in a crowded, but still growing market. Delivery methods also expanded from traditional classroom seminars to a wide variety of methods, ranging from informal "lunch and learn" sessions to full degree programs. Moreover, modern information and communication technologies (ICT) have opened up new ways for program deliveries, such as podcasts and distance learning.

Academic institutions were initially slow in adapting to the growing needs for project management education. In the mid-1990s, there were only two bachelor and nine master's programs in project management. Today, we can choose from a growing number of over a thousand degree and certificate programs around the world, with the strongest expansion in Asia and South America.

19.5.2 Developing Successful Programs

However, not all programs are created equal. Developing a solid project management degree program responsive to professional needs in the field, with high academic standards and integrity, is not a simple task. As a young discipline, the formal body of knowledge and underlying theories are still emerging. There is still confusion among many academics about the uniqueness of project management in comparison to other forms of management. This can lead to big arguments about the necessity and legitimacy of academic programs in project management.

Yet, in spite of these concerns and academic politics, nearly one hundred new project management programs are being introduced each year by academic institutions across the globe. The best of these programs, with the highest approval rate by students and managers in industry, are the ones responsive to the unique nature of project management. They create a curriculum and learning environment that helps students to gain the diverse knowledge in support of the skills needed in the field for effective role performance. The temporary nature of project management with its unconventional reporting relationships, shared authority, power, and resources requires different skills and therefore different knowledge, in contrast to managing a functional discipline. The best programs put a lot of emphasis on the human side. They teach project management process, tools, and techniques with focus on collaboration, conflict resolution, and team leadership. They also teach project management as a business model aligned with the enterprise.

Another challenge is the lack of existing templates or standard methods for developing project management curricula or programs. However, there are some guidelines available from academic and professional organizations, such as PMI's Global Accreditation Center (GAC) for Project Management Education Programs. These guidelines help to build curricula for specialized academic programs in business, engineering, architecture, or IT, as well as general project management programs applicable across multiple disciplines.

Some schools, like Capella University in Minneapolis, have made project management part of the core academic curriculum, offered both as a standalone subject and integrated with other areas of study. As explained by Dr. Sue Talley, Dean of Capella's School of Technology: "Project management covers one of the most significant core competencies that all IT professionals and business managers should have. This has been very successful for Capella, as well as for our graduates and corporate partners . . .it is a key asset in developing educational alliances with key corporations." This comment is typical for the increasing focus of educational programs on specific application areas of project management, and efforts to enhance the educational value and relevancy by collaborating with industry on curriculum development in support of the competencies needed in the field.

"Progressive schools recognize the profound changes taking place in the business and project management arenas—and the opportunities they present" says Dr. Edwin Andrews, former director, academic and educational programs and services at the Project Management Institute. "Educators are not only introducing programs to address the needs of today's students and professionals, they're looking for more innovative ways to integrate project management into the fabric of organizations." (Project Management Institute 2008).

Taken together, we are making progress in educating current and future project leaders. Yet, despite the worldwide increase in educational programs at all levels, many more are needed to support the increasing demand for project management expertise. Responding to this issue, many organizations across all industries and government agencies, from IBM to Boeing and NASA, have established in-house programs or corporate universities, often aligned with university partners in collaboration of research and curriculum development.

19.6 PROFESSIONAL CERTIFICATION AND ACCREDITATION

With the growing number of project managers worldwide, the need for professional standards and formal recognition is steadily increasing. Professional certification is often seen as a path toward establishing professional competency standards, credentials, and recognition. The growth of certification programs is also a reaction to the changing employment market. Many of the most popular certifications are portable—that is, independent of a particular company affiliation or position. A certification represents an endorsement of an individual's professional knowledge, experience, and competence, an important credential in today's competitive job market, looking good on a resume at any time.

19.6.1 Types of Professional Certification

Professional certifications are also known as professional accreditations, or designations. While there are semantic differences between these terms, especially for accreditation that is usually a license to practice, the most common name for this credential is certification. There are many different types of certification in any profession, including project management. Wikipedia suggests a useful classification that has been adopted for this chapter: (1) profession-wide, (2) product-specific, (3) corporate, and (4) university educational institutions.

Profession-wide Certification

This is the most general and most portable type of certification. It is being offered by many professional project management organizations, such as the Project Management Institute (PMI), International Project Management Association (IPMA), and Japan Project Management Forum (JPMF). In addition to strictly project management–focused certificates, field-related certifications are also available, such as offered by professional organizations, such as the American Association of Cost Engineers (AACE), Product Development and Management Association (PDMA), and Association of Information Technology Professionals (AITP), just to name a few.

Many of these organizations offer certification for different levels of competencies and different application areas. For example, PMI offers seven certifications, each aimed at a different audience: Certified Associate in Project Management (CAPM)®, Project Management Professional (PMP)®, Program Management Professional (PgMP)®, PMI Portfolio Management Professional (PfMP)^{SM}, PMI Agile Certified Practitioner (PMI-ACP)®, PMI Risk Management Professional (PMI-RMP)®, and PMI Scheduling Professional (PMI-SP)®.

Professional certifications are based on a variety of qualifiers that may include work experience, formal education, and professional knowledge that is usually tested in an exam. Once earned, professional certification must usually be renewed periodically with proof of maintained professional status, such as continuing practice and participation in professional development activities.

Product-Specific Certification

This certification focuses on product-specific proficiencies, such as a certification as *Microsoft Office Specialist (MOS) or Microsoft Certified Solutions Expert (MCSE)*. This certification is very common in the information technology (IT) industry and is portable to other locations but not to other products.

Corporate Certification

Many companies and government agencies have their own in-house certification programs for their employees that focus on project management or related areas. Often, these programs are structured after already existing certifications from outside sources, and modified to fit the specific in-house needs. For US companies, a popular model is PMI's Project Management Professional (PMP) certification. While these certificates have limited portability, they carry high value, recognition, and prestige within the organization.

University and Other Educational Certification

Many universities and other institutions award professional certificates for completing an educational program, covering a specific subject, such as project management. The breadth and depth of the educational program varies, ranging from a few hours of classroom lectures to multicourse graduate-level programs with exams and other forms of proficiency testing. These certificate programs provide processes for gaining knowledge, recognition, and entry-level credentials. They are often also used as stepping stones for higher-level certification.

19.6.2 Who Certifies Professional Proficiencies?

Certification is usually earned from professional societies, trade organizations, or educational institutes, not the government. This is different for professional licensure, which in the United States is usually issued by state agencies. In project management, virtually all of the broadly recognized, portable competency certifications are being offered by professional societies, such as PMI's seven certification classes or IPMA's four levels of competency certification. The qualifications for being a certifying organization are defined by national and international standards, such as Standard 1100 of the American National Standards Institute (ANSI) or 17024 of the International Organization for Standardization (ISO). All certifying organizations must adhere to established quality standards to ensure credibility and recognition of their credentials by the project management community.

19.6.3 Benefits of Certification

Any form of certification is a personal credential testifying to a level of professional competency and accomplishment. In addition to the value as a credential, the person gains new knowledge and professional perspective in the process of getting certified, which benefits the individual and any organization employing his/her services. Especially beneficial are the broadly recognized certifications with higher levels of qualifying threshold. These elevate the professional status of the credential holder within an organization and the project management community.

Professional certification is often seen as a stepping stone into a project management career and future advancement. The certification maintenance programs required by many certifying organizations encourage individuals' continuing professional development and growth via learning and practice. Some certifications are also important to employers to qualify for contract work or to comply with customer requirements. In future years, organizations and individuals are expected to value certifications even more as a means of confirming a certain level of specialized work experience, formal training, and education. Overall, despite ongoing debates of its value as a predictor of project management performance, professional certification is seen as an effective way to validate a level of competency in specialized areas, increasing marketability to employers, and as a stepping stone on the project management career path.

19.7 CAREER OPPORTUNITIES IN PROJECT MANAGEMENT

"In the 21th century the demand for skilled project managers is at an all-time high as organizations continue to focus on higher productivity and greater customer satisfaction with minimal resources." This is one of the conclusions reached by PMI (2011b). I concur. For many years, there is an increasing demand for professionals across a broad spectrum of industries who can effectively manage project-based assignments and can use project management to leverage business performance.

With advanced technology, globalization, and pressures toward rapid market response, opportunities for careers in project management have become even more plentiful. Virtually every business activity, in many of today's industrial, commercial, and governmental organizations, use project management systems and standardized methods to get their tasks accomplished. New developments must be planned and managed in spite of fast changing technology, markets, regulations, and socioeconomic factors. Modern project management provides the process template and metrics for effectively executing these ventures, while information technology provides many of the tools for dealing with the enormous complexities of tracking, integrating and controlling these projects, that have become not only more complex, but also more demanding regarding cost, schedule, and technical performance. All of these challenges are career opportunities for project-minded professionals, technical and nontechnical, in virtually every field of business and commerce.

Traditionally, project management was seen as a career primarily in certain industries, such as construction, engineering, manufacturing, and aerospace. Today, virtually every industry, from construction to real estate development and from IT to financial services, uses project management as an integrated part of their business processes. Projects range from computer developments to urban renewal, transportation, communications, finance, advertising, health care, consulting, education, and foreign assistance programs, with the service sector accounting for the largest increase of project-related activities. Many career opportunities exist also outside these defined areas. They include launching new products, developing new technologies, organizing trade shows, building alliances, and managing mergers and acquisitions.

Whether a project involves releasing a product or launching a new space program, project professionals make sure that the objectives are met and results are delivered in a timely, cost-effective manner. Responsibilities for these projects come at various levels and titles, such as scheduler, assistant, associate, team leader, project engineer, project manager, systems manager, program manager, and director, providing opportunities for on-the-job learning and career development.

Very few people start in their career as full-fledged project manager. Most entry positions are assisting a project manager or supporting a project team by updating the schedules, tracking progress, reviewing documents, maintaining project management software, and writing reports. As you gain experience, you may be assigned more tasks to manage, until you're ready to lead others in completing an entire project. Others start out with primarily "technical" assignments in such as engineering, marketing or finance, with project management assigned as an additional responsibility. A typical example is the appointment of an engineer or scientist as team leader of a small technology project. These one-time assignments give the individual and senior management a chance to observe and evaluate performance, likes and dislikes, and potential for advanced assignments. In other cases, new college graduates from any field get hired as assistants to a project manager, or as a coordinator for a rollout, trade show, or introduction of a new administrative procedure. General business and support functions are loaded with activities that need to be executed with specific on-time and budget deliverables. Business managers often hire personnel responsible for proper execution of these activities. They look for people at the beginning of their professional career with the ability for multitasking, critical thinking, and good communication skills. Although the job title might not spell "project manager," these people perform project management work with all the challenges of integrating multidisciplinary activities across functional lines without much formal authority, and dealing with changes, conflict, and uncertainty. This is an excellent learning environment for project managers and a chance for identifying larger project management opportunities for career advancement.

The growth of standards and certifications has fueled the recognition of project management as a profession with many career paths. Whether you are already in the profession or thinking of a career in project management, a broad spectrum of opportunities exists at various levels of responsibilities, titles, and salaries. But, each *next* career level must be earned through demonstrated solid performance on the current job. Therefore, as for any career, you should be prepared to work for your next promotion. However, the overall picture looks very good. With a strong demand for project management professionals across all industries worldwide, fueled by an estimated $20 trillion investment in major projects, there is no shortage of career opportunities.

19.8 SUMMARY OF KEY POINTS AND CONCLUSIONS

The following key points were made in this chapter:

- Specialized knowledge and skill sets necessary for effective functioning of project manager vary, depending on project size, complexity, and maturity of the project organization.
- Appropriate training and development of project leaders is essential to ensure effective project management.
- Soft skills like leadership, conflict resolution, collaboration, team building, and business management are much more difficult to learn than analytical skills.
- Knowledge supports the development of skills that together form the basis for competency but provide no guarantee of competency.

- Competency is the ability to make things happen by applying knowledge, skills, and talents, driven by courage, to move projects forward.
- Project management knowledge can be gained in many different ways, grouped into four categories: (1) experiential, (2) teaching, (3) self-directed learning, and (4) professional networking.
- Project management skills require the ability to apply knowledge. They are developed experientially through practice, supported by knowledge, and personal attributes like desire, drive, and persistence.
- Developing project managers takes systematic efforts of building knowledge, integrated with practice and mentoring.
- Developing a solid project management degree program is a complex undertaking. The best programs create a curriculum and learning environment that helps students to gain the diverse knowledge in support of the skills needed in the field. They emphasize the human side, teaching project management process, tools, and techniques with focus on collaboration, conflict resolution, and team leadership. They also emphasize the importance of aligning project management with the business process of the enterprise.
- Professional certification represents an endorsement of an individual's professional knowledge, experience, and competence, an important credential in today's competitive job market.
- Professional certification programs can be classified into four categories: (1) profession-wide, (2) product-specific, (3) corporate, and (4) university educational institutions.
- The qualifications for being a certifying organization are defined by national and international standards, such as ANSI Standard 1100 or ISO 17024.
- For many years, the demand for professionals who can effectively manage project-based assignments has been increasing. Career opportunities exist for project-minded professionals, technical and nontechnical, in virtually every field of business and commerce.
- Typical entry positions are supporting a project manager and his/her team. More management responsibility may be assigned with increasing experience and competency.
- Whether you are already in the profession or thinking of a career in project management, a broad spectrum of opportunities exists at various levels of project management responsibilities, titles, and salaries. But, each *next* career level must be earned through demonstrated solid performance on the current job.

19.9 QUESTIONS FOR DISCUSSION AND EXERCISES

1. What are some of the knowledge and skill requirements in project management that are different from traditional "functional" management?

2. Discuss some of the methods for developing the (1) knowledge, (2) skills, and (3) competencies needed for effective role performance as project manager.
3. Discuss the GE approach to developing management talent. Is it relevant to project management? Which part is or is not relevant? How does GE's approach differ from traditional management training/development?
4. How are knowledge, skill sets, and competencies linked together?
5. Discuss the approach you would take in developing a new master's program in project management that is responsive to the knowledge and skill requirements in the field.
6. The value of professional certification as a predictor of project management performance is often argued. Discuss. What is the value of professional certification?
7. What are the benefits of a career in project management in comparison to a career in functional or general management? What are the caveats?
8. You would like to shift your career as a professional individual contributor into project management. How would you approach this career move?

19.10 *PMBOK®* REFERENCES AND CONNECTIONS

The topic of professional development focuses most specifically on the PMBOK® knowledge area of project human resource management (#6) with strong connections to the PMBOK® processing groups of planning, executing, and monitoring/controlling. Similar to Chapter 3 on skills and values, much of this chapter deals with the context of project executing and monitoring/controlling, discussing the need for managerial skill building to ensure effective project management throughout its life cycle. The managerial perspectives presented in this chapter should be helpful in connecting the PMBOK standards with best practices of project management, and in studying effectively for PMP® certification. In preparing for the PMP® Exam, the following two PMBOK sections relate most especially to this chapter and should be studied: (1) organizational planning and (2) staff acquisition.

INTERNET LINKS AND RESOURCES

AACE, American Association of Cost Engineers. www.aacei.org/
AITP, Association of Information Technology Professionals. www.aitp.org/
ANSI, American National Standards Institute. http://webstore.ansi.org/
DOE, US Department of Energy., Project Management Career Development Program (website). http://energy.gov/management/office-management/operational-management/certifications-and-professional-development-1
IPMA, International Project Management Association. http://ipma.ch/

ISO, International Organization for Standardization. www.iso.org/iso/home.html

PDMA, Product Development and Management Association. www.pdma.org/

PMAJ, The Project Management Association Japan www.pmaj.or.jp/ENG/

PMI, Certification (website). www.pmi.org/Certification.aspx

PMI, Global Accreditation Center for Project Management Education Programs. http://gacpm.org/

PMI, Learning Education and Development (LEAD) Community of Practice. http://lead.vc.pmi.org/Public/Home.aspx

Wikipedia. 2013. "Certification and Accreditation." http://en.wikipedia.org/wiki/Certification_and_Accreditation

REFERENCES AND ADDITIONAL READINGS

Baldwin, T., W. Bommer, and R. S. Rubin. 2012. *Developing Management Skills*. New York: McGraw-Hill Irwin.

Bredin, K., and J. Söderlund. 2012. "Project Managers and Career Models: An Exploratory Comparative Study." *International Journal of Project Management* 31(6): 889–902.

Carbone, G., and S. Gholston. 2004. "Project Manager Skill Development: A Survey of Programs and Practitioners." *Engineering Management Journal* 16(3): 10–16.

Clegg, S., and A. Ross-Smith. 2003. "Revising the Boundaries: Management Education and Learning in a Postpositivist World." *Academy of Management Learning & Education* 2(1): 85–98.

Crawford, L. 2004. "Professional Associations and Global Initiatives." In G. Morris and J. Pinto (eds.), *The Wiley Guide to Managing Projects*. Hoboken, NJ: John Wiley & Sons.

Edwards, A. 2009. "Tap into the Amazing Growth of Project Management." PMI White Paper. Newtown, PA: Project Management Institute.

El-Sabaa, S. 2001. "The Skills and Career Path of an Effective Project Manager." *International Journal of Project Management* 19(1): 1–7.

Gasiorowski-Denis, E. (ed.). 2012. *New ISO Standard on Project Management*. ISO. http://www.iso.org/iso/home/news_index/news_archive/news.htm?refid=Ref1662.

GE. 2013. *GE 2012 Annual Report*. Fairfield, CT: General Electric Company.

Hicks, R. 1996. "Experimental Learning in a Postgraduate Project Management Program." *Education & Training* 38(3): 28–38.

Merriam, S. 2001. "Andragogy and Self-Directed Learning: Pillars of Adult Learning Theory." *New Directions for Adult and Continuing Education* 89: 3–14.

Nellore, R., and R. Balachandra. 2001. "Factors Influencing Success in Integrated Product Development (IPD) Projects." *IEEE Transactions on Engineering Management* 48(2) (May): 164–174.

Pratt, M. 2012. "10 Hot IT Skills For 2013." *Computerworld* (September 24, 2012), www.computerworld.com/s/article/9231486/10_hot_IT_skills_for_2013.

Project Management Institute (PMI). 2002. "Project Manager Competency Development (PMCD) Framework." White Paper. Newtown, PA: Project Management Institute.

———. 2009. "The Power of Project Management." PMI White Paper. Newtown, PA: Project Management Institute.

———. 2010. "Establishing a Project Management Degree." PMI White Paper #046–039–2010(9–10). Newtown, PA: Project Management Institute.

————. 2011a. *Handbook of Accreditation of Degree Programs in Project Management*. Newtown, PA: Project Management Institute.

————. 2011b. *Careers in Project Management*, White Paper. Newtown, PA: Project Management Institute.

————. 2013. *A Guide to the Project Management Body of Knowledge (PMBOK® Guide)*. Newtown Square, PA: Project Management Institute.

Chapter 20

The Future of Project Management

20.1 IS THE FUTURE PREDICTABLE?

Predicting the future is difficult and risky. History is full of sociopolitical, economic, and technological happenings, from the Industrial Revolution to the sudden collapse of the Soviet Union and the invention of the transistor as the precursor of the digital age. None of these events were predicted decades ahead of time. Similar examples can be given for project management. Who predicted the evolution of management approaches like agile, Stage-Gate®, virtual teams, extreme project management or Internet-supported dashboard controls, and their impact on the practice of project management in the 1980s? That is only 30 years ago, a very short time period in comparison to 4,000 years of project management practice. Yet despite the difficulties of predicting the future, some people seem to be less surprised and better prepared to deal with changes in the business environment when they occur. These are the leaders who understand their current environment, trends, and forces that shape the future. Nobody has the proverbial crystal ball to predict the future. However, I strongly believe that understanding historic developments, current dynamics, trends, and forces in the business environment are the best predictors of upcoming changes and preparation for the future.

20.2 CHANGES AND TRENDS IN THE PROJECT ENVIRONMENT

Just 50 years ago, project management emerged as a formal discipline, impacting virtually every operation of the modern enterprise in every industry. How did things change so fast after thousands of years of stable praxis with little or no changes in the work process, methods, and supporting tools and techniques? What are the forces that drove these paradigm shifts in project management, and what lessons can we learn for identifying possible trends for the future? Let's focus on the past 25 years.

KEY DRIVING FORCES AND TRENDS AFFECTING PROJECT MANAGEMENT

- Advances in technology, especially computers and communications
- Advances in the art and science of project management to a maturity level that can produce predictable results even under changing and dynamic conditions
- Alternative project team designs, such as virtual, extreme, agile
- Broad application of project management to virtually all industries, businesses, and segments of society
- Emergence of new management processes and practices, such as concurrent engineering, agile, user-centered design, virtual teams, reengineering, enterprise pm, gate review, rapid prototyping, spiral processes, out-of-bounds reviews, and extreme project management
- Globalization of business and project management
- Greater participation of suppliers, contractors, and customers in project execution
- Increased responsibility of project managers for business results
- Increasing competitive pressures toward faster, better, cheaper products and services
- Increasing need and ability for managing more complex projects
- Integration of project management into the business process of the enterprise
- More focus on human issues and emphasis of people skills
- Political and social changes across large geographic regions of the world
- Recognition of broad spectrum of stakeholders within and outside the project organization
- Recognition of project management as a formal discipline with its own body of knowledge, standards, and norms
- Shorter product and service life cycles
- Sustainability as a major concern
- Technology-based knowledge doubling every few years

Driven to a large extend by advances in computer and communication technologies and by worldwide sociopolitical changes, four major shifts in our business environment influenced project management and created the ambience that prompted many of the recent changes in the way we manage projects today. Understanding these paradigm shifts and the forces that drive them is critical for recognizing trend and possible future developments.

20.2.1 Shift from Locally Organized Projects to Globally Dispersed Project Organizations

Supported by modern communication technology, project teams can be dispersed over wide geographic areas, taking advantage of the best specialized skills, economics, and facilities anywhere in this world. This ability led to intricate multicompany alliances and highly complex forms of work integration that rely to a considerable extent on member-generated performance norms and work processes.

Managing these virtual team processes requires new tools and techniques, and a shift toward more team ownership, power sharing, accountability, collaboration, commitment, and self-direction at the local level. These trends are likely to continue in the future.

20.2.2 Shift from Linear Work Processes to Dynamic Systems

While in the past, project management was based on predominately linear models, typically exemplified by sequential product developments, scheduled services, and discovery-oriented R&D, today's project managers have to operate in a much more dynamic and interactive way to respond to the increased pressures for faster, more customer-focused and resource-limited delivery of results. The resulting processes, such as concurrent engineering, Stage-Gate®, agile, and integrated product development, are often nonlinear. They demand a more sophisticated management style that relies to a considerable extent on member-generated performance norms and evaluations, rather than on hierarchical guidelines, policies, and procedures.

Although this paradigm shift is driven by changing organizational complexities, capabilities, demands, and cultures, it also leads to radical departures from traditional management philosophy on organizational structure, motivation, leadership, and project control. As a result, traditional "hardwired" organizations, such as the traditional matrix, are modified or replaced by more flexible and nimble networks that are in most cases derivatives of the conventional matrix organization. While allowing more concurrent and flexible operations, these networks have more permeable boundaries that require broad power and resource sharing. These are trends likely to continue in the future.

20.2.3 Shift from Efficiency toward Effectiveness and Linkage to Business Strategy

Many companies have broadened their focus from *efficient* execution of their project operations—emphasizing job skills, teamwork, communications, time, and resource optimization at the operational level—to *include organizational effectiveness*. This shift responds to the need for better integration of ongoing project operation into the overall enterprise, linking project management with business strategy. As an example, companies are leveraging project management as a core competency, integrating project-oriented activities closely with other functions, such as marketing, R&D, field services, and strategic business planning; and to achieve accelerated product developments, higher levels of innovation, better quality, and better overall resource utilization.

Although this shift is enhancing the status and value of certain business functions within the enterprise, it raises the overall level of responsibility and accountability for project managers to perform as a full partner within the integrated enterprise system, a trend likely to continue in the future.

20.2.4 Shift from Processing Information to Fully Utilizing Information Technology

Today's technology provides managers anywhere in the enterprise and beyond with push-button access to critical information on operational status and performance. The availability and promise of technology has led to the development of an enormous variety of powerful IT-based project support tools and techniques, ranging from resource estimating to scheduling, risk analysis, and decision making, and from design to testing, system integration, and customer validation.

The future challenge is at the enterprise level for looking beyond the immediate application—such as project management or manufacturing resource planning—to integrate information systems among the various business processes, such as design, operations, field services, and project management. The objective, then, is to integrate project management with business processes of the enterprise, rather than just replacing traditional forms of communications, interactions, and problem solving. These issues are broadly recognized by management and started a trend that is likely to continue in the future.

20.3 WHAT DOES IT MEAN FOR THE FUTURE OF PROJECT MANAGEMENT?

Preparing for the future is not an easy feat. No magic formula guarantees success. However, conditioning for future success in project management is not a random process. A better understanding of the criteria and dynamics that affect our business environment today can help managers in recognizing the emerging trends that affect the future of project management. Here are some of the trends that are likely to continue and shape the future of project management:

- With some certainty we can predict that the current trend toward more professionalism and standardization will continue in project management, leading to additional growth in career positions, educational offerings, research, and published material in a variety of media. It will also lead to a broader acceptance of the body of knowledge and standards that will be applicable and recognized in future years by large segments of industry and government across the globe.

- Changes in management philosophy toward more empowerment of team members, stakeholder involvement, and a management style based on collaboration, commitment, and risk sharing are expected to be adopted more broadly throughout the profession of project management, replacing the traditional, authority-based "command and control" style that was found ineffective for many of today's complex project management situations.

- Geographically dispersed, "virtual" teams will continue to grow in importance to take advantage of specialized skill pools, economic situations, markets, and project logistics. The tools, techniques, and methods of unifying and managing these virtual teams and integrating their work is expected to continue to improve, leading to higher levels of overall project effectiveness.

- Technologies of many forms, from computers to communications and nanotechnology, will continue to grow, leading to new applications in support of the increasing project management challenges and opportunities of the future.

- We can expect an increase in project complexity across all areas of project management. This complexity is not just limited to the technical part of the project, but also includes customer interfaces, regulations, financing, political, and legal and environmental considerations. Having the appropriate skill sets, technology, and support systems in place will be critically important for being able to take advantage of upcoming opportunities and to execute them successfully.

- In addition to the general complexity, the need and opportunity for megaprojects will increase worldwide, These projects include infrastructure, energy, healthcare, nation-building, and aerospace, just to name a few of the megaprojects known to date.

- Sustainability is expected to become an issue of primary importance, with increased pressure on companies for more accountability regarding sustainable developments. This will affect the future of project management in the way we plan, execute, and deliver projects. It will influence project management methodologies, standards, and practices, including the way we measure project performance and distribute reward.

- Risk and uncertainty are expected to intensify in an increasingly changing and dynamic world. This will have strong impact on the way we plan, negotiate, and manage projects in the future. It will also drive the development of new tools, techniques, and management processes for dealing with uncertainties associated with the increasing complexities of future projects and their environment.

- Measures of project performance are expected to continue to shift from short-term efficiency metrics to longer-term effectiveness, which not only measures the contracted project performance but also goes beyond the quadruple constraint to include performance against overall business objectives and long-term enterprise benefits, including sustainability. This links project management to enterprise performance.
- Taken together, project management will be different in the future from the organizational systems, processes, and practices of today. However, progressive managers at all levels will recognize the current changes and driving forces in the business environment that create the future environment. These are the project managers and business leaders that will be prepared to deal with the challenges and opportunities of the future.

20.4 SUMMARY OF KEY POINTS AND CONCLUSIONS

The following key points were made in this chapter:

- Predicting the future is difficult and risky. However, some people seem to be better prepared than others to deal with changes in the business environment when they occur.
- Understanding historic developments and the forces that drive change in the current business environment are the best predictors of upcoming changes in the future.
- Over the history of project management, the discipline has most radically and rapidly changed during the past 50 years.
- Driven to a large extend by advances in computer and communication technologies and by worldwide sociopolitical changes, four major shifts in our business environment have influenced and changed the discipline of project management: shift from (1) local to global, (2) linear work processes to dynamic systems, (3) efficiency toward effectiveness and linkage to business strategy, and (4) processing information to fully utilizing IT.
- Many of the changes that will occur in the future will be extensions of current trends. Other changes will be more radical and difficult to predict.
- We can predict with some certainty that the current trend toward more professionalism and standardization in project management will continue, leading to additional growth in project-related jobs, career positions, educational, research and publications.
- Management style will change toward more empowerment of teams and stakeholder involvement. Collaboration, commitment, and risk sharing will be adopted more broadly as a basis of control, replacing the traditional authority-based "command and control" methods.
- The use of geographically dispersed, "virtual" teams is expected to grow further, supported by new tools, techniques, and methods for managing these virtual teams and integrating their work.

- We can expect an increase in project complexity across all areas of project management, from the technical part to customer interfaces, regulations, financing, political, and legal and environmental considerations.
- Sustainability will increase in importance. Pressure for more accountability will influence changes to project management methodologies, standards, and practices, including the way we measure project performance.
- Risk and uncertainty are both expected to intensify in an increasingly changing and dynamic world, affecting the way we plan, negotiate, and manage future projects. Appropriate skill sets and technology will be critically important to deal with the challenges and opportunities.
- Project performance is expected to include more long-term effectiveness measures beyond the quadruple constraint, linking project management with business objectives.
- Managers who recognize the driving forces that are likely to create changes will be prepared to deal with the challenges and opportunities of the future.

20.5 QUESTIONS FOR DISCUSSION AND EXERCISES

1. Discuss the major changes in project management practice, process, and concepts that you can identify (or have observed) over the past 10 years. What were the major drivers causing these changes?
2. Do you agree or disagree with the predictions made in this chapter regarding the future of project management? Why or why not? Select a few statements and discuss.
3. Select an industry you are familiar with. (a) How would you predict the future project management environment to look 10 years or 25 years from now? What method or approach would you use for your prediction? (b) What predictions would you make? (c) What changes in project management style and process do you predict as a result of your environmental forecast? (d) Do you feel that your conclusions reached in item (b) and (c) are also applicable to other industries? Discuss.
4. How would you as a (a) project manager and (b) senior manager/executive prepare for the future?

INTERNET LINKS AND RESOURCES

Gerush, M. 2009. "Project Management: The Next Generation." Posted on Forrester Blogs (Forrester Research, Inc.) on November 11. http://blogs.forrester.com/application_development/2009/11/project-management-the-next-generation.html
Kurzweil, R. 2006. "The Accelerating Power of Technology." posted on YouTube, November 2006. www.ted.com/talks/ray_kurzweil_on_how_technology_will_transform_us.html

LinkedIn 2013. Next Generation Project Management (website); http://www.linkedin
   .com/groups/Next-Generation-Project-Management-4463887
PMI. 2012. "Next Generation Project Managers." PMI-OC 2012 Project Management
   Conference: Leadership Panel—Next Generation Project Managers. Posted on
   YouTube. September 28. www.youtube.com/watch?v=a21iJXj3S3Q

REFERENCES AND ADDITIONAL READINGS

Cicmil, S., T. Williams, J. Thomas, and D. Hodgson. 2006. "Rethinking Project
   Management: Researching the Actuality of Projects." *International Journal of
   Project Management* 24(8): 675–686.
Cleland, D., and B. Bidanda. 2009. *Project Management Circa 2025*. Newtown Square,
   PA: Project Management Institute.
Cleland, D., and L. Ireland. 2007. *Project Management: Strategic Design and
   Implementation*. New York: McGraw Hill.
Harris, S. 2011. "Next Generation Project Management Thinking." Online publication.
   American Society for the Advancement of Project Management, posted April 2011.
   http://asapm.org/asapmag/articles/NextGenPM.pdf.
Loden, M. 2013. "The Future of Project Management." Online publication by PSMJ
   Resources. www.psmj.com/knowledge-community/articles/the-future-of-project-man
   agement.cfm.
Shenhar, A., and D. Dvir. 2007. *Reinventing Project Management: The Diamond
   Approach to Successful Growth and Innovation*. Cambridge, MA: Harvard Business
   School Press.
Winter, M., C. Smith, P. Morris, and S. Cicmil. 2006. "Directions for Future Research in
   Project Management: The Main Findings of a UK Government-Funded Research
   Network." *International Journal of Project Management* 24(8): 638–649.

Appendix 1

Policy and Procedure Examples

Four sample documents are shown in this appendix to illustrate the type of administrative guidelines that should be developed in support of project operations within the enterprise, providing the framework for managerial direction, communication and control:

EXAMPLE 1: CHARTER OF PROGRAM OR PROJECT MANAGER (MATRIX ORGANIZATION)

Alpha Technology Corporation
ABC Division
Charter No. 01.213456.14
Purpose: Define program management charter within ABC Division
Effective Date: September 1, 2014
Position Title: Program Manager*

Authority

The program manager* has the delegated authority from general management to direct all program activities. He or she represents the company in contacts with the customer and all internal and external negotiations. Project personnel have the typical dual-reporting relationship: to functional management for technical performance and to the program manager for contractual performance in accordance with specifications, schedules, and budgets. The program manager approves all project personnel assignments and influences their salary and promotional status via formal performance reports to their functional managers. Travel and customer contact activities must be coordinated and approved by the program manager.

Any conflict with functional management or company policy shall be resolved by the general manager or his or her staff.

---

*Both the program manager and the project manager are referred to as program manager in this charter.

Responsibility

The program manager's responsibilities are to the general manager for overall program direction according to established business objectives and contractual requirements regarding technical specifications, schedules, and budgets.

More specifically, the program manager is responsible for (1) establishing and maintaining the program plan, (2) establishing the program organization, (3) managing and controlling the program, and (4) communicating the program status:

1. **Establishing and maintaining the program plan.** Prior to authorizing the work, the program manager develops the program plan in concert with all key members of the program team. This includes master schedules, budgets, performance specifications, statements of work, work breakdown structures, and task and work authorizations. All of these documents must be negotiated and agreed upon with both the customer and the performing organizations before they become management tools for controlling the program. The program manager is further responsible for updating and maintaining the plan during the life cycle of the program, including the issuance of work authorizations and budgets for each work package in accordance with the master plan.

2. **Establishing the program organization.** In accordance with company policy, the program manager establishes the necessary program organization by defining the type of each functional group needed, including their charters, specific roles, and authority relationships.

3. **Managing and controlling the program.** The program manager is responsible for the effective management and control of the program according to established customer requirements and business objectives. He or she directs the coordination and integration of the various disciplines for all program phases through the functional organizations and subcontractors. He or she monitors Und controls the work in progress according to the program plan. Potential deficiencies regarding the quality of work, specifications, cost, or schedule must be assessed immediately. It is the responsibility of the program manager to rectify any performance deficiencies.

4. **Communicating the program status.** The program manager is responsible for building and maintaining the necessary communication channels among project team members to the customer community and to the firm's management. The type and extent of management tools employed for facilitating communications must be carefully chosen by the program manager. They include status meetings, design reviews, periodic program reviews, schedules, budgets, data banks, progress reports, and team colocation.

EXAMPLE 2: CHARTER OF FUNCTIONAL/RESOURCE MANAGER (MATRIX ORGANIZATION)

Alpha Technology Corporation
ABC Division
Charter No. 02.345678.14
Purpose: Define resource department charter within ABC Division
Effective Date: October 1, 2014
Position Title: Resource Department Manager

Authority

The functional resource manager has the delegated authority from the general manager or his or her functional director to establish, develop, and deploy organizational resources according to the business needs, both long and short range. This authority includes the hiring, training, maintaining, and terminating of personnel; the development and maintenance of the physical plant, facilities, and equipment; and the direction of the functional personnel with regard to the execution and implementation of the various disciplines according to specific project requirements from the program office.

Responsibility

The functional resource manager is accountable to the general manager or his or her functional director for all work within his or her functional areas in support of all programs. He or she establishes organizational objectives and develops the resources needed for effective performance regarding the cost, schedule, and technical requirements established by the program office, and seeks out and develops new methods and technology to prepare the company for future business opportunities.

EXAMPLE 3: POLICY FOR PROJECT MANAGEMENT (MATRIX ORGANIZATION)

Alpha Technology Corporation
ABC Division
Policy No. 03.654321.14
Effective Date: October 1, 2014

1. Purpose and Scope
   This policy provides the basis for the management of programs within the Alpha Technology Corporation. It defines the responsibilities,

authorities, and accountabilities for performance of assigned programs consistent with program requirements and company policies.

2. Applicability and Organizations Affected

This policy is applicable to all organizational units.

3. Definitions

   3.1. *Program Manager*—The individual who has been assigned responsibility for management of proposal or contract.

   3.2. *Task Manager*—The individual within a line or functional organization to whom responsibility has been assigned for fulfilling the requirement of a task authorization.

   3.3. *Functional or Line Manager*—These titles are used interchangeably to identify responsibilities such as manager of engineering, manufacturing, or product assurance.

   3.4. *Task*—A manageable portion of a total program that is consistent with items of customer accountability. It is usually progressively subdivided, to succeeding levels in the work breakdown structure.

   3.5. *Task Agreement*—A formal document issued by the procurement manager to authorize performance of a task, production of material, or furnishing of services.

   3.6. *Task Authorization*—A formal document issued by a program manager and agreed to by a functional manager within an operating division to authorize performance of specific tasks, time phase within that division as required to fulfill a customer contract.

   3.7. *Task Matrix*—A two-dimensional representation of a plan describing the relationship of who is responsible for what tasks in accomplishing the total job.

   3.8. *Accounting Charge Number*—A number used for identifying costs charged to a task or to a subtask which is shown on the task matrix.

4. Policy

   4.1. Responsibility for each contract awarded to the Alpha Technology Corporation will be assigned to the appropriate business area. The business area manager will assume overall responsibility to ensure that the requirements for each contract under his jurisdiction are successfully met.

   4.2. The business area manager, subject to the approval of the general manager, will appoint a qualified individual as program manager.

   4.3. The program manager will act as the senior management representative for all facets of the program utilizing all authorities as delegated to him by the business area manager to perform his function.

   4.4. The program office will be staffed with those skills necessary to ensure effective, competent, and professional direction and guidance of the program. Personnel so assigned will receive supervision on matters pertaining specifically to the program from the program manager or his designated representative.

4.5. The objectives of the program office are to ensure that program tasks are accomplished within cost, schedule, and performance requirements of the contract and that the full business potential of the program is exploited. The program office will not duplicate skills that belong in the functional organizations. The program office defines what to do (contract scope of work), when to do it (schedule requirements), and basic parameters (budgets and specifications). The functional organization directs the team with regard to who is going to perform (skills and talent distribution), where activities will take place (make or buy decisions), how things are to be done (methods and techniques), and when they are to be done (internal schedules).

4.6. The program office is to accomplish the following major functions:
- Prepare and maintain a master program plan.
- Divide the work into discrete and clearly defined tasks. Assign tasks to the functional organizations, other company locations, other outside sources, or perform them in the program office.
- Negotiate, establish, and allocate budgets, schedules, and technical requirements for the various tasks consistent with the work to be done and compatible with total contract requirements.
- Maintain continuing control and surveillance of schedule, cost, technical performance, and personnel to ensure progress on all planned tasks.
- Replan, redirect, or make tradeoffs between prime tasks if established criteria cannot be met, and adjust task authorizations.
- Carefully evaluate customer requests/directions to ensure proper contractual coverage.

4.7. The program office in managing the program shall utilize functional organizations. To the extent that existing capabilities do not fully satisfy the needs of the program, the program manager will arrange for their acquisition, consistent with company objectives and policies.

4.8. The functional organizations shall comply with direction from the program manager regarding all phases of the program, consistent with the contractual requirements, task authorizations, and subject to Paragraph 4.11. All program direction shall flow through the responsible task manager.

4.9. Task authorizations will be issued to the functional organization and the functional managers will be responsible for the proper performance of the tasks assigned to their organization. Task authorizations shall be negotiated between the appropriate program manager and the appropriate functional managers.

4.10. Each involved functional organization will appoint a task manager who will have responsibility for the overall planning, coordination, and control needed to successfully complete his task within the budget and schedule prescribed by the program office.

All programs will be performed utilizing the business area program task management concept whereby all programs are divided into tasks, each under the direction of a task manager. It will be the task manager's responsibility to see that all requirements of the task as defined by the business area program office are successfully met and are in accordance with specified budgets and schedules. Cost forecasting, weekly labor reporting, and various scheduling techniques will be employed to ensure that each task is progressing as scheduled.

a. Cost Forecasting

The cost forecast is a projection of the cost-at-completion. It is determined by adding the cost-to-complete forecast to the actual cost of resources expanded to date. The cost forecast is prepared by each task manager.

- It will be performed monthly.
- Basis-of-estimates are not required.
- It does not in itself culminate in an agreement with the program manager.

The cost forecast is used as an indicator to determine whether a formal cost-to-complete estimate is necessary or corrective actions are required. Cost forecast reports will be reviewed by the program manager monthly.

b. Cost-to-Complete

Estimates that reflect the work remaining to complete a task including commitments yet to be initiated. These estimates should be prepared in a specified level of detail, normally determined by the cost element. These estimates will be consistent with the latest program plan and established management directives (Project Reviews 08.03.015).

c. Weekly Labor Reporting

The weekly labor report depicts a detailed summary of all tasks within a contract in hours, and measures those hours against the time-phased hours that exist within the task agreements, in a weekly, monthly, and inception-to-date report. Its prime function is to give the program manager as well as task and functional managers a weekly up-to-date report of how they are performing against their tasks.

d. Scheduling Techniques

The required methods of control (PERT, LOB, milestone charts) will be specified in the task authorizations by the program office. The methods of control are normally specified in the contract.

4.11. Should problems arise that are not resolved at the program office task manager level, the program manager and the functional manager(s) will attempt in good faith and on a timely basis to resolve them in a manner consistent with the terms, conditions, and requirements of the contract and will be held accountable for so doing. Either the program manager or the functional manager(s) may, if necessary, request resolution of such problems by the business area manager and the general manager. Pending such resolution, however, the tasks, budgets, and schedules established by the program manager shall be adhered to.

EXAMPLE 4: JOB DESCRIPTION FOR R&D PROJECT MANAGER

Alpha Technology Corporation
ABC Division
Management Directive No. 04.546399.14
Effective Date: November 1, 2014

The project manager is the key individual charged with the responsibility for the total project and is delegated the authority by management. He is also assigned a supporting staff, which may include individuals directly responsible to him (i.e., administratively and technically) as well as others technically responsible to him though administratively located in other parts of the organization. The responsibilities and authorities of the project manager can be summarized as follows:

- Establish and effectively operate an integration effort that is based on rapid feedback from each element of project activity.
- Implement an appropriate philosophy of how project work will be done, avoiding cumbersome formality without sacrificing traceability and project intercommunications.
- Plan the work and break it down into understandable elements with well-defined technical, schedular, and financial aspects. Maintain an up-to-date plan that integrates and reflects the actual work status of these work elements.
- Analyze the total project work against allocated resources and establish an optimum project organization to achieve the project objectives. Reorganize this project organization as required to meet the changing needs of the project.
- Assign responsibility for discrete elements of project work (contract and in-house) to members of his project organization and redelegate sufficient of the project manager's own authority to these members to enable them to contribute effectively to the successful completion of the project.
- Serve as the focal point of responsibility for all actions relating to accomplishment of the total project, including both in-house and contract effort.
- Ensure, by direct participation and review of the work of others, that each contract effort in support of his project is well planned and fully defined during the preparation of the technical package, thus enabling

the solicitation through RFPs of technically responsive offers from responsible contractors.

- Ensure, by direct participation in negotiations, that the successful contractor and the company have a common understanding of the goals and requirements of each contract before contract execution.
- Maintain a continuous surveillance and evaluation of all aspects of the work being conducted by each contractor, including technical, schedular, and financial status.
- Identify, devise, and execute effective solutions to management and/or technical problems that arise during the course of the work.
- Ensure the timely detection and correction of oversights in any aspect of each contract to minimize cost overruns, schedule delays, and technical failures.
- Make final decisions within the scope of work of each contract.
- Give guidance and technical direction for all elements of the project work, or concur in contractor actions in accordance with provisions of each contract.
- Continually evaluate the quality of the work performed by each contractor and verify that the requirements are properly carried out by the contractor.
- Ensure that configuration management requirements are adhered to by each contractor in accordance with the requirements of the contract.
- Help to indoctrinate and regularly monitor contractor performance to ensure full reporting of all new technology evolved under each project contract.
- Participate in contract closeout or in termination proceedings to ensure that the best interests of the company are safeguarded.

Appendix 2

Professional Societies, Journals, and Conferences in Project Engineering, and Technology Management

With the enormous growth of technology and project management activities around the globe and the increased recognition of project management as a profession, a large number of professional societies emerged. Many of these societies are headquartered in one country, but service their worldwide membership by maintaining chapters in many locations across the globe. As an example, the Project Management Institute (PMI), headquartered in the United States, reaches over 500,000 professionals in 180 countries with 250 chapters around the world and offices in, Singapore, Belgium, India, and China.

This appendix lists professional societies that focus on the advancement of project management, engineering management or technology management. The listing includes mostly U.S.-based societies, but also includes others from the international field with connections to U.S. societies and professional networks in the U.S. The listing is for reference only. No attempt is made to rank or exclude any particular organization.

PROFESSIONAL SOCIETIES

Academy of Applied Science (AAS); Concord, NH; www.aas-world.org/
Academy of Management (AOM); Briarcliff Manor, NY; http://aom.org/
American Association for the Advancement of Science (AAAS); Washington, DC; www.aaas.org/
American Chemical Society (ACS); Washington, DC; http://www.acs.org/content/acs/en.html
American Institute of Aeronautics and Astronautics (AIAA); Reston, VA; www.aiaa.org/
American Institute of Chemical Engineers (AIChE); New York, NY; www.aiche.org/

American Institute of Mining, Metallurgical, and Petroleum Engineers (AIME); Littleton, CO; www.aimeny.org/

American Institute of Physics (AIP); One Physics Ellipse, College Park, Maryland 20740-3843; Ph (301) 209-3100; www.aip.org/index.html/

American Management Association (AMA); New York, NY; www.amanet.org

American Physical Society (APS); College Park, MD; www.aps.org/

American Society for Engineering Education (ASEE); Washington, DC; www.asee.org/

American Society for Engineering Management (ASEM); Rolla, MO; www.asem.org/home.html

American Society for Quality (ASQ); Milwaukee, WI; www.asq.org/

American Society for the Advancement of Project Management (ASAPM) – Affiliated with IPMA; Colorado Springs, CO; www.asapm.org/a_home.asp

American Society for Training and Development (ASTD); Alexandria, VA; www.astd.org/

American Society of Civil Engineers (ASCE); Reston, VA; www.asce.org/

American Society of Mechanical Engineers (ASME); New York, NY; www.asme.org/

American Society of Metals (ASM); Materials Park, OH; www.asminternational.org/

Association for Computing Machinery (ACM); New York, NY; www.acm.org/

Association for Consulting Chemists and Chemical Engineers (ACC&CE); Sparta, NJ; www.chemconsult.org/

Association for Facilities Engineering (AFE); Cincinnati, OH; www.afe.org/

Association for Federal Information Resources Management (AFFIRM); Washington, DC; www.affirm.org/

Association for Project Management (APM); Princes Risborough Bucks, UK; www.apm.org.uk/help

Association for the Advancement of Cost Engineering International (AACE); Morgantown, WV; www.aacei.org/

Association for Women in Science (AWIS); Washington, DC; www.awis.org/

Australian Institute of Project Management (AIPM); Sydney, Australia; www.aipm.com.au/

Decision Sciences Institute (DSI); Atlanta, GA; www.decisionsciences.org/

Electro-Chemical Society (ECS); Pennington, NJ; www.electrochem.org/

Industrial Relations Research Association (IRRA); Champaign, IL; www.irra.uiuc.edu/

Industrial Research Institute (IRI); Arlington, VA; www.iriinc.org/

Institute for Operations Research and the Management Sciences (INFORMS); Linthicum, MD; www.informs.org/

Institute of Electrical and Electronics Engineers (IEEE); New York, NY; www.ieee.org/

Institute of Industrial Engineers (IIE); Norcross, GA; www.iienet.org/

Institute of Management Consultants (IMC); Washington, DC; www.imcusa.org/

Instrumentation, Systems, and Automation Society (ISA); Research Triangle Park, NC; www.isa.org/

International Association for Management of Technology (IAMOT); Coral Gables, FL; www.iamot.com/

International Association of Contract and Commercial Managers (IACCM); Ridgefield, CT; www.iaccm.com/

International Project Management Association (IPMA); Nijkerk, The Netherlands; http://ipma.ch/

National Academy of Engineering (NAE); Washington, DC; www.nae.edu/

National Contract Management Association (NCMA); McLean, VA; www.ncmahq.org/

National Mining Association (NMA); Washington, DC; www.nma.org/

National Society of Professional Engineers (NSPE); Alexandria, VA; www.nspe.org/

Product Development and Management Association (PDMA); Mount Laurel, NJ; www.pdma.org/

Project Management Association Japan (PMAJ); Tokyo, Japan; www.pmaj.or.jp/

Project Management Research Committee, China (PMRC); www.pmrc.org.cn/do/index.php?&ch=6

Project Management Institute (PMI); Newtown Square, PA; www.pmi.org/

Project Management South Africa (PMSA); Rivonia Santon, South Africa; www.projectmanagement.org.za/

Society for the Advancement of Management (SAM); Corpus Christi, https://www.facebook.com/SAMnationall

Society of Automotive Engineers (SAE); Warrendale, PA; www.sae.org/

Society of Concurrent Product Development (SCPD); Dedham, MA; www.scpdnet.org/

Society of Project Managers, Singapore (SPMS); Singapore; www.sprojm.org.sg/

Society of Research Administrators International (SRA); Falls Church, VA; www.srainternational.org/

Society of Women Engineers (SWE); Chicago, IL; http://societyofwomenengineers.swe.org/

Technology Management Council (Division of IEEE); New York, NY;
http://ieee-tmc.org/
Technology Transfer Society (TTS); Austin, TX; www.cisalpino.eu/t2s/

PROFESSIONAL JOURNALS

The listing below represents professional journals dedicated, at least in part, to the advancement of knowledge in the field of project management, as well as engineering and technology management. The listing focuses on U.S.-based publications, but also includes publications from other countries with readership in the United States. Because of the similarities of managerial issues, challenges and support systems, many of these journals are being read world-wide, regardless of their origin. The listing is for reference only. No attempt is being made to rank or exclude any particular publication.

Academy of Management Journal. Published by the Academy of Management, Briarcliff Manor, NY; http://aom.org/amj/
Academy of Management Review. Published by the Academy of Management, Briarcliff Manor, NY; http://aom.org/AMR/
Aerospace America. Published by the American Institute of Aeronautics and Astronautics, Reston, VA;, http://arc.aiaa.org www.aerospaceamerica .org/Pages/TableOfContents.aspx
AIAA Journal. Published by the American Institute of Aeronautics and Astronautics, Reston, VA; http://arc.aiaa.org, http://arc.aiaa.org/loi/aiaaj
California Management Review. Published by the University of California at Berkley; http://cmr.berkeley.edu/
Cost Engineering Journal. Published by the Association for the Advancement of Cost Engineering International, Morgantown, WV; www .aacei.org/resources/ce
Creativity Research Journal. Published Taylor and Francis; www .tandfonline.com/loi/hcrj20
Decision Analysis. Published by the Institute for Operations Research and the Management Science (INFORMS), Linthicum, MD; http://pubsonline .informs.org/journal/deca
Decision Sciences Journal of Innovative Education. Published by the Decision Sciences Institute, Atlanta, GA; http://www.decisionsciences.org/
Decision Sciences Journal. Published by the Decision Sciences Institute, Atlanta, GA; www.decisionsciences.org/dsj/index.htm
Engineering Management Journal. Published by the American Society for Engineering Management; www.asem.org/publications/index.html, www .asem.org/home.html
Global Advanced Research Journal of Engineering, Technology and Innovation **(GARJETI).** Published by Global Advanced Research Journals; http://garj.org/garjeti/index.htm
Harvard Business Review. Published by Harvard University, Cambridge, MA; http://hbr.org

IBM Systems Journal. Published by IBM, White Plains, NY; www
.research.ibm.com/journal/sj/

IEEE Engineering Management Review. Published by the IEEE
Technology Management Council, New York, NY; http://ieee-tmc.org/emr

IEEE Transactions on Engineering Management. Published by the
IEEE Technology Management Council, New York, NY; http://ieee-tmc.org/
tem

Information Systems Research. Published by the Institute for
Operations Research and the Management Science (INFORMS), Linthicum,
MD; http://pubsonline.informs.org/journal/isre

***International Journal of Innovation and Technology Management
(IJITM).*** Published by World Scientific Publishing Co., Singapore; www
.worldscientific.com/worldscinet/ijitm

International Journal of Innovation Management (IJIM). Published
by World Scientific Publishing Co., Singapore; www.worldscientific.com/
worldscinet/ijim

International Journal of Innovation Management. Published by
World Scientific Publishing, Hackensack, NJ; www.worldscinet.com/ijim/
ijim.shtml

International Journal of Project Management (IJPM). Published by
Elsevier in collaboration with the Association for Project Management (APM)
and the International Project Management Association (IPMA), UK; www
.journals.elsevier.com/international-journal-of-project-management/

Journal of Engineering and Technology Management (JETM).
Published by Elsevier, New York, NY; http://www.journals.elsevier.com/
journal-of-engineering-and-technology-management

Journal of Management in Engineering. Published by the American
Society of Civil Engineers. Reston, http://ascelibrary.org/journal/jmenea

Journal of Manufacturing Science and Engineering. Published by
the American Society of Mechanical Engineers, Fairfield, NJ; www.asme.org/
products/journals/journal-manufacturing-science-and-engineering

Journal of Product Innovation Management (JPIM). Published by
the Product Development & Management Association, Mount Laurel, NJ;
http://www.blackwellpublishing.com/journal.asp?ref=0737-6782, http://online
library.wiley.com/journal/10.1111/(ISSN)1540-5885

***Journal of Professional Issues in Engineering Education and
Practice.*** Published by the American Society of Civil Engineers, Reston, VA;
http://www.asce.org/, http://ascelibrary.org/journal/jpepe3

Journal of the Association of Proposal Management Professionals.
Published by the Association of Proposal Management Professionals, www
.apmp.org/?page=PubsHome

Leadership and Management in Engineering. Published by the
American Society of Civil Engineers. Reston, VA; www.pubs.asce.org/journals/
lenews.html

Management and Organization Review. Published by the International
Association for Chinese Management Research, Hong Kong University of

Science and Technology and Peking University; http://onlinelibrary.wiley
.com/journal/10.1111/(ISSN)1740-8784

Management Science. Published by the Institute for Operations
Research and the Management Science (INFORMS), Linthicum, MD; www
.decisionsciences.org, http://pubsonline.informs.org/journal/mnsc

Operations Research. Published by the Institute for Operations Research
and the Management Science (INFORMS), Linthicum, MD; www.jstor.org/
journals/0030364X.html

Organizational Dynamics. Published by Emerald/Ingenta plc, Bath,
UK; www.ingentaconnect.com/content/mcb/502;jsessionid=9arr8xqnaybk
.victoria?

Perspectives. Published by the Academy of Management, Briarcliff
Manor, NY; http://aom.org/amp/

Plant/Operations Progress, Process Safety Progress (Quarterly).
Published by the American Institute of Chemical Engineers, New York, NY;
www.aiche.org/ccps/resources/publications/process-safety-progress

Project Management Journal. Published by the Project Management
Institute, Newtown Square, PA; www.pmi.org/Knowledge-Center/
Publications-Project-Management-Journal.aspx

Proposal Management. Published by the Association of Proposal
Management Professionals, www.apmp.org/, http://www.apmp.org/Pubs
APMP.asp

Quality Management Journal. Published by the American Society for
Quality, Milwaukee, WI; http://www.asq.org/pub/

Quality Progress. Published by the American Society for Quality,
Milwaukee, WI; http://asq.org/qualityprogress/index.html

R&D Management. Published by John Wiley & Sons, http://onlinelibrary
.wiley.com/journal/10.1111/(ISSN)1467-9310

Research-Technology Management. Published by the Industrial
Research Institute, Arlington, VA.

Six Sigma Forum Magazine. Published by the American Society for
Quality, Milwaukee, WI; http://asq.org/pub/sixsigma/

Sloan Management Review. Published by MIT, Cambridge, MA; http://
sloanreview.mit.edu/

Technology Review. Published by MIT, Cambridge, MA; www.tech
nologyreview.com/

The Futurist. Published by the World Future Society, Bethesda, MD;
http://www.wfs.org/futurist

PROFESSIONAL CONFERENCES

The listing below represents major professional conferences at national
or international level, focus on the advancement of project management,

engineering management or technology management. Most of the conferences listed are managed by U.S.-based organizations, but are often held in countries outside the United States. The listing also includes some conferences organized and managed by institutions outside the U.S. Because of the similarities of project management and technology issues world-wide, many of these conferences draw delegates internationally, regardless of their venue. The listing is for reference only. No attempt is being made to rank or exclude any particular conference.

Annual Meeting of AACE International. Organized by the Association for the Advancement of Cost Engineering International (AACE), Morgantown, WV; www.aacei.org/

Annual Meeting of the AAAS. Organized by the American Association for the Advancement of Science (AAAS), Washington, DC; http://meetings.aaas.org/

Annual Meeting of the Academy of Management, AOM. Organized by the Academy of Management (AOM), Briarcliff Manor, NY; http://aom.org/

Annual Meeting of the Decision Sciences Institute (DSI). Organized by the Decision Sciences Institute (DSI), Atlanta, GA; www.decisionsciences.org/

ASCE Civil Engineering Conference and Exposition. Organized by American Society of Civil Engineers (ASCE); Reston, VA; www.asce.org/

ASEE Annual Conference and Exposition. Organized by the American Society for Engineering Education (ASEE), Washington, DC; www.asee.org/

ASEE/AAAE Global Colloquium on Engineering Education. Organized by the American Society for Engineering Education (ASEE), Washington, DC; www.asee.org/

ASEM National Conference. Organized by the American Society for Engineering Management (ASEM); Rolla, MO, www.asem.org/home.html

ASTD International Conference and Exposition. Organized by American Society for Training and Development (ASTD), Alexandria, VA; www.astd.org/ASTD/conferences/ice/ice05/ice05_home

Hawaii International Conference of Systems Science, HICSS. Organized by the University of Hawaii; www.hicss.hawaii.edu/

IAMOT International Conference on Management of Technology. Organized by International Association for Management of Technology (IAMOT); Coral Gables, FL; iamot@miami.edu, www.iamot.com/

IIE Annual Conference & Exhibition. Organized by Institute of Industrial Engineers (IIE); Norcross, GA; http://www.iienet.org/ www.iienet2.org/Default.aspx

INFORMS Annual Meeting. Organized by Institute for Operations Research and the Management Sciences (INFORMS), Linthicum, MD; www.informs.org/

International Technology Management Conference, ITMC (IEEE). Organized by the Technology Management Council (Division of IEEE); New York, NY; http://ieee-tmc.org/

Management Roundtable. Organized by The Management Roundtable (Resource for Product & Technology Development), Waltham, MA; www.roundtable.com/

PDMA International Conference. Organized by Product Development and Management Association (PDMA), Mount Laurel, NJ; www.pdma.org/

PMI Global Congress. Multiple venues: North America, Europe, Asia, Latin America. Organized by the Project Management Institute (PMI), Newtown Square, PA; www.pmi.org/

PMI Project Management Research and Education Conference. Held every two years. Organized by the Project Management Institute (PMI), Newtown Square, PA; www.pmi.org/

Portland International Conference for Management of Engineering and Technology, PICMET. Organized by the International Center for Management of Engineering and Technology at Portland State University, Portland, OR; www.picmet.org/main/

SAM International Business Conference. Organized by Society for the Advancement of Management (SAM), Corpus Christi, TX; http://samnational.org/

CENTERS OF TECHNOLOGY MANAGEMENT AND OTHER RESOURCES

The listing below represents just a small sample of internet-accessible centers with technology and innovation management. These sites often provide links to other related resources, and hence provide a starting point for further research. The listing is for reference only, and not intended to be comprehensive.

Boeing Center for Technology, Information & Manufacturing: http://www.olin.wustl.edu/EN-US/Faculty-Research/research-centers/boeing-center-for-technology-information-and-manufacturing/Pages/default.aspx

IfM Institute for Manufacturing at the University of Cambridge: www.ifm.eng.cam.ac.uk/common/az.html.

Center for Innovation in Product Development at MIT: www.nsf.gov/pubs/2000/nsf00137/nsf00137k.htm

Centre for Management of Technology and Entrepreneurship at the University of Toronto: http://www.cmte.utoronto.ca/

Management of Innovation and New Technology (MINT) Research Centre at MacMaster University, Hamilton, Ontario, Canada: http://

mbastudent.degroote.mcmaster.ca/program-information/specializations/
management-of-innovation-and-new-technology-mint/

Management of Technology Program at the University of Minnesota, Minneapolis, Minnesota: http://tli.umn.edu/graduate/mot

Management of Technology Programs at University of Texas, San Antonio

MIT Media Lab: www.media.mit.edu/

US-Asia Technology Management Center at Stamford University: http://asia.stanford.edu/

Glossary

This glossary is just a small sample of acronyms and terms commonly used in project management. The listing is for reference only, and not intended to be comprehensive. One of the best ways to explore the meaning and application of a particular professional term is to search for its definition and application on the Internet. Many of the internet sites that explain the term also provide links to other related sources of information and knowledge.

A

Acceptance criteria   Contractual requirements associated with project deliverables that must be met before the customer will sign-off on a deliverable item.

Activity   A unit of work (also called task), defined by its scope, timeline, resource requirement and deliverable results. The specific role of an activity within the overall project is identified by its WBS number.

Actual cost (AC)   Total cost actually incurred during a given work period.

Actual cost of work performed (ACWP)   Resources expended so far (terminology of Earned Value Management, EVM).

Aggregate planning   Incremental planning process that often provides more accuracy at the beginning of the planning cycle, but allows for more details and updating to be provided later in the execution.

Agile project management   Projects execution in a highly flexible, adaptive and interactive manner (in opposite to *waterfall method*)

Assumptions   Factors that are believed to be true, but not known to be true.

B

Backward pass   PERT calculation determining the latest starting dates, backward from the required project completion date.

Baseline   The basic agreement on project scope, schedule, budget and quality.

Bid proposal   Offer to deliver specific goods or services based on a (formal) *request for proposal*.

Bottom-up estimating   Method of detailed cost estimating, aggregated or rolled-up into the total project budget.

Budget at completion (BAC)   Total planned project value.

Budget   Estimated cost of any part or the whole project.

Budgeted cost of work performed (BCWP)   Cost of work actually performed, equals *earned value*.

Budgeted cost of work scheduled (BCWS)   Allocated budget to complete work within a specified time period.

Business process modeling (BPM)   Breakdown of the business process into subsystems and activities for analysis and process improvement.

C

Change control   A formal process to ensure that necessary changes are introduced in to the project execution in a controlled and orderly manner, including documentation, cost negotiations and impact assessments.

Co-location   Project team members are located (or relocated) in close proximity to each another (e.g., in the same room or building).

Configuration management system   Procedures used to identify, track, document and control, project subsystems or deliverables. Also used for change management.

Constraint   Restriction or limitation on a project parameter, such as "earliest start" or "not to exceed budget."

Contract   Mutually binding agreement between parties.

Core team   Key members of a project team.

Corrective actions   Action item needed to correct an issue, often part of project review process.

Cost management   Estimating, planning, analyzing, and controlling costs.

Cost overrun   Actual cost exceeds established budget.

Cost performance index (CPI)   Cost efficiency measure, defined as EV divided by AC.

Cost variance (CV)   Cost performance measure, defined as $CV = EV - AC$.

Cost-plus-fixed-fee contract   Cost-reimbursable contract which includes actual cost plus a fixed fee.

Crashing   Project schedule compression technique (decrease of total project duration) achieved by adding more resources.

Critical chain project management (CCPM)   Method of planning and managing projects with focus on resources requirements and the critical path of the project.

Critical path (CP)   Any activity path that is equal or longer than the established or planned project duration.

Critical path method (CPM)   Tool for modeling and analyzing sets of interdependent project activities (similar to PERT).

D

Deliverable   Specific result to be produced from a task, activity, phase, or project.

Delphi technique   Method of reaching consensus of expert opinions on a subject, forecast or prediction.

Dependency   Links between project activities which restrict independent execution of these activities.

Duration   The total time required to complete an activity or total project

E

Early finish time (EF)   Earliest possible point in time a scheduled activity can finish, given the schedule network logic, timing, dependencies and constraints.

Early start time (ES)   Earliest possible point in time a scheduled activity can start, given the schedule network logic, timing, dependencies and constraints.

Earned value (EV)   Value of completed work.

Earned value management (EVM)   Technique for measuring project performance or progress based on cost, schedule and deliverables.

Enterprise project management (EPM)   Looking at project management from an enterprise perspective.

Estimate at completion (EAC)   Expected total project cost (possibly different from agreed-on budget).

Estimate to complete (ETC)   Expected cost to complete all the remaining project work.

Estimate   Approximation of a value or other data based on the best information available.

Extreme project management (XPM)   Contemporary concept of managing large, complex and uncertain projects. XPM emphasizes flexibility and stakeholder collaboration.

F

Fast tracking   A project schedule compression technique that focuses on executing activities in parallel.

Finish-to-finish (FF)   The succeeding activity cannot finish until the preceding activity is completed. This terminology is often used in PERT.

Finish-to-start (FS)   An activity cannot Start until the preceding activity has started. This terminology is often used in PERT.

Firm-fixed-price contracts.   Contract cost or price is fixed.

Forward pass   Calculation of early start and early finish dates in a network diagram such as PERT..

Free float or float Amount of time an activity can be delayed without delaying the project, relative to the actual time requirements of all other activities in the project.

Functional manager Manager in a resource department, usually responsible for managing all human and material resources toward established objectives.

Functional organization Hierarchical organization with clear lines of authority, command, communication and control.

G

Gantt chart Also known as *bar graph*. Graphic display of activities against time lines.

Graphical Evaluation and Review Technique (GERT) Network analysis technique similar to PERT.

K

Kickoff meeting Initial meeting at the beginning of a project, providing the project team and stakeholders with a project overview.

L

Late finish time (LF) Latest possible point in time an activity can finish, given the logic, timing, dependencies and constraints of the activity schedule.

Late start time (LS) Latest possible point in time that an activity may begin, given the logic, timing, dependencies and constraints of the activity schedule.

Lean manufacturing Also known as lean production, focuses on creation of value for the customer; all other expenditures should be minimized or eliminated.

Lessons learned Knowledge gained from past experiences, potentially useful for future work.

Linear scheduling method (LSM) Graphical scheduling method focusing on continuous resource utilization.

Line-of-balance (LOB) Also known as the *vertical production method*, LOB is a graphical technique used together with arrow or precedence diagrams.

M

Matrix conflict Conflict caused in matrix organizations due to dual accountability, and shared power and resources.

Matrix organization Organizational structure with two layers of management, resource and project layer.

Megaproject An extremely large and complex project.

Milestone A significant point or event in the project.

Milestone schedule Summary schedule listing just the major project milestones (i.e., events and dates).

Milestone Significant event associated with major results and deliverables.

Monitoring Collecting and processing of project performance information.

Monte Carlo analysis Computerized simulation technique to determine certain values (i.e. cost) under uncertainty.

N

Network analysis Methods for analysing various project-related networks, such as PERT, CPM or GERT.

Network diagram Model of activities, showing their sequencing, linkages and dependencies throughout the project lifecycle.

Nonlinear Refers to a system or event for which the output is not directly proportional to its input (superposition principle is not satisfied).

O

Organizational Project Management Maturity Model (OPM3)®. Published by the Project Management Institute (PMI), OPM3 provides a model for understanding organizational project management processes.

Out-of-bounds reviews. Process permitting any project team member to call for a review of issues that could be potentially strongly impact project success.

P

Parametric estimating Estimating technique based on historical data and the scalability of key parameters. Commonly used for project cost and time estimates.

Performance index (PI) Performance measure within the Earned Value Management (EVM) system. PIs are defined in two types, cost and schedule focused; cPI=EV/ACWP and sPI=EV/BCWS.

Phased management Management approach similar to Stage Gate®. The project is broken into phases, each with defined inputs, outputs, and gate criteria.

Portfolio management Selection, prioritisation and execution of a set of projects and programs linked to common enterprise objectives.

Portfolio, Program and Project Management Maturity Model (P3M3) Reference guide for structured best practice. P3M3 is endorsed and owned by The UK Office of Government Commerce (OGC).

Project Evaluation and Review Technique A statistical tool used in project management, commonly abbreviated PERT, that is designed to analyze and represent the tasks involved in completing a given project. First developed by the United States Navy in the 1950s, it is commonly used in conjunction with the critical path method (CPM).

Project Management Body of Knowledge (PMBOK®) A project management practice standard developed and maintained by the Project Management Institute (PMI).

Project Management Maturity Model (P3M) A model for defining project management processes.

R

Rapid prototyping Techniques for rapidly validating a design concept, such as using computer aided design (CAD), simulation, 3D printing or stereo lithography.

Reengineering Redesign or reorganize a system, process or organization; term is especially used for business process reengineering.

Requirements Contractual condition to be met.

Reserve Budget and/or schedule provision for covering risk and contingencies.

Resource leveling Method and philosophy of utilizing resources across the organization most effectively.

Resources Assets (i.e., funding, personnel, facilities) needed to execute a task or project.

Risk An uncertainty with the potential of affecting project performance positively or negatively.

Rolling wave planning Progressive planning, providing more detail for near-term activities, while long-term work is planned at a high level and detailed later.

Root cause analysis Determine underlying reason for actual or potential problems.

S

Schedules Tabular or graphical presentation of project activities, including start and finish dates.

Scope Project work to be accomplished to deliver contractual results.

Scope creep Unintended or unexpected changes in project scope.

Scrum An iterative incremental process of project execution commonly used with agile methods of project management.

Six Sigma Process, concept and method for quality improvement, aiming for 99.99966% reliability ($= 6\sigma$).

Spiral process A process model focused on software development project. Depending on the risk dynamics, the process guides the team toward various execution processes, such as incremental, waterfall, or evolutionary prototyping.

Stage Gate® A phase-stage process especially designed for new product development project planning and execution.

Stakeholders Persons or organizations with strong interest in the project and potential impact on project performance and vice versa.

Statement of work (SOW) Description of products or services to be provided.

Systems engineering An interdisciplinary area concerned with the design and management of complex engineering projects.

T

Task Element of work to be accomplished.

Timeline Start and finish dates associated with a specific task. It can also refer to a schedule.

Total slack (TS) Amount of time an activity can be delayed without affecting the required finishing date (schedule constraint).

V

Value engineering Management concept for optimizing project costs, time and overall value to enterprise and customer.

Variance Measurable deviation from a known baseline value.

Variance analysis Technique for measuring project performance or progress based on cost, schedule and deliverables. Same as earned value management (EVM).

Virtual team Term often used for geographically dispersed project teams connected via communication technology.

W

Work breakdown structure (WBS) Deliverable-oriented hierarchical breakdown of the total project into subsystems and task groups, providing the backbone for project budgeting and execution.

Work package Subset of a WBS.

Index